A Worthy Tradition

Other books by Harry Kalven, Jr.

The American Jury (with H. Zeisel)
The Negro and the First Amendment
Delay in the Court (with H. Zeisel & B. Buchholz)
Cases and Materials on Torts (with C. Gregory)
The Uneasy Case for Progressive Taxation (with W. Blum)

A
Worthy
Tradition

Freedom of Speech in America

Harry Kalven, Jr.
Edited by Jamie Kalven

An Edward Burlingame Book

Harper & Row, Publishers, New York

Grand Rapids, Philadelphia, St. Louis, San Francisco
London, Singapore, Sydney, Tokyo

A hardcover edition of this book was published in 1988 by Harper & Row, Publishers.

Lines from Pound's Canto from *The Pisan Cantos,* © copyright 1948 by Ezra Pound. Used by permission of New Directions Publishing Corporation.

The editor gratefully acknowledges the support of the Chicago Bar Foundation, the Playboy Foundation, and the J. Roderick MacArthur Foundation.

First PERENNIAL LIBRARY edition published 1989

Library of Congress Cataloging-in-Publication Data

Kalven, Harry.
  A worthy tradition.
  Bibliography: p.
  Includes index.
  1. Freedom of speech—United States. I. Kalven,
Jamie. II. Title.
KF4772.K35 1989   342.73'0853   347.302853   87-45059
ISBN 0-06-091622-2

89 90 91 92 93 FG 10 9 8 7 6 5 4 3 2 1

What thou lovest well remains,
                          the rest is dross
What thou lov'st well shall not be reft from thee
What thou lov'st well is thy true heritage

Ezra Pound
Canto LXXXI

Contents

Editor's Introduction   xi

PART ONE: THE REGULATION OF CONTENT

Preface   3
1   The Consensus on Untouchable Content   6

The Minor Jurisdictions of Censorship

2   Contempt by Publication   23
3   Obscenity   33
4   The Child Audience   54
5   Libel   60

The Major Jurisdictions of Censorship

Reflexive Disorder
6   The First Encounter   77
7   The Civil Rights Cases   96
8   *Chaplinsky* Redux   106
Subversive Advocacy
9   The Core Issue and the *Brandenburg* Answer   119

10 The Beginnings   125
11 The Great Debate—Sanford in *Gitlow* v. Brandeis
       in *Whitney*   150
12 Speech Starts to Win   167
13 The Heyday of Clear and Present Danger   179
14 The Great Confrontation—*Dennis v. United States*   190
15 The *Yates* Revision   211
16 *Brandenburg* Revisited   227

PART TWO: THE REGULATION OF ASSOCIATION

The Regulation of Political Groups

17 Sanctions Against Groups   241
18 The Nexus Issue: Is Membership Enough?   243
19 Compulsory Disclosure as a Group Sanction:
       The Civil Rights Cases   254
20 Compulsory Disclosure as a Group Sanction:
       The *SACB* Case   264
21 Stigmatization as a Group Sanction   288
22 Sanctions Against Individuals as a Group Sanction   297

Partial Sanctions: The Anti-Communist Inheritance

23 The Partial Sanction: A General Analysis   301
24 Partial Sanctions Keyed to Membership
       in Disfavored Groups   315
25 The Denial of Employment   318
26 The Loyalty Oath   340
27 The Security Calculus   368
28 The Allocation of Subsidies   384
29 The Multiplier Effect   391

Sanctions out from under the Constitution

30 Deportation   403
31 Denaturalization   423

32 Exclusion   437
33 The Regulation of Passports   449

Official Inquiry

34 Legislative Investigation: The Beginnings, 1880-1956   459
35 Legislative Investigation: The Period of
       First Amendment Challenge, 1957-1959   483
36 Legislative Investigation: The Law Unable
       to Work Itself Pure   506
37 The Principle of *Speiser v. Randall*   532
38 The Principle of *Shelton v. Tucker*   542
39 Wondrous Complexity: The Bar Admission Cases   548

Editor's Afterword   589
Notes   611
Table of Cases   673
Index   681

Editor's Introduction

Whatever else it may or may not be, it is turning out to be the book I always wanted to write." I find these words in a letter from my father dated September 1, 1973. Mailed from a vacation cottage on Martha's Vineyard, the letter crackles with characteristic gaiety:

I spent the first four weeks here post-sunrise slowly carefully rereading my 800 pages of manuscript and doing some shuffling of pieces. The news is that I found it just swell! . . . I am now clear that the effort to document *a tradition* is sound, especially for *this* tradition. Anyway I now estimate, I'm still 600 pages away from completion (but I can almost *touch* the end). With editing the total length should be 1300 plus ms pages or two nicely printed 375 page volumes! Now all I need do is to get [my] editors . . . out here to read it amidst swans, rabbits, and egrets! Anyway I'm promised Fall 1974 off, and with the six months starting next June, really hope to bring it to a close. Mother, I should add, liked all the many passages I read aloud to her!

The manuscript on which my father was working with such appetite was an essay on the American constitutional experience under the First Amendment: the book in your hands. Conceived early in his career, it had long been deferred while he worked on other things. He had ranged widely during his career as a law professor at the University of Chicago: he taught torts and was the co-author of a leading casebook in the field; he did pioneering work in the application of social science research techniques to legal institutions; and he had a lively interest in a range of other legal matters. Yet, by his own account, it was the constitutional law on freedom of speech that engaged him most deeply.

The First Amendment, he observed more than once, has "a charisma" that sets it apart from other rules of law. Whatever its merits as a generalization, this was certainly true for him. There is something telling about his choice of the word "charisma" from among the many he might have used to make a general point about the specialness of the First Amendment. It speaks to his experience, to what the subject summoned from him. He was a member of that select company of critics—whatever their fields, they have much in common—whom one values not only for their erudition and judgment but also for their heightened capacity for response: a sensitivity—a vulnerability—to the impact of their chosen genre coupled with the ability to report on what they have seen and felt.

Almost all his writings on freedom of speech, prior to this book, were produced in response to controversies of the moment. His agenda was set by his times. In the 1950s he wrote extensively about abuses of the legislative investigation process and about other loyalty-security issues of the day. In the 1960s, as the Warren Court extended the reach of the First Amendment, he scouted the new terrain. He wrote a book on the contributions of the civil rights movement to free speech doctrine, and in a series of influential articles explored the issues posed by public demonstrations, obscenity, and libel.

Finally in 1970 he cleared his desk of other commitments and set to work on the book he had "always wanted to write." His plan was to pull together in one place the analyses of various problems he had developed over the years in scattered articles and in class. He aspired to survey the entire corpus of the Supreme Court's work on issues of freedom of speech and association. To get it all into a single book. To see it whole.

This was not just another book in the life of a productive scholar. He began it in the aftermath of a heart attack and two years later suffered a stroke. He accepted these betrayals of his body with grace, but there is no question they deepened the importance the book held for him. It is my impression that he worked with a rare quality of attention during those years. I know he lived that way.

Before he wrote a word, he reread in chronological sequence all the First Amendment cases decided by the Supreme Court. Then he began to write—a bit uncertainly at first, then with gathering force.

He wrote without revising. Each summer he would reread his growing manuscript and write comments in the margins—sketching revisions, flagging additions, sometimes directly challenging the substance of the text. He did not act on these notes. Problems, once noted in the margin, could wait. He wanted to maintain his momentum, his forward sweep through the cases. ("I can almost *touch* the end.") Then, in the fall of 1974, at his desk, working on the manuscript, he died. He was sixty years old.

He bequeathed an unfinished first draft of over a thousand pages heavily embroidered with marginalia. This manuscript posed a dilemma to which there could be no fully satisfactory solution. Unpublishable in the form he left it, it was too good to put aside, too precious to cede to death. Working closely with Professor Owen Fiss of the Yale Law School, I have edited and, where necessary, supplemented the manuscript. This book is the product of that effort: my father's manuscript conveyed to the reader by other hands.

No effort has been made to complete the book. Nor have we updated it beyond the time of my father's death; this is a study of the First Amendment tradition through 1974. The objective of the editing has been to make it the clearest possible reflection of my father's thinking on the First Amendment—to recover, insofar as possible, his full meaning from the ambiguities and unresolved tensions of his first draft. In the afterword I describe some of the problems we encountered and some of the editorial strategies we employed in pursuit of that objective.

The balance of this introduction is devoted to prefatory points my father intended to make and to telling you a little about the mind you will encounter in these pages. In addition to his published work, I have drawn for this purpose on notes he generated in the course of working on this book and on lecture notes for the First Amendment courses he taught in 1971 and 1974—remnants of the animated conversation about freedom of speech he carried on from year to year with successive generations of students.

I

The First Amendment poses a question: what is "the freedom of speech" of which it speaks? On hundreds of occasions over the last sixty-odd years that question has been put to the United States Supreme Court. HK likens this body of experience to a Socratic dialogue:

There has been over the years at the level of the Supreme Court a sort of Socratic dialogue going on between the Court and the society as to the meaning of freedom of speech. "Tell us, Socrates, what is freedom of speech?" As with Socrates, the dialogue appears to be eternally open-ended—a definitive, fully understood answer will never be reached and so the process must go on with another and yet another question being put.[1]

This dialogue is, in some respects, peculiar. The Court, unlike the philosopher, is not free to pursue an inquiry of its own design; it is limited to answering the questions presented—often in haphazard, random sequence—by the society. And the pattern of questioning over time is odd. Some questions are asked again and again, while others, equally or more important, are rarely, if ever, raised.

The shape of the legal dialogue—what it takes in, what it does not—fascinated HK. He noted that the map of issues yielded by the dialogue is "skewed" when laid beside the map suggested by a philosophic discussion of freedom of speech such as John Stuart Mill's *On Liberty:*

It is skewed in the sense that the incidence of litigation and hence the expenditure of thought and effort by the justices have centered on problems the philosopher may well not have been aware existed.[2]

HK found this a pleasing datum. It underscored what he saw as distinctive about the legal perspective: its immersion in the problems that actually arise in the society, its direct experience with the practical requirements of the norm. The dialogue is, he observed, "marvelously seasoned by experience."

He also saw in the contrast between the legal and philosophic perspectives a reassuring reflection of how well-favored the American experience has been: certain questions have not arisen, because the answers have been largely assumed. It was with this perspective in mind that he chose to open this book with a chapter on "the consensus on untouchable content"—areas where there is substantial agreement that the content of speech cannot be reached by law.

There is, however, another perspective on the disproportions of the dialogue which is less reassuring. One of HK's notes reads: "it's a nice point that the *philosophic map* is so skewed; it is a disturbing point, however, that the *sociological map* is so skewed due to three facts: the sheer weight of broadcasting, the sheer weight of advertising, and the ownership of the means of communication." The centrality of broadcasting in American life—the fact that it embraces so much of our public discourse—is scarcely reflected in the Court's First Amendment oeuvre; there are only a few cases. Nor has the Court had much experience with the implications for freedom of speech of the economics of mass communications. Does the First Amendment, addressed as it is to government censorship, have any bearing on the power for private censorship that is conferred by concentrated ownership of the means of communication? The Court is yet to engage this question in a sustained way.

In another note HK listed areas in which the Court has, for one reason or another, been unable to give full expression to First Amendment values: immigration and deportation, where the government exercises virtually unqualified power; legislative investigation, where the Court is hobbled by the institutional realities of its relationship to Congress; and, again, "broadcasting!" and "economics." Surveying this list, he noted "the danger that all or almost all really important areas are left outside Court's 1st A scrutiny." Although this should perhaps be discounted somewhat as the sort of overstatement notes to oneself allow, it testifies to his awareness of the incompleteness of the dialogue—an awareness he sought to maintain, even as he celebrated the tradition that dialogue has engendered.

The law's experience is also, HK stressed, surprisingly recent. The First Amendment has been part of the Constitution and of American life since 1791. Yet it was only during World War I that the process of defining freedom of speech by means of judicial review really got started. Since then the legal dialogue has steadily accelerated. This can be dramatized in several ways. For example, as of the cutoff date of this book, 1974, more than 50 percent of all First Amendment cases had been decided since 1959—in other words, more than half were the work of the Warren Court. Justices Holmes and Brandeis, widely perceived as the "architects" of First Amendment doctrine, participated in some thirty-four cases; Justice Brennan has participated in well over three hundred. When Zechariah Chafee wrote the first edition of his influential *Free Speech in the United States* in 1920, there were about twenty cases.[3] When Alexander Meiklejohn in 1949 delivered the lectures that were to become *Free Speech and Its Relation to Self-Government*, there were roughly a hundred cases.[4] In 1974 HK, at work on this book, counted over four hundred. Finally, the recency of the dialogue can be characterized in more personal terms: it unfolded during HK's lifetime, most of it during his career as a legal scholar.

The dialogue has not only accelerated in recent years; it has also been fertile in generating a variety of problems to test the norm. Contemporary free speech issues are strikingly different from those that faced Holmes and Brandeis, Chafee and Meiklejohn. They were concerned almost exclusively with the issue posed by the use of criminal sanctions to prohibit subversive advocacy. That problem remains of central importance today, but it has been joined by a host of other issues posed by diverse categories of speech and by different sorts of sanctions.

The recency of the dialogue—and its exfoliation into new areas—have presented an inviting challenge to scholars. As HK put it in a note, "1st A recency permits total sweep as something more than history." Hence the desire to encompass it all in a single essay: the aspiration to find—amidst the great buzzing, blooming confusion of the field—an underlying unity.

The primary expression of that aspiration has been the quest for a unified general theory of the First Amendment. HK was sharply ambivalent about this quest. Indeed, he persuasively stated both the case for seeking such a theory and the case for not expecting to find one. In the introduction to *The Negro and the First Amendment* he puzzles over why the law, which in general displays a "great capacity to tolerate inconsistencies," should have such a strong "appetite for theory" in the First Amendment area. He then observes:

If my puzzle as to the First Amendment is not a true puzzle, it can only be for the congenial reason that free speech is so close to the heart of democratic organization that if we do not have an appropriate theory for our law here, we feel we really do not understand the society in which we live.[5]

It was in this spirit that he celebrated the Supreme Court's 1964 decision in *New York Times v. Sullivan*[6] as a great advance in clarity. In *Times* the Court, in reversing a libel judgment, made explicit the principle that seditious libel—criticism of government—cannot be made a crime in America and spoke in this connection of "the central meaning of the First Amendment." HK hailed the decision as perhaps "the best and most important" yet handed down in the First Amendment area and noted with delight that the Court appeared to be endorsing a particular theory of the First Amendment—Alexander Meiklejohn's thesis that freedom of speech is justified by the requirements of self-government.[7]

HK remains strongly identified with the *Times* decision and with Meiklejohn; properly so in both instances. Yet ironically this may also mislead by making this fox seem a hedgehog. Although it would be hard to overstate the importance he attached to the seditious libel point—it was a touchstone to which he often returned—he did not see "the central meaning of the First Amendment" as its only meaning. Indeed, his response to those words was, characteristically, as much literary as analytic: he found it striking the Court would use such language. And while he saw the Meiklejohn thesis as a major contribution—and was bound to the man by the deepest affection—he did not share Meiklejohn's insistence on a unified theory grounded on a single rationale.

The fact is that HK was highly skeptical about the quest for a general theory. The same year he wrote his article on *New York Times* he gave an exam in his First Amendment course in which he invited students to write "a reflective essay" on the following theme:

It is a mistake to pursue a unitary theory of freedom of speech under the United States Constitution. There are irreducible differences in the situations the Court is called upon to review and no legal principle can accommodate them all. The most we can aspire to is not a theory but specific solutions to a congeries of speech situations. This after all has been the genius of the Common Law.

HK, it is important to recall, taught torts throughout his career. The sensibility he brought to constitutional law was steeped in the culture of the common law. Distrustful of theory, he had great faith in the common law process. He valued its attention to particulars, its tolerance for inconsistencies, its capacity for growth and self-correction. These qualities are evoked by a favorite metaphor to which he frequently recurs: the image of "the law working itself pure." What drew him to First Amendment law was of a piece with what drew him to torts. The constitutional law on freedom of speech, he observed in class, is "a really great example of the common law process at work in a single jurisdiction—judge-made law, inch by inch, case by case."

HK was not anxious to generalize. He was concerned that the search for a unifying principle, if pursued with too much single-minded intensity, would blunt rather than deepen perception. He wanted to stay close to the ground of experience. In 1971 he told his students:

On my current view, one should seek not so much an organizing principle to answer all speech issues as an *organizing map* on which to place the problems. They are difficult to conceptualize and to relate to each other, depending in large part on the sociological *feel* of the situation—*genre* of the problem.

His central methodological commitment is to pay close attention to the *particularity* of different First Amendment problems. In this respect, his approach follows from his view of the nature of the Court's achievement. The Court may not have harmonized its answers to various questions, but it has, in his view, at its best, worked with patience and skill to discern the criteria appropriate to particular problems. Its achievement, as he sees it, resides in this close analysis of the particulars, whatever the cost in overall coherence. In a sense, he celebrates what others deplore. "In confusion and lack of overall formula," he told his students, "I see strength."

II

HK's emphasis on the particularity of First Amendment problems, his insistence on close attention to the contours of the given issue, his resistance to generalizations that flatten differences and collapse incommensurate phenomena into common categories—these features of his approach do not reflect a lack of interest in the larger question of what this body of experience, taken as a whole, amounts to. On the contrary, one of the striking things about his approach is how it combines this narrow focus on the precise character of particular problems with a broad perspective on what we are doing as a society when we engage in First Amendment controversies.

At the center of his approach is the concept of *tradition*. He conceived of the American experience under the First Amendment as something more than a body of legal precedent; he saw it as a tradition of the society. He seems to have found in this concept the sense of coherence, the sense of being securely grounded that others seek in theory. It offered him a way of talking in general terms without generalizing—without, that is, being reductive of rich experience, without blunting the particulars.

The concept is at once central and elusive, foundational and sketchy. What does HK mean when he speaks of "tradition" in connection with the First Amendment? In an article, written while he was working on this book, he brooded on the general theme of "tradition in law."[8] After discussing several relatively obvious instances of tradition—the use of precedent and various practices of the profession—he turned to "the difficult sense in which precedent and, in a way, practices embody values that transcend technical limits, an aspect perhaps associated most often with constitutional law."[9] There are, he wrote, "areas of law where the precedents taken as a whole, rather than in logical, precise, vertical sequences, carry a compulsion and inspiration that goes beyond literal holdings."[10]

As an example, he quoted Justice Frankfurter on the constitutional requirement of "due process." HK was not a great admirer of Frankfurter's work as a judge and, as this book makes clear, found him peculiarly insensitive to First Amendment values. Yet in his view it was Frankfurter who "best articulated the sense in which legal tradition can transmit a concept or norm that transcends precedent."[11] The occasion was *Joint Anti-Fascist Refugee Committee v. McGrath*, a 1951 case involving the Attorney General's list of subversive organizations:

The requirement of "due process" is not a fair-weather or timid assurance. It must be respected in periods of calm and in times of trouble; it protects aliens as well as citizens. But "due process," unlike some legal rules, is not a technical conception with a fixed content unrelated to time, place and circumstances. Expressing as it does in its ultimate analysis respect enforced by law for that feeling of just treatment which has been evolved through centuries of Anglo-American constitutional history and civilization, "due process" cannot be imprisoned within the treacherous limits of any formula. Representing a profound attitude of fairness between man and man, and more particularly between the individual and government, "due process" is compounded of history, reason, the past course of decisions, and stout confidence in the strength of the democratic faith which we profess.[12]

What is the role of the Court in relation to such a tradition? HK sharply disagreed with the view expressed in an earlier era by, among others, James Bradley Thayer—and echoed today by some who would constrict the role of the courts in American life—that constitutional values such as those embodied in the First Amendment are for the most part judicially unenforceable and must rely for their protection on the traditions of the society. One of his notes reads:

The Court and the tradition. Thayer is only 1/2 right. True, Ct. cannot single handedly save or keep liberal and tolerant a people. But a *tradition* can, and the role of the Court is to steadily enrich and nourish that tradition.

Judges do not create such a tradition—it resides ultimately in the society—but they do play a key role in articulating it, clarifying it, freshening it. It was in this spirit that HK, borrowing from Karl Llewellyn, saluted the judges who over time have given "living body, toughness, and inspiration" to "what is now for me the worthiest tradition in American law, the tradition of freedom of speech, press, and political action."[13]

HK's view of the Court's work in this area as the elaboration of a tradition had important implications for how he conceived and executed this book. If it is a tradition we are talking about and not simply a body of law, then the requirements of exposition are somewhat different: a matter of evocation as well as analysis, of narrative as well as logic. The objective is not simply to restate the most current answers to the issues the Court has encountered. It is to give a full account of the dialogue out of which they have emerged. In order to grasp the moral, one needs to know the story.

In this respect, HK's thinking about tradition was influenced by T. S. Eliot's essay "Tradition and the Individual Talent."[14] (I know this, in part, because he directed me to it when I began to write.) Eliot advises the apprentice poet to discipline his talent by steeping himself in the tradition of English poetry and thereby to develop "the historical sense"—"a perception, not only of the pastness of the past, but of its presence."[15] HK sees the requirements of the First Amendment tradition in similar terms: "We need, in Learned Hand's splendid phrase, to have a sense of our 'hardbought acquisition in the fight for freedom.' "[16]

Perhaps the most important implication of HK's orientation is that from the perspective of tradition, everything in the Court's First Amendment oeuvre is alive and available, regardless of its current status as precedent. New precedents may supersede old, but they do not erase the ideas and language and experience the latter contain. In the realm of tradition insights and arguments, once uttered, are indelible. As Eliot said of literary tradition, this is "a development which abandons nothing *en route.*"[17] Or to put it another way, HK distinguishes between precedent and intellectual history and emphasizes the latter.

His vision of the tradition is manifest in his style of approach. Virtually any First Amendment case is for him a potential source of rich narrative resources. And of language: he is always listening for the living voices of the tradition. He quotes extensively and makes generous use of italics in an effort to make those voices immediate—to bring them back alive. Foraging through the history, he encounters cases, whatever their precedential value, with the same energy of response—the same firsthandedness and density of perception—that he brought to controversies of the moment. In spirit, if not invariably in fact, he always writes in the present tense.

III

"A living tradition," Alasdair MacIntyre has observed, "is an historically extended, socially embodied argument, and an argument precisely in part about the goods which constitute that tradition."[18] HK's understanding of tradition is similar. He offers specific arguments as to what the content of the First Amendment tradition is or should be; above all, he sees rejection of the crime of seditious libel as essential. Yet his use of "tradition" does not reduce down (as is so often the case with this word) to a rhetorical device in the service of his own views. His essay is informed by a larger vision of the tradition-as-argument. As I understand it, he sees the essence of the tradition as residing not in one or another set of contending views but in the controversy itself. It is a matter of regarding these questions as central, of taking them seriously, of bringing to them a certain quality of attention.

He is thus disposed to see First Amendment controversies not only as inevitable but also (in most, though not all, instances) as desirable—to see them as evidence of the vitality of the tradition and as a means of maintaining that vitality. Altogether apart from resolution of the point at issue, such controversies serve a range of functions. By dramatizing the tradition, they serve as vehicles for its transmission. They often provide extended occasions for that "counterspeech" which classic First Amendment doctrine prescribes as the appropriate remedy for evil speech short of outright incitement to criminal action. (An irony: the counterspeech promoted by free speech doctrine as the alternative to censorship is frequently cast in the form of arguments for censorship.) Perhaps most important, they are occasions for renewing our understanding of the norm, for articulating it anew. Unwarranted censorship is not the only threat to freedom of speech. There is also the danger that a doctrinaire orthodoxy will harden around the norm. The intensity of the dialogue insures critical discussion of this principle designed to foster critical discussion. The principle is exemplified by the practice.

"To gain insight" into a First Amendment problem, HK advised his students, "it is necessary to have sympathy for the grievance against speech." One must "honor the countervalues." Such sympathy is an avenue to understanding the problem. It is also rhetorically effective: a demonstration to the aggrieved that their argument has been heard. And it is an antidote to the common tendency to argue against censorship on the ground that speech does not have any real impact on the world. One of HK's notes reads:

Speech has *a price*. It is a liberal weakness to discount so heavily the price. It is not always a "witchhunt," it is not always correct to win by showing danger has been exaggerated.

To be sure, the danger often *is* exaggerated; this is a common pattern. Rejoinder in these terms is thus often called for. Employed reflexively and thoughtlessly, however, this argument is self-defeating—a defense of the First Amendment that weakens it. For it rests on the unstated premise that speech is to be protected so long as it does not really matter. HK called this the "luxury civil liberty" view of the First Amendment and saw it as a major vulnerability in the tradition—a premise that can be turned against speech when the need for protection is greatest.

The high value HK places on the continual testing of the norm by experience is given engaging expression in one of his notes. It begins as a set of critical observations about the absolute reading of the First Amendment advanced by Justice Black. Although a great admirer of Black, HK had little enthusiasm for this argument and saw the debate it provoked as distracting and fruitless. He characterizes Black's absolutism as "a sad flaw, amidst so much gallantry." He can see "no reason why all use of words *per se* should be 100% immune." Moreover, he thinks the absolutist stance rhetorically weak: if the First Amendment position is that all use of words is protected, then the "debate is won by showing *any* instance where speech can be regulated." This sequence of reflections delivers him to a concentrated statement of his own view:

Finally, my personal view is that speech is "almost an absolute"—that is, it is highly unlikely in any instance that the argument v. regulation will win but that this is not an *a priori* conclusion known in advance of the concrete challenge but a result to be won by sweat in the individual case, time after time!

How much hangs on that "almost"! If you believe freedom of speech an absolute, you can state your position in a sentence. Believing it "almost an absolute," HK was moved to write this book; and, had he lived, he would have written much more. For, as he sees it, the dialogue between the society and the Court over the meaning of freedom of speech is not simply a succession of occasions for declaring an absolute. Nor is it only a means to the end of a general theory. It is, above all, an end in itself: a discipline of freedom, the ongoing work of a free society.

A similar conception of freedom was beautifully expressed by Ramsey Clark in a memorial tribute to HK. He said HK was "a free man" because "he questioned most severely the things he loved best."[19] Over the years I have thought a good deal about that remark—have thought about it, in part, from the perspective of one of the things he loved. It is not easy to characterize the tenor of his questioning. The word "severely" is not quite right. It does not convey the play of his mind. Also, there was an unconditional quality about his loyalty to the individuals and institutions he cared about. What is hard to convey is how his questioning did not threaten but was in the service of his love: the relationship between his endless questions and his underlying faith. Question followed question as easily as breath followed breath.

The least doctrinaire of men, HK embodied a relationship to the world—reflected in his writing style, his manner of teaching, and the very rhythms of his thought—that might best be described as conversational. Talk of "dialogue" and references to Socrates do not capture its flavor—the warmth and wit, the play of intelligence, the impulse to connect. One might say of him what he once said of his friend Meiklejohn: "I have always suspected that Socrates, however wise and admirable, would have made a trying and difficult companion. Alec was a Socrates who wore well, a Socrates it was fun to be with, a Socrates for all seasons."[20]

IV

HK's conversational style—the way he entertained a question—was to remain poised amid competing impulses and perspectives, holding them in productive tension: taut strings that gave out his distinctive notes and chords, his singular resonances. This style of mind was well suited to the subject of the Supreme Court. The fit was especially good with the Warren Court: the tensions in him corresponded to those among the justices. For some, a Court composed exclusively of Harlans might be the ideal; for others, a Court composed of Blacks; for some, a Court of Frankfurters; for others, a Court of Douglases.

But what HK valued was the mix and the resulting interplay: the way the tensions on the Court served to deepen understanding of the issues it was called upon to decide.

He was attentive as well to the tensions within individual judges. He once defined law as "disciplined passion"—with equal emphasis on both words. This sense of the law, at its best, as a demanding interaction between qualities of heart and mind strongly colored the lens through which he viewed the work of particular judges. He was fascinated by what he called "judicial style"—the mix of qualities peculiar to a judge's work—and a number of striking profiles emerge in the pages of this book. (Among them: Holmes, Jackson, Frankfurter, Harlan, Black, Brennan.) Indeed, the question at the center of the book—what is freedom of speech?—is shadowed by another: what makes a good judge, and more specifically, a good First Amendment judge?

There is no single answer, no single model. No one has a monopoly on insight; and, as HK puts it in a note, "everyone has a good day once in a while." The performances of individual justices over time and in response to diverse issues are uneven: "judicial profiles are mixed." The range of issues arising under the First Amendment is so broad and varied that it is inevitable an individual judge will respond more fully and sensitively to some than to others. Everyone's vision is partial. The tradition is the work of many hands.

For all his delight in the play of competing views, HK never lost sight of the fundamental character of adjudication: judges must decide. The conversation cannot remain forever in play. The dialogue must yield a judgment. And that judgment ultimately carries the coercive power of the state. Adjudication is not an exercise in pure criticism; it is not a free, unrestrained inquiry. It is a complex process, subject to political pressures and institutional constraints, removed from the realm of abstract discourse by the necessity of decision and the consequences of decision.

"The rest of us are fortunate indeed," HK once wrote of legal scholars, "that our job is so much easier and less responsible."[21] "He never lost his awe at the enormity of the justices' task nor his awareness of the weight of responsibility under which they act. His writing bears no trace of the subtle condescension—the archness—that colors much academic commentary on the Court. (A corollary: his anger, when he is so moved, has unimpeded fluency and force.)

Expressions of his temperament, the generosity and sympathy that animate his approach are also aspects of a demanding critical method. Central to that method is a reluctance to regard factors extrinsic to legal reasoning as sufficient explanations of the Court's decisions. A note reads:

The limits of realpolitik. Undoubtedly other factors also explain: cold war, balance in public criticism of the Ct, judicial personalities—but they do not deny rational content of problems; there is *always* this dimension.

HK acknowledges the force of the realist's critique, but he resists the conclusion that adjudication reduces down to that alone—that it is all at bottom a matter of politics and personalities. His orientation—the discipline he imposes upon himself—is to note such factors but for the most part to eschew relying on their explanatory power and to pursue instead the possibilities of intellectual analysis of the Court's work. He readily acknowledges that it is possible to exaggerate the role played by the compulsions of legal reasoning. Yet he is prepared to run that risk—to err in that direction—in the belief that such an approach is more likely to yield insight than the alternatives.

That is not to say that he is oblivious to extrinsic factors or that he excludes them from consideration. On the contrary, in his view, it is precisely the "interplay of public reason and 'real' reason" in the process of adjudication that "accounts for much of the fascination of law study."[22] But he will leave it to others to seize upon the presence of extrinsic factors as evidence that the process of adjudication is compromised. He is more interested in discerning how such factors may press the Court to constitutional insight and doctrinal innovation. As he sees it, the presence of extrinsic factors does not in itself impeach the integrity of the institution; rather, it defines the strenuous, problematic nature of its task.

HK writes from a perspective I have come to think of as that of the tenth justice. By this I do not mean to suggest qualities of self-importance but of collegiality—his passionate identification with the institution of the Court and his feel for the logic of evolving doctrine, for the problems it presents and the possibilities it holds. He does not hold himself above and apart; he does not engage in the sorts of criticism that are only possible because one is not in a position of responsibility. Confronted with a Supreme Court decision, his basic critical impulse is to *re-adjudicate* the case—to encounter anew the controversy it presents, to reconsider the alternatives open to the Court, to seek out the best available avenue for meeting the necessity of decision and advancing the development of the law.

He is interested in the full range of judicial tactics. Eloquence really matters here, he once observed; this tradition of protecting words lives by words. Much of the eloquence that has come to be invested in the tradition was first uttered in dissent. A dissenting opinion can be read as an essay by the individual justice. It is a form that allows for the full force of a singular voice and for the clear statement of a normative position. Indeed, there was a time when the widely held impression of a strong free speech tradition in American law rested almost entirely on the dissenting opinions of Holmes and Brandeis rather than on the decisions from which they dissented. It may well be, HK speculates, that one reason the tradition grew so strong was that it was able to mature in dissent relieved of the need to make accommodations in order to gain a majority.

It is easy to see an eloquent dissenting opinion as part of a grand public dialogue about the meaning of freedom of speech. Yet perhaps the strongest strain in this essay is HK's close attention to the quiet, non-eloquent exercise of judicial craftsmanship in the construction of majority opinions. He is often moved to celebrate the contributions of what he calls "judicial statesmanship": the tactical deftness that seeks, while honoring institutional constraints and navigating political cross-currents, to meet the need for decision in the particular case and to advance the development of the law.

It is not easy to fix the contributions of the judicial statesman with precision. If he has been successful in locating common ground and marshalling a majority upon it, he speaks for the institution of the Court, and his opinion is likely to be shaped (or misshaped) by the compromises and bargains, the concessions and tact required to build and maintain a majority. Such an opinion may represent a considerable intellectual achievement, but it is an achievement unlikely to declare itself in the form of surface brilliance or full-throated eloquence. The contributions of the judicial statesman are more likely to be discernible in the themes that shape the emerging law over time.

At this point the image of the dialogue between the society and the Court over the meaning of freedom of speech complicates. For the judicial statesman's moves can seem obscure and evasive. Concerned to protect the institution of the Court while responding to the claims of the parties in the particular controversy, he will often seek to avoid direct confrontation with the underlying constitutional issue, will dispose of the case on lesser grounds—will, to use a favorite HK word, "finesse" the situation. When he does address the underlying constitutional issue, he may do so obliquely rather than directly—by reorchestrating old precedents to yield new meanings, by rewriting but not openly repudiating disfavored precedents, by advancing via statutory construction toward a new constitutional formulation. As legal doctrine evolves under his hand, the argument tends to be muted and in extreme instances antithetical propositions are portrayed as cohering.

We touch here upon a central tension in HK's thought: a tension between his vision of the tradition-as-argument and his appreciation—and appetite—for the subtleties of judicial statesmanship. He does not frame this tension explicitly; nor does he address it directly. Yet there is a sense in which his distinctive role as a legal scholar arises out of it: he seeks to resolve the tension in narrative—to embed the fragile stratagems of the judicial statesman in an account that will give them weight and resonance. Amid obscurity, compromise and apparent contradiction, he delights in tracing the golden thread of "the law working itself pure."

HK's admiration for judicial statesmanship, though large, is not, however, boundless. He accepts that there are times when the Court's stewardship of the First Amendment may properly involve the avoidance of constitutional confrontation, the diplomatic correction of the particular injustice by means that do not reach the underlying issue, and the building of doctrinal bridges through strained readings of prior precedent. The question is: when are those times? Everything turns on an assessment of the expanding and contracting spheres of possible action, now and in the future. HK often notes the costs of misassessment: Diplomatic resolutions may prove short-lived—the problem soon returns. By obscuring what it is doing from the public, the Court may waste important educational opportunities. And the concessions the statesman makes in the course of building his doctrinal edifices may ultimately undo his work: it is possible to travel both ways on a bridge.

One product of judicial statesmanship about which HK had little ambivalence was what he called "the technical preferred position": various technical doctrines the Court has developed—and often used to avoid direct constitutional confrontation—in First Amendment cases. In other areas regulation may be accorded a certain latitude in order to insure it hits the evil at which it is aimed. By contrast, a strong—though by no means uncontested—strand of the First Amendment tradition insists that the boundaries of protected expression be drawn with the utmost clarity and precision: it demands that regulations in the speech domain hit their targets directly. Similarly, it has little patience with unnecessary burdens, no matter how small, on the exercise of First Amendment freedoms, and is willing to intervene on the basis of anticipated harm to those freedoms rather than waiting for the harm to mature.

In HK's view, the principle underlying these technical doctrines is that, while speech may be subject to censorship, any *waste* of First Amendment freedoms in the process will not be tolerated. This principle rests on a perception not only of the value of speech but also of its perishability—an awareness of how hard it can be to speak, how easy to keep silent. The Court has been alert to the dangers of self-censorship—a regulation may offend not because it directly censors speech but because it has features that may prompt citizens to censor themselves—and it has often spoken of "the breathing space" required by First Amendment freedoms.

The term "preferred position" figured prominently in debate during the 1940s over whether the First Amendment enjoyed preeminence in the hierarchy of constitutional values. The argument was that because of the great importance of First Amendment freedoms, legislation touching on speech should face a presumption of unconstitutionality. It is my impression that HK saw this as too sweeping an argument, too blunt an instrument. His use of the term "technical preferred position" thus carries the implication that the First Amendment is best served not by broad generalizations about its preeminence but by a set of habits and standards that insure we *take care* in our pursuit of answers to the question it poses.

In a way, these technical standards are the counterpart to HK's insistence on being open to the full force of the argument for censorship, on cultivating "sympathy for the grievance" against speech. Both contribute to the rigor and intensity of the dialogue. When the Court employs these doctrines, it does not foreclose the possibility of censorship, but it does challenge the government to define the scope of censorship in terms sufficiently clear and narrow to be consistent with the great value we place on First Amendment freedoms. In this respect, it more than ever resembles Socrates—turning an assertion back at an interlocutor in the form of a question.

V

This book is not complete. HK did not finish his grand design. There are isolated gaps, and a projected third section on non-content regulation remains unwritten. Yet there is a sense in which the map of the field that emerges is more revealing than an exhaustive survey of every First Amendment issue to reach the Court would have been. HK wrote first about the issues that mattered most to him. The shape of the book thus reflects what commanded his attention when he surveyed the full sweep of the American experience under the First Amendment.

Part One is devoted to regulation of the *content* of speech. It opens with a chapter on "the consensus" with regard to speech content which, it is generally agreed, should be beyond the reach of the law. HK thought it important to establish at the outset that there are elements of the tradition that are, so to speak, invisible, because they have so rarely given rise to litigation. Having made this point in its opening pages, he devotes the balance of the book to mapping contested terrain—areas where there has been ongoing controversy over whether or not speech is constitutionally protected. He first considers several "minor jurisdictions of censorship": contempt by publication, obscenity, libel. He groups these issues together in part to make a point about how *different* they are—no single analytic device, no single test or standard, is equal to such diversity. He then turns to the "major jurisdictions of censorship"—areas where the grievance against speech is that it is the cause of illegal action. There are two basic forms of the problem: speech that provokes others to disorder in retaliation against the speaker and speech that incites others to illegal action against a target selected by the speaker. The chapters on "reflexive disorder" deal with the former; those on "subversive advocacy" with the latter.

The discussion of the problem of subversive advocacy—that is, the issue posed by the advocacy of violence and lawlessness as political tactics—dominates Part One. HK characterizes this as "the core issue." Analytically, it goes to the heart of the First Amendment: the call to criminal action is typically part of a larger political critique; hence to set the boundaries of permissible advocacy is also to delineate the point beyond which political criticism may constitutionally be suppressed. Historically, this issue precipitated the birth of the legal tradition and has occasioned a series of cases, from World War I to the present, which provide rich materials for understanding the dynamics of dissent in a free society.

The architecture of this section explicitly dramatizes what HK is doing in the book as a whole. He "starts at the end of the story," with the Court's most recent statement of the constitutional boundaries of permissible advocacy, *Brandenburg v. Ohio* in 1969, a particularly opaque exercise in judicial statesmanship.[23] Then he returns to the earliest cases and embarks on a continuous account from the World War I period through the collapse of First Amendment protections during the 1950s to the efforts of the Court in recent decades to recover the ground surrendered by various anti-Communist decisions. When, in conclusion, he revisits *Brandenburg*, the opinion is resonant with meaning conferred by the narrative context he has created around it.

Part Two deals with freedom of association. The great majority of the cases covered arise out of the anti-Communist experience. The threat of domestic Communism, as perceived, posed a novel set of problems for American law. The concern had less to do with the content of Communist speech, though the issue was often framed that way, than with the threat of group action and attendant questions about the loyalty and reliability of individual members. HK traces the law's response to these perceived threats. He begins with the strategies by which the government has sought to impose sanctions directly on groups. Then he turns to the wide assortment of noncriminal sanctions imposed on individuals as members of groups. These take two basic forms: the denial of a privilege or benefit of some sort (e.g., a public job, a passport, a tax exemption, etc.); and official inquiry into the individual's political views and affiliations. In both instances the government typically argues that the regulation is not intended as a sanction but rather that the negative impact on speech and association is an unintended by-product of the pursuit of some other legitimate government objective. The overarching question for the law is whether, in view of the noncriminal nature of the sanction and the ambiguity of the state objective, the constitutional standards governing the use of criminal sanctions should apply.

It is striking that HK—his emphasis on the diversity of First Amendment issues notwithstanding—ended up writing a book so centrally concerned with freedom of association. His allocation of effort testifies to the importance these issues had for him and to his belief that we have not yet fully come to terms with them. The law—and the tradition—have found it easier to protect the isolated individual speaker than to protect the association of those who join together to achieve political ends. The latter has been harder to conceptualize; it has more sharply tested political tolerance; and it has posed issues at once basic and unresolved.

Much has happened in the years since HK's death. There have been changes in the composition of the Court and in the mood of the country; there have been marked changes in other areas of constitutional law. Yet the discussion of subversive advocacy and freedom of association that occupies the bulk of the book remains remarkably current. For whatever reasons, there has been surprisingly little Supreme Court activity bearing on this constellation of issues in recent years. Were HK writing today, his tone and distribution of emphasis would no doubt be different. Nonetheless this book, written more than a decade ago, remains an essentially up-to-date account of the body of precedent on advocacy and association that the present Court inherited and has as yet had little occasion to revise.

Although the issues that dominate the book have been dormant in recent years, the Court's First Amendment docket has remained full. In the "minor jurisdictions"—contempt by publication, obscenity, libel—there have been significant developments. We nonetheless felt it important to include these chapters. This is a personal essay: the effort of a singular mind to evoke the First Amendment tradition. Its overall design—HK's sense of the geography of the field—is an integral part of that effort. Moreover, the "minor jurisdictions" chapters introduce certain general themes that will resonate through the essay.

Centrally concerned with the 1950s and 1960s, written in the 1970s, and now published in the 1980s, this book interacts with its times in ways HK could not have anticipated. Death fixed his perspective. That limits the book but also gives it a special quality. At this distance in time it is perhaps easier to see the nature of his interaction with the cases, to see the surviving residue of the "disciplined passion" he brought to bear upon them, to see that in "documenting" the tradition he was also in a very real sense engaged in creating it.

Read today, his essay makes immediate questions about the relationship between law and tradition that only the future can answer. One cannot but be struck by an impression of disparity between the weight of the body of experience his intense retelling of the cases evokes and the fragility of the expressions that experience has found in law. Some of the achievements of judicial statesmanship he celebrates are vulnerable to being undone by the same means—the same rewriting and reorchestration of precedents—that were used to achieve them. There is nothing *in law* to prevent a Court that is so disposed from reviving the precedents they were designed to neutralize. Yet they do not exist in law alone; they also exist in the medium of tradition. Ironically, their vulnerability as precedent heightens one's awareness of the sturdiness of the tradition. It would be false to the spirit of this book to suggest that precedent does not matter. (HK: "We don't want victories that are too easy or doctrinaire, but we do want victories.") Yet it is also clear that the tradition does not reduce down to the precedents of the moment. Its authority resides elsewhere; its vitality issues from multiple sources. Changes in the law will not in themselves diminish its power to embolden citizens to speak their minds.

The judicial statesman works at the edge of a future he does not know. So does the writer. Reading HK's essay today, we know something of the future into which he spoke. In some respects the passage of time has undermined his words; in others it has conferred power upon them; and it has sharpened his questions about the relationship of law and tradition. Happily, it has also deepened the sense in which this book about tradition embodies tradition. That which survives is sustaining: the companionship of his lively, passionate, interested voice speaking to us, out of the past, in the present tense.

Jamie Kalven

PART ONE

THE REGULATION
OF CONTENT

Preface

The problem in running one's mind over the American tradition of freedom of speech is to find some point from which to begin the journey. The usual approach has been to start by evaluating the general principles announced by the Court and only then to look at the actual decision patterns. Although the law on freedom of speech is deeply interesting—perhaps the most interesting part of all law—precisely because it is so rich in philosophic resonance, I find it imprudent and uncongenial to begin on high ground. The Court has not fashioned a single, general theory which would explain all of its decisions; rather, it has floated different principles for different problems. It would therefore prove treacherous to plunge in at the level of principle. I would prefer to begin by examining the concrete pattern of problems the Supreme Court and the First Amendment have over time been asked to solve; and only then to consider the Court's general formulations.

If we are to begin with the concrete problems and not the general principles, we need a series of operational questions to put to the mass of decisions in order to gain a perspective on them. A first such question, a core question from which further inquiry can readily radiate is: When, if ever, may the content of speech be directly inhibited by the state? The key word here is "content." Surely that is the common sense of it; the basic objection to speech must reside in *what* is said.

Putting the question this way serves to underscore the require-

ment that the state *point to* what it is in the speech it objects to. In the
first great speech case in the American tradition, *Masses Publishing Co.
v. Patten*, [1] decided in 1917, Judge Hand of the District Court observed:

> The tradition of English-speaking freedom has depended in no small part
> upon the merely procedural requirement that the state point with exactness
> to just that conduct which violates the law. It is difficult and often impossible
> to meet the charge that one's general ethos is treasonable. . . .[2]

It is this precision that distinguishes a legal view of the matter from
a popular one. The popular view is that one disapproves of the whole
syndrome of a person's views without specification; the views come to
characterize the person—he is unreliable, not one of us, a freak, a
Red, a long hair, or, more recently, a "communist liberal." It is
against this popular model of a general objection to the syndrome of
the speaker's views that we set the model of a precise objection to the
content of particular messages considered one at a time.

As we shall see, American law in its pursuit of subversives has by
no means always been able to avoid shifting its concern from the
content of the speech to the character of the speaker. It is a revealing
test of the quality of a Supreme Court opinion on freedom of speech
to see whether or not the Court cites in detail or quotes the offensive
message. When it does not, we should be on guard.

Another advantage in taking the quest for forbidden content as
our starting point is that it makes it immediately apparent how close
the concept of freedom of speech may be to the concept of equal
protection of laws. Since the Equal Protection Clause has become so
dominant in contemporary thinking about constitutional matters, it
might prove helpful, at least rhetorically, to explore the possibility of
restating speech issues in equal protection terms. Today race and
religion have become "suspect" criteria for classification and presumptively violative of equal protection. Although the tradition has
not done so, it might well have considered classification of speech by
content to be equally suspect. From such a perspective, the key question would be: What is the difference between the content of the
messages we permit and the content of those we prohibit?[3]

It would be helpful to perceive at the outset how much speech
content we all agree is beyond the reach of censorship. There is both
in the law and in the society more consensus than there may at times
appear to be. Our first task in this section will be to document that

consensus, insofar as we can. Our second task, by far the more demanding one, will be to map the trouble zones where consensus has broken down or never been achieved—areas where there has been recurring challenge to the propriety of speech and hence recurring judicial experience.

1

The Consensus on Untouchable Content

American life has enjoyed a remarkably broad consensus on the kinds of messages the government should leave alone. Ironically, this consensus is difficult to document. The Supreme Court does not tend to get the easy cases. As a result, our sense of the free speech tradition may suffer from having paid too much attention to the incidence of litigation and hence to the actual pronouncements of the Court. Some of the strongest parts of the tradition have simply been taken for granted. Little precedent speaks directly to them, for they are rarely, if ever, challenged.

It is a paradox of modern life that speech, although highly prized, enjoys its great protection in part because it is so often of no concern to anyone. To an almost alarming degree, tolerance depends not on principle but on indifference. Why then are men ever sufficiently moved to want to limit speech? Talking at large, we can identify several general motivations: religion; patriotism in time of war; removing government policies and officials from aggressive, unfair criticism; elevating public taste; and avoiding stimuli to disruptive political action. On this rough map, we can quickly put several big points to rest.

Heresy and Blasphemy

First and most important, the freedom of speech clause of the First Amendment has been the beneficiary of the religion clauses. Throughout history, religion has played a dismal role as a source of motivations for censorship. If a community believes it is in possession of revealed truth and the salvation of man's soul is at stake, indifference will no longer protect and it becomes altogether rational to pay close attention to what people are allowed to say, especially publicly. From such a perspective, prohibitions of heresy and blasphemy make sense.

Perhaps we would all be happier in a society with more religion and less free speech. That is an issue I am not equipped to argue, except to note that the answer does not seem to me a foregone conclusion. Happily, we need not resolve it for present purposes. The American commitment to separation of Church and State has not only had benign consequences for freedom of religion, it has also made it impossible for the state to umpire religious controversies. Thus, a first great principle of the consensus emerges: *In America there is no heresy, no blasphemy.*

Cantwell v. Connecticut[1] in 1940 illustrates the tenor of the Court's approach. Cantwell, a Jehovah's Witness, accosted on the street two men who turned out to be Catholics. He asked and received permission to play a phonograph record which virulently attacked the Catholic Church. Incensed by the performance, the men were moved to strike Cantwell, but restrained themselves. Upon being told to leave—presumably in no uncertain terms—Cantwell did so. He was arrested and charged with soliciting without a license and inciting a breach of the peace. The Supreme Court invalidated his conviction on both counts. Although the precise legal issue has nothing to do with heresy, Justice Roberts's remarks are nevertheless relevant:

In the realm of religious faith, and in that of political belief, sharp differences arise. In both fields the tenets of one man may seem the rankest error to his neighbor. To persuade others to his own point of view, the pleader, as we know, at times, resorts to exaggeration, to vilification of men who have been, or are, prominent in church or state, and even to false statement. But the people of this nation have ordained in the light of history, that, in spite of the probability of excesses and abuses, these liberties are, in the long view, essential to enlightened opinion and right conduct on the part of the citizens of a democracy.[2]

More directly relevant is Justice Frankfurter's concurring opinion in *Burstyn v. Wilson*[3] in 1952, the case which established that movies come within the protection of the First Amendment. The controversy arose when New York denied a license to the Italian movie *The Miracle* on the ground that it was "sacrilegious." The Court unanimously reversed the action. Speaking through Justice Clark, the majority found that "sacrilege" was an impermissibly vague criterion by which to guide the discretion of the licensor. Moved to write a separate concurrence, Justice Frankfurter produced what is perhaps the most positive of his many opinions touching issues of freedom of speech.

The opinion is devoted to a careful study of the term "sacrilege." He finds that it has a narrow, technical meaning of physical damage to religious personnel or symbols and a loose general meaning of "insult to sacred things." The fatal flaw of the New York statute is that it has departed from the technical meaning and has set the censor adrift to deal with matters offensive to any of the religious sects in the United States. Drawing on history for illustrations, Frankfurter underscores the treacherous character of the expanded definition:

If "sacrilegious" bans more than the physical abuse of sacred persons, places, or things, if it permits censorship of religious opinions, which is the effect of the holding below, the term will include what may be found to be "blasphemous." England's experience with that treacherous word should give us pause, apart from our requirements for the separation of Church and State. The crime of blasphemy in Seventeenth Century England was the crime of dissenting from whatever was the current religious dogma. King James I's "Book of Sports" was first required reading in the churches; later all copies were consigned to the flames. To attack the mass was once blasphemous; to perform it became so. At different times during that century, with the shifts in the attitude of government towards particular religious views, persons who doubted the doctrine of the Trinity (*e.g.*, Unitarians, Universalists, etc.) or the divinity of Christ, observed the Sabbath on Saturday, denied the possibility of witchcraft, repudiated child baptism or urged methods of baptism other than sprinkling, were charged as blasphemers, or their books were burned or banned as blasphemous. Blasphemy was the chameleon phrase which meant the criticism of whatever the ruling authority of the moment established as orthodox religious doctrine.[4]

In sharp contrast to his personal tolerance, Justice Frankfurter was among the most cautious and restrained of all justices in intervening to protect speech. This extended discourse on "sacrilege" and "blasphemy" is impressive, because we sense that even for him this case touches a nerve of the free speech tradition. He says, in effect, that American society would have to be reconstituted, if we were to give "sacrilege" the broad meaning carelessly ascribed to it by the New York courts. Thus, although he speaks only for himself and Justice Jackson and the decision itself is placed on the neutral ground of vagueness, *Burstyn* is an important datum about the consensus that in America there can be no heresy or blasphemy.

For our purposes, the most interesting of the Court's encounters with the issue is *Epperson v. Arkansas*[5] in 1968, a case involving a slightly modified version of the "anti-evolution" law which had precipitated the celebrated *Scopes* case in 1927.[6] Although the "Monkey Trial" had been a major cultural event and is celebrated today as a victory for intellectual freedom, the law had been held unconstitutional only by ridicule and never by a court of law. In *Scopes* the Tennessee court had upheld the law, while upsetting the conviction on technical grounds, thereby mooting the controversy prior to review by the Supreme Court. Forty years later in *Epperson* the unanimous Court finally invalidated the statute which made it a misdemeanor for a teacher in a public school "to teach the theory or doctrine that mankind ascended or descended from a lower order of animals."

In an opinion by Justice Fortas, the Court both eschewed placing its ruling simply on vagueness grounds, as was suggested by Justices Black and Stewart, and avoided opening an awesome vista of judicial review of public school curricula. It did so by relying on the tradition that there is no heresy in American life. It read the statute as forbidding evolutionary doctrine only because it was thought to conflict with particular religious teachings. The state was guilty therefore of violating the Establishment Clause by giving preference to the truths of one religion over the truths of others. Justice Fortas was thus able to strike down the statute without suffering the embarrassment of arbitrating whether or not the theory of evolution is true.

Again, the issue touches a nerve of the American tradition. Justice Fortas writes:

> The antecedents of today's decision are many and unmistakable. They are rooted in the foundation soil of our Nation. They are fundamental to freedom.
>
> Government in our democracy, state and national, must be neutral in matters of religious theory, doctrine, and practice. It may not be hostile to any religion or to the advocacy of no-religion; and it may not aid, foster, or

promote one religion or religious theory against another or even against the militant opposite. The First Amendment mandates governmental neutrality between religion and religion, and between religion and nonreligion.

As early as 1872, this Court said: "The law knows no heresy, and is committed to the support of no dogma, the establishment of no sect". . . . [7]

The result in itself is not surprising. *Epperson* makes official and emphatic what we had, somewhat hazily, assumed was the rule all along. But such resort to the Establishment Clause has enormous implications for freedom of speech. It eliminates the possibility of state intervention keyed to objections of a religious origin, and that covers a lot of ground. Moreover, the manner in which the Court has handled this issue suggests an approach of even wider application. Conceivably, the religion clauses of the First Amendment might serve as a model for the speech and press clauses. The point would be that the state is not to umpire the truth or falsity of doctrine; it is to remain neutral. Under such an approach, the Court in speech controversies would be like the wife in Lincoln's anecdote who looks on while her husband fights a bear: "Go it, husband! Go it, bear!"

It will suffice for present purposes to look at one further case, *Torcaso v. Watkins*[8] in 1961. *Torcaso* makes explicit a point touched on by Justice Fortas in *Epperson:* The state is not only forbidden from preferring one religion to another; it is also forbidden from preferring religion to no-religion. Technically, the case involved not the advocacy of atheism but a challenge to the validity of an oath for public office which required a simple declaration of belief in God. The Court unanimously upset the requirement. Justice Black stated:

We repeat and again reaffirm that neither a State nor the Federal Government can constitutionally force a person "to profess a belief or disbelief in any religion." Neither can constitutionally pass laws or impose requirements which aid all religions as against non-believers. . . .[9]

Although the Court has no occasion to say so, presumably Torcaso, who could not be barred from office for refusing to assert belief in God, also could not be subjected to sanctions for asserting disbelief in God or advocating atheism.

Taken together, these decisions converge on a deeply held position and produce a major core of fully protected speech. Today this sort of tolerance may no longer excite or delight us, but a measure of perspective might be gained if we return for a moment to Mill's essay *On Liberty*. In arguing his defense of free speech, Mill imagines the hardest, most extreme case against which to test his argument:

. . . I choose, by preference, the cases which are least favorable to me—in which the argument against freedom of opinion, both on the score of truth and on that of utility, is considered the strongest. Let the opinions impugned be the belief in a God and in a future state, or any of the commonly received doctrines of morality. To fight the battle on such ground gives a great advantage to an unfair antagonist, since he will be sure to say (and many who have no desire to be unfair will say it internally), Are these the doctrines which you do not deem sufficiently certain to be taken under the protection of law? Is the belief in a God one of the opinions to feel sure of which you hold to be assuming infallibility?[10]

False Doctrine

The consensus regarding the immunity of religious doctrine and theory can today be said to extend to non-religious doctrine and theory as well. Once again we have to approach the matter obliquely, for apart from its brush with the theory of evolution in *Epperson,* the Court has never had occasion directly to confront an effort by the state to suppress a doctrine on the ground that it is false.

Considerable light has been thrown on this element of the consensus from an unlikely quarter—the controversy over the movie version of *Lady Chatterley's Lover, Kingsley Pictures v. Regents*[11] in 1959. Once again the administration of the New York licensing statute furnished the occasion for the insight. New York, in a somewhat obscure fashion, had denied the movie a license. Although there was an aura of obscenity about the film, the state did not place its ban flatly on that ground but rather invoked a statutory clause about "immorality." The Court unanimously reversed the action. The unanimity, however, ended with the decision; there were six different opinions as to just what the fatal flaw in the state's action was. Justice Clark repeated his point from *Burstyn* about vagueness; Justices Black and Douglas held that all prior licensing, regardless of the criterion, is bad; Justices Frankfurter and Harlan found the statute valid and confined their objection to this particular application. It is the opinion of the Court, written by Justice Stewart, and joined by Justices Brennan and Whittaker, which is of enduring interest.

Justice Stewart reads the court below as having found the movie "immoral" because the statute "requires the denial of a license to any motion picture which approvingly portrays an adulterous relationship, quite without reference to the manner of its portrayal."[12] Like Justice Frankfurter in *Burstyn* and Justice Fortas in *Epperson*, he perceives the issue as a great one transcending concerns with prior restraints, vagueness, or obscenity. It would be difficult to improve upon the clarity and gallantry with which he states the underlying principle:

> What New York has done, therefore, is to prevent the exhibition of a motion picture because that picture advocates an idea—that adultery under certain circumstances may be proper behavior. Yet the First Amendment's basic guarantee is of freedom to advocate ideas. The State, quite simply, has thus struck at the very heart of constitutionally protected liberty.
>
> It is contended that the State's action was justified because the motion picture attractively portrays a relationship which is contrary to the moral standards, the religious precepts, and the legal code of its citizenry. This argument misconceives what it is that the Constitution protects. Its guarantee is not confined to the expression of ideas that are conventional or shared by a majority. It protects advocacy of the opinion that adultery may sometimes be proper, no less than advocacy of socialism or the single tax. And in the realm of ideas it protects expression which is eloquent no less than that which is unconvincing.[13]

We will have occasion elsewhere to look at the tactics of the justices, but we cannot leave these cases without observing that constitutional principles would be more firmly perceived by the legal community, and the public generally, if the justices would be a little less clever and statesmanlike, and would agree to confront and decide important constitutional points which are fully upon them and on which there is no disagreement among them. Surely in *Burstyn* and in *Kingsley Pictures* they improvidently let pass opportunities to express their agreement with Justice Frankfurter on sacrilege and with Justice Stewart on thematic obscenity.

One final indication that the Court truly takes the principle for granted is afforded by *Street v. New York*[14] in 1969. Decided a few months after *Epperson*, *Street* involved the criminal conviction of a Negro who, upset by the news that civil rights leader James Meredith had been shot by a sniper in Mississippi, rushed out to a street corner in New York and burned his American flag. As he did so, he said to a small crowd that had gathered, "We don't need no damn flag," and then a moment later to a policeman, "If they let that happen to

Meredith, we don't need an American flag." In an impressive performance by Justice Harlan, the Court reversed the conviction out of concern that the jury might have been permitted to convict the defendant for what he said as distinct from the act of burning the flag.

This decision illustrates how treacherous it is to force members of the Court into liberal and conservative molds, at least where values of free speech are concerned. The vote was 5 to 4. Among the dissenters from Justice Harlan's view were Justices Black and Fortas and Chief Justice Warren.

Our interest here is in just one component of the intricate Harlan analysis. He is considering whether Street's remarks about the flag can be censored. He writes:

Appellant's words, taken alone, did not urge anyone to do anything unlawful. They amounted only to somewhat excited public advocacy of the idea that the United States should abandon, at least temporarily, one of its national symbols. It is clear that the Fourteenth Amendment prohibits the States from imposing criminal punishment for public advocacy of peaceful change in our institutions.[15]

Taste

Another major source of anxiety over what is communicated is the desire to elevate public taste and to eliminate the tawdry, the vulgar, the worthless. This is an appealing objective, indeed a seductive one. We all aspire to have our children appreciate excellence. We all wish that the society made better use of its communication resources, that the TV shows and movies, the books and magazines were of higher quality. The question is whether we are to make the state a literary critic. This is another point on which there is a consensus, although, setting obscenity to one side, there has been almost no direct judicial confrontation with the principle.[16]

Once again insight comes by an eccentric route. As in *Burstyn* and *Kingsley Pictures,* it is a quasi-obscenity case, *Hannegan v. Esquire*[17] in 1946, that triggers the statement of an important principle. One is tempted to generalize that obscenity cases pose a narrow and relatively uninteresting problem for the student of free speech, but near-obscenity cases bristle with basic insights.

The controversy was joined when the Postmaster General attempted to revoke the second class mailing permit of *Esquire* magazine. He contended that, although the magazine was not obscene, its quality was so low and it so flirted with obscenity that it was "morally improper" and hence failed to satisfy the statutory condition for second class mail, namely, that it be "published for the dissemination of information of a public character or devoted to literature, the sciences, arts or some special industry." Much as New York had expanded the meaning of "sacrilege" in *Burstyn,* the Postmaster read the statutory requirement regarding "literature" and the "arts" to mean *good* literature, *good* art. And here as there, the new meaning shook the foundations of the American speech tradition. A unanimous Supreme Court responded by striking it down.[18]

The Court did not place its ruling on constitutional grounds; rather, it decided that the statutory scheme properly construed did not delegate such authority to the Postmaster. In brief, the Postmaster was wrong because he had misread his authority under the statute. In theory the decision leaves open the question of what would have happened had he been right, but in reality the decision and the opinion of the Court by Justice Douglas supply another basic datum about the American consensus on untouchable content.

Justice Douglas uses the familiar and powerful logical tactic of arguing that the exercise of such authority over popular taste by a public official would be so contrary to American traditions as to make it unlikely that Congress had intended it. The statement of congressional intent, he writes, "would have to be far more explicit for us to assume that Congress made such a radical departure from our traditions." He continues:

Under our system of government there is an accommodation for the widest varieties of tastes and ideas. What is good literature, what has educational value, what is refined public information, what is good art, varies with individuals as it does from one generation to another. There doubtless would be a contrariety of views concerning Cervantes' Don Quixote, Shakespeare's Venus and Adonis, or Zola's Nana. But a requirement that literature or art conform to some norm prescribed by an official smacks of an ideology foreign to our system. The basic values implicit in the requirements of the [statutory condition for second class mail] can be served only by uncensored distribution of literature. From the multitude of competing offerings the public will pick and choose. What seems to one to be trash may have for others fleeting or even enduring values.[19]

Two years later this statement is echoed in *Winters v. New York,*[20] a case involving an effort to prohibit "massed stories of bloodshed and lust likely to incite to crimes of violence." In a sharply divided decision, the Court held the statute unconstitutional. Speaking through Justice Reed, the majority stated:

> We do not accede to appellee's suggestion that the constitutional protection for a free press applies only to the exposition of ideas. The line between the informing and the entertaining is too elusive for the protection of that basic right. Everyone is familiar with instances of propaganda through fiction. What is one man's amusement, teaches another's doctrine. Though we can see nothing of any possible value to society in these magazines, they are as much entitled to the protection of free speech as the best of literature. Cf. *Hannegan v. Esquire.* [21]

In 1971 this principle received a major endorsement in *Cohen v. California,* [22] a case which at first glance seems an unlikely source of insight. The defendant was convicted of disturbing the peace by wearing in the corridors of a courthouse building—but not, it should be noted, in the courtroom itself—a jacket on which the slogan "Fuck the Draft" was clearly visible. The Court reversed the conviction, deprived of unanimity by the dissents of Justices Black and Blackmun and Chief Justice Burger. Writing for the majority, Justice Harlan devoted his very considerable analytic powers to this nominally trivial and faintly embarrassing controversy. The opinion, one of his last, exemplifies the best of the judicial tradition as to the First Amendment.

Harlan begins his analysis by carefully establishing that, although conduct in a public place is involved, the issue is speech. "The conviction quite clearly rests upon the asserted offensiveness of the *words* Cohen used to convey his message to the public."[23] He then adds a sentence which underscores our thesis that the core question about freedom of speech in general is *content:* "The only 'conduct' which the State sought to punish is the fact of communication."[24]

He next concludes that the message itself as to "the inutility or immorality of the draft"[25] could not be subjected to sanctions by the government. It follows therefore that Cohen's conviction could be supported, if at all, "only as a valid regulation of the manner in which he exercised that freedom, not as a permissible prohibition of the substantive message it conveys."[26]

Not yet ready to put the case to rest, Justice Harlan continues to pare away unrelated issues. Cohen's speech does not involve obscenity, although the popular mind would be quick to assert that it did. With high judicial irony, Harlan concludes that Cohen's statement was not erotic: "It cannot plausibly be maintained that this vulgar allusion to the Selective Service System would conjure up such psychic stimulation in anyone likely to be confronted with Cohen's crudely defaced jacket."[27] Nor is the statement an instance of "fighting words" uttered face-to-face. Nor finally did it involve inflicting offense upon a captive audience: "Those in the Los Angeles courthouse could effectively avoid further bombardment of their sensibilities simply by averting their eyes."[28]

Harlan then turns to the precise issue before him. The question, he says, is whether the states, "acting as guardians of public morality," can punish public utterance of "this unseemly expletive in order to maintain what they regard as a suitable level of discourse within the body politic."[29] He answers this question with assurance. The trivial case before him has sent him back to first principles. The result is an important contribution to the anthology of worthy judicial utterances:

. . . The constitutional right of free expression is powerful medicine in a society as diverse and populous as ours. . . .

To many, the immediate consequence of this freedom may often appear to be only verbal tumult, discord, and even offensive utterance. These are, however, within established limits, in truth necessary side effects of the broader enduring values which the process of open debate permits us to achieve. That the air may at times seem filled with verbal cacophony is, in this sense, not a sign of weakness but of strength. We cannot lose sight of the fact that, in what otherwise might seem a trifling and annoying instance of individual distasteful abuse of a privilege, these fundamental societal values are truly implicated. . . .

Against this perception of the constitutional policies involved, we discern certain more particularized considerations that peculiarly call for reversal of this conviction. First, the principle contended for by the State seems inherently boundless. How is one to distinguish this from any other offensive word? Surely the State has no right to cleanse public debate to the point where it is grammatically palatable to the most squeamish among us. Yet no readily ascertainable general principle exists for stopping short of that result were we to affirm the judgment below. For, while the particular four-letter word being litigated here is perhaps more distasteful than most others of its genre, it is nevertheless often true that one man's vulgarity is another's lyric. Indeed, we think it is largely because governmental officials cannot make principled distinctions in this area that the Constitution leaves matters of taste and style so largely to the individual.[30]

Once again we are at the parameters of a deeply held consensus. The state is no more the arbiter of taste than it is the arbiter of religious truth. But before we conclude that there is an unqualified consensus against all state intervention on behalf of good taste, we must consider two points touched on by Justice Harlan's *Cohen* opinion, the special problems of "fighting words" and obscenity. In both instances the law permits regulation, and in both the Court has talked of "worthless" speech. To what extent, if any, does this concept of the *worthless* in speech qualify the consensus?

The story begins with another Jehovah's Witness case, *Chaplinsky v. New Hampshire*[31] in 1942. Although there was some dispute as to the precise facts, it appears that while Chaplinsky distributed his literature, a restless crowd gathered, and the City Marshall intervened. Chaplinsky was charged with a breach of peace for saying to the Marshall: "You are a God damned racketeer" and "a damned Fascist."

In a brief, effortless opinion by Justice Murphy, the Court unanimously upheld the conviction and announced the so-called "fighting words" doctrine, a judicial ratification of the well-known *bon mot* from Owen Wister's *The Virginian*, "When you call me that, smile!" Justice Murphy quoted the opinion of the New Hampshire Supreme Court, which put it this way:

The test is what men of common intelligence would understand would be words likely to cause an average addressee to fight. . . . The English language has a number of words and expressions which by general consent are "fighting words" when said without a disarming smile. . . . Such words, as ordinary men know, are likely to cause a fight. . . . The statute, as construed, does no more than prohibit the face-to-face words plainly likely to cause a breach of the peace by the addressee. . . .[32]

Today *Chaplinsky* strikes a quaint, almost nostalgic note. One wonders, alas, if there are any fighting words left. Our concern, however, is with Justice Murphy's rationale for thus limiting speech. He justifies the decision in language which goes well beyond the facts of the particular case:

There are certain well-defined and narrowly limited classes of speech, the prevention and punishment of which have never been thought to raise any Constitutional problem. These include the lewd and obscene, the profane, the libelous, and the insulting or "fighting" words—those which by their very utterance inflict injury or tend to incite an immediate breach of the peace. It has been well observed that such utterances are no essential part of any exposition of ideas, and are of such slight social value as a step to truth that any benefit that may be derived from them is clearly outweighed by the social interest in order and morality.[33]

If it is permissible for this purpose to consider that speech is "an essential part of any exposition of ideas," or has the requisite "social value," is it permissible for other purposes? The passage is unfortunate, and, as we shall see, it has haunted constitutional law in more than one later instance. It also testifies to how deep and plausible the desire to improve the quality of speech can be, for it was written by a justice who was famed, almost notorious, for his enthusiastic support of freedom of speech.

Apart from this broad dictum, however, the narrow "fighting words" holding does not have much impact on the consensus. It applies only to situations where the speaker is responsible for a face-to-face invitation to a fight. The overriding motivation for the state's intervention is not the desire to improve the level of public taste, or to cleanse public discourse, but to preserve order and prevent breaches of peace. Doubtless, Justice Murphy would have been appalled, had he been confronted with an effort to apply his general premise outside the context of an immediate threat to order. Finally, *Chaplinsky,* decided in 1942, can today be said to stand in the shadow of the Court's 1971 decision in *Cohen.*

A more complex problem is presented by the Court's reflections on obscenity. For the moment, our interest is not in obscenity as a technical speech problem but as an occasion for disclosure by the Court of its thinking about "worthlessness" as a predicate for regulation.

Starting with *Roth v. United States*[34] in 1957, the Court has developed a three-pronged test of the constitutionally obscene: pruriency, patency, and utterly without redeeming social importance. It is the third element of the test that concerns us here. In my view, the Court in *Roth* failed to perceive that obscenity deals not with ideas but with stimuli to the imagination, with imagery and fantasy. It therefore attempted to accommodate the regulation of the obscene with the non-regulation of ideas generally. Justice Brennan stated:

All ideas having even the slightest redeeming social importance—unorthodox ideas, controversial ideas, even ideas hateful to the prevailing climate of opinion—have the full protection of the guaranties, unless excludable because they encroach upon the limited area of more important interests. But implicit in the history of the First Amendment is the rejection of obscenity as utterly without redeeming social importance.[35]

The premise is that obscenity may be regulated not because it is dangerous but because it is worthless. If the worthless treatment of sex can be regulated, does it follow that the worthless treatment of any other subject can therefore be regulated? Or is the Court implicitly holding the engaging thesis that nothing can be so worthless as the worthless treatment of sex, that no other topic admits of comment which is utterly without social importance?

I would argue that here, as in *Chaplinsky,* the Court, happily, does not have the courage of its major premise. In view of the enormity and pressures of its task, it is understandable that the Court has not yet harmonized its many observations about free speech. It would be astonished, I suspect, by any effort to apply this premise to other forms of worthless speech. It sees obscenity as a special problem unlike other speech issues and has consistently ignored the warnings of Justices Black and Douglas that the regulation of obscenity is a first step toward the regulation of political speech. Sex is different.

Moreover, it should be recognized that the Court's recurrent emphasis on the criterion of "utterly without redeeming social importance" evidences not a preoccupation with ridding society of the worthless in speech but rather a shrewd tactic for limiting the regulation of the obscene. It is a pro-free speech tactic which has been used repeatedly as a basis for upsetting regulation. Thus, the special case of obscenity does not impeach the consensus about the role of government with respect to matters of taste. Rather, it provides evidence, of which there will be much more as we go along, that the Court is a political institution with its own strategies in a practical world.

Finally, there is strong evidence in the record that the Court will not readily permit the idea of obscenity to expand to the non-erotic. It said "no" to the effort to suppress the sexually-toned "sacrilege" in *Burstyn;* it said "no" to the effort to suppress thematic obscenity in *Kingsley Pictures;* it said "no" to the effort to suppress obscene violence in *Winters;* it said "no" to the effort to suppress the near-obscene from the mails in *Hannegan;* and, perhaps most important, it said "no" to the effort to suppress the non-erotic use of the classical language of obscenity in *Cohen.* One might even contend that the regulation of obscenity, partly because it is worthless, is an instance of that mysterious principle by which the exception proves the rule.

The Minor Jurisdictions
of Censorship

2

Contempt by Publication

The consensus on protected content is so broad and reassuring that one is tempted to ask: What else is there? What is left to regulate? The answer is: less than has popularly been thought, but still quite a bit. And it is of course in the areas at the frontiers of the consensus that the vital tensions in the tradition arise.

The American tradition is curiously skewed if laid against a philosophic tradition such as that suggested by Mill's essay *On Liberty*. It is skewed in the sense that the incidence of litigation and hence the expenditure of thought and effort by the justices have centered on problems the philosopher may well not have been aware existed. Or to put this another way, there has been over the years at the level of the Supreme Court a sort of Socratic dialogue going on between the Court and the society as to the meaning of freedom of speech. "Tell us, Socrates, what is freedom of speech?" As with Socrates, the dialogue appears to be eternally open-ended—a definitive, fully understood answer will never be reached and so the process must go on with another and yet another question being put. In terms of this metaphor, we can say that since the dialogue began a half-century ago, the pattern of questioning shows a curious strain; some questions are asked again and again with dogged persistence; others, arguably more important, are never raised.

In this section we will consider three speech problems: contempt by publication, obscenity, and libel. These disparate problems share two basic features. First, each represents a point on which the popular view has been that speech surely is subject to regulation. Second, the Supreme Court, while acknowledging in each instance a domain subject to regulation, has devoted its energies to rendering that domain as narrow as possible. In the end, what is striking about the Court's response is not the nominal concession to censorship but rather the dramatic protection of the bulk of such communications.

An appropriate point of departure for our inquiry is provided by the problem of contempt by publication. The cases in this area offer a chance to examine in detail the *content* of the messages at issue. They are the occasion for recurring debate over speech policy. And most important, they involve a countervalue everyone takes seriously—the right to a fair trial.

The precise legal issue presented by these cases is: To what extent may a court punish publication of comment about a matter *pending* in court? The rationale for the regulation of such speech is to prevent interference with the outcome of the judicial proceeding. These cases thus involve an apparent collision between two prized values: on one hand, freedom of speech; on the other, the need to preserve the independence and tranquility of the judicial mind while at work on its special task.

Generalization at this level, however, does not capture the flavor of the speech problem posed. The regulation of out-of-court comment has several distinctive features. First, its effect is to keep the communication from everyone in order to insulate a very narrow audience composed of the judge, jury, and witnesses.[1] Second, it involves a peculiar relationship between the speech and the evil. The outcome feared is not overt action but the special action of making a decision. Third, the legal sanction most often used to regulate out-of-court comment is the contempt citation. Given its summary nature and the fact that the offending conduct takes place outside the courtroom, this form of regulation is peculiarly subject to abuse.

Yet there are two powerful counter-considerations. First, the censorship is only temporary. It is an adaptation of *Robert's Rules of Order;* while the trial is pending, the publication is "out of order." Once the trial is over, comment on it enjoys the full protection afforded comment on other issues. Second, the adjudication of a case is the one type of public business on which public opinion is irrelevant; no one wants such matters decided by majority vote.

The Court has distinguished between the two types of communication which may arise while a matter is pending in court: disclosure

of evidence outside the record and general comment. The first, especially where a jury is involved, may tell the trier something we do not
want him to hear. The second, by expressing criticism or a view about
the merits, may influence the trier's judgment when we wish it to
remain independent.

Disclosure of Evidence

The disclosure of evidence outside the record occurs most often in
connection with highly publicized crimes and is sometimes referred
to as "trial by newspaper." In a series of cases, starting with *Irvin v.
Dowds*[2] in 1961, the Supreme Court has granted new trials because the
publicity attending the initial trial had in one way or another produced
a violation of due process. These cases pose an obvious question. If
the publicity was serious enough to warrant the conclusion that the
defendant's constitutional rights were impaired, must the Court find
that generating such publicity is an abuse of free speech which the law
can properly seek to inhibit? Justice Frankfurter, concurring in *Irvin*,
posed the issue in memorable form:

This Court has not yet decided that the fair administration of criminal justice
must be subordinated to another safeguard of our constitutional system—
freedom of the press, properly conceived. The Court has not yet decided
that, while convictions must be reversed and miscarriages of justice result
because the minds of the jurors or potential jurors were poisoned, the poi-
soner is constitutionally protected in plying his trade.[3]

Insight into the Court's stance is provided by *Sheppard v. Maxwell*,[4] a 1966 decision in which it reversed the conviction of a Cleve-
land doctor for the murder of his wife because of the "massive,
pervasive, and prejudicial publicity" which attended his trial. The
opinion of the Court is by Justice Clark. After recounting in great
detail the improprieties and excesses of the press, he turns to the
performance of the trial judge. He finds that the judge failed to exercise his powers to ensure a fair trial and enumerates a series of steps
he might have taken. These include controlling out-of-court statements by the parties, counsel, officials and witnesses; limiting the
intrusion of the press into the courtroom; insulating witnesses; granting continuances; sequestering the jury; and "warning" the press.
Clark concludes: "these procedures would have been sufficient to
guarantee Sheppard a fair trial and so [we] do not consider what

sanctions might be available against a recalcitrant press."[5] The tenor of the opinion thus suggests that the Court is determined to postpone as long as possible the confrontation with the press which Justice Frankfurter in *Irvin* seemed so eagerly to await.

Out-of-Court Comment

The other strand of the problem—out-of-court expression of opinion on a pending case—has been considered by the Court in a remarkable line of cases. An impressive block of precedent indicates that such commentary must be afforded protection quite analogous to that given criticism of public officials other than judges. The firmness of the Court's position, which has by no means been universally admired by commentators, has been underscored by the strong dissent from it repeatedly entered by Justice Frankfurter.

For our purposes, the most revealing and important of these cases is the first, *Bridges v. California*[6] in 1941. Two cases were consolidated for decision in *Bridges*. The first involved a *Los Angeles Times* editorial on the trial of two union members who had been convicted of assault on non-union truck drivers and awaited sentencing. The editorial opposed probation "for gorillas" and stated that the judge "will make a serious mistake if he grants probation. . . . This community needs the example of their assignment to the jute mill."

The second case arose out of a fierce jurisdictional dispute between the International Longshoremen's and Warehousemen's Union and the International Longshoremen's Association. Members of the local I.L.A. affiliate had obtained a court order enjoining the officers of the local from working on behalf of the I.L.W.U. While a motion for a new trial was pending, Harry Bridges, the president of the I.L.W.U., sent a wire of protest to the Secretary of Labor. The wire found its way into the press, apparently with Bridges's approval and cooperation. It stated that the I.L.W.U. had the overwhelming majority of union members, that "attempted enforcement of the . . . decision will tie up port of Los Angeles and involve entire Pacific Coast," and that the I.L.W.U. "does not intend to allow state courts to override the majority vote of members in choosing its officers and representatives and to override the National Labor Relations Board."

For these communications, the newspaper and the labor leader were cited for contempt of court. In a sharply divided decision, the Supreme Court reversed both convictions. Justice Black, writing his first opinion in a speech case, was the spokesman for the five-member majority; Justice Frankfurter wrote for the four dissenters. Their conflicting responses to the facts give bold definition to the underlying issue.

Justice Frankfurter reads the publications against the etiquette which has traditionally surrounded statements to a court and finds them to be serious breaches. His dissent begins:

Our whole history repels the view that it is an exercise of one of the civil liberties secured by the Bill of Rights for a leader of a large following or for a powerful metropolitan newspaper to attempt to overawe a judge in a matter immediately pending before him.[7]

While he acknowledges that the Constitution protects the right to comment on pending judicial proceedings, Frankfurter argues that the extent of such protection must be limited by the requirements of fair administration of justice: "Comment however forthright is one thing. Intimidation with respect to specific matters still in judicial suspense, quite another."[8] In his view, the editorial and the publication of the telegram were efforts at "intimidation" and were properly punished as contempt of court.

Justice Black and the majority, by contrast, focus primarily on the impact of the contempt judgments on freedom of speech. Black stresses that comment on a particular judicial proceeding may figure in the discussion of important public issues and hence punishment of the former may constrict the latter:

Since they punish utterances made during the pendency of a case, the judgments below therefore produce their restrictive results at the precise time when public interest in the matters discussed would naturally be at its height. Moreover, the ban is likely to fall not only at a crucial time but upon the most important topics of discussion. Here, for example, labor controversies were the topics of some of the publications. Experience shows that the more acute labor controversies are, the more likely it is that in some aspect they will get into court. It is therefore the controversies that command most interest that the decisions below would remove from the arena of public discussion.[9]

Black also notes that, although restrictions on out-of-court comment only apply while a case is pending and thus are "limited in time," it cannot be assumed that such moratoria on public discussion will be of brief duration: "the 'pendency' of a case is frequently a matter of months or even years rather than days or weeks."[10]

Although Black does not foreclose the possibility of regulating out-of-court comment, he does insist that, in view of the impact of such regulation on free speech, a stringent standard must be met before comment may be punished: the clear and present danger test. We will have much to say later in this book about the strange career of this celebrated test, but for the moment we need only note that it conditions regulation of speech on a showing of a clear and present danger of some evil the state has the power to prevent. In applying the test to the problem of contempt by publication, Black places particular emphasis on the requirement that the evil be serious:

. . . we are convinced that the judgments below result in a curtailment of expression that cannot be dismissed as insignificant. If they can be justified at all, it must be in terms of some serious substantive evil which they are designed to avert.[11]

What, he asks, are the evils involved in these cases? He discerns two possibilities: "disrespect for the judiciary" and "disorderly and unfair administration of justice." He dismisses the first of these possible evils out of hand:

The assumption that respect for the judiciary can be won by shielding judges from published criticism wrongly appraises the character of American public opinion. For it is a prized American privilege to speak one's mind, although not always with perfect good taste, on all public institutions. And an enforced silence, however limited, solely in the name of preserving the dignity of the bench, would probably engender resentment, suspicion, and contempt much more than it would enhance respect.[12]

Black thus strikes a theme to which we will return many times in the course of this book: In a free society government may not use legal sanctions to silence criticism of its policies and officials. And he makes clear that this principle applies with equal force to judges—even while litigation is pending before them—as to other public officials.

Black acknowledges that the second evil—"disorderly and unfair administration of justice"—is unquestionably serious enough to justify regulation. He thus concedes a jurisdiction to censorship: Publications which create a clear and present danger of disorderly or unfair administration of justice may be punished as contempt of court. But when he turns to the particular publications in question, he finds that neither falls within that jurisdiction.

With respect to the editorial, he emphasizes that the judge must already have known of the militant, anti-union stance of the paper:

Hence, this editorial, given the most intimidating construction it will bear, did no more than threaten future adverse criticism which was reasonably to be expected anyway in the event of a lenient disposition of the pending case. To regard it, therefore, as in itself of substantial influence upon the course of justice would be to impute to judges a lack of firmness, wisdom, or honor— which we cannot accept as a major premise.[13]

Black thus reads the editorial as he would read any other expression of political opinion; it is simply a strong assertion of preference, a sharp expression of criticism. It does not, in his view, cast a serious shadow over judicial independence.

The bite of the principle announced by the majority is even more apparent when measured against the second set of facts, those centering on the publication of the Bridges telegram. The telegram, it will be recalled, stated that there would be a strike, if the pending decision went against Bridges's union. Justice Frankfurter, writing for the dissenters, construed this as an overt effort to intimidate the judge and argued that the state had properly exercised its "power to protect its courts from being bludgeoned by serious threats while a decision is hanging in the judicial balance."[14] But Justice Black again finds that the comment falls short of the clear and present danger standard. He stresses that the contents of the wire were appropriate for its addressee, the Secretary of Labor, and that the judge must have realized that in so tense a labor situation there was the high risk of a strike, which, in any event, would not, in Black's view, have been illegal. The threat, if any, resided in the facts, not the telegram:

If [the judge] was not intimidated by the facts themselves, we do not believe that the most explicit statement of them could have sidetracked the course of justice. . . . If there was electricity in the atmosphere, it was generated by the facts; the charge added by the Bridges telegram can be dismissed as negligible.[15]

Justice Black's response to the facts gives precise meaning to the majority principle. If Bridges's telegram did not fall within the jurisdiction of the censor, then the protection afforded out-of-court comment is very generous indeed. *Bridges* thus makes clear the Court's intention to protect serious criticism of judicial action while it is pending and not to permit it to be alchemized into "intimidation."

The bite of the *Bridges* principle has held firm in a series of later applications. In *Pennekamp v. Florida*[16] in 1946 it was applied to protect newspaper editorials which criticized sharply and with some inaccuracies the handling of a series of criminal cases. This case, even more than *Bridges,* illustrates how treacherous a rule deferring to the special aura of the judicial office and leaving the judge with large discretion in preserving his independence from outside pressures can be. For, although some of the cases were still technically pending, the newspaper's criticisms were directed at judicial actions already taken. Thus the only possible interest served by punishment of the paper was protection of the reputation of the courts. The Supreme Court, speaking through Justice Reed, unanimously reversed the contempt conviction against the paper. Applying the clear and present danger test, Reed found that "the danger under this record to fair judicial administration has not the clearness and immediacy necessary to close the door of permissible public comment."[17] He also observed:

> In the borderline instances where it is difficult to say upon which side the alleged offense falls, we think the specific freedom of public comment should weigh heavily against a possible tendency to influence pending cases.[18]

Justice Frankfurter concurred in the decision on the ground that the cases were not really pending, but entered a lengthy opinion disputing the relevance of the clear and present danger test both in general and as applied to the problem of out-of-court publication.

The argument was continued with the same outcome in *Craig v. Harney*[19] in 1947. This case arose in a small Texas town over civil litigation concerning the leasehold rights to one "Playboy Cafe." The trial judge, brushing aside requests for argument, twice refused to accept a jury finding on behalf of one of the litigants, who was at the time serving in the armed forces. The event aroused considerable unrest because a serviceman's rights were at stake. The judge, who was a layman, used his summary contempt power to punish the town's one newspaper for an editorial published while a motion for a new trial was pending. Adhering to *Bridges,* the Court upset the conviction, with Justices Jackson and Frankfurter in dissent.

The editorial had been strongly worded. It described the judge's performance as "highhanded," "a tragedy," and "a travesty of justice." Justice Frankfurter, stressing the newspaper's dominance in the town and the emotion-laden issue of a serviceman's rights, saw the editorial as an effort to whip up popular opinion against the judge in order to secure reversal of his action. If this did not constitute a clear and present danger to the administration of justice, he argued, nothing ever would, and the formula was simply a cover for a "novel, iron constitutional doctrine."[20]

The majority, in an opinion by Justice Douglas, reaffirmed the basic point that serious criticism of judicial handling of pending matters will not readily be interpreted as threat and intimidation. Justice Douglas said of the editorial: "This was strong language, intemperate language, and, we assume, an unfair criticism." But he concluded that it fell short of the *Bridges* standard:

The vehemence of the language used is not alone the measure of the power to punish for contempt. The fires which it kindles must constitute an imminent, not merely a likely, threat to the administration of justice. The danger must not be remote or even probable; it must immediately imperil.[21]

The Warren Court's one major encounter with the issue—*Wood v. Georgia*[22] in 1962—introduced some variations on the familiar pattern. It involved a contempt conviction for comments aimed not at a judge but at members of a grand jury; and this time the speaker was a public official, not a newspaper or a private citizen. In the midst of a political campaign, a county judge had instructed the grand jury to investigate "the inane and inexplicable pattern of Negro bloc voting" in the county. The local sheriff, a candidate for re-election, issued a press release in which he sharply criticized the judge's action as "one of the most deplorable examples of race agitation to come out of middle Georgia in recent years" and expressed the hope that "the present Grand Jury will not let its high office be party to any political attempt to intimidate the Negro people in this community." He also sent an open letter to the grand jury in which he suggested that if voting fraud had been committed, the likely culprit was the local Democratic committee. Cited for contempt for these statements, he issued a third statement, in which he repeated his earlier criticisms and asserted that his defense would be that he spoke the truth. The contempt citation was then amended to include a third count, which charged that this statement obstructed the disposition of the earlier citation. The Supreme Court reversed in a 5 to 2 decision.

Justice Harlan, in a dissent joined by Justice Clark, argued that the special circumstances of the case justified punishment of Wood's statements. He stressed in particular the added danger of speech by a public official and the vulnerability to influence of the laymen who made up the grand jury. But Chief Justice Warren, writing for the majority, did not find either of these points persuasive. In his view, the fact that Wood was sheriff was irrelevant: "we do not believe this fact provides any basis for curtailing his right of speech."[23] And he insisted that Wood's comments were not rendered more dangerous by the fact that they were directed at a grand jury rather than a judge. He noted in passing that different standards might apply to comments directed at a petit jury: "we need not pause here to consider the variant factors that would be present in a case involving a petit jury."[24] But he emphasized that in this case the grand jury was engaged in a general investigation and hence the rights of individual litigants were not at stake.[25] Indeed, he found Wood's comments not only tolerable but consistent with the distinctive function of the grand jury:

When the grand jury is performing its investigatory function into a general problem area, without specific regard to indicting a particular individual, society's interest is best served by a thorough and extensive investigation, and a greater degree of disinterestedness and impartiality is assured by allowing free expression of contrary opinion.[26]

These cases thus bear out our initial observation. While the area of contempt by publication is technically an exception to the consensus on protected content, the Court has endeavored to keep that exception as narrow as possible. The principal device it uses to determine the boundaries of protection for out-of-court comment remains the clear and present danger test. This is ironic, for, as we shall see, the test has fallen out of use in other areas. Moreover, it seems ill-suited to analysis of this particular problem. Arguably, it has led the Court to conceptualize the issue awkwardly. Yet the Court's instinct has been sound. Despite the distraction of the test, it has located and embraced a fundamental principle: in America judges, no less than other public officials, must bear their full brunt of public criticism.

3

Obscenity

In the contempt by publication cases the grievance against speech was clear and powerful. Whatever their disagreements over the propriety of regulation in the particular case, none of the justices questioned the legitimacy of the state interest in preventing interference with the administration of justice. When we turn to the issue of obscenity, however, the state interests in regulation prove more elusive and questionable.

What are the evils which the regulation of obscenity seeks to prevent? One major concern, which we will address in the next chapter, is the impact of obscenity on children. Few contest the legitimacy of this concern. It does not, however, provide a rationale for general regulation, for the Court, as we shall see, has isolated the problem of the child audience; that is, it has permitted the regulation of materials sold directly to children, but has not allowed protection of the child audience to be used as a predicate for adult regulation.

If we put the problem of the child audience to one side, the possible evils of obscenity are at most four: (i) The material will move the audience to anti-social sexual action; (ii) the material will offend the sensibilities of many in the audience; (iii) the material will advocate or endorse improper doctrines of sexual behavior; and (iv) the material will inflame the imagination and excite, albeit privately, a sexual response from the body.

On analysis, these purported evils quickly reduce to a single one. The first, although still voiced by occasional politicians and "decency" lobbies, lacks scientific support. The second may pose a problem for captive audiences, but obscenity regulation has been largely aimed at willing, indeed all too willing, audiences. The third, thematic obscenity, falls within the consensus regarding false doctrine; unsound ideas about sex, like unsound ideas about anything else, present an evil which we agree not to use the law to reduce.

So we are left with the evil of exciting the sexual fantasies of adults. It may well be true that our imaginations are more vulnerable to fantasies about sex than to fantasies about anything else. In any event, there has long existed a genre of writing assiduously devoted to feeding this taste, often to the exclusion of any other objective. And there should be no dispute that some such material does in fact excite the sexual imagination. This dimension of the obscenity issue dates from an earlier day; it was stressed by such champions of regulation as Anthony Comstock. Presumably, the underlying concern, although contemporary lawmakers, unlike Comstock, have rarely been candid enough to say so, is with masturbation. The question is whether this state interest is sufficient, in the case of consenting adults, to justify the solemn intervention of the law.

This unlikely issue has proved uniquely stubborn and resistant. The Court has been handicapped by a treacherous political undertow: The justifications for obscenity regulation may be faint, but the political passions invested in the issue are fierce.[1] Moreover, of all the issues that come before the Court, obscenity is surely the one least suited to its style and competence and most unnerving of its self-respect. As Thurman Arnold pointed out some years ago in defending *Playboy* magazine before the Vermont Supreme Court:

The spectacle of a judge poring over the picture of some nude, trying to ascertain the extent to which she arouses prurient interests, and then attempting to write an opinion which explains the difference between that nude and some other nude has elements of low comedy. Justice is supposed to be a blind Goddess. The task of explaining why the words "sexual relations" are decent and some other word with the same meaning is indecent is not one for which judicial techniques are adapted.[2]

Indeed, the idea of regulating obscenity by law while permitting case by case challenges in the courts sometimes seems like an invention of the Devil designed to embarrass and unhinge the legal system.

The Constitutional Definition

It is one of the oddities of Supreme Court history that the Court was not forced to adjudicate the constitutionality of obscenity regulation until *Roth v. United States*[3] in 1957. When it finally addressed the question in *Roth* the Court affirmed the constitutionality of the federal obscenity statute and thereby acknowledged the assumption that had prevailed throughout our constitutional history: *Some* regulation of obscenity is permissible. But the Court also made the *definition* of obscenity a matter of constitutional law, and during the decade following *Roth* it endeavored to narrow the scope of the censor's jurisdiction by adding limiting conditions to that definition.

Prior to *Roth,* the Court had two noteworthy encounters with the issue. The first—*Doubleday v. New York*[4] in 1948—was rather ominous. The case involved a novel, *Memoirs of Hecate County,* by the distinguished literary critic Edmund Wilson. The New York Court of Appeals had held unanimously that the book was obscene, and the Supreme Court accepted the case for review. But expectations that the Court in deciding the case would determine the constitutionality of obscenity regulation were not realized. The Court divided 4 to 4, thereby affirming the conviction, and, following tradition in evenly divided decisions, there was no opinion.[5] The result was thus both unnerving and inconclusive.

The Court's next encounter with the issue—*Butler v. Michigan*[6] in 1957—was more reassuring. *Butler* involved a conviction under a statute which made it a crime to "publish materials tending to the corruption of the morals of youth." The Court read this statute as making it an offense to sell to the general public a book that might have a deleterious influence on the young. The case thus posed the question of whether, in order to prevent unsuitable materials from coming into the hands of the vulnerable, the state may prohibit them generally. The Court's answer was a loud, clear, and unanimous "no." Justice Frankfurter stated:

The State insists that, by thus quarantining the general reading public against books not too rugged for grown men and women in order to shield juvenile innocence, it is exercising its power to promote the general welfare. Surely, this is to burn the house to roast the pig. . . . The incidence of this enactment is to reduce the adult population of Michigan to reading only what is fit for children. It thereby arbitrarily curtails one of those liberties of the individual, now enshrined in the Due Process Clause of the Fourteenth Amendment, that history has attested as the indispensable conditions for the maintenance and progress of a free society.[7]

Thus, *Butler*, while leaving open the possibility of regulation aimed at the sale of materials directly to the young, firmly established the principle that protection of the vulnerable may not be used as a rationale for restricting the rest of the public. It thereby substantially narrowed the potential scope of obscenity regulation. And it served to sharpen the issue of the constitutionality of general obscenity statutes: If materials not specifically aimed at children were to be banned, it could only be because of their impact on adults.

When the Court reached the constitutional issue in *Roth*, a year later, it was confronted with a dilemma. The general impression at the time was that the measure of permissible regulation of speech was the clear and present danger test. To uphold regulation of the obscene, the Court appeared obligated to point to the substantive evil of which obscenity presented a clear and present danger. It thus seemed doomed to invoking the danger of stimulating the sexual fantasies of willing adults.

Speaking through Justice Brennan, the Court managed to finesse this dilemma. "The dispositive question," stated Brennan at the outset, "is whether obscenity is utterance within the area of protected speech."[8] Having thus framed the question, he proceeded to answer it with ease:

All ideas having even the slightest redeeming social importance—unorthodox ideas, controversial ideas, even ideas hateful to the prevailing climate of opinion—have the full protection of the guaranties, unless excludable because they encroach upon the limited area of more important interests. But implicit in the history of the First Amendment is the rejection of obscenity as utterly without redeeming social importance.[9]

Relying on *Chaplinsky*, [10] Brennan concluded that obscenity is "outside" the protection of the First Amendment and hence *per se* subject to reasonable regulation. He thus found it unnecessary to apply the clear and present danger test or any other distinctive First Amendment standard, and so was relieved of the close analysis of the rationales for regulation which ordinary First Amendment analysis would have required.

In addition to raising the clear and present danger point, the defendant had also challenged the statute on grounds of vagueness. But again Justice Brennan saw no constitutional difficulties. Although the terms of obscenity statutes are "not precise," he stated, the Court "has consistently held that lack of precision is not itself offensive to the requirements of due process."[11]

The effect of Justice Brennan's evasive manuever in *Roth* was to shift the focus of constitutional interest to the *definition* of obscenity. Everything now turned on the question of what speech fell within the category of "obscenity" and hence was "outside" the protection of the First Amendment. The definition that emerged from *Roth* replaced the traditional definition, articulated in 1868 in *Queen v. Hicklin,* the leading common law case.[12] Under the *Hicklin* test, the material was measured in terms of its impact on the vulnerable and excerpts could be considered standing alone. Justice Brennan rejected this approach as "unconstitutionally restrictive of the freedoms of speech and press," and replaced it with a definition keyed to an obscure English word, "prurient." The new test was: "whether to the average person, applying contemporary community standards, the dominant theme of the material taken as a whole appeals to prurient interest."[13]

This test was a major improvement over the *Hicklin* test in two respects: It focused on the "dominant theme" of the material as a whole rather than on particular passages considered in isolation; and it was keyed to "the average person" rather than to the vulnerable. But, despite these improvements, the Court's definition did not escape the logical difficulties and the vagueness which had characterized earlier efforts to define the obscene. It suffered from an awkward circularity in that a prurient interest might well be defined as an interest in the obscene. Moreover, the key term—"pruriency"—was highly subjective. The *Roth* test was thus potentially broad in scope and unpredictable in application.

Although the Court in subsequent cases was unable to cure the circularity and vagueness of its definition, it did manage substantially to narrow the jurisdiction of the censor by elaborating that definition. In *Manual Enterprises v. Day*[14] in 1962 the Court's strange vocabulary was enriched by the addition of another term—"patently offensive." The case involved the exclusion from the mails of a magazine catering to a homosexual audience and featuring photographs of nude males. In a notable instance of the employment of neutral principles, Justice Harlan, writing for the Court, found that the male nudes were no "more objectionable than many portrayals of the female nude that society tolerates."[15] He found them therefore not obscene, since whatever their specialized appeal to pruriency, they lacked "patent offensiveness."[16]

In the next major case—*Jacobellis v. Ohio*[17] in 1964—Justice Brennan made two further additions to the definition. First, he made it clear that "the contemporary community standards" by which obscenity was to be judged under the *Roth* test were *national*, not local, standards; otherwise, he said, "the constitutional limits of free expression in the Nation would vary with state lines."[18] Second, he stated that the rationale he had offered in *Roth* for excluding obscenity from First Amendment protection—that it was "utterly without social importance"—was also an element of the constitutional definition. It is worth noting that both patency and lack of social significance were, arguably, implicit in the original *Roth* formula. Thus, the Court, responding to the dialectic of subsequent cases, can be said to have developed its central idea, and in the process to have narrowed the scope of regulation.

Finally, in 1966 in the *Memoirs* case—known officially as *A Book Named "John Cleland's Memoirs of a Woman of Pleasure" v. Attorney General of Massachusetts*[19]—the Court, again speaking through Justice Brennan, orchestrated the disparate elements of the definition into a demanding three-part test:

. . . three elements must coalesce: it must be established that (a) the dominant theme of the material taken as a whole appeals to a prurient interest in sex; (b) the material is patently offensive because it affronts contemporary community standards relating to the description or representation of sexual matters; and (c) the material is utterly without redeeming social value.[20]

The terms of this test suggest a metaphysics of their own. It is possible apparently to have valuable, patently offensive pruriency. More important, it is possible to have all sorts of materials which are utterly without redeeming social importance or are patently offensive but which are nevertheless beyond the reach of the law because they do not deal with sex. The upshot is that in this area the Court tolerates criteria such as offensiveness and lack of significance which it would not tolerate for a moment as predicates for regulation in other areas. But because all three criteria must be met independently in order to satisfy the test, the concession to censorship is minimal and very little material is left within the reach of the law.

The bite of the test is illustrated by its application in *Memoirs*. At issue was an effort by Massachusetts to suppress John Cleland's *Fanny*

Hill. For two centuries this book had enjoyed a reputation as a classic in the underground literature of pornography. The distance between it and, say, *Lady Chatterley's Lover* was enormous. It had been written by Cleland in a deliberate effort to make money by exploiting the market for the obscene. Were the Court to protect this book, it would not simply be intervening to defend an item of serious literature from misguided censorship, it would rather be entering the customarily acknowledged domain of the obscene to pull out an item for protection. Yet despite its almost endless descriptions of sexual intercourse, *Fanny Hill* strikes a quaint note to the modern ear. Written in the graceful prose of the eighteenth century, it does not contain ostentatious vulgarity. Moreover, it conveys a rather enthusiastic view of sex as a truly pleasurable activity. For an urbane and sophisticated justice, it would be embarrassing to take it too seriously. In view of its reputation as a "dirty book," however, it would also be embarrassing to upset the censor's claims. The Court chose the second of these embarrassments. In a 6 to 3 decision, it protected the book.

The majority opinion by Justice Brennan is brief. The case had arisen under a Massachusetts procedure that permits the use of experts, and a number of literary scholars had testified. In an engaging footnote Justice Brennan summarizes their contributions: The book was a piece of "social history"; Cleland displayed a sense of "deliberate, calculated comedy"; the style was not without grace; the language served to create "a distance, even when sexual experiences are portrayed"; and students of eighteenth century English fiction could draw instructive comparisons among Cleland, Richardson, and Fielding in the handling of certain themes. At least one expert, however, stated that the book "is obscene, impure, hardcore pornography, and is patently offensive."[21]

In light of this data, the Massachusetts court had found the book obscene, stating: "the fact that the testimony may indicate this book has some minimal literary value does not mean that it is of any social importance." While treating it as not controverted that *Fanny Hill was* prurient and patently offensive, Justice Brennan found a constitutional impediment to banning the book in the trial judge's acknowledgement of minimal literary value. He could not have made the point more clearly:

A book cannot be proscribed unless it is found to be *utterly* without redeeming social value. This is so even though the book is found to possess the requisite prurient appeal and to be patently offensive. Each of the three federal constitutional criteria is to be applied independently; the social value of the book can neither be weighed against nor canceled by its prurient appeal or patent offensiveness. Hence, even on the view of the court below that *Memoirs* possessed only a modicum of social value, its judgment must be reversed as being founded on an erroneous interpretation of a federal constitutional standard.[22]

There is a sense in which this ringing declaration displays high diplomacy. The Court carefully avoided expressing its own opinion on the status of *Fanny Hill;* it is enough that the court below found it had a modicum of value. Nevertheless, the fact remains that the Court braved public displeasure to announce to the world that *Fanny Hill* was not obscene.

While the Court managed to save the book, it had less success in mustering a majority in support of the doctrine announced. Justice Brennan's opinion was joined only by Justice Fortas and Chief Justice Warren; and even the apparent consensus among these three masked points of disagreement. For Chief Justice Warren, though he did not write an opinion in *Memoirs,* had earlier expressed concern, dissenting in *Jacobellis,* about the burden the Court had imposed on itself by treating obscenity as a constitutional fact, thus placing itself under pressure to review an endless number of individual cases. He would have preferred to eschew *de novo* review in obscenity cases and to limit the Court's role to consideration of whether there was "sufficient evidence" in the record to support a finding of obscenity.

What does the diversity of opinion among the other members of the Court indicate? Three Justices—Stewart, Black, and Douglas—concur in the result, but do not subscribe to Justice Brennan's approach. Justice Stewart's objections go to the complexity of the tripartite formula. He would simplify matters by replacing "obscenity" with the term "hard-core pornography." He has been realistic and gallant enough to admit that, given the nature of the subject matter, such terms are extraordinarily difficult to define. As he put it in a memorable passage in *Jacobellis* to which he recurs in *Memoirs:*

. . . I imply no criticism of the Court, which . . . was faced with the task of trying to define what may be indefinable. I have reached the conclusion . . . that under the First and Fourteenth Amendments criminal laws in this area are constitutionally limited to hard-core pornography. I shall not today attempt further to describe the kinds of material I understand to be embraced within that shorthand description; and perhaps I could never succeed in intelligibly doing so. But I know it when I see it, and the motion picture involved in this case is not that.[23]

Justices Douglas and Black repeat the position they had maintained with steady integrity since *Roth: No* censorship keyed to obscenity is permissible under the First Amendment. In my view, their argument against regulation is not as persuasive as it might be, because they ignore the special appeal of obscenity to imagery rather than ideas and so continue to speak of "no power in government over *expression of ideas*"[24] and of "governmental censorship over *views.*"[25] But, be that as it may, their more liberal view, like that of Justice Stewart, assuredly reinforces the not-quite-so-liberal position articulated by Justice Brennan.[26]

When we turn to the three dissenters, there is, of course, sharp disagreement. Dismayed by the proliferation of judicial views on obscenity, Justice Harlan advances the views on federalism and the First Amendment which he had earlier expounded in *Roth.* He would distinguish between the power of the state and the power of the federal government to regulate obscenity. At the federal level, he would agree with Justice Stewart that the test is limited to hard-core pornography. But he would allow the states the latitude of reasonable regulation. Thus, in his view, it was not "unreasonable" for Massachusetts to label *Fanny Hill* obscene, since, as he pointedly notes, the majority has so cautiously abstained from giving *its own* appraisal of the book. In view of the fact that obscenity regulation, apart from the Post Office and Customs, is largely a state matter, the Harlan position would give a significantly different incidence to censorship of the obscene.

Justice White's dissent breaks with the scope of the formula put forward by Justice Brennan. He would not make "social importance" a third and independent variable in the constitutional definition; if there is both dominant prurient appeal and patent offensiveness, that is enough. He voices the commonsense objection that if the test is taken as literally as the Court takes it in *Memoirs,* the insertion of one or two historical facts will salvage an otherwise prurient work. But the essential problem with his alternative approach is that it would once again expose literature to censorship. There are classics which have prurient appeal and are offensive to many ears. Perhaps White would import such considerations into his weighing of pruriency, but the point of the principle applied in *Memoirs* is to place literature beyond *the risk* of censorship, while preserving some chance for the regulation of sheer commercial pornography.

Finally, there is the dissent of Justice Clark. He agrees with Justice White that social importance is not part of the constitutional definition of obscenity and pointedly traces the evolution of this notion in the opinions of Justice Brennan. The special flavor of his opinion, however, resides not in doctrinal argument but in his description of the book itself and his ironic dissection of the expert testimony.[27] Indeed, it is only with Clark's dissent that the full impact of the step taken in *Memoirs* is felt. His opinion is refreshing in its candor. In contrast to Justices Harlan and White, who carefully placed their dissents on doctrinal grounds and, like the majority, avoided personal response to the book, Clark lets us know with verve and wit exactly how *he* feels about *Fanny Hill:* "I have 'stomached' past cases for almost 10 years without much outcry. Though I am not known to be a purist—or a shrinking violet—this book is too much even for me."[28]

As if the complexity of the tripartite *Roth-Memoirs* test and the diversity of views among the justices were not enough, obscenity doctrine was further complicated by two decisions handed down on the same day as *Memoirs*—*Mishkin v. New York*[29] and *Ginzburg v. United States*.[30] Both of these cases prompted further elaborations of the test; and in both the Court—for the first time since *Roth*—affirmed the convictions. As in *Memoirs,* Justice Brennan wrote the prevailing opinions, but this time he had the support of a clear majority of the Court. Justices Clark, White, and Fortas and Chief Justice Warren subscribed to his opinions in both cases, and Justice Harlan concurred separately in *Mishkin.*

The materials at issue in *Mishkin* catered to a sadomasochistic audience; they did not have any impact, except perhaps revulsion, on the ordinary adult. The defendant argued that they did not fall within the constitutional definition of obscenity because they did not appeal to a prurient interest of "the average person" in sex. Not surprisingly, the Court rejected this argument. It held that the prurient appeal of the materials was to be judged by their impact on the audience at which they were so deliberately aimed and found them obscene. Presumably, this decision was not intended to limit the general public to what is proper for those with sadomasochistic tastes to read. The violence and cruelty of much general literature is fully protected whatever its impact on the vulnerable. Rather, the point is that when a genre of pornography is conspicuously tailored to the tastes of a special audience the law may take notice of that audience and seek to protect it.

The *Ginzburg* decision was more surprising and disturbing. The case involved an obscenity prosecution for distribution of the magazine *Eros*, a sophisticated, expensive venture in eroticism. It was not clear whether the material standing alone would have satisfied all three prongs of the test, but this time the prosecution had added evidence of the way in which the magazine had been promoted and marketed. The Court ruled that the material need not be judged standing alone but could be placed in the context of its advertising, and on that basis held it obscene. The result was to introduce a new concept into the field: "pandering." In effect, the principle was that if a defendant advertised his wares as obscene he would not be heard to deny his advertising. But even this is not quite the formula, for the Court held that evidence of pandering would only be relevant in what were, under the three-pronged test, "close cases."

The decision is troubling. Arguably, the defendant was denied due process. As the dissenters were quick to point out, the Court had, in effect, "rewritten" the federal obscenity statute with the result that Ginzburg's conviction was sustained on the basis of a theory different from the one on which he had been charged and tried. Moreover, from a First Amendment perspective, the Court's reasoning in *Ginzburg* appears to undercut *Memoirs* in that the censor might still reach material protected by the tripartite test by means of the pandering concept.

One can only wonder why the Court was so determined to punish Ginzburg, even at the cost of due process and First Amendment values. Perhaps a partial explanation resides in the political pressures under which it operates in this area. In light of its record since *Roth* of rejecting the claims of censorship and its contemporaneous decision to protect *Fanny Hill*, the Court may have felt the need to reassure advocates of regulation that it was still possible to secure a conviction for obscenity. If so, Ginzburg may unwittingly have presented himself as the ideal candidate for sacrifice. In a footnote the Court quotes from one of the advertisements it found relevant in reaching its decision:

Eros is a child of its times. . . . [It] is the result of recent court decisions that have realistically interpreted America's obscenity laws and that have given to this country a new breadth of freedom of expression. . . . EROS takes full advantage of this new freedom of expression. It is *the* magazine of sexual candor.[31]

In effect, Ginzburg declared a partnership with the Court in the selling of pornography. And the Court responded by emphatically dis-
solving that partnership.

Taken together, the three 1966 cases—*Memoirs, Mishkin,* and
Ginzburg—reflect the ambivalent and unsettled state of obscenity doctrine a decade after *Roth*. There is no question that the Court, by
elaborating the constitutional definition of obscenity, had managed
substantially to narrow the *Roth* concession to censorship. But the
resulting spiral of doctrine, coupled with the extreme lack of consensus among the justices, can hardly be said to have yielded clear and
stable rules in this area. As Justice Black, dissenting in *Ginzburg,* observed, "after the fourteen separate opinions handed down" in the
1966 trio of cases, "no person, not even the most learned judge much
less a layman, is capable of knowing in advance of ultimate decision
in his particular case by this Court whether certain material comes
within the area of 'obscenity.' "[32]

A New Beginning?

In the aftermath of the 1966 trilogy, the Court appeared to move by
degrees away from the *Roth-Memoirs* definitional approach. Instead, it
began to direct its attention toward the rationales for regulation, and
there were signs that a new and simpler approach was emerging—an
approach that would define the censor's domain in terms of the *purposes* of regulation. In view of the elusiveness of the evils of obscenity,
such scrutiny of the state interests in regulation promised to contract
further—and perhaps to eliminate altogether—the censor's jurisdiction over materials addressed to consenting adults.

The first hint of a change in direction was contained in *Redrup v.
New York*[33] in 1967, a *per curiam* reversal of several obscenity convictions. *Redrup* reflected the Court's lack of consensus—the brief opinion reported that four different views were advanced by the seven
justices who made up the majority—but it also suggested the possibility that a new approach might be emerging. The Court gave the
following reasons for reversing the convictions:

In none of the cases was there a claim that the statute in question reflected
a specific and limited state concern for juveniles. . . . In none was there any
suggestion of an assault upon individual privacy by publication in a manner
so obtrusive as to make it impossible for an unwilling audience to avoid

exposure to it. And in none was there evidence of the sort of "pandering" which the Court found significant in *Ginzburg v. United States.*[34]

The Court does not talk here of obscenity being *per se* outside the protection of the First Amendment; nor does it say that the materials at issue fail to satisfy the tripartite *Memoirs* test. Rather, it specifies three state interests that justify regulation—the protection of children, the protection of the captive audience, and the prevention of pandering. Apparently, a majority of the justices, whatever their other points of disagreement, agreed as to the legitimacy of these state interests. The terse *per curiam* opinion thus raised two related questions. Were these the *only* state interests that justified regulation? If not, what was the justification for regulation aimed at consenting adults?

Two years later in *Stanley v. Georgia*[35] these questions were sharply posed by a novel fact situation. In the course of an investigation of the defendant's alleged bookmaking activities, police officers, acting under the authority of a search warrant, searched his home. Although the search yielded little evidence of illegal gambling, it did turn up several reels of film. After viewing the films, the police concluded they were obscene, seized them, and charged Stanley with violation of the state obscenity law. It was stipulated by the parties that the films fell within the *Roth-Memoirs* definition of obscenity. The case thus boldly presented the question of whether the mere possession of obscene material in one's home could be made a crime.

In a unanimous decision the Court reversed Stanley's conviction. Justices Stewart, Brennan, and White saw no need to engage the First Amendment question; in an opinion by Stewart they concurred on the ground that the seizure of the films violated the Fourth Amendment. But the other members of the Court rested their decision squarely on the First Amendment. The opinion of the Court was written by Justice Marshall, who had replaced Justice Clark in 1967, and it was joined by Chief Justice Warren and Justices Harlan, Fortas, and Douglas. Justice Black, concurring separately, reiterated his view that all obscenity regulation is unconstitutional.

Georgia, relying on *Roth,* had argued that since obscenity was not within the protection of the First Amendment, the state was free to deal with it, subject to the limits of other constitutional provisions, in any way it deemed necessary, just as it might deal "with other things thought to be detrimental to the welfare" of its citizens. Justice Mar-

shall meets this argument by distinguishing *Roth* on the ground that
it dealt with the "regulation of commercial distribution of obscene
material," not possession. He emphasizes that the regulation of mere
possession challenges fundamental values:

It is now well established that the Constitution protects the right to receive
information and ideas. . . . This right to receive information and ideas,
regardless of their social worth, is fundamental to our free society. Moreover,
in the context of this case—a prosecution for mere possession of printed or
filmed matter in the privacy of a person's own home—that right takes on an
added dimension. For also fundamental is the right to be free, except in very
limited circumstances, from unwanted governmental intrusions into one's
privacy. . . . If the First Amendment means anything, it means that a State
has no business telling a man, sitting alone in his own house, what books he
may read or what films he may watch. Our whole constitutional heritage
rebels at the thought of giving government the power to control men's
minds.[36]

Marshall then goes on to appraise, more directly than the Court
has ever done before, the rationales for regulation advanced by the
state. He sharply dismisses the state's argument that it has an interest
in protecting "the individual's mind from the effects of obscenity" as
"wholly inconsistent with the philosophy of the First Amendment."[37]
Nor does he find the asserted state interest in regulating possession
as an aid to the regulation of distribution any more persuasive; such
an interest, he argues, is insufficient to justify "infringement of the
individual's right to read or observe what he pleases."[38] Finally, he
rejects the argument that "exposure to obscene materials may lead to
deviant sexual behavior or crimes of a sexual nature" on the grounds
that it lacks empirical support and that, in any event, quoting Brandeis, "among free men, the deterrents ordinarily to be applied to
prevent crime are education and punishment for violations of the
law."[39] Marshall acknowledges that *Roth* "rejected the necessity of
proving that exposure to obscene material would create a clear and
present danger of antisocial conduct," but he emphasizes again that
Roth "dealt with public distribution of obscene materials and such
distribution is subject to different objections."[40] Echoing *Redrup*, he
adds: "For example, there is always the danger that obscene material
might fall into the hands of children or that it might intrude upon the
sensibilities or privacy of the general public. No such dangers are
present in this case."[41]

Despite Justice Marshall's insistence that *Roth* was "not impaired" by the *Stanley* decision, his opinion seemed to sabotage the *Roth* premise that obscenity is *per se* outside the protection of the First Amendment. Moreover, it seemed that, if the Court did not abandon *Roth*, it would be left in the logical difficulty of asserting that a citizen has an inalienable right to possess obscenity in his library, but that no one has a right to supply him with it. Thus, the expectation was that the logic of *Stanley* must inevitably extend beyond the possession to the distribution of obscene materials.

The moment of truth came in 1971 in *United States v. Reidel*,[42] a case which posed the question of whether the federal mail obscenity statute was unconstitutional insofar as it applied to the distribution of obscene materials to willing adults. The court below had held that it was. Relying on *Stanley*, it had reasoned that "if a person has the right to receive and possess" obscene material, "then someone must have a right to deliver it to him." In an opinion by Justice White, the majority rejected this interpretation of *Stanley* and reaffirmed its allegiance to *Roth*. Justice White stated:

The District Court gave *Stanley* too wide a sweep. To extrapolate from Stanley's right to have and peruse obscene material in the privacy of his own home a First Amendment right in *Reidel* to sell it to him would effectively scuttle *Roth*, the precise result that the *Stanley* opinion abjured. . . . *Roth* has squarely placed obscenity and its distribution outside the reach of the First Amendment and they remain there today. *Stanley* did not overrule *Roth* and we decline to do so now.[43]

Justice Marshall, the author of *Stanley*, took issue with the Court's interpretation of his opinion. The assessment of state interests in *Stanley*, he argued, applied to distribution as well as possession. True, the *Stanley* Court had not overruled *Roth*, but it had declined to do so because of "the validity of regulatory action taken to protect children and unwilling adults,"[44] not because the state had a legitimate interest in regulating the distribution of obscenity to consenting adults. Nevertheless, Marshall concurred in the result on the limited ground that, in the absence of more stringent controls than were present in this case, distribution of obscene material through the mails "poses the danger that obscenity will be sent to children."[45]

Reidel was decided during a transitional period between the Warren and the Burger Courts. In 1969 the Chief Justiceship had passed from Warren to Burger, and Justice Fortas had been replaced by Justice Blackmun. But these personnel changes do not explain the decision, for in addition to the new Chief Justice and Justice Black

mun, Justices Harlan, Stewart, and Brennan also joined Justice
White's opinion. Only Justices Black and Douglas dissented. Thus, by
the end of the Warren Court era, after fifteen years of experience with
the problem of obscenity, the Court had been carried by the dialectic
momentum of its decisions to the threshold of the conclusion that the
First Amendment does not permit the regulation of obscenity for
consenting adults. But it was not quite ready to take the final step
across that threshold.

The Burger Court Revisions

The gradual, tentative movement of the Court toward deregulation
of obscenity was abruptly halted by a group of decisions handed down
in 1973. In large part, this reversal of the liberalizing trend was due
to changes in personnel. During the years since *Stanley* Burger had
replaced Warren, Blackmun had replaced Fortas, Powell had replaced
Black, and Rehnquist had replaced Harlan. In 1973 these new members of the Court joined with Justice White—one of the *Memoirs* dissenters—to form a new majority which undertook, in the Chief
Justice's words, to make a "re-examination" of obscenity doctrine and
to "formulate standards more concrete than those in the past."[46]

The change in direction was announced in two decisions handed
down on the same day—*Paris Theatre I v. Slaton*[47] and *Miller v. California.* [48] The majority opinions in these cases, both of which were written by the Chief Justice, can be read as a single, unified statement. The
Paris Theatre opinion is largely devoted to a discussion of the rationales for obscenity regulation; the *Miller* opinion announces the
new test. Taken together, they effect a retreat from the frontier established by *Stanley* and a return to a definitional approach similar to but
looser than the *Memoirs* approach.

The basic strategy of the new majority is to revive the *Roth* premise that obscenity is *per se* outside the protection of the First Amendment. The Chief Justice declares: "This much has been categorically
settled by the Court, that obscene material is unprotected by the First
Amendment."[49] He is equally firm in rejecting the argument, based
on *Stanley,* that the state lacks a legitimate interest in regulating obscenity for consenting adults:

. . . we hold that there are legitimate state interests at stake in stemming the
tide of commercialized obscenity, even assuming it is feasible to enforce
effective safeguards against exposure to juveniles and passersby.[50]

Burger specifies two sorts of "legitimate state interests." He resuscitates the proposition that there is a relationship between exposure to pornography and anti-social behavior: "there is at least an arguable correlation between obscene material and crime."[51] And he advances a second, more diffuse rationale: "the interest of the public in the quality of life and the total community environment."[52]

In *Stanley* the Court had appraised similar state interests and had found them insufficient to justify censorship. Although it had not openly disavowed *Roth,* the *Stanley* Court had subjected the asserted state interests to precisely the sort of stringent First Amendment scrutiny that the logic of *Roth* had been designed to avoid. But Chief Justice Burger, having revived *Roth,* sees no need to engage in a similar analysis. Because obscenity *per se* is outside the protection of the First Amendment, it is enough that the state have a rational basis for concluding that regulation would serve the ends of maintaining "the public safety" and "the quality of life":

The sum of experience, including that of the past two decades, affords an ample basis for legislatures to conclude that a sensitive, key relationship of human existence, central to family life, community welfare, and the development of human personality, can be debased and distorted by crass commercial exploitation of sex. Nothing in the Constitution prohibits a State from reaching such a conclusion and acting on it legislatively simply because there is no conclusive evidence or empirical data.[53]

Before announcing the new test, Burger reviews the Court's earlier efforts. He regards *Memoirs* as a critical juncture in the development of the law; it is, as he sees it, the point at which "the Court veered sharply away from the *Roth* concept."[54] He is especially critical of the "utterly without redeeming social value" component of the *Memoirs* test: "even as they repeated the words of *Roth,* the *Memoirs* plurality produced a drastically altered test."[55] In view of these comments and the tone of the opinion as a whole, one would expect the new test to differ markedly from the tripartite *Memoirs* test. In fact, it proves quite similar:

. . . we now confine the permissible scope of such regulation to works which depict or describe sexual conduct. That conduct must be specifically defined by the applicable state law, as written or authoritatively construed. . . . The basic guidelines for the trier of fact must be: (a) whether "the average person, applying contemporary community standards" would find that the work, taken as a whole, appeals to the prurient interest; (b) whether the work depicts or describes, in a patently offensive way, sexual conduct specifically defined by the applicable state law; and (c) whether the work, taken as a whole, lacks serious literary, artistic, political, or scientific value.[56]

This test differs from the *Memoirs* test in three major respects, each of which is likely to generate future problems for the new majority:

(i) The pruriency and patency wings of the test—though, significantly, not the "social value" wing—are to be judged by local rather than national standards. This aspect of the new test is likely to give rise to formidable problems of administration, for in a society so pervaded by mass communications it will be difficult to isolate the local community.

(ii) In an apparent effort to cure the chronic vagueness of obscenity regulations, the Court has added the requirement that regulation be limited to descriptions and depictions of "sexual conduct specifically defined by the applicable state law." This requirement, which may have the paradoxical effect of invalidating much obscenity legislation, will not solve the vagueness dilemma, however, for it will still be necessary to distinguish between permissible and impermissible representations of explicit sexual conduct by means of the pruriency, patency, and social value wings of the test.

(iii) The most notable change in the test is the substitution of "lacks serious literary, artistic, political, or scientific value" for "utterly without redeeming social value." This dilution of the third component of the test appears to broaden the scope of permissible regulation. It is of course unlikely that *Ulysses* will again be banned, but there *is* a danger under the new test that a second-rate *Ulysses* which the Court does not regard as sufficiently "serious" will be.

In view of the new majority's determination to make a change and its criticism of the *Memoirs* approach, the most striking thing about the new test is that it is so similar to what has come before. Moreover, it is significant that the Court did not take one of the more extreme alternative approaches which had been advanced in earlier cases. The roads not taken include Justice Harlan's approach, which would have given a greater degree of latitude to regulation by the states; Chief Justice Warren's suggestion that the Court forego *de novo* review in obscenity cases; and the revision of the *Memoirs* test advocated by Justice White, which would have deleted the social value wing altogether. The fact that the Court eschewed these alternative approaches suggests that at least one member of the majority balked when presented with each alternative.

The emergence of a new majority favoring vigorous enforcement of obscenity regulations was not the only development in the 1973 cases. Of equal—if not greater—significance was the coalescing of a solid four-member minority unified behind the position that regulation aimed at consenting adults is unconstitutional. This dissenting bloc was composed of Justices Douglas, Stewart, Marshall, and Brennan. Justice Douglas wrote a separate dissent reiterating his view that *all* regulation of obscenity—even that keyed to the child audience—is unconstitutional. The other dissenters joined in an opinion which argued that regulation is unconstitutional in the absence of child audience or captive audience considerations. Appropriately, the author of that opinion was Justice Brennan, the chief architect of the *Roth-Memoirs* approach.

Brennan's dissent can be read as the epilogue to the Warren Court's efforts in the field of obscenity and, as the final stage in the evolution of his own thinking about the issue, an evolution which began with *Roth* sixteen years earlier. He begins by observing:

No other aspect of the First Amendment has, in recent years, demanded so substantial a commitment of our time, generated such disharmony of views, and remained so resistant to the formulation of stable and manageable standards. I am convinced that the approach initiated 16 years ago in *Roth v. United States,* and culminating in the Court's decision today, cannot bring stability to this area of the law without jeopardizing fundamental First Amendment values, and I have concluded that the time has come to make a significant departure from that approach.[57]

The majority's approach, argues Brennan, does not represent such a "significant departure." For the most part, the majority has simply followed the *Roth-Memoirs* approach, and insofar as the new test departs from that approach, it is a step backwards. He is particularly critical of the dilution of the social value component of the test:

. . . the definition of "obscenity" as expression utterly lacking in social importance is the key to the conceptual basis of *Roth* and our subsequent opinions. In *Roth* we held that certain expression is obscene, and thus outside the First Amendment, precisely *because* it lacks even the slightest redeeming social value. . . . The Court's approach necessarily assumes that some works will be deemed obscene—even though they clearly have *some* social value— because the State was able to prove that the value, measured by some unspecified standard, was not sufficiently "serious" to warrant constitutional protection. That result is not merely inconsistent with our holding in *Roth;* it is nothing less than a rejection of the fundamental First Amendment premises and rationale of the *Roth* opinion and an invitation to wide-spread suppression of sexually oriented speech. Before today, the protections of the First Amendment have never been thought limited to expression of *serious* literary or political value.[58]

Brennan's dissent is not limited to the approach initiated in *Miller* and *Paris Theatre.* Even if the *Roth-Memoirs* approach had been preserved intact, he would, he says, "nevertheless be compelled to reject it."[59] His rejection of the approach he devoted so much energy to designing does not represent a repudiation of the view he expressed in *Roth* that there is such a thing as unprotected obscenity. Rather, it reflects his conclusion, based on long experience with the issue, that there is no way to regulate obscenity for consenting adults without offending the First Amendment.

The basic dilemma, as Brennan sees it, is that obscenity statutes are inevitably either overbroad or vague. On one hand, the Court might draw a clear, bold line between protected and unprotected speech; for example, it might hold that "any depiction or description of human sexual organs, irrespective of the manner or purpose of the portrayal, is outside the protection of the First Amendment."[60] Such an easily understood line would certainly solve the vagueness problem, but only at the cost of "permitting the suppression of a vast range of literary, scientific, and artistic masterpieces."[61] On the other hand, the Court might seek to fashion more "sensitive tools" for distinguishing between protected and unprotected speech. This is what the Court has in fact elected to do, but experience has shown that, while this approach avoids the overbreadth problem, it requires the use of highly subjective terms, such as "prurient interest," "patent offensiveness," and "social value." The Court's rules are thus infected with an intolerable degree of vagueness. Moreover, because the unavoidable vagueness of constitutional obscenity standards necessitates *de novo* review in every case, it imposes severe "institutional stress" on the judicial machinery of the nation, including the Supreme Court.[62]

In light of these "inevitable side effects of state efforts to suppress what is assumed to be *unprotected* speech," Brennan argues, regulation can only be justified if the state can show "some very substantial interest in suppressing such speech."[63] He is thus brought back to the question of the rationales underlying regulation, the question he had sidestepped sixteen years earlier in *Roth*. After quoting extensively and with approval from Justice Marshall's appraisal of the state interests asserted in *Stanley*, he concludes:

In short, while I cannot say that the interests of the State—apart from the question of juveniles and unconsenting adults—are trivial or nonexistent, I am compelled to conclude that these interests cannot justify the substantial damage to constitutional rights and to this Nation's judicial machinery that inevitably results from state efforts to bar the distribution of even unprotected materials to consenting adults. I would hold, therefore, that at least in the absence of distribution to juveniles or obtrusive exposure to unconsenting adults, the First and Fourteenth Amendments prohibit the State and Federal Governments from attempting wholly to suppress sexually oriented materials on the basis of their allegedly "obscene" contents.[64]

For the moment, the hard-won clarity of Justice Brennan's view is confined to dissent. This should not, however, be allowed to obscure the central fact that over time the Court has dramatically narrowed the jurisdiction of the censor in this volatile area. It is worth recalling that twenty-five years ago an evenly divided Court permitted the censorship of a novel by Edmund Wilson. Today the Court is still divided, but the debate is over the precise scope of permissible regulation of commercialized hard-core pornography. If we must end this chapter on a small note of disappointment, it is because a bare majority of five justices continues to resist the conclusion that even the narrowest concession to censorship cannot be justified in the case of consenting adults, in view of the cost of regulation and the absence of any compelling state interest in policing the sexual fantasies of adults.

4

The Child Audience

One of the issues touched on in the preceding chapter deserves more extended treatment—the problem of obscenity and the child. As we have seen, there is almost universal agreement that the state has a legitimate interest in insulating children from exposure to pornography. With the exceptions of Justices Black and Douglas, even those members of the Court who have argued that regulation aimed at consenting adults is unconstitutional have endorsed regulation of material sold directly to children. Yet such regulation is in its way no less problematic than regulation for adults.

The protection of children as a vulnerable audience in the field of obscenity rests on the premise that freedom of speech necessarily presupposes some degree of maturity, intelligence, and discipline on the part of the audience; and further, that state intervention is appropriate in situations where the audience is likely to lack those qualifications. John Stuart Mill gives expression to this premise in his essay *On Liberty*. Speaking not only of free speech but of liberty in general, he writes:

It is, perhaps, hardly necessary to say that this doctrine is meant to apply only to human beings in the maturity of their faculties. We are not speaking of children or of young persons below the age which the law may fix as that of manhood or womanhood. Those who are still in a state to require being taken care of by others must be protected against their own actions as well as against external injury. For the same reason we may leave out of consideration those backward states of society in which the race itself may be considered as in its nonage. . . . Despotism is a legitimate mode of government in dealing with barbarians, provided the end be their improvement and the means justified by actually effecting that end. Liberty, as a principle, has no application to any state of things anterior to the time when mankind have become capable of being improved by free and equal discussion. Until then, there is nothing for them but implicit obedience to an Akbar or a Charlemagne, if they are so fortunate as to find one.[1]

As this quote illustrates, the vulnerable audience concept is at once plausible and treacherous. It appeals to common sense. Yet its potential scope is alarmingly broad. Carried to an extreme, it can provide an argument against free speech on the ground that the general public is simply not ready for it. We would do well to remember that the American tradition had its first dismal experience with the concept during the period of slavery, when it was so fiercely held that it was impermissible to teach a slave to read.

In the context of obscenity, concern over the vulnerability of the child audience generates two distinct issues. First, may materials be prohibited generally in order to prevent them from coming into the hands of children? Second, may communications directly to the child audience be prohibited, and, if so, what are the limits? What, in other words, are the First Amendment rights of the child?

As we have seen, the Court answered the first of these questions with admirable firmness in *Butler v. Michigan*[2] in 1956 when it held that protection of the vulnerable may *not* be used as a predicate for restricting the rest of the population. Although the *Butler* Court did not directly address the second question, the implication was present in its opinion that the state could prohibit sales aimed directly at children. In 1968 implication became fact in *Ginsberg v. New York*,[3] a 6 to 3 decision which authoritatively established what had long been suspected: The First Amendment rights of children are different and, in a sense, less than those of adults.

Ginsberg was convicted (and given a suspended sentence) for selling two girlie magazines to a minor, a sixteen-year-old boy. The statute under which he was convicted reads like a caricature of legal craftsmanship. It is drafted so as to employ the three-pronged test of obscenity: The material must appeal to the "prurient . . . interest . . . of minors," be "patently offensive to prevailing standards in the adult community as a whole with respect to what is suitable material for minors," and "utterly without redeeming social importance for minors."

The majority found no constitutional impediments to this strat-

egy of regulation. It held that, though the magazines were not constitutionally obscene for an adult audience, that did not dispose of the
specific offense of selling them to a minor. The majority opinion by
Justice Brennan is a disappointing one from a judge who has been so
sensitive to First Amendment values. Relying somewhat flatfootedly
on the proposition from *Roth*[4] that obscenity is not protected expression, he apparently sees no dangers in the general premise that minors can be made a disfavored audience if the state finds it reasonable
to do so. Further, he points out that under the statute parents are free
to buy the material and distribute it to their children. Finally, he
rejects the contention that the statute is impermissibly vague.

Justice Stewart, concurring, offers the novel idea that the child
audience, at least with respect to obscenity, is like a captive audience—it "is not possessed of that full capacity for individual choice
which is the presupposition of First Amendment guarantees." He
continues:

It is only upon such a premise, I should suppose, that a State may deprive
children of other rights—the right to marry, for example, or the right to
vote—deprivations that would be constitutionally intolerable for adults.[5]

Presumably, Justice Stewart would scrutinize very carefully any effort
to extend the *Ginsberg* paternalism to other areas of speech, as, for
example, to radical politics.

The opinion most sensitive to the constitutional risks involved in
setting children apart is that of Justice Fortas in dissent. While he
agrees that the First Amendment will permit some concessions on
behalf of the young, he is at odds with the Court's handling of the case
on two basic grounds. First, neither the statute nor the ruling was
confined to cases where there was pandering directly to children. He
would draw the line for state intervention at that point. Second, the
Court failed to confront directly the hard question of whether the two
girlie magazines were obscene when measured by the diluted standard set for the juvenile audience. On this point, he invites quotation:

The Court certainly cannot mean that the States and cities and counties
and villages have unlimited power to withhold anything and everything that
is written or pictorial from younger people. . . .
I agree that the State in the exercise of its police power—even in the First
Amendment domain—may make proper and careful differentiation between
adults and children. But I do not agree that this power may be used on an

arbitrary, free-wheeling basis. . . . It begs the question to present this undefined, unlimited censorship as an aid to parents in the rearing of their
children. This decision does not merely protect children from activities which
all sensible parents would condemn. Rather, its undefined and unlimited
approval of state censorship in this area denies to children free access to
books and works of art to which many parents may wish their children to have
unlimited access. For denial of access to these magazines, without any standard or definition of their allegedly distinguishing characteristics, is also
denial of access to great works of art and literature.[6]

Two other cases announced during the same term as *Ginsberg*—
Rabeck v. New York[7] and *Interstate Circuit, Inc. v. Dallas*[8]—suggest that
the Court intends only a narrow exception for the young in the field
of obscenity. In both cases the Court struck down efforts at "adults
only" regulation on grounds of vagueness.

Rabeck, which was disposed of in a one paragraph *per curiam*
opinion, deserves to be remembered only for the statutory formula
which the Court found too vague. The statute, another section of the
New York law used in *Ginsberg,* prohibited the sale to minors "of any
magazine . . . which would appeal to the lust of persons under the age
of eighteen years or to their curiosity as to sex or to anatomical
differences between the sexes." The Court went to the trouble to find
this too vague, despite the fact that the statute had been repealed. It
brushed aside any claims on behalf of protecting children with the
reassuring comment: "The permissible extent of vagueness is not
directly proportional to, or a function of, the extent of the power to
regulate or control expression with respect to children."[9]

In *Interstate* the ban on minors was incorporated into a movie
licensing scheme. The licensor was limited to classifying movies as
suitable or unsuitable for minors. The ordinance, however, made it
a misdemeanor knowingly to admit a minor to a movie classified as
unsuitable. Thus, despite the added nuance of prior restraint, the
scheme was much like that in *Ginsberg.* The criteria provided included
depictions of "brutality, criminal violence or depravity such as to
incite or encourage crime or delinquency on the part of young persons," and the censors made some passing references to violence in
their adverse comments on the movie in question. But the Court did
not claim this chance to reexamine the important issue of violence
stimuli aimed at juvenile audiences, a question it had dealt with
obliquely in *Winters v. New York*[10] in 1948. It focused instead on a
provision forbidding the portrayal of "sexual promiscuity or ex-

tramarital . . . sexual relations in such a manner . . . as to encourage
sexual promiscuity on the part of young persons." In upholding this
provision, the Texas court read it as covering "the portrayal . . . of
sexual promiscuity as acceptable." The Supreme Court, in an opinion
by Justice Marshall, held that it was impossible to say what the term
"sexual promiscuity" meant in this context and hence found the ordinance impermissibly vague. Thus, once again the Court stressed that
the child like the adult is entitled to utter precision in any efforts to
limit his First Amendment rights.

The opinion, however, disappoints. It underscores again that the
tactic of placing a decision on vagueness grounds may cost the Court
a valuable chance to strengthen a principle it has already adopted.
The Court did not appear to recognize that it was dealing with thematic obscenity—a point on which Justice Stewart had been both lucid
and eloquent in *Kingsley Pictures* [11] in 1959. By placing its objection of
vagueness, it left the disturbing implication that the state might be
able to protect children from thematic obscenity. But if children can
be protected because of their youthfulness from exposure to what are
thought to be unsound ideas about sexual mores, must it not follow
that they can also be protected from what are considered unsound
ideas about, say, war or capitalism?

Justice Brennan voiced concern about this possibility in his concurring opinion in *Rowan v. United States Post Office* [12] in 1970. *Rowan*
arose under a statute which set up machinery whereby a householder
who received what he considered "pandering" advertising could no-
tify the Post Office of his displeasure. It, in turn, was empowered to
order the sender to discontinue and to delete the objector's name
from his mailing lists. In an opinion by Chief Justice Burger, the Court
unanimously upheld the statute, holding that this form of regulation
avoided the flaw of an absolute ban on door-to-door solicitation,
because it depended entirely on the individual householder's judgment that he did not want the mail. Further, the Court held that
properly construed the statutory prohibition applied not only to mail
of a similar character from the particular sender, but to all "future
mailings independent of any objective test."[13]

Justice Brennan was troubled by a provision which allowed the
addressee to cut off mail addressed to his children under the age of
nineteen:

In light of the broad interpretation that the Court assigns to [section] 4009
. . . , the possibility exists that parents could prevent their children, even if

they are 18 years old, from receiving political, religious, or other materials
that the parents find offensive. In my view, a statute so construed and applied
is not without constitutional difficulties.[14]

    This series of cases points up a troubling aspect of the Court's
general response to obscenity. It is apparent that the Court has come
to regard obscenity as a special *ad hoc* exception to its basic notions
about free speech. There is, to be sure, something to be said for this
as a diplomatic solution to a political problem, and certainly the Court
has done a great deal to narrow the scope of obscenity regulation.
Hence I am not disposed to fault its performance. The problem is,
rather, that in seeking to rationalize its *ad hoc* exception, the Court has
not simply asserted that obscenity is somehow different, but has gone
on to offer reasons *general* in form. It has thus placed in the tradition
premises that could be acutely awkward if applied to other areas of
speech. The notion of material that forfeits its constitutional status
because it is deemed by the courts to be "utterly without redeeming
social importance" or lacking in "serious social value" is one such
instance. And the notion that the state may use sanctions to limit the
flow of messages to the young is another. However trivial the occasion
of obscenity, it contains the seed of a solemn ratification in constitutional terms of the "generation gap."

5

Libel

When the Supreme Court first brought the elegant complexities of the common law of libel under constitutional scrutiny in *New York Times v. Sullivan*[1] in 1964, it located a new genre of First Amendment problem. This problem arises when discussion of public issues is interlaced, as it often will be, with statements about individuals which carry a risk of being false in fact. If the aggrieved individual is given an unqualified tort remedy, he will have the power to veto or inhibit the discussion of the public issue. The free speech issue is thus how best to accommodate the individual interest in reputation and the public interest in unrestrained debate of public issues. Like obscenity, this is a speech problem that cannot readily be conceptualized within a clear and present danger framework. Perhaps as a result, it too has produced great diversity of opinion among the justices and a doctrinal metaphysics all its own.

The common law of libel has not, as the layman might suppose, simply involved money damages for malicious falsehoods which caused injury to an individual's reputation. Three rules, developed over a century, gave it far wider sweep. First, defamatory statements were presumed to be false. This placed the burden of proving truth upon the publisher, and truth turned out to be a most difficult item to prove firmly in court. Second, it did not matter whether the falsehood was the result of malice, negligence, or bad luck. You published defamation at your peril; and, as the old law put it, malice was presumed from the fact of publication. Third, the aggrieved party did not have to prove *actual* harm to his reputation; it too was inferred or presumed from the fact of publication, making possible the award of what were technically called *general* damages. Taken together, these "galloping" presumptions, as a critic once called them,[2] meant that the publisher of a serious criticism was, in effect, required by law to insure the absolute accuracy of what he said.

The common law recognized that these rules had a chilling effect on speech in certain valued communication situations and offset their harshness with a series of *privileges,* such as those for fair comment in literary criticism, for speeches by legislators on the floor of the house, for reprinting from official public records, and for fair comment on public officials or candidates for public office. It is this final category of privilege that is of interest to us here. American law had developed two versions of the privilege for fair comment on public office. Under the rule in a majority of states a distinction was made between fact and opinion, and opinion was protected only so long as there was no inaccuracy in the underlying facts. The risk of such factual error was on the publisher of the defamation; he lost his privilege even though the errors of fact were the result of inadvertence. Under a minority view, the privilege covered erroneous statements of fact if made in good faith. It was this common law calculus of individual interest in reputation weighed against public interest in speech that the Supreme Court undertook to evaluate against the mandate of the First Amendment in *New York Times v. Sullivan.*

Prior to *New York Times,* the Court had had an earlier skirmish with libel in *Beauharnais v. Illinois*[3] in 1952. Beauharnais, the president of a white supremacist group, had published and distributed a leaflet which protested "Negro aggression and infiltration into all white neighborhoods" and stated:

If persuasion and the need to prevent the white race from becoming mongrelized by the negro will not unite us, then the aggressions . . . rapes, robberies, knives, guns and marijuana of the negro, surely will.[4]

In a 5 to 4 decision, the Court affirmed Beauharnais's conviction under an Illinois statute prohibiting group libel. Speaking through Justice Frankfurter, the Court relied on the *Chaplinsky*[5] classification of libel, along with fighting words, obscenity, and profanity, as belonging to a second level of speech. "Libelous utterances," declared Frankfurter, are not "within the area of constitutionally protected speech." Thus, the Court in *Beauharnais*—as in *Roth*[6] five years later—

found it unnecessary to apply First Amendment standards to the regulation at issue. In a sharp dissent Justice Douglas argued that the decision represented "a philosophy at war with the First Amendment" and predicted:

Today a white man stands convicted for protesting in unseemly language against our decisions invalidating restrictive covenants. Tomorrow a Negro will be hauled before a court for denouncing lynch law in heated terms.[7]

Douglas's words proved prophetic. The next time the Court encountered the libel issue—in *New York Times*—it was in the context of the civil rights movement. The case arose as a libel action brought by the police commissioner of Montgomery, Alabama, against the *New York Times* for publishing an advertisement sponsored by a civil rights group. Titled "Heed Their Rising Voices," the advertisement recited various hardships Dr. Martin Luther King, Jr., and his followers had undergone in the South and appealed for funds. Although he was not mentioned by name, the plaintiff claimed that the advertisement cast a derogatory light on his performance of his official duties by inference. The Alabama court found the allegations defamatory and disallowed the defense of truth on the ground the statement was not *perfectly* true—it had contained several minor inaccuracies. Moreover, there was no privilege of fair comment since there were errors in the statement of underlying facts. The jury awarded general damages of $500,000, and the Alabama Supreme Court affirmed.

The uncanny thing about *New York Times* was that it pushed to their extremes the harsh technical rules which for centuries had made up the Anglo-American law of defamation. Although the case had a certain appearance of sham and of Southern revenge on the *Times* for intruding into local affairs,[8] Alabama had not made up any new law for the occasion, but had simply applied its customary rule as to fair comment, a rule which was found in the majority of the states. Yet, as a political reality, the case clamored for readjustment.

In this posture of events, the Court, compelled by the realities of the case to rescue the *Times* and equally compelled by its role to seek high ground in justifying its result, arrived at some very high ground indeed. Speaking through Justice Brennan, it unanimously held that the Alabama rule as to fair comment violated the First Amendment, because by holding the speaker strictly liable for any errors of fact it tended to inhibit too seriously criticism of public officials. In effect, the decision gave constitutional status to the minority common law rule as to the level of privilege to be afforded comments on public officials. An aggrieved official could only recover damages, wrote Brennan, if he could prove that the remark was made with " 'actual malice'—that is, with knowledge that it was false or with reckless disregard of whether it was false or not."[9]

In reaching this conclusion, the Court broke entirely new ground. It took its bearings from the fate of the Sedition Act of 1798. Although it had been one of the great ironies of our free speech history that we had never satisfactorily put to rest the fundamental question of whether the Sedition Act was constitutional, the Court in effect now found it unconstitutional. And in the controversy which had followed passage of the Act, it found the clue, as Justice Brennan put it, to "the central meaning of the First Amendment."[10]

The *New York Times* case is thus of major significance on two levels. First, its underlying rationale makes a major contribution to speech theory. By authoritatively declaring the unconstitutionality of seditious libel, it clears the air as to one of the key rationales underlying First Amendment policy. Second, by providing a constitutional dimension to what had long been regarded as a purely private law matter left to the common law of each state, *Times* and subsequent decisions have had considerable impact on the tort law of defamation.

"The Central Meaning of the First Amendment"

Seditious libel is the doctrine that flourished in England during and after the Star Chamber. It is the hallmark of closed societies throughout the world. Under it criticism of government is viewed as defamation and punished as a crime. The treatment of such speech as criminal is based on an accurate perception of the dangers in it; it is likely to undermine confidence in government policies and in the official incumbents. But political freedom ends when government can use its powers and its courts to silence its critics. In my view, the presence or absence in the law of the concept of seditious libel defines the society. A society may or may not treat obscenity or contempt by publication as legal offenses without altering its basic nature. If, however, it makes seditious libel an offense, it is not a free society, no matter what its other characteristics.

The curious career of seditious libel in the American constitutional tradition began with the passage of the Sedition Act in 1798, only seven years after the adoption of the First Amendment. In effect, the Act made it a crime to defame the government or its officials. In its precise terms, it provided:

> . . . if any person shall write, print, utter, or publish . . . any false, scandalous and malicious writing or writings against the government of the United States, or either house of the Congress of the United States, with intent to defame the said government, or either house of the said Congress, or the said President, or to bring them, or either of them, into contempt or disrepute; or to excite against them or either or any of them, the hatred of the good people of the United States . . . then such person being thereof convicted . . . shall be punished by a fine not exceeding two thousand dollars, and by imprisonment not exceeding two years.[11]

The apparent qualifications on the face of the Act as to falsity and malice were illusory, since, as we have noted, under the common law of defamation, if a statement was judged defamatory, malice and falsity were assumed, leaving the burden of proof on the defendant. Moreover, most statements would be expressions of opinion for which the defense of truth would be unavailable. The import of the Act therefore was to convert serious criticism of government into defamation, thereby arming the government with criminal sanctions with which to silence its critics.

The Act expired by its own terms two years after enactment and was never revived. None of the handful of cases prosecuted under it left a serious precedent. When Jefferson came to power in 1800 in a sharp switch of political fortunes between Federalists and Jeffersonian Democrats, he pardoned the violators still in prison and some years later Congress repaid the fines. The Sedition Act thus appeared to be the one great exception to de Tocqueville's shrewd dictum that in the United States all great issues of policy sooner or later become justiciable. It disappeared from view before its status could be confronted by the Court and as a result it disappeared from the American discussion of free speech. From many points of view the central question for the law of the First Amendment was whether the Sedition Act had been constitutional. If the answer was "yes," as many commentators thought as late as the start of World War I, then the free speech tradition would be feeble indeed.

In this regard, it is instructive, if a little unnerving, to consider a case we will discuss at length later in this essay, *Abrams v. United States*[12] in 1919. The defendants had printed and distributed leaflets condemning the government for sending troops into Russia following the Revolution. They were charged under the Espionage Act of 1917. As amended in 1918, the Act made it a felony (punishable by up to twenty years in prison) to publish, while the United States was at war, among other things:

any disloyal . . . scurrilous or abusive language about the form of government of the United States, or the Constitution, or the flag, or the uniform of the Army or Navy.

any language intended to bring the form of government of the United States . . . into contempt, scorn, contumely, or disrepute.[13]

The defendants were tried and convicted under a four-count indictment. Two of the counts charged obstruction of the draft and of the war effort; the other two charged violation of these provisions which sound in seditious libel. The Court was thus brought to the brink of confronting whether this echo of the Sedition Act of 1798 was constitutional. Indeed, the government counsel argued from the premise that the Act had been constitutional. And it was quite possible that the Court in 1919 would have agreed. But it turned instead to the counts involving obstruction of the draft and of the war effort, where the evidence of violation seemed clearer. Since the conviction under each ran concurrently, the Court found it unnecessary to pass on the other two counts. Thus, we were saved from its judgment as to the validity of punishing seditious libel.

The performance of Justice Holmes in dissent is puzzling. He has a major chance to set the tradition straight and put the constitutionality of seditious libel to rest, but he does not *quite* do so. He confines himself to a brief comment:

I wholly disagree with the argument of the Government that the First Amendment left the common law as to seditious libel in force. History seems to me against the notion. I had conceived that the United States through many years had shown its repentance for the Sedition Act of 1798, by repaying fines that it imposed.[14]

In any event, it is not necessary to choose between competing views of history. My point is simply that for over 150 years it was not thought necessary to clarify the status of the Act as a first step in getting to the meaning of the First Amendment. In view of this awk-

ward history, a coherent approach to issues of free speech was handicapped, if not impossible.

It is this shadow that *New York Times* decisively dispels. The critical passage in Justice Brennan's opinion reads:

If neither factual error nor defamatory content suffices to remove the constitutional shield from criticism of official conduct, the combination of the two
elements is no less inadequate. This is the lesson to be drawn from the great
controversy over the Sedition Act of 1798 . . . which first crystallized a
national awareness of the central meaning of the First Amendment.[15]

There follows an extended discussion of "the great controversy" with
appropriate quotations from Madison, whose views are summarized
thus by the Court: "The right of free public discussion of the stewardship of public officials was thus, in Madison's view, a fundamental
principle of the American form of government."[16] Then, some 164
years after the expiration of the Sedition Act, the Court turns to
confront the question of its constitutionality and states: "Although
the Sedition Act was never tested in this Court, the attack upon its
validity has carried the day in the court of history."[17]

This use of history is arresting. Apparently, the constitutionality
of the Act when it was passed was indeterminate, but when the subsequent outcry "crystallized a national awareness of the central meaning
of the First Amendment," it also crystallized the constitutional status
of the Act. Whatever difficulties there may be in the notion that the
Sedition Act, possibly constitutional when enacted, became unconstitutional with the passage of time and that its unconstitutionality was
adjudicated in effect by public opinion, the Court's answer is clear and
unequivocal. After citing the views of various men from Jefferson to
Chafee, Brennan concludes:

These views reflect a broad consensus that the Act, because of the restraint
it imposed upon criticism of government and public officials, was inconsistent
with the First Amendment.[18]

In short, seditious libel, like heresy, is now firmly outside the American tradition.

Although Justice Brennan's opinion is scarcely a straightforward
exposition of the basic theme, it seems to me to convey the following
crucial syllogism. The central meaning of the First Amendment is that
seditious libel cannot be made the subject of government sanction.

The Alabama rule on fair comment is closely akin to making seditious libel an offense. The Alabama rule, therefore, violated the central meaning of the Amendment. The talk about the Sedition Act is not merely graceful rhetoric; it is truly the rationale for the decision.

There are three other portions of the opinion that confirm the impression that the Court is being carried along by a momentum of insight about the democratic necessities for free speech. First, Justice Brennan concludes a preliminary review of existing law with what is to my ear a perfect and splendid sentence:

Thus we consider this case against the background of a profound national commitment to the principle that debate on public issues should be uninhibited, robust, and wide-open, and that it may well include vehement, caustic, and sometimes unpleasantly sharp attacks on government and public officials.[19]

Then, he draws an analogy between the case at bar and *Barr v. Matteo*[20] in 1959, in which the Court had ratified the privilege of the high-ranking public official when sued for libel of a private citizen. If the *official* was to be given protection when acting in the course of his duties, argued Justice Brennan, then it followed that the *citizen* should be given comparable protection when *he* was acting in the course of *his* duties. "It is as much his duty to criticize as it is the official's duty to administer."[21] At this point in its rhetoric and sweep, the opinion almost literally incorporated Alexander Meiklejohn's thesis that in a democracy the citizen as ruler is our most important public official.

Finally, there is Justice Brennan's response to the circumstance that the defamation at issue did not refer explicitly to the plaintiff but was an inference drawn from criticism of government action. If such a connection to individuals is made too easily, all criticism of government policy will carry *implicit defamation* of the officials in charge of the policy attacked. Such a rule of construction, says Justice Brennan,

would sidestep this [constitutional] obstacle by transmuting criticism of government, however impersonal it may seem on its face, into personal criticism, and hence potential libel, of the officials of whom the government is composed. There is no legal alchemy by which a State may thus create the cause of action that would otherwise be denied. . . .

And then to leave no doubt about the point, he adds:

Raising as it does the possibility that a good-faith critic of government will be penalized for his criticism, the proposition relied on by the Alabama courts strikes at the very center of the constitutionally protected area of free expression.[22]

When the opinion is read as a whole, it becomes evident that the Court was not simply uttering, as the Court is wont to do, the occasional sentence that reads felicitously even out of context. It was clearly being driven by a concern for the central meaning of the First Amendment.

The Impact of Times on the Law of Defamation

The underlying rationale of *New York Times* has implications which reach beyond the narrow field of libel, and it has served to illuminate a variety of other issues. We will have occasion to discuss some of these applications of the *Times* insight elsewhere in this book. For the moment, however, our concern is with the impact of *Times* on the law of defamation. During the years since *Times* came down, there has developed a formidable body of Supreme Court precedent amplifying the new constitutional law of defamation. In effect, the Court has been forced to rewrite and federalize a considerable part of the state common law of libel in its efforts to disentangle the component of public issue discussion from the private redress of the law of libel.

The nature of the Court's response will, as always, be illuminated by consideration of a particular case. *Rosenblatt v. Baer*[23] in 1966 was among the first occasions the Court had to apply the rule it had announced in *Times*. A relatively homely controversy, it illustrates how deeply the constitutional criticism of libel law now cuts into the handling of routine local disputes. Baer had been the supervisor of a county-operated recreation area in New Hampshire; he was employed by and responsible to three county commissioners. A local controversy over the way the recreation area was operated as a tourist attraction resulted in a change of administrations and Baer's dismissal. Rosenblatt ran an opinion column in the local newspaper in which he noted the "fantastic" improvement in income from the recreation area under the new management and asked: "What happened to the money last year? and every other year?" Baer sued, alleging that the column had "greatly exaggerated" the facts as to the degree of improvement, and that, although he had not been mentioned by name, many people in the community had understood the column to impute "mismanagement and peculation" to him. A local jury awarded $31,500. The case had gone to trial before *New York Times* came down, and the jury had been instructed that mere negligent mis-statement of fact would defeat the defendant's claim of privilege. Armed with the new criterion furnished by *Times*, Rosenblatt levied a constitutional challenge against this apparently routine application of New Hampshire libel law. And he prevailed.

In an 8 to 1 decision, the Court reversed the award and remanded the case to the New Hampshire courts for a new trial. The lone dissenter was Justice Fortas, who was disturbed by the fact that the case had been tried prior to the date of *Times* and that, as a result, the record was not tailored to meet the issues made relevant by *Times*. He would have dismissed the writ of *certiorari* as improvidently granted, thus letting the award below stand. Although the other justices were in essential agreement on the result, *Rosenblatt* was the occasion for six separate opinions. Of particular interest is the pattern formed by the opinions of Justices Brennan, Black, and Stewart.

Justice Brennan wrote the opinion of the Court. As he saw it, the case presented two questions. First, did the defendant's column—a comment about the management of the recreation area without reference to particular individuals—sufficiently refer to the plaintiff? The trial court had instructed the jury that "an imputation of impropriety or a crime to one or some of a small group that casts suspicion on all is actionable." But Justice Brennan found this instruction in error, for it ran the risk, noted in *Times*, of permitting impersonal criticism of government policy to be converted into personal defamation:

A theory that the column cast indiscriminate suspicion on the members of the group responsible for the conduct of this governmental operation is tantamount to a demand for recovery based on libel of government, and therefore is constitutionally insufficient.[24]

A second question presented by the case was whether the plaintiff—the former manager of a recreation area—was a "public official" within the *Times* rule. Justice Brennan found the record unclear on this point.[25] Therefore he remanded the case to the state courts to give the plaintiff a chance to show if his grievance fell outside the *Times* privilege, either because he was a private person or because "actual malice" could be shown as to the defendant's errors of fact.

Justice Brennan's explanation of the relevant criteria for determining the status of the plaintiff under *Times* illustrates the Court's resolve to ferret out the public issue implications of routine libel cases. He sees implicated in this dispute the central values of speech policy:

The motivating force for the decision in *New York Times* was twofold. We expressed "a profound national commitment to the principle that debate on public issues should be uninhibited, robust, and wide-open, *and* that [such debate] may well include vehement, caustic, and sometimes unpleasantly sharp attacks on government and public officials." . . . There is, first, a strong interest in debate on public issues, and, second, a strong interest in debate about those persons who are in a position significantly to influence the resolution of those issues. Criticism of government is at the very center of the constitutionally protected area of free discussion. Criticism of those responsible for government operations must be free, lest criticism of government itself be penalized.[26]

Justice Black shares these values, but he departs from Justice Brennan in the matter of their implementation. No accommodation of the competing interests will satisfy him or his fellow critic of the *Times* rule, Justice Douglas. In a concurring opinion, joined by Douglas, Black states his criticism of *Times* with power:

. . . To be faithful to the First Amendment's guarantees, this Court should free private critics of public agents from fear of libel judgments for money just as it has freed critics from fear of pains and penalties inflicted by government.

This case illustrates I think what a short and inadequate step this Court took in the *New York Times* case to guard free press and free speech against the grave dangers to the press and the public created by libel actions. Half-million-dollar judgments for libel damages like those awarded against the *New York Times* will not be stopped by requirements that "malice" be found, however that term is defined. Such a requirement is little protection against high emotions and deep prejudices which frequently pervade local communities where libel suits are tried. . . . The only sure way to protect speech and press against these threats is to recognize that libel laws are abridgments of speech and press and therefore are barred in both federal and state courts by the First and Fourteenth Amendments. I repeat what I said in the *New York Times* case that "An unconditional right to say what one pleases about public affairs is what I consider to be the minimum guarantee of the First Amendment."[27]

Justice Stewart's concurring opinion stresses the bite of the *Times* principle into the countervalue of personal reputation:

The right of a man to the protection of his own reputation from unjustified invasion and wrongful hurt reflects no more than our basic concept of the essential dignity and worth of every human being—a concept at the root of any decent system of ordered liberty. The protection of private personality, like the protection of life itself, is left primarily to the individual States under the Ninth and Tenth Amendments. But this does not mean that the right is entitled to any less recognition by this Court as a basic of our constitutional system.

We use misleading euphemisms when we speak of the *New York Times* rule as involving "uninhibited, robust, and wide-open debate," or "vehement, caustic, and sometimes unpleasantly sharp" criticism. What the *New York Times* rule ultimately protects is defamatory falsehood. No matter how gross the untruth, the *New York Times* rule deprives a defamed public official of any hope for legal redress without proof that the lie was a knowing one, or uttered in reckless disregard of the truth.

That rule should not be applied except where a State's law of defamation has been unconstitutionally converted into a law of seditious libel. The First and Fourteenth Amendments have not stripped private citizens of all means of redress for injuries inflicted upon them by careless liars. . . .

Surely if the 1950's taught us anything, they taught us that the poisonous atmosphere of the easy lie can infect and degrade a whole society.[28]

Read together, these opinions highlight the tension that will always attend the *New York Times* rule—the tension between protection of robust criticism on public matters and protection of individual reputations. On one hand, there will always be an impulse to make the level of privilege afforded by *Times* more absolute—it is, after all, still defeasible by showing knowledge or reckless disregard of falsity. On the other, there will always be an impulse to circumscribe such very generous protection of speech out of deference to personal reputation.

During the years since *Times* debate among the justices has reflected this tension. It has centered on two issues: What is the *ambit* of the *Times* privilege, that is, who will be treated as being in the same shoes as the public official? What is the *level* of the privilege, that is, does it vary as the subject of the defamation varies and moves away from the literal public official?

In response to the first issue, the Court has steadily expanded the *ambit* of protection to the point that today the privilege extends to anyone enmeshed in the discussion of a public issue, whether he is a public official, a public figure, or a private citizen involuntarily newsworthy. The second issue has proved more controversial. The question is: Does the *level* of the privilege vary as we move from the public official to the public figure to the newsworthy private individual? This issue has evoked a complex pattern of positions among the justices. Indeed, the diversity of views on this point is reminiscent of the Court's lack of consensus in the field of obscenity. As of the early 1970s, the following views had emerged:

At one extreme was the position identified with Justices Black and Douglas, who opposed any imposition of liability for defamation and hence would accord an absolute privilege in all three situations. At the other extreme was the position elaborated by Justice Harlan. He would accord a different level of privilege in each of the three situations in order to achieve the requisite accommodation of the competing interests involved. The strongest privilege to the speaker and the least protection to the subject would be given in the public official case; the weakest privilege to the speaker and the most protection to the subject would be given in the private citizen case; and in between would be the privilege and protection given in the public figure case. He would achieve these levels by using the *New York Times* "reckless disregard" test for the first level; a "gross negligence" test for the middle level; and finally, a simple negligence test to defeat the speaker's privilege in the third situation.

Justices Brennan and Marshall occupy positions in the center. Brennan would apply the "knowing and reckless disregard" standard of *New York Times* in all three situations. Marshall agrees with Brennan that the "reckless disregard" standard is appropriate in cases involving public officials and public figures. Like Justice Harlan, however, he argues that a different accommodation is called for in cases involving private individuals who have become involuntarily newsworthy. In such cases he would allow the state to apply whatever standard it thought appropriate, but would restrict the damages awarded the plaintiff to "actual losses," that is, he would not allow punitive or presumed damages. In his view, such an approach would eliminate the most significant factor in producing self-censorship—the threat of huge damage judgments—while affording individual reputation a greater degree of protection than is provided by the "reckless disregard" standard.

That the Court should have devoted so much time and energy and argument to these nuances is both disturbing and splendid. It may be read as a sign that the justices now simply cannot agree on anything and we are approaching the day when there will be nine rules of constitutional law on every point. But surely it is better read affirmatively as an indication of the Court's concern with and commitment to the values of the First Amendment. Moreover, the disagreements among the justices over the level of privilege to be afforded publications about newsworthy private individuals should not be allowed to deflect our attention from the degree of consensus they have achieved in this area. All of the justices subscribe without qualification to the *New York Times* standard as applied to public officials; and a substantial majority agree that the *Times* standard applies to public figures and that publications about private individuals are subject to *some* degree of constitutional protection. Thus, once again, while conceding a narrow jurisdiction to the censor, the Court has managed largely to recover an important category of speech from the sphere of traditional censorship.

Looking back over these three jurisdictions of censorship, what is impressive about the Court's performance is the momentum with which it has pursued First Amendment policy—into the hallowed precincts of judicial authority in the contempt by publication cases, into the province of an anxiously held social taboo in the obscenity cases, and into a dusty hyper-technical corner of the common law of private remedies in the libel cases. In each area the Court, after granting that there can be some basis for censorship, thereby blunting large doctrinal disputes, has been sensitive to the threats involved in the concession and patient with the particulars. Thus, at the expense perhaps of sweeping doctrinal clarity and certainly at the price of very considerable work at the case by case level, it has disengaged from these areas a core of freedom for public discussion in politics and art.

What then remains of the censor's jurisdiction in these areas? The direct and immediate threat to the impartial administration of justice; the hard-core pornography of the commercial dealer; the special concern with the child audience; and the knowing or reckless falsehood damaging to reputation. There remain of course questions of tactics. Free speech policy may in the end turn on the strategy of overprotecting speech in order to protect the speech that matters. But certainly the Court has not done badly in leaving, as it were, only the husks of censorship.

The Major Jurisdictions
of Censorship

6

Reflexive Disorder:
The First Encounter

The primary battleground for the American tradition of free speech has been provided by a cluster of problems in which speech is alleged to be the unmediated cause of fairly immediate improper action. In these cases the ostensible justification for censoring speech is to control the action thought to result from it. As we shall see, the whole process is often more complex and the ostensible justification for censorship may not always be the true one, but for the moment this crude characterization will serve us as a point of departure.

The relationship of speech to illegal action may take two basic forms. It is important to distinguish between them. On one hand, there is the problem posed by speech that threatens to *incite* others to illegal action against a target selected by the speaker. On the other, there is the problem that arises when speech threatens to *excite* others to disorder in retaliation against the speaker. Our concern here is with the latter.

This genre of speech is difficult to define with precision. It occurs in public places such as streets and parks before what is likely to be a transient audience. In this fluid situation the primary agent of censorship is the policeman seeking to keep public order, and the legal mechanisms used tend to be breach of peace and disorderly conduct statutes. Such laws are aimed at minor disorders such as brawls, traffic snarls, and drunks rather than at speech as such and are customarily loosely drafted. Like obscenity and libel, this is an area in which common sense has long conceded some degree of censorship. The task of the Supreme Court has been to disentangle speech values from the high value of maintaining order in the public forum.[1]

The relationship of the law to the content of the message in this area is not as direct as it has been in those we have examined thus far. Ostensibly the state is motivated by neutral objectives independent of the content of the speech; its aim is simply to keep order on the streets. But the street corner rostrum is most likely to be claimed by spokesmen for aggrieved and minority viewpoints who do not have ready access to more established channels of communication. And most, if not all, of the disorder threatened in these cases arises not from the urgings of the speaker but from the irritations of the audience. The essential problem is thus that of reflexive disorder. If the police restore order at the expense of the speaker, they arm the audience with a heckler's veto, and hence by a circuitous route the law collaborates in the *content* regulation sought by the hostile audience.

These cases thus illustrate the power, as analytic tool, of our basic question: When can the content of messages be regulated? For unless one focuses on the suppression of content, he may miss what makes them so much more troublesome than the ordinary breach of peace. Indeed, they can be seen as posing the question: When can content which is generally permissible be suppressed?

Between 1940 and 1952 the Supreme Court had occasion to consider this question in a series of six cases: *Cantwell v. Connecticut* (1940), *Chaplinsky v. New Hampshire* (1942), *Terminiello v. Chicago* (1949), *Feiner v. New York* (1951), *Kunz v. New York* (1951), and *Beauharnais v. Illinois* (1952).[2] These cases present several variants of the reflexive disorder problem. For the sake of analytic clarity, we will begin with the simplest form of the problem, the fighting words issue posed by *Chaplinsky*.

Fighting Words

We had occasion earlier to discuss *Chaplinsky*, a case which bespeaks the gentility of a bygone era, as the source of the two-level approach to speech problems. Here our concern is with the narrow issue posed by the case: whether a state could constitutionally convict a man for using insulting language to another in public. The Supreme Court held that it could and ratified the fighting words doctrine developed by the New Hampshire Supreme Court: If in a face-to-face encounter, you use language—"classical epithet"—which would render the reasonable man angry enough to hit you and thereby breach the peace, *you* have breached the peace.

Chaplinsky was a unanimous decision by a Court which included among its members Justices Black and Douglas; and the opinion was written by Justice Murphy, a judge acutely sensitive to First Amendment values. Apart from Murphy's broad dictum about worthless speech, it seems on first reading a narrow and sensible concession to censorship. The statute involved is not the usual loose breach of peace interdiction, but the relatively precise prohibition of addressing "any offensive, derisive, or annoying word to any other person who is lawfully in any street or other public place."[3] And the fighting words doctrine adopted by the Court is apparently limited in three respects: to face-to-face encounters, to public places, and to a narrow category of words conventionally regarded as serious insults. In this limited context what would seem to be at stake is more a breach of etiquette than the challenge of an unorthodox point of view.

Closer examination, however, reveals *Chaplinsky* to be a disturbing decision. Here is Justice Murphy's summary of the facts:

. . . Chaplinsky was distributing the literature of his sect on the streets of Rochester on a busy Saturday afternoon. Members of the local citizenry complained to the City Marshal, Bowering, that Chaplinsky was denouncing all religion as a "racket." Bowering told them that Chaplinsky was lawfully engaged, and then warned Chaplinsky that the crowd was getting restless. Some time later, a disturbance occurred and the traffic officer on duty at the busy intersection started with Chaplinsky for the police station, but did not inform him that he was under arrest or that he was going to be arrested. On the way, they encountered Marshal Bowering, who had been advised that a riot was under way and was therefore hurrying to the scene. Bowering repeated his earlier warning to Chaplinsky, who then addressed to Bowering the words set forth in the complaint.

Chaplinsky's version of the affair was slightly different. He testified that, when he met Bowering, he asked him to arrest the ones responsible for the disturbance. In reply, Bowering cursed him and told him to come along. Appellant admitted that he said the words charged in the complaint, with the exception of the name of the Deity.[4]

It *is* odd that Bowering should repeat his warning about the unrest of the crowd to a speaker who is on his way to the police station under police escort, but whichever version we accept, it is clear that the controversy arises from *earlier* police handling of a street corner

speech in which ideological differences and not insults were the
source of the disturbance. Moreover, Chaplinsky does little more than
comment bitterly on how the police have handled the whole affair. If,
as seems to be the case, the police had violated his rights by stopping
him, the episode, including the cursing of the policeman, takes on a
different complexion. Further, it should be noted that Chaplinsky's
words were: "You are a God damned racketeer" and "a damned
Fascist and the whole government of Rochester are Fascists or agents
of Fascists." In context these are not simply epithets and nothing
more; nor are they within that vocabulary of classic insult likely to
arouse any normal man to violence.[5]

In any event, putting aside our uneasiness about the facts, it is
clear that the doctrine announced in *Chaplinsky*, whatever its merits,
is sharply limited. It is an exception keyed to face-to-face insults and
therefore cannot by its nature apply either to written communications
nor, I would suggest, to a speaker addressing an audience of any size.

Ideological Fighting Words?

The *Chaplinsky* concession to censorship represents a narrow and
manageable recognition by law of the speaker's responsibility for the
unrest of his audience. But it raises a larger question: Might the same
rationale for censorship—the inherently provocative character of the
speech—be extended from personal epithets to speech with ideological content?

This possibility was touched on in an earlier decision, *Cantwell v.
Connecticut* in 1940. In *Cantwell* the defendant, a Jehovah's Witness,
went from person to person on the street, as if he were distributing
leaflets, and requested permission to play a phonograph record. The
record, which contained a virulent attack on Catholicism, deeply
offended two listeners, who said that they felt like hitting Cantwell.
Thus, once again speech on the public street threatened to provoke
retaliatory violence. But this time there were no personal insults involved. The offense was purely ideological. On these facts the Connecticut courts found Cantwell guilty of a common law breach of
peace. In a thoughtful opinion by Justice Roberts the Supreme Court
unanimously reversed.

Justice Roberts makes much of the circumstance that breach of
peace was a common law crime in Connecticut. He would like the
Court to have the benefit of the legislature's judgment as to the risks
posed by this category of speech. For him, it is the absence of a

narrow, deliberate expression of state policy that tips the balance in favor of the defendant.[6] Thus, although he upsets the conviction, Roberts raises the possibility that the Constitution *might* permit regulation of speech likely to arouse reflexive violence on ideological grounds, if the legislature will crystallize that judgment into a precise and narrow statute. He carefully leaves open, that is, the possibility of *ideological fighting words.* Having done so, however, he then proceeds to express tolerance for excesses in religious and political speech in a passage which is the direct precursor of Justice Brennan's "robust, uninhibited, and wide-open" language in *New York Times v. Sullivan:*[7]

In the realm of religious faith, and in that of political belief, sharp differences arise. In both fields the tenets of one man may seem the rankest error to his neighbor. To persuade others to his own point of view, the pleader, as we know, at times, resorts to exaggeration, to vilification of men, who have been, or are, prominent in church or state, and even to false statement. But the people of this nation have ordained in the light of history, that, in spite of the probability of excesses and abuses, these liberties are, in the long view, essential to enlightened opinion and right conduct on the part of the citizens of a democracy.[8]

During the late 1940s and the early 1950s the Court had two major encounters with the reflexive disorder problem and with the possibility of ideological fighting words: *Terminiello v. Chicago* in 1949 and *Kunz v. New York* in 1951. Both cases involved extremist speakers vigorously expressing ugly views about religious minorities and in both there was a threat of retaliatory violence. But because of the way the legal issue was postured in each, they fail to put the question satisfactorily to rest. In both cases the Court "saves" the speaker, but it does so by means of tactical maneuvers that deprive the decisions of value as precedents on the reflexive disorder problem. Bitterly divided, it can only manage a majority for *ad hoc* resolution of these cases and is unable to agree on any statement for future handling of the problem.

Terminiello and *Kunz* are made memorable, however, by the contributions of Justice Jackson in dissent. In effect, he submits a brief on behalf of the concept of ideological fighting words. Having recently returned to the Court from the Nuremberg trials, where he had served as Allied prosecutor, he is acutely sensitive to the horrors of fascism, anti-Semitism, and Communist extremism. In two eloquent, angry dissents he furnishes a realistic account of the facts and warns that,

in light of the dismal experience in other countries, small episodes of
street unrest may be tactics in the large-scale revolutionary strategies
of extremist groups. Although he does not in the end provide much
help toward the statement of the appropriate principle, Justice Jackson is brilliant in the role of Cassandra.

Father Terminiello, a suspended Catholic priest, was a spokesman for the anti-Semitic, fascist faction in American life during the
late 1940s associated with such names as Father Coughlin and Gerald
L. K. Smith. He was a professional rabble-rouser. The case arose as
a result of a public speech he gave at an auditorium in Chicago.
Advertisement of the event had aroused widespread resentment, and
by the time he rose to speak to an audience of eight hundred, there
was a police cordon around the auditorium. A hostile crowd of at least
a thousand milled around outside, and there were sporadic episodes
of brick throwing and other violence. In this tense setting Terminiello
gave a speech which, though it had a surface restraint, was rich in
horror stories about what some Jewish doctors had done to German
war prisoners and was dotted with remarks such as: "That's what they
want for you, that howling mob outside"; "Some of the scum got in
by mistake"; "Why should we tolerate them?"; "We don't want them
here, we want them to go back where they came from." The sympathetic crowd inside the auditorium, which was excited before he
began, was visibly stirred by his words. Thanks presumably to the
efforts of the police, the speech was completed without an outbreak
of violence, Terminiello was able to leave in safety, and the crowds
dispersed. For making the speech Terminiello was charged with disorderly conduct under the Chicago breach of peace ordinance and
was fined $100. The Illinois courts affirmed the conviction as an
application of the fighting words doctrine and the appeal was argued
to the Supreme Court on those grounds.

The Court was thus directly confronted with the critical issue of
ideological fighting words in the context of an explosive fact situation.
Speaking through Justice Douglas, the five-man majority reversed the
conviction on constitutional grounds, but did so in a way that sidestepped the issue so boldly presented by the facts. "We do not reach
that question," Justice Douglas stated at the outset, "for there is a
preliminary question that is dispositive of the case."[9] The preliminary
question was an error discovered in the instructions the trial judge
had given the jury, an error which had not been argued by the defendant below and was put forward by the Supreme Court on its own
motion.

The fatal instruction had included the comment that the breach of peace ordinance covered speech "which stirs the public to anger, invites dispute, brings about a condition of unrest, or creates a disturbance." Justice Douglas argued that by the instruction the Illinois courts had authoritatively set the meaning of the ordinance and that, so defined, it was too broadly restrictive of speech since it interdicted the mere stirring to anger, dispute or unrest. It was thus possible that the jury might have placed its decision on the impermissible parts of the instruction; hence, under accepted doctrine, the conviction could not stand.

None of the justices disagree with the principle that speech may invite dispute and even anger in our society. Indeed, the restatement of *this* principle was not worth making. But Justice Frankfurter and Chief Justice Vinson in dissent are appalled that the Court would "ferret out" an error so buried in the record. Frankfurter would join Justice Jackson in affirming on the merits. Vinson would prefer to place the decision on two points not mentioned in the Douglas opinion: (i) whether Terminiello's remarks were "fighting words" to those *inside* the hall; and (ii) whether it was permissible to keep him from speaking because of the hostility of those outside.

The case is thus a rich example of the subtleties of judicial review and judicial role. Justice Douglas, perhaps with conscious irony, is making the minimum decision and leaving virtually everything else for a later day. His opinion is the perfect execution of the Frankfurter etiquette of judicial economy, and it renders Jackson's magnificent dissent out of order. Frankfurter is anything but pleased by Douglas's restraint. He complains that the Court is stepping outside its "delicate role" by redressing grievances not pressed upon it by litigants. Behind the formalism of this protest lies a gut point which is left unspoken: If the Court cannot make a more serious point on behalf of Terminiello, it should let his conviction stand; this is trifling with serious issues.

Justice Jackson's dissent is a twenty-five-page essay which deserves to be read in its own right. He wrote so well, especially when angry, that it is hard to select representative excerpts. Anxious to disclose what the case is really about, he leaves us unclear as to how he disposes of Justice Douglas's error in the instruction and hence dilutes a bit the power of his dissent. Similarly, although he makes it abundantly clear that on these facts he would permit the police to arrest the speaker, he never quite tells us what the correct rule or principle should be. Nevertheless, his anger and eloquence force a sobering realization of how high the stakes are in cases of this genre.

Jackson emphasizes the facts. He evokes the unrest around the auditorium when Terminiello rose to speak and quotes the speech extensively. He sees this episode as part of a larger extremist strategy of "fighting for the streets" as a first step toward revolution. Since instances of calculated disorder like this one will, as he sees it, arise steadily given the brutal political struggles afoot in the world, he would permit the police to stop and if necessary arrest the speaker when in their judgment the speech carries a considerable risk of disorder. Listen to him for a moment:

. . . the local court that tried Terminiello was not indulging in theory. It was dealing with a riot and with a speech that provoked a hostile mob and incited a friendly one, and threatened violence between the two.[10]

This was not an isolated, spontaneous and unintended collision of political, racial or ideological adversaries. It was a local manifestation of a world-wide and standing conflict between two organized groups of revolutionary fanatics, each of which has imported to this country the strong-arm technique developed in the struggle by which their kind has devastated Europe.[11]

. . . we must bear in mind also that no serious outbreak of mob violence, race rioting, lynching or public disorder is likely to get going without help of some speech-making to some mass of people. A street may be filled with men and women and the crowd still not be a mob. Unity of purpose, passion and hatred, which merges the many minds of a crowd into the mindlessness of a mob, almost invariably is supplied by speeches. It is naive, or worse, to teach that oratory with this object or effect is a service to liberty. No mob has ever protected any liberty, even its own, but if not put down it always winds up in an orgy of lawlessness which respects no liberties.[12]

As a people grow in capacity for civilization and liberty their tolerance will grow, and they will endure, if not welcome, discussion even on topics as to which they are committed. . . . But on our way to this idealistic state of tolerance the police have to deal with men as they are.[13]

There is danger that, if the Court does not temper its doctrinaire logic with a little practical wisdom, it will convert the constitutional Bill of Rights into a suicide pact.[14]

In view of the majority's evasive disposition of the case, the challenge posed by *Terminiello* is to make peace with Jackson's dissent. He has added three complications to our perception of the problem.

First, the situation may be one which is being *manipulated* as a conscious strategy of inducing disorder, even against the speaker. This is the dilemma posed by contemporary tactics of confrontation designed to trick "the system" into overreacting, thereby precipitating disorder and disenchantment. Second, the speech must be placed in the context of tensions that exist at the moment the speaker chooses to speak or to continue speaking; the speaker may inherit a situation in which further speaking will be the trigger of disorder. On this view, the situation was already impossibly tense when Terminiello started to speak. Third, in a tense situation with factions in the audience, language which is neutral in form may take on meaning as incitement. Thus, Jackson was disposed to read some of Terminiello's remarks in context as inciting *his* audience to aggressive action.

Whatever our gratitude to Jackson for properly sobering the issue, there are several great difficulties with his reaction to the *Terminiello* facts. The content of Terminiello's speech was not in itself within the reach of the law. Had it been written, it would have raised little question. Also, his remarks, however offensive to those outside, were not fighting words to the audience he was addressing within the hall. Hence even if the fighting words doctrine were extended to ideological insults, it would have no bearing on these facts. Finally, the problem of disorder is precipitated exclusively by the hostility of the mob outside. This is not a speech on a street corner; it is in a hall. There is no shadow of a captive audience problem present. The mob outside is attempting censorship by the naked exercise of physical force.

The problem is tough, and one must sympathize with the police, but the rule selected may set the tenor of the society. While it makes sense to "take men as they are" in recognizing and penalizing the risks involved in uttering fighting words intending to insult, it makes profoundly less sense to "take men as they are" with respect to the risks involved in uttering offensive ideas. It is difficult to see that form of moral outrage as a fact of life which the law must accommodate. In the end, Justice Jackson's argument in *Terminiello* seems to rest on the reaction of the hostile audience whatever the merits of the audience's views; it is the *fact* of their reaction that tips the balance against speech. But it seems to me that sometimes even when the danger of disorder is high, the society must protect the speaker and insist that the audience endure the offense of an unpleasant idea.

Perhaps there is a middle ground. There may be implicit in a situation like *Terminiello* a kind of second-class speech which is generally permissible but which is not so valuable that the right to utter it will be protected regardless of the likely impact on a hostile audience. But, if so, we are back full circle to Justice Roberts's insistence in *Cantwell* that, if there are such categories of speech, the legislature must locate and evaluate them.

Like *Terminiello, Kunz v. New York,* decided in 1951, sharply poses the possibility of ideological fighting words. This time the issue is raised not by a conviction for breach of peace but by the defendant's speaking on the streets of New York without a license. Kunz was a Baptist minister who went out on the highways to preach the word of Christ. A New York ordinance required a permit for public meetings in the streets. Kunz had been granted such a permit in prior years, but it had been revoked because of his attacks on other religions. Denied a permit for the present occasion, he spoke without one. For this offense, he was fined $10. It is the validity of this sanction that brings the case before the Supreme Court. The Court, with only Justice Jackson in dissent, reverses.

Kunz is primarily a precedent on prior restraints. The issue it posed was whether a licensing system which left apparently unlimited discretion in the licensor was valid. The Court disposes of the matter firmly in a brief opinion by Chief Justice Vinson: The merits are covered by clear precedents. The use of the streets for public meetings is a fundamental liberty. Although such forums are subject to some regulation keyed to other customary uses, the Court has "consistently condemned licensing systems which vest in an administrative official discretion to grant or withhold a permit upon broad criteria unrelated to proper regulation of public places";[15] and it has held that such a scheme could be challenged by a speaker proceeding without a license. Nor is the case saved by the special facts as to the disorder caused by Kunz in the past. The Court is careful not to express an opinion as to whether subsequent punishment might be applied to Kunz for the speech he made. All that it need speak to is the absence of appropriate standards to guide the action of the licensor. On the view of the majority, Kunz, even though he may have made a speech which the state could validly subject to sanctions, can play the role of vicarious champion and challenge for all the validity of an imprecise licensing scheme. Thus, although the Court again ignores the problem of ideological fighting words, it reaffirms an important principle in the speech field about attacking measures "on their face."

Justice Frankfurter, concurring, reinforces the underlying principle ("The vice to be guarded against is arbitrary action by officials"),[16] but carries matters a step beyond the majority opinion. A properly drafted licensing scheme could, he thinks, validly bar a speaker because of the likelihood that he "would outrage the religious sensibilities of others."[17] Kunz is saved solely because the licensing scheme was too loosely drafted. On this view, it would not only be possible to punish a speaker for triggering the reflexive violence of the audience, it would also be possible to deny him a permit on the prediction, if the criteria were fully set forth, that he was likely to provoke such a reaction. This goes well beyond the notion that the policeman on the immediate scene should be permitted some leeway in predicting audience disorder.

Justice Jackson in angry dissent is, if anything, even more eloquent than he was in *Terminiello*. He does not really join issue with the majority or with Frankfurter. Ignoring the niceties of their positions, he appears to read them as having barred the states from using licensing keyed to the likelihood of disorder. Also, he appears to be less concerned, at least as regards a speaker like Kunz, with the discretion granted administrative officials. Kunz, he feels, "must win on the strength of his own right."[18]

Much of Jackson's anger is directed at the principle, the very good principle indeed, of scrutinizing with special care the discretion allotted administrative censors under schemes for prior restraints. Although stunning in his prose, he is not persuasive on this point. Also, Jackson is emphatically in accord with Justice Frankfurter that prior restraints could validly be keyed to predictions of reflexive disorder. Indeed, he insists this is the only sane way to administer the streets as public forums. Since the majority carefully abstained from expressing any opinion on this issue, he seems to be lambasting a straw man. But his opinion may reflect a tension that developed during the judicial conference on the case; perhaps he is angry precisely because the majority has refused to indicate that this method of control through licensing would be constitutional.

Jackson's most effective point is that when uttered on the streets of New York with its population of Jews and Catholics Kunz's speeches are fighting words—ideological fighting words:

This Court today initiates the doctrine that language such as this, in the environment of the street meeting, is immune from prior municipal control. We would have a very different question if New York had presumed to say that Kunz could not speak his piece in his own pulpit or hall. But it has undertaken to restrain him only if he chooses to speak at street meetings. There is a world of difference. The street preacher takes advantage of people's presence on the streets to impose his message upon what, in a sense, is a captive audience. A meeting on private property is made up of an audience that has volunteered to listen. The question, therefore, is not whether New York could, if it tried, silence Kunz, but whether it must place its streets at his service to hurl insults at the passer-by.[19]

He then quotes from *Chaplinsky* and continues:

Equally inciting and more clearly "fighting words," when thrown at Catholics and Jews who are rightfully on the streets of New York, are statements that "The Pope is the anti-Christ" and the Jews are "Christ-killers." These terse epithets come down to our generation weighted with hatreds accumulated through centuries of bloodshed. They are recognized words of art in the profession of defamation. They are not the kind of insult that men bandy and laugh off when the spirits are high and the flagons are low. They are not in that class of epithets whose literal sting will be drawn if the speaker smiles when he uses them. They are always, and in every context, insults which do not spring from reason and can be answered by none. Their historical associations with violence are well understood, both by those who hurl and those who are struck by these missiles. Jews, many of whose families perished in extermination furnaces of Dachau and Auschwitz, are more than tolerant if they pass off lightly the suggestion that unbelievers in Christ should all have been burned. Of course, people might pass this speaker by as a mental case, and so they might file out of a theater in good order at the cry of "fire." But in both cases there is genuine likelihood that someone will get hurt.[20]

Justice Jackson's eloquent dissent should be read against the opinions of Chief Justice Vinson and Justice Frankfurter and against Justice Roberts's opinion in *Cantwell*. The Court has not yet decided that the state may *not* reach such speech even though the disorder it causes is reflexive. What it has decided, both for subsequent restraints in *Cantwell* and for prior restraints in *Kunz,* is that it will not permit the policeman or the censor to stop such speech without the guidance of a carefully drafted legislative mandate. Despite the power of Justice Jackson's rhetoric, such a statute has not been forthcoming. I suspect the difficulties of drafting reveal a point of principle—the worthless offending speech cannot be safely disentangled.

The Speaker Is Silenced

Soon after the *Terminiello* decision in 1949 Justices Murphy and Rutledge, who had joined Justices Black and Douglas to form an unprecedentedly powerful liberal bloc, died and were replaced by Justices Clark and Minton. Although these personnel changes did not affect the outcome in *Kunz*, they did have an impact on two other major reflexive disorder cases decided during this period—*Feiner v. New York* in 1951 and *Beauharnais v. Illinois* in 1952. In both instances the Court underwrote broad censorship of street corner speech and established precedents that remain to be reckoned with down to the present day.

Feiner can perhaps best be understood as a reaction against the *Terminiello* decision two years earlier. The facts are relatively tame. Feiner was arrested, while making a street corner speech to a restless crowd, for violation of the New York breach of peace statute. His offense did not reside in the content of his message in any direct sense. In the course of a speech urging the audience to attend a meeting of the "Young Progressives" later that night at a nearby hotel, he had made derogatory remarks about President Truman, the American Legion, the Mayor of Syracuse, and other local officials. But it was agreed that these remarks—"Mayor Costello is a champagne-sipping bum"; "The American Legion is a Nazi Gestapo"—were not beyond the protection of the First Amendment. Nor was it contended that Feiner's speech constituted fighting words. Rather, his offense was that he was speaking to a "mixed audience" of Negroes and whites, some of whom liked what he was saying and some of whom detested it. One angry listener told the police, "If you don't get that son of a bitch off, I'll go in and get him off myself." The police judged that Feiner's speech was stirring up the crowd against him, and perhaps more important, against one another. Twice they requested him to stop, but he persisted. After he had been talking for half an hour, they arrested him. The Court by a vote of 6 to 3 affirmed the finding of the New York courts that the condition of the crowd coupled with Feiner's refusal to obey the police justified the termination of his speech and his conviction for disorderly conduct. The police were "faced with a crisis," wrote Chief Justice Vinson; their on-the-spot judgment as to the means necessary to preserve order must be given leeway.

Feiner thus endorses a heckler's veto. The speech at issue is not classic epithet; nor is the argument seriously advanced that it constitutes ideological fighting words. The risk of disorder arises because

the audience, or some of it, does not like what the defendant is saying
and wishes to stop it. In the abstract, if the state did not like what he
was saying, it would be powerless to silence him. In this situation,
however, it can claim neutrality. Chief Justice Vinson states:

Petitioner was . . . neither arrested nor convicted for the making or the
content of his speech. Rather, it was the reaction which it actually engendered.[21]

But by giving the police wide discretion to stop the speaker because
of audience hostility, the state—and the *Feiner* Court—in effect trans-
fers the power of censorship to the crowd. Moreover, the police are
likely to share the views of the angry audience; hence, their perception
of the unrest may be colored by their assessment of the speaker's
message. In any event, whatever the motivations of the police, the end
result is the censorship of wholly permissible content. *Feiner* thus
emerges as one of the Court's least satisfactory efforts—a decision
which endorses conduct deeply offensive to free speech values. The
man who has his way and emerges unscathed is the one who calls the
defendant a "son of a bitch" and threatens to hit him.

The bland Vinson opinion provokes sharp dissents from Justices
Black and Douglas; and Justice Frankfurter contributes a concurring
opinion. Several points emerge from the interplay of their views.

First, there is the question of "incitement." Vinson states:

It is one thing to say that the police cannot be used as an instrument for the
suppression of unpopular views, and another to say that, when as here the
speaker passes the bounds of argument or persuasion and undertakes incitement to riot, they are powerless to prevent a breach of the peace.[22]

Justice Frankfurter in his summary of the facts states that the defendant told part of his audience that it "should rise up in arms."[23] Neither
quotes what Feiner actually said. Justice Douglas does: "The negroes
don't have equal rights; they should rise up in arms and fight for their
rights."[24] (Feiner, it should be remembered, was inviting people to
attend a political meeting that evening.) Justice Black penetrates still
further. In a footnote he cites parts of the record that raise serious
doubt that Feiner had in fact used "in arms" this way. Then putting
evidentiary dispute aside, he adds: "In any event, the statement ascribed to petitioner by the officers seems clearly rhetorical when read

in context."[25] There was no indication that anyone in the audience was being moved to "rise up in arms."

The second point goes to the heckler's veto issue. Chief Justice Vinson pays lip service to it, but finds it irrelevant because Feiner was engaged in "incitement to riot." Justice Frankfurter seriously addresses the issue. He stresses that all the judges below had accepted the finding that "Feiner was stopped not because the listeners or police officers disagreed with his views but because these officers were honestly concerned with preventing a breach of the peace."[26] Aware that this hardly disposes of the issue of whether the police were enforcing the censorship of content sought by the crowd, Frankfurter acknowledges that the police "are peace officers for the speaker as well as for his hearers."[27] But having gone this far, he would defer to the practicalities of police administration of order on the streets. He adds the admonition: "It is not a constitutional principle that, in acting to preserve order, the police must proceed against the crowd, whatever its size and temper, and not against the speaker."[28]

Justice Black is highly effective in rebuttal. He states the controlling principle somewhat differently:

The police of course have power to prevent breaches of the peace. But if, in the name of preserving order, they ever can interfere with a lawful public speaker, they must first make all reasonable efforts to protect him.[29]

He then argues that on the record the police did "not even pretend to try to protect petitioner," and notes that the "one isolated threat" against the speaker was uttered by "a man whose wife and two small children accompanied him."[30] It is not enough that the police act in good faith; Justice Black would require that they exhaust other means of preserving order before silencing the speaker.

The third point goes to the degree to which the Court will assume the burden of making a fresh evaluation of the facts in such cases. It is agreed that First Amendment questions may involve constitutional facts and that where they do, as in obscenity, the Court will make a *de novo* review. Justice Black complains that the Court has shirked this responsibility in *Feiner*. The task, however, is more troublesome here than in obscenity, for there is likely to be more ambiguity in the record. Perhaps what is required is not so much that the Court reappraise the record as that it show patient interest in the particulars. The opinions of Chief Justice Vinson and Justice Frankfurter are unpersuasive not so much because of dispute over principle, although there may well be some, but because of their apparent indifference to the twin facts stressed by Justice Black, namely, that the disorder was threatened by the hostile audience not the speaker, and that the police made no effort to keep order before moving to silence the speaker.

Finally, although the Court does not address the point in *Feiner,* it may be helpful to bring into the discussion the concept of the *captive audience.* To some degree the street corner orator inflicts his message on unwilling ears, and that is surely a point against protecting it. But the time period of the "capture" is very brief and is, in my view, an appropriate price to extract from society in order to keep open the possibility of attracting the *attention* of a potential audience. Moreover, in *Feiner* nothing kept those members of the audience who were unhappy from simply walking away. The captive audience dilemma arises only because the unhappy insist on staying to be offended.

Two sociological realities compete with the abstract normative analysis of the issue posed by a case like *Feiner.* First, we may be asking the police to perform an impossible task—not merely to allow freedom for the thought they hate but to go down fighting on the side of the utterer of that thought. Second, there is the question of whether the Court, so far from the street corner, can really supervise the norm. In view of these realities, it is tempting to respond to the problem as the Court does in *Feiner* by piously admonishing against the suppression of unpopular views while underwriting broad police discretion. Yet that answer seems wrong. The Court should not underestimate its symbolic and educative role. It can affect the attitude and training of the police, and it can influence the popular attitude, which in turn will affect the police. Moreover, although it is tempting to see the *Feiner* episode as trivial, recent years have taught us the value of the streets and parks as places for public protest and the airing of grievances. The public forum should be protected not out of nostalgic regard for bygone days when leaflets and soapbox orators were important, but because it may again be central to the dynamics of dissent among free men. In the end, I think Justice Black had it exactly right. The police must make a serious effort to keep order before silencing the speaker; and the Supreme Court must remain open to review of that effort.

In *Beauharnais v. Illinois,* decided a year after *Feiner,* the Court once again endorses broad censorship of street corner speech. This time the defendant is prosecuted not for breach of peace or disorderly conduct but for violation of an Illinois statute making it a crime to publish, present, or exhibit in any public place material which portrays depravity, criminality, unchastity, or lack of virtue of a class of citizens, of any race, color, creed or religion which said publication or exhibition exposes the citizens of any race, color, creed or religion to contempt, derision, or obloquy or which is productive of breach of the peace or riots.[31]

The defendant was the president of an organization called the White Circle League. On a downtown Chicago street corner he and members of the League distributed a leaflet, in the form of a petition to the Mayor and City Council, which called on the City "to halt the further encroachment, harassment and invasion of white people, their property, neighborhoods and persons, by the Negro." The most pungent paragraph stated:

THE WHITE CIRCLE LEAGUE OF AMERICA is the only articulate white voice in America being raised in protest against negro aggressions and infiltrations into all white neighborhoods. The white people of Chicago MUST take advantage of this opportunity to become UNITED. If persuasion and the need to prevent the white race from becoming mongrelized by the negro will not unite us, then the aggressions . . . rapes, robberies, knives, guns, and marijuana of the negro, SURELY WILL![32]

The *Beauharnais* fact situation does not pose the reflexive violence issue squarely. Although the communication takes place on a street corner, it is by the written word. And, while the statute might be read as interdicting ideological insults in public places, it sounds in libel. As a result, there is little momentum for the Court to pursue the reflexive disorder issue and much discussion of the law of criminal libel.

The Court affirms the conviction in a 5 to 4 decision. The majority opinion is by Justice Frankfurter. His justification for upholding the conviction rests not on the views he expressed in *Feiner* and *Kunz* but on the assimilation of group libel to individual libel. Since there has been a long tradition of criminal sanctions against libel of individuals, "we cannot," he argues, "deny to a State power to punish the same utterance directed at a defined group, unless we can say that this is a wilful and purposeless restriction unrelated to the peace and well-being of the State."[33] Using this peculiar test, he devotes his opinion to marshalling data on racial tensions and disorder over Illinois history in order to establish that prohibition of racial group libel is not a "wilful and purposeless restriction." Nor is there any distinctive First Amendment standard that must be met, he argues, for libel belongs in the same family of speech as the fighting words in *Chap-linsky.*

Despite the talk of disorder and the citation of *Chaplinsky,* the focus has changed. The violence feared is not the reflexive violence of angry Negro audiences; it is the violence against Negroes generated by willful falsehoods about race. And the reference to *Chaplinsky* does not mean that Frankfurter saw Beauharnais's leaflet as containing fighting words; it means rather that he saw this kind of speech as belonging in the same "bottom drawer" of communications as the fighting words in *Chaplinsky.* [34]

On the basis of his dissents in *Terminiello* and *Kunz,* one might expect Justice Jackson to applaud the *Beauharnais* decision, but this time he ends up in dissent on the side of the speaker. He is centrally concerned with reconciling the deep tradition against seditious libel with the state criminal libel laws. He finds resolution in the argument that the First Amendment applies more stringently against federal regulation of speech than it does against state regulation. Then, despite this hard-won premise, he goes on to find that the Illinois statute transgressed even the less stringent standards for the states because it failed to provide adequate safeguards for the speech involved. Among other things, he would require the state to establish that the likelihood of disorder was high enough to satisfy the clear and present danger test before permitting it to convict a speaker. He is thus brought back to the issue of disorder in the streets. Application of the clear and present danger test, he argues, would require the trier to

consider whether a leaflet is so emotionally exciting to immediate action as the spoken word, especially the incendiary street or public speech [citing *Kunz* and *Terminiello*]. It will inquire whether this publication was obviously so foul and extreme as to defeat its own ends, whether its appeals for money—which has a cooling effect on many persons—would not negative its inflammatory effect, whether it would not impress the passer-by as the work of an irresponsible who needed mental examination. [35]

For a variety of reasons, Justice Frankfurter's opinion has always seemed to me a singularly illiberal and unpersuasive effort. Justice Jackson's dissent, after yielding so much to state regulation and in light of his special concern with ideological fighting words, is a powerful corroboration of that evaluation.

Two other aspects of *Beauharnais*—one of the Court's most complex, if dismal, free speech contributions—are of interest. First, in an exceptionally able dissent Justice Reed argues that the Illinois statute is unconstitutionally vague in its description of the proscribed material as that which "portrays . . . the lack of virtue of a class of citizens . . . which exposes [them] to . . . derision or obloquy." His opinion is a powerful reminder that if we are to have ideological fighting words, it will be a delicate and difficult task to draft them with the requisite precision. Second, Justice Black enters a stirring dissent which is sensitive to the seditious libel implications of the majority opinion. "The conviction rests," he reminds us, "on the leaflet's contents."[36]

7

Reflexive Disorder:
The Civil Rights Cases

For more than a decade after *Beauharnais* this area of the First Amendment field lay fallow. During the 1950s the Court was centrally concerned with various issues generated by official anti-Communism; by contrast, the problems of street corner speech seemed a bit quaint. Then during the heyday of the Warren Court in the early 1960s the phenomenon of speech in the public forum and the attendant problem of reflexive disorder once again claimed the Court's attention. This time the cases were presented not by ugly speakers like Terminiello and Kunz but by civil rights activists protesting segregation. And they involved not simply literal speech but other forms of expression such as parades and residential picketing.

The first of these cases, *Edwards v. South Carolina*[1] in 1963, arose out of a demonstration on the grounds of the South Carolina legislature. As a group of 187 young Negro students peacefully picketed to protest to the legislature various aspects of segregation, a crowd of two to three hundred whites gathered. A special contingent of police was on the scene. After about half an hour of observation, they expressed concern for public order and requested the demonstrators to disband. The demonstrators chose to remain and began to sing patriotic and religious songs, including "The Star-Spangled Banner." They were arrested and convicted of a breach of peace, a common law crime in South Carolina. In a confident opinion by Justice Stewart, the Court firmly rejected the judgment of the police and reversed the convictions. A lone dissent was entered by Justice Clark.

Several points in Justice Stewart's disposition of the controversy should be underscored. First, he has no difficulty in recognizing that public issue picketing is speech; indeed, he describes the demonstration as an exercise of First Amendment rights "in their most pristine and classic form."[2] Second, he explicitly states that in this area, as in obscenity, the Court has the power and the "duty" of *de novo* review of the facts. Third, he easily distinguishes *Chaplinsky*: "the record is barren of any evidence of 'fighting words.'"[3] Fourth, he emphasizes that, as in *Cantwell*, the state, by utilizing breach of peace as a common law crime "not susceptible of exact definition," has failed to give the courts, including the Supreme Court, the benefit of guidance from a narrow, deliberately drafted statute, evaluating the counter-interests against demonstrations like this.[4]

Finally, although this was arguably a great opportunity to do so, the Court does not confront *Feiner* head on and reappraise the cardinal principle that reflexive disorder may provide the basis for sanctioning the speaker. Rather, it elects to distinguish *Feiner* on the facts. That situation may have been dangerous; this one clearly was not. Culling from the *Feiner* opinion, Justice Stewart states:

This . . . was a far cry from the situation in *Feiner v. New York* where two policemen were faced with a crowd which was "pushing, shoving, milling around," where at least one member of the crowd "threatened violence if the police did not act," where "the crowd was pressing closer around petitioner and the officer," and where "the speaker passes the bounds of argument or persuasion and undertakes incitement to riot."[5]

The Court thus leaves the underlying question of principle unresolved and carefully keeps *Feiner* alive as a precedent. Despite the poignancy of its facts and Justice Stewart's empathy for the new rhetoric of the demonstration, *Edwards* leaves little more residue than did *Terminiello*. We learn only that where the hostile reaction of the audience *does not in fact threaten disorder,* the police may not constitutionally halt the speaker.

Justice Stewart concludes by reaffirming the non-controversial principle promulgated in *Terminiello* that the Constitution does not permit the suppression of views that are "unpopular," "provocative and challenging," that "invite dispute," or "stir people to anger." Although it is always good to have this principle reaffirmed, the Court leaves the impression of having reaffirmed what everyone agrees to, while cautiously stopping short of the real problem: May the dis-

affected non-captive audience, by threatening disorder, silence with
the aid of the police the speaker whose views they dislike?

Like *Edwards, Cox v. Louisiana*[6] in 1965 involved a mass demonstration
of Negroes—this time roughly fifteen hundred—in a Southern locale.
The situation was, however, more complex than in *Edwards* in that the
leader of the demonstration was charged with three different offenses:
breach of peace; obstructing public passageways; and picketing near
a courthouse in violation of a statute prohibiting such conduct. The
Court marshalled a majority for reversing the convictions on each of
these counts, but in the process indicated sharp disapproval of courthouse picketing and potential sympathy for flat bans of such massive
demonstrations on public streets. More than once references to
"mobs" and "mob law" creep into the opinions.

    The Louisiana court had found the defendant's conduct a breach
of peace because

[It] must be recognized to be inherently dangerous and a breach of the peace
to bring 1,500 people, colored people, down in the predominantly white
business district in the City of Baton Rouge and congregate across the street
from the courthouse and sing songs as described to me by the defendant as
the CORE national anthem carrying lines such as "black and white together"
and to urge upon those 1,500 people to descend upon our lunch counters
and sit there until they are served. That has to be an inherent breach of the
peace. . . . [7]

    The Supreme Court, speaking through Justice Goldberg, re-
sponds much as it did in *Edwards.* It makes its own review of the record
and finds that the vigorous singing and hand clapping of the demonstrators did not in fact amount to disorder. It notes that "the fear of
violence seems to have been based upon the reaction of the group of
white citizens looking on from across the street." There are various
references to this crowd "grumbling," "muttering," and becoming "a
bit agitated." But the Court concludes that this too is "a far cry" from
Feiner. [8] It is therefore unnecessary to reexamine the premise underlying *Feiner.* Once again, the Court is satisfied merely to distinguish
Feiner on its facts; here there simply was no real risk of reflexive
disorder. Also, the Court finds the Louisiana breach of peace statute
as construed to be unconstitutionally vague in that "it sweeps within
its broad scope activities that are constitutionally protected free
speech and assembly."[9] The categories of protected speech so endan-

gered consist, as they did in *Edwards,* of speech which may invite dispute and unrest and be provocative and challenging. Finally, as in *Edwards,* the Court finds no evidence of "fighting words."

The Court's disinclination to come to grips with the dilemmas of reflexive disorder threatened by audience hostility become still more pronounced in *Gregory v. Chicago* [10] in 1969. This case arose out of a celebrated demonstration in which the comedian and civil rights leader Dick Gregory led a group of Negroes to the home of Mayor Richard Daley, where they picketed in protest of segregation in the Chicago public school system and urged the firing of the Superintendent of Schools. Although the picketers were peaceful and orderly, their presence in the white neighborhood in which the Mayor lived and at the very doorstep of the Mayor's home was deeply annoying. After several hours, during which the police, who appear to have handled matters professionally and neutrally, were able to maintain order, the crowd of white onlookers became increasingly hostile and restive. The police decided dispersal was necessary to preserve order. When the protesters refused to move, they were arrested for violating the Chicago disorderly conduct ordinance—the same ordinance involved in *Terminiello* twenty years earlier.

Gregory posed the underlying issue sharply. The threat of disorder was real, and there was reason to respect the judgment of the police, who had "chaired" the meeting with skill and patience. Hence the tactic used in *Edwards* and *Cox* was not available to the Court. Moreover, the picketing of the private residence of a public official raised challenging countervalues, and in this instance the speaker had in effect "invaded" the environment of the hostile audience. Not since *Terminiello* had the Court been confronted with so powerful a fact situation. As in *Terminiello,* however, it elected to dispose of the case tactically, upsetting the conviction while avoiding confrontation with the question of principle. Its ambivalent response is all the more striking because it is unanimous in upsetting the convictions.

Chief Justice Warren, writing for the Court, sets the tone at the outset of his one-and-a-half-page opinion: "This is a simple case." He then offers a capsule restatement of the facts which serves to highlight the heckler's veto issue:

Although petitioners and the other demonstrators continued to march in a completely lawful fashion, the onlookers became unruly as the number of bystanders increased. Chicago police, to prevent what they regarded as an impending civil disorder, demanded that the demonstrators, upon pain of arrest, disperse. When this command was not obeyed, petitioners were arrested for disorderly conduct.[11]

Having so neatly framed the reflexive violence problem, the Chief Justice disposes of the case in three paragraphs without ever finding it necessary to refer to the problem again. From his examination of the record he concludes that there is no evidence to support a finding that the defendants' conduct was "disorderly," ignoring apparently the contention that it was responsible for triggering the reflexive disorder of the crowd. He also notes the possibility that the demonstrators were convicted for their failure to obey the police request to disperse. He disposes of this point, which has never been fully settled by the Court, on the ground that the defendants were not charged with refusing to obey an officer. Finally, he adds, without discussion, that the "trial judge's charge permitted the jury to convict for acts clearly entitled to First Amendment protection."[12] Apparently the judge had read the ordinance to the jury. Justices White, Stewart, and Harlan in brief concurring opinions rest their decision solely on the overbreadth of the ordinance and the judge's charge pursuant to it. Thus, twenty troubled years after *Feiner,* the Court is still anxious to decide as little as possible about the limits of censorship when the countervalue is the risk of disorder.

Gregory is saved from oblivion only by the vigor and seriousness of Justice Black's seventeen-page concurrence. His opening statement contrasts sharply with that of the Chief Justice:

This I think is a highly important case which requires more detailed consideration than the Court's opinion gives it. It in a way tests the ability of the United States to keep the promises its Constitution makes to the people of the Nation.[13]

The opinion makes fascinating reading as Justice Black struggles nobly with his ambivalence. On one hand, as he has made clear on several earlier occasions, he does not like public issue picketing and demonstrations. He sees in them the seeds of mob violence. He concurs in the decision of the Court because the ordinance is not sufficiently narrow to safeguard the speech component in such behavior. But he makes it abundantly clear that the state could stringently regulate this type of protest, especially when it invades the privacy of the home, by means of a carefully drafted, narrow statute. On the other hand, he is sensitive to the style and poise of the Gregory protesters and pauses to pay them a compliment:

Indeed, in the face of jeers, insults, and assaults with rocks and eggs, Gregory and his group maintained a decorum that speaks well for their determination simply to tell their side of their grievances and complaints.[14]

He is also sensitive to the fact that the risk of disorder is created exclusively by the hostility of the audience:

. . . both police and demonstrators made their best efforts to discharge their responsibilities as officers and citizens, but they were nevertheless unable to restrain the hostile hecklers within decent and orderly bounds.[15]

But finally even Justice Black does not resolve the issue he poses so carefully and fairly: May the demonstrators present their grievance to the Mayor and the public in this dramatic fashion or must they defer to the hostility of the audience? Rather, he finds the root of the trouble in the picketing and not the message. He vigorously reasserts that

the Constitution does not bar enactment of laws regulating *conduct*, even though connected with speech, press, assembly, and petition, if such laws specifically bar only the conduct deemed obnoxious. . . . [Emphasis added.][16]

Later he repeats that the states are not "powerless to regulate the conduct of demonstrators and picketers, conduct which is more than 'speech,' more than 'press,' more than 'assembly,' more than 'peti- tion.' "[17] Justice Black appears to be suggesting that the disorder in *Gregory* arises because picketing rather than leaflets or soapbox ora- tory is the medium of expression. Certainly this act of communication, given its notoriety and coverage by the news media, conveys—and is meant to convey—a complex and highly charged message that goes beyond the flat assertion that the Superintendent of Schools must be changed. In any event, the point to note here is that the added ele- ment of residential picketing in *Gregory* greatly complicates the al- ready complex issue of reflexive disorder, with the result that even the serious effort of Justice Black to unravel the dilemmas posed does not frame a solution.

Justice Black's opinion recalls a striking passage in *Miami and the Siege of Chicago* by Norman Mailer.[18] As a member of a large audience

kept waiting half an hour by a civil rights leader, Mailer finds himself
growing angry and reflects that if even he is moved to anger by so
petty an annoyance, think what tides of rage the Negro protests and
their concomitant annoyances must be stirring in those throughout
the country who are less friendly to the Negro cause than he is. One
is tempted to see a comparable omen in Justice Black's response to
the new rhetoric of demonstration. If so valiant and steadfast a friend
of freedom of speech can get this upset over the annoyances and risks
which attend demonstrations, it must give us all pause. Listen to this
passage from his *Gregory* opinion:

> But to say that the First Amendment grants those broad rights free from any
> exercise of governmental power to regulate conduct, as distinguished from
> speech, press, assembly, or petition, would subject all the people of the
> Nation to the uncontrollable whim and arrogance of speakers, and writers,
> and protesters, and grievance bearers.[19]

Gregory suggests another issue which deserves our attention: Can
refusal to obey a police order to disperse or move on be made an
independent, non-challengeable ground for criminal sanction? The
demonstrators, it will be recalled, were arrested when they refused to
obey such an order. Chief Justice Warren found it unnecessary to
appraise this as a possible basis for the conviction, because neither the
disorderly conduct ordinance nor the judge's charge had specified it
as an offense. Thus the question remains: Might the troublesome
issues of censorship posed by street corner speech be "finessed" by
moving to the neutral ground of penalizing refusal to cooperate in the
judgment of the police officer on the scene? Or in this sensitive area
is the policeman's order, like the action of a licensor denying a permit,
necessarily subject to the collateral attack of direct disobedience?

Considerable light is cast on the point, although not precisely in
this context, by *Shuttlesworth v. Birmingham*[20] in 1965. This case arose
out of a civil rights boycott. The Reverend Shuttlesworth and a group
of ten or twelve were standing in front of a Birmingham store when
requested to disperse by a policeman. The others moved on, leaving
Shuttlesworth standing there alone. When he refused a second request to move, he was arrested and convicted of violating two city
ordinances prohibiting obstruction of the sidewalk, refusal to obey a
police request to move on, and refusal to obey "any lawful order" of
the police. The Court unanimously upset the conviction.

The opinion of the Court by Justice Stewart definitively rejects the notion that the state may delegate to the police *full* discretion in regulating behavior on the public streets:

Literally read . . . the second part of this ordinance says that a person may stand on a public sidewalk in Birmingham only at the whim of any police officer of that city. . . . Instinct with its ever-present potential for arbitrarily suppressing First Amendment liberties, that kind of law bears the hallmark of a police state.[21]

Could the state, however, narrow the discretion of the policeman but still make him the final arbiter of what is necessary to prevent inconvenience or disorder on the streets? The Alabama court had attempted to salvage the statutes under which Shuttlesworth was convicted by restricting the one to the prevention of obstruction and the other to the management of vehicular traffic. The Court rejects the first because the narrowing construction came too late in the case; and it rejects the second because there is no evidence that the policeman who ordered Shuttlesworth to move on was directing traffic at the time. Thus, it does not reach the question of whether under limited circumstances the refusal to obey the police in and of itself could be made the offense.

Justice Black has spoken eloquently to this question on two occasions—in his concurring opinions in *Cox* and *Gregory*. In *Cox* the question of the finality of the police judgment arises in the form of a challenge to the vagueness of the statute and not to the separate offense of disobeying a police command. Justice Black states:

In the case before us Louisiana has by a broad, vague statute given policemen an unlimited power to order people off the streets, not to enforce a specific, nondiscriminatory state statute forbidding patrolling and picketing, but rather whenever a policeman makes a decision on his own personal judgment that views being expressed on the street are provoking or might provoke a breach of the peace. Such a statute does not provide for government by clearly defined laws, but rather for government by the moment-to-moment opinions of a policeman on his beat.[22]

In *Gregory* he meets the issue head on. In response to the contention that the refusal to obey the police order to disperse was "the diversion tending to a breach of the peace," he states:

The "diversion" complained of on the part of Gregory and the other marchers was not any noise they made or annoyance or disturbance of "other persons" they had inflicted. Their guilt of "disorderly conduct" therefore turns out to be their refusal to obey instanter an individual policeman's command to leave the area of the Mayor's home. Since neither the city council nor the state legislature had enacted a narrowly drawn statute forbidding disruptive picketing or demonstrating in a residential neighborhood, the conduct involved here could become "disorderly" only if the policeman's command was a law which the petitioners were bound to obey at their peril. But under our democratic system of government, lawmaking is not entrusted to the moment-to-moment judgment of the policeman on his beat. . . . To let a policeman's command become equivalent to a criminal statute comes dangerously near making our government one of men rather than of laws.[23]

Neither the force nor the clarity of this statement can be improved upon. If the policeman is to be allowed to play the role of chairman at street corner meetings at all, he may only do so under a detailed set of *Robert's Rules of Order* provided for him by the legislature.

When placed against the background of the Court's earlier experiences with street corner speech, the civil rights cases invite several reflections.

First, these cases show that the street corner forum is anything but obsolete. Indeed, the sophistication of modern communication technology enhances rather than diminishes the impact of street corner speech. The old-fashioned forms of protest and the new mass media collaborate. The former supply the colorful, newsworthy episode; the latter supply the national and global coverage. The street corner forum thus continues to occupy an important part of the free speech field.

Second, by studiously avoiding reexamination of the *Feiner* rationale the Court keeps *Feiner* available as a principle—there remains the possibility of a risk of reflexive disorder sufficiently high to justify the silencing of the speaker by the police. The Court, however, steadfastly protects the speech in the particular case by making its own review of the facts and concluding that the risk of disorder was not high enough in fact, that the case before it is "a far cry from *Feiner.*"

Third, in appraising the risk of disorder, the Court appears to place reliance on the presence at the scene of a sizeable contingent of police. It sees the presence of the police not as a corroboration of the risk of disorder but as an indication that there is sufficient power available to maintain order. This leaves open the troublesome question of what happens when insufficient police are provided. May the state substitute arresting the speaker for providing the police?

Fourth, the Court has rejected efforts by the states to delegate solution of the street corner speech problem to the policeman by making the refusal to obey a police order an independent criminal offense. The citizen is permitted to challenge the authority of the police command by directly disobeying it; the illegality of such an act of disobedience depends upon the validity of the policeman's act of censorship. In brief, the Court has granted to the citizen on the public streets review of the policeman's efforts to chair the meeting.

Fifth, in appraising the propriety of silencing the speaker, the Court seems affected, though it does not say so, by its own evaluation of the merits of the speaker's views. It is one thing to become restless at the vulgar fulminations of a Father Terminiello or a Reverend Kunz; it is quite another to become restless over the graceful protests of the Negro young in a Southern city.

Finally, there is the irony that *Terminiello,* which seemed so empty as a precedent, has been selected by the Court for repeated citation. The Court announces the bland principle that the audience must undergo some discomfort without help from the police; it must endure views that are unpopular, challenging, provocative, and likely to stir unrest and anger and invite dispute. While it is possible to read too much into levels of judicial rhetoric, surely this formula lacks the hearty resonance of the "robust, uninhibited, and wide-open" phrase which has come ringing down from *New York Times v. Sullivan.* [24]

8

Reflexive Disorder: *Chaplinsky* Redux

———————◆———————

The character of the street corner speech problem changed once again in the early 1970s as a series of cases generated by the escalating rhetoric of the anti-war and civil rights movements reached the Court. These cases were decided during a period of transition between the Warren and Burger Courts. In every instance the majority protected the speaker, but it did so in the face of increasingly sharp dissents by the new members of the Court. At issue was the scope of the "fighting words" doctrine announced three decades earlier in *Chaplinsky*. The majority insisted that the doctrine applied only to provocative personal insults uttered face-to-face, while the dissenters argued that *Chaplinsky* covered not only fighting words but offensive speech in public places as well.

The Court's first encounter with the offensive language issue came in 1971 in *Cohen v. California,*[1] a case we have discussed elsewhere. Cohen was convicted under a statute prohibiting "offensive conduct" for wearing a jacket bearing the slogan "Fuck the Draft" in the corridors of a Los Angeles courthouse. The California Court of Appeals, in affirming the conviction, defined "offensive conduct" as "behavior which has a tendency to provoke *others* to acts of violence or to in turn disturb the peace," and concluded that the conviction was justified, for it was "reasonably foreseeable" that others might be provoked to violent reaction by Cohen's jacket. The Supreme Court reversed the conviction in an opinion by Justice Harlan. Chief Justice Burger and Justices Blackmun, Black, and White dissented.

Justice Harlan's opinion remains the most powerful statement of the majority view of the scope of *Chaplinsky* and of the status of offensive speech under the First Amendment.[2] At the outset he stresses that the content ("the inutility or immorality of the draft"),[3] as distinct from the manner, of Cohen's message is clearly beyond the reach of government sanction. He then considers in turn a number of issues which are *not* presented by the case. Cohen's message was not obscene, for it was in no way erotic. Nor did it fall within the narrow category of fighting words. Harlan distinguishes *Cohen* from *Chaplinsky* with admirable rigor:

While the four-letter word displayed by Cohen in relation to the draft is not uncommonly employed in a personally provocative fashion, in this instance it was clearly not "directed to the person of the hearer." No individual actually or likely to be present could reasonably have regarded the words on appellant's jacket as a direct personal insult.[4]

He also distinguishes *Feiner*, adding an intriguing gloss to it in the process:

Nor do we have here an instance of the exercise of the State's police power to prevent a speaker from *intentionally* provoking a given group to a hostile reaction. Cf. *Feiner v. New York* (1951); *Terminiello v. Chicago* (1949). There is . . . no showing that anyone who saw Cohen was in fact violently aroused or that appellant intended such a result. [Emphasis added.][5]

This restatement of *Feiner* is double-edged. On one hand, it appears to be an attempt to curtail the scope of that troublesome precedent. On the other, it suggests a possible strategy for dealing with situations in which the speaker makes a deliberate effort to induce reflexive disorder.

Harlan next turns to the captive audience considerations which have so often troubled the Court in the street corner context. Did the state have a legitimate interest in protecting "unwilling or unsuspecting viewers" from "otherwise unavoidable exposure to appellant's crude form of protest"?[6] Harlan acknowledges that regulation of street corner speech may sometimes be warranted in order to protect a captive audience, but he establishes a high threshold for such regulation:

The ability of government, consonant with the Constitution, to shut off discourse solely to protect others from hearing it is . . . dependent upon a showing that substantial privacy interests are being invaded in an essentially intolerable manner. Any broader view of this authority would effectively empower a majority to silence dissidents as a matter of personal predilections.[7]

This standard was not met in *Cohen,* he concludes, for those in the courthouse "could effectively avoid further bombardment of their sensibilities simply by averting their eyes."[8]

Having dealt with these satellite issues, Harlan reaches the crux of the case:

Against this background, the issue flushed by this case stands out in bold relief. It is whether California can excise . . . one particular scurrilous epithet from the public discourse, either upon the theory of the court below that its use is inherently likely to cause violent reaction or upon a more general assertion that the States, acting as guardians of public morality, may properly remove this offensive word from the public vocabulary.[9]

The first of these rationales for censorship brings Harlan back to the problem of audience hostility. The California court had, in effect, extended the rationale underlying the regulation of fighting words to offensive speech. Harlan rejects this strategy in a passage of great power and clarity. Again, one is struck by what a remarkable contribution to free speech theory the apparently trivial *Cohen* case has become in his hands:

The rationale of the California court is plainly untenable. . . . We have been shown no evidence that substantial numbers of citizens are standing ready to strike out physically at whoever may assault their sensibilities with execrations like that uttered by Cohen. There may be some persons about with such lawless and violent proclivities, but that is an insufficient base upon which to erect, consistently with constitutional values, a governmental power to force persons who wish to ventilate their dissident views into avoiding particular forms of expression. The argument amounts to little more than the self-defeating proposition that to avoid physical censorship of one who has not sought to provoke such a response by a hypothetical coterie of the violent and lawless, the States may more appropriately effectuate that censorship themselves.[10]

The underlying logic of *Chaplinsky* is that the utterer of fighting words is responsible for the violent response of the person to whom his words are addressed. But Harlan refuses to apply such a line of reasoning to offensive speech. Had others reacted violently to Cohen's jacket, they—"the violent and lawless"—would have been guilty of a breach of peace, not Cohen himself.

Harlan also rejects the alternative rationale for censoring offensive speech—the argument that the states may regulate such speech "in order to maintain what they regard as a suitable level of discourse within the body politic."[11] In his view, the dangers which attend such regulation far outweigh any benefits that might be derived from it. First, there is the difficulty of distinguishing offensive words:

. . . while the particular four-letter word being litigated here is perhaps more distasteful than most others of its genre, it is nevertheless often true that one man's vulgarity is another's lyric. Indeed, we think it is largely because governmental officials cannot make principled distinctions in this area that the Constitution leaves matters of taste and style so largely to the individual.[12]

Second, as the statement "one man's vulgarity is another's lyric" suggests, Harlan recognizes that regulation of offensive speech might have the effect of limiting the participation in public discourse of those for whom such language is an accepted vernacular.

Third, Harlan observes that "words are often chosen as much for their emotive as their cognitive force."[13] Cohen's choice of language was not gratuitous; he was attempting to convey the depth of his feelings about the draft. Had he been barred from using the particular word he chose, the content of his message would have suffered:

We cannot sanction the view that the Constitution, while solicitous of the cognitive content of individual speech, has little or no regard for that emotive function which, practically speaking, may often be the more important element of the overall message sought to be communicated.[14]

In view of the "emotive force" of his language, Cohen's message is the epitome of seditious libel. It speaks with limitless criticism and disgust of a government policy. And Harlan is sensitive to the contribution Cohen's diction makes to that political message.

Finally, Harlan warns that the censorship of particular words might serve as a cover for the censorship of ideas:

. . . we cannot indulge the facile assumption that one can forbid particular words without also running a substantial risk of suppressing ideas in the process. Indeed, governments might soon seize upon the censorship of particular words as a convenient guise for banning the expression of unpopular views.[15]

The net effect of Justice Harlan's opinion is thus to curtail the potential scope of *Chaplinsky* and to extend the protection of the First Amendment to offensive speech. Although the actual decision in *Chaplinsky* was limited to fighting words, Justice Murphy's opinion contained some loose language about other categories of speech, the "punishment of which has never been thought to raise a constitutional question."[16] In addition to fighting words, he mentioned "the lewd and obscene," "the libellous," and "the profane." As we have seen, the Court in *Roth* and *Beauharnais* accepted the *Chaplinsky* invitation and placed obscenity and group libel outside the protection of the First Amendment. But the *Cohen* Court declines to do the same with respect to "the profane." Justice Harlan insists that *Chaplinsky* applies only to personal insults, "directed to the person of the hearer," which are inherently likely to provoke a breach of peace. And he flatly refuses to extend the fighting words rationale for censorship—the risk of reflexive disorder—to offensive speech. Moreover, he explicitly rejects other possible rationales for the censorship of such speech: Neither the vulgarity of the speech nor captive audience considerations, short of invasion of privacy in "an essentially intolerable manner," are sufficient justifications for censorship.

In a brief opinion by Justice Blackmun, the dissenters dismiss the Court's "agonizing over First Amendment values" as "misplaced and unnecessary." In their view, "Cohen's absurd and immature antic" fell "well within the sphere of *Chaplinsky.*"[17]

Gooding v. Wilson[18] in 1972 further reinforces the majority's narrow reading of *Chaplinsky.* The facts in *Gooding,* unlike those in *Cohen,* fall directly within the classic fighting words format. The defendant was a participant in an anti-war demonstration in front of an Army building in Georgia. When inductees arrived at the building, the demonstrators blocked the entrance and refused to obey a police order to move. The police then attempted to remove them forcibly and a scuffle ensued in the course of which the defendant said to one policeman, "White son of a bitch, I'll kill you," and to another, "You son of a bitch, if you ever put your hands on me again, I'll cut you all to pieces." He was convicted under a Georgia statute that made it a misdemeanor to use "to or of another, and in his presence . . . opprobrious words or abusive language, tending to cause a breach of the peace." In a 5 to 2 decision the Supreme Court invalidated the statute

on its face on the ground that it was capable of reaching protected as
well as unprotected speech. Justices Powell and Rehnquist did not
participate. Chief Justice Burger and Justice Blackmun vigorously
dissented.

The majority, in an opinion by Justice Brennan, applied the overbreadth doctrine. Under this doctrine, which was elaborated and saw
frequent use during the heyday of the Warren Court, a defendant is
permitted to challenge an overly broad speech statute on its face, even
though his own conduct might be subject to regulation under a more
narrowly drawn statute. In effect, the defendant is allowed to act as
a vicarious champion on behalf of others to whom the law might be
unconstitutionally applied. Thus, although the defendant in *Gooding*
may in fact have engaged in unprotected expression, he is allowed to
challenge the facial validity of the Georgia statute. The rationale for
this relaxation of traditional rules of standing is, as Justice Brennan
puts it, "the transcendent value to all society of constitutionally protected expression."[19] The very existence of an overly broad statute is
harmful, for it may inhibit those whose speech is protected from
exercising their First Amendment rights. It also may provide a pretext
for discriminatory enforcement against unpopular speakers. The
practical effects of the overbreadth technique are that it enables the
Court to invalidate such a law on its face and to do so in the earliest
possible case—it need not wait for an unconstitutional application.

The state contends that the statute under which Gooding was
convicted had been construed by the Georgia courts to be limited to
fighting words and hence did not suffer from overbreadth. Justice
Brennan rejects this argument. On the basis of his own examination
of the Georgia cases, he finds that the statute was not limited "as in
Chaplinsky, to words that 'have a direct tendency to cause acts of
violence by the person to whom, individually, the remark is addressed' ";[20] it was applied as well to language which, though vulgar
and offensive, was clearly protected. The statute is thus unconstitutional on its face, for it is susceptible of being applied to protected
expression.

The dissenters are sharply critical of the majority's use of the
overbreadth technique and, by extension, of its narrow reading of
Chaplinsky. Chief Justice Burger characterizes the result as "bizarre"
and observes:

If words are to bear their common meaning, and are to be considered in
context, rather than dissected with surgical precision using a semantic scal-

pel, this statute has little potential for application outside the realm of "fighting words." . . . [21]

Justice Blackmun, in an opinion joined by the Chief Justice, remarks that he finds the decision "strange indeed" and adds: "I feel that by decisions such as this one and, indeed, *Cohen v. California,* the Court, despite its protestations to the contrary, is merely paying lip service to *Chaplinsky.* "[22]

On June 26, 1972 the Court made cultural history of a sort by deciding three cases involving the word "motherfucker." The three cases follow a roughly similar pattern. In *Rosenfeld v. New Jersey*[23] the defendant was convicted under a statute that proscribed "loud and offensive or profane or indecent language" in any public place; in the course of addressing a school board meeting he had, as the Court put it, used the adjective "m——f——" to describe the teachers, the school board, the town, and the country. In *Lewis v. New Orleans*[24] an ordinance made it a breach of peace "wantonly to curse or revile or to use obscene or opprobrious language toward or with reference to" a policeman; the defendant had addressed policemen who were arresting her son as "g—d——m—— f——police." And in *Brown v. Oklahoma*[25] the defendant was convicted under a statute prohibiting the utterance of "any obscene or lascivious language or word in any public place or in the presence of females"; during a political meeting held in a university chapel Brown, a Black Panther, had referred to some policemen as "m—— f——fascist pig cops" and to a particular policeman as that "m—— f——pig."

In each instance the majority, adhering to the narrow interpretation of *Chaplinsky* embodied in *Cohen* and *Gooding,* summarily vacates the conviction and remands the case to the state courts—*Rosenfeld* and *Brown* for reconsideration in light of *Cohen* and *Gooding; Lewis* for reconsideration in light of *Gooding* alone. Chief Justice Burger and Justices Blackmun and Rehnquist dissent in all three cases, with Burger and Rehnquist both entering opinions. Justice Powell, drawing interesting distinctions between the three cases, dissents in *Rosenfeld* and concurs in *Lewis* and *Brown;* he writes a separate opinion in each case.

Lewis is the only one of the three cases that falls within the fighting words pattern. The Court's remand of the case for reconsideration in light of *Gooding* indicates that it is concerned with the possible overbreadth of the ordinance's prohibition of "obscene and opprobrious language." Justice Powell, concurring, does not share the majority's concern with overbreadth: "I see no genuine over-breadth problem in this case."[26] But he finds the conviction vulnerable on another ground. He emphasizes that the defendant's words were addressed not to the average citizen but to a policeman on duty:

> If these words had been addressed by one citizen to another, face to face and in a hostile manner, I would have no doubt that they would be "fighting words." But the situation may be different where such words are addressed to a police officer trained to exercise a higher degree of restraint than the average citizen.[27]

Powell would thus remand the case for reconsideration in light of *Chaplinsky*. Ironically, if his principle were adopted by the Court, it would tend to impeach the decision that launched the fighting words doctrine—Chaplinsky, it will be recalled, was convicted for addressing fighting words to a policeman.[28]

    Rosenfeld and *Brown* involve not fighting words but offensive speech. The dissenters offer several different rationales for punishing such speech. Like the California court in *Cohen*, the Chief Justice does not distinguish between the use of offensive language in public and the direct verbal assault of fighting words. He argues that both categories of speech are more likely to provoke breaches of peace and both should be regulated in the interest of preserving public order:

> It is barely a century since men in parts of this country carried guns constantly because the law did not afford protection. In that setting, the words used in these cases, if directed toward such an armed civilian, could well have led to death or serious bodily injury. When we undermine the general belief that the law will give protection against fighting words and profane and abusive language such as the utterances involved in these cases, we take steps to return to the law of the jungle. These three cases, like *Gooding*, are small but symptomatic steps. If continued, this permissiveness will tend further to erode public confidence in the law—that subtle but indispensable ingredient of ordered liberty.[29]

    Justice Rehnquist's rationale for censoring offensive speech is simply that such speech is worthless. He pointedly quotes the passage from *Chaplinsky* in which Justice Murphy suggested that "the lewd and obscene" and "the profane," as well as fighting words, are outside the First Amendment. As he sees it, Lewis's words were fighting words, and those of Rosenfeld and Brown were lewd, obscene, and profane.

He thus refuses to recognize not only the gloss added to *Chaplinsky* by *Cohen* but also the Court's many decisions setting stringent standards for the regulation of obscenity.

Justice Powell, dissenting in *Rosenfeld,* offers a narrower and more closely reasoned rationale for censorship. He concedes that Rosenfeld's language did not constitute fighting words, for it was not directed at a particular individual, and "the good taste and restraint" of the audience at the school board meeting "made it unlikely that physical violence would result."[30] Like the other dissenters, however, he rejects the majority view that *Chaplinsky* is limited to fighting words:

. . . the exception to First Amendment protection recognized in *Chaplinsky* is not limited to words whose mere utterance entails a high probability of an outbreak of physical violence. It also extends to the willful use of scurrilous language calculated to offend the sensibilities of an unwilling audience.[31]

Powell would thus affirm the conviction in *Rosenfeld* on the ground that the defendant's utterances constituted "a verbal assault on an unwilling audience."[32] He concludes:

The preservation of the right to free and robust speech is accorded high priority in our society and under the Constitution. Yet, there are other significant values. One of the hallmarks of a civilized society is the level and quality of discourse. We have witnessed in recent years a disquieting deterioration in standards of taste and civility in speech. For the increasing number of persons who derive satisfaction from vocabularies dependent upon filth and obscenities, there are abundant opportunities to gratify their debased tastes. But our free society must be flexible enough to tolerate even such a debasement provided it occurs without subjecting unwilling audiences to the type of verbal nuisance committed in this case. The shock and sense of affront, and sometimes the injury to mind and spirit, can be as great from words as from some physical attacks.[33]

Powell's personal distaste for the speech at issue is unmistakable in this passage, but he does not appear to share the premise implicit in the opinions of the other dissenters that the state has a legitimate interest in raising the level of public discourse. Nor does he appear to subscribe to Chief Justice Burger's premise that offensive language, like fighting words, is productive of disorder. He does, however, insist that the censorship of such speech is justified under certain circumstances in the interest of protecting the sensibilities of the audience.

Powell's concurrence in *Brown* makes it clear that he is serious about trying to find a basis for principled distinctions in this area. He finds *Brown* a "significantly different" case from *Rosenfeld* in that the captive audience considerations which were for him decisive in the latter are not present in the former. Brown had been invited to "a political meeting . . . to present the Black Panther viewpoint"; hence the language he used "might well have been anticipated by the audience."[34] This distinction is, however, pretty subtle. Indeed, in important respects the two cases are identical. Both Brown and Rosenfeld used offensive language in the course of explicitly political speeches and in both instances those offended could simply have left. Thus, Powell's effort, though interesting, is not altogether persuasive.

Unlike the other dissenters, Powell does not openly disavow *Cohen.* It is not clear, however, how he would square his approach with that precedent. Justice Harlan in *Cohen,* while leaving open the possibility of regulating offensive speech in the interest of protecting a captive audience, had established a high threshold for such regulation. It was only warranted, he said, when "substantial privacy interests are being invaded in an essentially intolerable manner."[35] Justice Powell does not quote or cite this strong language. In the absence of such a standard, the expansion of *Chaplinsky* he advocates might prove difficult to contain and might allow a "sensitive audience veto" over public discussion. For, as Justice Harlan warned in *Cohen,* too broad a view of the privacy rights of the audience in the public forum "would effectively empower a majority to silence dissidents as a matter of personal predilections."[36]

No doubt pressure to expand *Chaplinsky* will continue in the future. But in this series of cases the Warren Court majority holds, though just barely. *Chaplinsky* remains an extremely narrow concession to censorship; and *Cohen,* which explicitly extends protection to offensive speech, remains good law.[37]

What can be said by way of summarizing assessment about the Court's experience with the problem of disorder in the public forum? The single dominating fact is that in all of the numerous street corner speech cases the Court has decided over the last three decades the threat of disorder has come from the reaction of a hostile audience *to* the speaker, not from the incitement of an empathetic audience *by* the speaker. There is nothing in the nature of things that would keep street corner speech from involving incitement. The simple datum from cases at the level of the Supreme Court, however, is that the problem of public disorder has arisen where the audience and not the speaker threatens the disorder.

Public order is a paramount value for a society, and once it is breached the consequences are likely to set off a chain reaction. The Court has thus been confronted with a troublesome question of policy: When, if ever, may the speaker be silenced for the sake of preserving order? The ideal answer to this question, which is that the crowd should never be permitted to censor the speaker, when apart from its threats the law has no claim to silence him, is at war with the practical realities and the necessity of maintaining order on the public streets. It runs against the hard common sense that we must not expect too much tolerance from the random audiences of the street and that we must not expect too much of the policeman thrust by events into the role of chairing the meeting.

The Supreme Court has reflected these tensions in its handling of the problem. It has thus far declined to answer definitively the underlying policy question about the censorship rights of the hostile audience. And it has repeatedly quoted the mild dictum from *Terminiello* that the First Amendment protects speech which invites unrest and anger and is challenging and provocative—rhetoric which carefully avoids mention of speech which invites not merely dispute but the risk of retaliatory disorder. Nevertheless, in the vast majority of cases it has managed by one constitutional route or another to find a basis for upsetting the particular conviction. Indeed, the speaker has won in *every* case decided during the last twenty-five years. Thus, whatever its reticence toward bold, clear assertions of principle in this area, the Court has shown remarkable empathy for dissident speech, however vulgar, unpatriotic, or abrasive.

There are, however, three early cases—*Chaplinsky, Feiner,* and *Beauharnais*—in which the Court permitted the conviction of the speaker to stand. These cases form an interesting pattern. All three permit an audience veto. It is sharpest and narrowest in *Chaplinsky,* where it is limited to fighting words—face-to-face insults likely to stir the average man to retaliatory violence. The Court continues to cite *Chaplinsky* with approval, but always readily distinguishes it from the case at hand. In retrospect, it seems to enjoy an undeserved reputation and prestige as a precedent. Although in recent years several members of the Court have urged that the fighting words exception be expanded to cover offensive speech in public, *Chaplinsky,* as interpreted by the majority, marks off only a tiny corner of the speech field.

The concession to censorship is least clear and least limited in *Feiner.* Chief Justice Vinson's opinion in *Feiner* contains some loose and misleading language about incitement, but in the end it represents a holding that, if the risk of disorder is great enough, the police may silence the speaker, and may do so before they have exhausted other means of keeping the peace. It permits, that is, a heckler's veto. Although impeached at the time by Justice Black's exceptional dissent, it has continued in good standing down to the moment. Indeed, the reluctance of the Court to overrule *Feiner* is itself a major point about the development of doctrine in this area. Yet in cases such as *Edwards* and *Cox* the Court has firmly protected the speaker by making its own review of the facts and concluding that the case before it is "a far cry from *Feiner.*" Arguably, these cases indicate that *Feiner* has been overruled *sub silento* and that the Court will simply refuse to find in any future case a sufficient risk of disorder. Certainly it seems likely that *Feiner* itself would be decided differently were it to arise today.

Finally, *Beauharnais,* the group defamation decision, may indicate that something akin to "group fighting words" will be acceptable as a rationale for censorship, if there is a statute so providing. *Beauharnais* is not tied directly to the risk of retaliatory disorder, as are *Chaplinsky* and *Feiner.* Rather, it rests on an analogy between group and individual libel. Although the Court has never again been confronted with the group defamation question, the continued vitality of *Beauharnais* is highly questionable, in view of the Court's discovery in *New York Times*[38] of the free speech values implicated in private libel cases.

While the Court has left this trio of precedents intact, it has limited their scope by two tactics. First, it has asserted its privilege, indeed its duty, to make an independent review and evaluation of the facts. Since the issues in these cases are likely to be imbedded in factual detail, the Court adds immeasurably to the bite of its principles by so intimately supervising their application; and it adds too to its flexibility in processing grievances.

Second, following *Cantwell,* it has insisted on precision in the legislative banning of speech. It has thus virtually barred the traditional, all-purpose breach of peace statute from use in this context. Before street corner speech can be disciplined by law, the Court requires that the legislature think about the problem, isolate precisely what it is about the speech it does not like, and give the police, the jury, *and* the Supreme Court of the United States the benefit of its advice. The alternative, as Justice Black has so eloquently warned, is censorship by the policeman on his beat.

Cantwell, the very first case in the sequence, thus emerges in the end as perhaps the most powerful precedent in the field and as an especially powerful resource on the side of the speaker. It should be remembered, however, that Justice Roberts's careful opinion left open the possibility of the legislature specifying ideological fighting words, that is, statements other than personal insults which might move men to retaliatory violence. But he insisted that if censorship of offensive opinions is ever to occur in this society, the censorial judgment must be made deliberately by the legislature and not *ad hoc* by the crowd in the street.

One final turn of the screw has been suggested not only by the character of certain contemporary demonstrations but also by Justice Harlan's restatement in *Cohen* of the holding in *Feiner*. He stated in *Cohen* by way of distinguishing *Feiner:* "Nor do we have here an instance of the exercise of the State's police power to prevent a speaker from intentionally provoking a given group to hostile reaction."[39] We have heard a lot in recent years about confrontation tactics designed to goad authorities into overreacting and thus producing a larger grievance to exploit. May the law make it an offense to *intentionally* stir an audience to retaliatory violence against oneself? This time we may have a gap between realism and what practically can be isolated by legal draftsmanship and safely entrusted to juries to pass on. In any event, *Cantwell* would surely require extraordinary precision in the drafting of such a measure.

In the end, the Court's hesitation to commit itself further on principle in this area may reflect not only the intransigence of the reflexive disorder issue in a turbulent, real world but also a certain political shrewdness in keeping its options open. As the *dramatis personae* have changed over the past three decades from Jehovah's Witnesses to Young Progressives to crypto-fascists to Negro civil rights groups to anti-Vietnam protestors, there has been abundant indication that street corner speech remains close to a vital nerve in the society and that it is treacherous to attempt to classify with finality the form the reflexive disorder problem is likely to assume when protest takes to the streets.

9

Subversive Advocacy:
The Core Issue
and the *Brandenburg* Answer

———◆———

The last stage in our review of the regulation of content is, appropriately, both the most important and the most difficult of the First Amendment issues we have surveyed. It is the problem of speech that *incites* to violence and illegal action as a political tactic. Analytically, this problem complements the problem of reflexive disorder. In both instances society regulates speech as a tactic in maintaining order. Speech is seen as a stimulus to undesirable action; censorship is seen as part of a strategy for controlling that action. In the reflexive disorder area the concern is that the speaker will move a hostile audience to disorder in retaliation against him; in this area the concern is that the speaker will move a sympathetic audience to violent action against a target he has selected.

We reach here the ultimate battleground for free speech theory—the area in which the claims of censorship are at once most compelling and most dangerous to key values in an open society. The case for speech is that it is, in a profound sense, *the* alternative to force as a way of changing men's actions. The question is: Does speech at some point become so closely linked to force that we perceive it as the exercise of force? The commonsense answer has always been "yes," and there has always been general agreement that at some point of proximity to violent action words can be reached by law. Indeed, even so ardent a champion of free speech as John Stuart Mill conceded that his theory would permit punishing the statement that corn dealers are starvers of the poor "when delivered orally to an excited mob assembled before the house of a corn dealer."[1]

In part, the concession to the censor in this area has rested on an analogy to ordinary crimes, such as theft, arson, and murder. The common law has long accepted the concepts of incitement and solicitation to such crimes. A moment's reflection, however, makes it apparent that the matter is not so simple. Surely there is a profound difference between inciting to arson by the use of words and inciting to revolution by the use of words. We do not have a ready word for the distinction, yet it is a deep and obvious one. And the basic fact about the Supreme Court's encounters with incitement is that *in every instance they have involved incitement as a political tactic.* This fact does not make the analogy to routine criminal incitement irrelevant. It does, however, complicate it.

The primary complication is that cases of incitement as a political tactic involve a uniquely important countervalue: radical criticism of the government and the society. This countervalue emerges most clearly in the extreme instance, the crime of violent overthrow of the government. While it might be possible to incite another to arson by private persuasion, it is unlikely that premises so private could move him to revolution. If a man is seriously enough at odds with the society to advocate violent overthrow, his speech has utility not because advocating violence is useful but because the premises underlying his call to action should be heard. He says something more than "Revolt! Revolt!" He advances premises in support of that conclusion. And those premises are worth protecting, for they are likely to incorporate serious and radical criticism of the society and the government. To state in capsule form a point to which we shall frequently recur, there is a fundamental tension between the principle that seditious libel cannot be proscribed by law and the common sense of stopping free speech at the boundary of incitement to crime. The accommodation between these two notions is perhaps the central issue for the American tradition of free speech.

It is singularly difficult to find a formula that will serve to separate the valuable radical premises—the criticism—from the not-so-valuable radical action conclusion. Yet there is a dilemma if we do not try to do so. On one hand, were we to solve the problem by holding that all radical action rhetoric is immune, the affront to community common sense might well be greater than it would be were we to immunize all pornography. On the other hand, if we acknowledge the risk of disorder that such speech carries as the rationale for some censorship, it will be difficult to keep the law from reading that risk into all serious dissident criticism.[2]

A strategy for reaching an accommodation which grants a jurisdiction to censorship, while confining it as narrowly as possible, might include the following elements:

(i) to require, somewhat pedantically, that the message contain *explicit action words*. If we do not draw the line here, it will prove impossible to control the inclination to perceive implicit action commands and urgings in all serious criticism of government.

(ii) to require that the action words be urgings of direct, immediate, concrete action.

(iii) to read the message as a whole, and to develop sensitivity in reading the metaphors of violence which are frequent in radical rhetoric.

(iv) to view the problem from the perspective of the countervalues to be protected; and to read the message against a tradition of robust criticism and political tolerance.

Although the Supreme Court has followed these tactics unevenly, its most recent actions reflect a very close approach to them. It is to these recent developments that we turn first; thereafter we shall trace the Court's tortuous path to this last stage.

One final prefatory observation before we embark: The problem does not arise as purely as we will treat it. It does not, that is, arise with *lone individual speakers;* only *groups* employ or contemplate employing violence and illegality as a political tactic. The incitement issue therefore merges with the problems of vicarious advocacy, freedom of assembly, and political conspiracy. Those problems shall occupy much of our attention in this book, as they have occupied the attention of the Court. For the moment, however, we shall concentrate on the content of the inciting messages, at the risk of distorting the size and strength of the speakers.

We begin at the end of the story, with *Brandenburg v. Ohio*[3] in 1969, one of the oddest performances in the Court's history. *Brandenburg* involved the conviction of a Ku Klux Klan leader for violating the Ohio Criminal Syndicalism Statute. This law had been enacted in 1919 in response to the use of selective violence as a means of industrial change, a tactic primarily associated with the rise of the Industrial Workers of the World. It prohibited "advocating . . . the duty, necessity, or propriety of crime, sabotage, violence or unlawful methods of terrorism as a means of accomplishing industrial or political reform."

An almost identical statute had been upheld by the Court in *Whitney v. California*[4] in 1927.

The Klan meeting had taken place at a farm outside Cincinnati and had been filmed by newsmen. Although the films showed hooded figures, guns, and a burning cross, the meeting was notably docile, at least for a protest in 1969. There were some mutterings about "burying the nigger" and "sending the Jews back to Israel," and the defendant made a short speech, the most provocative sentence of which was:

We're not a revengent organization, but if our President, our Congress, our Supreme Court, continues to suppress the white, Caucasian race, it's possible that there might have to be some revengeance taken.[5]

Nothing in the case offered an occasion for rethinking basic doctrine. Neither the speech nor the surrounding fact situation contained any suggestion of violence or of the advocacy of violence. Unless the Court was to take judicial notice of the violent propensities of the Klan thirty years too late, the Ohio statute as applied appeared clearly to have violated the Constitution. One would have expected, therefore, a *per curiam* reversal of the conviction.

That expectation would have been half correct. The Court unanimously upset the conviction, and it did so in a *per curiam* opinion. But it then went on to find the Ohio statute unconstitutional on its face and to overrule *Whitney v. California,* thereby resetting, albeit in somewhat delphic fashion, the boundary line for radical speech. Moreover, as we shall see, it engaged in "revision" of the prior precedent. And it did all this in a four-and-a-half-page opinion, two pages of which were simply devoted to stating the facts of the case.

The Court's reasoning is important enough to warrant quoting in its entirety:

The Ohio Criminal Syndicalism Statute was enacted in 1919. From 1917 to 1920, identical or quite similar laws were adopted by 20 States and two territories. . . . In 1927, this Court sustained the constitutionality of California's Criminal Syndicalism Act, the text of which is quite similar to that of the laws of Ohio. *Whitney v. California* (1927). The Court upheld the statute on the ground that, without more, "advocating" violent means to effect political and economic change involves such danger to the security of the State that the State may outlaw it. Cf. *Fiske v. Kansas* (1927). But *Whitney* has been thoroughly discredited by later decisions. See *Dennis v. United States,* 341 U.S. 494, at 507 (1951). These later decisions have fashioned the principle that the constitutional guarantees of free speech and free press do not permit a State to forbid or proscribe advocacy of the use of force or of law violation except where such advocacy is directed to inciting or producing imminent lawless action and is likely to incite or produce such action. As we said in *Noto v. United States* (1961), "the mere abstract teaching . . . of the moral propriety or even moral necessity for a resort to force and violence, is not the same as preparing a group for violent action and steeling it to such action." See also *Herndon v. Lowry* (1937); *Bond v. Floyd* (1966). A statute which fails to draw this distinction impermissibly intrudes upon the freedoms guaranteed by the First and Fourteenth Amendments. It sweeps within its condemnation speech which our Constitution has immunized from governmental control. Cf. *Yates v. United States* (1957); *DeJonge v. Oregon* (1937); *Stromberg v. California* (1931). . . .

Measured by this test, Ohio's Criminal Syndicalism Act cannot be sustained. The Act punishes persons who "advocate or teach the duty, necessity, or propriety" of violence "as a means of accomplishing industrial or political reform"; or who publish or circulate or display any book or paper containing such advocacy; or who "justify" the commission of violent acts "with intent to exemplify, spread or advocate the propriety of the doctrines of criminal syndicalism"; or who "voluntarily assemble" with a group formed "to teach or advocate the doctrines of criminal syndicalism." Neither the indictment nor the trial judge's instructions to the jury in any way refined the statute's bald definition of the crime in terms of mere advocacy not distinguished from incitement to imminent lawless action.

Accordingly, we are here confronted with a statute which, by its own words and as applied, purports to punish mere advocacy and to forbid, on pain of criminal punishment, assembly with others merely to advocate the described type of action. Such a statute falls within the condemnation of the First and Fourteenth Amendments. The contrary teaching of *Whitney v. California* cannot be supported, and that decision is therefore overruled.[6]

This then is the Court's latest word on the problem of accommodating radical political criticism and incitement. Unfortunately, the facts neither add insight into the Court's meaning nor provide a measure of the principle asserted. Almost any principle, however bland, would have sufficed to protect the speech at issue. Moreover, the gesture of the *per curiam* opinion, which is customarily a warning not to make too much of the Court's action, suggests that it did not regard what it was doing as especially important.

Yet *Brandenburg* is of great significance. As I read the opinion, the Court has done two things. First, in much the fashion that it protected the advocacy of adultery in *Kingsley Pictures*,[7] it has placed beyond censorship the "mere advocacy" of violence. The Ohio statute is addressed to a doctrine—the doctrine of criminal syndicalism—in much the same way that the Arkansas law in *Epperson* was addressed to the doctrine of evolution.[8] At this level there may appear to be a distinction between advocating a *doctrine* of industrial terrorism and advocating an *act* of industrial terrorism, but the Court makes no such distinction. Rather, it extends protection to all advocacy of violence, including the advocacy of particular acts.

Second, having so emphatically rejected the proposition that advocacy of violence is unprotected, it was necessary for the Court to reset the boundary line of permissible censorship. This seems to me the most striking aspect of *Brandenburg*. The new line is located "where such advocacy is directed to inciting or producing imminent lawless action and is likely to incite or produce such action." The magic words are now "incitement to imminent lawless action." Perhaps there is no way to capture the boundary in words that will please everyone or sound the same to all ears. But for me, "incitement" has the ring of a term of art and is the best word for marking the minimal jurisdiction over political speech that concern with public order requires be ceded to censorship. It marks the last term in a series.

10

Subversive Advocacy: The Beginnings

———◆———

The Hand Legacy

The story of the development of the law up to *Brandenburg* lies close to the heart of the American free speech tradition. Perhaps the law's most complex example of doctrinal evolution, it retains irresistible fascination as intellectual history. And it provides us with an occasion to survey the most extraordinary anthology of judicial utterances ever. Among the most remarkable of the essays in this anthology is the first—Judge Learned Hand's opinion, as a District Court judge, in *Masses Publishing Co. v. Patten.* [1]

Decided on July 24, 1917, *Masses* antedates the Supreme Court's first major speech decision, *Schenck v. United States* [2] by two years. Three factors, however, have conspired to lessen its salience in the tradition. First, Judge Hand chose to place his decision on the basis of statutory construction alone. Second, his construction of the statute was rejected by the Court of Appeals which reversed his decision. Third, his opinion was overtaken and overwhelmed by the prestige and prominence which came to be attached to the opinion of Justice Holmes in *Schenck* two years later. There is in the fate of *Masses* a stunning irony about the building of a tradition. Judge Hand's opinion is to my mind vastly superior to Holmes's effort. Had it been the dominant initial document, our legal history would almost certainly have been better. Indeed, as I see it, part of the achievement of the inelegant *Brandenburg per curiam* opinion is that it recovers an insight into the nature of the problem of speech triggering action first advanced by Learned Hand's elegant opinion fifty-two years earlier.

The legislation involved in *Masses*—and in most of the other speech cases which arose during World War I—was the Espionage Act of 1917. The Act was primarily concerned with espionage and the protection of military secrets, but it also included the following provisions:

Whoever, when the United States is at war, shall willfully make or convey false reports or false statements with intent to interfere with the operation or success of the military or naval forces of the United States or to promote the success of its enemies and whoever, when the United States is at war, shall willfully cause or attempt to cause insubordination, disloyalty, mutiny, or refusal of duty, in the military or naval forces of the United States, or shall willfully obstruct the recruiting or enlistment services of the United States, shall be punished by a fine of not more than $10,000 or imprisonment for not more than twenty years, or both.[3]

The Act also provided for the punishment of conspiracy to violate these provisions; authorized the issue of search warrants for the seizure of property used in committing a violation of the Act; and empowered the Postmaster General to declare "non-mailable" materials he judged to be in violation of the Act.

The Masses was a radical journal which flourished during the decade 1910-1920, featuring such names as Max Eastman, John Reed, John Sloan, Art Young, Sherwood Anderson, and George Bellow. The litigation arose over an effort by the magazine to enjoin the Postmaster from barring an issue from the mails on the ground that it contained material which violated the provisions of the Act quoted above. The items objected to were four political cartoons, titled "Liberty Bell," "Conscription," "Making the World Safe for Capitalism," and "Congress and Big-business," a poem in tribute to Emma Goldman and Alexander Berkman, who were then in prison, and three editorial comments on the draft and conscientious objection, which quoted letters by English conscientious objectors on the brutality of prison life. Judge Hand granted the injunction.

Hand's opinion is a classic example of the power the statutory construction tactic can have. At the outset he emphasizes that "no question arises touching the war powers of Congress." Indeed, he is willing, almost anxious, to concede broad powers of censorship to Congress in light of wartime necessities:

It may be that the peril of war, which goes to the very existence of the state, justifies any measure of compulsion, any measure of suppression which Congress deems necessary to its safety, the liberties of each being in subjection to the liberties of all.[4]

But the decisive question for him is to what extent Congress has in fact exercised these powers. And the statute is to be read against the background of American traditions of political tolerance which Congress will be assumed to be following in the absence of unequivocal expression to the contrary.

The leverage of this tactic is apparent in the following passage. Judge Hand is weighing the Government's contention that the items under challenge would "cause" insubordination in the armed forces by generating discontent and disaffection with the war in the general public:

This, too, is true; men who become satisfied that they are engaged in an enterprise dictated by the unconscionable selfishness of the rich, and effectuated by a tyrannous disregard for the will of those who must suffer and die, will be more prone to insubordination than those who have faith in the cause and acquiesce in the means.[5]

He then applies his canon of construction:

Yet to interpret the word "cause" so broadly would . . . involve necessarily as a consequence the suppression of all hostile criticism, and of all opinion except what encouraged and supported the existing policies, or which fell within the range of temperate argument. It would contradict the normal assumption of democratic government that the suppression of hostile criticism does not turn upon the justice of its substance or the decency and propriety of its temper. Assuming that the power to repress such opinion may rest in Congress in the throes of a struggle for the very existence of the state, its exercise is so contrary to the use and wont of our people that only the clearest expression of such a power justifies the conclusion that it was intended.[6]

Hand then proceeds to locate the point at which the Postmaster would be justified in barring the magazine. I do not believe it is possible to improve upon his statement of the principle:

Yet there has always been a recognized limit to such expressions, incident indeed to the existence of any compulsive power of the state itself. One may not counsel or advise others to violate the law as it stands. Words are not only the keys of persuasion, but the triggers of action, and those which have no purport but to counsel the violation of law cannot by any latitude of interpretation be part of that public opinion which is the final source of government in a democratic state. The defendant asserts not only that the magazine indirectly through its propaganda leads to a disintegration of loyalty and a disobedience of law, but that in addition it counsels and advises resistance to existing law, especially to the draft. . . . To counsel or advise a man to an act is to urge upon him either that it is his interest or his duty to do it. While, of course, this may be accomplished as well by indirection as expressly, since words carry the meaning that they impart, the definition is exhaustive, I think, and I shall use it. Political agitation, by the passions it arouses or the convictions it engenders, may in fact stimulate men to the violation of law. Detestation of existing policies is easily transformed into forcible resistance of the authority which puts them in execution, and it would be folly to disregard the causal relation between the two. Yet to assimilate agitation, legitimate as such, with *direct incitement to violent resistance,* is to disregard the tolerance of all methods of political agitation which in normal times is a safeguard of free government. The distinction is not a scholastic subterfuge, but a hard-bought acquisition in the fight for freedom, and the purpose to disregard it must be evident when the power exists. If one stops short of urging upon others that it is their duty or their interest to resist the law, it seems to me one should not be held to have attempted to cause its violation. If that be not the test, I can see no escape from the conclusion that under this section every political agitation which can be shown to be apt to create a seditious temper is illegal. I am confident that by such language Congress had no such revolutionary purpose in view. [Emphasis added.][7]

There are several things to underscore in this remarkable passage, a passage which seems all the more impressive when read in the hindsight of later judicial efforts to talk about freedom of speech. First, it would seem to make little difference that Hand is not talking about the meaning of the First Amendment. He ascribes the principle he is using to "the use and wont of our people," and he works with it not as the finding of a public opinion survey but as a normative philosophic principle. Second, he is acutely sensitive to the urgency of protecting vigorous, effective, and even damaging political criticism. He warns that if we draw the line of censorship more generously, we will cut off "the tolerance of all methods of political agitation which in normal times is a safeguard of free government." Third and most important, he writes like a man working with a living distinction. This distinction may not be easy to capture in fixed words, but one can express a feel for it and can come at it in different ways. The terms pile up: "counsel," "advise," "urge upon others it is their duty or interest," "direct incitement," "triggers of action."

The facts in *Masses,* unlike those in *Brandenburg,* give meaning to the principle being applied. Judge Hand patiently reviews the various items and finds that each falls short of being a "trigger of action." The most bitter of the four cartoons was the one titled "Conscription," which Hand describes as follows:

The second cartoon shows a cannon to the mouth of which is bound the naked figure of a youth, to the wheel that of a woman, marked "Democracy," and upon the carriage that of a man, marked "Labor." On the ground kneels a draped woman marked "Motherhood" in a posture of desperation, while her infant lies on the ground. The import of this cartoon is obviously that conscription is the destruction of youth, democracy, and labor, and the desolation of the family. No one can dispute that it was intended to rouse detestation for the draft law.[8]

Having flatly acknowledged that the cartoon is a deliberate effort to engender detestation of the law, Hand applies his "incitement" test to it:

As to the cartoons it seems to me quite clear that they do not fall within such a test. Certainly the nearest is that titled "Conscription," and the most that can be said of that is that it may breed such animosity to the draft as will promote resistance and strengthen the determination of those disposed to be recalcitrant. There is no intimation that, however hateful the draft may be, one is duty bound to resist it, certainly none that such resistance is to one's interest. I cannot, therefore, even with the limitations which surround the power of the court, assent to the assertion that any of the cartoons violate the act.[9]

He then turns to the texts which express strong admiration for draft resisters and conscientious objectors, treating them, in his words, as "heroes worthy of a freeman's admiration." He is a stickler for explicit incitement:

That such comments have a tendency to arouse emulation in others is clear enough, but that they counsel others to follow these examples is not so plain. Literally at least they do not, and while, as I have said, the words are to be taken, not literally, but according to their full import, the literal meaning is the starting point for interpretation. One may admire and approve the course of a hero without feeling any duty to follow him. There is not the least implied

intimation in these words that others are under a duty to follow. The most
that can be said is that, if others do follow, they will get the same admiration
and the same approval. Now, there is surely an appreciable distance between
esteem and emulation; and unless there is here some advocacy of such emulation, I cannot see how the passages can be said to fall within the law.[10]

In the closing paragraphs of the opinion, Judge Hand, in a passage we quoted in the preface, disposes of the government's attempt
to rest its case in the end not on particular items so much as on the
"general tenor and animus of the paper as a whole." With speech
crimes as with other crimes, Hand insists, the state must "point with
exactness to just that conduct which violates the law."[11]

It must be remembered that Judge Hand was dealing with the
written word in a magazine of general circulation, not with an excited
crowd already on the scene. Hence he concentrates on an exegesis of
the words used and seems uninterested in the surrounding circumstances. One can object that his test may invite something akin to tax
avoidance by clever speakers who convey their meaning without using
the fatal action words. At this remove, we cannot be certain, for
example, how Hand would have decided a case like the Mill example
in which the speaker addresses the "opinion that corn dealers are
starvers of the poor" to "an excited mob assembled before the house
of a corn dealer." Perhaps he would have found that under those very
special circumstances the "literal" words did not exhaust the "full
import" of the speaker's message. But he would certainly have insisted that the basic problem is one of safely extracting incitement
from vigorous political criticism and that for that purpose it is a good
idea to begin with exactly what the man said. As he puts it in his very
great sentence, the distinction between political agitation and incitement "is not a scholastic subterfuge, but a hard-bought acquisition in
the fight for freedom."

The Holmes Legacy

If the intellectual history starts with Judge Hand's opinion in *Masses*
in 1917, the Supreme Court history starts with Justice Holmes's opinion in *Schenck v. United States,* decided on March 3, 1919. For our
purposes, *Schenck* is best read, not only against *Masses,* but also together with *Debs v. United States,* [12] decided one week later, on March
10, 1919.

Both *Schenck* and *Debs* arose out of Socialist Party opposition to the war and to conscription. Schenck, a party official, had participated in the preparation and distribution of a leaflet to men who were awaiting induction into the armed forces. Eugene Debs, a nationally prominent leader of the party, had addressed a general audience at a Socialist convention. Both were convicted under the Espionage Act for their communications. Schenck was sentenced to six months; Debs, who a year later, while in prison, was to poll almost a million votes as the Socialist candidate for President, was sentenced to ten years. Both convictions were affirmed unanimously by a Supreme Court which numbered among its members Justices Holmes and Brandeis. And both opinions were written by Justice Holmes.

By modern standards the *Schenck* leaflet is startlingly mild. One side simply presented an argument that conscription violated the involuntary servitude prohibition of the Thirteenth Amendment. It contained references to "venal capitalist newspapers," "gang politicians," and "monstrous wrongs against humanity." The action words were:

. . . join the Socialist Party in its campaign for the repeal of the Conscription Act. Write to your congressman. . . . You have a right to demand the repeal of any law. Exercise your rights of free speech, peaceful assemblage and petitioning the government for a redress of grievances. . . . sign a petition to congress for the repeal of the Conscription Act. Help us wipe out this stain upon the Constitution!

The other side of the leaflet was a bit more militant. Headed "Assert Your Rights," it argued that officials acted unconstitutionally if they refused to "recognize your right to assert your opposition to the draft." Its most strongly worded sentence—"Will you let cunning politicians and a mercenary capitalist press wrongly and untruthfully mould your thoughts?"—was followed by this: "Do not forget your right to elect officials who are opposed to conscription." For this communication, Schenck and another Party official were convicted of conspiracy to cause "insubordination" in the armed forces and to "obstruct" the recruiting and enlistment services.[13]

Prior to *Schenck* there had been some controversy over whether the First Amendment stood for anything more that the abolition of prior restraints, the Blackstonian definition of freedom of speech. It is the unqualified, if little heralded, achievement of Justice Holmes's opinion to establish that the Amendment applies to subsequent as well as prior restraints. He disposes of the matter in a single sentence:

It may well be that the prohibition of laws abridging the freedom of speech is not confined to previous restraints, although to prevent them may have been the main purpose, as intimated in *Patterson v. Colorado*. [14]

The opinion then proceeds to the defendants' challenge under the First Amendment to the subsequent restraint imposed in the case at hand:

We admit that in many places and in ordinary times the defendants in saying all that was said in the circular would have been within their constitutional rights. But the character of every act depends upon the circumstances in which it is done. The most stringent protection of free speech would not protect a man in falsely shouting fire in a theater and causing a panic. It does not even protect a man from an injunction against uttering words that may have all the effect of force. The question in every case is whether the words used are used in such circumstances and are of such a nature as to create a clear and present danger that they will bring about the substantive evils that Congress has a right to prevent. It is a question of proximity and degree. When a nation is at war many things that might be said in time of peace are such a hindrance to its effort that their utterance will not be endured so long as men fight and that no court could regard them as protected by any constitutional right. It seems to be admitted that if an actual obstruction of the recruiting service were proved, liability for words that produced that effect might be enforced. The statute of 1917, in [section] 4 punishes conspiracies to obstruct as well as actual obstruction. If the act (speaking, or circulating a paper,) its tendency and the intent with which it is done are the same, we perceive no ground for saying that success alone warrants making the act a crime. *Goldman v. United States.* Indeed that case might be said to dispose of the present contention if the precedent covers all *media concludendi.* But as the right to free speech was not referred to specially, we have thought fit to add a few words. [15]

This passage invites a number of reactions. First, there is the casualness of the tone. Holmes tells us that *Goldman,* a decision affirming the convictions of Emma Goldman and Alexander Berkman for conspiring to violate the Selective Draft Act, is dispositive of the case before him. [16] He is merely adding "a few words" about free speech.

  Second, the clear and present danger formula is announced as a premise to support the conviction, not to impeach it. Apparently the *Schenck* leaflet presented a clear and present danger within Holmes's meaning of the words. Also, there is the unnoticed puzzle that, if this is the test, then Schenck could scarcely have been tried under it; surely this is not what the jury was asked to decide.

Third, Holmes makes no effort to limit the statute. He holds that success is not necessary for a conviction and that it is sufficient if the speech be made with the intent and have the tendency to cause obstruction. Then he is willing to infer the "intent" and the "tendency" from the mere distribution of the leaflet to those eligible for the draft:

Of course the document would not have been sent unless it had been intended to have some effect, and we do not see what effect it could be expected to have upon persons subject to the draft except to influence them to obstruct the carrying of it out.[17]

This would be a questionable exercise with respect to any statute, but it is especially disturbing in the First Amendment area, and it stands in striking contrast to Judge Hand's effort to give a narrow construction to the same provisions of the Espionage Act.

Finally, the concern expressed by Hand for preserving to the uttermost the possibilities of political criticism is, to my ear, altogether missing. Holmes verges on saying that any serious criticism of the war and the draft sent to men who are eligible for service would violate the statute. The fundamental poverty of his analysis is that he treats the problem of political speech as he might any crime. And even this is too generous an assessment, I am afraid, for he does not accord such speech the care in analysis and the stringency of standards he would have applied to, say, a solicitation to arson.

Schenck—and perhaps even Holmes himself—are best remembered for the example of the man "falsely shouting fire" in a crowded theater. Judge Hand said in *Masses* that "words are not only the keys of persuasion, but the triggers of action." Justice Holmes makes the same point by means of the "fire" example, an image which was to catch the fancy of the culture.[18] But the example has long seemed to me trivial and misleading. It is as if the only conceivable controversy over speech policy were with an adversary who asserts that *all* use of words is absolutely immunized under the First Amendment. The "fire" example then triumphantly impeaches this massive major premise. Beyond that, it adds nothing to our understanding. If the point were that *only* speech which is a comparable "trigger of action" could be regulated, the example might prove a stirring way of drawing the line at incitement, but it is abundantly clear that Justice Holmes is not comparing Schenck's leaflet to the shouting of "fire." Moreover, because the example is so wholly apolitical, it lacks the requisite complexity for dealing with any serious speech problem likely to confront the legal system. The man shouting "fire" does not offer premises resembling those underlying radical political rhetoric—premises that constitute criticism of government.

Another important aspect of the *Schenck* opinion is the premise about the impact of wartime upon political tolerance: "In ordinary times" the leaflet would have been constitutionally protected, but "when a nation is at war many things that might be said in time of peace are such a hindrance to its effort that their utterance will not be endured so long as men fight." Does Holmes mean, as the result in *Schenck* suggests, that when a nation is at war public morale is so delicate a matter that seditious libel cannot be permitted? Judge Hand too had considered the impact of speech during wartime but had concluded that the American tradition of freedom of dissent required that the statute be construed so as to permit speech which generated detestation of the war. Perhaps Justice Holmes was making Hand's point that the war powers of Congress might permit legislation that censored utterances damaging to morale, if Congress made its intention to do so sufficiently explicit, that in a showdown the war powers might limit the prohibitions of the First Amendment. But if so, he selected a notably cryptic way of presenting a complex issue.[19]

Above all, *Schenck* bequeaths the principle of clear and present danger as a condition for censorship. There is, of course, a kinship between this principle and the one announced by Judge Hand in *Masses*. Yet the distance between the two analyses is considerable. Undoubtedly it would be forcing matters to assert that Holmes ignores the words, while Hand ignores the surrounding circumstances. Nevertheless, there remains a key difference between them. Hand would require as a threshold test that the state point to words of incitement. He is acutely aware that any less stringent test will foreclose too much serious dissent. Holmes in *Schenck* appears to ignore this countervalue altogether; his approach is rooted in an appraisal of the surrounding circumstances rather than of the words used. If we push the two approaches to their extremes, the coverages crisscross in the minority of instances in which they do not overlap. Under the Holmes approach, speech which contained no concrete advocacy of action might be reached, if the danger was deemed great enough. His application of the principle to the *Schenck* facts underscores this difficulty. By contrast, the Hand approach might fail to reach speech which was imminently dangerous but cleverly worded; and it might also fail to protect speech which was militantly worded but not in fact dangerous. Each would leave some political speech unprotected. My own feeling is that the Hand approach serves to interpose a weightier barrier against the state's impulse in times of tension to intercept serious radical criticism because it is dangerous. In any event, it is important to note that *Brandenburg* carefully combines the two approaches. It draws the line at "advocacy directed to inciting or producing imminent lawless action" *and* "likely to incite or produce such action."[20]

Although the American traditions of political and intellectual tolerance are enormously indebted to Justice Holmes for the contributions his pen and prestige are to make during the next decade, the awkward fact is that the legal tradition gets off to a limping start with his opinion in *Schenck*. This impression deepens when we look at his opinion a week later in *Debs*.

In *Debs* the communication is not addressed to a special audience of men awaiting the draft as in *Schenck*, but to a general audience at a public meeting; and this time there are even fewer direct action words. The dominant theme of Debs's speech was the growth of socialism and a prophecy of its ultimate success. In passing he expressed sympathy and strong admiration for several "loyal comrades" who had been convicted of obstructing the draft and of aiding others in failing to register. He indicted war on general socialist grounds, stating that "the master class has always declared the war and the subject class has always fought the battles . . . the working class, who furnish the corpses, have never yet had a voice in declaring the peace." He concluded with the exhortation: "Don't worry about the charge of treason to your masters; but be concerned about the treason that involves yourselves." Further, during the trial he addressed the jury, professing his innocence and declaring: "I have been accused of obstructing the war. I admit it. Gentlemen, I abhor war. I would oppose the war if I stood alone."[21]

Debs was convicted under the "insubordination" and "obstruction" provisions of the Espionage Act and was sentenced to a prison term of ten years. There should, of course, be no special immunity for political leaders, but the imprisoning—for ten years—of a man who has run for President four times for the offense of making a public speech is so alien to American expectations that it clamors for a close look by the Court at the premises supporting so startling a conclusion.

The stage was thus set for the first great Supreme Court opinion exploring the First Amendment. But the chief issues with which the brief Holmes opinion deals are the admission of two items into evidence: the record of the convictions of various persons Debs had named with admiration; and an Anti-War Proclamation adopted by the party on another occasion and not mentioned by Debs in his speech. Justice Holmes finds it possible to connect both of these items with the case against Debs. He dismisses the free speech issue curtly:

The chief defenses upon which the defendant seemed willing to rely were the denial that we have dealt with and that based upon the First Amendment to the Constitution, disposed of in *Schenck v. United States.* [22]

Later there is this further sentence:

We should add that the jury were most carefully instructed that they could not find the defendant guilty for advocacy of any of his opinions unless the words used had as their natural tendency and reasonably probable effect to obstruct the recruiting service, etc., and unless the defendant had the specific intent to do so in his mind.[23]

That is all Holmes has to say. He does not devote even a sentence to the circumstance that the special audience of *Schenck* is no longer present, that he is dealing with a speech to the general public. The jury instruction quoted with apparent approval is keyed to "natural tendency" and "reasonably probable effect." Are these for Holmes synonyms of clear and present danger? Equally troublesome, there is no effort to curb the misunderstanding likely to be aroused by the decision itself. If Eugene Debs can be sent to jail for a public speech, what, if anything, can the ordinary man safely say against the war? Although subsequent World War I cases are to provide close competition, *Debs* marks a low point in the Court's performance in speech cases.

The Benign Conspiracy

In his influential book *Free Speech in the United States,* Professor Chafee casts Justice Holmes—not Learned Hand—as the architect-hero of First Amendment doctrine.[24] It remains for us to consider Chafee's defense of these two precedents which have read so dismally to us.

The task is an ungrateful one. Chafee was a fine teacher and a first-class scholar who did distinguished and durable work in a number of fields. He was also quite possibly the best stylist the law teaching profession has yet produced. And throughout his life he was a passionate champion of free speech. Indeed, he can be said, through his writings, single-handedly to have created the field as a law topic. The debt to him is incalculable. Yet today his reading of the early law seems strained. Several brief excerpts should be sufficient to mark his approach:

The first decision . . . and the most influential upon the later development of constitutional law was *Schenck v. United States*. This was one of the few reported prosecutions under the [Espionage] Act where there clearly was incitement to resist the draft. The defendants had mailed circulars to men who had passed exemption boards, which not only declared conscription to be unconstitutional despotism, but urged the recipients in impassioned language to assert their rights. Such utterances could fairly be considered a direct and dangerous interference with the power of Congress to raise armies, and were also counselling unlawful action within Judge Hand's interpretation of the statute. Consequently, no real question of free speech arose.[25]

The Supreme Court's opinion in the *Schenck* case lends much support to the views of Judge Learned Hand in the *Masses* case. Justice Holmes does interpret the Espionage Act somewhat more widely than Judge Hand, in making the nature of the words only one element of danger, and in not requiring that the utterances shall in themselves satisfy an objective standard. Thus he loses the great administrative advantages of Judge Hand's test.[26]

[In *Schenck*] the concept of freedom of speech received for the first time an authoritative interpretation in accord with the purposes of the framers of the Constitution.[27]

Several perplexities attach to this reading of *Schenck:* How can the case be said to involve "no real question of free speech," in view of the content of the leaflet? Does the difference between the Hand and Holmes tests really reduce down to no more than a matter of "administrative advantages"? Above all, how can Chafee's celebration of *Schenck* be squared with the *Debs* decision one week later?

    Chafee acknowledges the awkwardness of *Debs:*

Deb's utterances are hard to reconcile with the Supreme Court test of "clear and present danger," but Justice Holmes was willing to accept the jury's verdict as proof that actual interference with the war was intended and was the proximate effect of the words used.[28]

After noting that the decision came as "a great shock" to many in
whose eyes Justice Holmes "had long taken on heroic dimensions,"[29]
Chafee offers an explanation:

> . . . Looking backward, however, we see that Justice Holmes was biding his
> time until the Court should have before it a conviction so clearly wrong as
> to let him speak out his deepest thoughts about the First Amendment.
>
> Meanwhile the cause of freedom of speech surely profited from his
> serving as spokesman for all the Justices in the *Schenck* case, far more than
> if he had voted for reversal. For subsequent decisions prove that he would
> then have been in a small minority and would not have been able (as he
> actually was) to announce with the backing of a unanimous Supreme Court
> the rule of clear and present danger. . . .
>
> The opportunity for which Justice Holmes had been waiting came eight
> months after Debs went to prison, in *Abrams v. United States*. . . . [30]

In *Abrams*,[31] to which we shall turn in a moment, Justice Holmes,
joined by Justice Brandeis, dissents. Drawing on his opinion for the
Court in *Schenck*, he seeks to capitalize on the casual language about
clear and present danger. Chafee sees in this a retrospective explanation of *Schenck*, and he joins with Holmes and Brandeis in an effort
to alchemize clear and present danger into *the* test, a test ratified by
a unanimous Court.[32]

We confront therefore a benign conspiracy. With the advent of
the Holmes eloquence in *Abrams*, *Schenck* is infused with new vitality
and *Debs* is conveniently forgotten. The tradition is read as though the
Abrams dissent had in fact been the opinion for the unanimous Court
in *Schenck*. No doubt this has had beneficial results for tolerance in the
long run. Indeed, in view of the politics of the judicial process, it may
well be that the step taken in *Brandenburg* in 1969 was possible only
because of the insistence of Holmes and Brandeis, reinforced by
Chafee, that the First Amendment tradition starts with *Schenck* and
with the formula requiring a clear and present danger as a condition
for censorship. We are, however, left with a nagging question: What
does it mean about law, about political tolerance, and about Justice
Holmes that it was *Abrams* and not *Debs* which stirred him to speak "his
deepest thoughts" about freedom of speech?

"The Opportunity for Which Justice Holmes Had Been Waiting"

There was, to be sure, plenty in *Abrams* to stir indignation. Decided on November 10, 1919, it arose under legislation which differs from that in *Schenck* and *Debs*. The Espionage Act of 1917 had not been explicitly directed at speech, but in 1918 the Act was amended and several new sections added, including the four under which the *Abrams* indictment lay: (i) publishing "disloyal, scurrilous and abusive language about the form of Government of the United States"; (ii) publishing language "intended to bring the form of Government of the United States into contempt, scorn, contumely and disrepute"; (iii) publishing language "intended to incite, provoke and encourage resistance to the United States in said war"; (iv) "by utterance, writing, printing and publication, to urge, incite and advocate curtailment of production of things . . . necessary . . . to the prosecution of the war."[33]

These sections greatly broadened the evils which censorship sought to intercept. Sections (i) and (ii) are really seditious libel statutes, acutely reminiscent of the Sedition Act of 1798. Section (iii) is tantamount to a prohibition of statements which might lower public morale during a war. Section (iv) refers to specific conduct—interference with wartime production—and yet it too remains alarmingly broad in scope. It is almost a certainty that none of them as drafted would survive constitutional scrutiny today.

The *Abrams* facts are in the sharpest "social" contrast to *Debs*. Abrams and his associates, Russian Jewish emigres living in New York, were self-styled "rebels," "revolutionists," and "anarchists." They participated in the printing of some five thousand leaflets condemning the United States for sending troops into Russia following the revolution and calling for a general strike of workers in munitions factories. Perhaps the most telling fact is that some of the leaflets were distributed by dropping them out of a window. Chafee has left an indelible account of the conduct of the trial which shows it to have been a scandal—a political trial of the defendants for the excesses of the Russian Revolution.[34]

Speaking through Justice Clarke, the majority of the Supreme Court affirms the convictions in an opinion which is primarily concerned with meeting the defendants' challenge that there was no evidence to support the charges. Although the Court closely examines the contents of the leaflets, it shows little sensitivity in the reading of radical rhetoric. For example, one of the leaflets reads:

> The Russian Revolution cries: Workers of the World! Awake! Rise! Put down your enemy and mine!
> Yes! friends, there is only one enemy of the workers of the world and that is CAPITALISM.[35]

Justice Clarke's construction runs as follows:

> This is clearly an appeal to the "workers" of this country to arise and put down by force the Government of the United States, which they characterize as their "hypocritical," "cowardly," and "capitalistic" enemy.[36]

Another instance is drawn from a leaflet printed in Yiddish:

> Workers, Russian emigrants, you who had the least belief in the honesty of *our* Government must now throw away all confidence, must spit in the face the false, hypocritic, military propaganda which has fooled you so relentlessly, calling forth your sympathy, your help, to the prosecution of the war.[37]

Justice Clarke's construction reads:

> The purpose of this obviously was to persuade the persons to whom it was addressed to turn a deaf ear to patriotic appeals in behalf of the Government of the United States, and to cease to render it assistance in the prosecution of the war.[38]

Despite the pathetic aspects of the defendants' show of revolutionary energy, a passage in one of the leaflets comes closer to advocacy of concrete action than any of the language reviewed by the Court in *Schenck* or *Debs:*

> *Workers, our reply to the barbaric intervention has to be the general strike! An open challenge* only will let the Government know that not only the Russian Worker fights for freedom, but also *here in America lives the spirit of Revolution.* [39]

This language, it should be noted, falls far short of a specific plan of action; it does not call for a general strike in terms that can be directly translated into action.[40] In any event, the majority does not isolate this statement, but rather treats it simply as one among several examples of excessive language on par with the two instances previously quoted.

After its detailed summary of the leaflets, the Court puts aside the counts under sections (i) and (ii), thereby postponing adjudication on the status of the Sedition Act of 1798 until *New York Times v. Sullivan*[41] in 1964. But it readily finds evidence to support the remaining two counts, which charge that the leaflets were "intended to incite, provoke and encourage" resistance to the government during wartime and that they urged "curtailment of production of things" necessary to the war effort.

Relying on *Schenck*, the Court disposes of the First Amendment challenge in two sentences:

On the record . . . it is argued, somewhat faintly, that the acts charged against the defendants were not unlawful because within the protection of that freedom of speech and of the press which is guaranteed by the First Amendment to the Constitution of the United States, and that the entire Espionage Act is unconstitutional because in conflict with that Amendment. This contention is sufficiently discussed and is definitely negatived in *Schenck v. United States.* . . . [42]

Justice Holmes, the author of *Schenck*, dissents, joined by Justice Brandeis. His opinion is the most sustained statement he is ever to make on free speech; it is almost twice as long as his opinion for the majority in *Schenck*. Like the best of Justice Jackson's writing, it is ennobled by a deep anger at what his government and his law have done. And it contains some surprises. The famous dissent devotes more space and energy to a technical discussion of intent than it does to free speech.

The special "equity" of the defendants in Holmes's eyes seems to have been the puzzle about their pro-Russian motivations. Their animus was directed against United States intervention in Russia. They were not pro-German; they were simply interested in protecting Russia. The majority acknowledges this, but argues that since their "primary purpose" could only be achieved by impairing the American war effort as a means to that end, they were still guilty under the statute of "urging curtailment of production of things" necessary to the war effort. Holmes admits that

the suggestion to workers in the ammunition factories that they are producing bullets to murder their dearest, and the further advocacy of a general strike . . . do urge curtailment of production of things necessary to the prosecution of the war. . . .[43]

The chief burden, and the chief strategy, of his argument is to seek a way out of the problem created by this direct language.

His first tactic is to construe the statute so as to require a distinctive intent to "cripple the United States" in the prosecution of the war. There was no such intent, he argues, because injury to the United States was "not the aim of the deed."[44] This analysis is not altogether persuasive, for, as the majority points out, the defendants could only achieve their aim of protecting Russia by impairing the war productive capacity of the United States. Hence by ordinary legal analysis, they had the requisite intent. In fact, Holmes seems on the verge of confusing motive and intent.

After wrestling with the point for a page or so, he suddenly abandons construction tactics, leaving the point unsettled in order to pass to "a more important aspect of the case," the First Amendment. He reiterates that *Schenck* and *Debs* were "rightly decided" on the questions of law that "alone" were before the Court, and he offers another analogy:

I do not doubt for a moment that by the same reasoning that would justify punishing persuasion to murder, the United States constitutionally may punish speech that produces or is intended to produce a clear and imminent danger that it will bring about forthwith certain substantive evils that the United States constitutionally may seek to prevent.[45]

Once again, as was the case with the "fire" example, the effect of this analogy is to wash out the political context in which the problems arise and to straitjacket them into the frame of common law analysis of individual crime.

Still proceeding to set up his major premise, Holmes adds an interesting gloss to his comments in *Schenck* about the impact of wartime on freedom of speech:

. . . The power [of Congress] undoubtedly is greater in time of war than in time of peace because war opens dangers that do not exist at other times.

But, as against dangers peculiar to war, as against others, the principle of the right to free speech is always the same. It is only the present danger of immediate evil or an intent to bring it about that warrants Congress in setting a limit to the expression of opinion where private rights are not concerned.[46]

Holmes appears to be making the same point he made in *Schenck:* Although the "principle" of free speech is "always the same," war presents unique dangers and hence speech which would be protected in ordinary times may be impermissible during wartime. But the distribution of emphasis here differs from that in *Schenck.* This passage conveys a commitment to speech values "as against dangers peculiar to war" which was not apparent in the earlier opinion.

Holmes is now ready to apply *the* test on behalf of Abrams. He begins:

Now nobody can suppose that the surreptitious publishing of a silly leaflet by an unknown man, without more, would present any immediate danger that its opinions would hinder the success of the government arms or have any appreciable tendency to do so.[47]

This remark leaves the impression that the test was designed to protect the occasional, trivial radical speech to which no one should, or would, pay any attention. In the end, it seems that Abrams moved Holmes because he was so trivial a critic. Debs should have moved him because he was such an important one.

At this point in the opinion, Holmes returns to his concern with intent. The lack of danger alone is not enough to save Abrams. It would alter matters if the ineffectual speaker had the requisite intent, whatever his power. That "at any rate would have the quality of an attempt"—even apparently in the case of "the surreptitious publication of a silly leaflet by an unknown man." "So," he continues, "I assume that the second leaflet, if published for the purposes alleged in the fourth count, might be punishable. But it seems pretty clear to me that nothing less than that would bring these papers within the scope of this law." And such an intent was absent, he argues once again, because the defendants' "only object" was "to help Russia . . . not to impede the United States in the war that it was carrying on."[48]

Insofar as I follow the argument, it runs something like this: The test is two-pronged. There must be either the requisite danger or the requisite intent. The explanation for the outcomes in *Schenck* and *Debs* inferentially is that while the danger was lacking, the intent could be said by a jury to have been present. In *Abrams,* by contrast, not only is the danger missing but there is no intent.

This thesis bristles with perplexities. And it alters the comparison between the Hand and Holmes approaches. If intent alone is enough, then the Holmes test will no longer protect in any case where the Hand approach would not also have protected—it no longer protects the militant speaker who does not present the requisite danger. Moreover, if, as Holmes suggested in *Schenck,* the intent may be derived simply from the fact that the speaker uttered radical criticism, then it is difficult to see just what threat of censorship his approach is aimed at reducing.

If Holmes's opinion had ended at this point, as logically it might have, it would rate as a confused and unpersuasive performance by a great justice. But it does not end, and in that circumstance is found the effective birth of the American tradition of freedom of speech. Sensing that his argument does not persuade, Holmes cannot leave it at this. He is indignant at the twenty-years sentences imposed on the defendants for such an abortive, well-intentioned, trivial, radical effort:

Even if I am technically wrong and enough can be squeezed from these poor and puny anonymities to turn the color of legal litmus paper; I will add, even if what I think the necessary intent were shown; the most nominal punishment seems to me all that possibly could be inflicted, unless. . . .[49]

He now turns to a new, more general target and releases the full force of his eloquence:

. . . unless the defendants are to be made to suffer not for what the indictment alleges but for the creed they avow—a creed that I believe to be the creed of ignorance and immaturity when honestly held, as I see no reason to doubt that it was held here, but which, although made the subject of examination at the trial, no one has a right even to consider in dealing with the charges before the Court.[50]

There then follows the famous peroration which alchemizes the muddled opinion into durable gold:

Persecution for the expression of opinions seems to me perfectly logical. If you have no doubt of your premises or your power and want a certain result with all your heart you naturally express your wishes in law and sweep away all opposition. To allow opposition by speech seems to indicate that you think the speech impotent, as when a man says that he has squared the circle, or that you do not care whole-heartedly for the result, or that you doubt either your power or your premises. But when men have realized that time has upset many fighting faiths, they may come to believe even more than they believe the very foundations of their own conduct that the ultimate good desired is better reached by free trade in ideas—that the best test of truth is the power of the thought to get itself accepted in the competition of the market and that truth is the only ground upon which their wishes safely can be carried out. That at any rate is the theory of our Constitution. It is an experiment, as all life is an experiment. Every year, if not every day, we have to wager our salvation upon some prophecy based upon imperfect knowledge. While that experiment is part of our system I think that we should be eternally vigilant against attempts to check the expression of opinions that we loathe and believe to be fraught with death, unless they so imminently threaten immediate interference with the lawful and pressing purposes of the law that an immediate check is required to save the country. I wholly disagree with the argument of the Government that the First Amendment left the common law as to seditious libel in force. History seems to me against the notion. I had conceived that the United States through many years had shown its repentance for the Sedition Act of July 14, 1798, by repaying fines that it imposed. Only the emergency that makes it immediately dangerous to leave the correction of evil counsels to time warrants making any exception to the sweeping command, "Congress shall make no law . . . abridging the freedom of speech." Of course I am speaking only of expressions of opinion and exhortations, which were all that were uttered here, but I regret that I cannot put into more impressive words my belief that in their conviction upon this indictment the defendants were deprived of their rights under the Constitution of the United States.[51]

This statement, although durably eloquent and a wonderful gesture of passion by the seventy-nine-year-old justice, is puzzling. If the First Amendment is this stringent, then how is one to explain the decisions in *Schenck* and *Debs*? Surely Holmes does not mean that Schenck's leaflet and Debs's speech "so imminently threatened immediate interference with the lawful and pressing purposes of the law that an immediate check was required to save the country."

Also puzzling is the logical relationship of the passage to the argument that precedes it. Holmes has just conceded that *intent* qualifies the level of danger required by the clear and present danger test and has done his best to rebut the argument that Abrams had the requisite intent. One cannot be altogether sure, but my strong impression is that the great peroration is addressed not to the precise charge against the defendants but to the broad issue of persecuting a man for his radical opinions or creed. In realist's terms, it is addressed to the submerged issue of *Abrams*—it was a political trial of Bolsheviks. In the peroration, liberated from the precise issues of the case and no longer fussing about intent, Holmes can deal with free speech policy in great broad strokes.

Whatever the overall coherence of the curious and wonderful Holmes performance in *Abrams*, Chafee's thesis is in some respects correct. Justice Holmes's splendid indignation over the shabby draconian treatment of the radicals in *Abrams*, whom he saw as distributors of "these poor and puny anonymities," supplies a blood transfusion for the *Schenck* dictum. This is the view of Chafee, writing in 1920:

The decision of the majority worked injustice to the defendants, but its effect on the national ideal of freedom of speech should be temporary in view of its meager discussion and the enduring qualities of the reasoning of Justice Holmes. Although a dissenting opinion, it must carry great weight as an interpretation of the First Amendment, because it is only an elaboration of the principle of "clear and present danger" laid down by him with the backing of a unanimous Court in *Schenck v. United States*. This principle is greatly strengthened since the *Abrams* case by Justice Holmes' magnificent exposition of the philosophic basis of this article of our Constitution.[52]

The strategy is thus to read the burst of eloquence at the end of the *Abrams* dissent into the casual *Schenck* dictum and then to claim that it was there all the time, that it was this intense commitment to a stringent test for freedom of speech that the whole Court underwrote in *Schenck*. And in a curious extra-precedential way it works. Although the test is virtually ignored by the majority after *Schenck*, it comes to acquire enormous prestige. The process of evolution from *Schenck* to *Abrams*, and ultimately to *Brandenburg*, has indeed been a mysterious and instructive one showing that the First Amendment has a charisma that sets it apart from other rules and principles of law.

The Other World War I Cases

With *Abrams* the free speech tradition divides sharply. On one hand, there is the exciting "unwritten law" of the Holmes dissent; on the other, there is the official law represented by the majority opinion, the first opinion on free speech not written by Justice Holmes. Both traditions appeal to *Schenck* as a starting point. The Holmes view reads *Schenck* as incorporating clear and present danger, taken stringently, as *the* constitutional test under the First Amendment. The official view, by contrast, has nothing whatsoever to do with clear and present danger. The phrase is never even mentioned by the majority in the other speech cases decided during the World War I period. The point is not, as has sometimes been said, that the Court adopted the test in *Schenck,* then for a time departed from it; the point is rather that during this period the Court *never* adopted the test. For the majority, the meaning of *Schenck* is simply that freedom of speech is not absolute, and that the Espionage Act is fully constitutional. Thus, it will be recalled, Justice Clarke, writing for the *Abrams* majority, curtly disposes of the defendants' First Amendment claims by stating that they were "definitively negatived" in *Schenck.* And he asserts this readily, although the precise statutory provisions involved in *Abrams* were quite different from those approved in *Schenck.* In short, the majority sees *Schenck* as *the* precedent for denying First Amendment claims.

The remaining World War I cases make the majority view abundantly clear. *Schaefer v. United States* (1920)[53] affirms the convictions of the officers of a German-language newspaper under the "false statements" and "obstruction" provisions of the Espionage Act for the offense of translating and editing articles reprinted from other newspapers in such a way as to serve a pro-German bias. *Pierce v. United States* (1920)[54] affirms the convictions under the "false statements" and "insubordination" provisions of three Socialists who had distributed a pamphlet condemning war and conscription. *Gilbert v. Minnesota* (1920)[55] affirms the conviction under a state sedition law of a man who had given a speech critical of the war and of conscription. And *United States ex rel Milwaukee Social Democratic Publishing Company v. Burleson* (1921)[56] affirms the Postmaster General's denial of second-class mailing privileges to a German-American newspaper, edited by the Socialist leader Victor Berger, which had repeatedly criticized the war and conscription.

These decisions leave no doubt as to the majority rule: While the nation is at war serious, abrasive criticism of the war or of conscription is beyond constitutional protection. They are dismal evidence of the degree to which the mood of society penetrates judicial chambers. The Court's performance is simply wretched. It displays no patience, no precision, and no tolerance. Consider, for example, the majority's response in *Gilbert v. Minnesota.*

Gilbert was convicted under a Minnesota statute which prohibited "in any public place or at any meeting where more than five people are present, to advocate . . . that men should not enlist in the military or naval forces of the United States or the State of Minnesota." His offense was a public speech in which he said:

We are going over to Europe to make the world safe for democracy, but I tell you we had better make America safe for democracy first. You say, what is the matter with our democracy. I tell you what is the matter with it: Have you had anything to say as to who should be president? Have you had anything to say as to who should be Governor of this state? Have you had anything to say as to whether we would go into this war? You know you have not. If this is such a good democracy, for Heaven's sake why should we not vote on conscription of men. We were stampeded into this war by newspaper rot to pull England's chestnuts out of the fire for her. I tell you, if they conscripted wealth like they have conscripted men, this war would not last forty-eight hours.[57]

Justice McKenna, writing for the Court, is indignant that the author of such a speech would have the effrontery to appeal to the Constitution. After citing *Schenck, Debs* and *Abrams,* he declares:

In *Schaefer v. United States,* commenting on those cases and their contentions it was said that the curious spectacle was presented of the Constitution of the United States being invoked to justify the activities of anarchy or of the enemies of the United States, and, by a strange perversion of its precepts it was adduced against itself. And we did more than reject the contention, we forestalled all repetitions of it, and the contention in the case at bar is a repetition of it.[58]

McKenna's irritation with the defendant is not yet exhausted. His peroration—written some thirteen months after Justice Holmes's eloquent peroration in *Abrams*—reads as follows:

Gilbert's speech had the purpose [the statutes] denounce. The Nation was at war with Germany, armies were recruiting, and the speech was the discouragement of that. . . . It was not an advocacy of policies or a censure of actions that a citizen had the right to make. The war was flagrant; it had been declared by the power constituted by the Constitution to declare it, and in the manner provided for by the Constitution. It was not declared in aggression, but in defense, in defense of our national honor, in vindication of the "most sacred rights of our Nation and our people" [citing President

Wilson's War Message to Congress, April 2, 1917].

This was known to Gilbert, for he was informed in affairs and the operations of the Government, and every word that he uttered in denunciation of the war was false, was deliberate misrepresentation of the motives which impelled it, and the objects for which it was prosecuted. He could have had no purpose other than that of which he was charged. It would be a travesty on the constitutional privilege he invokes to assign him its protection.[59]

Besides showing how patriotism can unsettle the judicial mind, Justice McKenna's response to Gilbert's speech illustrates how quickly the issue of incitement elides back into seditious libel. My personal judgment is that so long as cases of this genre are approached by judges alert to the evils of making seditious libel an offense, the exact formula for testing whether there is sufficient proximity to action matters relatively little. The lawyer's impulse, however, has been to engage in Talmudic analysis of competing formulae and to forget the point of protecting this genre of speech—the value of radical criticism of society.

Despite the majority's refusal even to acknowledge the existence of the clear and present danger test, the counter-tradition, initiated by Holmes's *Abrams* dissent, gathers momentum in these final World War I cases. Justice Brandeis, the silent partner in the *Abrams* dissent, now speaks in his own voice. Joined by Holmes, he enters dissenting opinions in *Schaefer, Pierce,* and *Burleson,* and in *Gilbert* he dissents alone. In each case he carefully dissects the majority opinion and in each he insists that the Court has departed from the rule of clear and present danger adopted in *Schenck.* By the end of the World War I period the seeds of change have been firmly planted. Although Holmes and Brandeis have not yet had any apparent impact on the majority view, their dissents have lent prestige and eloquence to a counterview and have generated an enduring tension within the Court. Indeed, one reason the countertradition becomes so powerful may be that it is permitted to flower in dissent, relieved of the constraints imposed by the necessity of accommodating other views in order to gain a majority.

11

Subversive Advocacy: The Great Debate—Sanford in *Gitlow* v. Brandeis in *Whitney*

The first speech decision by a Supreme Court unhampered by war-time pressures, *Gitlow v. New York*[1] in 1925 marks a critical point in the development of the tradition. It is the first sustained effort by a Court *majority* to speak to issues of free speech, and in some respects it represents an advance over the prior cases.

The case originated in a split in the American Socialist Party between radical and old-line Socialists, a split from which the origin of the American Communist Party can be traced. Gitlow, an official of the newly formed Left Wing Faction of the Socialist Party and three associates were convicted of violating the New York criminal anarchy statute which prohibited advocating the doctrine that organized government should be overthrown by force, violence, or assassination. They had participated in the publication of a pamphlet titled "Left Wing Manifesto," which sponsored "revolutionary socialism" and the ultimate overthrow of democratic capitalism by a series of actions based on the class struggle and culminating in "mass political strikes and revolutionary mass action." The Supreme Court, speaking through Justice Sanford, affirmed the convictions.

At one point in his opinion Justice Sanford remarks in a rhetorical burst that passages of the "Manifesto" contain "the language of direct incitement."[2] This statement, coupled with the oft-quoted ironic assessment of the pamphlet by Justice Holmes in dissent—"whatever may be thought of the redundant discourse before us it had no chance of starting a present conflagration"[3]—has tended to make Sanford's handling of the case appear ludicrous. Yet this is one of those minor unfairnesses of history. Sanford is an important architect of First Amendment doctrine during these decades. In *Gitlow* he is not at all guilty of the foolish exaggeration so distressingly obvious in Justice McKenna's *Gilbert* opinion. Nor does he dismiss the defendants' challenge as a frivolous claim of constitutional right. Rather, he patiently examines what the defendants said and points to the language which in his judgment offends the statute. Moreover, he provides a coherent justification of the decision in policy terms.

Before we turn to Justice Sanford's statement of First Amendment policy, we should note that *Gitlow* was the first decision holding that the First Amendment applies via the Fourteenth to the states as well as to the federal government. Although some thoughtful students question this development, it has made possible the nationalizing of the free speech norm. By greatly multiplying the occasions on which the Court would have to confront speech issues, it has been of great importance to the development of a seasoned constitutional interpretation. This great step is taken quickly; only a summary paragraph of the long opinion is devoted to it.

Several circumstances combine in *Gitlow* to yield an unusually luminous holding as to the precise boundaries of permissible speech. First, the statute was explicitly addressed to the advocacy of *doctrine;* it made the advocacy of "the criminal anarchy doctrine" a felony. Second, the trial court had denied a request by the defendants for an instruction requiring for conviction advocacy of " 'some definite or immediate act or acts' of force, violence or unlawfulness directed toward the overthrowing of organized government."[4] Third, the New York Court of Appeals in affirming had acknowledged: "It is true that there is no advocacy in specific terms of the use of . . . force or violence."[5] Thus, *Gitlow* put sharply into issue the question of whether advocacy of some concrete, immediate act—in brief, incitement—was the constitutional line.

In order to identify the speech at issue in *Gitlow,* it will be helpful to distinguish three different types of speech, moving away from seditious libel and approaching action: (i) The "pure" seditious libel case where there is abrasive, damaging criticism of existing law and policy but no urging of action of any sort. (ii) The same case except that there is now urging of action, but only in a general, non-concrete way. (iii) The same case except that it is now coupled with concrete, immediate advocacy of a plan of action.

Something about the style of Communist rhetoric gave life to the second category, in which criticism of the existing order is coupled with discussion of the necessity for radical tactics to change it and with advocacy of such tactics. The *Gitlow* "Manifesto," which argues the case for the mass strike as a tactic without ever calling concretely for a strike, falls within this second category. However dull and ponderous, it does advocate in general terms a program of "revolutionary mass action," the conquest and destruction of the parliamentary state, and the development of the "mass political strike" as a revolutionary tactic.

The desire of the legislature to reach this category of speech is intelligible. A general militant program which argues for the use of violence as a necessary means to a desired social change may generate over time a climate in which the use of specific violent means becomes possible. Such speech would seem to resemble group libel in that it can be said gradually to alter or erode the goodwill of society toward an important value—in one instance, toward a racial or religious minority; in the other, toward the government itself.

Justice Sanford's answer to the issue posed in *Gitlow* is clear and firm: When there is a statute proscribing a class of speech and the speech contains general advocacy of violence, the boundaries of free speech have been reached. This holds true regardless of the degree of danger in fact from the speech. Sanford would give great weight to the legislative judgment and would apply the test of substantive due process:

> We cannot hold that the present statute is an arbitrary or unreasonable exercise of the police power of the State unwarrantably infringing the freedom of speech or press; and we must and do sustain its constitutionality.
>
> This being so it may be applied to every utterance—not too trivial to be beneath the notice of the law—which is of such a character and used with such intent and purpose as to bring it within the prohibition of the statute. . . . [citing *Abrams, Schaefer, Pierce,* and *Gilbert*] In other words, when the legislative body has determined generally, in the constitutional exercise of its discretion, that utterances of a certain kind involve such danger of substantive evil that they may be punished, the question whether any specific utterance coming within the prohibited class is likely, in and of itself, to bring about the substantive evil, is not open to consideration. It is sufficient that the statute itself be constitutional, and that the use of the language comes within its prohibition.[6]

The *Gitlow* statute is valid, Sanford argues, because it reflects a rational legislative judgment about a category of speech, namely, that

which advocates violent overthrow of the government. His argument
has the ring of common sense:

That utterances inciting to the overthrow of organized government by unlawful means, present a sufficient danger of substantive evil to bring their punishment within the range of legislative discretion, is clear. Such utterances,
by their very nature, involve danger to the public peace and to the security
of the State. They threaten breaches of the peace and ultimate revolution.
And the immediate danger is none the less real and substantial, because the
effect of a given utterance cannot be accurately foreseen. The State cannot
reasonably be required to measure the danger from every such utterance in
the nice balance of a jeweler's scale. A single revolutionary spark may kindle
a fire that, smouldering for a time, may burst into a sweeping and destructive
conflagration. It cannot be said that the State is acting arbitrarily or unreasonably when in the exercise of its judgment as to the measures necessary to
protect the public peace and safety, it seeks to extinguish the spark without
waiting until it has enkindled the flame or blazed into the conflagration. It
cannot reasonably be required to defer the adoption of measures for its own
peace and safety until the revolutionary utterances lead to actual disturbances of the public peace or imminent and immediate danger of its own
destruction; but it may, in the exercise of its judgment, suppress the threatened danger in its incipiency.[7]

It would appear that Justice Sanford is drawing the line at general
advocacy. He is saying that general advocacy marks the end of free
speech and the beginning of censorship. There must be, that is, at
least that much stimulus to unlawful action in the speech, and arguably there must also be a legislative judgment that speech of that sort
is to be banned. Thus, the majority principle has evolved. In *Gitlow*
for the first time we get a speech precedent that has parameters.

Justice Sanford's opinion also contains important commentary
on the dissenters' principle. Indeed, it is the first majority opinion
since *Schenck* to make any mention at all of the clear and present
danger formula. Sanford acknowledges that there was "no evidence
of any effect resulting from the publication and circulation of the
Manifesto."[8] But he argues that in a case such as *Gitlow,* where the
legislature has specified the category of speech it wishes to intercept,
the danger of the particular utterance is immaterial. In reaching this
conclusion he makes some shrewd criticisms of the Holmes-Brandeis
test: How is a judge to weigh the danger of the particular utterance?
Why must the state wait until the utterance threatens immediate danger, especially when the danger is the overthrow of the state itself?

Most important, however, Sanford sees a limited role for the formula. He would distinguish two types of speech cases: first, those such as *Gitlow* where the statute proscribes a given class of speech; and second, those such as *Schenck* where the statute forbids a class of actions and says nothing about speech. In cases of the first type, argues Sanford, the legislature itself has found the danger of the category of speech and there is no reason to reconsider its judgment in the particular case.[9] That is not to say that *any* legislative judgment that a category of speech is dangerous will be sufficient, but rather that substantive due process, not clear and present danger, is the measure of the validity of such judgments. Sanford would, however, find a place for clear and present danger in cases of the second type, "where the statute merely prohibits certain acts involving the danger of substantive evil, without reference to language itself":

There, if it be contended that the statute cannot be applied to the language used by the defendant because of its protection by the freedom of speech or press, it must necessarily be found, as an original question, without any previous determination by the legislative body, whether the specific language used involved such likelihood of bringing about the substantive evil as to deprive it of the constitutional protection. . . . [The clear and present danger test]—upon which great reliance is placed in the defendant's argument—was manifestly intended, as shown by the context, to apply only in cases of this class, and has no application to those like the present, where the legislative body itself has previously determined the danger of substantive evil arising from utterances of a specified character.[10]

After a dozen cases the formula has finally won a toehold in the official doctrine.

The majority opinion in *Gitlow* then was both lucid enough and rational enough to provide a proper occasion for a full-blown debate among the justices over free speech policy. Justice Sanford had made three effective points that deserved a rejoinder: (i) Why is it not a satisfactory adjustment between speech and censorship to draw the line at advocacy of crime, violence, and overthrow of government? In brief, what is so valuable about such speech? (ii) How could a test requiring judicial appraisal of the danger of the utterance in the individual instance possibly be practicable? How would the judge know what the danger was? (iii) Was it not valid to distinguish *Schenck* as applying only to cases where the statute had not directly created a speech crime and where the issue was therefore one of estimating

how close speech had come to the acts which the statute had proscribed?

Justices Holmes and Brandeis, however, do not rise to the occasion. They enter a one-page dissent written by Justice Holmes.
Although another wonderful burst of eloquence from the eighty-four-
year-old justice, the opinion does not respond to the points raised by
the majority. Holmes ignores the distinction Justice Sanford had
drawn between *Schenck* and the case at bar. He simply asserts that "the
criterion sanctioned by the full Court in *Schenck v. United States* applies," and states:

It is true that in my opinion this criterion was departed from in *Abrams v.
United States,* but the convictions that I expressed in that case are too deep
for it to be possible for me as yet to believe that it and *Schaefer v. United States*
have settled the law.[11]

Holmes is equally unresponsive to Sanford's other points. He
does not deny that the pamphlet contains words of general advocacy,
and does not reply to Sanford's commonsense claim that such speech
may, if a legislature is so persuaded, be censored. Nor does he respond to Sanford's point about the difficulty of assessing the danger
of the particular utterance. He simply makes the vigorous and plausible assertion that the "Manifesto" carried no danger—a point Justice
Sanford and the majority do not contest:

If what I think the correct test is applied, it is manifest that there was no
present danger of an attempt to overthrow the government by force on the
part of the admittedly small minority who shared the defendant's views.[12]

Justice Holmes is distracted by Sanford's rhetorical statement
that the "Manifesto" contained "the language of direct incitement,"
and most of his eloquence is spent on that point:

It is said that this manifesto was more than a theory, that it was an incitement.
Every idea is an incitement. It offers itself for belief and if believed, is acted
on unless some other belief outweighs it or some failure of energy stifles the
movement at its birth. The only difference between the expression of an
opinion and an incitement in the narrower sense is the speaker's enthusiasm
for the result. Eloquence may set fire to reason. But whatever may be thought
of the redundant discourse before us it had no chance of starting a present
conflagration. If in the long run the beliefs expressed in proletarian dictatorship are destined to be accepted by the dominant forces of the community,

the only meaning of free speech is that they should be given their chance and have their way.[13]

This famous passage points up the ironies in tradition building. The basic problem of finding an accommodation between speech too close to action and censorship too close to criticism might, we have argued, have been tolerably solved by settling on "incitement" as the key term. It is a term which came easily to the mind of Learned Hand. But for Holmes it does not resonate as it did for Hand. It strikes his ear as a loose, expansible term. At an inopportune moment in the history of free speech the great master of the common law turns poet: "Every idea is an incitement." There is of course a sense in which this is true and in which it is a "scholastic subterfuge" to pretend that speech can be arrayed in firm categories. But the defendants' proposed instruction had offered a sense in which it was not true, in which incitement required advocacy of some definite and immediate acts of force. The weakness of the prosecution's case was not that the defendants' radicalism was not dangerous; it was that their manifesto was not concrete enough to be an incitement.

Justice Holmes's dissent in *Gitlow,* like his *Abrams* peroration, is extraordinary prose to find in a judicial opinion, and I suspect it has contributed beyond measure to the charisma of the First Amendment. But it also carries the disturbing suggestion that the defendants' speech is to be protected precisely because it is harmless and unimportant. It smacks, as will the later protections of Jehovah's Witnesses, of a luxury civil liberty.

The full counter-argument, which the dissenters failed to make in *Gitlow,* is entered by Justice Brandeis in *Whitney v. California*[14] two years later. Indeed, *Whitney* is close enough to *Gitlow* in its statute and on its facts that Brandeis's opinion can properly be read as though he were responding directly to the Sanford opinion in *Gitlow.* Although his opinion has no immediate impact on the majority view, it marks a considerable further evolution of the dissenters' principle, which has now passed through three distinct stages: the original statement in *Schenck;* the philosophic peroration by Justice Holmes in *Abrams;* and the extensive and eloquent gloss now added by Justice Brandeis in *Whitney.*

The statute under which Miss Whitney was convicted made it a felony to organize, assist in organizing, or knowingly become a member of "any organization, society, group or assemblage of persons organized or assembled to advocate, teach or aid and abet criminal syndicalism." It defined "criminal syndicalism" as "the commission of crime, sabotage . . . or unlawful acts of force and violence or unlawful methods of terrorism as a means of accomplishing a change in industrial ownership or control or effecting any political change."

Like *Gitlow*, *Whitney* arose out of the splintering of the American Socialist Party. Miss Whitney, who had joined the more "radical" Communist Labor Party, attended a meeting at which a California branch of the party was organized. Considerable ambiguity attaches to her role at the meeting. She sponsored a resolution favoring use of the ballot which was defeated, and she denied at trial that it was her purpose that the "new" party use terrorism. The Court, however, declined to look into this issue, arguing that it was foreclosed by the jury verdict affirmed by the Court of Appeals below, and that, in any event, she had remained at the meeting after the defeat of her resolution without protesting. Thus, *Whitney* put into issue the constitutionality of using criminal sanctions to penalize advocacy of terrorism despite the fact that it was far from clear that Miss Whitney had so advocated.

Gitlow had been indicted for what he had done personally, that is, for participating directly in the publication of the "Manifesto." Miss Whitney was indicted for participating in organizing a group to teach criminal syndicalism. At this juncture we reach a major transition in the nature of the speech problem, from one of regulating the content of speech to one of regulating what are best called "political conspiracies." This is the form in which the legion of anti-Communist cases will come to the Court in the next decades, and we shall devote considerable attention to it in later chapters. For the moment, it need not distract us, though we should note that Justice Brandeis remarks on the "novelty" of the statute at the start of his opinion.[15]

The majority, relying on *Gitlow*, requires only a page and a half to dispose of the free speech issue. The opinion by Justice Sanford indicates once again how little the clear and present danger test means to the majority at this time. Sanford does not refer to it; he relies on a strong presumption of the constitutionality of the statute; and he refers to utterances which tend "to incite to crime" and to "endanger the foundations of organized government."[16] Although there is no proof in the record that the advocacy with which Miss Whitney was charged created a high degree of danger, the majority dismisses such a consideration as immaterial. In its view, advocating the syndicalist doctrine of selective violence is enough.

Justice Brandeis, in an opinion joined by Justice Holmes, launches an eloquent protest against the bland analysis of the majority opinion. In durable rhetoric he explores the policy basis of our commitment to free speech and analyzes with care when, in light of that policy, a danger can be said to be imminent enough and serious enough to warrant restriction.

Although *Whitney* marks the sixth consecutive decision in which the majority has either ignored the clear and present danger test or found it inapplicable, Justice Brandeis asserts at the outset:

That the necessity which is essential to a valid restriction does not exist unless speech would produce, or is intended to produce, a clear and imminent danger of some substantive evil which the State constitutionally may seek to prevent has been settled. See *Schenck v. United States.* [17]

The stamina and tactics of these classic dissents are remarkable. In professional lawyering terms, the performance of Justices Holmes and Brandeis is outrageous. They keep insisting that they are adhering to the Court's true rule adopted in *Schenck.* They have been told by the majority that clear and present danger is not now and never was the general test and that it is applicable only in cases where speech is punished under statutes aimed at acts. They have conveniently forgotten *Debs,* and, in the face of the majority's skepticism, they have never paused to explain how *Schenck* itself comported with the test. Yet we are all deeply in their debt for their outrageous behavior. They have kept alive a counter-tension in the tradition, and their towering prestige has invested the slogan with almost mesmerizing force. Like twin Moses come down from Mount Sinai bearing the true Commandment, they see little need to argue that the formula is rightly derived from the First Amendment, merely that it is.

Although possibly a mite less eloquent than Justice Holmes, Justice Brandeis constructs his argument in a much more lawyer-like fashion. In response to the majority's deference to the legislative judgment as to the danger of criminal syndicalist advocacy, he argues that in constitutional law the legislature cannot pull itself up by its own bootstraps:

The legislature must obviously decide, in the first instance, whether a danger exists which calls for a particular protective measure. But where a statute is valid only in case certain conditions exist, the enactment of the statute cannot alone establish the facts which are essential to its validity.[18]

This answer is powerful. If the legislature could make conclusive findings of constitutional facts, the function of judicial review of legislation on First Amendment grounds would virtually disappear. But Justice Sanford in *Gitlow* had not eschewed all judicial review of the application of pure speech statutes; rather, he had said that in cases involving such statutes the appropriate standard of review was substantive due process, and he had confined the clear and present danger test to *Schenck*-like cases, where the statute proscribes acts, not words.[19] Thus, Brandeis does not fully meet Sanford's argument. He does not explain why we must read *Schenck* as having launched a principle so much broader than the facts required. Yet when he has finished his full argument, it will be apparent that he has not begged the question but has dealt seriously with all aspects of it.

Brandeis begins his exegesis of the clear and present danger standard by posing a series of questions:

This Court has not yet fixed the standard by which to determine when a danger shall be deemed clear; how remote the danger may be and yet be deemed present; and what degree of evil shall be deemed sufficiently substantial to justify resort to abridgement of free speech and assembly as the means of protection.[20]

The agenda is to prove a splendid one. But how extraordinary to say that the Court has "not yet" attended to resolving ambiguities in the test, when the Court has so steadfastly refused to grant the test the status Holmes and Brandeis claim for it. It is the two dissenters who have not yet determined these features of their formula.

Before answering his three questions about the test, Justice Brandeis pauses to examine the underlying policy which dictates such stringent control over the regulation of speech. The passage is quite wonderful and provides, among other things, a rejoinder to Sanford's query as to why the state must leave alone speech which advocates in general terms tactics of force, terrorism, and sabotage:

Those who won our independence believed that the final end of the State was to make men free to develop their faculties; and that in its government the deliberative forces should prevail over the arbitrary. They valued liberty both as an end and as a means. They believed liberty to be the secret of happiness and courage to be the secret of liberty. They believed that freedom to think as you will and to speak as you think are means indispensable to the discovery and spread of political truth; that without free speech and assembly discussion would be futile; that with them, discussion affords ordinarily adequate protection against the dissemination of noxious doctrine; that the greatest menace to freedom is an inert people; that public discussion is a political duty; and that this should be a fundamental principle of the American government.[21]

To intrude for a moment: Here at last is an effort to work the test back to the Constitution itself. Justice Brandeis supplies the statement that was so noticeably lacking in *Schenck*. The basic American premise, embodied in the basic document of government, is that "freedom to think what you will and to speak what you think are means indispensible to the discovery and spread of political truth." He continues:

They recognized the risks to which all human institutions are subject. But they knew that order cannot be secured merely through fear of punishment for its infraction; that it is hazardous to discourage thought, hope and imagination; that fear breeds repression; that repression breeds hate; that hate menaces stable government; that the path of safety lies in the opportunity to discuss freely supposed grievances and proposed remedies; and that the fitting remedy for evil counsels is good ones. Believing in the power of reason as applied through public discussion, they eschewed silence coerced by law—the argument of force in its worst form. Recognizing the occasional tyrannies of governing majorities, they amended the Constitution so that free speech and assembly should be guaranteed.[22]

This passage serves to correct the ill-fitting private crime analogy Justice Holmes automatically reached for. What is at stake is not the false shouting of "fire" in a theater or the counselling of murder; rather, it is a matter of providing maximum opportunity for "the power of reason as applied through public discussion." And what is to be guarded against, in Brandeis's memorable phrase, is the ugliness of "silence coerced by law." With these grand premises made explicit, Justice Brandeis turns to the question of how *clear* and *present* the danger must be:

Fear of serious injury cannot alone justify suppression of free speech and assembly. Men feared witches and burnt women. It is the function of speech to free men from the bondage of irrational fears. To justify suppression of free speech there must be reasonable ground to fear that serious evil will result if free speech is practiced. There must be reasonable ground to believe that the danger apprehended is imminent. There must be reasonable ground to believe that the evil to be prevented is a serious one.[23]

Again we intrude. There is plausibility to the clear and present danger test as Justice Brandeis derives it from the basic architecture of American values. The point is simple: Freedom of speech is so essential to the American way of life and thought, and confidence in its power is so deep, that only an extraordinary threat to the safety of the community justifies departing from those expectations by employing the law to coerce silence.

Being the careful lawyer, Justice Brandeis now turns to the practical task of distinguishing among admittedly risky forms of speech. At this point his opinion bears an arresting resemblance to Judge Hand's opinion in *Masses,* which he cites. Both seek to locate words which are "triggers of action." One talks in terms of "incitement"; the other in terms of "clear and present danger." As I see it, despite the differences in idiom, both are making the same point:

> Every denunciation of existing law tends in some measure to increase the probability that there will be violation of it. Condonation of a breach enhances the probability. Expressions of approval add to the probability. Propagation of the criminal state of mind by teaching syndicalism increases it.[24]

Note that in this last sentence Justice Brandeis fully acknowledges the common sense of Justice Sanford's view in *Gitlow.* He is, however, firmly convinced that we cannot stop there:

> Advocacy of law-breaking heightens it still further. But even advocacy of violation, however reprehensible morally, is not a justification for denying free speech where the advocacy falls short of incitement and there is nothing to indicate that the advocacy would be immediately acted on. The wide difference between advocacy and incitement, between preparation and attempt, between assembling and conspiracy, must be borne in mind. In order to support a finding of clear and present danger it must be shown either that immediate serious violence was to be expected or was advocated, or that the past conduct furnished reason to believe that such advocacy was then contemplated.[25]

As in Hand's opinion, the analytic device is to array categories of dangerous speech, and the effort is to locate the last term in the series, whatever the precise label given to it. It would seem to matter little whether we talk of "clear and present danger" or of "incitement." What is sought is concrete advocacy of direct and immediate criminal action; and what is to be guarded against is censorship of "denunciation," "condonation," "expressions of approval," "teaching of radical doctrine." In Brandeis's terms, which recall *Masses* and anticipate *Brandenburg,* what is to be guarded against is censorship "where advocacy falls short of incitement."

Justice Brandeis goes on to underscore with zest another strand of the argument for free speech: the efficacy of counter-speech as the remedy for evil speech. In the case of speech harms there is a distinctive self-help remedy that makes the intervention of law less urgent than in the case of physical harms—more speech:

Those who won our independence by revolution were not cowards. They did not fear political change. They did not exalt order at the cost of liberty. To courageous, self-reliant men, with confidence in the power of free and fearless reasoning applied through the processes of popular government, no danger flowing from speech can be deemed clear and present, unless the incidence of the evil apprehended is so imminent that it may befall before there is opportunity for full discussion. If there be time to expose through discussion the falsehood and fallacies, to avert the evil by the processes of education, the remedy to be applied is more speech, not enforced silence. Only an emergency can justify repression. Such must be the rule if authority is to be reconciled with freedom. Such, in my opinion, is the command of the Constitution. It is therefore always open to Americans to challenge a law abridging free speech and assembly by showing that there was no emergency justifying it.[26]

One might hope that the splendid admonition of this last sentence, although uttered in the spirit of dissent, has served to expunge from the memory of the society, if not from the records of the Court, the nastiness of Justice McKenna's dictum about the defendant's challenge in *Gilbert:* "It would be a travesty on the constitutional protection he invokes to assign him its protection."[27]

Justice Brandeis was seventy-one years old when he wrote this remarkable opinion; Justice Holmes was seventy-nine years old when he wrote his eloquent peroration in *Abrams;* Alexander Meiklejohn was seventy-eight years old when he wrote his stirring essay on free speech. It is the mark of the topic that it recruits such distilled wisdom from the concerned elders of the society, and it is the special blessing of the American heritage that it has had such elders to rise and speak.

Justice Brandeis has answered his question as to how clear and how present the danger must be to warrant restriction of speech. As I read the opinion, his answers come at the matter in three different ways. First, there is the policy underpinning: it is highly unlikely in any given case that the danger will be sufficient to overcome the national commitment to liberty. Second, there is the effort to distinguish advocacy which falls short of incitement. Third, there is the suggestion that only when there is no longer time for counter-speech is the danger imminent enough.

The opinion has achieved a great deal thus far. While remaining loyal to the *Schenck* formula, Justice Brandeis has completely reformulated the matter. He has made it clear that no tidy formulaic answer is possible, that incitement and clear and present danger are two different ways of saying the same difficult thing. Moreover, he has cured the test of the tendency it had in the hands of Justice Holmes to conceive its function as the protection of trivial speech by the pathetic and the dull. One can only wonder what the history of freedom of speech in American constitutional law would have been like had Justice Brandeis uttered his *Whitney* opinion in *Schenck* itself.

There is still one more turn to the opinion, one final question to answer: "What degree of evil shall be deemed sufficiently substantial to justify resort to abridgement of free speech and assembly as the means of protection?"[28] One of the weaknesses of the clear and present danger test as first articulated by Justice Holmes was that it would allow punishment of speech which created an imminent danger of virtually any substantive evil, no matter how trivial. Justice Brandeis now undertakes to cure this flaw in the test:

Moreover, even imminent danger cannot justify resort to prohibitions of these functions essential to effective democracy, unless the evil apprehended is relatively serious. Prohibition of free speech and assembly is a measure so stringent that it would be inappropriate as the means for averting a relatively trivial harm to society. A police measure may be unconstitutional merely because the remedy, although effective as a means of protection, is unduly harsh or oppressive. Thus, a State might, in the exercise of its police power, make any trespass upon the land of another a crime, regardless of the results or of the intent or purpose of the trespasser. It might, also, punish an attempt, a conspiracy, or an incitement to commit the trespass. But it is hardly conceivable that this Court would hold constitutional a statute which punished as a felony the mere voluntary assembly with a society formed to teach that pedestrians had the moral right to cross unenclosed, unposted, waste lands and to advocate their doing so, even if there was imminent danger that advocacy would lead to a trespass. The fact that speech is likely to result in some violence or in destruction of property is not enough to justify its suppression. There must be the probability of serious injury to the state. Among freemen, the deterrents ordinarily to be applied to prevent crime are education and punishment for violations of the law, not abridgment of the rights of free speech and assembly.[29]

From the tenor of the opinion thus far one would anticipate that Justice Brandeis must end up in dissent. In fact, however, he concurs in affirming the conviction of Miss Whitney. This outcome leaves us with a train of puzzles as to what he has been saying. There are at least four such puzzles.

(i) In view of the argument he has made, why does he not find the California statute unconstitutional on its face? The statute would reach and penalize the non-concrete urging of terrorist tactics as a strategy for basic long-term industrial change. Thus, it would by definition sweep within regulation much of the speech which Brandeis has just argued must be placed beyond the reach of censorship. In brief, why did he not come to the conclusion the whole Court was to arrive at four decades later in *Brandenburg*?

The answer may lie in the preamble to the statute. In it the California legislature recited that an emergency had arisen because large numbers of persons were "going from place to place in this state advocating, teaching and practicing criminal syndicalism." For Brandeis, this finding apparently created a "rebuttable presumption" of the validity of the statute.[30] Moreover, I suspect that in 1927 there was no tradition of finding speech statutes bad on their face.

(ii) Why does Brandeis not find the statute unconstitutional as applied to Miss Whitney? The function of the clear and present danger test, as he explains it, is to measure the validity of the *application* of a valid statute in the particular case. As a matter of constitutional law, the test introduces an *equity* into the application of general laws regulating speech. It "must remain open to a defendant to present the issue whether there actually did exist at the time a clear danger." No matter how the general rule is worded, the defendant retains the chance of impeaching its application to him.[31] Thus, Miss Whitney might have made the existence of clear and present danger "the important issue in the case" and have required that it be determined either by the court or the jury. But her fatal error was that she failed to request at trial that the existence of these conditions be passed upon. Since "there was evidence on which the court or jury might have found that such danger existed,"[32] the Court, given its limited powers of review, cannot upset the conviction. Presumably, if the issue had been preserved below, the Court could then have reviewed the level of danger.

(iii) If particular danger is the constitutional test, why was it incumbent on the defendant to preserve the point? Why was it not part of the prosecution case? Perhaps at this stage in the development of the test, it is regarded as a special mitigating circumstance to be shown by the defense; or perhaps Justice Brandeis is indicating that there was enough evidence of danger in the record to shift the burden of explanation back to Miss Whitney. In any event, it is apparent that clear and present danger raises puzzles not only at the philosophical level, but also at the trial level.

(iv) What evidence of danger was there in the record sufficient to satisfy the very stringent standards Brandeis had laid down in principle? The answer foreshadows a shift in focus that will preoccupy us when we turn in later chapters to direct anti-Communist control measures; it is a shift from concern with the danger of the content of speech to concern with the danger of the organized group of speakers. Justice Brandeis states:

I am unable to assent to the suggestion in the opinion of the Court that assembling with a political party, formed to advocate the desirability of a proletarian revolution by mass action at some date necessarily far in the future, is not a right within the protection of the Fourteenth Amendment. In the present case, however, there was other testimony which tended to establish the existence of a conspiracy, on the part of members of the International Workers of the World, to commit present serious crimes; and likewise to show that such a conspiracy would be furthered by the activity of the society of which Miss Whitney was a member.[33]

Although only obliquely a speech issue, the problem of the political conspiracy has proved to be inextricably tied to speech issues and has posed the most troublesome First Amendment issues for the Court. Like war, the existence of a conspiracy adds a factor to the social environment, making too dangerous speech that might otherwise be permissible. As we shall see, this premise, which has a certain power, is latched onto in the Communist cases, although there is no longer a conspiracy shown to commit *present* serious crime.

In conclusion, we should note that when the Court overruled *Whitney* in *Brandenburg* it did not even mention the Brandeis concurrence that had done so much to weaken and undermine the precedent it was striking down. Two possible explanations come to mind for this curious failure to acknowledge an obvious debt. First, the Court may have felt that in the end Brandeis had not drawn the line precisely where they wanted to place it and thus did not wish by erasing the majority view to make the competing Brandeis exposition the official view. Perhaps the Court balked at Brandeis's statement of the principle:

In order to support a finding of clear and present danger it must be shown either that immediate serious violence was to be expected or was advocated, or that the past conduct furnished reason to believe that such conduct was then contemplated.[34]

Under this test *either* the danger of "immediate serious violence" or the advocacy of such violence, that is, incitement, would be sufficient to convict, but *Brandenburg* requires *both* danger and incitement. Moreover, the final clause of this statement suggests a dangerous concession to censorship. Second, even if the Brandeis opinion were read to embody the *Brandenburg* principle, the Court may have found it too tied to the idiom of clear and present danger. Thus, in *Brandenburg* the Court brought the bifurcated tradition to an end by eliminating both the majority and the dissenting branches of that tradition.

12

Subversive Advocacy: Speech Starts to Win

The Professional Touch

When Charles Evans Hughes was appointed Chief Justice in 1930, Justices Holmes and Brandeis gained a powerful ally. This became apparent when the new Chief Justice wrote the majority opinion in *Stromberg v. California* [1] in 1931, the first case in the history of the Court in which there was an explicit victory for free speech. The Hughes opinion marks the beginning of a strand in the tradition which is to become very powerful in later years—the ultra-technical defense of free speech. If the dissents of Holmes and Brandeis are memorable because of their extraordinary bursts of eloquence, an eloquence which transcends the judicial role, Hughes's opinion in *Stromberg* is memorable as a prime example of a legal professional employing all his technical skill on behalf of liberty. It also marks a change in the mood and stance of the Court toward speech issues. Henceforth the Court will be more patient and precise in its analysis of the particular case and will do its best to save the particular defendant.

The defendant in *Stromberg* was a young woman who served as a counsellor at a summer camp where children were taught, among other things, "class consciousness, the solidarity of the workers, and the theory that the workers of the world are of one blood and brothers all." The camp library contained radical literature, which, as the state court put it, carried incitements to violence and to "armed uprisings"; and Miss Stromberg herself owned similar books and pamphlets. It was stipulated, however, that none of this material was used in teaching the children. Rather, the gist of the offense charged against the defendant was that she had participated in a daily ceremony, a reveille for radicals, at which "a camp-made reproduction of the flag of Soviet Russia, which was also the flag of the Communist Party in the United States" was raised, while the children saluted and pledged allegiance "to the worker's red flag, and to the cause for which it stands; one aim throughout our lives, freedom for the working class."[2]

Stromberg is unusual, if not unique, in that the California statute involved is addressed explicitly to the message conveyed by the symbol of the flag. In later symbolic speech case, such as *O'Brien v. United States*[3] in 1968, the draft card burning case, conduct is regulated despite the fact that it is symbolic. Here it is regulated because it is symbolic. The statute provides:

Any person who displays a red flag, banner or badge or any flag, badge, banner, or device of any color or form whatever in any public place or in any meeting place or public assembly, or from or on any house, building or window as a sign, symbol or emblem of opposition to organized government or as an invitation or stimulus to anarchistic action or as an aid to propaganda that is of a seditious character is guilty of a felony.[4]

The trial court had instructed the jury that they could convict only if they found that the red flag had been publicly displayed "for any one or more" of the three purposes proscribed by the statute: as an emblem of opposition to organized government, as a stimulus to anarchistic action, or as an aid to propaganda of a seditious character. The jury had returned a general verdict of guilty without specifying which of these purposes it had ascribed to the flag.

After meticulously examining the statute and the instruction, Chief Justice Hughes concludes that the three proscribed purposes are in the disjunctive so that the jury could convict on the basis of any one standing alone. He then goes on to find the first clause prohibiting display of the flag as "a symbol of opposition to organized government" unconstitutional in that it is so vague and indefinite as to permit the punishment of such innocuous conduct as the opposition of the party out of government to the party in power or the urging of changes in government by legal and constitutional means. The state court, in affirming, had conceded the possibility that this clause might be unconstitutional, but had rested its decision on the second and third clauses; in effect, it had held that if any of the clauses were valid, the conviction could stand. Hughes, however, insists that the conviction must be reversed, for the verdict was a general one and hence there is no way of knowing whether or not it was based on the invalid portion of the statute. His altogether non-eloquent handling of this point bequeaths an important technical tool. Over time *Stromberg* is to become one of the Court's most frequently cited decisions.

Apart from its central holding, the Hughes opinion is also of interest for the succinct summary it provides of the prior law on free speech. In the course of upholding the second and third clauses of the statute dealing with anarchistic action and propaganda of a seditious character, Hughes states:

The principles to be applied have been clearly set forth in our former decisions. It has been determined that the conception of liberty under the due process clause of the Fourteenth Amendment embraces the right of free speech. The right is not an absolute one, and the State in the exercise of its police power may punish the abuse of this freedom. There is no question but that the State may thus provide for the punishment of those who indulge in utterances which incite to violence and crime and threaten the overthrow of organized government by unlawful means. There is no constitutional immunity for such conduct abhorrent to our institutions. [citing *Gitlow* and *Whitney*] We have no reason to doubt the validity of the second and third clauses to the statute as construed by the state court to relate to such incitements to violence.[5]

Although Hughes uses the idiom of incitement, this passage leaves little doubt that the official rule as of 1931 was that speech containing *general* advocacy of violence and illegality could be proscribed without violating the First Amendment. Indeed, in light of the World War I decisions, the only question about the rule was whether it might not prove much less generous to speech should the occasion arise.

The Hardest Case

The next case, *Herndon v. Lowry*[6] in 1937, arose from the abortive effort by the Communist Party in the 1930s to organize the American Negro, an effort which, had it been successful, would have profoundly altered American life. Angelo Herndon, a Negro and a Party organizer, had been sent to Atlanta, where he had held three meetings and enrolled at least five members. At the time of his arrest he had in his possession membership blanks and Communist literature. The litera-

ture included a booklet advocating "self-determination" for the Black
Belt—that is, the establishment of a separate, autonomous Negro
state—by means of confiscation of white land holdings, strikes, boy-
cotts, and a "revolutionary struggle for power even if the situation
does not yet warrant raising the question of uprising."

Professor Chafee has said of Herndon:

> I have let my mind run over all the chief sedition defendants . . . from Debs
> down to date—Abrams, Berger, Gilbert, Gitlow, Miss Whitney, and the rest—
> and tried to decide which of them I myself honestly think did create a "clear
> and present danger" of unlawful acts under the circumstances surrounding
> his words. The upshot is, all but one seem to me fairly harmless. The one
> exception is Herndon.[7]

Chafee's hunch that Herndon was really dangerous is based on the
perception that the Negro population which formed his target audience was especially vulnerable to his fantastic proposal of literal
Negro autonomy. On this view, the oppressed Southern Negro resembles the crowd gathered outside the corn dealer's house in the Mill
example.

Herndon was indicted under an old Georgia slave insurrection
statute, which could possibly carry the death penalty. Convicted, he
was sentenced to eighteen-to-twenty years in prison. After a complex
effort to reach the Supreme Court,[8] he secured reversal of his conviction on constitutional grounds. The vote was 5 to 4; Justice Roberts
wrote the majority opinion.

Despite the blow it strikes for political tolerance, *Herndon* is a
difficult and frustrating precedent. In large part this is due to the
obliqueness of the Georgia statute. As Chafee pointedly notes, this
law was inspired by Nat Turner's Rebellion in 1832 and had remained
unused until it was applied to a Communist organizer a century later.
Designed for another purpose, it fits the facts awkwardly and skews
Herndon as a speech case. The section under which Herndon was
indicted provides:

> Any attempt, by persuasion or otherwise, to induce others to join in any
> combined resistance to the lawful authority of the State shall constitute an
> attempt to incite insurrection.[9]

The State argued that, given the Black Belt proposal, Herndon's
efforts to induce people to join the Communist Party constituted

"combined resistance to the lawful authority of the State." This positioning of the case makes it difficult to isolate the speech at issue.[10] The charge is not membership in a group which advocates unlawful action as in *Whitney;* rather, it is recruiting members for an insurrection. Thus, when Justice Roberts concludes that the application of the statute to Herndon is "an unwarranted invasion of the right of freedom of speech," I find it unclear what speech he is talking about. Is it the speech of soliciting members, or is it Herndon's vicarious share in the speech of the Communist Party, as was the case in *Whitney?*

The parties offer Justice Roberts sharply opposed readings of the prior precedent. The defendant contends that the legislative power to regulate speech is limited to measures protecting against clear and present danger of the use of force against the state. The State contends that *Gitlow* controls and that it is sufficient if utterances have a "dangerous tendency" toward subversion of the state. Justice Roberts carefully abstains from fully endorsing either view. He reaffirms the *Gitlow* distinction, thereby rejecting the defendant's contention that clear and present danger is the measure of the validity of all restrictions on speech; under *Gitlow* the test is limited to cases where speech is punished under statutes dealing with acts. Then he goes on to reject the State's contention that the *Gitlow* standard in cases involving pure speech statutes is the "dangerous tendency" of the speech:

The power of a state to abridge freedom of speech and of assembly is the exception rather than the rule and the penalizing even of utterances of a defined character must find its justification in a reasonable apprehension of danger to organized government. The judgment of the legislature is not unfettered. The limitation upon individual liberty must have appropriate relation to the safety of the state. Legislation which goes beyond this need violates the principle of the Constitution.[11]

This passage suggests a tightening of the *Gitlow* standard. The test for pure speech statutes is something more than substantive due process; it is "reasonable apprehension of danger."

Turning to the case before him, Roberts finds the record ambiguous as to whether Herndon had distributed the Black Belt literature, believed it, or had even shown it. He concludes that the evidence is inadequate to establish an attempt to incite to violent insurrection:

The appellant induced others to become members of the Communist Party. Did he thus incite to insurrection by reason of the fact that they agreed to abide by the tenets of the party, some of them lawful, others, as may be assumed, unlawful, in the absence of proof that he brought the unlawful aims to their notice, that he approved them, or that the fantastic program they envisaged was conceived of by anyone as more than an ultimate ideal? Doubtless circumstantial evidence might affect the answer to the question if appellant had been shown to have said that the Black Belt should be organized at once as a separate state and that that objective was one of his principal aims. But here circumstantial evidence is all to the opposite effect. The only objectives appellant is proved to have urged are those having to do with unemployment and emergency relief which are void of criminality. His membership in the Communist Party and his solicitation of a few members wholly fails to establish an attempt to incite others to insurrection. Indeed, so far as appears, he had but a single copy of the booklet the State claims to be objectionable; that copy he retained. The same may be said with respect to the other books and pamphlets, some of them of more innocent purport.[12]

We cannot say, unfortunately, that Herndon wins because the Black Belt program itself must be viewed simply as political action, a holding which would have important implications for radical agitation. Rather, he appears to win because all the State has proved is that he induced a few people to become members of the Communist Party and this alone is insufficient to establish an attempt to incite insurrection—a holding which hinges on facts as to participation and *scienter*.

As an alternative basis for decision, Justice Roberts finds the Georgia statute, as construed, too vague to meet constitutional standards. In an effort to make sense of the statute, the trial court had instructed the jury that the defendant could not be convicted unless it appeared "clearly from the evidence that immediate serious violence against the State of Georgia was to be expected or advocated." The jury having convicted, Herndon appealed on the ground that there was no evidence to support *this* charge, a very good point indeed. The appellate court, apparently reluctant to give up the conviction, attempted to salvage it by providing a new construction of the statute:

Force must have been contemplated, but the statute does not include either its occurrence or its imminence as an ingredient of the particular offense charged. Nor would it be necessary to guilt that the alleged offender should have intended that an insurrection should follow instantly or at any given time, but as to this element it would be sufficient if he intended that it should happen at any time within which he might reasonably expect his influence to continue to be directly operative in causing such action by those whom he sought to induce.[13]

Under such a "proximate cause test," any mention of forcible change, however general and unfocused, could be reached by law, because it would be impossible for the defendant to show that his influence might not still be expected to be "directly operative." Nor was it clear that force need even be mentioned; it was enough if it were "contemplated."

Justice Roberts will have none of this. He finds the law too vague to warn the actor and too vague to inform the judge and jury. It fails to provide "an ascertainable standard of guilt," and so, like the instruction in *Stromberg,* violates the First Amendment by giving the jury the power of censorship. We have stressed the technique of Hand and Brandeis of arraying categories of dangerous speech and seeking to locate the last term in such a series. Justice Roberts's approach is similar:

To be guilty under the law, as construed, a defendant need not advocate resort to force. He need not teach any particular doctrine to come within its purview. Indeed, he need not be active in the formation of a combination or group if he agitate for a change in the frame of government, however peaceful his own intent. If, by the exercise of prophesy, he can forecast that, as a result of a chain of causation, following his proposed action a group may arise at some future date which will resort to force, he is bound to make the prophesy and abstain, under pain of punishment, possibly execution. Every person who attacks existing conditions, who agitates for a change in the form of government, must take the risk that if a jury should be of opinion he ought to have foreseen that his utterances might contribute in any measure to some future forcible resistance to the existing government he may be convicted of the offense of inciting insurrection.[14]

A standard so vague makes the jury the unfettered censor of speech it does not like. And in this particular instance there was a great deal in Herndon's assertions about Negro equality that a Southern jury in the 1930s might deeply dislike.

A detail in Justice Roberts's handling of the vagueness point deserves further comment. He emphasizes that the alleged incitement is without referent or focus and notes that the statute differs sharply from the Espionage Act provisions involved in the earlier cases "in that it does not deal with a wilful attempt to obstruct a described and defined activity of the government."[15] Later he speaks of "a law general in its description of the mischief to be remedied."[16] Finally, he complains:

> The Act does not prohibit incitement to violent interference with any given activity or operation of the state. By force of it, as construed, the judge and jury trying an alleged offender cannot appraise the circumstances and character of the defendant's utterances or activities as begetting a clear and present danger of forcible obstruction of a particular state function. Nor is any specified conduct or utterance of the accused made an offense.[17]

There is the germ of an interesting idea here. He is suggesting that within the framework of the *Gitlow* distinction, statutes which proscribe acts, not words, cannot be made the predicate of speech "attempts" unless they are precise enough to permit measurement of how close the defendant came to the substantive evil. And the crime likely to have the least precision for the purposes of such measurement is violent overthrow of the government.

In the end, despite it opaqueness, *Herndon* emerges as an important precedent in five respects. First, following *Stromberg,* it adds momentum to the reversal of the trend of decisions on radical speech. If *Stromberg* made the nominal point that opposition to government as such cannot be proscribed, *Herndon* adds the more substantial point that advocacy of *forcible* opposition to government, when remote and unfocused, also cannot be proscribed. Second, it clarifies any possible ambiguity left by Justice Sanford's distinction in *Gitlow* by emphasizing that even pure speech statutes are subject to judicial review, and it suggests that the standard of review in such cases may be somewhat more stringent than substantive due process. Third, it reaffirms the role of clear and present danger in cases where the statute does not reflect a legislative judgment as to the danger from a specific class of utterances. Fourth, Roberts's vagueness analysis foreshadows a tradition which is to become powerful in subsequent decades—the requirement of the utmost precision in legislation impinging on speech. Fifth, the decision itself is an act of tough-minded liberalism in what must be regarded as the first genuine Communist confrontation in the Supreme Court of the United States.

Finally, we should note that *Herndon* is not only the Court's first encounter with American Communism, but also anticipates the cases generated during the 1960s by the Negro civil rights movement. Chafee observes:

My guess is that the men concerned in this prosecution were not worried in the slightest about any plotted insurrection or the possibility of a new Liberia between the Tennessee Valley Authority and the Gulf of Mexico. But they were worried, I suspect, about something else that Herndon really wanted—his demand for equal rights for Negroes. If he got going with that, there was was a clear and present danger of racial friction and isolated acts of violence by individuals on both sides. They were afraid, not that the United States Constitution would be overthrown, but that it might be enforced.[18]

Thus, *Herndon*, like *New York Times v. Sullivan*[19] thirty years later, presented the Court with a problem of judicial statesmanship: to absorb and respond to the realpolitik of the case without corrupting the ceremony of giving public reasons. In such instances the Court cannot be candid and call the prosecution's sham, but it can be realistic in its decision. In *Herndon* it was.

The Erosion of Gitlow

Hughes's tenure as Chief Justice lasted from 1930 until 1940 and proved a busy period for the Court in the First Amendment field. In addition to *Stromberg* and *Herndon*, the Court handed down a number of other major decisions during these years. In *Near v. Minnesota* (1931),[20] speaking through the Chief Justice, it firmly rejected prior restraint as a form of regulation in all but "exceptional cases," and in terms which anticipate *New York Times v. Sullivan* warned of the danger of restraining criticism of public officials. In *Grosjean v. American Press Co.* (1936)[21] it unanimously struck down a Louisiana tax on the advertising revenues of newspapers, which it characterized, in light of the history of "taxes on knowledge," as a particularly "odious" form of prior restraint. In *DeJonge v. Oregon* (1937),[22] an important decision on freedom of assembly which we will have occasion to discuss elsewhere, the unanimous Court, again speaking through Hughes, held unconstitutional the application of a state criminal syndicalism statute to a Communist for his participation in a meeting held under Communist Party auspices at which, it was agreed, there was no advocacy of criminal syndicalism. And in *Lovell v. Griffin* (1938)[23] and *Hague v. CIO* (1939)[24] the Court invalidated municipal ordinances which required permits for the distribution of leaflets (*Lovell*) and for assemblies (*Hague*) in public places, thereby establishing important precedents on speech in the public forum.

These decisions reflect a profound change in the Court's stance toward speech cases. This is apparent not only in the fact that the speech side wins, but also in the process by which the Court reaches that result. Most often its decisions rest on the application of various technical doctrines, such as the aversion to prior restraint as a form of regulation, strict construction of statutes, the insistence that speech statutes be narrowly drawn, and the vagueness rule. Taken together, these decisions suggest that a majority of the Court has come to share the view that First Amendment cases demand especially close judicial scrutiny.

That view is explicitly articulated in two cases decided toward the end of the decade: *United States v. Carolene Products Co.* [25] in 1938 and *Schneider v. State* [26] in 1939. Neither of these cases involves subversive advocacy, and *Carolene Products* is not even a speech case. But both are relevant to our inquiry, for they signal a shift in the Court's stance toward the First Amendment, a shift which has implications for the future of both the clear and present danger test and the *Gitlow* distinction.

Carolene Products marks a watershed in the history of the Court. It was one of the series of decisions during the mid-1930s in which the Court withdrew by degrees from intervention in the economic sphere, thereby bringing to an end a thirty-year period during which many government efforts at economic regulation had been struck down. At issue in *Carolene Products* was a federal statute which declared that "filled milk"—skimmed milk to which fats other than milk fats had been added—is "injurious to public health" and "a fraud upon the public" and which prohibited the shipment of such milk in interstate commerce. The defendant argued that in passing the statute Congress had exceeded its power over interstate commerce and that the statute violated the due process clause of the Fifth Amendment. In rejecting these contentions, Justice Stone, writing for the Court, shows great deference to the legislative judgment:

. . . the existence of facts supporting the legislative judgment is to be presumed, for regulatory legislation affecting ordinary commercial transactions is not to be pronounced unconstitutional unless in the light of the facts made known or generally assumed it is of such a character as to preclude the assumption that it rests upon some rational basis within the knowledge and experience of the legislators. [27]

In a footnote keyed to this passage, Stone suggests that a different standard of judicial review—a narrowing of the presumption of constitutionality—may be called for in cases involving basic personal liberties protected by the Bill of Rights. The footnote reads in part:

⁴ There may be narrower scope for operation of the presumption of constitutionality when legislation appears on its face to be within a specific prohibition of the Constitution, such as those of the first ten amendments, which are deemed equally specific when held to be embraced within the Fourteenth. . . .

It is unnecessary to consider now whether legislation which restricts those political processes which can ordinarily be expected to bring about repeal of undesirable legislation, is to be subjected to more exacting judicial scrutiny under the general prohibitions of the Fourteenth Amendment than are most other types of legislation. On restrictions upon the right to vote, see *Nixon v. Herndon, Nixon v. Condon;* on restraints upon the dissemination of information, see *Near v. Minnesota, Grosjean v. American Press Co., Lovell v. Griffin;* on interference with political organizations, see *Stromberg v. California, Fiske v. Kansas, Whitney v. California* [citing Justice Brandeis's concurrence], *Herndon v. Lowry,* and see Holmes, J., in *Gitlow v. New York;* as to prohibition of peaceable assembly, see *DeJonge v. Oregon.* ²⁸

Although his phrasing is tentative, Justice Stone's comments and citations are suggestive. A decade earlier Stone had joined in the opinions of the Court in *Gitlow* and *Whitney*—opinions which held that the constitutional standard for restrictions on speech was a "rational basis" for the legislative judgment. But now, citing the Holmes dissent in *Gitlow* and the Brandeis concurrence in *Whitney* as well as the more recent opinions of the Hughes Court, he suggests that such cases may demand "more exacting judicial scrutiny."

This view is expressed more forcefully a year later by Justice Roberts in *Schneider v. State,* a case in which the Court found unconstitutional a group of municipal ordinances restricting the distribution of leaflets on public streets. After observing that the Court "has characterized the freedom of speech and that of press as fundamental personal rights and liberties," Roberts declares:

In every case, therefore, where legislative abridgment of the rights is asserted, the courts should be astute to examine the effect of the challenged legislation. Mere legislative preferences or beliefs respecting matters of public convenience may well support regulation directed at other personal activities, but be insufficient to justify such as diminishes the exercise of rights so vital to the maintenance of democratic institutions. And so, as cases arise, the delicate and difficult task falls upon the courts to weigh the circumstances and to appraise the substantiality of the reasons advanced in support of the regulation of the free enjoyment of the rights.[29]

Neither Stone nor Roberts confronts—or even mentions—the majority opinions in *Gitlow* and *Whitney*, but both express a general orientation which would seem to be directly at odds with the *Gitlow-Whitney* standard. Thus, by the end of the 1930s developments in areas far removed from the problem of subversive advocacy had called into question the majority view of that problem.

13

Subversive Advocacy:
The Heyday of Clear
and Present Danger

In 1941 Chief Justice Hughes died and was replaced by Justice Harlan Stone, the author of *Carolene Products*. This change in the leadership of the Court coincided with a dramatic change in its composition: Between 1937 and 1945 every seat on the Court changed occupants. Among those to join the Court during this period was a group of justices who were to form a powerful liberal bloc—Black, Douglas, Murphy, and Rutledge—as well as their chief critics, Frankfurter and Jackson. Although Holmes and Brandeis had only recently departed—Holmes in 1935, Brandeis in 1939—this new generation of justices regards them with veneration, and there soon emerges a majority on the Court which sees their test of clear and present danger as the touchstone of First Amendment policy.

The transformation of the Holmes-Brandeis dissents into majority doctrine occurs with startling suddenness. For a full decade after *Whitney,* the Court had been silent about clear and present danger. Although the Hughes Court handed down a number of speech decisions during this period, it apparently felt no need to refer to the test. The silence was broken only by Justice Roberts's mention of the test in *Herndon* in 1937. Then in *Thornhill v. Alabama*[1] in 1940 Justice Murphy, writing for the Court, announces:

Abridgement of the liberty of . . . discussion can be justified only where the clear danger of substantive evils arises under circumstances affording no opportunity to test the merits of ideas by competition for acceptance in the market of public opinion.[2]

Thereafter clear and present danger is invoked in a variety of cases. By 1943 it is possible for Justice Jackson, no great friend of the test, to declare on behalf of the Court in *West Virginia Board of Education v. Barnette:*[3]

It is now a commonplace that censorship or suppression of expression of opinion is tolerated by our Constitution only when the expression presents a clear and present danger of action of a kind the State is empowered to prevent and punish.[4]

The Court does not disavow or even confront *Gitlow* and *Whitney;* rather, it rests its use of the test on the authority of the Holmes-Brandeis dissents. For a majority of the Court the underground tradition of the dissent has become more powerful precedent than the official majority opinions. The clear and present danger test, having lost each of the battles, wins the war.

The sudden change in the fortunes of the test is all the more striking in that it occurs in areas far removed from subversive advocacy, the problem Holmes and Brandeis had addressed in their dissents. Clear and present danger becomes, in effect, the general, all-purpose First Amendment test. *Thornhill* involves labor picketing. *Barnette* arises from the refusal of Jehovah's Witnesses' children to participate in compulsory flag salute ceremonies in public schools. In other cases decided during this period the test is applied to a variety of other problems, including some we have discussed elsewhere, such as reflexive disorder (*Cantwell v. Connecticut*) and contempt by publication (*Bridges v. California, Pennekamp v. Florida,* and *Craig v. Harney*).[5]

As it is applied to diverse speech problems, the test is subtly altered by usage. So long as it was limited to the problem of subversive advocacy, considerations regarding the gravity of the evil, introduced by Brandeis in his *Whitney* concurrence, were of little relevance: no one questioned the seriousness of the evil of violent overthrow. But once the test is exported to other areas—where the evil is more questionable—"gravity" emerges as a central consideration. The logic of Brandeis's *Whitney* concurrence would seem to require that the "gravity" criterion operate as a precondition which must be met before the "clear" and "present" criteria are applied. The Court, however, never pauses to explain the relationship between the different elements of the test, and there is a tendency to absorb "gravity" directly into the test.[6] Indeed, the operative meaning of the test in many of these cases is simply that only a grave evil can justify the restriction of speech—a point which could easily be made without reference to the test.

The Court is by no means unanimous in its allegiance to the clear and present danger test. Only the liberal four—Black, Douglas, Rutledge, and Murphy—are fully committed to the test and invoke it consistently. In order to form a majority, they depend on the vote of one or another of their colleagues, none of whom can be said to be an enthusiast for the test. The chief critic of the test is Justice Frankfurter, who dissents repeatedly and at length. Frankfurter chides the majority for its "doctrinaire overstatement" and charges that, as used by the majority, clear and present danger is a "pat formula" which embodies "vague and uncritical generalizations" and frustrates close analysis of the particular case before the Court. Appointing himself the true spokesman for Holmes and Brandeis, he argues that the majority misconceives the "origin and purpose of the concept of clear and present danger," and that it has taken "a felicitous phrase out of the context of the particular situation where it arose and for which it was adapted." Above all, Frankfurter is critical of the majority's emphasis on the gravity requirement, which he characterizes as "absolutist." In this respect, his comments in dissent provide a mirror image of the importance the gravity point has assumed for the majority.[7]

The Subversive Advocacy Cases

Although the Court adopted a stringent version of clear and present danger during this period, it had few occasions to apply it to the core issue of subversive advocacy. In large part, this was due to an irony in the dialogue between the society and the Court: Although the nation was at war, few speech cases of the sort generated by World War I reached the Court.[8] Conceivably this may reflect an increase in political tolerance over the intervening decades. The central explanation, however, appears to be the wartime stance of the American Communist Party. In light of the alliance between the United States and the Soviet Union, American Communists were enthusiastic supporters of the war effort. This was reflected in the transformation of the militant Party into the relatively tame Communist Political Association; and it appears to have cut the other way as well by checking the government's impulse to prosecute Communists.

In any event, whatever the reason for the hiatus in subversive advocacy prosecutions, there were only three cases during this period which touched on the issue: *Taylor v. Mississippi* and *Schneiderman v. United States* in 1943, and *Hartzel v. United States* in 1944.[9] While these cases do not produce major statements such as *Gitlow* and *Whitney,* they leave little doubt that in the subversive advocacy context, as in various other areas, clear and present danger is *the* test.

Taylor v. Mississippi arose out of a controversy involving the refusal on religious grounds of Jehovah's Witnesses' children to participate in compulsory flag salute ceremonies in the public schools. The defendants were convicted of violating an omnibus Mississippi statute passed during the war. The provisions under which they were charged were aimed at communications which reasonably tend "to create an attitude of stubborn refusal to salute, honor or respect the flag or government of the United States, or of the state of Mississippi" and at communications "calculated to encourage . . . disloyalty to the government of the United States, or to the State of Mississippi."

The defendants had distributed literature condemning flag saluting as a direct violation of God's commandment, as "a contemptible form of primitive idol worship," and as the stratagem of a "desperate Satan." Also, in an interview with several women, two of whom had lost sons in the war, they stated that "it was wrong for our President to send our boys across in uniform to fight our enemies" and that "these boys were being shot down for no purpose at all." The Supreme Court, speaking through Justice Roberts, unanimously reversed the convictions.

Justice Roberts treats the Court's contemporaneous decision in *Barnette* as disposing *a fortiori* of the flag salute aspect of *Taylor.* If the state cannot compel people to salute the flag, as the Court held in *Barnette,* it must also, he argues, lack the power to punish them for urging others on religious grounds not to salute. This point may be more complex and important than it appears. However one approaches the problem of speech which triggers action, there is a puzzle as to whether the state may intervene when the target action is not itself criminal, as for example, not volunteering for military service, not working at a munitions job, or, as in *Taylor,* refusing to salute the flag. The majority in *Abrams,* without noting the point, had decided that the state could reach such speech; and neither Holmes nor Brandeis had ever touched on the matter in their dissents.

Justice Roberts in *Taylor* comes close to asserting that whenever the state leaves the individual free to decide for himself whether or not to do certain acts, it must be open to others to urge, advocate, or incite him either to act or not to act. This idea could be far-reaching; it could yield the premise that the state can enlist the criminal law against speech only as an adjunct to its enforcement of the criminal law itself. Such a premise would make sense so long as the state's objection to the speech was in terms of it triggering specific action. It is, however, not at all clear that Justice Roberts is committing himself and the Court to such large premises. He sees the case in light of the controversy over compulsory flag salutes and thus may be deciding no more than that Jehovah's Witnesses and others with objections to compulsory flag salutes may voice those objections.[10]

The other wing of the case, involving the provision aimed at communications "calculated to encourage disloyalty," is more directly relevant to the problem of speech triggering action. Although the statutory prohibition is obviously vague and the defendants had stressed the vagueness challenge, Justice Roberts rests his decision on the clear and present danger test:

> The statute as construed . . . makes it a criminal offense to communicate to others views and opinions respecting governmental policies, and prophecies concerning the future of our own and other nations. As applied to the appellants it punishes them although what they communicated is not claimed or shown to have been done with an evil or sinister purpose, to have advocated or incited subversive action against the nation or state [citing *Schenck, Abrams,* and *Whitney*], or to have threatened any clear and present danger to our institutions or our Government [citing *DeJonge* and *Herndon*]. What these appellants communicated were their beliefs and opinions concerning domestic measures and trends in national and world affairs.
>
> Under our decisions criminal sanctions cannot be imposed for such communication.[11]

This passage is striking. *Taylor* is the first subversive advocacy case to come before the Stone Court and *Gitlow* is still on the books, but Roberts's use of clear and present danger seems almost automatic. The test has indeed become "a commonplace." Yet it is not altogether clear from Roberts's terse statement just what the content of his version of the test is—he uses the idioms of incitement and advocacy, as well as that of clear and present danger, and he also talks of "evil purpose." He does not, however, pause to explain the relationship between these terms.

A clearer statement of the line between protected and unprotected speech is provided by Justice Murphy's opinion for the Court in *Schneiderman v. United States,* a decision handed down during the same term as *Taylor. Schneiderman* arose out of one of the many denaturalization proceedings initiated by the Government during World War II. The Russian-born Schneiderman had become a naturalized citizen in 1927. Twelve years later he was threatened with the loss of his citizenship under a provision of the Naturalization Act of 1906, which empowered the Government to revoke naturalization papers which had been fraudulently or illegally procured. Among the conditions for acquiring citizenship was the requirement that the applicant demonstrate that at the time of his application and during the preceding five years he was "attached to the principles of the Constitution." The Government charged that Schneiderman had illegally procured his citizenship in that he had been a member of the Communist Party at the time of his naturalization and hence had not satisfied this condition.[12]

Justice Murphy, writing for the Court, begins by construing the Naturalization Act in such a way as to require a high standard of proof. He states that because American citizenship is "precious" and is "conferred by solemn adjudication," it can be revoked only on a showing of "clear, unequivocal, and convincing" evidence of violation of the Act. Thus, the question is whether membership in the Party constitutes "clear, unequivocal, and convincing" proof of lack of attachment to the principles of the Constitution.[13]

The Government had argued that Schneiderman was unattached in two respects. First, he was committed to various policies of the Party—such as socialization of the means of production and dictatorship of the proletariat—which were fundamentally incompatible with the Constitution. Murphy flatly rejects this contention, arguing that "the many important and far-reaching changes made in the Constitution since 1787 refute the idea that attachment to any particular provision or provisions is essential, or that one who advocates radical changes is necessarily not attached to the Constitution."

Second, the Government contended that Schneiderman's lack of attachment was shown by his membership in an organization which advocated violent overthrow of the government. After an extended review of Marxist literature, Murphy finds that a reasonable man might conclude that the Party in 1927 urged violent overthrow. But he also cites excerpts from the literature which support the conclusion that "the Party in 1927 desired to achieve its purposes by peaceful and democratic means, and as a theoretical matter justified the use of force and violence only as a method of preventing an attempted forcible counter-overthrow . . . or as a method of last resort." There is, Murphy argues, a profound difference between these two possible interpretations of the Party's program:

There is a material difference between agitation and exhortation calling for present violent action which creates a clear and present danger of public disorder or other substantive evil, and mere doctrinal justification or prediction of the use of force under hypothetical conditions at some indefinite future time—prediction that is not calculated or intended to be presently acted upon, thus leaving opportunity for general discussion and calm processes of thought and reason. Cf. *Bridges v. California* and Justice Brandeis' concurring opinion in *Whitney v. California.* See also *Taylor v. Mississippi.* [14]

Although those who call for "present violent action" are clearly unattached to the Constitution, those who engage in "mere doctrinal justification" of violence enjoy the protection of the First Amendment, and there is no reason to conclude that they are unattached to the Constitution. Murphy concludes that two interpretations of the Party's program are possible—the one protected, the other unprotected—and that the Government has not met the burden of proving that Schneiderman subscribed to the latter interpretation.

Given its special procedural context, *Schneiderman* is not a ruling on the propriety of Communist speech. Yet the language it uses in distinguishing between protected and unprotected advocacy is suggestive. Although cast in the idiom of clear and present danger, Murphy's statement of the line displays the equal emphasis on the speaker's words ("agitation and exhortation calling for present violent action . . .") and their probable consequences (" . . . which creates a clear and present danger") that is essential to the *Brandenburg* principle. Unfortunately, the Court never developed the point, for it was sharply divided both on the merits of the clear and present danger test and on the issue of subversive advocacy.

The depth of those divisions is revealed by *Hartzel v. United States* in 1944. The only World War II prosecution under the Espionage Act of 1917 to reach the Court, *Hartzel* almost proved a replay of *Schenck.* The defendant had published and distributed three pamphlets which the Court describes in the following terms:

In substance, they depict the war as a gross betrayal of America, denounce our English allies and the Jews and assail in reckless terms the integrity and patriotism of the President of the United States. They call for an abandonment of our allies and a conversion of the war into a racial conflict. They further urge an "internal war of race against race" and "occupation [of America] by foreign troops until we are able to stand alone."[15]

Mimeographed copies of these pamphlets were mailed anonymously to a wide range of institutions and individuals whom Hartzel considered influential. Among the recipients were several high-ranking military officers, a journal addressed primarily to a military audience, and various civilian groups, such as the American Legion, the Lions International, and Kiwanis International. At the offices of the military journal, the pamphlets were read by two members of the military; elsewhere they were read by several individuals eligible for the draft, among them a twenty-year-old mail clerk at the Lions International headquarters. Like Schenck twenty-five years earlier, Hartzel was convicted under the provisions of the Espionage Act directed at those who during wartime "willfully cause or attempt to cause insubordination, disloyalty, mutiny, or refusal of duty in the military or naval forces" or who "willfully obstruct the recruiting or enlistment service." He was sentenced to five years in prison.

The Court reverses, but the vote is 5 to 4, and the majority is unable to agree on an opinion. Justice Murphy, in an opinion joined by Black, Rutledge, and Stone, construes the statutory requirement of "willfullness" so as to require a specific intent. If specific intent is shown, then the question is whether the speech created a clear and present danger of the evils proscribed by the statute. But there is no need to reach this question, Murphy says, because the evidence is insufficient to establish that Hartzel had a specific intent to obstruct the draft. Justice Roberts concurs in the judgment separately, saying only that he agrees that the evidence is insufficient.

Justice Reed writes for the dissent, and his emphasis on the exigencies of wartime vividly recalls the majority opinions of the World War I period. Although Hartzel's target audience was not limited to those connected with or eligible for the military, Reed resurrects Justice Holmes's argument in *Schenck* that the fact that some of the pamphlets were sent to members of the military establishes the requisite intent:

To adopt the language of Mr. Justice Holmes speaking for a unanimous Court in *Schenck v. United States,* of course the documents would not have been sent unless they had been intended to have some effect, and we do not see what effect they could be expected to have upon persons in the military service except to influence them to obstruct the carrying on of the war against Germany when petitioner deemed that a betrayal of our country.[16]

Reed's dissent is joined by Frankfurter, Jackson, and, inexplicably, Douglas. There is thus a sense in which the Court in 1944 was but one vote away from reviving *Schenck*.

The Dawn of the Cold War

The heyday of clear and present danger proved short-lived. In 1945 Burton replaced Roberts, and a year later Vinson replaced Stone as Chief Justice. Over the next few years the vigor and appetite with which the Court approached First Amendment matters began to wane.[17] Finally, in 1949 the deaths of Murphy and Rutledge and their replacement by Clark and Minton broke the liberal bloc and cast a shadow over the future of the test.

These changes in the composition of the Court coincided with a shift in the Court's First Amendment workload. With the conclusion of World War II and the dissolution of the United States-Soviet Union alliance, the militant Communist Party was revived, and concern with domestic subversion began to dominate American life. In 1950—soon after the deaths of Murphy and Rutledge—the first big anti-Communist case, *American Communication Association v. Douds*, [18] reached the Court.

In *Douds*, as in *Schneiderman*, the confrontation with Communist speech is oblique. The case involved a challenge to a provision of the Taft-Hartley Act which denied the benefits of the National Labor Relations Act to any union whose officers failed to submit affidavits to the National Labor Relations Board swearing that they were not members of the Communist Party and that they did not believe in violent overthrow of the government. The purpose of this legislation was said to be to protect the flow of interstate commerce against disruptions caused by "political strikes," and the affidavit requirement was justified as a means of identifying those likely to promote such strikes. The Court, in an opinion by Chief Justice Vinson, upheld the constitutionality of this requirement. In a later chapter we will have occasion to discuss *Douds* as an important precedent on the problem of partial sanctions against speech. But from our present perspective the most interesting thing about the case is what the Court has to say about the clear and present danger test.

Chief Justice Vinson does not doubt that Congress possesses the power to regulate interstate commerce, and he is satisfied that there is a rational relationship between the evil the statute seeks to prevent and the remedy it provides. But he acknowledges that the case poses a First Amendment issue: The statute has the indirect effect of "discouraging the lawful exercise of political freedoms." Vinson would, however, distinguish this issue from the one "that Justices Holmes and Brandeis found convenient to consider in terms of clear and present danger."[19] The essence of the Holmes-Brandeis doctrine, argues Vinson, is that

. . . ideas and doctrines thought harmful or dangerous are best fought with words. Only, therefore, when force is very likely to follow an utterance before there is a chance for counter-argument to have effect may that utterance be punished or prevented.[20]

But *Douds* presents a different sort of issue:

Government's interest here is not in preventing the dissemination of Communist doctrine or the holding of particular beliefs because it is feared that unlawful action will result therefrom if free speech is practiced. Its interest is in protecting the free flow of commerce from what Congress considers to be substantial evils of conduct that are not the products of speech at all. Section 9(h), in other words, does not interfere with speech because Congress fears the consequences of speech; it regulates harmful conduct which Congress has determined is carried on by persons who may be identified by their political affiliations and beliefs.[21]

The affidavit requirement is not aimed at speech; rather, it is a device for identifying those who are likely to engage in conduct—political strikes—which is not caused by speech and cannot be countered by speech. The rationale underlying the Holmes-Brandeis requirement of imminence, argues Vinson, is irrelevant, for counter-speech affords no remedy to the evil of political strikes: "force may and must be met with force."[22] He concludes that clear and present danger is inapplicable to cases such as *Douds,* where the impact of regulation is "an indirect, conditional, partial abridgement of speech."[23] In such cases the duty of the Court is to balance the conflicting interests.

Douds thus marks a curious turn in the career of the test. It is now 1950. There is no longer a majority prepared to use clear and present danger to protect speech. Yet the test survives. Not only has it been announced as the constitutional standard in numerous cases during this decade, but it retains the authority of the Holmes-Brandeis dissents that gave it birth. However much he might like to, Vinson simply cannot ignore the test. And in order to avoid applying it to the case before him, he is forced to a conclusion that would have astonished Justice Sanford, the author of *Gitlow*, namely, that clear and present danger is the appropriate test in cases involving direct restrictions on speech.

14

Subversive Advocacy:
The Great Confrontation—
Dennis v. United States

Joseph Wood Krutch has a passage somewhere comparing Eugene O'Neill and Shakespeare. O'Neill, he thought, possessed great powers as a dramatist, but fell short of supreme greatness because he lacked Shakespeare's gift for matching the height of his poetry to the height of his drama. In much the same way, one keeps expecting, and hoping, as the First Amendment tradition unfolds, that great events will provoke great doctrinal confrontations which in turn will stir the Court to great statement. *Dennis v. United States*[1] in 1952 is a prime example of the defeat of that expectation.

Everything conspired to make *Dennis* a great moment. It involved the direct criminal prosecution of eleven leaders of the Communist Party. The trial, which lasted nine months, was almost certainly the great American political trial. The case reached the Supreme Court during the height of the country's preoccupation with domestic subversion. And the Court responded to it as a great case. In a 6 to 2 decision, upholding the convictions, the Court produced five opinions, totalling one hundred pages. Chief Justice Vinson wrote for the majority; Justices Frankfurter and Jackson added elaborate concurrences; and Justices Black and Douglas entered sharp dissents. But in the end *Dennis* does not prove a great case, and today, after twenty years, it has no doctrinal significance in its own right.

Dennis does, however, retain considerable interest as the climax of the career of the clear and present danger test. It is at once the finest and the last hour of the test. The majority acknowledges clear and present danger as the constitutional measure of free speech, but in the process, to meet the political exigencies of the case, it officially adjusts the test, giving it the kiss of death.

The Posture of the Case

The *Dennis* defendants were convicted under the Smith Act, a sweeping federal sedition law passed in 1940.[2] Although enacted at a time when the Communist threat was paramount, the Act shows little sophistication about the nature of contemporary radical tactics. In effect, it combines the 1902 New York criminal syndicalism used in *Gitlow* with the conspiracy to advocate tactic used in *Whitney*. In its precise terms, the Act makes it a crime

. . . to knowingly or willfully advocate, abet, advise, or teach the duty, necessity, desirability, or propriety of overthrowing or destroying any government in the United States by force or violence, or by the assassination of any officer of any such government;

. . . to organize or help or to organize any society, group, or assembly of persons who teach, advocate, or encourage the overthrow or destruction of any government in the United States by force or violence; or to be or become a member of, or affiliate with, any such society, group, or assembly of persons, knowing the purposes thereof.[3]

The defendants in *Dennis* are charged with conspiring to violate the "advocacy" and "organizing" provisions of the Act.

We will not at this point make an elaborate analysis of the issues raised by the effort to prosecute the Communist Party. Those issues are best handled as a topic in their own right—the problem of group advocacy. We must, however, note one aspect of this larger topic: the Government's reliance on conspiracy doctrine in the framing of the *Dennis* prosecution. The exact charge is not advocating overthrow. Nor is it conspiring to overthrow, no doubt the Government's real grievance. Rather, it is *conspiring to advocate overthrow* and *conspiring to organize a group to advocate overthrow*.

The awkwardness of this charge is underscored if we compare it to the charges in earlier cases, such as *Schenck* and *Whitney*. For the sake of analytic clarity, we have thus far separated the single speaker from the group. In fact, however, the individual speaker has not been Thoreau-like entirely alone; nor is he likely to be if the speech touches political concerns of general public interest. In *Schenck* the leaflet was the product of a general Socialist Party campaign against the war and the draft; Schenck himself was the secretary of the Party in charge of the headquarters from which the leaflets were sent. He did not write the leaflet; he merely arranged to have fifteen thousand printed and mailed. As a technical matter, the charge was *conspiracy* to obstruct the draft, and a second defendant, another official, was also charged. But the vast difference between *Schenck* and *Dennis* is in the focus. Although a collaborative effort is involved in *Schenck,* the charge is not against the Socialist Party or the local chapter; it is against the actors who in a familiar common law sense "published" the leaflet. The focus accordingly is on the propriety of the leaflet itself, and it matters little that Schenck did not actually write it.

Whitney is somewhat closer to *Dennis.* Indeed, the statutes are strikingly similar. Miss Whitney is charged with violating the California Criminal Syndicalism Act in that she did "willfully . . . organize and assist in organizing and was, is, and knowingly became a member of an organization . . . assembled to advocate, teach, aid and abet criminal syndicalism." Although the focus in *Whitney* is still on a fairly specific set of messages, the charge is explicitly concerned with the defendant's role in supporting the group. The term "conspiracy" is not used, but one could easily restate the statute: The offense proscribed is advocacy by a group, and Miss Whitney's crime resides in her assisting in the organizing of the group. She is, in effect, a member of a conspiracy. Neither the Court nor the defendants pause to make much of this step and the questions to which it gives rise: At what point does one become legally responsible for the speech of another? Is not vicarious responsibility being attached more easily to speech crimes than it could be attached to action crimes under conventional criminal law? This bastard form of conspiracy does, however, trouble Justice Brandeis. He observes at the outset of his great concurring opinion:

The felony which the statute created is a crime very unlike the old felony of conspiracy or the old misdemeanor of unlawful assembly. The mere act of assisting in forming a society for teaching syndicalism, of becoming a member of it, or of assembling with others for that purpose is given the dynamic quality of crime. There is guilt although the society may not contemplate immediate promulgation of the doctrine. Thus the accused is to be punished, not for contempt, incitement or conspiracy, but for a step in preparation, which, if it threatens the public order at all, does so only remotely. The novelty in the prohibition introduced is that the statute aims, not at the practice of criminal syndicalism, nor even directly at the preaching of it, but at association with those who propose to preach it.[4]

When we turn to *Dennis,* Justice Brandeis's uneasiness proves prophetic. The "conspiracy to advocate" charge in *Dennis* is essentially the same as the charge in *Whitney;* in both instances the defendants are charged with organizing a group to commit a speech crime. But in *Dennis* another dimension has been added: The defendants are also charged with "conspiracy to organize"—a charge which comes precariously close to a conspiracy to organize a conspiracy to commit a speech crime.

The application of conspiracy doctrine to speech crimes raises difficult First Amendment questions. The difficulties are generated by the twin aspects of conspiracy: It involves not only the pooling of the efforts of several people, but also preparation and planning prior to action. On one hand, the multiple-person, combination aspect of conspiracy may make it unrealistic to treat such cases as though they involved only a single speaker. It is a proper question whether with speech, as with other conduct, action which would be tolerable standing alone is rendered criminal by the presence of conspiracy. On the other hand, the preparation aspect of conspiracy makes it a slippery notion to apply to speech crimes. The First Amendment has favored a policy of waiting for the evil to mature, but conspiracy doctrine enables the government to "move the clock back" so as to reach a prior stage of preparation to speak. Further, it is doubtful that we can judge the propriety of the target crime of a speech conspiracy until we hear what the message is. It is thus a live question whether conspiracy doctrine can be used, consistently with the First Amendment, to enlarge the jurisdiction of the censor.

Dennis should have been the occasion for a major decision on the constitutional limits of conspiracy doctrine applied to speech. But the Court virtually ignores the question. Although the majority weighs the conspiracy factor heavily in its assessment of the danger of Communist advocacy, it makes no effort to reconcile conspiracy doctrine with the First Amendment. Justices Black and Douglas in dissent and Justice Jackson, concurring, are more concerned about the conspiracy issue, but—perhaps because the case has generated so many other pressures—they tend to talk at cross-purposes and what might have been a fruitful debate among them never occurs.

In addition to the conspiracy complication, *Dennis* is further skewed by another factor—the Court's remove from the record. As we noted in the preface, the soundness and utility of a speech decision is likely to vary directly with the attention paid to particular messages. From this perspective, the most striking thing about *Dennis* is that no specific messages whatsoever are discussed, or even mentioned, in the opinion of the Court. For undisclosed reasons, the Court decided to limit its grant of *certiorari* to consideration of whether the Smith Act was unconstitutional either on its face or as applied. As Chief Justice Vinson put it:

The trial of the case extended over nine months, six of which were devoted to the taking of evidence, resulting in a record of 16,000 pages. Our limited grant of the writ of certiorari has removed from our consideration any question as to the sufficiency of the evidence to support the jury's determination that petitioners are guilty of the offense charged. Whether on this record petitioners did in fact advocate the overthrow of the Government by force and violence is not before us, and we must base any discussion of this point upon the conclusions stated in the opinion of the Court of Appeals, which treated the issue in great detail.[5]

As a consequence of this move, the justices are cut off from the political realities of the speech they are adjudicating, and we get a curiously abstract discussion of the limits of political dissent. It is true that the trial judge, Harold Medina, made a careful and lucid summation of the evidence in his charge to the jury and that Judge Hand, speaking for the Court of Appeals, reviewed the evidence in some detail. Nevertheless, the central fact about this most important of speech cases is that the justices do not have the slightest idea of what the defendants said. The one exception is Justice Douglas, who sneaked a look at the trial record and thereby lent a special flavor and power to his dissent. After acknowledging the possibility that the teaching of techniques of sabotage and terror could be reached by law, he adds:

So far as the present record is concerned, what petitioners did was to organize people to teach and themselves teach the Marxist-Leninist doctrine contained chiefly in four books: Stalin, Foundations of Leninism (1924); Marx and Engels, The Communist Manifesto (1848); Lenin, State and Revolution (1917); History of the Communist Party of the Soviet Union (B) (1939).[6]

In a footnote keyed to this passage Justice Douglas adds:

Other books taught were Stalin, Problems of Leninism, Strategy and Tactics of World Communism (H Doc. No. 619, 80th Cong. 2d Sess.) and Program of the Communist International.[7]

As Justice Douglas goes on to point out, none of these books are banned by the Court's decisions. Indeed, they remain in full and free circulation during the entire period of intense anti-Communist feeling in the 1950s.

Six years after *Dennis*, in *Yates v. United States*,[8] another Smith Act prosecution of Communist Party leaders, the Court, having looked at the trial record, will announce with astonishment how little it contains and will make the highly unusual gesture of directing the acquittals of several of the defendants. In view of the fact that the trial in *Dennis* was completed in 1949 and the indictment in *Yates* was handed down in 1951, it is difficult to believe that the prosecution in *Yates* did not have access to the *best* evidence used in *Dennis*. Accordingly, the Court's response to the quality of proof in *Yates* must also be read as a commentary on the quality of proof in *Dennis*. It is, therefore, likely that the conviction was an injustice, insofar as it was a conviction for a speech crime.

The Majority Opinion

One puzzle about *Dennis* is why the Court had to work so hard to affirm the convictions. It was accepting the lower court's judgment that the defendants were guilty of conspiring to advocate violent overthrow; it was not going to review the factual basis of that judgment; it was not going to address itself to the First Amendment perplexities raised by the Government's sweeping use of conspiracy doctrine; the Smith Act had been modelled after the statutes sustained in *Gitlow* and *Whitney;* and, finally, but not least, the defendants were not nonentities—they were the leaders of the Communist Party. Why then was *Dennis* not an open and shut case?

There are two answers. First, the trial had been a highly visible public event and had prompted charges that America was finally indulging in political trials. Thus the Court may have felt that the importance of the occasion required at least the ceremony of painstakingly reconciling the Government's anti-Communist strategy with the traditions of free speech and political tolerance. After all, the Govern-

ment itself had elected to frame the case in speech terms; the charge
was not that the Communists were conspiring to overthrow the government, but that they were conspiring to talk about doing so. The
second answer, however, is more relevant to our present concerns. It
is that all the justices felt that they had to make their peace with the
stringent version of the clear and present danger test they had inherited from Holmes and Brandeis by way of the Stone Court. On my
view, the supreme achievement of the test in American constitutional
law, and perhaps its only achievement, was that it made the Court
sweat so much to affirm the conviction in *Dennis*—a case in which the
danger posed by the defendants' advocacy, however "clear" and
"grave," could hardly be said to be "present."

From this vantage point, the majority opinion of Chief Justice
Vinson makes fascinating reading. Apart from a nod to the challenge
that the Smith Act was unconstitutionally vague and a brief essay at
construing it, Vinson's eighteen-page opinion is devoted entirely to
showing that this application of the Act fully satisfied the clear and
present danger test. He begins with an elaborate review of the prior
cases, discussing in some detail *Schenck, Abrams, Debs, Gitlow, Whitney,*
and *Douds.* In the course of this survey he carefully notes and restates
the distinction Justice Sanford had relied on in *Gitlow* in distinguishing *Schenck,* namely, that the *Gitlow* statute had proscribed a particular
category of speech:

The majority [in *Gitlow*] refused to apply the "clear and present danger" test
to the specific utterance. Its reasoning was as follows: The "clear and present
danger" test was applied to the utterance itself in *Schenck* because the question was merely one of sufficiency of evidence under an admittedly constitutional statute. *Gitlow,* however, presented a different question. There a
legislature had found that a certain kind of speech was, itself, harmful and
unlawful. The constitutionality of such a state statute had to be adjudged by
this Court just as it determined the constitutionality of any state statute,
namely, whether the statute was "reasonable." Since it was entirely reasonable for a state to attempt to protect itself against violent overthrow, the
statute was perforce reasonable.[9]

As this passage makes evident, *Gitlow* would solve the Court's problems. All it would have to do to dispose summarily of this and any
other constitutional challenge of the Smith Act would be to follow
precedent. But the decisions of the 1940s which transformed the

Holmes-Brandeis dissents into majority doctrine block the Court's access to *Gitlow:*

Although no case subsequent to *Whitney* and *Gitlow* has expressly overruled the majority opinions in those cases, there is little doubt that subsequent opinions have inclined toward the Holmes-Brandeis rationale.[10]

Thus, Vinson makes explicit what had been implicit during the 1940s—the *Gitlow* distinction is no longer operative. He then goes on to note that in *Douds,* in the course of finding the clear and present danger test inapplicable in cases where a regulation has an *indirect* impact on speech, the Court had stated that in cases involving *direct* restrictions on speech the First Amendment "requires that one be permitted to advocate what he will unless there is a clear and present danger that a substantial public evil will result therefrom."[11]

The Chief Justice thus finds himself bound—in part by his own opinion in *Douds*—to apply the clear and present danger test to the case before him. By way of preface he warns that speech is not "an absolute," that Holmes and Brandeis never intended that "a short-hand phrase should be crystallized into a rigid rule to be applied inflexibly without regard to the circumstances of each case," and finally that "to those who would paralyze our Government in the face of impending threat by encasing it in a semantic straitjacket we must reply that all concepts are relative." Having softened the rigor of the test by these caveats, he then moves to the confrontation: "In this case we are squarely presented with the application of the 'clear and present danger' test and must decide what that phrase imports."[12]

Vinson first makes the trivial point that the interest in this case, unlike littering the streets, is substantial enough to meet the test: revolution is a weightier "substantive evil" than littering! He then engages the real embarrassment—the revolution is set for the indefinite future. The danger, however clear and weighty, is not present. He makes the commonsense point that the government need not "wait until the *putsch* is about to be executed."[13] Then he asserts that this case is not like the situations with which Holmes and Brandeis were concerned—this is really serious. He thus sounds a note which will echo in the concurring opinions of Justices Jackson and Frankfurter: Holmes and Brandeis simply had not been addressing themselves to speech that carried grave risks. Clear and present danger, although indisputably the test according to the Vinson Court, was the test only for speech that did not matter, the luxury civil liberty.

The Chief Justice is now ready to solve the dilemma posed by the lack of immediacy of the danger. Judge Hand in the Court of Appeals had provided the key by rephrasing the test, as the torts judge would put it:

In each case [courts] must ask whether the gravity of the "evil;" discounted by its improbability, justifies such invasion of free speech as is necessary to avoid the danger.[14]

With a sigh of relief, the Court adopts "this statement of the rule." There is no attempt to show that this is what Holmes and Brandeis meant, no acknowledgment that under this rule any talk of revolution, however unlikely, must weigh as a requisite danger.

As explained by Brandeis in *Whitney*, the mission of the "gravity" requirement was to avoid the anomaly of finding a clear and present danger of an insubstantial evil, and during the 1940s it served that purpose in a number of decisions. While it is true that the Court did not fully explain the relationship of "gravity" to the other elements of the test, it never suggested that the gravity of the evil was to be weighed against the imminence of the danger. Yet that is the effect of the Hand-Vinson restatement. By fastening on the gravity requirement the *Dennis* Court is able to loosen the imminence requirement and thereby to remove the obstacle to conviction which the clear and present danger test would otherwise have presented. The upshot is that, having eschewed explicit reliance on *Gitlow* and *Whitney*, the Court by means of the modified test manages, in effect, to reach back to the *Gitlow-Whitney* standard of general advocacy.[15]

Having resolved the problem of the lack of immediacy, Vinson proceeds to apply the discounted test. Not surprisingly, he finds that the trial court was correct in finding that the requisite danger existed. The exact statement warrants quotation, since it indicates that the Court's attention has shifted from the danger of the *speech* for which the defendants were indicted to the danger of the *speakers* themselves:

The formation by petitioners of such a highly organized conspiracy, with rigidly disciplined members subject to call when the leaders, these petitioners, felt that the time had come for action, coupled with the inflammable nature of world conditions, similar uprisings in other countries, and the touch-and-go nature of our relations with countries with whom petitioners were in the very least ideologically attuned, convince us that their convictions were justified on this score.[16]

He then adds the only reference in the majority opinion to the use of conspiracy doctrine in framing the prosecution:

And this analysis disposes of the contention that a conspiracy to advocate, as distinguished from the advocacy itself, cannot be constitutionally restrained, because it comprises only the preparation. It is the existence of the conspiracy which creates the danger.[17]

Apparently, as the Court reflects on the case, the plot has, perhaps unconsciously, become this: The defendants, a cadre of committed revolutionaries, were conspiring to overthrow the government. The constitutional measure of the validity of their convictions is the clear and present danger test. Surely the existence of such a conspiracy presents the requisite danger.

Since the defendants are envisaged as a conspiracy to overthrow, there is no need to look at the speech for which they were indicted. Thus, the anomaly of *Dennis* is that the defendants were charged with talking but convicted for acting. If indeed they were guilty of acting, we would have had at worst an anomaly; but the deep suspicion is that the Government could not have satisfied anyone with its proof of a literal conspiracy to overthrow. Somehow the legal legerdemain has made it possible to punish speech when one could not punish action.

We can only speculate as to what the outcome would have been had the Communist defendants been bluntly charged with conspiring to overthrow the government. It is, I suppose, doubtful that they would have been convicted. But it would be a mistake to assume that they were therefore not something for the law to worry about. Perhaps the law should be able to deal distinctively with the political conspiracy, a matter we look at more closely in future chapters. If it is to do so, however, the tactics used must be more precise, more realistic, and, above all, more candid than those employed to secure the convictions in *Dennis*.

Justice Douglas

The shift in focus from the danger of the speech to the danger of the speaker explains the difference between Justice Douglas and the majority. Having looked at the record, Douglas argues with eloquence that the *speech* presented no danger. It is one of his most memorable utterances:

Communism in the world scene is no bogeyman; but Communism as a political faction or party in this country plainly is. Communism has been so thoroughly exposed in this country that it has been crippled as a political force. Free speech has destroyed it as an effective political party. It is inconceivable that those who went up and down this country preaching the doctrine of revolution which petitioners espouse would have any success. In days of trouble and confusion when bread lines were long, when the unemployed walked the streets, when people were starving, the advocates of a short-cut by a revolution might have a chance to gain adherents. But today there are no such conditions. The country is not in despair; the people know Soviet Communism; the doctrine of Soviet revolution is exposed in all of its ugliness and the American people want none of it.

How it can be said that there is a clear and present danger that this advocacy will succeed is, therefore, a mystery. Some nations less resilient than the United States, where illiteracy is high and where democratic traditions are only budding, might have to take drastic steps and jail these men for merely speaking their creed. But in America they are miserable merchants of unwanted ideas; their wares remain unsold. The fact that their ideas are abhorrent does not make them powerful.[18]

One suspects that the majority does not really disagree with Douglas's appraisal of the dangers from Communist *speech*. But, as they see it, the problem is no longer the danger of speech moving an audience against a target the speaker has selected; it is the danger of the speaker himself moving. Thus, Justice Douglas is arguing a different case from the one the majority has in mind.

There are two other points of disagreement between Justice Douglas and the majority: the use of conspiracy doctrine and the handling of the clear and present danger formula. Douglas argues with respect to conspiracy:

The doctrine of conspiracy has served divers and oppressive purposes and in its broad reach can be made to do great evil. But never until today has anyone seriously thought that the ancient law of conspiracy could constitutionally be used to turn speech into seditious conduct. Yet that is precisely what is suggested. I repeat that we deal here with speech alone, not with speech *plus* acts of sabotage or unlawful conduct. Not a single seditious act is charged in the indictment. To make a lawful speech unlawful because two men conceive it is to raise the law of conspiracy to appalling proportions.[19]

He goes on to say that such use of conspiracy doctrine violates "one of the cardinal principles of our constitutional scheme"—free speech. He does not, however, stick with the point and analyze precisely how conspiracy doctrine offends the First Amendment. Instead, he shifts his attention to the Court's handling of clear and present danger and enters two objections. First, as would be expected, he will not abide the discounted test. But, although he presents an extended quote from Brandeis's explanation of clear and present danger in *Whitney*, he does not pause to argue against Hand's derivation of the discounted test. He appears more interested in his second objection, an objection triggered by the trial judge's handling of the clear and present danger issue. Judge Medina had withdrawn from the jury the question of whether the acts charged created a clear and present danger and had treated it as a question of law; that is, he had instructed the jury as to the sort of speech prohibited by the Smith Act and had ruled that *if* the defendants engaged in such speech, that would constitute a clear and present danger. In so doing, he unearthed a hitherto unnoticed ambiguity in the formula. Douglas insists that the issue should have been left to the jury, although it would appear to be an absurdly impractical issue for a jury. In any event, Douglas argued, whether or not the question is submitted to the jury, it cannot be left to judicial notice; there must be some evidence put into the record by the prosecution as to the danger. If we add the *Gitlow* distinction at this point, it can be said that as of 1951, more than three decades after *Schenck,* it is a matter of deep controversy whether the danger is to be found by the legislature, by the court, or by the jury.

Justice Black and Justice Jackson

Equally interesting in juxtaposition are the opinions of Justice Black in dissent and Justice Jackson concurring. On the surface, they would seem to have nothing in common, but in fact they share a central theme: both see the conspiracy charge as the crux of the case.

Justice Black, in language echoing Justice Brandeis in *Whitney*, begins:

At the outset I want to emphasize what the crime involved in this case is, and what it is not. These petitioners were not charged with an attempt to overthrow the Government. They were not charged with overt acts of any kind designed to overthrow the Government. They were not even charged with saying anything or writing anything designed to overthrow the Government. The charge was that they agreed to assemble and to talk and publish certain ideas at a later date: The indictment is that they conspired to organize the

Communist Party and to use speech or newspapers and other publications in the future to teach and advocate the forcible overthrow of the Government.[20]

He then goes on to make a curious impeachment of the whole Government enterprise. At first one thinks he has somehow misspoken, but reflection on the tensions between conspiracy doctrine and the First Amendment makes it evident why he phrases his objection as he does:

No matter how it is worded, this is a virulent form of prior censorship of speech and press, which I believe the First Amendment forbids. I would hold [section] 3 of the Smith Act authorizing this prior restraint unconstitutional on its face and as applied.[21]

The point, I take it, is that the First Amendment requires that the state at least wait until a person has spoken before seeking to cut off his speech!

Justice Black is also critical of the majority's handling of the clear and present danger test. He repeats once more his view that the test does not mark "the furthermost constitutional boundaries of protected expression." And he adds that the majority has downgraded even this "minimal compulsion of the Bill of Rights": "Such a doctrine waters down the First Amendment so that it amounts to little more than an admonition to Congress."[22] But, like Douglas, he makes no effort to rebut the discounted test by analyzing the prior precedents from which the clear and present danger formula itself is alleged to have been derived. He joins Douglas's objection to the withdrawal of the danger issue from the jury and adds a final complaint against the limited grant of *certiorari*. His closing words strike a note of despair:

Public opinion being what it now is, few will protest the conviction of these Communist petitioners. There is hope, however, that in calmer times, when present pressures, passions and fears subside, this or some later Court will restore the First Amendment liberties to the high preferred place where they belong in a free society.[23]

In retrospect, Justice Black's dissent in *Dennis* wears well. He has touched all the points, has sounded the long-term concern with the value of free speech against the anti-Communist excitements of the moment, and has compressed it all into a statement of just two pages.

For Justice Jackson, too, the decisive fact about the case is that it involves conspiracy. As in *Terminiello* and *Kunz*, he contributes a realist's essay—this time on the dangers of Communism, the subtlety of its tactics, and the outmoded nature of the statutes used to counteract its threat. He stresses that modern Communists practice revolution more by stealth and strategic infiltration than by blunt use of violence. His pen, as always, is brilliant: "The Communist Party advocates force only when prudent and profitable. . . . They resort to violence as to truth, not as a principle but as an expedient."[24] In view of the tactics of modern Communism, he concludes that it would be suicidal to compel the Government to wait until there is a clear and present danger of violence. The burden of his opinion is thus to render the formula inapplicable.

He begins by repeating in exaggerated form the theme that Holmes and Brandeis devised their test in more tranquil times before the sophisticated techniques of modern revolutionaries, and intended it only for quaint cases in which the charges often rested "on farfetched inferences which, if true, would establish only technical or trivial violations." He adds:

I would save it, unmodified, for application as a "rule of reason" in the kind of case for which it was devised. When the issue is criminality of a hot-headed speech on a street corner, or circulation of a few incendiary pamphlets, or parading by some zealots behind a red flag, or refusal of a handful of school children to salute our flag, it is not beyond the capacity of the judicial process to gather, comprehend, and weigh the necessary materials for decision whether it is a clear and present danger of substantive evil or a harmless letting off of steam.[25]

Jackson's view of the origins of the doctrine, like that of the Chief Justice, offends in its implicit assumption that the function of the Amendment is to protect speech which does not matter, "the harmless letting off of steam." He crystallizes the theme in one last epigram:

Unless we are to hold our Government captive in a judge-made verbal trap, we must approach the problem of a well-organized, nation-wide conspiracy, such as I have described, as realistically as our predecessors faced the trivialities that were being prosecuted until they were checked with a rule of reason.[26]

He then moves on to make a more persuasive point against use of the
test in this context. It is not only suicidal, it is also utterly unworkable:

. . . [The Court] must appraise imponderables, including international and
national phenomena which baffled the best informed foreign offices . . . No
doctrine can be sound whose application requires us to make a prophecy of
that sort in the guise of a legal decision. The judicial process simply is not
adequate to a trial of such far-flung issues.[27]

It is hard to avoid the conclusion which both the Douglas dissent and
the Jackson concurrence underscore: if the issue of danger is taken
seriously and exposed to adversary attack and defense, the test imposes extraordinary burdens on the trial process. Its survival as a
formula in legal and popular culture resides in no small part, I suspect, on the circumstance that prior to *Dennis* it was never really put
to the test of a rigorous application.

Jackson's assault on the test is not yet exhausted. Without so
much as acknowledging *Gitlow,* he starts on a new tack: "even an
individual cannot claim that the Constitution protects him in advocating or teaching overthrow of government by force or violence."[28] He
adds that in cases of advocacy of violent overthrow, the speech can be
reached "without also providing that the odds favored its success by
99 to 1, or some other extremely high ratio."[29] The test is thus
inapplicable, on his view, when there is explicit advocacy of violence;
and this is true even in the case of the individual speaker.

Finally, Jackson reaches his central concern—conspiracy:

What really is under review here is a conviction of conspiracy, after a trial for
conspiracy, on an indictment charging conspiracy, brought under a statute
outlawing conspiracy. With due respect to my colleagues, they seem to me
to discuss anything under the sun except the law of conspiracy. One of the
dissenting opinions even appears to chide me for "invoking the law of conspiracy." As that is the case before us, it may be more amazing that its reversal
can be proposed without even considering the law of conspiracy.[30]

Jackson is aware that conspiracy is often treacherous doctrine, but he
finds it has been the chief means at the Government's disposal for
dealing with the problem of "permanently organized, well-financed,
semisecret and highly disciplined political organizations."[31] He adds:
"I happen to think it is an awkward and inept remedy, but I find no
constitutional authority for taking this weapon from the Govern-

ment."[32] He makes pointed reference to anti-trust conspiracy cases and notes: "In conspiracy cases the Court has not only dispensed with proof of clear and present danger but even of power to create a danger."[33]

Jackson's performance in *Dennis* is very similar to his opinions in *Terminiello* and *Kunz*. He is a very special kind of judge. He writes perhaps better than any of his peers, and he is admirably realistic about what is going on in the world, but he is impatient with legal doctrine and analysis to a degree that would make each of these opinions a flunking answer in any reputable law school. Yet he always locates and wrestles with a real problem. In *Terminiello* and *Kunz* it is the problem of ideological fighting words; and in *Dennis* it is the problem of the tightly knit political conspiracy that is planning, not tomorrow, but in its own sweet time to overthrow the government by infiltration, guile, and the selective use of force. Twenty years after *Dennis* the law still awaits an answer to the question: What is the constitutionally appropriate countermove, if any, against an organization with the power, purpose, and teachings which Justice Jackson ascribed to the Communist Party in 1951? Jackson may well not have been right on the facts, but whether he was right or not, he put a question we need a rule of law to answer.

Justice Frankfurter

The opinions thus far have formed arresting patterns on the issues of conspiracy and clear and present danger. All the justices have touched the conspiracy element. For Chief Justice Vinson, conspiracy supplied the danger that satisfied the clear and present danger test; for Justice Jackson, the presence of conspiracy was among the factors that made the test inapplicable; while for Justices Black and Douglas, the use of conspiracy doctrine put special strains on the First Amendment, strains so severe they caused Black to condemn the Smith Act as a prior restraint.

The clear and present danger test provoked equally diverse reactions. Black and Douglas would apply the test in its full vigor as a bar to this conviction; Douglas stressed that there was no danger of these speakers moving an audience; and, finally, the two dissenters joined in urging that precedent required that the issue of proximity to danger from the Communist speech be submitted to the jury. Chief Justice Vinson agreed that the case was controlled by the clear and present danger test, but argued that the test was properly restated as

gravity discounted by improbability, that the trial judge was correct
to have handled the issue himself, and that he was correct in holding
that the requisite danger existed. Justice Jackson appeared to agree
with Black and Douglas that the test should not be discounted, but he
argued that it should not be applied to a case such as this because it
would be unworkable and suicidal and because this was conspiracy.

The concurring opinion of Justice Frankfurter adds one more
variant and offers final proof that in 1951 there was no common
understanding among the justices as to the role of the clear and
present danger test—or the First Amendment. Justice Frankfurter
contributes by far the longest opinion, a thirty-four-page essay. As
was the case with Justice Jackson, the opinion exhibits certain distinctive qualities of its author's First Amendment judgments in general.

Justice Frankfurter begins by acknowledging that this is a great
case—"Few questions of comparable import have come to this Court
in recent years"[34]—and also that it is a difficult case. Apart from
Justices Black and Douglas, it is Frankfurter who seems most aware
that the conviction may disturb popular impressions of political tolerance in the United States. He sees the case as a crucial confrontation
between the free speech tradition and the needs for security and
order. "If adjudication is to be a rational process," he insists, "we
cannot escape a candid examination of the conflicting claims with full
recognition that both are supported by weighty title-deeds."[35]

The case is complicated for him by two considerations. First, as
we have seen, he has never been persuaded that the clear and present
danger formula has, or should have, any constitutional status. This is
a battle he has long waged, and he sees *Dennis* as a decisive occasion
for ridding the law of the myth of the test. Unlike Jackson, he would
not preserve the test as the constitutional measure of *any* speech, but
would erase it altogether as a gloss on the First Amendment. Second,
his integrity as a judge is offended by the majority's pretense that the
discounted test they have borrowed from Judge Hand below *is* the test
of Holmes and Brandeis. He is concerned that the Court will appear
to have made up a new rule in order to satisfy the political need to
"get" the Communist Party: "In all fairness, the [defendants'] argument cannot be met by reinterpreting the Court's frequent use of
'clear' and 'present' to mean an entertainable 'probability.' "[36] Thus,
his mission is to show that clear and present danger was never the
"true" rule; and that under the true rule these Communist defendants
were properly convicted.

To find the true principle after all the loose rhetoric the Court has added requires considering the corpus of First Amendment adjudications as a whole:

Unless we are to compromise judicial impartiality and subject these defendants to the risk of an *ad hoc* judgment influenced by the impregnating atmosphere of the times, the constitutionality of their conviction must be determined by principles established in cases decided in more tranquil periods. If those decisions are to be used as a guide and not as an argument, it is important to view them as a whole and to distrust the easy generalizations to which some of them lend themselves.[37]

Justice Frankfurter then proceeds with a seventeen-page review of the major precedents, doing in microcosm what we have been doing throughout this essay.[38] From his reading of the cases, he draws three conclusions: Speech cases are not exceptions to the principle that the justices are not legislators; by and large, the same results would have been reached in speech cases without the distraction of the formula by a "careful weighing of the conflicting interests"; and, finally, not all speech weighs equally and advocacy of violence ranks low on any scale of speech values. As to his *bete noir,* the formula itself, it does not attend to all the factors that proper balancing requires. To apply it to this case is to distort it:

So it is with the attempt to use the direction of thought lying behind the criterion of "clear and present danger" wholly out of the context in which it originated, and to make of it an absolute dogma and definitive measuring rod for the power of Congress to deal with assaults against security through devices other than overt physical attempts.[39]

Once again we are reminded that Holmes in *Abrams* spoke of "puny anonymities." Apparently, we are to believe Holmes and Brandeis had in mind only the luxury civil liberty had of protecting eccentric and harmless dissent. Finally, the epitaph is uttered:

It were far better that the phrase be abandoned than that it be sounded once more to hide from the believers in an absolute right of free speech the plain fact that the interest in speech, profoundly important as it is, is no more conclusive in judicial review than other attributes of democracy or than a determination of the people's representatives that a measure is necessary to assure the safety of government itself.[40]

The most curious aspect of Justice Frankfurter's performance is his handling of the *Gitlow* distinction. He has argued that speech cases are just like other instances of judicial review, that balancing of interests is called for, and that the primary responsibility for balancing rests with the legislature. Moreover, throughout the 1940s he repeatedly dissented from decisions which accorded clear and present danger a broader role than that conceded by the *Gitlow* majority. Thus, the Sanford opinion in *Gitlow* would seem to embody his argument. In his review of the cases he notes that the *Gitlow* distinction, if accepted here, "would make decision easy."[41] Yet he does not rest his case on *Gitlow.* The reason, I suspect, is that he cannot desert his hero: Holmes thought it absurd to convict Gitlow for the tiresome pamphlet. Frankfurter perforce must think so too, although the pamphlet contained words of direct advocacy and a state supreme court had held that its statute was violated. In the course of his review of prior precedents, he remarks: "It requires excessive tolerance of the legislative judgment to suppose that the *Gitlow* publication in the circumstances could justify serious concern."[42] It is not easy to see how Frankfurter can reject the legislative judgment as applied in *Gitlow* without introducing a criterion of danger in the particular circumstances. Thus, his nod to Holmes seems to impeach the whole rationale of his opinion.

Having written this lengthy preface, he is finally ready to apply "these general considerations" to the case at hand. He proceeds dutifully to weigh the competing interests: security and public order against the values of speech advocating violent overthrow when the advocate is a well-organized, well-disciplined group of substantial size conditioned to embark on unlawful activity on command. With due regard to the judicial function in such matters, he cannot bring himself to say that the legislature has overstepped its bounds. "It is not for us to decide how we would adjust the clash of interests which the case presents were the primary responsibility for reconciling it ours."[43] Thus, the Smith Act as applied to the Communist Party is constitutional.

Frankfurter closes with an epilogue on the difference in constitutional law between power and wisdom. He pointedly quotes George Kennan to the effect that for America Communism is primarily an external danger; the danger from within is that we will destroy the quality of American life in a frantic quest for scapegoats. Finally, we are admonished again: "Much that should be rejected as illiberal, because repressive and envenoming, may well be not unconstitutional."[44]

If, having reviewed Justice Frankfurter's long, agonizing performance, we step back and ask again why *Dennis* proved such a difficult case for him, several explanations suggest themselves. First, as we have stressed, he feels the need to deflate the myth that clear and present danger is the test, for it is of high importance in so politically charged a case that the Communist leaders be convicted only under the true principles of the First Amendment. Second, as his quoting of Kennan intimates, he is uneasy about the excesses of the current anti-Communist mood in America; the Kennan passage carries echoes of Justice Douglas's "miserable merchants of unwanted ideas" theme. Finally, he is troubled by the free speech implications of the case. It is a striking reminder of Frankfurter's strengths as a justice that he alone addresses himself to the value of revolutionary speech:

A public interest is not wanting in granting freedom to speak their minds even to those who advocate the overthrow of the Government by force. For, as the evidence in this case abundantly illustrates, coupled with such advocacy is criticism of defects in our society.[45]

And to the dangers of suppressing it:

Suppressing advocates of overthrow inevitably will also silence critics who do not advocate overthrow but fear that their criticism may be so construed. . . . It is a sobering fact that in sustaining the convictions before us we can hardly escape restriction on the interchange of ideas.[46]

The Residue of Dennis

We have been dealing with *Dennis* on two levels: as part of the intellectual history of the clear and present danger test, and as a precedent on the boundaries of censorship for speech which moves an audience to action.

On the first level, the *Dennis* opinions are a source of endless fascination. Chief Justice Vinson, writing for the Court, applies the test as modified by Hand and sustains the convictions; Justices Black and Douglas, dissenting, would apply the test as proposed and would reverse the convictions because there is no showing of danger from

the Communist speech; Justice Jackson, concurring, would save the
test intact but would not apply it to cases of this genre; and Justice
Frankfurter, concurring, would disavow the test as a constitutional
measure in all forms and for any speech. The test never recovers.

On the second level, *Dennis* can be said, in effect, to restore the
Gitlow-Whitney standard—at least in the instance of group speech. The
Court does not do this directly. Indeed, it explicitly eschews resting
its decision on *Gitlow* and *Whitney*. Nor does the opinion of the Court
contain a clear statement of the location of the constitutional line. But
the combined effect of the majority's uncritical acceptance of the
conspiracy framework and its reformulation of the clear and present
danger test is to enlarge the censor's domain so that it once again
includes general advocacy of violent overthrow.

15

Subversive Advocacy: The *Yates* Revision

On June 17, 1957 the Cold War came to an end in the Supreme Court of the United States. On that day the Court announced four striking decisions in cases generated by official anti-Communism. In *Watkins v. United States* [1] and *Sweezy v. New Hampshire* [2] it barred particular legislative investigations into subversion. In *Service v. Dulles* [3] it upset an unfavorable finding in a famous loyalty-security dismissal from federal employment. And in the case which concerns us here, *Yates v. United States,* [4] it reversed the convictions under the Smith Act of the leaders of the California branch of the Communist Party.

During the six years between *Dennis* and *Yates* there were several changes in Court personnel: Chief Justice Vinson was replaced by Earl Warren, and Justices Reed, Minton, and Jackson were replaced by Justices Brennan, Whittaker, and Harlan. *Yates* is a 6 to 1 decision; Justices Brennan and Whittaker do not participate; Justice Black concurs in part and dissents in part; and Justice Clark is the lonely full dissenter. In the end, the decision is the achievement of Justice Harlan, who writes the opinion of the Court and carries Justices Frankfurter and Burton with him. The Harlan opinion now appears to be architectonic for the First Amendment. Yet a more unlikely "great" precedent would be hard to imagine; at first acquaintance it seems a sort of *Finnegans Wake* of impossibly nice distinctions. [5]

Yates is the sequel to *Dennis.* Again leaders of the Communist Party are prosecuted under the Smith Act for conspiring to teach and advocate violent overthrow and for conspiring to organize a group to

teach and advocate violent overthrow. Indeed, the plots of the two
cases are so similar that the *Dennis* defendants are named as unin-
dicted co-conspirators. As Justice Clark remarks in dissent, the *Yates*
defendants "served in the same army and were engaged in the same
mission" as the defendants whose convictions were affirmed in *Dennis.*
This time, however, the Court finds two fatal errors in the trial. First,
the "organize" wing of the Government's case is barred by the statute
of limitations. Justice Harlan, relying on *Stromberg v. California,* [6] rules
that the convictions must therefore be reversed, for it is possible that
the jury's verdict may have rested on the invalid "organize" grounds.
Second and more important, Harlan finds another independent
ground for reversal in the "advocacy" wing of the case: The trial judge
in his instructions to the jury had incorrectly described the type of
speech proscribed by the Smith Act. And to give bite to the constitutional boundary line of permissible advocacy the Court carefully reviews the record and directs acquittals for five of the fourteen
defendants because of the total failure of the Government's proof to
show a conspiracy to engage in illegal advocacy.

The dispute over the statute of limitations on the "organize" charge
is worth a moment's pause. Part of the Government's ingenuity in
framing the *Dennis* prosecution had been to date the conspiracy to
organize from the post-World War II shift in American-Soviet relations, a shift which was reflected in a sharp and visible reorientation
by the American Communist Party: In July of 1945 the Communist
Political Association was disbanded and reconstituted as the Communist Party of the United States. The Government was thus able to
prosecute in *Dennis* for "organizing" in 1945, although in a loose
sense the Party had been in existence since 1919. The indictment in
Yates, however, is not until 1951, or six years after the 1945 baseline,
and there is a three-year statute of limitations.

The Government in *Yates* tries to get around this obstacle by
arguing that organizing is "a continuing process which goes on
throughout the life of an organization" as new members are recruited
and new units are formed. Otherwise, it insists, the Smith Act when
passed in 1940 would not have covered the organization of the Communist Party, which Congress could not *then* have predicted would
recur in 1945. The Court's rejection of this reasoning is impressive.
It strikes a note which had been lacking in the earlier anti-Communist
cases, namely, that the law is dealing with general rules, not solely
with rules for the Communist Party:

While the legislative history of the Smith Act does show that concern about communism was a strong factor leading to this legislation, it also reveals that the statute, which was patterned on state anti-sedition laws directed not against Communists but against anarchists and syndicalists, was aimed equally at all groups falling within its scope.[7]

As a matter of statutory construction and policy, Justice Harlan can see no reason to give "organize" a special meaning. If the Government seeks to reach people who have actively supported the Party, there remain the membership and the conspiracy to advocate provisions.

The Government also argues that, even if the trial court had been mistaken in its construction of "organize," the error was harmless. The jury had been instructed, the Government contends, that in order to convict it must find a conspiracy extending to *both* "advocating" and "organizing," and hence could be assumed to have found the defendants guilty of conspiring to advocate. Justice Harlan rejects this contention. He finds the instruction unclear as to whether both objectives of conspiracy were required to convict; and he notes that the "overt acts" in furtherance of the conspiracy alleged in the record might equally be associated with advocacy and organizing.[8] He concludes that the *Stromberg* rule requires reversal of the convictions, for it is possible that the verdict may have rested on the invalid "organize" ground.

The upshot of Justice Harlan's ruling on the "organize" wing of the case is that henceforth no one can be prosecuted for organizing the Communist Party; and the Government's rhetoric of dark conspiracy will have lost a touch of menace, since it sounds more evil to organize a group than to be an active member of it. A second consequence of Harlan's ruling is purely internal to the judicial process: Having this ground for necessary reversal, he is liberated to deal with the other, more important, issue presented by the case—the precise location of the boundaries of permissible advocacy.

The "advocacy" wing of the case centers on the trial court's instruction to the jury. Although requested to do so by the Government, the trial judge in *Yates* had declined to give *in haec verba* the instruction given by the trial judge in *Dennis*. Instead, he drafted his own version. This small detail affords Justice Harlan a technical base which he skillfully exploits. He is able to find in the variations between the two instructions—variations which to the uninitiated might appear trivial—the essential parameters of political censorship.

Harlan accomplishes this without ever reaching the First Amendment. The issue is treated entirely, albeit somewhat disingenuously, as a matter of statutory construction of the Smith Act. His opinion is thus a replay of the technique Judge Hand used so powerfully in *Masses* a half-century earlier. And it yields a similar result. Although *Dennis* had been permeated by concerns about the clear and present danger test, Harlan fashions a fresh interpretation of *Dennis* and applies it to the case at hand without making a single reference to the famous formula. Moreover, he manages to extract from *Dennis* a new idiom unencumbered by the historic mortgage of the Holmes test— the idiom of "incitement." He thus effects a bloodless revolution in the reading of the First Amendment, while ostensibly doing no more than construing the Smith Act in light of *Dennis*.

In order to understand how Harlan accomplishes his revision of the doctrine on subversive advocacy, it is necessary to backtrack for a moment to take a look at the jury instruction given in *Dennis*. The trial judge, Harold Medina, instructed the jury as follows:

In further construction and interpretation of the statute I charge you that it is not the abstract doctrine of overthrowing or destroying organized government by unlawful means which is denounced by this law, but the teaching and advocacy of action for the accomplishment of that purpose, by language reasonably and ordinarily calculated to incite persons to such action. Accordingly, you cannot find the defendants or any of them guilty of the crime charged unless you are satisfied beyond a reasonable doubt that they conspired to organize a society, group and assembly of persons who teach and advocate the overthrow or destruction of the Government of the United States by force and violence and to advocate and teach the duty and necessity of overthrowing or destroying the Government of the United States by force and violence, with the intent that such teaching and advocacy be of a rule or principle of action and by language reasonably and ordinarily calculated to incite persons to such action, all with the intent to cause the overthrow or destruction of the Government of the United States by force and violence as speedily as circumstances would permit.[9]

On first reading, this instruction reminds one of an item in *The New Yorker* under the rubric "The Legal Mind at Work." It is perfectly absurd that the all-important boundary between tolerable and censorable dissent should be stated in so crabbed, opaque, and inaccessible a form. Yet one cannot help being struck by how clever and skillful Judge Medina was in accommodating the pressures that bore down on him. On the one hand, there was the political need to provide a formula that would permit conviction of the Communist Party, despite the shabbiness of the Government's proof and despite the fact that the Party urged action, if at all, only in the indefinite future. On the other hand, there was the need to make that formula compatible with the First Amendment. Medina extricates himself by placing the constitutional line at advocacy of "rules and principles of action," expressed in language reasonably calculated "to incite" to the action of violent overthrow "as speedily as circumstances would permit."

This language, buried in the Medina instruction, will provide Justice Harlan in *Yates* with the means to push back the boundaries of protected advocacy. Yet in Chief Justice Vinson's opinion for the Court in *Dennis,* upon which Harlan purports to rely, the Medina instruction receives little attention. Although Vinson, in effect, ratifies the instruction as a correct reading of the Smith Act and the First Amendment, he does not isolate or comment upon the language which is to prove so important to Harlan six years later. Nor is there any suggestion in his opinion that the *Dennis* Court regarded the instruction as significantly narrowing the Smith Act's bald prohibition of advocacy. Indeed, the only explicit limitation Vinson extracts from the instruction is, as he puts it, that the Act is "directed at advocacy, not discussion."

The trial judge in *Yates* declined to give the Medina instruction. Instead, he drafted his own. He stressed three points: The advocacy must include the urging of action; it must urge "not merely a desirability but a necessity," "not merely a propriety but a duty";[10] and it must be uttered with the specific intent to bring about violent overthrow of the government "as speedily as circumstances would permit."[11]

Justice Harlan finds this instruction unacceptable in that it ignores the emphasis on *concreteness,* which he sees as the essential point of *Dennis.* Largely ignoring the reasoning of the Court in *Dennis,* he focuses on the Medina instruction and asserts that "the essence of the *Dennis* holding" was that advocacy directed to violence "as a rule or principle of action" and "employing the language of incitement" is not constitutionally protected. He continues:

This is quite a different thing from the view of the District Court here that mere doctrinal justification of forcible overthrow, if engaged in with the intent to accomplish overthrow, is punishable *per se* under the Smith Act. That sort of advocacy, even though uttered with the hope that it may ultimately lead to violent revolution, is too remote from concrete action to be regarded as the kind of indoctrination preparatory to action which was condemned in *Dennis*. [12]

The subtlety of the distinction between advocacy of doctrine with evil intent and advocacy as a principle of action in the future is agonizing, but Justice Harlan is pursuing a real point:

We think that the trial court's statement that the proscribed advocacy must include the "urging," "necessity," and "duty" of forcible overthrow, and not merely its "desirability" and "propriety," may not be regarded as a sufficient substitute for charging that the Smith Act reaches only advocacy of action for the overthrow of government by force and violence. The essential distinction is that those to whom the advocacy is addressed must be urged to *do* something now or in the future, rather than merely to *believe* in something.[13]

The standard that emerges from Harlan's analysis might best be termed "incitement-to-future-action." This elusive concept represents an intermediate step between the general advocacy standard implicitly endorsed in *Dennis* and the *Brandenburg* standard. Incitement to violence, as defined in *Brandenburg*, is distinguished from general advocacy of violence as a doctrine by two attributes: concreteness and immediacy. General advocacy of violence is neither concretized as a plan of action nor carries any expectation of immediate action. It is, therefore, still possible to think of it as political discourse. Incitement, the last term in a series, requires both concreteness and immediacy—a given course of action *now*. It is possible to think of it as political discourse only if violence itself is an acceptable political tactic. There is thus a meaningful distinction between general unfocused advocacy of violence and incitement to it. And it will be the achievement of *Brandenburg* to establish this distinction as the constitutional boundary.

The effect of Harlan's opinion in *Yates* is to alchemize the language in the *Dennis* instruction into a stringent requirement of *concreteness*, although it is far from clear that this is what Judge Medina and the *Dennis* Court had in mind. Harlan does not, however, take the next step and restore the *immediacy* requirement, which was abandoned in *Dennis*. Rather, he continues to view the problem within the *group advocacy* framework established in *Dennis*. He is clear, I think, in his own mind that political tolerance requires that the individual speaker not be censored until the stimulus of his speech has crossed over to the immediacy and concreteness of incitement. As I read him, he is unwilling to apply quite so generous a standard in the instance of group speech. Perhaps there is no justification for making this concession to the dangers of group advocacy; arguably, the line for both individual and group speech should be drawn at incitement to immediate action. But the Court and Justice Harlan are not willing to go that far. Thus, they set the line for group speech at incitement-to-future-action.

The pragmatic test of Harlan's meaning is his response to the record. His close scrutiny of the evidence confirms the impression that he is in command of a real distinction. There is no doubt that the Party preached a doctrine of violent change, but Harlan can find little in its speech that suggests planning for concrete action now or in the future. He observes:

The need for precise and understandable instructions on this issue is further emphasized by the equivocal character of the evidence in this record. . . . Instances of speech that could be considered to amount to "advocacy of action" are so few and far between as to be almost completely overshadowed by the hundreds of instances in the record in which overthrow, if mentioned at all, occurs in the course of doctrinal disputation so remote from action as to be almost wholly lacking in probative value.[14]

Once Justice Harlan has disclosed that the emperor has no clothes, it is difficult not to be scandalized by some aspects of official anti-Communism during the 1950s. I am not here concerned with the extravagant claims of Senator McCarthy; rather, what astonishes is that when the Government, after years of investigation, was finally called upon to put up its proof in the Smith Act cases, it came up with the proof Justice Harlan reviews in *Yates*. Harlan devotes some seven pages to this task, and those pages ought to be preserved in a more accessible form for government officials and the public.

Although the fourteen-thousand-page record rivals the length of the *Dennis* record, the Court feels obligated not only to look at it, but also—in a move which Justice Clark charges is altogether unprecedented—to see whether it should "foreclose further proceedings against those of the petitioners as to whom the evidence . . . would be palpably insufficient upon a new trial."[15] Justice Harlan emphasizes that he is reviewing the record under a specially lenient standard, as favorable as possible to the Government proof, and that he is assuming that all doubts are to be resolved in the Government's favor. As he rephrases the task he has set himself, it is "to see whether there are individuals as to whom acquittal is unequivocally demanded."[16]

Using this very low threshold for measuring the adequacy of the Government's proof, he finds that five defendants require acquittals directed by the Supreme Court. It is true that one reason he finds the record so sparse is that he has, as he puts it, barred "evidence relating to the 'organizing' aspect of the alleged conspiracy, except insofar as it bears upon the 'advocacy' charge." He concedes that this "dilutes in a substantial way a large part of the evidence," for "the Government relied heavily on its 'organizing' charge."[17] More important, however, the Government, apparently thinking that general advocacy is enough, had rested its case on proof that the doctrine of forcible overthrow is a tenet of the Communist Party and that the defendants were active Party members. But Justice Harlan wants something more, and it is here that his appraisal of the record is deadly:

. . . when it comes to Party advocacy or teaching in the sense of a call to forcible action at some future time we cannot but regard this record as strikingly deficient. At best this voluminous record shows but a half dozen or so scattered incidents which, even under the loosest standards, could be deemed to show such advocacy. Most of these were not connected with any of the petitioners, or occurred many years before the period covered by the indictment.[18]

Justice Harlan feels the need to remind us:

We need scarcely say that however much one may abhor even the abstract preaching of forcible overthrow of government, or believe that forcible overthrow is the ultimate purpose to which the Communist Party is dedicated, it is upon the evidence in the record that the petitioners must be judged in this case.[19]

Apparently the era of judicial notice of the evils of Communism has ended too.

Once mere connection with the Communist Party has been held insufficient to convict the individual defendants, it becomes difficult to find any other evidence which more specifically incriminates them. As to five, Justice Harlan simply cannot find anything else, and so directs acquittals. One detail here is worth noting. Two of these defendants, Connelly and Richmond, were editors of *The Daily People's World*, the West Coast Communist newspaper. The Government offered as part of its proof material from the paper. Justice Harlan dismissed it in a curt sentence—"we can find nothing in the material introduced into evidence from that newspaper which advances the Government's case"[20]—but Justice Clark sees in it proof of the defendants' guilt. In a footnote Clark states:

> There can be no question that the proof sustained the charges against Richmond and Connelly in the conspiracy. Their newspaper was the conduit through which the Party announced its aims, policies, and decisions, sought its funds, and recruited its members. It is the height of naiveté to claim that the People's World does not publish appeals to its readers to follow Party doctrine by seeking the overthrow of the Government by force, but it is stark reality to conclude that such a publication provides an incomparable means of promoting the Party's aim of forcible seizure when the time is ripe.[21]

Apart from Justice Douglas's references to the four Marxist-Leninist classics in *Dennis,* books which remained available in libraries and bookstores, this is the only reference in these two great cases of Communist speech to what the speech was. Here it was a newspaper available at newsstands. Thus, had the decision gone the other way, *Yates* would have been perversely memorable in the annals of free speech as a conviction for conspiracy based in part on the evidence of items published in a newspaper of general circulation.

As to the other nine defendants whom Harlan sends back for a new trial, his comments on the Government's proof damn with faint praise. He notes that there is evidence tying these defendants to classes "where there occurred what might be considered to be the systematic teaching and advocacy of illegal action."[22] He then describes the sort of proof he is looking for:

> It might be found that one of the purposes of such classes was to develop in the members of the group a readiness to engage at the crucial time, perhaps during war or during attack upon the United States from without, in such activities as sabotage and street fighting, in order to divert and diffuse the resistance of the authorities and if possible to seize local vantage points.[23]

He is thus willing to permit a jury to try to find a conspiracy within the larger "conspiracy" of the Communist Party. But even here he has a notably uncharitable view of the quality of the Government's proof:

In short, while the record contains evidence of little more than a general program of educational activity by the Communist Party which included advocacy of violence as a theoretical matter, we are not prepared to say, at this stage in the case, that it would be impossible for a jury, resolving all conflicts in favor of the Government and giving the evidence its utmost sweep, to find that advocacy of action was also engaged in when the group involved was thought particularly trustworthy, dedicated, and suited for violent tasks.[24]

Once Justice Harlan has finished his review of the evidence little remains of the Government's proof. Of the eleven overt acts charged in the indictment, nine are barred by his ruling with respect to evidence bearing on the "organize" charge. Of the two acts remaining, one involves nothing more than a meeting at which it is agreed nothing unlawful was said or done. Nevertheless, Harlan, in the teeth of a sharp protest on this point by Justice Black, holds that this could have been an overt act in furtherance of the conspiracy sufficient to satisfy the statute.

Justice Harlan's close scrutiny of the facts as to the Communist conspiracy has two consequences. First, it has the remarkable effect of simply eliminating the Smith Act as a weapon in the campaign against American Communism. On the remand of the nine, the Government drops the charges, and thereafter it initiates no new Smith Act prosecutions.[25] Second, and in the long run perhaps even more important, Justice Harlan's response to the facts gives content and bite to the analytic distinctions he makes in finding the trial judge's instructions in error. By touching earth with the factual record, he transforms an apparently metaphysical exercise into a tough-minded setting of boundaries to censorship of radical dissent.

The opinions of Justices Clark and Black, each in its own way, provide an appropriate final perspective on Harlan's complex diplomacy. Justice Clark, in dissent, underscores how radical Justice Harlan's revision of *Dennis* has been. He cannot understand why this is not a routine application of *Dennis.* The evidence in this case, he says, with unintended irony, "paralleled that in *Dennis* . . . and was equally strong."[26] He is incredulous at the directed acquittals: "In [the Court's] long history I find no case in which an acquittal has been ordered solely on the *facts.* "[27] And he insists that the Smith Act was passed primarily to curb the growth of the Communist Party and that the Court's construction of "organize" frustrates that purpose. But he saves his chief fire for Harlan's analysis of advocacy:

I have studied the section of the opinion concerning the instructions and frankly its "artillery of words" leaves me confused as to why the majority concludes that the charge as given was insufficient.[28]

He then quotes Harlan's restatement of *Dennis:*

The essence of the *Dennis* holding was that indoctrination of a group in preparation for future violent action, as well as exhortation to immediate action, by advocacy found to be directed to "action for the accomplishment" of forcible overthrow, to violence "as a rule or principle of action," and employing "language of incitement," is not constitutionally protected when the group is of sufficient size and cohesiveness, is sufficiently oriented towards action, and other circumstances are such as reasonably to justify apprehension that action will occur.[29]

Clark laments: "I have read this statement over and over but do not seem to grasp its meaning for I see no resemblance between it and what the respected Chief Justice wrote in *Dennis.*"[30]

Justice Black, concurring in part and dissenting in part, underscores how differently he and Justice Harlan, those best of adversaries, approach First Amendment matters. It is a contrast in judicial styles more interesting than the celebrated difference between Justice Black and Justice Frankfurter. Black simply has no patience with the niceties and technicalities so congenial to the Harlan analysis. He would sweep the Smith Act prosecutions away in one broad, exhilarating constitutional stroke. And he would reject the boundary line Harlan has so laboriously drawn between advocacy and incitement. His position comes through with stark clarity:

. . . I cannot agree that the instruction which the Court indicates it might approve is constitutionally permissible. The Court says that persons can be punished for advocating action to overthrow the Government by force and violence, where those to whom the advocacy is addressed are urged "to *do* something, now or in the future, rather than merely to *believe* in something." Under the Court's approach, defendants could still be convicted simply for agreeing to talk as distinguished from agreeing to act. I believe that the First Amendment forbids Congress to punish people for talking about public affairs, whether or not such discussion incites to action, legal or illegal.[31]

There is much to be said for both the Harlan and the Black approaches, and we will have occasion to appraise them in other contexts. But *Yates* should be remembered, above all, as an instance of the Harlan technique operating at full complexity and full power. His opinion is a brilliant example of legal craftsmanship and judicial statesmanship on the side of the angels.

The Membership Cases: Scales *and* Noto

In our excitement over the five directed acquittals in *Yates,* we may overlook the evidence on which Justice Harlan was willing to let the other nine defendants stand retrial. In this respect, *Scales v. United States* [32] in 1961, one of the two final Smith Act prosecutions to reach the Court, is sobering. In *Scales* Justice Harlan, again writing for the Court, reaffirms the boundary line of incitement-to-future-action he had worked so hard to set in *Yates,* but then he goes on to cite evidence as satisfactory to show incitement which tends seriously to dilute the test. Indeed, his performance leaves an impression opposite to that left by *Yates.* There the concrete citations of evidence gave bite to the verbal formulae; here they appear to loosen the verbal formulae.

Scales differs from *Dennis* and *Yates* technically in that another portion of the Smith Act is invoked. The defendant is not charged under the "advocate" or "organize" provisions, but rather under a provision proscribing *membership* in a group which advocates violent overthrow. In its precise terms, the so-called membership clause interdicts: "whoever . . . becomes or is a member of, or affiliates with, any such society, group, or assembly, knowing the purposes thereof." The Court affirms Scales's conviction in a 5 to 4 decision. [33] Justices Black, Douglas, Brennan, and Chief Justice Warren dissent.

The Government's use of the membership clause sharply poses an issue which was not present in *Dennis* and *Yates:* What degree of connection or association with the speech of the group is sufficient to charge the individual with legal responsibility for it? *Scales* proves an important precedent on this question, and we will have occasion to discuss this aspect of Justice Harlan's opinion in the section of this book that deals with associational freedoms. For the moment, however, we are concerned with another portion of the opinion. The Government's strategy of reaching Scales solely through his ties to the Communist Party required that it first establish that the Party engaged in illegal advocacy. *Scales* is thus directly in line with *Dennis* and *Yates,* and adds a further gloss to the First Amendment on the matter of the limits of permissible group advocacy.

Before beginning his extended review of the evidence, Justice Harlan restates with vigor the criteria laid down in *Yates:* The distinction is "between theoretical advocacy and advocacy of violence as a rule of action";[34] evidence of the teaching of Marxist-Leninist "classics" is "not in itself sufficient to show illegal advocacy,"[35] but evidence of the teaching of revolutionary "techniques"[36] is. Having emphatically reaffirmed the *Yates* standard, Harlan, in order to affirm the conviction, must find some additional strength in the proof in this record which was missing in *Yates*. Much of the evidence is strictly comparable to that in *Yates,* but Harlan argues that this evidence, while insufficient in itself, is relevant as background, if there is other more concrete evidence with which it can be joined. Then, he proceeds to find the proof he needs in specific evidence about Scales's activities and contacts in the Party—evidence which depends on treating Scales "as a Party official" and not as "the defendant in this case" charged with membership. In what seems to me a considerable irony, this evidence is used not to establish that Scales himself engaged in illegal advocacy but to show the true character of the Party of which he is charged with being a member.

The particular proof about Scales which for Justice Harlan tips the balance in favor of conviction involves three witnesses, Clontz, Childs, and Reavis. The following are the most vivid items cited by Harlan and presumably constitute the "cream" of the long trial record:

(a) Clontz, while a law school student, arranged with the FBI to "penetrate" the Party and to furnish information about its activities. He came under the tutelage of Scales, who was "Chairman" of the "Carolina District Communist Party." Several times Scales told him that it would not be possible to proceed by education and voting, "but that forceful revolution would be necessary."

(b) In conversation with Clontz, Scales set out "the basic strategy" of the Party, a strategy which, in Justice Harlan's words, went beyond predicting the "theoretical inevitability of revolution" to "give concrete foundation to the theory, *i.e.* to bringing about the revolution." The strategy was based on the concept that there were two groups in American society that could be "used by the Communist Party to foment a revolution": the working class and the Negroes.

(c) Scales told Clontz that revolution would be "easier" in America than it had been in Russia in 1917 because now there was the Soviet Union to help, although he added that "the Soviet Union could not be expected to land troops to start a revolution here."

(d) Scales arranged a "scholarship" for Clontz at the Jefferson School in New York, where he was tutored by one Doxey Wilkerson.

Wilkerson told Clontz that due to the Smith Act the Party was now officially concealing its espousal of violent revolution and that "in the future many things would be left unsaid that previously had been said, many things would be left unwritten that previously had been written." He also instructed Clontz to conceal his Party membership and "to go underground" in order to be most useful to the Party.

(e) Childs testified that he went to a "Party Training School" in South Carolina run by Scales. The school met on a farm under strict security measures. Childs was told among other things that the Communists aimed to place people in key jobs in key industries "so that the Communist Party members in a particular plant will have a cell . . . in which they will be able to more effectively plan for such things as attempting to control the union in that particular plant." Reavis testified that he was instructed to get a job at Western Electric in Winston-Salem and to falsify his Taft-Hartley anti-Communist affidavit.

(f) During "a compulsory recreation period" Childs was instructed in jujitsu and was shown how to make a quick jab with a pencil in order to kill by stabbing in the heart, a maneuver which the students were told they "might be able to use on a picket line."

For Justice Harlan these thin examples seem to have had the requisite concreteness to satisfy the standard of incitement-to-future-action. He concludes:

. . . we think that the jury, under instructions which fully satisfied the requirements of *Yates,* was entitled to infer from this systematic preaching that where the *explicitness and concreteness,* of the sort described previously, seemed necessary and prudent, the doctrine of violent revolution—elsewhere more a theory of historical predictability than a rule of conduct—was put forward as a guide to future action, in whatever tone, be it emotional or calculating, that the audience and occasion required; in short, that "advocacy of action" was engaged in. [Emphasis added.][37]

In view of the directed acquittals in *Yates,* Justice Harlan's patience with the *Scales* evidence is puzzling. Perhaps a partial explanation is provided by the difference between the technical postures of the cases: In *Yates* the ruling on the "organize" charge and the error in the jury instruction made a new trial necessary in any event; here there are no other reasons for upsetting the conviction and so Harlan must squarely confront the question of whether or not there was a case for the jury. Also, it should be remembered that the Court in these cases is not treating the quality of incitement as a constitutional fact subject to *de novo* review as in obscenity cases. It is engaged in statutory construction, and, as a consequence, Justice Harlan in his extended reviews of the record is attempting only to see whether a jury could rationally find against the defendant.[38] Finally, it should be recalled that Harlan did not direct acquittals for all the defendants in *Yates;* he allowed nine of the fourteen defendants to be retried. Implicit in that judgment was the view that a reasonable jury could convict on the basis of the evidence in the record—evidence which, as we noted, was quite meager. Thus, despite the apparent contrast between the directed acquittals in *Yates* and the *Scales* decision, there is a continuity between the cases Harlan sent back to trial in *Yates* and the *Scales* affirmance.

The pattern of precedent on permissible group advocacy under the Smith Act, which is already under considerable tension, is given another turn of the screw in *Noto v. United States,* [39] a companion case to *Scales*. In *Noto* the Court, again speaking through Justice Harlan, unanimously reverses a conviction under the membership clause on evidentiary grounds. The evidentiary weakness concerns the failure of the Government to prove *in this case* that the Party did indeed incite to action in the future. There is an elegant evenhandedness about Justice Harlan's disposition of the point:

> The kind of evidence which we found in *Scales* sufficient to support the jury's verdict of present illegal Party advocacy is lacking here in any adequately substantial degree. It need hardly be said that it is upon the particular evidence in a particular record that a particular defendant must be judged, and not upon the evidence in some other record or upon what may be supposed to be the tenets of the Communist Party.[40]

This insistence that the illegal advocacy of the Party must be proved again in each individual prosecution is heartening. But Justice Harlan's judgment of what constitutes sufficient evidence of illegal advocacy remains unnerving—the differences between the evidence that failed in *Noto* and the evidence that persuaded in *Scales* are pretty subtle. Thus, *Noto,* despite the decision in favor of the speaker, does not significantly alter the gloss added to *Yates* by *Scales*.

The net effect of *Scales* and *Noto* is to reduce the force of *Yates* and to demonstrate the vulnerability of the line for group speech. Although Justice Harlan endorses the thrust of *Yates,* his handling of his evidentiary embarrassment in *Scales* dilutes that endorsement and

leaves a potential flaw in the architecture he has so carefully erected—
a flaw which the anxieties of some future day may exploit. It is this
which adds a final complication to the story of "hardbought acquisi-
tions in the fight for freedom" which we are tracing. We have noted
on several occasions that the bite of a principle rests not only on what
the Court said, but also on the facts to which it was applied. The
particular case, as the common law had it, gave meaning and breadth
to the principle by which it was decided. In *Scales* the application
warns of a narrowness of the principle and suggests that incitement-
to-future-action may not be a viable idea after all, that once we surrender the "immediacy" requirement we will find ourselves necessarily
reducing the "concreteness" requirement as well.

16

Subversive Advocacy: *Brandenburg* Revisited

At this juncture it is appropriate to pause and locate where we are in our journey. We are concerned with the final, and most troublesome, genre of speech in which the regulation of content is to some extent permissible—speech that carries the risk of moving the audience against a target selected by the speaker. The constitutional question is how great that risk must be before the censor may step in. And the central fact about the Court's experience with this question is that in every instance it has been posed in a political context.

We began, somewhat perversely, at the end of the story with the answer finally given in *Brandenburg v. Ohio* in 1969 that radical speech cannot be cut off until it reaches "incitement to imminent lawless action." We then returned to the Court's first precedent, *Schenck v. United States* in 1919, and embarked on a lengthy review of the evolution of doctrine that ultimately yields the *Brandenburg* answer. Beginning with Justice Holmes's dissent in *Abrams,* we found ourselves tracing the development of two competing approaches: the majority approach, most fully articulated in *Gitlow* and *Whitney,* which held that general advocacy of violence was unprotected; and the approach of the dissenters, Holmes and Brandeis, who argued that censorship of radical speech could only be justified by a showing of clear and present danger. During the 1940s the clear and present danger test finally made its way into majority doctrine, displacing, though not explicitly erasing, the *Gitlow-Whitney* standard. For several years it was frequently invoked to protect speech. This brief heyday of clear and

present danger as a speech-protective device came to an abrupt end,
however, in *Dennis* in 1951, when the Court, confronted with the
advocacy of the Communist Party, reformulated the test in such a way
as to deprive it of its stringency. Although the *Dennis* Court did not
rely directly on *Gitlow* and *Whitney,* the effect of its decision was once
again to expose general advocacy of violence to censorship. Thereafter, the Court's idiom changed, as Justice Harlan in *Yates,* purport-
ing to engage in statutory construction of the Smith Act in light of
Dennis, fashioned the standard of incitement-to-future-action. Although this standard was a significant improvement over general advocacy, it proved in practice—in *Scales* and *Noto* in 1961—to be elusive
and unpredictable. In the aftermath of *Scales* and *Noto,* it was thus
difficult to say with any certainty precisely where the boundaries of
permissible advocacy lay.

During the years between *Scales* and *Brandenburg,* the air was
cleared considerably by a decision we have discussed elsewhere, *New
York Times v. Sullivan*[1] in 1964. Decided by the Warren Court at the
height of its powers, *New York Times* establishes a critically important
perspective on issues of political speech. The narrow holding in *Times,*
it will be recalled, was that it violated the First Amendment to impose
liability for defamation of a public official unless the aggrieved party
showed that the damaging comment had been made with "actual
malice." The broad implications of this decision for speech issues
other than libel flow from its underlying rationale—the principle that
in America seditious libel cannot be made a crime. As Justice Brennan
put it, the protection of such speech follows from "a profound national commitment to the principle that debate on public issues
should be uninhibited, robust, and wide-open,"[2] and from the recognition that such debate "may well include vehement, caustic, and
sometimes unpleasantly sharp attacks on government and public officials."[3] The Court's choice of language in *Times* was unusually apt. It
spoke of "the central meaning of the First Amendment"[4]: a core of
protection of speech without which democracy cannot function.

Various factors have contributed to the difficulties experienced
by the Court in determining the boundaries of constitutional protection for radical speech. But surely central among them has been the
unresolved status of seditious libel in American law. So long as the
countervalue of protecting serious radical criticism was open to question, the law on subversive advocacy seemed destined to remain un-
stable. Occasional opinions—such as Judge Hand's *Masses* opinion

and Justice Brandeis's *Whitney* concurrence—evidenced acute sensitivity to this countervalue and attempted to define a core of protected criticism and advocacy short of incitement. But *Masses* was almost immediately eclipsed by the majority view during World War I and Justice Brandeis's *Whitney* approach, although adopted for a while by the Court during the 1940s, was uprooted by *Dennis*. Justice Harlan's revision of *Dennis* in *Yates* recovered the *Masses* orientation, but it represented at best a precarious toehold. The great contribution of *New York Times* is to eliminate this underlying uncertainty. By authoritatively declaring the unconstitutionality of seditious libel, it transforms the premise upon which the "incitement" approach rests—the importance of protecting serious radical criticism—into constitutional doctrine.

The Court's new perspective is apparent in a number of cases decided during the years between *Times* and *Brandenburg*. Most of these cases were generated by the civil rights and anti-war movements of the 1960s. During World War I they would probably have been conceptualized as questions of subversive advocacy, but the Warren Court's clarity about the countervalues involved largely forecloses the issue from arising in that form.[5]

A dramatic illustration of the Court's stance is provided by *Bond v. Floyd*[6] in 1966. This case was precipitated by the refusal of the Georgia House of Representatives to seat Julian Bond because of statements he had made critical of Vietnam policy and the draft. Bond, a Negro and prominent civil rights activist, had been elected to the Georgia House by an overwhelming majority. Shortly before the convening of the House, the Student Nonviolent Coordinating Committee [SNNC], an organization of which he was an officer, issued a sharply worded anti-war statement, which emphasized the analogy between oppressed peasants in Vietnam and oppressed Negroes in the United States. The statement charged the government with being "deceptive" in its expression of concern for the freedom of the Vietnamese people, since it had never been "truly determined to end the rule of terror and oppression within its own border." It equated the recent murder of a civil rights leader with the murder of peasants in Vietnam and concluded that in each case the "United States government bears a great part of the responsibility." It complained of the lax enforcement of voting rights here and questioned the "ability and even the desire" of the United States to guarantee free elections elsewhere in the world. It noted sharply that 16 percent of the draftees

were Negroes "called on to stifle the liberation of Vietnam, to preserve a 'democracy' which does not exist for them at home." And, in
its most active paragraph, it stated:

We are in sympathy with, and support, the men in this country who are
unwilling to respond to a military draft which would compel them to contribute their lives to United States aggression in Vietnam in the name of the
"freedom" we find so false in this country.[7]

In various informal statements to the press, Bond stated unequivocally that he endorsed the SNCC statement and that he could not
support the war. At a House committee hearing, he explained that he
had not burned his draft card and did not counsel others to do so, but
that he "admired the courage of someone who could act on his convictions knowing that he faces pretty stiff consequences."[8]

The Georgia House found the statements verging on treason.
Seventy-five members filed petitions challenging Bond's right to take
his seat on the grounds that his remarks were "totally and completely
repugnant to and inconsistent with" the oath of allegiance required
of House members. Bond stated that he stood ready and willing to
take the oath. After a hearing, the House voted not to seat him. The
Court of Appeals, in affirming the action of the House, spoke of the
SNCC statement as going beyond strong criticism of government
policy and "as being a call to action based on race."

Taking its bearings from *New York Times,* the Supreme Court
unanimously holds the refusal to seat Bond unconstitutional. The
opinion is by Chief Justice Warren. He insists that, despite the special
circumstances of Bond's role, the measure of his rights are those of
the citizen-critic of government. Bond can say these things about the
war and American race policy, *because any American can say them.* The
Chief Justice concludes:

The central commitment of the First Amendment, as summarized in the
opinion of the Court in *New York Times v. Sullivan,* is that "debate on public
issues should be uninhibited, robust, and wide-open." We think the rationale
of the *New York Times* case disposes of the claim that Bond's statements fell
outside the range of constitutional protection.[9]

Bond thus demonstrates the power of the *New York Times* principle. It also foreshadows *Brandenburg.* After carefully summarizing the
exact nuances of Bond's statements, Chief Justice Warren observes:

Certainly this clarification does not demonstrate any incitement to violation of the law. No useful purpose would be served by discussing the many decisions of this Court which establish that Bond could not have been convicted for these statements consistently with the First Amendment.[10]

Note how easily the term "incitement" seems to leap to the Chief Justice's lips as he seeks to communicate, without formal discussion and citation, the location of the constitutional line.

Two years later in *Brandenburg* the Court does not cite *New York Times*. Yet the two decisions must be read together. When one does so, the brief *Brandenburg per curiam* takes on great resonance. For *Times* provides the ringing declaration of underlying rationales which is assumed but not articulated in *Brandenburg*.

We have now come full circle and have returned to our starting point, the Court's intriguing performance in *Brandenburg*. In our retelling of the history, we have stressed that Justice Harlan in *Yates*, while ostensibly doing no more than construing the Smith Act in light of *Dennis*, somewhat narrowed the jurisdiction ceded to censorship by *Dennis*. Whatever the opaqueness of his metaphysics, Harlan was in a very pragmatic way moving the Court toward a liberal revision of the boundary line for censorship of radical dissent. *Brandenburg* completes this revisionist movement by announcing "incitement to imminent lawless action" as the constitutional line. It is an easy step in *Brandenburg* to adopt the Harlan emphasis on "incitement" as the constitutional measure, since *Yates* is read as simply restating as statutory construction what *Dennis* had held as a matter of constitutional law. But the *Brandenburg* Court goes further. Not only does it adopt the incitement focus; it also restores the requirement of *immediacy* which had been all but eliminated by the *Dennis* Court's restatement of the clear and present danger test.

The revision of the doctrine is set forth in two passages of the *Brandenburg* opinion, one in the text and the other in a footnote. After stating that *Whitney* stands for the proposition that general advocacy of violent change may be censored, the Court goes on to observe:

But *Whitney* has been thoroughly discredited by later decisions. See *Dennis v. United States*, 341 U.S. 494, at 507 (1951). These later decisions have fashioned the principle that the constitutional guarantees of free speech and free press do not permit a State to forbid or proscribe advocacy of the use of force or of law violation except where such advocacy is directed to inciting or

producing imminent lawless action and is likely to produce such action.[2] As
we said in *Noto v. United States*, "the mere abstract teaching . . . of the moral
propriety or even moral necessity for a resort to force and violence, is not
the same as preparing a group for violent action and steeling it to such
action." A statute which fails to draw this distinction impermissibly intrudes
upon the freedoms guaranteed by the First and Fourteenth Amendments.[11]

Footnote 2 reads:

It was on the theory that the Smith Act . . . embodied such a principle and
that it had been applied only in conformity with it that this Court sustained
the Act's constitutionality. *Dennis v. United States.* That this was the basis for
Dennis was emphasized in *Yates v. United States* in which the Court overturned
convictions for advocacy of the forcible overthrow of the Government under
the Smith Act, because the trial judge's instructions had allowed conviction
for mere advocacy, unrelated to its tendency to produce forcible action.[12]

The upshot is that the Court in *Yates,* while engaged only in statutory
construction of the Smith Act, effected an alteration in the reading of
the First Amendment which now requires that *Whitney* be flatly overruled. In so doing, the *Brandenburg* Court, although it purports to rely
on *Dennis,* explicitly rejects the general advocacy standard which *Dennis* implicitly endorsed—the perfect ending to a long story!

Yet there remain some unresolved chords. For one thing, there
is the Court's emphatic silence about the clear and present danger
test. *Whitney* was an instance of explicit refusal by the majority to
accept the Holmes-Brandeis argument for clear and present danger,
and it was made memorable by Brandeis's eloquence on behalf of the
formula. One would expect that, if the Court were now striking down
Whitney, it must necessarily be raising the clear and present danger
standard and ratifying the Brandeis argument. Moreover, the new
standard announced by the Court—"incitement to imminent lawless
action"—incorporates the emphasis on immediacy which is the distinctive feature of the Holmes-Brandeis test. But the brief opinion
does not so much as mention the words "clear and present danger."
What are we to make of this studied silence? Why did the Court not
use the idiom of clear and present danger as a way of harmonizing the
complex and somewhat messy prior doctrine behind the principle
announced in *Brandenburg?*

There are two possible explanations. The first is substantive: The
Brandenburg standard is not merely a synonym for clear and present

danger; it is a significant advance in clarity and precision. Conceivably, the words "clear and present danger" could have served as a vehicle for the *Brandenburg* principle, but over time those words had become encrusted with conflicting meanings and had proved treacherously elastic in practice. Rather than graft yet another layer of meaning onto the battle-scarred phrase, the Court elected to inter it once and for all. Thus, although the Court retains the Holmes-Brandeis emphasis on immediacy, the effect of its opinion is to reduce the phrase "clear and present danger" to what Justice Frankfurter had so long and stubbornly insisted was all it ever was—a felicitous expression from the pen of Justice Holmes.

The second explanation for the silence about the test is strategic. It rests on the Court's evident reluctance to overrule *Dennis*. Assuming for the moment that the Court wanted to restore the more speech-protective version of the clear and present danger test articulated by Brandeis in *Whitney*, it could do so only by overruling *Dennis*. For, as of 1969, clear and present danger, at least as applied to the problem of subversive advocacy, meant what the *Dennis* Court said it meant. One can only speculate as to the reasons for the Court's unwillingness to overrule *Dennis*. Perhaps so radical a course would not have commanded a majority. Perhaps the Court wanted to preserve *Dennis*, so that it would be available as a precedent in the future should a case arise involving a group possessing the characteristics ascribed to the Communist Party in the 1950s. Whatever the reason, the Court's reluctance to overrule *Dennis* has the effect of foreclosing it from using the clear and present danger idiom as the vehicle for a more stringent test.

Moreover, the revisionist strategy that the Court in fact elects to follow requires that it keep silent about clear and present danger. In order to make use of *Yates*, which recovered the focus on content and initiated a new idiom, the Court must of necessity preserve *Dennis*, for *Yates* was ostensibly no more than statutory construction of the Smith Act in light of *Dennis*. But the last thing the Court wants to do is to resurrect the *Dennis* version of clear and present danger. The maneuvers behind the brief *per curiam* opinion are thus wondrous indeed.[13]

A second puzzle left unresolved by the terse opinion is the question of whether the *Brandenburg* line is to apply to the group as well as the individual speaker. The Court, as we have seen, faced the problem of group speech in *Whitney* in 1927, in *Dennis* in 1951, in *Yates* in 1957, and in *Scales* and *Noto* in 1961. *Brandenburg* officially erases *Whitney*. Its impact on the Smith Act cases, however, is more oblique.

The standard that emerged from those cases was incitement, but incitement adjusted to meet the problem of a group that is being organized to act not immediately but in the future—to meet, that is, what was taken to be the threat presented by the Communist Party. The resulting legal concept we have called incitement to *future action*. But the standard announced in *Brandenburg* is incitement to *immediate action*. What then has become of the distinction between group and individual speech which seemed implicit in the earlier decisions?

One possibility is that the *Brandenburg* Court intended to erase any such distinction, and that it was deliberately, if obscurely, revising *Yates*. Such a reading of the opinion is suggested by the footnote quoted above. In it the Court accurately restates *Yates* in support of a principle which differs from the *Yates* standard in that it incorporates a requirement of immediacy. It is also possible, however, that the Court regarded *Brandenburg* as an instance of individual speech and hence has preserved the group/individual distinction. Under such an approach the *Yates* incitement-to-future-action standard would apply to group speech and the *Brandenburg* incitement-to-immediate-action standard would apply to the individual speaker. This possibility is suggested by the quotation from *Noto* which immediately follows the statement of the new standard:

. . . the mere abstract teaching . . . of the moral propriety or even moral necessity for a resort to force and violence, is not the same as preparing a group for violent action and steeling it to such action.[14]

This statement resonates to the concern with the dangers of group advocacy that informed *Dennis*.

The question of whether a group, on analogy to conspiracy, is governed by different standards than the individual speaker when it is a matter of regulating content is a critically important one. For, as we saw in *Scales*, the *Yates* standard of incitement-to-future-action, although a marked improvement over unfocused general advocacy, proves treacherously subtle in practice. Unfortunately, this question cannot be said to be settled by *Brandenburg* and so must await future clarification.

The Lawyer and the Philosopher

Having traced the tortuous path by which the law and the tradition worked themselves pure from *Schenck* to *Brandenburg*, we can now attempt to put the issue of subversive advocacy into final perspective.

The central problem of free speech is to determine when, if ever, the *content* of communications may be interdicted by law. American law has attained a very considerable consensus on what we have called untouchable content. And over time it has worked through various categories of censorable content with pretty fair success. Although it has failed to find a single test by which to resolve all speech problems, it has functionally held the censor to minimal jurisdiction in each category while abstaining from philosophic sweep. What the opinions have lacked in philosophic tone and eloquence, they have to my mind more than made up in pragmatic results.

There is a striking difference now apparent between the incidence of problems in the American constitutional experience under the First Amendment and their salience in a philosophic discussion of free speech such as John Stuart Mill's essay *On Liberty*. For Mill, the great issues were those presented by radically unpopular doctrines such as disbelief in God, and the central thrust of his argument was against the censorship of false or unsound doctrine. Almost casually he concedes that at some point of proximity a speech inciting a mob is within the reach of the law. If we lay the American legal experience against such a map of the issues, the contrast is startling. We have experienced almost no efforts to suppress false doctrine and have virtually taken for granted that there can be no censorship on that premise. But the law has been centrally preoccupied with the problem of speech inciting to violence, which to the philosopher must seem a fringe issue.

There is, I think, an explanation for this marked difference in perspective. In the real world it has not been easy to conceptualize and capture different kinds of radical dissent. The lawyer has taken as self-evident the truth that words can on occasion be the triggers of action; and the core problem for him has been to accommodate that insight with the essential value of robust, abrasive, uninhibited dissent. Or to put this another way, the problem has been to keep in mind always that the instances of inciting speech the law will in fact confront arise in a political context. Hence the law's almost obsessive preoccupation with distinctions and gradations in speech urging violence has arisen in cases involving radical dissent and has been in the end closer to the heart of the philosopher's concerns than the arid legal formulae suggest.

With the cases behind us, the following scheme may offer some insight. Think of arraying three kinds of abrasive speech: seditious libel, general unfocused advocacy of violence as a tactic of social change, and incitement. It would seem at first that the crucial distinction lies between seditious libel and the other two, and that the distinction between kinds of urging of action is a finicky lawyer's point. What American constitutional law—after *Yates, New York Times,* and *Brandenburg*—is, I think, saying is that the crucial distinction lies between incitement and the other two, and that the difference between seditious libel and general advocacy of violent change is a finicky theoretical point that the law need not attend to. To put this as a diagram, the question is which is the true perspective, A or B?

A	seditious libel	general advocacy	incitement
B	seditious libel	general advocacy	incitement

In a sense, it is all much like the issue of advocating that adultery might sometimes be proper which stirred Justice Stewart to memorable utterance in *Kingsley Pictures.* [15] If the propriety of adultery is, as he said, just another idea like the single tax, then so too is the propriety of violence. It is a point which can be discussed, argued, and debated. But just as the urging of adultery becomes quite a different matter when the urging is concrete and immediate, so it is with the advocacy of violence when it becomes concrete and immediate. That, it seems to me, is the meaning of the *Brandenburg* line. Finally, those who oppose adultery and those who oppose violence would be well advised, in the interest of their cause, to permit discussion so that the strength of their arguments might better be appreciated. And that, I take it, is what free speech is all about.

PART TWO

THE REGULATION
OF ASSOCIATION

The Regulation
of Political Groups

17

Sanctions Against Groups

The erratic, almost random, course of the Socratic dialogue between American society and the Supreme Court over the meaning of freedom of speech is such that we have been forced, while en route to answering the nuclear question of the permissible content regulation of *individual* speech, to deal substantially as well with the question of the limits of censorship of *group* speech.

It is helpful, yet misleading, to conceptualize the topic as group *speech*. It is helpful in that it focuses attention on the fact that people organize to present opinions to the public. Indeed, it is likely that most speech in our society today is group speech. Moreover, the concept enables us to locate rather tidily two key questions: (i) Does the group enjoy the same degree of free speech as the individual? (ii) What degree of connection or association with the speech of another is sufficient to charge the individual with legal responsibility for it, with what might be called *vicarious liability* for speech? It is important to isolate these questions and to appraise the answers the Court has thus far provided to them.

It is misleading, however, to put the questions only in this form. Individuals join together to present opinions to the public not simply as an exercise in speech but as a complex gesture of political action. We find ourselves short of concepts for capturing the phenomena with which the law is dealing, phenomena that have to do with organizations, with conspiracies, with the right of assembly, and with freedom of association. The focus of our inquiry thus shifts to what the

First Amendment tradition has to say about *associational freedoms* in American life.

There is a formidable amount of precedent to review. Overall it is probable that the Supreme Court has spent the bulk of its time and energy on group First Amendment rights. Five kinds of groups have generated most of the cases and most of the radical history of twentieth-century America: the socialist-pacifists of the World War I period; the radical industrial groups of the 1920s; the Jehovah's Witnesses; the Communist Party and its alleged satellites; and the NAACP. The record of the law's response to the two early groups is, as we have seen, erratic. And it is striking that the myriad Jehovah's Witness cases have been framed as involving only individuals and not the group, while the opposite emphasis has characterized the law's confrontations with the Communists, and even more, with the NAACP.

Our concern in this section is with instances in which the law applies sanctions directly to the group. There are three ways in which the issue has been put into litigation: (i) The law may seek to apply criminal sanctions to the *organizing* of the group, as in *Dennis* and *Yates*. [1] (ii) It may seek to make *membership* in the group a crime, as in *Scales*. [2] (iii) It may seek to inhibit the group by the use of non-criminal sanctions, such as compulsory disclosure of membership and stigmatization. We will start with the efforts to impose criminal sanctions and then will turn to the efforts to use non-criminal sanctions.

It is not easy to map a path through this body of precedent. One must resist the temptation to over-conceptualize or to coerce the data into deceptively neat patterns. For the moment, we would only note how complex it becomes to keep the functional realities of law in mind and yet trace systematically the body of answers the Court has given over time to the meaning of the First Amendment. The Court's world, as it must know better than the rest of us, is incurably untidy.

18

The Nexus Issue:
Is Membership Enough?

We have already covered what the Court has had to say about the application of criminal sanctions to the *content* of group speech. The important cases are *Whitney* in 1927, *Dennis* in 1951, *Yates* in 1957, and *Brandenburg* in 1969.[1] As we have seen, *Brandenburg* explicitly overruled *Whitney,* but its impact on the Smith Act decisions was more ambiguous. Thus, *Yates,* which substantially revised *Dennis,* emerges as the pivotal precedent on the limits of permissible group advocacy. It establishes that group speech cannot be made a crime unless something more than general advocacy is involved. Justice Harlan purported to find that "something more" in the elusive concept of incitement-to-future-action, a concept tailored to meet what was thought to be the threat to American society posed by the Communist Party.

Our concern in this chapter is with the second of our core questions about group speech—the question of the individual's nexus to the group, of vicarious responsibility for the speech of another. This question can be posed in various ways. Can nominally political organizations of radical bent be treated as conspiracies in their entirety so that mere membership in them is equivalent to participating in a conspiracy? If the organization has within it a smaller conspiratorial core, how can the law get at that core without causing side effects that are damaging to political freedom?

The question, however it is phrased, is architectonic for a large part of the law of the First Amendment. In a rational system the answer to it provides a necessary baseline for measuring the host of other issues stirred by the government's anti-Communist tactics. During the 1940s and 1950s American law spawned a wide variety of legal constraints on those who were members of or had some nexus to "the Communist conspiracy." It was a chief characteristic of these constraints that they did not involve the use of direct criminal sanctions but always—and in a wondrous variety of ways—involved some other and lesser form of sanction. We will turn in the following section of this book to these indirect "partial sanctions." We would stress here that it is of great help, although possibly not dispositive, to get our bearings by seeing how far the criminal law itself can constitutionally extend the conspiracy notion.

The Early Cases

Scales v. United States,[2] the Smith Act membership case, is the key precedent on the question of individual nexus to the proscribed group activity. But the idea of treating membership in an organization as itself a crime, thus turning the organization into a conspiracy, did not originate with the Smith Act. Although it was not until *Scales* in 1961 that the Court squarely confronted the propriety of this tactic, it figured in a number of early cases.

The nexus issue was, for example, present in *Whitney* in a poignant form. Miss Whitney had opposed the group's program of violence and had submitted a resolution favoring use of the ballot which had been defeated. She had, however, remained at the meeting after the defeat of her resolution, and this the Court thought was enough to justify holding her criminally responsible for the program of the group.[3] The point does not appear to have been pushed in argument; it receives little attention in the majority opinion and none in the celebrated Brandeis concurrence. The issue was also present in *Herndon.*[4] Justice Roberts, it will be recalled, stressed the lack of evidence that Herndon had ever read or knew the contents of the Communist pamphlets found in his room or that he understood them to advocate Communism.

Perhaps the most striking of the early precedents is *DeJonge v. Oregon*[5] in 1937. This case appears to have been a prosecutor's mistake, but mistake or not it furnishes Chief Justice Hughes with the occasion for some characteristic technical lawyering and some oft-quoted eloquence on freedom of assembly. DeJonge, a member of the Communist Party, had spoken to a meeting called by the Party. The meeting had been open to the public; only a small minority of the audience were Communists; and the discussion concerned a long-shoremen's strike then in progress. DeJonge, speaking in the name of the Party, had addressed himself largely to the issues of the strike. Although he was alleged to have urged the purchase of certain Communist literature, there was no showing that this material advocated any unlawful conduct. He was indicted under a state criminal syndicalist statute which made it a crime to "preside at or conduct . . . any assemblage of persons, or any organization . . . which teaches or advocates the doctrine of criminal syndicalism." DeJonge challenged the conviction on the ground that there was simply no evidence that criminal syndicalism was advocated at the meeting. The state court, in an effort to salvage the conviction, construed the indictment as charging the defendant with assisting at a meeting of the Communist Party which itself, the meeting apart, taught and advocated criminal syndicalism. Focusing on this narrow charge, Chief Justice Hughes confidently found the statute as applied unconstitutional.

Hughes stresses that DeJonge's complicity has not been made to depend on his membership in the Party; rather, it depends solely on his participation at the public meeting:

A like fate might have attended any speaker, although not a member, who "assisted in the conduct" of the meeting. However innocuous the object of the meeting, however lawful the subjects and tenor of the addresses, however reasonable and timely the discussion, all those assisting in the conduct of the meeting would be subject to imprisonment as felons, if the meeting were held by the Communist Party.[6]

He goes on to declare that freedom of assembly is a right so fundamental as to be protected against the states under the Fourteenth Amendment, just as *Gitlow* a decade earlier had held the speech and press clauses of the First Amendment incorporated in the Fourteenth. He concludes with a stirring assertion of the importance of free assembly:

It follows from these considerations that . . . peaceable assembly for lawful discussion cannot be made a crime. The holding of meetings for peaceable political action cannot be proscribed. Those who assist in the conduct of such meetings cannot be branded as criminals on that score. The question, if the rights of free speech and peaceable assembly are to be preserved, is not as to the auspices under which the meeting is held but as to its purpose. . . .[7]

Despite its idiosyncratic facts, *DeJonge* stands tall as a precedent for the proposition that the link between the individual and the group speech crime must be substantial to avoid unconstitutionality.

Scales v. United States

Scales, it will be recalled, was a 5 to 4 decision affirming a conviction under the clause of the Smith Act that made it a crime to be a member of an organization that advocated violent overthrow of the government. Justice Harlan wrote the majority opinion. Chief Justice Warren and Justices Black, Douglas, and Brennan dissented. Earlier we discussed the troubling gloss *Scales* added to the *Yates* standard of permissible group advocacy; here we are concerned with the challenge to the membership clause.

The defendant attacked the membership clause on three fronts: (i) its incompatibility with the 1950 Subversive Activities Control Act [SACA], which, he argued, immunized "membership *per se*" from legal sanctions; (ii) its violation of the due process clause of the Fifth Amendment as a form of guilt by association; and (iii) its violation of the First Amendment as a "chilling" of the right of political association.

The first point need not long detain us. It is the occasion for a sustained debate over statutory construction between Justices Harlan and Brennan. Section 4(f) of the 1950 Act provided that neither "the holding of office nor membership in any Communist organization shall constitute per se a violation" of the Act or "of any other criminal statute." This provision has a rich political history and reflects the lawmakers' unease over "outlawing" the Communist Party by making mere membership in it a crime. It also reflects the extraordinary difficulty the government was having coordinating its various anti-Communist strategies, especially the Smith Act strategy of direct criminal sanctions and the SACA strategy of compulsory disclosure. In combination these strategies gave rise to a dilemma: If the membership clause of the Smith Act remained in force, the compulsory disclosure of membership required by the SACA would compel disclosure of a crime and hence would run afoul of the Fifth Amendment privilege against self-incrimination.

Justice Brennan, in a dissent joined by Chief Justice Warren and Justice Douglas, argues that Section 4(f) was Congress's solution to this dilemma and was intended to bar prosecutions under the membership clause. But Justice Harlan reads Section 4(f) as "a mandate to the courts" that the Smith Act is not to be "*construed* so as to make 'membership' in a Communist organization 'per se a violation.' "[8] He is thus able to save the membership clause from repeal by the 1950 Act.[9]

Harlan then turns to the question of just what "membership" means under the Smith Act. This is the key step in his opinion. It is necessitated by his handling of the Section 4(f) challenge; and it provides the basis for his response to the challenges under the Fifth and First Amendments. Endorsing the jury instructions of the trial judge, he adds to "membership" the following qualifying and narrowing terms: (i) *active* and not merely "nominal" or "passive"; (ii) *knowledge* of the Party's illegal advocacy; and (iii) *a specific intent* to bring about overthrow "as speedily as circumstances would permit."[10]

Harlan stresses that any other construction of the membership clause would raise constitutional questions and that therefore Congress must be presumed to have intended the narrower, more stringent meaning of "membership." Characteristically, it is here in his effort to narrow the definition of "membership" by means of statutory construction rather than in the constitutional arguments which follow that Harlan makes his moves in favor of freedom of association. As we will see, *Scales* has turned out to be a major, liberating precedent on precisely this point. But one feels a twinge of regret that Justice Harlan was so exquisitely patient and did not instead let the membership clause carry into the constitutional challenge the uncomplicated, unqualified, and vulnerable meaning Congress must in fact have intended for it. This is especially true since *Scales* is muddied on this point by its facts. Scales was not simply a member of the Party; he was a high-ranking Party official and hence the ambiguities lurking in other membership cases are less salient in his case. In any event, as the Harlan opinion proceeds, the constitutional challenge is to be measured against a membership clause that has had the benefit of a narrowing construction.

Interestingly, the more elaborate constitutional challenge, at least as reflected in Harlan's response, comes under the Fifth Amendment, not under the First. The challenge is thus addressed not only to associational ties to speech crimes but to associational ties to any type of crime. As Harlan restates it:

In our jurisprudence guilt is personal, and when the imposition of punishment on a status or on conduct can only be justified by reference to the relationship of that status or conduct to other concededly criminal activity (here advocacy of violent overthrow), that relationship must be sufficiently substantial to satisfy the concept of personal guilt in order to withstand attack under the Due Process Clause of the Fifth Amendment. Membership, without more, in an organization engaged in illegal advocacy, it is now said, has not heretofore been recognized by this Court to be such a relationship. This claim stands, and we shall examine it, independently of the claim made under the First Amendment.[11]

Justice Harlan begins his answer by reminding us that "familiar concepts of the law of conspiracy and complicity" show that guilt has never been personal in a literal, simplistic sense. He next deals with the circumstance that the Smith Act does not invoke conventional conspiracy or complicity concepts but talks rather of knowing membership in illegal organizations:

The fact that Congress has not resorted to either of these familiar concepts means only that the enquiry here must direct itself to an analysis of the relationship between the fact of membership and the underlying substantive illegal conduct, in order to determine whether that relationship is indeed too tenuous to permit its use as the basis of criminal liability. In this instance it is an organization which engages in criminal activity, and we can perceive no reason why one who actively and knowingly works in the ranks of that organization, intending to contribute to the success of those specifically illegal activities, should be any more immune from prosecution than he to whom the organization has assigned the task of carrying out the substantive criminal act.[12]

Somehow this passage, despite its lucidity and willingness to take the challenge head on, does not quite persuade. We cannot but wonder why, if the government could have achieved the same results by using conspiracy doctrine, it did not elect to do so. Would the case have come out the same way, had a conspiracy been charged and knowing membership in the Party been employed only as proof of participation in the conspiracy? If the law for centuries could handle collective crimes with the rule of conspiracy, why is it suddenly necessary to employ the new tool of knowing membership? Moreover, are not special freedoms endangered when this new tool is used only for speech crimes? No prosecution has found useful the circumlocution of "membership in a group" when the organization is designed for bank robbery. Since, as Justice Harlan has stressed, the speech crime involved here is "subtle," there seems an inevitable loosening of the nexus required for criminal imputability when the membership link is used to tie the individual to a diffuse, subtle speech crime. Justice Harlan acknowledges and replies to the point:

Nor should the fact that Congress has focussed here on "membership," the characteristic relationship between an individual and the type of conspiratorial quasi-political associations with the criminal aspect of whose activities Congress was concerned, of itself require the conclusion that the legislature has traveled outside the familiar and permissible bounds of criminal imputability. In truth, the specificity of the proscribed relationship is not necessarily a vice; it provides instruction and warning.[13]

The confrontation proceeds to its climax, and it is an impressive one:

What must be met, then, is the argument that membership, even when accompanied by the elements of knowledge and specific intent, affords an insufficient quantum of participation in the organization's alleged criminal activity, that is, an insufficiently significant form of aid and encouragement to permit the imposition of criminal sanctions on that basis. It must indeed be recognized that a person who merely becomes a member of an illegal organization, by that "act" alone need be doing nothing more than signifying his assent to its purposes and activities on one hand, and providing, on the other, only the sort of moral encouragement which comes from the knowledge that others believe in what the organization is doing. It may indeed be argued that such assent and encouragement do fall short of the concrete, practical impetus given to a criminal enterprise which is lent for instance by a commitment on the part of a conspirator to act in furtherance of that enterprise. A member, as distinguished from a conspirator, may indicate his approval of a criminal enterprise by the very fact of his membership without thereby committing himself to further it by any act or course of conduct whatever.[14]

Having stated the counter-argument so lucidly and powerfully, he proceeds to bring matters to the constitutional brink:

In an area of criminal law which this Court has indicated more than once demands its watchful scrutiny [citing *Dennis, Yates,* and *Noto*], these factors have weight and must be found to be overborne in a total constitutional assessment of the statute.[15]

The passage is made even more arresting by a footnote reference to the passage in Brandeis's *Whitney* opinion in which he comments

sharply on how disturbingly unlike conventional criminal statutes the
California Criminal Syndicalism Act was. It is exactly the right passage
to have selected. One cannot but feel at this point that Justice Harlan
has confronted the full weight of the counter-argument, that the defendant's point has been heard.

The moment is, I think, an important one in American law. It is
1961; the anti-Communist fevers have long since abated. Justice Harlan writes as though he were within inches of finding the whole complex strategy of membership ties to group speech crimes and the
subtleties of incitement-to-future-action unconstitutional. Had he
persuaded the Court to do so, he would have relieved American law
and tradition of the awkward and potentially dangerous mortgage that
anti-Communism has placed upon the future. But he cannot quite
take the step:

> We think, however, they ["these factors"] are duly met when the statute is
> found to reach only "active" members having also a guilty knowledge and
> intent, and which therefore prevents a conviction on what otherwise might
> be regarded as merely an expression of sympathy with the alleged criminal
> enterprise, unaccompanied by any significant action in its support or any
> commitment to undertake such action.[16]

We are thus left with half a loaf. The law stands. The conviction of
Junius Scales, which becomes almost unique, stands. And the strategy
of sanctioning membership in group speech crimes remains available.
But as an offset there is the solemn reminder that this strategy has
pushed the censor's power to the uttermost boundary under the Constitution, and the whole scheme remains constitutional only if the
three qualifications of the membership tie—knowledge, specific intent, activity—are taken seriously and applied honestly.

It is instructive that so lengthy a discussion of the *Scales* opinion
has been highly relevant to the purposes of this study even though the
First Amendment has yet to be mentioned! And it is ironic that meeting the First Amendment challenge to the membership clause requires little more than a single page of the fifty-six-page opinion.
Harlan regards the matter largely disposed of by *Dennis*. The legal
algebra is difficult to impeach: *Dennis* and *Yates* have interdicted this
form of group speech; further, *Dennis* held unprotected "association"
for the purpose of organizing a group to promote criminal speech. He
continues:

We can discern no reason why membership, when it constitutes a purposeful form of complicity in a group engaging in this same forbidden advocacy should receive any greater degree of protection from the guarantees of that Amendment.[17]

There is, of course, a reason. Even in the eyes of its harshest critics, a radical political organization is not a pure conspiracy and nothing more. It is at worst a conspiracy overlaid on a political organization which also has legal objectives and talks importantly to public issues. Membership, as Harlan acknowledges, is the characteristic form of affiliation with such groups. There is therefore a considerable risk that the legal process and jury trial will not be calibrated finely enough in times of high feeling when such prosecutions are likely to be brought to make the necessary distinctions and to disentangle the inner conspiratorial group from the outer radical political association. Once again it would seem that depriving the prosecution of the rhetorical advantage of proceeding against membership rather than against participation in a conspiracy is precisely the sort of "bonus" the law has accorded defendants in other First Amendment areas. Justice Harlan is, as always, admirable in weighing the counter-argument:

It is, of course, true that quasi-political parties or other groups that may embrace both legal and illegal aims differ from a technical conspiracy, which is defined by its criminal purpose, so that *all* knowing association with the conspiracy is a proper subject for criminal proscription as far as First Amendment liberties are concerned. If there were a similar blanket prohibition of association with a group having both legal and illegal aims, there would be a real danger that legitimate political expression or association would be impaired. . . . [18]

He has seen the point, but again is not quite persuaded by it. The sentence continues:

. . . but the membership clause, as here construed, does not cut deeper into the freedom of association than is necessary to deal with "the substantive evils that Congress has a right to prevent." The clause does not make criminal all association with an organization which has been shown to engage in illegal advocacy. There must be clear proof that a defendant "specifically intend[s] to accomplish [the aims of the organization] by resort to violence." Thus the member for whom the organization is a vehicle for the advancement of legitimate aims and policies does not fall within the ban of the statute: he lacks the requisite specific intent "to bring about the overthrow of the government as speedily as circumstances would permit." Such a person may be foolish, deluded, or perhaps merely optimistic, but he is not by this statute made a criminal.[19]

This answer is much the same as the answer to the Fifth Amendment challenge. Using First Amendment scales has not altered the way the balance comes to rest. Justice Harlan's references to "quasi-political parties" have brought the Court closer than it has ever been to focusing on the problem. His lucidity and analytic stamina have contributed invaluably to the discussion of the problem, but in the end he lacks the last measure of sensitivity to First Amendment values and needs. And he makes heroic assumptions about the capacity of either the ordinary citizen or the ordinary trial court to draw the gossamer distinctions on which he chooses to rely. It remains a puzzle why he was moved to such extraordinary expenditures of energy and skill to save this one conviction—which, as it turns out, is the last gasp of efforts to apply criminal sanctions to the Communists.

Justices Brennan, Douglas, and Black file dissenting opinions. Brennan, as we have seen, concentrates his fire on the awkward relationship between Smith Act prosecutions under the membership clause and the strategy of compulsory disclosure under SACA. Douglas takes another tack. After charging that the Court has ratified the idea of guilt by association and criticizing the thinness of the evidence on Scales's participation in any illegality, he pitches the main thrust of his dissent in terms of penalizing "belief." This is to my ear an odd way to put it, but the point is arresting. Just what does a man do who endorses group speech by joining a group? Justice Harlan had wrestled with the point searching for something more than "merely an expression of sympathy with the alleged criminal enterprise." He thought he had found it in the requirement of active membership, guilty knowledge and specific intent. Justice Douglas's answer is that all the man does is profess a belief:

Not one single illegal act is charged to petitioner. That is why the essence of the crime covered by the indictment is merely belief—belief in the proletarian revolution, belief in Communist creed.[20]

The Douglas dissent verges on punning on belief in the sense in which we today take religious beliefs to be inviolate. It would have been more useful had he elected to defend his position in the idiom of freedom of association rather than freedom of belief.

Justice Black states that the Brennan and Douglas opinions cover his primary reasons for dissent and that his own opinion is only a sort of footnote. He devotes it to one more complaint about the Court's use of the "balancing" test. This reaction strikes me as misplaced and unfortunate. In the sense that, say, *Barenblatt* and *Konigsberg* can be said to involve balancing, it is not at all clear that *Scales* does.[21] The evil Justice Black has so steadfastly fought would now seem to have expanded in his mind to include any concession whatsoever to censorship no matter how arrived at. More important, it is a distraction. *Scales* was the Court's first full dress confrontation with the strategy of applying conspiracy notions to membership in "quasi-political parties," a question of the greatest import for political freedom in America. Rejoinder to the Harlan analysis in these terms should have commandeered all the dissenters' energy.

19

Compulsory Disclosure as a Group Sanction: The Civil Rights Cases

The strategy of controlling troublesome groups through the direct use of criminal sanctions has unsuspected complexities. It is not easy to outlaw a group. The law can seek to punish specific acts by individuals on the group's behalf, such as the publication of censorable material; or it can try to inhibit the group by making organizing a crime. But the blunt treating of the group itself as criminal requires, as *Scales* underscores, that it be alchemized into something akin to a conspiracy with the consequence that knowing membership in it becomes a crime.

One effect of the effort to control radical political and quasi-political groups by means of criminal sanctions was to pervert American law by forcing the "crime" into speech terms. As we have seen, the government in the Smith Act cases adopted the pretense that it was deeply concerned with Communist *speech;* and the Court painfully worked out a complex, artificial analysis of permissible censorship of group speech.

During the 1950s another strategy for containing domestic subversion became salient—the use of compulsory disclosure. At first blush it seems odd that disclosure could ever be viewed as or would work as a sanction against speech, or if it did, that it would create any constitutional difficulties. Indeed, it would invite a deep paradox to maintain that freedom of speech incorporates a freedom to keep silent. But, as we shall see in later chapters, the issue has been a frequent source of constitutional controversy in connection with leg-

islative investigating committees, the character and fitness committees of the legal profession, various anti-subversive affidavits, and the
like.

Our concern here is with a narrower issue: the use of disclosure
when intended as a sanction. This is to be distinguished from situations
where the impact of disclosure is said to be the unintended by-product of the pursuit of some other legitimate state purpose. Also, we are
concerned here with the use of disclosure as a sanction against *groups,*
not individuals. It may well be that somewhat different questions arise
in the two cases. In any event, the Court has had no doubt that when
applied to a group to force it to make public its membership, disclosure is a formidable sanction, the use of which raises important First
Amendment questions.

Before turning to the handful of cases which speak to this issue,
it may prove helpful to pause for a moment to consider *Talley v.
California,* [1] a 1960 case involving anonymous pamphlets. *Talley* is one
of those trivial cases that somehow provide an occasion for major
generalizations about freedom of speech. Although not directly on
point, it evoked important discussion among the justices about privacy and political speech. It may therefore serve as an appropriate
preface to the topic of compulsory disclosure.

At issue was the imposition of a $10 fine for violation of a Califor-
nia ordinance which prohibited the distribution of handbills unless
the names of the author, publisher, printer, and sponsor were disclosed on them. The handbills in question were part of a boycott
campaign against manufacturers who did not offer "equal employment opportunities to Negroes, Mexicans, and Orientals"; and, although they did not disclose individual names, they were not in fact
anonymous, but carried the name, address, and phone number of the
sponsoring organization. The Court held the ordinance void on its
face in a 6 to 3 decision. The facts stir the suspicion that the prosecution was hyper-technical and vindictive—a tactic in the battle over
racial bias in employment. But the Court in an opinion by Justice
Black elects to go to high ground and to condemn the identification
requirement as a violation of the First Amendment.

Justice Clark in a dissent joined by Justices Frankfurter and Whittaker provides an effective counterpoint, a kind of commonsense be-
wilderment that anonymity is protected by free speech norms. "The
Constitution," he observes, "says nothing about freedom of anonymous speech."[2] There is, in his view, nothing objectionable about the
Los Angeles ordinance:

All that Los Angeles requires is that one who exercises his right of free speech through writing or distributing handbills identify himself just as does one who speaks from the platform. The ordinance makes for the responsibility in writing that is present in public utterance.[3]

The argument is, in effect, that disclosure is justified as a complement to free speech. The majority, however, does not see it that way. Justice Black contributes a felicitous essay on the importance of protecting anonymity in political discourse:

Anonymous pamphlets, leaflets, brochures and even books have played an important role in the progress of mankind. Persecuted groups and sects from time to time throughout history have been able to criticize oppressive practices and laws either anonymously or not at all. The obnoxious press licensing law of England, which was also enforced on the Colonies was due in part to the knowledge that exposure of the names of printers, writers and distributors would lessen the circulation of literature critical of the government. The old seditious libel cases in England show the lengths to which government had to go to find out who was responsible for books that were obnoxious to the rulers. John Liliburne was whipped, pilloried and fined for refusing to answer questions designed to get evidence to convict him or someone else for secret distribution of books in England. Two Puritan Ministers, John Penry and John Udal, were sentenced to death on charges that they were responsible for writing, printing or publishing books. Before the Revolutionary War colonial patriots frequently had to conceal their authorship or distribution of literature that easily could have brought down on them prosecutions by English-controlled courts. Along about that time the Letters of Junius were written and the identity of their author is unknown to this day. Even the Federalist Papers, written in favor of the adoption of our Constitution, were published under fictitious names. It is plain that anonymity has sometimes been assumed for the most constructive purposes.[4]

Justice Black's eloquence in *Talley* about the great services to freedom performed by anonymity stands in striking contrast to *Bryant v. Zimmerman,* a 1928 decision in which the Court endorsed the use of compulsory disclosure as a deterrent against the Ku Klux Klan.[5] The plaintiff in *Bryant* was charged under a New York statute requiring "every existing unincorporated association having a membership of twenty or more persons, which corporation or association requires an oath as a prerequisite or condition of membership" to file its membership list with the Secretary of State. The statute provided further that any person who became a member or attended a meeting of such an oath-bound organization knowing it had failed to file was guilty of a misdemeanor. The Supreme Court in an opinion by Justice Van Devanter upheld the compulsory registration requirement by an 8 to 1 vote; the lone dissent was on jurisdictional grounds.

At this early stage in the development of free speech doctrine no direct appeal is made to the First Amendment. The plaintiff does, however, argue in terms of "a right of association," first under the privileges and immunities clause, and then under the due process clause. The first point is summarily dismissed as not involving a federal privilege:

If to be and remain a member of a secret oath-bound association within a state be a privilege arising out of citizenship at all, it is an incident of state rather than United States citizenship.[6]

The due process contention evokes a more elaborate answer:

The relator's contention under the due process clause is that the statute deprives him of liberty in that it prevents him from exercising his right of membership in the association. But his liberty in this regard, like most other personal rights, must yield to the rightful exertion of the police power.[7]

After noting that the state has a right to be informed about the nature of organizations operating within its territory, the Court adds:

. . . requiring this information to be supplied for the public files will operate as an effective or substantial deterrent from the violations of public and private right to which the association might be tempted if such disclosure were not required.[8]

The New York statute, it will be noted, imposes the burden on all unincorporated associations without specifying characteristics other than the requirements of an oath. But when the Court turns to the plaintiff's final contention under the equal protection clause it becomes evident that the law is explicitly aimed at undesirable groups. The statute exempts certain oath-bound groups, such as labor unions, the Masons, the Knights of Columbus, etc. The Court upholds this discrimination by finding a reasonable difference between the exempt and the covered groups:

... the difference consisted (a) in a manifest tendency on the part of one class to make the secrecy surrounding its purposes and membership a cloak for acts and conduct inimical to personal rights and public welfare, and (b) in the absence of such a tendency on the part of the other class.[9]

This argument might fail today, since the Court would be more sensitive to the fact that not all "desirable" groups had been excluded by the exemption; hence the disclosure sanction as provided by the statute would be perceived as overbroad.

The more important matter, however, is the Court's readiness to hold that a group like the Klan, which "functions largely at night, its members disguised by hoods and gowns and doing things calculated to strike terror into the minds of people," could be sanctioned directly.[10] Although the point is not fully articulated, the chilling impact of the disclosure in *Bryant* is justified *not as a necessary by-product of some other proper state purpose, but as the very point of the statute.*

Bryant raises several questions that will plague the Court in later years: Must an organization, if it is to be subject to direct sanctions, rise to the evil status of a conspiracy or can organizations which in some looser sense are undesirable be reached and discouraged? Is the jurisdiction of the censor enlarged when the sanction is merely compulsory disclosure and not a criminal penalty? Is this true in any event where the deterrent impact of the disclosure is intended as a sanction? The Court does not directly engage these questions in *Bryant,* but its decision, based on a loose judicial notice of the nature of the Klan, suggests that organizations which in some sense are merely undesirable can be sanctioned directly, at least by the sanction of compulsory disclosure.

One last insight from *Bryant.* The grievance against the association, although the Klan certainly had political significance, had nothing to do with freedom of speech. It would have been confusing to force the case, as the Court will do in *Dennis,* into the mold of a conspiracy to commit a speech crime.

Disclosure and the NAACP

During the early years of the civil rights movement the Court had occasion to reconsider the propriety of the compulsory disclosure tactic in a series of cases in which Southern states—citing the use of disclosure against white supremacists in *Bryant*—sought to compel the NAACP to disclose its membership. These cases arise out of what has been called the counterattack of the South. After the school desegregation decision in *Brown v. Board of Education*[11] the South sought by various strategies to slow down and turn back the civil rights movement. One of the strategies was to seek by legal means to hobble the gadfly of the movement, the NAACP. From the vantage point of that part of the South whose social order was being unsettled, the analogy between the NAACP and the Communist Party was persuasively close—both were subversive organizations. Although the Southern legal strategists must have felt that the NAACP was a quasi-conspiracy, they did not for the most part have the daring to attack it directly. Rather, they sought nominally neutral reasons to force the NAACP to make public its membership. Thus, the chilling impact of disclosure in the NAACP cases is ostensibly a by-product of some other legitimate state purpose. But in fact these cases are—in spirit, if not in letter—instances of compulsory disclosure of membership as a direct sanction. Indeed, they strike a certain note of high comedy, because the South cannot find a strong enough "proper" rationale for disclosure of the information it seeks for improper reasons.

The Court, although it does not openly impeach official motivation, decides these cases in favor of the NAACP. The empathy for the First Amendment challenge it displays is in striking contrast to its response when the Communist Party challenges the disclosure tactic. It is tempting to join the "realist" and state the operative principle bluntly: The Communists cannot win, the NAACP cannot lose.

The first episode is *NAACP v. Alabama*[12] in 1958. Alabama initiated the controversy by moving to oust the NAACP from the state for its failure to comply with certain registration requirements for out-of-state corporations doing business in Alabama. These requirements involved filing the corporate charter with the Secretary of State and designating a place of business and an agent for service of legal process; they did not include disclosure of membership. As the controversy unfolded in the state courts, however, the requirement to supply membership lists was added, and the quarrel came to a head over the imposition of a $100,000 fine on the NAACP for refusing to do so, although it offered all other information normally requested of out-of-state corporations. The Supreme Court in a unanimous decision reversed the contempt conviction. Justice Harlan wrote the opinion.

There is at the outset a procedural nicety. The state argues that any right of associational privacy belongs to the individual members and thus the NAACP itself lacks standing to assert those rights. Justice

Harlan rejects this contention. He finds it utterly impractical to expect the individual members to make the challenge and finds the organization an appropriate representative of their claim. This answer meets the need of petitioners and perhaps it has to be put so circumlocutiously because the NAACP itself is not on the face of things the direct target. It would not seem a big step, however, to have held that the right to resist chilling of membership by disclosure was a right belonging directly to the organization as well as to its individual members.

Turning to the constitutional issue, Justice Harlan begins by endorsing association as a basic freedom:

Effective advocacy of both public and private points of view, particularly controversial ones, is undeniably enhanced by group association, as this Court has more than once recognized by remarking upon the close nexus between the freedoms of speech and assembly. It is beyond debate that freedom to engage in association for the advancement of beliefs and ideas is an inseparable aspect of the "liberty" assured by the Due Process Clause of the Fourteenth Amendment. . . . Of course it is immaterial whether the beliefs sought to be advanced by association pertain to political, economic, religious or cultural matters, and state action which may have the effect of curtailing the freedom to associate is subject to the closest scrutiny.[13]

Harlan acknowledges that Alabama "has taken no direct action to restrict the right of petitioner's members to associate freely."[14] But this does not resolve the matter, because *even "unintended" abridgements require the closest scrutiny.* That disclosure of membership may produce such abridgement of associational freedoms is, he thinks, obvious. "It is hardly a novel perception," he writes, "that compelled disclosure of affiliation with groups engaged in advocacy may constitute as effective a restraint on freedom of association" as various other sorts of sanctions.[15] He notes the example of adherents of a particular religion or political party being compelled to wear identifying arm bands, and adds:

Compelled disclosure of membership in an organization engaged in advocacy of particular beliefs is of the same order. Inviolability of privacy in group association may in many circumstances be indispensable to preservation of freedom of association, particularly where a group espouses dissident beliefs.[16]

Justice Harlan proceeds to bring the argument to its inexorable conclusion. There is no doubt under the circumstances of the day that disclosure will have a heavy deterrent impact on the NAACP in Alabama. It is immaterial that the inhibiting pressures will come from private action since the government action has triggered the social response. Such impact on associational freedoms can only be justified, writes Harlan, if the state has "a subordinating interest which is compelling."[17] That is not the case in this instance. Weighing the ostensible state interest against the deterrent impact, he finds that the scales tip decisively in favor the NAACP.

The game between the South and the Court is replayed in *Bates v. Little Rock*[18] in 1960. At issue are two identical ordinances levying a license tax on corporations doing business within the municipal limits of two Arkansas cities. The ordinances, which had had unexceptionable lives for years, were amended in 1957 to require the furnishing of additional information, including the purpose of the corporation, the names of its officers, and a full financial statement "including dues, fees, assessments and/or contributions paid, by whom, and the date thereof." The NAACP officials who were custodians of its records were fined for their noncompliance and the appeal of the fine worked its way to the Supreme Court. Again, the Court unanimously reversed the conviction. Justice Stewart wrote the opinion of the Court; and Justices Black and Douglas appended a brief concurring opinion arguing that the right of association is beyond abridgement, direct or indirect.

The logic of Justice Stewart's opinion is the same as that of the Harlan opinion in *NAACP v. Alabama,* which he quotes at length. What is remarkable is how readily and emphatically the Court in these cases endorses what might be thought a "social science" insight. The harm here is after all not the product of a conventional sanction but the consequence of a behavioral sequence. "Freedoms such as these," Justice Stewart tells us, "are protected not only against heavy-handed frontal attack, but also from being stifled by more subtle governmental interference."[19]

The case is, of course, easy. There is simply no connection between the state's ostensible interest in taxation and information as to the identities of the organization's members. Any kind of balancing test would end up in the NAACP's favor. Justice Stewart restates with force the balancing formula from *Alabama:*

Decision in this case must finally turn. . . on whether the cities as instrumentalities of the State have demonstrated so cogent an interest in obtaining and making public the membership lists of these organizations as to justify the substantial abridgement of associational freedom which such disclosures will effect. Where there is a significant encroachment upon personal liberty, the State may prevail only upon showing a subordinating interest which is compelling.[20]

Shelton v. Tucker[21] in 1960 comes at the disclosure problem from a different angle and furnishes a major precedent for other purposes. This time the state does not address itself to the NAACP at all, and superficially not even to NAACP membership. Yet it is apparent that Arkansas has engaged in one more gesture of harassment of the organization.[22] In form the Arkansas law requires that each school-teacher disclose all organizations to which he has belonged in the last five years. The Court is thus at the threshold of a genuine difficulty, for the state's nominal interest is persuasive—a concern with teacher qualifications and dedication. Hence the formula of *Alabama* and *Bates* will not work. Moreover, the Court has steadfastly declined to impeach official motivation, a policy of general importance not to be set aside lightly. Can it then, consistently with other precedents and values, protect against this compulsion to disclose NAACP membership to a hostile audience?

The dilemma splits the Court. The disclosure is again frustrated, but only by a 5 to 4 decision, with Justices Frankfurter and Harlan filing vigorous dissents. Justice Stewart, for the majority, concedes that *Alabama* and *Bates* do not control the case, for in this instance "there can be no question of the relevance of a State's inquiry into the fitness and competence of its teachers."[23] Rather, he finds the constitutional flaw in the sheer diseconomy of the state's method of inquiry. He relies on the series of public forum cases—such as *Lovell* and *Schneider*[24]—in which the Court invalidated flat bans on the distribution of handbills in the interest of preventing littering:

In a series of decisions this Court has held that, even though the governmental purpose be legitimate and substantial, that purpose cannot be pursued by means that broadly stifle fundamental personal liberties when the end can be more narrowly achieved. The breadth of legislative abridgement must be viewed *in the light of less drastic means for achieving the same basic purpose* . . . .[25] [Emphasis added.]

He concludes:

The unlimited and indiscriminate sweep of the statute now before us brings it within the ban of our prior cases. The statute's comprehensive interference with associational freedom goes far beyond what might be justified in the exercise of the State's legitimate inquiry into the fitness and competency of its teachers.[26]

The Court is thus once again able to defeat the Southern tactics without openly impeaching official motivation. And in the process it adds a powerful new tool to its arsenal: even where the state's interest is legitimate and substantial, it cannot be pursued by unnecessarily broad means. This economy principle complements the balancing formula fashioned in *Alabama* and *Bates*. The state could cure the evil of breadth found in *Shelton* by asking only whether the employee was a member of the NAACP. But were it to do so, it would confront the difficulty that it has no legitimate interest in this information and the balancing rule of *Alabama* and *Bates* would apply.

Thus, the Court by one means or another manages in each instance to protect the NAACP from the demand for its membership lists. The impression left by this sequence of cases is that the Court is acutely sensitive to the First Amendment values implicated in the use of compulsory disclosure as a group sanction. Yet in a roughly contemporaneous decision virtually the same Court characterizes a challenge by the Communist Party to an official demand for disclosure of its membership as "a travesty" of the First Amendment. It is to that case—*Communist Party v. Subversive Activities Control Board*[27]—that we now turn.

20

Compulsory Disclosure as a Group Sanction: The *SACB* Case

We have commented several times on the ironies of timing in the flow of cases to the Supreme Court. The process is obviously complex and is influenced by a variety of factors. But whatever the causes, the results are clear: cases can come to the Court at the wrong time. In the area of First Amendment law the supreme example of a case out of its proper time is *Communist Party v. Subversive Activities Control Board*,[1] decided in 1961.

SACB should have been the architectonic case for freedom of association. It involved a complex government strategy—the Subversive Activities Control Act—that was explicitly aimed at sanctioning association and thus openly posed the issue that had been disguised as a speech problem in *Dennis*. It was the paradigm of the anti-Communist legal strategies which had dominated the 1940s and 1950s. It was in a real sense the major government attack on Communism in the United States and hence a political development of high import. And it evoked some 212 pages of opinions from the justices. Yet it comes too late. As the Court goes through its elaborate reasonings, there is the sense that no one is listening any longer. None of the excitement that greeted *Dennis* attends *SACB;* it invites relatively little commentary and today plays only a minor role in the casebooks on which lawyers are trained. It is treated as outside the mainstream of First Amendment precedent; it involved legislation so specifically tailored to hit the Communist Party that it seems to have been thought of as limited to that one question. Hence, as the Communist issue has receded, so too has the salience of *SACB*. Moreover, the length, tedium, and complexity of the opinions have deterred most lawyers from anything but the most casual acquaintance with the case. Yet it is quite possibly the precedent which carries the greatest threat to political freedoms in the future. Any effort to map the work of the Court in building a tradition around the First Amendment must allow it a central place.

The Subversive Activities Control Act

The statutory scheme is complicated. After an elaborate preamble of legislative findings about the dangers of the worldwide Communist movement, the Act defines two categories of organizations, "Communist-action" and "Communist-front." The Attorney General is empowered to initiate proceedings against a suspect organization which is then, in effect, "tried" before the Subversive Activities Control Board, an administrative agency created by the Act. If the organization is found after the hearing to be an improper organization, the Board enters an order requiring it to register as such with the Attorney General. Normal appeals to the courts are provided for, but once the registration order becomes final a series of satellite sanctions against the organization and its members come into play. Also, curiously severe penalties are provided for failure to register after an order has been entered; each day of failure is treated as a separate offense subject to a $10,000 fine.[2] Subsequent to registration distinctions are drawn in the treatment of "Communist-action" and "Communist-front" organizations. The key distinction is that action groups are required to disclose the names of both officers and members, while front groups are required to disclose only the names of officers. Finally, both action and front groups are required to provide a full financial accounting and a listing of all printing presses in the possession of the group or its members.

The various satellite sanctions imposed after the registration order becomes final leave one with a mixed impression of a rational effort to inhibit the Party and sheer Congressional petulance. There are a dozen different disabilities.

(i) Use of the mails is forbidden the organization unless the publication and envelope bear the legend: "Disseminated by [organization's name], a Communist organization."

(ii) There is a parallel prohibition of broadcasting unless the message is preceded by the announcement: "The following program is sponsored by [organization's name], a Communist organization."

(iii) The organization loses any federal income tax exemption it might have had; and, correlatively, contributions to it are not deductible.

(iv) There is a ban on the giving of classified information by any employee of the federal government to any member of such an organization; and as a correlative, it is unlawful for any member of such an organization to receive classified information.

(v) It is made unlawful for any member of such an organization to be employed by the United States. (This provision is worded to ban employment or the holding of "non-elective office." With an interesting sense of delicacy, it thus leaves open the possibility of holding elective office, which perhaps indicates the lawmakers' uneasiness about the premises of the whole enterprise.)

(vi) Members of action groups are barred from employment "in any defense facility." Members of front groups are required to disclose their membership in the organization "in seeking, accepting or holding employment in any defense facility."

(vii) It is made unlawful for any member of such an organization to be employed by any labor organization as defined by the National Labor Relations Act.

(viii) It is made a crime for a member of either an action or a front group to apply for a passport. In the case of a member of an action group, it is made a crime for any officer or employee of the United States knowingly to issue him a passport.

(ix) Aliens who have been members of such an organization "during the time it is registered or required to be registered" are ineligible for visas, excluded from admission to the United States, and, if in the United States, made subject to deportation.

(x) There is a provision barring from naturalization anyone who within the ten years prior has been a member of such an organization.

(xi) A parallel provision renders subject to revocation the naturalization of anyone who within five years after being naturalized becomes a member of such an organization. Membership is to be regarded as "*prima facie* evidence that such person was not attached to the principles of the Constitution," and, in the absence of countervailing evidence, is a sufficient basis for denaturalization.

(xii) The disabilities are also extended to the Social Security Act. Employment by such an organization does not count as employment for the purposes of Social Security.

One last detail. Anticipating self-incrimination problems in the compulsion to register, Section 4(f) of the Act provides that member-ship *per se* in a Communist organization shall not constitute a violation of the penal provisions of the Act "or of any other criminal statute," and further that the fact of registration shall not be received in evidence in any prosecution.

The Act thus brings to bear three different types of sanctions on a "Communist-action" group: (i) compulsory disclosure of member-ship; (ii) official stigmatization as a subversive group; and (iii) an extended set of special disabilities. Each of these provides a predicate for First Amendment challenge; and taken together as an articulated scheme, the combined impact of the three forms of sanction provides a further basis for First Amendment controversy.

It will serve to bring this scheme into sharper focus if we compare it to the Smith Act. There the conspiracy was pursued with criminal sanctions; it was defined in terms of planning to commit a speech crime; and active, knowing, evilly intended membership in the group subjected the individual member to criminal responsibility for the group offense. Here, by contrast, the conspiracy is more elaborately and less stringently defined; it is pursued by means of non-criminal sanctions—disclosure, stigmatization, and various disabilities; and membership in the group subjects the member to these sanctions. The upshot is that the new law still imposes sanctions on groups as "conspiracies," but the idiom of conspiracy has been dropped and the sanctions are complex and non-criminal. Equally important—and indeed a step forward in making clear what the controversy between the Party and the government is really about—the evil of the group is seen as residing not in group speech but in potential group action.

Although the *SACB* case deals only with the constitutionality of the Act as applied to "Communist-action" organizations, we should also say a few words about the application of the Act to "Communist-front" groups. For this aspect of the Act is arguably its most disturbing feature.

One of the congressional findings in support of the Act was that the Communist movement operates through "front" organizations created so as to conceal their true character, with the result that the "fronts" are able "to obtain support from persons who would not extend their support if they knew the nature of the organizations with which they dealt." The Act defines "front" organizations as those which are "substantially directed, dominated, or controlled by a Communist-action organization" and are "primarily operated for the purpose of giving aid and support to a Communist-action organization,

a Communist foreign government, or the world Communist movement." Such organizations are subject to registration and the consequent publicity; and although, unlike action organizations, they are
not required to disclose their membership, many of the satellite sanctions apply equally to them.

The potential reach of these provisions into ordinary political life
is enormous. We are no longer dealing with the relatively rigorously
profiled "conspiracy" of the Communist Party, which, after all,
touched only a tiny minority of Americans. The "front" provisions of
the Act bring within the purview of the law a large number of organizations which on the surface espouse liberal causes. The screening of
these organizations to see whether they are dominated by a "Communist-action" group must affect a sizeable fraction of the population.
Whatever the difficulties of defining the "action" group so as to delimit the target in deference to First Amendment values, they are
increased enormously when attention moves to the "front" group.

It is dismal to note how many grades of conspiracy the law has
now worked out: (i) conspiracy to overthrow the government by force;
(ii) conspiracy in the *Yates* sense of incitement now to overthrow at
some propitious future date; (iii) conspiracy in the SACA sense of a
Communist-*action* organization; and (iv) conspiracy in the sense of a
Communist-*front* organization.

It is a final irony in the crazy sequence of these issues to the Court
that in the mid-1960s it chooses on several occasions to postpone
confronting the validity of the Communist front provisions of the
Act—chooses, that is, to leave this vitally important ambiguity unresolved. We shall take these cases up in the next chapter.

The Posture of the Issues

The background of the 1961 case is convoluted. The apparently simple factual issue of whether the Communist Party, the existence of
which had inspired the statute, was indeed a "Communist-action"
organization within the terms of the statute was to take eleven years
to put to rest with an affirmative answer. The Attorney General had
initiated proceedings in 1950 to compel the registration of the Party.
Hearings before the Board took more than a year and produced a
record of over fourteen thousand pages. It then took the Board almost
a year to make its decision and write its report which it issued in 1953.
While the appeal was pending the Party moved to adduce additional
evidence to show that three key government witnesses had committed

perjury in their testimony before the Board. The Court of Appeals denied the motion, and the appeal on that question was taken to the Supreme Court. In *Communist Party v. Subversive Activities Control Board*[3] in 1956 the Supreme Court reversed the Court of Appeals and remanded the case to the Board to make certain that it had based its findings on untainted evidence. In an opinion by Justice Frankfurter, the Court said that it was acting out of "a fastidious regard for the honor of the administration of justice." The Board, acting pursuant to the remand, issued a modified report at the end of 1956 expunging the alleged perjury and reaffirming its conclusion that the Communist Party was a "Communist action" group. A second appeal on various evidentiary rulings by the Board was successful in the Court of Appeals and the case was once again remanded to the Board. After a further hearing the Board—for the third time—issued its decision and report. It is this adjudication by the Board which is the subject of the 1961 Supreme Court decision.

One cannot recite this history without feeling some ambivalence about the performance of the legal system. On one hand, one feels admiration for the impartiality and integrity that will deal so patiently with the procedural and evidentiary challenges of so hated and disfavored a challenger. On the other, it is surely comic that a law designed to provide urgent protection against domestic subversion should require more than a decade to gain final approval.

When the controversy finally reaches the Supreme Court in 1961 the Court by a vote of 5 to 4 upholds the constitutionality of the Board's order requiring the Party to register. The majority opinion is a 115-page essay by Justice Frankfurter which embodies both the best and the most debatable features of his judicial work. There are dissents by Chief Justice Warren and Justices Black, Brennan, and Douglas.

It is noteworthy that the Court hands down its decision in *SACB* on the same day that it announces its decision in *Scales*. Surely these are the Court's two basic statements on freedom of association. They are complementary. One covers the range of permissible regulation of groups when the sanction is criminal; the other when the sanction is non-criminal. And both precedents are established in the teeth of vigorous dissents by Warren, Black, Brennan, and Douglas.

In *SACB* the justices divide on three kinds of issues: (i) a series of evidentiary points; (ii) whether the compulsory registration requirement violates the Fifth Amendment privilege against self-incrimination; and (iii) whether the Act, in any of several ways, infringes First

Amendment rights. Our primary concern, of course, is with (iii), but the pattern among the justices on the other points requires some comment, for it tends to obscure the First Amendment issues and to make it difficult to locate the heart of the controversy.

The case is skewed, above all, by Justice Frankfurter's insistence on not reaching questions that are in his view prematurely raised. He rules that neither the Fifth Amendment challenge nor the challenge to the various satellite sanctions is ripe for decision and hence postpones consideration of these issues for another day. The Fifth Amendment challenge had been aimed at the order to register and at a provision of the Act which required the officers of a designated organization to register it in the event that the organization itself failed to do so. With respect to the challenge to the latter provision, Justice Frankfurter tells us:

. . . it is prematurely raised in the present proceeding. The duties imposed by those provisions will not arise until and unless the Party fails to register. At this time their application is wholly contingent and conjectural.[4]

Surely the contingency and conjecture are unreal here. The Fifth Amendment claim, as the dissenters forcefully argue, is a serious and substantial one. If successful, it would obviate the need to disclose membership—surely an important stake for both the government and the Party. Moreover, the Act itself is predicated on the legislative finding that the Party is a dedicated group of subversives deeply hostile to the United States government, and Frankfurter accepts that finding without reservations.[5] Under the circumstances to treat as conjectural whether the Party will elect to comply voluntarily with the registration requirement is fantasy. And Justice Frankfurter's resort to it must involve an exercise in political diplomacy, an effort to forestall public and congressional criticism of the Court. By tabling the Fifth Amendment issue he achieves the appearance for the moment of having the Court render an anti-Communist decision in an undiluted form.

Even less realistic is Frankfurter's refusal to consider the satellite sanctions. These become operative once the order to register has become final and do not depend on whether registration is forthcoming; the order is final once the Supreme Court renders its decision. Frankfurter relies heavily on the precedent set in *Electric Bond & Share Co. v. Securities Exchange Commission,*[6] a 1938 decision involving the constitutionality of the Public Utilities Holding Company Act, a New

Deal reform measure. There are structural analogies between the two statutes in that both involve a registration step as a prelude to the operation of satellite sanctions. In the *Electric Bond & Share* case the Court rejected as premature issues as to the constitutional status of the satellite sanctions. Thus, Frankfurter is nicely consistent when he insists that a case involving economic liberties is dispositive of parallel issues in a case involving political liberties. This, however, does not save him from looking foolish:

We do not know that, after such an order is in effect, the Party will wish to utilize the mails or any instrumentality of interstate commerce for the circulation of its publications. . . . It is wholly speculative now to foreshadow whether, or under what conditions, a member of the Party may in the future apply for a passport, or seek government or defense-facility or labor union employment, or, being an alien, become a party to a naturalization or a denaturalization proceeding. None of these things may happen.[7]

The vulnerabilities of the Frankfurter stance are not overlooked by Justice Black in dissent:

All of these enormous burdens, which are necessarily imposed upon the Party and its members by the act of registration, are dismissed by the Court on the basis of an alleged conflict with the Court-created rule that constitutional questions should be avoided whenever possible. Thus, the Court engages in extended discussions as to whether the people involved will ever want to do the things the Act says they cannot do and whether they will ever object to doing the things the Act says they must do, suggesting among other things, that the members of the Communist Party may never object to providing the evidence needed to send them to prison for violating the Smith Act; that they may never protest because they are forced to give up tax deductions that other people receive; that they may be willing to stamp all the Party's mail as coming from an evil organization; that they may never want to hold the jobs from which the Act disqualifies them; and that they may never want to get a passport to get out of the country. On the basis of all these "uncertainties" the Court seems to consider its hands tied because, it says, these are as yet only potential impairments of constitutional rights. In its view, there is no "justiciable" issue at all between the United States and the Communist Party except the bare requirement of registration.[8]

The controversy is further skewed by the strategies of the dissenters. Although the case is, as we see it, a great confrontation over freedom of association, only Justice Black pitches his dissent to this theme. The other dissenters attack the Frankfurter opinion along different fronts.

Chief Justice Warren argues for abstaining from *any* of the constitutional issues. Instead he would reverse the Board's order for errors in construing the Act and ruling on evidence. Yet ironically it is Warren who in the context of statutory construction most clearly makes the point we regard as central: all *direct* sanctions, non-criminal as well as criminal, should be judged by the same constitutional standards.

The Act defines an "action" group as one which "operates primarily to advance the objectives" of the world Communist movement. It does not, however, provide an explicit definition of those "objectives." The Court of Appeals adopted a construction which included the objective of the "overthrow of existing government by any means necessary, including force and violence."[9] The Party argued that this must be read as reaching only illegal advocacy as defined by *Yates.* The Board had failed to do so, it contended, and hence its order to register was not supported by its findings.

Justice Frankfurter flatly rejects this argument on the ground that the Act does not involve direct sanctions: "The Subversive Activities Control Act is a regulatory, not a prohibitory statute. It does not make unlawful pursuit of the objectives which [section] 2 defines."[10] Hence *Yates* does not apply.

Warren counters that the Party's argument is "eminently correct."[11] He argues, in effect, that the jurisdictions of non-criminal sanctions, such as those provided by the SACA, and criminal sanctions, such as those provided by the Smith Act, should be one and the same: "the Court should hold that the Board cannot require a group to register as a Communist-action organization unless it first finds that the organization is engaged in advocacy aimed at inciting action."[12] He continues:

. . . it blinks reality to say that this statute is not prohibitory. There can be little doubt that the registration provisions of the statute and the harsh sanctions which are automatically imposed after an order to register has been issued make this Act as prohibitory as any criminal statute.[13]

He would thus remand the case in order to have the Board determine whether the Party is "engaging in advocacy aimed at inciting the forceful overthrow of Government."[14]

The balance of Warren's opinion is devoted to a series of points about the handling of the evidence. As a result, a goodly fraction of the total Court opinions is taken up by a debate between Warren and Frankfurter. Like the Court's 1956 remand of the perjury challenge, this has the uncanny effect of solemnizing the nominal issue of fact here: is the Communist Party a Communist-action organization? To my taste, the essential flaw in the Frankfurter-Warren response to the basic confrontation posed by the case is that they treat it as though it were primarily a tough issue of fact like a murder case so that the primary obligation of the Court is to show fastidious regard for procedural regularity in finding the facts.

Looking back on *SACB* now, one is moved to say in tribute that only Justice Black perceived the major import of the case for the First Amendment tradition. Justices Brennan and Douglas elect to concentrate their dissents on the Fifth Amendment claim and not along First Amendment lines. There is force to their position, and, as we shall see, it will prevail in *Albertson v. Subversive Activities Control Board* [15] several years later. But like Chief Justice Warren's insistence on resting on evidence points, it strikes me as somewhat imprudent. Their move does not, however, appear to be tactical. Nor is it simply that they would prefer to argue the easier point first. They focus on the Fifth Amendment issue because they feel forced to concede the First Amendment issue. Since Justices Douglas and Brennan have been singularly empathetic in their response to First Amendment challenges over the years, this is a datum of high importance for us.

As I see it, there are four distinct First Amendment issues posed by the case:

(i) The official use of stigma as a sanction.

(ii) The use of Communist positions on public issues as evidence of foreign control and domination.

(iii) The impact of the *total* strategy of the Act as an effort to *outlaw* the Party.

(iv) The use of compulsory disclosure of membership as a sanction against an association not charged as a criminal conspiracy.

The majority opinion acknowledges only (iv) as a First Amendment issue and does not speak directly to the First Amendment implications of issues (i), (ii), and (iii). Nor do Justices Brennan and Douglas address these issues; they too treat the case as though compulsory disclosure was the only First Amendment issue generated by the Act. Even Justice Black, who is admirable in his direct perception of (iii) and (iv) as issues, pays only glancing attention to (i) and (ii).

Stigmatization

We can dispose of the stigma issue briefly at this point; we will return to it in the next chapter. A little noticed feature of the Act is that, altogether apart from registration, it envisages a final solemn public adjudication, after hearing, that a political group is "evil." It represents a sort of Pure Food and Drug venture into the political sphere; under an elaborate procedure the government is now empowered to *label* political groups. It is true of course that moral condemnation has often been remarked upon as a function of the criminal law. The finding that a man is guilty of murder or perjury or fraud is not only a step toward the use of criminal sanctions; it is also a statement about the man. But under our traditions the legal process has never been employed solely for the purpose of attaching the condemnatory label; whatever condemnation has resulted has normally been a by-product of the application of criminal sanctions.

More important, the Act is not keyed to the premise that a Communist-action or a Communist-front group is a criminal enterprise, a criminal conspiracy. The Act was surely conceived by its proponents as complementing, not repealing and replacing, the Smith Act. It does not involve establishing that an organization which falls within its terms is a criminal conspiracy to commit a speech crime in the careful sense the Court worked out in *Yates* and far less that it is a literal conspiracy to overthrow the government. The Act thus takes a step in a dangerous direction. It creates a twilight zone in which disfavored political groups, not reachable by criminal law, can be defamed out of existence by official government action.

Only Justice Black addresses this point. In an earlier case—*Viereck v. United States* in 1943—Black, dissenting, had strongly supported the disclosure requirements of the Foreign Agents Registration Act.[16] Adopted on the eve of World War II, that Act requires anyone acting in a public relations capacity for "a foreign principal" to register with the Secretary of State and at regular intervals thereafter to provide information regarding his role as publicist. In attempting to distinguish the SACA registration requirement, Black emphasizes the different way this registration-cum-sanction works:

When Viereck registered under the earlier and genuine registration statute [the Foreign Agents Registration Act], he was not thereby branded as being engaged in an evil, despicable undertaking bent on destroying this Nation. But that is precisely the effect of the present Act.[17]

He then proceeds to recite the characteristics which the Act ascribes to a Communist-action organization and its members: disloyalty; foreign domination; use of espionage; sabotage, treachery, deceit, etc. Later in his dissent he restates the point, arguing that the purposes of a legitimate registration statute—"the need of Government to provide means by which the people can obtain useful information"—can "certainly be accomplished without resort to official legislative pronouncements as to the treasonable nature of those compelled to register."[18]

It is regrettable that the Court did not confront this issue squarely. Perhaps the sanction of official stigmatization should be available to government under special circumstances. It may indeed be one kind of legal answer to the problem of the almost-conspiracy which so vexed Justice Jackson in *Dennis*. But if so, it is imperative that the special circumstances under which its use is constitutionally permissible be stated with the same care that was displayed in *Yates* and, it should be added, handled with the same awareness and concern that the government is trenching on the uttermost limits of tolerable political censorship.

Party Positions as Proof of Foreign Domination

The First Amendment issue everyone ignored—the use of Party positions on public issues as evidence of Soviet domination—also strikes me as being of major import. The government was required by the Act to show that the organization was under the control and domination of "the foreign government controlling the world Communist movement." One line of proof authorized by the Act was consideration of "the extent to which its views and policies do not deviate" from those of that foreign government. In brief, the Act made official use of the logic that Senator Joseph McCarthy had employed so vigorously, namely, testing the loyalty of a person by tracing the number of public issues on which his views coincide with those of the Soviet Union. In the gross form used by McCarthy it was enough to kill any position to show that the Soviets had endorsed it. Its use in the *SACB* case was far more circumspect and rational. The Government put on an expert witness, Dr. Moseley of Columbia University, who testified that he had examined the position of the Party on forty-five major international issues over thirty years and had found no substantial deviation between the Party position and that taken by the Soviet Union.

The Party challenged this line of proof, but only on narrow evidentiary grounds. It contended that the Board had made two errors in its handling of the evidence of non-deviation. First, it had not required the Government to show that the Party took its position on a given issue "subsequently to, and not independently of" the announced Soviet policy. In fact, the Party argued, in many of the instances cited by Moseley the statement of the Party position was made prior to that of the Soviet Union. Second, the Board had refused to let the Party introduce evidence to show that many non-Communists shared the views of the Party and the Soviets on particular issues.

Justice Frankfurter responds by arguing that the inference of foreign control from such a pattern of parallelism was rational and that the Board was not required to hear the Party's evidence in rebuttal. The dissenters are apparently satisfied with this answer.[19] The attitude of the Court is evident in the following passage from Frankfurter's opinion:

> The most that the Party could have proved, had it been allowed to make the offered showings, was that on the subject of each specific, isolated one among the forty-five international issues enumerated, a considerable number of persons not Soviet-dominated took positions parallel to those of the Soviet and the Party. This is only to be expected in the case of issues of this character. The Party never offered to show, despite wide latitude allowed by the hearing panel . . . that a continuing substantial body of independent groups and persons concurred with the Party on a significant aggregate number of policies among the forty-five.[20]

The Court thus ratified, without even seeming to be aware of it, a devastating technique for chilling discussion of public issues. It gave the Communist Party the power to capture any public issue it wished simply by embracing one side of it. The Government was announcing publicly that the way to stay out of trouble was to avoid taking the Soviet side of any public issue on which the Soviet Union had expressed an opinion. We are not told what the forty-five issues were, but Justice Frankfurter discloses some in a footnote. Among them are the North Atlantic Pact, the control of atomic energy, the election of Yugoslavia to the Security Council, the seating of Communist China in the United Nations, the case of Cardinal Mindszenty, and peace in Korea.

The point does not really depend upon whether, if the sample is good enough and the coincidence of views is high enough, an inference of non-independent thinking or worse may logically be ascribed to the group. It is rather that such a line of proof can never be worth what the legal system must pay for it in First Amendment values. It is difficult to think of any step more miseducating of public tolerance, more in contradiction of the traditions of the First Amendment, than this. It is a scandal that it passes unnoticed in the two hundred pages of judicial opinion in *SACB*.

The Total Impact of the Act: An Effort to Outlaw the Party?

The first of the First Amendment issues evokes considerable attention and argument from Justice Black. The question is whether the Act must not be appraised as an effort to *outlaw* the Party. It is not necessarily bad if it is such an effort, but the Court must pass upon the issue: *Under the First Amendment can an organization which is not a criminal conspiracy be outlawed by the use of other sanctions?*

The "outlawry" challenge depends upon viewing the Act, as its sponsors had surely intended, as a single coherent strategy for crippling the Party. For this purpose the Act must be considered as a whole. It does not merely impose upon the Party the burdens of registration and disclosure; it also officially labels it as evil and subjects it to a host of satellite sanctions. To evaluate the constitutionality of the Act its sanctions must be added up and weighed in the aggregate. The fundamental flaw of Justice Frankfurter's analysis is that he insists on atomizing the statute into separate, discrete steps, each of which he either evaluates in isolation or finds justification for not passing on now. Thus, he never confronts the cumulative impact of the Act.

His avoidance of the "outlawry" challenge is facilitated by the odd way the defendants elected to argue the point. The Party sought to build its argument upon the remarkably stringent penalty provisions which treated each day of non-registration as a new offense subject to a $10,000 fine. They argued that the Act considered as a whole was so onerous that it was never the real motivation of Congress that the Party come under it and register; rather, the hope was that the Party could not afford to register and that it would thus be placed in a position where it could be fined out of existence. Frankfurter acknowledges that the issue raised by the Party's "conspiracy" thesis is ripe:

Our determination that in the present proceeding all questions are premature which regard only the constitutionality of the various particular consequences of a registration order to a registered organization and its members,
does not foreclose the Party from arguing—and it does argue—that in light
of the cumulative effect of those consequences the registration provisions of
[section] 7 are not what they seem, but represent a legislative attempt, by
devious means, to "outlaw" the Party.[21]

Frankfurter finds the argument in this narrow form easy to meet. He
reviews the various satellite disabilities and finds a rational regulatory
purpose in them. "None of this," he writes, "is so lacking in conso-
nance as to suggest a clandestine purpose behind the registration
provisions"[22]; the Act is not "a ruse by Congress to evade constitutional safeguards."[23]

    In retrospect this may mark the critical step in his reasoning
about the constitutional status of the Act. He appears to have met the
brunt of the outlawry challenge. But he has met it *only* as it bears on
Congressional motivation to enact "a mere pressuring device meant
to catch an organization between two fires."[24] Let us agree *arguendo*
that the Party is unpersuasive about Congressional motivation and
that Congress honestly expected the Party to register. This does *not*
answer the key question of whether Congress can levy a coordinated
scheme of sanctions—disclosure, stigma, and various disabilities—
against an association without impairing First Amendment rights.
Perhaps the rhetoric of "outlawry" has thrown the argument out of
focus. There was much Congressional debate at the time about
whether Congress should "outlaw" the Party and a final decision not
to do so directly. Justice Frankfurter speaks of "the crucial constitutional significance of what Congress did when it rejected the approach
of outlawing the Party by name and accepted instead a statutory
program regulating not enumerated organizations but designated activities."[25]

    Whether or not Congress thought it was avoiding outlawry by
regulating only specific activities of the organization's membership,
such as use of the mails, travel, and employment, when all these
moves are made in a single legislative measure and are directed not
at the activities in general but only at those activities when done by
the members of the organization, there is, I submit, no way to evaluate
the First Amendment challenge without considering the scheme as a
whole and adding up the sanctions.

    What is so distressing about Justice Frankfurter's ingenuity in avoiding the challenge is that it is by no means clear that the challenge would or should prevail. A powerful argument can be made for sanctioning in this complex way an organization with the attributes which the Board after hearing has attached to the Party. It is, however, a disservice to refuse to face the question and answer it openly.

The major virtue of Justice Black's dissent is that he sees this point so clearly and aims his fire so powerfully at it. He emphasizes that it is freedom of association that is at stake:

The freedom to advocate ideas about public matters through associations of the nature of political parties and societies was contemplated and protected by the First Amendment. The existence of such groups is now, and for centuries has been, a necessary part of any effective promulgation of beliefs about governmental policies. And the destruction of such groups is now and always has been one of the first steps totalitarian governments take.[26]

As he sees it, the Act, however, parsed, is tantamount to outlawry: "The plan of the Act is to make it impossible for an organization to continue to function once a registration order is issued against it."[27] He notes the "crushing" penalty provisions and continues:

Having thus made it mandatory that Communist organizations and individual Communists make a full disclosure of their identities and activities, the Act then proceeds to heap burden after burden upon those so exposed.[28]

He then inventories the satellite sanctions and observes:

The Act thus makes it extremely difficult for a member of the Communist Party to live in this country and, at the same time, makes it a crime for him to try to get a passport to get out.[29]

In his view, the "outlawry" of the Party effected by the Act cannot be reconciled with the First Amendment:

The question under that Amendment is whether Congress has power to outlaw an association, group or party either on the ground that it advocates a policy of violent overthrow of the existing Government at some time in the distant future or on the ground that it is ideologically subservient to some foreign country. In my judgment, neither of these factors justifies an invasion of rights protected by the First Amendment.[30]

Justices Black and Frankfurter were famous adversaries over their long and distinguished careers on the Court. However one finally totals the score on all of their encounters, this time it is difficult to see how Frankfurter could have failed to hear Black's point.

Compulsory Disclosure

Having made our way through the thicket of other issues generated by *SACB*, we can now return to our point of departure—the controversy over compulsory disclosure of membership. The question is: May the state employ disclosure of membership as a *direct* sanction against a disfavored group? That is, may the state compel disclosure when it *intends* that the disclosure will generate social pressures to inhibit and discourage membership in the group?

It is important to distinguish this question from the quite different question raised by disclosure for some other purpose which as a by-product has the effect of inhibiting and chilling membership. When disclosure is intended as a direct sanction, I see little, if any, difference in terms of First Amendment concerns between it and any other sanction, be it a criminal penalty or, as in *New York Times v. Sullivan*, [31] say, tort damages. The jurisdiction of censorship should be the same for all direct sanctions. The central concern of the Amendment is with state action aimed directly at discouraging speech or association; the precise tactic used by the state for this purpose is something of a technical detail. On this view, a critical precedent on the disclosure issue in *SACB* would be *Yates*, in which the Court had so painstakingly defined the parameters of censorship of groups advocating violent overthrow of the government. Yet neither Justice Frankfurter for the Court nor Justice Black in dissent positions the argument this way, and neither makes use of *Yates*.

Justice Frankfurter, having worked so long and hard to strip the controversy of all other issues, is finally set at the end of his lengthy opinion to address the validity of the registration order. His conclusion is that there is absolutely no First Amendment difficulty:

The Communist Party would have us hold that the First Amendment prohibits Congress from requiring the registration and filing of information, including membership lists, by organizations substantially dominated or controlled by the foreign powers controlling the world Communist movement and which operate primarily to advance the objectives of that movement: the overthrow of existing government by any means necessary and the establishment in its place of a Communist totalitarian dictatorship. We cannot find such a prohibition in the First Amendment. So to find would make a travesty of that Amendment and the great ends for the well-being of our democracy that it serves.[32]

Not since the World War I cases have we heard the Court characterize a First Amendment challenge as a "travesty" of the Amendment.

The problem is not with the registration step, which, standing alone, is at most a nuisance, but with the disclosure of membership. Justice Frankfurter readily acknowledges that the Court in the NAACP membership cases was sensitive and responsive to the need of organizations for privacy. He also concedes that disclosure of membership "may in certain instances infringe constitutionally protected rights of association." But he stresses that this alone does not dispose of the case; it is rather only "one of the points of reference from which analysis must begin."[33]

The test on his view is the balancing of interests. This was the explicit formula in the NAACP cases. But his reliance on those precedents here is troubling in two respects. First, he restates them in a narrow and ungenerous fashion. He does not quote Justice Harlan's rhetoric in *NAACP v. Alabama* about the deep values of associational privacy. Nor does he mention the stringent balancing formula fashioned in that case and *Bates v. Alabama.* That formula, it will be recalled, required that in order to justify the chilling impact of disclosure on freedom of association the state must show "a subordinating interest which is compelling."[34] Justice Frankfurter's test is a good deal less demanding:

Against the impediments which particular governmental regulation causes to entire freedom of individual action, there must be weighed the value to the public of the ends which the regulation may achieve.[35]

No doubt Frankfurter could, on his view of the posture of the issues, have met the more stringent test; the different phrasing of his test is perhaps no more than a rhetorical nuance. But it is a nuance pointing in the wrong direction.

Second and more important, the NAACP cases, on the surface at least, did not involve efforts to impose direct sanctions on the organization. The Court had taken the South at its word when it claimed that the inhibiting impact on freedom of association was an unintended by-product of efforts to obtain disclosure for other, legitimate state

purposes. Thus, Justice Frankfurter's use of a balancing test to determine the constitutionality of disclosure as a *direct* sanction in *SACB*
requires a considerable step which he does not openly acknowledge.
Indeed, the burden of his argument is to show that the SACA disclosure requirement is not directed at the group as such and hence, like
the NAACP cases, involves a by-product chill of association.

Once Frankfurter has stated his test, the argument unfolds pre-
dictably: In weighing the public interest in regulation it is important
to consider both the "magnitude" of that interest and the "perti-
nence" of disclosure to its protection. The public interest is great
indeed and is carefully sketched in the Congressional findings set
forth in the Act. It is the security of the nation as it is threatened by
the world Communist movement. This movement utilizes organizations controlled from abroad and dedicated to overthrow by force if
necessary. These organizations use concealment, infiltration, and se-
cretive tactics, and they obtain support from people who would not
lend support if they understood their true nature. If we accept, as we
must, this "not unentertainable" appraisal by Congress of the threat,
"we must recognize that the power of Congress to regulate Communist organizations of this nature is extensive."[36]

Moreover, the argument continues, the very nature of the
threat—secrecy, concealment and infiltration employed by the Communist movement—makes disclosure peculiarly appropriate as a legal
counter-measure. The rationale for using disclosure is not that the
government hopes and intends thereby to destroy the Party, but that
it hopes and intends to prevent political fraud. If the prevention of
fraud entails as a by-product some chilling of membership, that is a
cost that is overborne by the public interest. Analogies are readily
marshalled—legislation such as the Corrupt Practices Act, the Lobbying Act, and the Foreign Registration Act have provided registration
and disclosure as the solution to a variety of "situations in which
secrecy or the concealment of associations has been regarded as a
threat to public safety and to the effective, free functioning of our
national institutions."[37] Frankfurter also cites *Bryant v. Zimmerman:* "It
was the nature of the organization regulated, and hence the danger
involved in its covert operation" which justified the statute. In the
NAACP cases, by contrast, "there was no showing of any danger
inherent in concealment, no showing that the State, in seeking disclosure, was attempting to cope with any perceived danger."[38] He concludes effectively:

Where the mask of anonymity which an organization's members wear serves the double purpose of protecting them from popular prejudice and of enabling them to cover over a foreign-directed conspiracy, infiltrate into other groups, and enlist the support of persons who would not, if the truth were revealed, lend their support, it would be a distortion of the First Amendment to hold that it prohibits Congress from removing the mask.[39]

Frankfurter thus argues in effect that where concealment serves both benign and sinister purposes, the latter may be regulated at the cost of sacrificing the former.[40]

The dissenting opinions are of little help in circumscribing the majority holding on the disclosure issue. Justice Black refuses to atomize the issues as Justice Frankfurter has done and aims his dissent, I think persuasively, at the cumulative impact of the Act as a whole upon the Party; he does not as a result debate the compulsory disclosure issue as such. Justices Douglas and Brennan pitch their dissents on Fifth Amendment grounds. Douglas has this to say about the scope of the decision:

. . . a group engaged in lawful conduct may not be required to file with the Government a list of members, no matter how unpopular it may be. For the disclosure of membership lists may cause harassment of members and seriously hamper their exercise of First Amendment rights. The more unpopular the group, the greater the likelihood of harassment. In logic then it might seem that the Communist Party, being at the low tide of popularity, might make out a better case of harassment than almost any other group on the contemporary scene.[41]

But, having so vividly captured the power of disclosure as a sanction, he goes on to agree that its use is justified in this instance in light of the findings of the Board about the disciplined, Soviet-dominated character of the organization:

These findings establish that more than debate, discourse, argumentation, propaganda, and other aspects of free speech and association are involved. An additional element enters, *viz.*, espionage, business activities, or the formation of cells for subversion, as well as the use of speech, press, and association by a foreign power to produce on this continent a Soviet satellite.[42]

When all is said and done, *SACB* does not add much to what we learned from *Bryant v. Zimmerman* thirty years earlier: groups whose characteristics fall somewhat short of those required for the imposi-

tion of criminal sanctions can at least be compelled to disclose membership. Two large ambiguities remain. For one thing, the rationale
for compulsory disclosure is never fully stated; at least four somewhat
different justifications are in the air:

(i) There is the argument that compulsory disclosure is justified
by the finding that the Party is controlled and directed by a foreign
power.

(ii) As Justice Frankfurter's reference to "a foreign-dominated
conspiracy" suggests, there lurks the notion that the Party is after all
a criminal conspiracy and that the law must be allowed to use lesser
sanctions whenever it would be proper to use criminal ones.

(iii) There is the idea that the Party, as Justice Jackson so eloquently argued in *Dennis,* is a new kind of group threat which the law
has not yet caught up with. Therefore, while it falls short of a criminal
conspiracy in the traditional sense, it is proper for the law now to
adjust our notions of "conspiracy" so as to make this complex international group reachable by legal sanction.

(iv) There is Frankfurter's argument that whatever the merits of
compulsory disclosure as a direct sanction in general, this group is set
apart by its use of secrecy and concealment. Disclosure is proper,
because it is a legal countermove perfectly tailored to the evil.

The other ambiguity is the question of just what other groups
would fall under the principle of the case. Perhaps the most disturbing
feature of the case is that the Court is so preoccupied with the idiosyncratic evils of the Communist Party that the decision seems to set out
a rule for the Party alone. Justice Frankfurter emphasizes that the
holding is not easily to be extended to other unpopular groups:

It is argued that if Congress may constitutionally enact legislation requiring
the Communist Party to register, to list its members, to file financial statements, and to identify its printing presses, Congress may impose similar
requirements upon any group which pursues unpopular political objectives
or which expresses an unpopular political ideology. Nothing which we decide
here remotely carries such an implication.[43]

But his effort to explain why the decision does not carry that implication is not altogether satisfying:

The Act compels the registration of organized groups which have been made
the instruments of a long-continued, systematic, disciplined activity directed
by a foreign power and purposing to overthrow existing government in this

country. Organizations are subject to it only when shown, after administrative hearing subject to judicial review, to be dominated by the foreign power or its organs and to operate primarily to advance its purposes.[44]

The distinguishing characteristic is not so much the objective of overthrow of the government or its proximity as it is the foreign domination. This factor makes the case easy for Frankfurter for the moment, but surely the Court is not holding that the use of such sanctions against a group is justified only when the group is foreign controlled and dominated. The dilemma which the Court first faced a decade earlier in *Dennis*—the non-immediate quality of the Communist revolutionary tactics—remains unresolved. The dilemma is how to delimit a category of near-conspiracy, given that under traditional Anglo-American notions of conspiracy the Party is not at the moment subject to prosecution, conviction, and punishment as a conspiracy to overthrow the government. This is the problem on which the Court worked so stubbornly and seriously in *Yates* and *Scales*. The opinion of Justice Frankfurter in *SACB*, however, reflects little of this background and little of this sense of general difficulty. It has bequeathed to us a most troublesome First Amendment precedent.

What can be said by way of summary about the Court's experience from *Bryant* through the NAACP cases to *SACB* with the use of compulsory disclosure of membership as a sanction against disfavored organizations?

First, there is no argument over whether disclosure *is* a sanction. The Court has unequivocally acknowledged the chilling effect of disclosure. While the note is stronger in the NAACP cases, it is not altogether missing from *SACB*. Thus, the argument is not over whether disclosure is a deterrent but rather is over whether the use of such a deterrent is justified.

Second, the Court will permit the use of the sanction against organizations that are sufficiently evil. This is the holding in both *Bryant* and *SACB*. The problem is that the Court has given little attention as yet to the question of what is a sufficiently evil organization. Once we have left the criminal law and its concepts of conspiracy, and more specifically once we have left the boundary set in *Yates*, we are pretty much at sea in appraising organizations in terms of their political virtue. Since both *Bryant* and *SACB* involved "secret" organizations, it is arguable that the Court will permit disclosure only where it is a rational antidote to concealment and political fraud. Whether or not this is a satisfactory policy poses a difficult question. It may be that almost any unpopular group operating in a hostile environment will attempt to conceal its membership, and that consequently what at first appears to be a narrow premise will in actual practice broaden ominously.

Third, the NAACP sequence, despite the eloquence about associational privacy, does not generate much tension when laid beside *SACB*. The ineptness of the South made those easy cases. There was simply no plausible state interest put forward, and the effort to conceal the true official motivation made the state interests proffered seem almost ludicrous. On this point Justice Frankfurter, whatever his rhetoric, was correct in *SACB;* the cases are very different.

Fourth, the Court has not yet made explicit what seems to me the preferable method of analysis of such problems. In a case such as *SACB* I would recognize the use of disclosure as an intended sanction against the group and then turn to the question of whether the group could be sanctioned consistently with the First Amendment. I would argue that in a rational constitutional system the propriety of disclosure as a direct sanction must be governed by the same criteria as the use of criminal sanctions. As a corollary, it would follow that the balancing formula used in instances of indirect sanctioning such as the NAACP cases would not be the appropriate tool for analysis of disclosure as a direct sanction. *Yates* is the relevant precedent.

Epilogue: Unfinished Business

Happily, the story of the legal fate of the Subversive Activities Control Act does not end with the 1961 decision. In 1965 one of the challenges postponed by Justice Frankfurter's exercise in judicial economy—the Fifth Amendment challenge—returns to the Court in *Albertson v. SACB*, and this time it prevails.

After the Court handed down its 1961 decision and thereby finalized the Board's registration order, the Party failed to register. At the request of the Attorney General, the Board issued orders requiring certain named individuals to register themselves as members of the Party. In *Albertson* the Court unanimously upsets the order as self-incrimination in violation of the Fifth Amendment. Other strategies to compel registration are held invalid by the Court of Appeals. Thus, the registration effort has been effectively paralyzed by the Fifth Amendment, leaving the anti-Communist strategy of the Act without this key step. As a result, the compulsory disclosure requirement, which the Court had held valid against First Amendment challenge in 1961, became inoperative; as it turns out, there is no practical way compatible with the Fifth Amendment and the non-repeal of the Smith Act to compel the disclosure. Moreover, *Albertson* suggests what may prove a general flaw in the disclosure tactic: where the rationale for disclosure is substantial, it is likely that criminal laws will bear on the subject of disclosure and hence that the disclosure requirement will run afoul of the Fifth Amendment.

The paralysis of the registration provision did not render the Act a futility in its entirety. The stigmatizing adjudication of Party status and the operation of the satellite sanctions were unaffected, since they depended, perhaps presciently, not on registration in fact but on an order to register becoming final. Two of the satellite provisions live, as it were, to fight and die another day. In *Aptheker v. Secretary of State* in 1964 the interdiction against applying for passports was held invalid on constitutional grounds; and in *United States v. Robel* in 1967 the provision barring employment at a defense facility met the same fate.[45]

It is gratifying that the complex strategy of the Act has over the years run into so many constitutional points of resistance. But the Act was a single coordinated scheme of attack on domestic subversion. We would have a much clearer image of what is and what is not permissible censorship of radical political associations today, a question of major importance, had the Court not yielded to the judicial economy strictures of Justice Frankfurter.

In the end, the solemn opening of Justice Black's dissent remains the fitting last word on the case:

The first banning of an association because it advocates hated ideas—whether that association be called a political party or not—marks a fateful moment in the history of a free country. That moment seems to have arrived for this country.[46]

21

Stigmatization
as a Group Sanction

In the course of discussing *SACB* we noted that one aspect of the case, attended to only by Justice Black in dissent, was the use of official stigmatization as a sanction against disfavored organizations. The Subversive Activities Control Act would still have imposed grave sanctions on Communist organizations had there been no registration and disclosure provisions, for the adjudication of "evil status" deserving stigma would still have been operative. Whatever the impact of this sanction on an individual, its bite is especially sharp for an organization. Nothing will be so likely to inhibit membership retention and growth as government labelling of an organization as in some sense unsound.

The issue of the propriety of official stigmatization under the First Amendment, although perplexing and inviting, has not yet really been engaged by the Court. The *SACB* decision does not deal with the point, although it should have. Apart from *SACB,* there are several other instances of the issue coming within reach of the Court: *Joint Anti-Fascist Refugee Committee v. McGrath* in 1951, *American Committee for Protection of Foreign Born v. Subversive Activities Control Board* and *Veterans of the Abraham Lincoln Brigade v. Subversive Activities Control Board* in 1965, and *DuBois Clubs of America v. Clark* in 1967.[1] In each instance, however, the Court manages to avoid full confrontation with the issue.

The Joint Anti-Fascist *Case*

Joint Anti-Fascist Refugee Committee v. McGrath, which is decided just a few months prior to *Dennis,* is another amusing and disturbing instance of the tensions generated for the Court by the anti-Communist legal strategies of the 1950s. Once again there is a vast outpouring of opinions; this time five justices add another ninety pages to the *Reports,* bringing the total for just the big cases—*Dennis, Yates, Scales, SACB,* and *Joint Anti-Fascist*—to some six hundred pages. Despite this expenditure of judicial energy, however, *Joint Anti-Fascist* yields a singularly frustrating and unhelpful precedent.

The case arises out of President Truman's Executive Order 9835, which in 1947 set up the Loyalty Program for federal employees. That program and its successors provided for the screening of the loyalty-security reliability of federal employees by means of an administrative process. The first major challenge to the program—*Bailey v. Richardson*[2]—was passed on by the Court on the same date the *Joint Anti-Fascist* decision was handed down. In *Bailey* the Court split 4 to 4, with the result that the decision below denying Miss Bailey's challenge was affirmed and no opinion was provided by the Court. Thus, *Joint Anti-Fascist* has chiefly been of interest for the light it sheds on the justices' positions on the Loyalty Program, which were left undisclosed by the brief *per curiam* opinion in *Bailey.* It has, however, considerable interest in its own right.

Executive Order 9835 empowered the Attorney General to compile and publish a list of suspect organizations for the sole purpose of assisting the loyalty screening of federal employees: Membership in a listed organization provided a non-conclusive datum to be weighed in the screening of a given employee. The Order provided that the list was to be compiled "after appropriate investigation and determination" by the Attorney General and that the organizations were to be designated in six categories: "totalitarian, fascist, communist or subversive, or as having adopted a policy of advocating or approving the commission of acts of force or violence to deny others their rights under the Constitution of the United States, or as seeking to alter the form of government of the United States by unconstitutional means." No legal consequences for the organization flow from the fact of listing. The 1947 Order was clearly conceived of as an exercise of the Executive's power to regulate federal employment; unlike the Subversive Activities Control Act of 1950, it was not intended to impose sanctions directly on the listed organizations.

The procedures by which the Attorney General compiled his lists were so informal as to make the Subversive Activities Control Act, as more than one justice noted, look like a model of decency. No provision was made prior to listing for notice or a hearing at which the organization might appear and offer evidence on its behalf. Nor was the employee-member allowed in his loyalty hearing to challenge the listing of the organization.

The *Joint Anti-Fascist* case arose when three organizations which had been designated "communist"—the Joint Anti-Fascist Refugee Committee, the National Council of Soviet-American Friendship, and the International Workers Order—sought declaratory and injunctive relief. In a 5 to 3 decision, with Justice Clark abstaining, the Court held that the organizations were entitled to relief. There was no opinion of the Court. Each member of the majority—Burton, Black, Douglas, Frankfurter, and Jackson—found it necessary to file a separate opinion; and there was a lengthy dissent by Justice Reed in which Chief Justice Vinson and Justice Minton joined.

The "victory" turned on the vote of Justice Burton, who in *Bailey* had voted with the three *Joint Anti-Fascist* dissenters to produce the 4 to 4 tie and the consequent defeat of Miss Bailey's challenge. There is something almost comic about this switch in vote, since the fact that moved Burton was so trivial. If it is possible to win a big civil liberties case on what in the world of sports would be called "a fluke," *Joint Anti-Fascist* is such a case.

When the organizations sought injunctive and declaratory relief, the Attorney General understandably sought to test the legal sufficiency of their challenge. He moved to dismiss their complaints, a procedural step which admits the allegations for the moment only for the sake of argument. Each organization had, however, alleged positive facts about its virtues and its patriotism and had denied that there was any basis for designating it as "communist." Justice Burton held that by moving to dismiss the Attorney General had positioned the issue so that the allegations of the complaints had to be taken as true: "By his present procedure he has claimed authority so to designate them upon the very facts alleged by them in their own complaints." But on the facts stated in the complaints a hostile designation would be wholly arbitrary. Burton therefore concluded that the Attorney General had pleaded himself into a corner. The question, as he chose to narrow it, was almost tautological: could the Attorney General designate at irrational whim? Given the political realities that surrounded the Attorney General's list in the real world at that time, it is breathtaking to have the question of its validity, by an exercise in the niceties of seventeenth century pleading, reduced to so formal, empty, and pointless an inquiry.

What makes Justice Burton's position appear so futile is not so much his analysis of the pleading point, which after all enlisted the agreement of Justices Black and Douglas; it is rather his insistence that the decision be fastidiously rested upon this point alone. If only the Attorney General will not insist he has the power to act wholly unreasonably, any procedure he uses to investigate the organization prior to listing will presumably satisfy Justice Burton. To perfect the artificiality of his disposition of the controversy, Justice Burton proceeds to hold that the designation is invalid because the Executive Order cannot be construed to have authorized such purely irrational designations. An important issue of political freedom is thus disposed of by a kind of word play that is unworthy of the occasion or the Court.

The bare-boned Burton opinion takes on a bit more flesh, however, when it is read against the dissent of Justice Reed. Justice Burton was at least taking the first step toward bringing this type of governmental action under legal scrutiny and discipline. He recognized that the listing did injure the organizations and their members and spoke of it as "defamation" by government.[3] He therefore found no problem as to the standing of the organizations to complain in court. Justice Reed, by contrast, holds that nothing has happened to the organizations because of state action:

This designation . . . does not prohibit any business of the organizations, subject them to any punishment or deprive them of liberty of speech or other freedom.[4]

Elsewhere he remarks, "They are in the position of every proponent of unpopular views. Heresy induces strong expressions of opposition."[5]

Thus, Justice Reed and the dissenters insist blindly that nothing has happened, while Justice Burton acknowledges the reality of harm to the organizations, but hypertechnically narrows his review of the propriety of the governmental action inflicting that harm.[6] What significance the *Joint Anti-Fascist* case retains resides in the unwillingness of the other members of the Court to be as carefully blind as the dissenters or as artificially narrow as Justice Burton. Of particular interest are the opinions of Justices Frankfurter and Black.

Justice Frankfurter begins with an extended and helpful essay on the issue of standing, which he decides in favor of the organizations. He then turns to the merits. He emphasizes that a designation such as this inflicts real harm:

They have been designated "communist" by the Attorney General of the United States. This designation imposes no legal sanction on these organizations other than that it serves as evidence in ridding the Government of persons reasonably suspected of disloyalty. It would be blindness, however, not to recognize that in the conditions of our time such designation drastically restricts the organizations, if it does not proscribe them.[7]

This observation constitutes, I think, an important datum. It lends a weighty endorsement to the insight that official stigmatization is a sanction and therefore is subject to judicial review under the Constitution.

For Justice Frankfurter the essential constitutional flaw in the Attorney General's listing procedure resides in its violation of Fifth Amendment guarantees of procedural due process. The Attorney General has acted without notice, hearing, or the possibility of challenge. Although Frankfurter acknowledges that the situation is novel and difficult, he insists that more procedural safeguards must be provided before official designations carrying such consequences for the organizations designated may be permitted. This theme sparks one of the great Frankfurter opinions. There is, as there will be a few months later in *Dennis* with respect to the First Amendment, an essay reviewing "our whole experience," this time with the Due Process Clause. Moreover, there is an arresting difference in tone between this Frankfurter opinion and those in *Dennis* and *SACB*. It arises, I suspect, because in *SACB* there was an elaborate procedure provided before registration, and because in *Dennis* the issue was free speech and not due process. The First Amendment tradition would have been strengthened immeasurably had Justice Frankfurter had the same empathy toward freedom of speech as a constitutional norm that he displayed toward procedural due process as a constitutional norm. His eloquence about due process compels quotation:

The requirement of "due process" is not a fair-weather or timid assurance. It must be respected in periods of calm and in times of trouble; it protects aliens as well as citizens. But "due process," unlike some legal rules, is not a technical conception with a fixed content unrelated to time, place and circumstances. Expressing as it does in its ultimate analysis respect enforced by law for that feeling of just treatment which has been evolved through centuries of Anglo-American constitutional history and civilization, "due process" cannot be imprisoned within the treacherous limits of any formula. Representing a profound attitude of fairness between man and man, and more particularly between the individual and government, "due process" is compounded of history, reason, the past course of decisions, and stout confidence in the strength of the democratic faith which we profess. Due process is not a mechanical instrument. It is not a yardstick. It is a process. It is a delicate process of adjustment inescapably involving the exercise of judgment by those whom the Constitution entrusted with the unfolding of the process.[8]

Procedural regularity, however, is not enough when the whole scheme is as much at war with political freedom as is this loose labelling of political organizations. The heart of the matter is the First Amendment challenge: Can the state do it at all, even if it does it right? Here, as in *SACB* a decade later, only Justice Black cuts through to the essential constitutional confrontation. He is indignant that the Government would not only defend the power of the Attorney General "to pronounce such deadly edicts" without notice or hearing,[9] but would also argue that the organizations so condemned lack standing to seek a judicial test of their grievance. He expresses his agreement with both Justice Burton and Justice Frankfurter. Then he turns to his central concern:

More fundamentally, however, in my judgment the executive has no constitutional authority, with or without a hearing, officially to prepare and publish the lists challenged by petitioners. . . . the system adopted effectively punishes many organizations and their members merely because of their political beliefs and utterances, and to this extent smacks of a most evil type of censorship. This cannot be reconciled with the First Amendment as I interpret it.[10]

Unfortunately Black goes on to dilute his opinion by elaborating his objections not in terms of First Amendment considerations but in terms of one of his favorite constitutional safeguards, the provisions against bills of attainder. The opinion ends with another appeal to history, this time a long quote from Macaulay on the bill of attainder against Protestants issued in 1688 by the Irish Parliament.

The "Communist-Front" Cases

The Court gets other opportunities to confront the stigmatization problem in the two "Communist-front" cases which reach it in 1965, *American Committee for Protection of Foreign Born v. Subversive Activities Control Board* and *Veterans of the Abraham Lincoln Brigade v. Subversive Activities Control Board,* and in *DuBois Clubs of America v. Clark* in 1967. The Subversive Activities Control Act, it will be recalled, covered two types of Communist organizations: "action" organizations and "front" organizations. The 1961 *SACB* case dealt with the Communist Party as an "action" organization; it was not concerned with the "front" provisions and left open the question of the validity of that part of the Act. It is obvious that this question carries the more far-reaching implications for political freedom, for these "fronts" are farthest removed from traditional concepts of conspiracy. "Fronts" are defined, in effect, as political subsidiaries dominated and directed by a Communist-action parent. Among the criteria set out for measuring the nexus of a group to a Communist-action organization are the extent of active membership in common, the extent of financial support, and "the extent to which the alleged front's positions on matters of policy do not deviate from the Communist line." Thus, any organization which had some Communists among its members and took radical positions on political issues came within the shadow of the Act. Finally, the consequences of being classified as a "front" differed from those of being classified as an "action" organization; disclosure of membership was not called for and hence the stigma of the label was a more salient sanction. The "front" provisions were thus both vitally important politically and highly dubious constitutionally. Nevertheless, in both of the 1965 cases the Court finds a way to finesse the confrontation.

In *American Committee for Protection of Foreign Born* the Court finds it necessary to remand the case for further proceedings because the record has become stale. The evidence on which the order to register was based had been taken in 1955; a key Communist member of the group had died in 1959, and there was no evidence on the status of the group since his death. The Court in a brief *per curiam* opinion acknowledges that the *SACB* decision had left open serious constitutional questions about the "front" provisions and in a footnote quotes pointedly from President Truman's veto message, which had distinguished sharply between the action and front provisions:

Insofar as the bill would require registration by the Communist Party itself, it does not endanger our traditional liberties. However, the application of the registration requirements to so-called Communist-front organizations can be the greatest danger to freedom of speech, press and assembly, since the alien and sedition laws of 1798.[11]

But the Court holds that it is inappropriate to pass on these questions when the record as to the organization's current status is unclear.

The remand sparks dissents from Justice Douglas, joined by Justice Harlan, and from Justice Black. The dissenters are eager to get to the constitutional issues. Justice Black is particularly uncompromising. After observing that among other things the Act "stigmatizes people for their beliefs, associations and views about politics, law, and government,"[12] he concludes his opinion:

Previous efforts to have this Court pass on the constitutionality of the various provisions of this freedom-crushing law have met with frustration on one excuse or another. I protest against following this course again. My vote is to hear the case now and hold the law to be what I think it is—a wholesale denial of what I believe to be the constitutional heritage of every freedom-loving American.[13]

The *Veterans of the Abraham Lincoln Brigade* case is dealt with the same way. The record is based "almost exclusively on events before 1950, and very largely on events before 1940."[14] The hearing had concluded in 1954. The very recital of these facts suggests the constitutional difficulties in determining "front" organizations. But again the Court finds it inappropriate to adjudicate constitutional challenges on so stale a record and remands the case. And again Justices Black, Douglas, and Harlan dissent. A poignant note is struck by the opening of Justice Douglas's dissent:

This is the famous brigade of Americans who fought in the Spanish Civil War against Franco. Approximately 3,000 American youths were members; and of these only about 1,800 survived.[15]

Finally, *DuBois Clubs of America v. Clark* in 1967 continues the pattern. The case arose when the Attorney General petitioned the SACB for an order requiring the DuBois Clubs to register as a "Communist-front" organization. The group sought injunctive relief, arguing that the Act was unconstitutional and that the pending hearings by the SACB chilled its freedom of association. The Court in a *per curiam* opinion affirmed the District Court's dismissal of the suit, holding that the organization must exhaust the administrative remedies provided by the Act. Justice Douglas in a dissenting opinion joined by Justice Black argued that the Court should confront the merits and find the registration provisions unconstitutional on their face.

The Court's reluctance to take these cases should give us pause. The dissenters, who in the 1965 cases included significantly Justice Harlan, could not muster two more votes from a Court which numbered among its members Chief Justice Warren and Justices Brennan, Goldberg, and Stewart. Perhaps the First Amendment invalidity of stigmatization of organizations is not so crystal clear after all. In any event, it has been left officially undecided by the Court.

22

Sanctions Against Individuals
as a Group Sanction

———◆———

We have been concerned in these chapters with the imposition of
sanctions directly against groups, a problem which in contemporary
America may well be the basic arena of First Amendment controversy.
It comes as something of a surprise that there are not in the end many
ways to sanction a group. We have isolated three different strategies:
(i) treating the group as a criminal conspiracy, which in operation
means treating individual members as criminal conspirators; (ii) compulsory disclosure of membership; and (iii) official stigmatization.

It remains for us to consider a fourth possibility—the sanctioning
of individual members as a group sanction. Although the Court has
not conceptualized it cleanly, this has, arguably, often been the underlying strategy. As we saw, the Subversive Activities Control Act could
be read as an effort to inhibit or outlaw the group by imposing sanctions on individual members. The various satellite sanctions affecting
such things as employment and travel by the individual members
could be thought of as a strategy to make membership so unattractive
as to destroy the group. Clearly the imposition of criminal sanctions
for conspiracy will, if pursued, have this effect. And taken together,
the satellite disabilities approach the total inhibiting impact of the
criminal law even though they do not employ criminal sanctions.

It will be recalled that the Court in *SACB* had an opportunity to
confront this issue, but Justice Frankfurter insisted that the question
of the validity of the satellite sanctions was prematurely raised and
hence not yet ripe for decision. Although the matter is not fully

addressed, he also appeared to hold that Congress could not be taken to have attempted to outlaw the Party by means of the twelve satellite sanctions; rather each sanction was to be viewed as an independent answer to a separate problem. Only Justice Black read the Act, correctly in my view, as a scheme for applying sanctions to the group.

The issue has not been addressed directly since. When one of the satellite sanctions—the prohibition against members applying for passports—is finally tested and invalidated in *Aptheker v. Secretary of State* [1] in 1964, the majority finds it sufficient to treat the sanction as infringing the rights of the individual and does not discuss the impact on the group. Justice Black, while concurring in the result, takes pains to reject the majority rationale about the power to allocate passports, and argues instead that "for reasons stated in my dissenting opinion in *Communist Party v. Subversive Activities Control Board,* I think the whole Act . . . is not a valid law, that it sets up a comprehensive statutory plan which violates the Federal Constitution." [2] This time, however, even he talks in terms of its impact on individuals and not of its impact on the group.

The point is more important, I think, than the Court's lack of experience, and concern, with it would suggest. It haunts the legion of cases involving the use of non-criminal sanctions against the individual that arose during the anti-Communist decades. These cases were generated by a common mood but not by a common coordinated strategy; they arose in different forms and from different sources. It was not possible therefore to challenge their cumulative impact as it might have been had they been the product not of piecemeal moves but of a single comprehensive legislative scheme. In retrospect, they seem to have been a sort of SACA informal but writ large. They were preoccupied almost exclusively with disqualifying the individual for this or that privilege because of his membership in a suspect organization. And they provided a vast amount of work for the Supreme Court. It will be the business of the next section of this book to review the Court's response to the First Amendment challenge in this oblique and complex form. In so doing, the perspective suggested here of viewing the law as at least in part sanctioning the group by sanctioning the individual member may prove helpful.

Partial Sanctions:
The Anti-Communist
Inheritance

———————◆———————

23

The Partial Sanction:
A General Analysis

———◆———

In our effort to map the Supreme Court's dialogue over freedom of speech and association, we have surveyed in turn the limits of censorship of individual speech, the limits of censorship of group speech, and the regulation of groups themselves as political associations, speech apart. We are now at the threshold of a new topic: the vast network of non-criminal restraints imposed upon individuals because of their affiliation with disfavored groups which occasioned the expenditure of so much legal energy during the anti-Communist decades. Before we move on, it will be helpful to pause for a new concept, the idea of *the partial sanction.*

The classic sanction for speech, prior licensing apart, has been the criminal sanction. A principal characteristic of modern speech problems is how far they have moved from this simple model to more complex and oblique sanctions. The criminal sanction is not ambiguous as to the objective of the state. Its purpose is to prevent the publishing of the disfavored message; it has no other purpose than to dissuade the speaker from saying *that.* In contrast, there is another set of situations in which only a privilege of some sort is at stake, and the state objective—and motivation—may be highly ambiguous.

A sufficient illustration of the formal point is provided by Justice Holmes's *bon mot* in the *McAuliffe* case[1] in 1892, back in the days when he was on the Massachusetts Supreme Court. McAuliffe had been fired by the city of New Bedford for violating a municipal regulation limiting the political activities of policemen. In an opinion upholding

the dismissal, Holmes observed: "The petitioner may have a constitutional right to talk politics, but he has no constitutional right to be a
policeman."[2] Viewed from one perspective, depriving a man of a job
because the state does not like a speech he has made is a powerful
form of censorship, possibly more painful and effective than a criminal fine. From another perspective, however, it may not represent the
pursuit of censorship but the pursuit of some other objective with
respect to public employment. Moreover, although Justice Holmes
was too simplistic in his wit, he did have an insight. The sanction in
such a case is *partial*. The state is not making an effort to prevent the
speech altogether; the speaker can continue to speak, albeit at the cost
of his job; and if someone else makes the same speech, the state need
not intervene. The problem is: Does this "degree of freedom"
afforded the speaker alter the normative judgment as to the propriety
of the state's action? Or to restate the problem in terms familiar to
our analysis: Is the jurisdiction of partial sanctions identical with that
of direct total sanctions? And if not, how does one determine what
that jurisdiction should be? What accommodations, that is, should
constitutional law make for the fact that the sanction is only partial?

To some extent the answer must turn on an appraisal of official
motivation, at least as it can be garnered from the face of the legal
measure. If the objective of the partial sanction is to censor speech or
to restrict associational liberty, it should be judged precisely as a
direct criminal sanction would be. If, however, the prejudice to speech
or association can be said to be a by-product of the pursuit of some
other legitimate state objective, we are again confronted with the
puzzling question of how to delimit the use of the partial sanction.

A further complexity of the partial sanction problem is that it
permits a double view of what liberty is being infringed. To recur to
Holmes's policeman, the imposition of the partial sanction can be
seen as (i) infringing the privilege of working as a policeman by
adding this condition to it, or (ii) as infringing the right to speak by
attaching disabilities such as the loss of employment to it. There
would seem to be no canon for detecting "which side is up," but the
question is whether it alters the analysis of propriety any, if we shift
from the perspective of infringing employment to the perspective of
infringing speech.

We should also note a clarifying analysis that has taken place in
recent decades. Normally the partial sanction will involve the withholding of a government privilege of some sort—a chance to work, to
travel, to get a tax exemption, to use the mails, etc. At one time there

was a tradition of distinguishing sharply between *rights* and *privileges,* and of holding that unless the opportunity or advantage at issue had the status of a right, its abridgement did not warrant constitutional scrutiny. The allocation of privileges was conceived of as a matter of grace. In recent decades this has changed.[3] Today almost any level of advantage is weighty enough to qualify for judicial review. Little any longer follows from the distinction between rights and privileges; privileges too can now be unconstitutionally abridged. This clarification, of course, does not in itself answer the question of when interference with a privilege is invalid.

The Court has not as yet developed an explicit scheme of analysis for problems of this sort. Bearing this array of questions in mind, we shall content ourselves with a sampling of the principal cases in which it has passed on the propriety of a partial sanction. And in this prefatory chapter we shall look only at the issue in its simplest form—cases where the sanction is applied to individuals and where there is no concern with membership in a subversive group. Just as the analysis of individual speech was a necessary prerequisite to the analysis of the more complex phenomenon of group speech, so the analysis of the partial sanction, subversive groups apart, is a prerequisite to the analysis of the more complex phenomenon of the application of partial sanctions to those who are members of a disfavored group.

We begin with *United Public Workers v. Mitchell*[4] in 1947, a case which poses the problem of the partial sanction in a clear and accessible form. It involved an effort by several individual public employees and a union of public employees to challenge by declaratory judgment the constitutionality of the Hatch Act. The Act, the latest in a series of legislative measures designed to "purify" the civil service, forbids, subject to dismissal, employees in the executive branch of the federal government from taking "any active part in political management or in political campaigns." Another provision explicitly exempts the right to vote and the right to express opinions on political subjects from the coverage of the Act. It appears that at the time as many as three million employees were affected by the limitation on political activity. The Court in a 4 to 3 decision, with Justices Murphy and Jackson not participating, upheld the provision.[5] Justices Black and Douglas filed dissenting opinions.

There is a procedural dispute at the outset over whether all the complainants present justiciable questions or whether in some cases they are not merely seeking an advisory opinion. It is, however, agreed that at least one employee, Poole, has violated the Act and thus presents a full blown controversy for adjudication by the Court. So the Act is tested against the case of Poole, who was a low-echelon employee on the industrial, not the administrative, side. A roller in the United States Mint in Philadelphia, he had also been working as "a ward executive committeeman of a political party."

The facts thus pose the partial sanction issue sharply. On one hand, there is a major abridgement of an important First Amendment activity—the right to engage actively in partisan politics; on the other, the objective of the Act is clearly not to censor political activity, but to improve the civil service by relieving it of partisan political pressures, a policy which has recommended itself to many people. The abridgement of political freedom is thus a by-product of the pursuit of an otherwise legitimate purpose. Once again Holmes's policeman is in point: Poole is left perfectly free to engage in politics, but he cannot at the same time work for the federal government.

Also, we should underscore one other characteristic of the Act: it is an instance of non-content regulation, that is, the regulation of political activity is *neutral* as between political parties or causes.

Justice Reed, writing for the majority, acknowledges that the Act interferes with political freedom:

The right claimed as inviolate may be stated as the right of a citizen to act as a party official or worker to further his own political views. Thus we have a measure of interference by the Hatch Act. . . with what otherwise would be the freedom of the civil servant under the First, Ninth and Tenth Amendments.[6]

Moreover, he concedes that some criteria for selecting federal employees would be unconstitutional, and that the matter is thus an appropriate one for judicial review:

Appellants urge that federal employees are protected by the Bill of Rights and that Congress may not "enact a regulation providing that no Republican, Jew or Negro shall be appointed to federal office, or that no federal employee shall attend Mass or take any active part in missionary work." None would deny such limitations on congressional power. . . .[7]

But, he continues, the fact that there are some limitations on the employment power, does not mean that the particular exercise of that power involved in this case is invalid. The test is balancing the competing interests:

Again this Court must balance the extent of the guarantees of freedom against a congressional enactment to protect a democratic society against the supposed evil of political partisanship by classified employees of government.[8]

Justice Reed then proceeds to apply the test. While it is true that political neutrality is not indispensable to a merit system of employment, Congress is not thereby precluded from deciding that it is desirable. The test is not that stringent. Moreover, much of the employee's political freedom is left untouched; he may vote and express political opinions. Further, such restrictions are supported by tradition; the Court in 1882 had upheld a prohibition on government employees "giving or receiving money contributions for political purposes from or to other employees of the government."[9] That was a prohibition of contributions of money; this is directed at "political contributions of energy."[10] Finally, whether the Act is too broad in that it includes under the ban industrial as well as administrative employees is, in his view, "a matter of detail for Congress."[11] He is now ready to strike the balance as the majority sees it:

We have said that Congress may regulate the political conduct of government employees "within reasonable limits," even though the regulation trenches to some extent upon unfettered political action. The determination of the extent to which political activities of governmental employees shall be regulated lies primarily with Congress. Courts will interfere only when such regulation passes beyond the generally existing conception of governmental power. That conception develops from practice, history, and changing educational, social and economic conditions. . . . When actions of civil servants in the judgment of Congress menace the integrity and the competency of the service, legislation to forestall such danger and adequate to maintain its usefulness is required. The Hatch Act is the answer of Congress to this need. We cannot say with such a background that these restrictions are unconstitutional.[12]

Although the Court acknowledges a duty of judicial review of such government employment criteria and although it acknowledges too that there is a substantial diminution of political freedoms here, once it perceives this as the by-product of an otherwise legitimate objective, the game is virtually over. It is enough that this is a plausible way to select federal employees.

But the case cannot be rendered quite that tranquil. Justice Douglas in dissent expresses a sympathetic understanding of the objective of creating a politically neutral civil service available on a continuing basis to serve whatever party is in power. He would agree, therefore, that some political sterilization of government employment is proper. But as he sees it, the Hatch Act goes further than is necessary to achieve that objective in that it applies to industrial as well as administrative employees: "To sacrifice the political rights of the industrial workers goes far beyond any demonstrated or demonstrable need."[13] Hence he would find the Act unconstitutional as to industrial employees like Poole. The formula for handling such cases for Justice Douglas too apparently is the balancing of interest, with the proviso that the state's interest be carefully scrutinized and no more put on the state side of the scales than is necessary to meet the professed need.

Although *Mitchell* is decided during the heyday of the liberal bloc of Murphy, Rutledge, Black, and Douglas and at the high point of the rhetorical affirmations of clear and present danger as the principle for all First Amendment controversies, there is no disposition to measure the propriety of the partial sanction at issue by a literal application of the clear and present danger test. The Douglas opinion does, however, contain one reference to the test:

If those rights are to be qualified by the larger requirements of modern democratic government, the restrictions should be narrowly and selectively drawn to define and punish the specific conduct which constitutes a clear and present danger to the operations of government.[14]

He thus finds it possible to combine in the same case the idiom of balancing with the idiom of clear and present danger.

Once again, as will be the case in *SACB* and *Joint Anti-Fascist Refugee Committee*, it is Justice Black who is most disturbed by the possible First Amendment abridgements involved. He restates the facts at the outset:

The number of federal employees thus barred from political action is approximately three million. Section 12 of the same Act affects the participation in political campaigns of many thousands of state employees [working in federally funded projects]. No one of all these millions of citizens can, without violating this law, "take any active part" in any campaign for a cause or candidate if the cause or candidate is "specifically identified with any National or State political party." Since under our common political practices most causes and candidates are espoused by political parties, the result is that, because they are paid out of the public treasury, all these citizens who engage in public work can take no really effective part in campaigns that may bring about changes in their lives, their fortunes, and their happiness.[15]

Black carefully inventories precisely what conduct the Act classifies as "taking an active part" in political campaigns and notes the possibility that an employee might be held responsible for his family's activities. The result is that the sum of partisan political activity permitted government employees and their families seems to him to be this: "They may vote in silence; they may carefully and quietly express a political view at their peril; and they may become 'spectators'. . . at campaign gatherings."[16]

If the Douglas tactic was to protect political freedom by narrowing the state's interest, thus lightening one side of the scales, the Black tactic is to elaborate on the magnitude of the First Amendment interference and abridgement, thus weighting the other side of the scales. Black will not concede that the Act is valid even if the category of "sterilized" employees is narrowed, as suggested by Douglas. He challenges the basic strategy of prophylactic legislation in this context, that is, the strategy of barring all to ensure that some will not abuse or corrupt. The point is, I suspect, a fundamental one: *The First Amendment does not permit such administrative convenience in achieving an objective.* It is too wasteful of First Amendment rights. In this case, as Black sees it, millions are deprived of vital political rights because a minority may abuse those rights:

It would hardly seem to be imperative to muzzle millions of citizens because some of them, if left their constitutional freedoms, might corrupt the political process. . . . It hardly seems consistent with our system of equal justice to all to suppress the political and speaking freedom of millions of good citizens because a few bad citizens might engage in coercion.[17]

In pursuit of its objective the state must, he argues, aim directly at the specific evil it fears:

If the possibility exists that some. . . public employees may, by reason of their more influential positions, coerce other public employees or other citizens, laws can be drawn to punish the coercers. . . . if the practice of making discharges, promotions, or recommendations for promotions on a political basis is so great an evil as to require legislation, the law could punish those public officials who engage in the practice.[18]

The point may be one of great generality. Black's stance is similar to that of Justice Roberts in *Schneider v. State.* [19] It was not, Roberts held, permissible for the state, seeking to prevent littering, to employ the strategy of flatly prohibiting the distribution of leaflets. It could, he argued, punish those who actually threw them away.

It seems to me that Justice Black's great affection for First Amendment values led him to see the case squarely, and in the end to see through the very plausible reasons advanced on behalf of the government regulation. The final sentence of his dissent gets it right: "Laudable as its purpose may be, it seems to me to hack at the roots of a Government by the people themselves; and consequently I cannot agree to sustain its validity."[20]

Torcaso v. Watkins [21] in 1961 provides an instance in which the Court unanimously finds a partial sanction invalid under the First Amendment. Although the case in form involves the profound freedom of speech infringement of compelling utterance, the Court relies on the religion and not the speech clauses. Its mode of analysis, however, is relevant to our purposes. The precise controversy involved the refusal of an appointee to the office of Notary Public in Maryland to declare his belief in God. The Maryland Constitution had a clause barring religious tests for public office "other than a declaration of belief in the existence of God." The Maryland court saw no problem at all and repeated in a slightly altered form Holmes's *bon mot* about the policeman:

The petitioner is not compelled to believe or disbelieve, under threat of punishment or other compulsion. True, unless he makes the declaration of belief he cannot hold public office in Maryland, but he is not compelled to hold office.[22]

The Supreme Court disagreed. Although the Maryland requirement is neutral as among religious sects, the Court, speaking through Justice Black, has no trouble in requiring that the state also be neutral between believers and atheists:

We repeat and again reaffirm that neither a State nor the Federal Government can constitutionally force a person "to profess a belief or disbelief in any religion." Neither can constitutionally pass laws or impose requirements which aid all religions as against non-believers, and neither can aid those religions based on a belief in the existence of God as against those religions founded on different beliefs.[23]

It is easier then to handle the partial sanction issue under the traditions of the religion clause than under the traditions of the speech, press, and assembly clauses. There is a firmer formula for the religion case. The state is prohibited from favoring in any way one set of religious beliefs over another. It is not necessary to argue that the true motivation of the state is to withhold public office from atheists as a direct sanction against atheism. Nor is it necessary to balance the state interest in God-fearing public officials against the interference with religious freedom. It is sufficient that the state to some degree by this measure favors believers over atheists; the state may not distinguish between the two for any purpose. A case like *Mitchell* simply cannot be recast into such a mode. It makes little sense to speak of the state favoring politically passive citizens over active.

In both *Torcaso* and *Mitchell* the partial sanction is the same: the withholding of public employment. Only the criteria for withholding are different, although both affect First Amendment freedoms. *Torcaso* tells us that partial sanctions keyed to religious distinctions are *automatically* invalid.[24] *Mitchell,* even in the dissent of Justice Black, tells us that partial sanctions keyed to speech and association distinctions are by no means automatically bad.

Bond v. Floyd[25] in 1966 furnishes a striking example for our purposes. A *cause celebre* at the time, it arose over the refusal of the Georgia legislature to seat Julian Bond, the young civil rights leader, because of remarks he had made opposing the Vietnam War and supporting draft resisters. The Georgia legislature decided that these statements made it evident that Bond could not in good faith take the oath to support the Constitution required of legislators, thus turning the routine oath of allegiance into a loyalty test oath. It also contended that Bond's speech tended to bring "discredit" upon the legislature. The Supreme Court in a unanimous decision held that the Georgia House had violated Bond's First Amendment rights.

The case appears to have originated in a borderline area between partial and total sanctions. The Georgia legislators had been outraged by Bond's remarks, and although one cannot ignore the racial overtones in the controversy, had presumably acted on the angry premise that no American should be allowed to talk that way about a war his country was engaged in. Thus initially the ouster of Bond may have been grounded on the view that the First Amendment did not protect remarks of that sort. Once Bond took the controversy to court, however, the state elected to defend on narrower grounds, making the case explicitly a partial sanction problem. Chief Justice Warren restates Georgia's argument as follows:

> The State declines to argue that Bond's statements would violate any law if made by a private citizen, but it does argue that even though such a citizen might be protected by his First Amendment rights, the State may nonetheless apply a stricter standard to its legislators.[26]

The state thus once again offers the essential defense of the partial sanction: It is not that private citizens may not engage in partisan political activity, but a stricter standard may be applied to civil servants; it is not that private citizens may not be atheists, but a stricter standard may be applied to public employees.

The Court's rejection of this argument involves two steps. First, Chief Justice Warren establishes with care that Bond's statements did not violate any valid law and were within the traditions of political tolerance. The baseline for this part of the analysis is the freedom of speech enjoyed by those who are not Georgia legislators, that is, the rest of the public. Second, Warren rejects the claim that the legislator's freedom of speech can constitutionally be made less than that of anyone else. The argument, however, is not, as I read it, that the jurisdiction of partial and total sanctions must as an axiom always be the same. It is rather that no rational basis can be found for so limiting the legislator whose very function requires maximum freedom of speech:

> The manifest function of the First Amendment in a representative government requires that legislators be given the widest latitude to express their views on issues of policy. . . . The State argues that the *New York Times* principle should not be extended to statements by a legislator because the policy of encouraging free debate about governmental operations only applies to the citizen-critic of his government. We find no support for this distinction in the *New York Times* case or in any other decision of this Court. The interest of the public in hearing all sides of a public issue is hardly advanced by extending more protection to citizen-critics than to legislators. Legislators have an obligation to take positions on controversial political questions so that their constituents can be fully informed by them, and be better able to assess their qualifications for office; also so they may be represented in governmental debates by the person they have elected to represent them.[27]

The decision, in the end, rests on the distinctive functions of a legislator as a spokesman for the views of his constituents; if they have anti-war views which they could validly express, he must be free to speak their views for them. The possibility thus remains that there may be occasions where it is proper to expect and demand special reticence on the part of a speaker. Certainly a cabinet member who vigorously and persistently disagrees with his Administration is not having his freedom of speech curtailed, in the constitutional sense, if he is asked to leave the cabinet. In such an instance it makes sense to talk of the loyalty owed by the speaker. Although the issue is more complex, it may also make sense to demand some sort of loyalty from military personnel during a war, at least at the officer level. But, as *Bond* makes utterly clear, no such duty can be imposed upon the legislator whose very function is to speak for the citizen in that "uninhibited, robust, wide-open" debate on public issues which is our constitutional heritage.

Again the contrast with *Torcaso* is arresting. *Torcaso* holds that there can be no state purpose for which it is permissible to disfavor a man who is an atheist. *Bond* does not address the broader question; it holds that the state may not cut the speech of a *legislator* back below that of the ordinary citizen.

Bond and *Mitchell* are also worth juxtaposing. They are reconcilable on the basis of functional differences between legislators and civil servants; and presumably also on the basis of the different reasons for limiting the rights in each case. Arguably, the civil servant too would be protected in saying what Bond said. What is more striking, however, is that the dissent of Justice Black in *Mitchell* and the opinion of Chief Justice Warren in *Bond* converge to suggest that, if a serious analysis is made, few if any rationales for partially limiting the First Amendment rights of public employees will survive scrutiny. In the end, we must stumble over the question of how lowering the exercise of First Amendment rights could be seen as a *rational* qualification for public office or employment—rational, that is, for a society that cherishes its traditions of freedom of speech and association.

The point is corroborated by one final illustration, *Pickering v. Board of Education*[28] in 1968. Pickering, a public school teacher, was dismissed for writing a letter to the local newspaper critical of the school board and the district superintendent of schools. The dismissal came after a hearing at which the letter was found "detrimental to the efficient operation and administration of the schools of the district."

The Supreme Court, again in a unanimous decision,[29] upheld the claim that Pickering's First Amendment rights had been violated by the dismissal.

Pickering's letter, which at this remove from the local controversy seems mild enough, was an entry into a public discussion of school financing precipitated by the defeat at the polls of two referenda on bond issues. Pickering criticized the Board of Education for misallocating funds between educational and athletic programs and for misleading the public by its promises; he also charged that the superintendent of schools had attempted to prevent teachers from speaking out in opposition to the proposed tax increase. It was found at the hearing that several of the statements in the letter were false, although in an appendix to his opinion Justice Marshall examined and considerably deflated the falsity charges. The Board, in effect, analogized the letter to defamation. The case thus presented a variant of seditious libel—this time a subordinate uttering seditious libel of his superiors.

It was agreed on all sides that had Pickering been a private citizen and not a teacher, his participation in the discussion of the public issue of school financing would have been fully protected, despite some marginal falsehoods in his statement, by the principle of *New York Times*. Thus, the sole issue was whether the state could qualify his rights of free speech *because* he was a teacher.

Although the Court had made the point clear in a number of prior cases, the state persisted in arguing—and the Illinois Supreme Court agreed—that Pickering's "acceptance of a teaching position in the public schools obliged him to refrain from making statements about the operation of the schools 'which in the absence of such position he would have an undoubted right to engage in.' "[30] The right/privilege tactic is thus put in a slightly different way: Pickering has agreed as a matter of contract to these conditions of employment. But the Court's answer is the same, and it is vigorously asserted: Teachers may not be compelled to surrender First Amendment rights as a condition of employment.

This shadow point out of the way, Justice Marshall turns to the merits: To what extent may the state require stricter standards from a teacher in comment on school affairs than from a member of the general public where the school affairs impinge upon a public issue? He is careful not to give the question too sweeping an answer:

Because of the enormous variety of fact situations in which critical statements by teachers and other public employees may be thought by their superiors, against whom the statements are directed, to furnish grounds for dismissal, we do not deem it either appropriate or feasible to attempt to lay down a general standard against which all such statements may be judged.[31]

Marshall then proceeds to evaluate the competing interests. Implicit in his analysis is the perception that the problem arises only because the public issue Pickering has discussed is one which bears so much on school affairs. Presumably, if it were almost any other public issue, Pickering would stand in the shoes of the private citizen. Marshall does not, unfortunately, refer to the *Bond* case, but it seems reasonably safe to assume that had Pickering made anti-war statements, the decision would follow *Bond.* The case would, however, be more complex, if he made statements supporting draft resistance by his own students.

Marshall notes first that Pickering's relationships with the Board and with the superintendent "are not the kind of close working relationships for which it can persuasively be claimed that personal loyalty and confidence are necessary."[32] Hence his true statements, no matter how critical of his remote superiors, would offer no rational basis for the dismissal, although in a footnote Marshall leaves open the possibility of a need for confidentiality so great "that even completely correct public statements might furnish a permissible grounds for dismissal."[33]

Marshall next takes up the false statements. He weighs the importance of having public issues such as these fully aired and concludes that the state interest "in limiting teachers' opportunities to contribute to public debate is not significantly greater than its interest in limiting a similar contribution by any member of the general public."[34] In the process, he explicitly enters a caveat about situations where the teacher might be thought by the public to have special access to the facts and where accordingly because of this supposed expertise his opinions would be harder to counter. Given that the state interest with respect to teachers is about the same as that with respect to the general public and that dismissal is a sanction roughly comparable to tort damages for libel, *New York Times* controls. Hence, since there was no showing that Pickering made the false statements either knowingly or with reckless disregard for the truth, the First Amendment prohibits this imposition of a sanction on his speech on a public issue.

Pickering is thus a powerful example of the approach the Court has evolved to the partial sanction problem. As in *Bond,* it declines to reduce the matter to a simplistic general formula, and it notes several possible situations in which a teacher might reasonably be restricted in his exercise of free speech. But the freedom an ordinary citizen would enjoy provides a crucial baseline for evaluating the partial sanction case, and the Court in cases such as *Bond* and *Pickering* has shown a disposition to scrutinize closely and patiently the state's rationale in the particular case for departing from that baseline.

If the judicial process in the partial sanction case can be viewed as a form of balancing, it is imperative to note that in cases involving partial sanctions on individuals, such as *Bond* and *Pickering,* the contemporary Court has kept a First Amendment thumb on the scales. And in any event, while it may be helpful to approach the problem through formal categories like partial vs. total sanctions, they obviously do not solve the problem. The hallmark of the Court's performance in these cases has been its sensitivity to the particular factual context.

24

Partial Sanctions Keyed to Membership in Disfavored Groups

We are now ready to enter what amounts to a virtual jungle of precedent in an effort to trace the underlying scheme of the Court's response to the problem of partial sanctions applied to individuals because of their membership in disfavored groups. Most of these cases were generated by the anti-Communist apprehensions of the 1940s and 1950s. They can be characterized in various competing ways. One characterization would be that they represent the law's translation of McCarthyism into official action. Another is that they represent the society's gradual and piecemeal response to the puzzling and serious threat to domestic order widely believed to have been created by the Communist Party. They are, I think, analytically, the most complex cases the Court has had to confront, for they combine the perplexities of partial sanctions with the perplexities of sanctioning membership in groups which fall short of criminal conspiracies.

The issues can of course be stated less formally and more in terms of flesh and blood political realities. We will be dealing with such familiar institutions as loyalty oaths, loyalty programs, and legislative investigating committees. Whether the threat in the future will be perceived as coming from the Communist Party or as emanating from some new radical coalition, these are institutions the constitutionality of which requires serious scrutiny in times of relative tranquility; for they are institutions that will be called upon again.

It will be helpful to return to the Subversive Activities Control

Act of 1950 as a source of perspective. The Act, which received such belated and incomplete consideration by the Court in *Communist Party v. SACB* in 1961, can be viewed as *an official blueprint* for regulating the threat of subversion presented by the Communist Party and its "Communist-front" supporters. It employed, it will be recalled, four types of non-criminal sanctions: (i) compulsory disclosure of membership; (ii) stigmatization; (iii) a set of partial sanctions affecting, among other things, use of the mails, passports, tax exemptions, and public employment; and (iv) deportation in the case of aliens and denaturalization in the case of naturalized citizens. If the law had developed in a rational time sequence, the Act would have been the architectonic tactic and the *SACB* case the definitive precedent on the constitutional limits governing the use of such non-criminal sanctions against political groups.

The cases we are about to examine can best be viewed as a sort of amateur or prehistoric effort to employ the tactics of the Subversive Activities Control Act. They represent, so to speak, the tactic without the coordinating blueprint, the tactic directed by the invisible hand of anti-Communism. The result was to spawn some one hundred cases—almost a third of the Court's First Amendment work load since 1919—each of which involved the imposition in one form or another of a partial sanction. The imposition of the sanctions was necessarily somewhat random and chaotic, since there was no authority giving overall direction to the strategy. Moreover, in sharp contrast to the 1950 Act, there was no procedure provided through which to establish the assumptions about the nature, activities, and aspirations of the Communist Party, which assumptions were always the foundation for the use of partial sanctions against individual members.

The task of the Court in processing these cases was complicated further by several additional circumstances. The first we have traced in the last chapter. It is the genuine difficulty analytically of the partial sanction issue, even when the sanction is applied cleanly against the individual. The second is that the Court was to require the entire decade 1950-1960 to work out the application of *direct* criminal sanctions to the Communist "conspiracy."

The third circumstance is that, because there was no coordinated strategy, the partial sanction was viewed by the Court simply as a sanction against the individual and not as a sanction against the group. This, it will be remembered, was an unresolved problem in *SACB*. It may be that the answer comes out the same whichever perspective is adopted. But to bar persons from, say, public employment, because they are members of a disfavored group, is a powerful sanction against the group, and the amount of interference with political freedom is best confronted if the matter is put that way.

The absence of explicit coordination also meant that the Court never added up the impact of the partial sanctions. It went on dealing with case after case as though the sanction imposed in each was an isolated event to be judged only in terms of its own impact. To return for a moment to the idiom the Court so fastidiously avoided in *SACB*, the loose network of partial sanctions which characterized the anti-Communist strategy of the 1940s and 1950s was a *de facto* attempt, however atomized and fragmented, to *outlaw* the Party.

Finally, many of these cases retain a preoccupation with speech, with advocacy of violent overthrow of the government, which seems anachronistic. The danger of the Party continues to be forced into the mold of saying it talks too much. The cases are thus cut off from more rational and realistic grounds for worrying about the existence of the Party, such as that it uses tactics of infiltration into strategic posts, etc.

Recent cases, such as *Keyishian, Robel, Elfbrandt, Aptheker,* and *Wadmond,* [1] have somewhat in the fashion of *Brandenburg* provided fairly clear-cut answers to the problems posed by the use of partial sanctions. It may therefore seem unnecessary to burden this essay with a detailed account of the Court's earlier answers. Our objective, however, is not simply to restate the most contemporary answers to the issues the Court has faced; it is also to make a rounded study of the dialogue the Court has had over the past half-century on First Amendment matters. Evaluation of the strength of the tradition we now have and of the Court's record as institutional guardian of First Amendment values requires, I think, that its very uneven performance on these problems be passed carefully in review. These cases represent, we would repeat, almost a third of the Court's total First Amendment work load.

25

The Denial of Employment

We begin our survey of partial sanctions keyed to membership in disfavored groups with cases in which public employment is the privilege being withheld. In general, the argument in these cases will be over an apparently simple issue: To what extent may the state as employer condition employment in terms of the employee's loyalty? Common sense would seem to dictate the answer that the state is surely entitled to refrain from employing the disloyal. On this view, the state's objective is not to regulate loyalty; it is simply to protect the public service in much the same way the prohibition against partisan political activity was designed to do in *Mitchell*. But perplexities quickly arise when we look for practicable criteria of disloyalty. The tendency has, understandably, been to use simple indices such as membership in disfavored groups. Hence an initial concern with some sort of generic loyalty is soon truncated to a concrete concern with the fact of membership. It thus becomes difficult to say whether the appropriate analogy is *Mitchell* and concern for the public service, or *Bond* and concern with freedom of speech and association.

There are two ways in which the state acts to limit public employment. The first is by making the proscribed membership in itself the basis for dismissal, or even the basis for criminal sanctions for holding public employment while a member. The second is the loyalty oath, which requires that the employee come forward and swear he is not a member of the group, so that failure to take the oath becomes the ground for discharge. The two approaches pose the same core issue, namely, whether the state may bar the member of the disfavored group from the public job. The loyalty oath, however, has a sociology and a coloration all its own; and its use generates distinctive grievances. We will therefore treat it independently in the next chapter.

In this chapter we will discuss two early partial sanction cases. The first of these—*United States v. Lovett*[1] in 1946—involves a clumsy, overt effort by Congress to remove particular individuals from government employment because of their views and associations. Although not argued on First Amendment grounds, *Lovett* is a revealing datum about the legal strategies of anti-Communism. The second case—*American Communication Association v. Douds*[2] in 1950—is of great interest because the partial sanction problem is treated so explicitly. Chief Justice Vinson, writing for the Court, offers an extended analysis of the distinctive issues raised by the use of partial sanctions, while Justice Black in a powerful dissenting opinion enters cogent objections. Indeed, in a sense, *Douds* can be said to "create" the partial sanction problem as an analytic matter.

United States v. Lovett

Lovett is the poetically right case with which to begin our survey of partial sanctions keyed to membership, for it involved the most primitive of all efforts to discipline domestic subversion. The controversy arose out of a well-publicized effort by Representative Martin Dies of Texas, the first chairman of the House Un-American Activities Committee, to rid government service of specific individuals he thought unfit because subversive in their views and associations. This effort culminated in a rider attached to an appropriation measure which barred salary or compensation to three employees who were singled out by name. The Supreme Court in a unanimous decision affirmed a holding by the Court of Claims that the three were entitled to a judgment for services rendered. In an opinion by Justice Black, the Court rested its judgment on the unconstitutionality of the rider as a bill of attainder. Justice Frankfurter in a concurring opinion, joined by Justice Reed, rested his vote on a narrowing construction of the rider by which he sought to avoid any constitutional question.

The *Lovett* facts indicate that at this early date the House Un-American Activities Committee was ingenuously candid about its aspirations: it envisaged its legislative hearings as the first step in removing undesirable individuals from government. Established by the House in 1938 as an expression of its concern with subversives, the Committee under Chairman Dies had undertaken to compile lists of people and organizations it thought subversive. At one point in this general campaign Dies had made a speech on the floor of the House in which he attacked thirty-nine named persons as "irresponsible, unrepresentative, crackpot, radical bureaucrats." He urged the Appropriations Committee to take "immediate and vigorous steps" to eliminate these people from public office. The Appropriations Committee dutifully reported out an amendment to the Treasury-Post Office Appropriation Bill which barred use of any funds thereby appropriated to pay the persons Dies had attacked. The amendment precipitated heated debate, and eventually it was decided that the Committee should first hold hearings at which the charges could be aired and the persons named could have a chance to defend themselves.

A subcommittee held hearings and formulated the following definition of "subversive activity":

Subversive activity in this country derives from conduct intentionally destructive of or inimical to the Government of the United States—that which seeks to undermine its institutions, or to distort its functions, or to impede its projects, or to lessen its efforts, the ultimate end being to overturn it all. Such activity may be open and direct as by effort to overthrow, or subtle and indirect as by sabotage.[3]

The subcommittee then proceeded to find that under this extraordinarily loose definition three of the named individuals—Dodd, Lovett, and Watson—were guilty of having engaged in "subversive activity" and recommended that they be held "unfit" for government employment. The subcommittee's findings with respect to Watson— similar to its findings as to the other two—stated that his "membership and association . . . with the organizations mentioned, and his views and philosophies as expressed in various statements and writings, constitute subversive activity."

The measure proposed by the Appropriations Committee was then passed by the House. It ran into difficulties, however, with the Senate, which rejected the proviso five times before yielding to the necessity of having an appropriations bill. It was also resisted by the President, who stated publicly that, like the Senate, he was forced to yield but thought the measure "not only unwise and discriminatory, but unconstitutional."

Reading these facts with his customary realism, Justice Black assesses the legislation as a measure designed to remove and bar persons from government as punishment for their political beliefs. Ironically, he does not rely on the First Amendment, although in retrospect the abridgement of First Amendment rights seems unmistakable. Had he done so, we would in 1946 have had an important precedent on the partial sanction under the First Amendment. Instead, Black, following plaintiff's counsel, elects to invoke the prohibition against bills of attainder, a cryptic and technical constitutional provision which was to become a curiously special favorite of his.[4] Thus, while his indignation at the shabbiness of this government action is splendid and warming, his handling of the case bequeaths a very narrow precedent with only the most limited application to matters of political freedom.

Bills of attainder, as Black defines them, are "legislative acts, no matter what their form, that apply either to named individuals or to easily ascertainable members of a group in such a way as to inflict punishment on them without a judicial trial."[5] He writes:

No one would think that Congress could have passed a valid law, stating that after investigation it had found Lovett, Dodd, and Watson "guilty" of the crime of engaging in "subversive activities," defined that term for the first time, and sentenced them to perpetual exclusion from any government employment. Section 304, while it does not use that language, accomplishes that result. The effect was to inflict punishment without the safeguards of a judicial trial and "determined by no previous law or fixed rule."[6]

What tension there is in the case is generated by the opposition between Justices Black and Frankfurter, even though both agree that the petitioners are entitled to be paid. The opposition is very like that which arises fifteen years later in *SACB*, where Black is the realist insisting that the Act must be taken as Congress had obviously intended and that the essential constitutional issue must be confronted, while Frankfurter is almost fiercely committed to the long-term institutional values in avoiding constitutional confrontation wherever possible and in avoiding impeaching official motivation always.

As Justice Frankfurter sees the case, the measure is not a bill of attainder, even if it is read as Black contends. In singling out the plaintiffs by name, however, it does raise serious constitutional issues of another sort—due process and separation of powers. He argues that the Court should favor a construction which avoids constitutional doubts and that such a construction is available: to read the legislation not as terminating employment but simply as prohibiting payment for it. Under that construction the plaintiffs had validly performed services for which the government's obligation to pay remained. Thus, if Justice Black handles the case so as to leave no residue of precedent on political freedom, although he is deeply attentive to the political realities, Justice Frankfurter, while as a matter of principle ignoring the political realities, manages to convert it into a foolish, arid, technical dispute, which in fact it so clearly was not.

Although the point is not essential to his decision, since he does not adopt Black's construction of the law, Justice Frankfurter goes to heroic lengths to refute Black's bill of attainder argument. Even accepting Black's reading that the law *bars* employment to those named, he questions whether the bar can be said by the Court to have been intended by Congress as *punishment* for past associations. His avoidance of the political realities is so deliberate that it must be taken not as insensitivity to the obvious facts, but as commitment to a different principle of constitutional adjudication. Justice Frankfurter at this moment is indeed, to borrow Thoreau's famous phrase, marching to the beat of a different drummer:

Is it clear then that the respondents were removed from office, still accepting the Court's reading of the statute, as a punishment for past acts? Is it clear, that is, to that degree of certitude which is required before this Court declares legislation by Congress unconstitutional? The disputed section does not say so. So far as the House of Representatives is concerned, the Kerr Committee, which proposed the measure, and many of those who voted in favor of the Bill . . . no doubt considered the respondents "subversive" and wished to exclude them from the Government because of their past associations and their present views. But the legislation upon which we now pass judgment is the product of both Houses of Congress and the President. The Senate five times rejected the substance of [section] 304. It finally prevailed, not because the Senate joined in an unexpressed declaration of guilt and retribution for it, but because the provision was included in an important appropriation bill. The stiffest interpretation that can be placed upon the Senate's action is that it agreed to remove the respondents from office (still assuming the Court's interpretation of [section] 304) without passing any judgment on their past conduct or present views.

Section 304 became law by the President's signature. His motive in allowing it to become law is free from doubt. He rejected the notion that the respondents were "subversive," and explicitly stated that he wished to retain them in the service of the Government. Historically, Parliament passed bills of attainder at the behest of the monarch. The Constitution, of course, provides for the enactment of legislation even against disapproval by the Executive. But to hold that a measure which did not express a judgment of condemnation by the Senate and carried an affirmative disavowal of such condemnation by the President constitutes a bill of attainder, disregards the historic tests for determining what is a bill of attainder.[7]

I think I understand the long-term values Justice Frankfurter is seeking to protect here, but somehow his display of energy and ingenuity—and one is tempted to add, enthusiasm—for this technical point, which is for him dicta, in this context, confronted by these facts, is unnerving. To turn statements of outrage by the Senate and the President that they are being blackmailed by the House into approving indecent legislation—the Senate's first rejection of the bill was 69 to 0—into sources of ambiguity as to the motivation of the legislation is, I admit, highly ingenious. It is also absurd.

American Communication Association v. Douds

It is characteristic of the uneven flow of problems to the Court that the next major case after *Lovett*—*American Communication Association v. Douds* in 1950—presented the partial sanction issue in a highly complex form.[8] *Douds* was the first of the Court's "big" anti-Communist precedents. It was perceived by the justices as a major confrontation and elicited seventy-five pages of opinions—a contribution to that special and peculiar shelf that includes *Dennis, Yates, Scales, SACB,* and *Joint Anti-Fascist Refugee Committee.* In retrospect, one is struck by how difficult the *Douds* case must have been for the justices. On one hand, there were the pressures generated by the mood of the country and the lawmakers; on the other, the Court had had little experience with the oblique First Amendment issues generated by the use of partial sanctions. Moreover, it was still a year away from *Dennis* and the effort to think through First Amendment norms when direct criminal sanctions were used against the Communist Party and its members. It thus had no baseline against which to place the partial sanction issue.

Douds is not, strictly speaking, a public employment case; rather, it involves a government effort to regulate employment in the private sector—officership in unions—by means of the allocation of certain benefits. At issue is the constitutionality of Section 9(h) of the Taft-Hartley Amendments to the National Labor Relations Act. Designed to curb the influence of Communists in labor unions and thereby to inhibit "political strikes," Section 9(h) required unions to "purge" themselves, if they wished to obtain the protection of the right to organize and bargain collectively afforded by the Act. The legal device was to require the *union* to file with the National Labor Relations Board an affidavit executed by each of its officers to the effect that "he is not a member of the Communist Party or affiliated with such party, and that he does not believe in, and is not a member of or supports any organization that believes in or teaches, the overthrow of the United States Government by force or by any illegal or unconstitutional methods." The Court upheld the affidavit requirement in a 5 to 1 decision, with Justices Clark, Minton, and Douglas not participating. Chief Justice Vinson wrote the opinion of the Court. Justices Frankfurter and Jackson, disturbed by the references to belief in the oath, concurred in part and dissented in part. And Justice Black filed the lone full dissent.[9]

It is noteworthy how gingerly the lawmakers approached the problem. There is no effort to tackle the grievance head on by making "political strikes" a crime. The approach is prophylactic after the fashion of conflict of interest legislation. The strategy is to reduce the risk of political strikes by removing from positions of leadership in the labor arena those thought likely, on the evidence of their beliefs and associations, to foment them. There is no effort to bar Communists from labor unions. The target of the affidavit requirement is selective; it is aimed at officers only, and the concern is with *present* membership only. Section 9(h) does not even directly bar Communists from being officers of unions; it simply withholds the benefits of the National Labor Relations Act from unions where this is the case. And finally, the form of regulation used to achieve this purpose is not direct but is the oblique device of the loyalty oath. Like the Subversive Activities Control Act of 1950, the Taft-Hartley anti-Communist affidavit requirement is the product of what we customarily admire as legal craftsmanship.

Douds touches on a number of distinct issues. It is, among other things, a decisive precedent on the constitutionality of loyalty oaths. We will consider this aspect of the case in the next chapter. Here our central concern is with the question of whether the partial sanction of denying the benefits of the NLRA to unions whose officers do not execute the anti-Communist affidavit can be squared with the First Amendment. But before we turn to this question two idiosyncratic issues raised by the wording of the affidavit require attention. The union officer was required to swear that he was not a member of or affiliated with the *Communist Party,* and that he did not *believe in* and was not a member or supporter of any organization that *believed in* or taught the overthrow of the government by force or by illegal or unconstitutional methods. The Act thus presented the anomaly in Anglo-American law of legislation which (i) used *proper names*—"the Communist Party"—and not simply general terms; and which (ii) touched at least verbally on matters of "belief."

The Proper Naming of the Communist Party

In their anxiety to get at Communist labor leaders, the draftsmen of the Act did not content themselves with requiring a disavowal of the political strike as an objective nor with the disavowal of membership in or support for organizations favoring the violent overthrow of the government; rather, they required, in so many words, non-membership in the Communist Party itself. The Act thus provided sanctions for membership in a particular organization without any finding by a court that the organization had proscribed characteristics. The "finding" about the Communist Party had been made solely by Congress. If the sanctions imposed had been criminal, the anomaly would have been shocking. Congress could not find that the Communist Party was a conspiracy so that membership in it was a crime. The Court was to spend much time and analysis on the Government's efforts to establish the evil of the Communist Party in such cases as *Dennis, Yates, Scales,* and especially *Noto.* And the draftsmen of the 1950 Subversive Activities Control Act had been careful to provide for adversary administrativ e hearing procedures to establish that the Communist Party was a "Communist-action" group. *Douds* thus posed the question of whether Congress could short-circuit the traditional processes of law when the question was one of applying partial sanctions to individuals because of their affiliations with the Communist Party.

The answer given by the Court in *Douds* was yes, and in retrospect the point seems to have received surprisingly little discussion. Chief Justice Vinson finds it sufficient to argue that the Act is not a bill of attainder since, unlike measures such as the one at issue in *Lovett,* it does not impose *punishment* for *past* conduct:

. . . in the previous decisions the individuals involved were in fact being punished for *past* actions; whereas in this case they are subject to possible loss of position only because there is substantial ground for the congressional judgment that their beliefs and loyalties will be transformed into *future* conduct.[10]

Vinson says nothing about the use by Congress of proper names. Nor does the anomaly appear to have bothered Justices Frankfurter and Jackson, both of whom concur in this part of the decision.

Although Justice Frankfurter had insisted in *Lovett* that the legislation there did not fall within the technical profile of a bill of attainder, he nevertheless noted that "the singling out of three government employees for removal" might violate some other constitutional prohibition, and had thought such constitutional doubts strong enough to require the Court to avoid them if it could by adopting a narrower construction of the legislation. In *Douds,* however, he does not comment on "the singling out" of the Communist Party.

The Jackson opinion is in a perverse way responsive to the problem. He begins his discussion by stating that if this legislation required union officials to forswear membership in the Democratic, Republican, or Socialist Party, "all agree that it would be unconstitutional."[11] The difference for him resides in *the findings by Congress* that set the Communist Party apart from ordinary political parties and justify the government intervention into the labor arena. He proceeds to summarize these findings in a celebrated essay profiling the Communist Party. He concludes that, while guilt is of course personal, "personal guilt may be incurred by joining a conspiracy."[12] It is all, he adds, a question of the sufficiency of the evidence. There is sufficient evidence so that Congress "on familiar conspiracy principles"[13] could charge each member of the Party with responsibility for the Party's aims. For Justice Jackson then the Party has been found by Congress to be a criminal conspiracy; hence the application of noncriminal sanctions to it and its members does not raise a problem.

Even Justice Black in dissent cannot be said to meet the point head on. Although he objects eloquently to the whole idea of sanctioning "beliefs and political associations," he does not key his attack to *the naming* of the Communist Party. He is, however, sharply critical of the looseness of the ascription to all members of the Party. After noting the vulnerability of minor parties, such as the Socialist Party, he says this about the reach of the law's rationale:

. . . Under today's opinion Congress could validly bar all members of these parties from officership in unions or industrial corporations; the only showing required would be testimony that some members in such positions had, by attempts to further their party's purposes, unjustifiably fostered industrial strife which hampered interstate commerce.

It is indicated, although the opinion is not thus limited and is based on threats to commerce rather than to national security, that members of the Communist Party or its "affiliates" can be individually attainted without danger to others because there is evidence that as a group they act in obedience to the commands of a foreign power. This was the precise reason given in Sixteenth Century England for attainting all Catholics unless they subscribed to test oaths wholly incompatible with their religion.[14]

The point has an interesting subsequent history. In 1965 the Court has occasion to revisit the issue of proper name reference to the Party in *United States v. Brown,*[15] a case involving a later incarnation of the *Douds* legislation. And this time the issue erupts as the central focus of the case.

In 1959 the oath provisions of the Labor Act, having proved unsatisfactory both because of the offense they caused labor leaders and because of their manifest inefficiency, were replaced with a provision making it a crime for anyone to be a union officer who was a member of the Communist Party, or had been one within the previous five years. The Court in a 5 to 4 decision found this bar on union leadership unconstitutional. It based its decision on the prohibition against bills of attainder and thus did not reach the First Amendment issue. The opinion of the Court by Chief Justice Warren was joined by Justices Black, Douglas, Brennan, and Goldberg; and Justice White entered a dissenting opinion in which he was joined by Justices Harlan, Stewart, and Clark.

At the heart of the controversy over attainders is an issue about the nature of lawmaking. The legislature, it is agreed, cannot adjudicate guilt and punish particular persons. It can, however, regulate conduct preventively by stating that persons with certain characteristics are not entitled to certain benefits or advantages. It can, for example, in order to prevent economic conflicts of interest, provide that employees of underwriting firms may not serve as directors of national banks. On one view, it has thus "punished" such employees by depriving them of the advantages of bank directorships. It has, however, named no individuals and has left all involved free to avoid penalties by giving up either employment in underwriting or directorships in banks. The dissenters in *Brown* insist that the labor statute is simply a variant on conflict of interest legislation designed to avoid the risk of political strikes. The designation of members of the Communist Party is, they argue, the same as the designation of employees of underwriting firms. In each case there is a significantly increased risk of trouble if the individual is a member of the group; and in neither case is past conduct decisive.

The majority, however, will have none of this. Chief Justice Warren argues that the attainder prohibition was taken very seriously as a safeguard by the framers of the Constitution and must be read generously and not as a narrow, archaic measure. Warren reads the prohibition as implementing the separation of powers and confining legislatures to their proper task of passing laws in general terms. Repeatedly he addresses the vice of legislating about the Communist Party by name:

We do not hold today that Congress cannot weed dangerous persons out of the labor movement, any more than the Court held in *Lovett* that subversives must be permitted to hold sensitive government positions. Rather, we make again the point made in *Lovett:* that Congress must accomplish such results by rules of general applicability. It cannot specify the people on whom the sanction it prescribes is to be levied. Under our Constitution, Congress possesses full legislative authority, but the task of adjudication must be left to other tribunals.[16]

In sharp contrast to the *Douds* Court's reading of *Lovett,* which limited the bill of attainder prohibition to situations in which individuals are "being punished for *past* actions," Chief Justice Warren employs a broad definition of "punishment":

It would be archaic to limit the definition of "punishment" to "retribution." Punishment serves several purposes: retributive, rehabilitative, deterrent—and preventive. One of the reasons society imprisons those convicted of crimes is to keep them from inflicting future harm, but that does not make imprisonment any the less punishment.[17]

In the end, the Court does not explicitly overrule *Douds* on this issue; rather, it distinguishes it on the basis of the five-year ban on *past* membership in *Brown,* a factor not present in *Douds.* It does, however, explicitly state that the Court in *Douds* "misread" *Lovett*[18]: the prohibition against attainders is *not* confined to sanctions imposed on past conduct.

The dispute probably cuts deeper than the nagging technical

controversy over the scope of the attainders provision. It is also, I suspect, more intimately connected with the use of partial sanctions than might first appear. Full analysis of the scope of the prohibition against attainders would require a marshalling of history and precedent that goes beyond our purposes, but a few final observations may be ventured.

First, in *Brown* the issue is debated in a curious way, as though some great importance attached to the exact contours of attainders. But this would only be true if the *sole* basis for constitutional objection were an appeal to this one provision of the Constitution. It is obvious that the prohibition against attainders embodies values similar to those set forth in the great generic amendments such as the First and the Fifth. The prohibition itself, however, is narrow and rarely applicable. It is therefore somewhat unfortunate, I think, that the majority in *Brown* elected to place its impeachment of the anti-Communist ban on this rationale. And it is a serious shortcoming of the otherwise carefully argued dissent of Justice White that, having disposed to his satisfaction of the attainder point, he feels no obligation to consider the labor statute against other constitutional objections that could be made to it.

Second, the anomaly of the proper naming of the Party is perhaps best seen if it is viewed against the background of strategies to control subversion. To ban members of X from certain government benefits is then seen *inter alia* as a strategy for limiting organization X and as hence requiring as an indispensable step establishing in a proper way the flaw in organization X.

Third, what may be at the root of things is the desire to utilize prophylactic or preventive regulation. The model, as the dissenters make clear in *Brown,* is that of conflict of interest legislation. It is not a matter of punishment; it is a matter of prudence, of a rational reduction of risks that have an actuarial basis. It may well be that this tactic, which relies on attributing the characteristics of *some* members of the group to *all* members on a probabilistic calculus, will prove impermissible where First Amendment values are concerned. The tactic would seem inevitably to suffer from overbreadth.

The Use of the Idiom of "Belief"

The second idiosyncratic issue raised by the wording of the *Douds* oath generates the sharpest debate, although the point strikes me as far less significant than the proper naming of the Party. The controversy arises because section 9(h) required, among other things, that the union official swear that he did not "believe" in, and was not a member of any organization that "believed" in the overthrow of the government by force.[19]

It is not apparent why the oath slipped into the idiom of "belief." The model of the Smith Act had been available for years at the time section 9(h) was drafted, and it solved the problem by use of "teach" and "advocate." Moreover, since section 9(h) was aimed at Communist union leaders, there was no serious objective of also restricting the individual radical who was not a Communist. Hence, as Justices Frankfurter and Jackson argue, the language about "belief" is readily detachable without hampering the oath, and looks now like surplusage in any event. I have no desire to appear indifferent to the values involved in the norm that beliefs are inviolate, but in this context I find it difficult to ascribe that meaning to "belief." What is the difference between being a member of an organization that *believes* in violent overthrow and an organization that *teaches* it? Surely since the grave issue of the constitutionality of part of a federal statute was involved, it was possible to construe these uses of "belief" so as to eliminate the controversy on this ground and to force it on to the more serious First Amendment considerations.

The reactions of the justices to the "belief" puzzle are fascinating. Chief Justice Vinson follows the strategy of construing the term narrowly, limiting it to those committed to overthrow now as an objective. But his construction does not quite do the trick and he is left arguing that under extreme circumstances, as for example, the barring from the Secret Service of those who believe in the assassination of Presidents, the sanctioning of belief would be permissible. Justice Black in dissent has much to say about sanctioning beliefs. His argument, however, does not turn on the actual use of the term in the oath but on the more fundamental point that the law invades "beliefs *and* political affiliations."

It is Justices Frankfurter and Jackson who are excited about the transgression involved.[20] They find no constitutional flaw in the effort as a whole, but their tolerance is exceeded by this effort to sanction "belief." Both are eloquent on behalf of freedom of belief, and one must always be grateful to have the principle reaffirmed. But in the context of the big issues of freedom of speech and association raised in *Douds* I do not find their fastidious regard for the inviolability of belief, and that alone, especially heartening.

Justice Jackson argues, in effect, that the use of partial sanctions where belief is involved is absolutely forbidden. It is not a matter of weighing the infringement of liberty against the rational purpose of reducing the risks of political strikes. The calculus of individual versus state interests which Jackson finds persuasive in the case of speech and association is totally out of place when it is belief that is touched:

I think that under our system, it is time enough for the law to lay hold of the citizen when he acts illegally, or in some rare circumstances when his thoughts are given illegal utterance. I think we must let his mind alone.[21]

Thus, in the Jackson scheme belief is given a preferred position over speech and association.

Justice Frankfurter's rationale for rejecting the belief provisions of the oath is not only that they touch belief; it is also that they touch belief in a vague and uncertain manner likely to deter a man of conscience from taking the oath. He seizes upon the circumstance that the oath proscribes belief in overthrow of the government "by force or by any illegal or unconstitutional methods." The terms "illegal or unconstitutional" are, Frankfurter argues, impermissibly vague.[22] Vagueness is a fatal flaw here for two reasons. First: "It should not be assumed that oaths will be lightly taken; fastidiously scrupulous regard for them should be encouraged."[23] Second:

A man can be regarded as an individual and not as a function of the state only if he is protected to the largest possible extent in his thoughts and in his beliefs as the citadel of his person. Entry into that citadel can be justified, if at all, only if strictly confined so that the belief that a man is asked to reveal is so defined as to leave no fair room for doubt that he is not asked to disclose what he has a right to withhold.[24]

The Frankfurter opinion, it should be noted, can be said to lay the basis for what in later cases is to become the chief method of attack on oaths: *Oaths are to be construed as they would be read by a man of conscience who does not swear lightly.* If this premise is taken seriously, it becomes possible to find ambiguity in almost any language. As we shall see, the price the Court will exact for use of the oath format will be to require that oaths be drafted with almost superhuman lucidity.

Neither Justice Jackson nor Justice Frankfurter acknowledges the insight which causes Justice Black to link belief and association. When a man is charged with being a member of an organization that advocates certain positions, what are we asserting about him? What has he done beyond *believing* in those positions? It is not that he himself has advocated those positions; presumably he has not said a word. Is the act of joining a group so overt a manifestation of belief as to make it different in kind from beliefs held only inwardly? Justices Frankfurter and Jackson clearly find a decisive difference at this point; equally clearly, Justice Black does not.

This is as appropriate a juncture as any to puzzle over the relationship between freedom of belief and freedom of speech. We like the ring of the classic formula that a man should be free to think what he pleases and to say what he thinks. Obviously for the most part the two ideas are inseparable. Freedom to believe what one wishes but not to voice those beliefs would be illusory. The question is whether any meaningful additional protection is afforded to liberty beyond that given by freedom of speech by holding that beliefs are inviolate. When a belief is translated into words, it loses any distinctive immunity as belief; when belief is silent, it would seem protected not by law but by the sheer impracticality of policing it. This suggests that the one occasion where talk of inviolate beliefs makes sense is when we deal with religion. And, as Justice Black argues from history, the chief, if not the only, way the law can reach such inner activities is by way of the oath, by compelling affirmance of that which the true believer cannot affirm. It is important to have safeguards in our constitutional system against this claim of government; but, religion apart, it is difficult to see inviolability of belief as adding to the protections afforded by proper norms as to freedom of speech and association. In the end, the surfacing of the belief issue in the political arena in *Douds* seems to me to have been an unimportant accident.

The Merits of the Partial Sanction

The lengthy discussion thus far of *Douds* has in a very real sense been prefatory to the core issue posed by the case—the propriety under the First Amendment of the use of the partial sanction keyed to political association. The bulk of Chief Justice Vinson's opinion for the Court is devoted to this subtle, perplexing issue. And he deals with it squarely, thus providing in 1950 what may still be the fullest judicial exposition on partial sanctions and the First Amendment.

At the outset Vinson firmly rejects the Government's argument that the case presents no First Amendment issue because no sanction is involved, that it was merely withholding a "privilege" which it was not obligated to furnish. He recognizes that, whatever the jurisprudential classification of the advantage furnished to unions by the NLRA, "it may well make it difficult for unions to remain effective if their officers do not sign the affidavits."[25] The advantage, whether a right or a privilege, is weighty enough to raise a substantial First Amendment question:

The difficult question that emerges is whether, consistently with the First Amendment, Congress, by statute, may exert these pressures upon labor unions to deny positions of leadership to certain persons who are identified by particular beliefs and political affiliations.[26]

With remarkable care and precision, Vinson then proceeds to position the partial sanction issue, avoiding one temptation after another to short-circuit the analysis and reduce the issue to some other, more tractable form. These moves are worth retracing, for they furnish an analytic map of just where the partial sanction, as a distinctive issue, falls.

(i) Vinson does not take the shortcut that appears to have appealed to Justice Jackson. He does not, that is, for the purposes of this case, explicitly treat the Communist Party as a criminal conspiracy to overthrow the government. Such an approach would reduce the question before him to whether a member of that conspiracy could be barred from union office. My guess is that in fact he sees the merits this way and that this perception controls his decision. The point is only that he does not elect to make it his *public* reason for upholding the partial sanction. The partial sanction issue, it should be underscored, only emerges as a problem in its own right when the state attempts by means of partial sanctions to regulate beyond what is permissible for direct sanctions.

(ii) Vinson also avoids the trap of viewing the case simply as a restriction of economic opportunities so as to bring it into line with other instances of such regulation, such as regulations designed to avoid conflicts of interest. We noted earlier that most, if not all, partial sanction cases have a *twin* aspect. A law providing that you cannot be a Y, if you are a member of X, can be viewed either as an abridgement of the freedom to be a Y or as an abridgement of the freedom to belong to X. With admirable clarity, Vinson traces the consequences under each view. He is clear that if we are concerned with the limiting of the freedom to be a Y, in this case a union official, the case is easy. All that is required is that there be a reasonable relation between the ban and the apprehended evil. Here the risk of political strikes reason-

ably warrants the banning from union positions of men thought especially prone to calling such strikes. The case neatly fits a prior precedent in which the Court upheld a ban on members of securities
underwriting firms serving as directors of national banks.[27] "If no
more were involved than possible loss of position," notes Vinson,
"the foregoing would dispose of the case."[28] But he recognizes that
more *is* involved. The regulation must also be appraised in its other
aspect—as a limitation on the freedom to belong to X, in this case to
be a member of the Party or of an organization that teaches violent
overthrow:

. . . the more difficult problem here arises because, in drawing lines on the
basis of beliefs and political associations, though it may be granted that the
proscriptions of the statute bear a reasonable relation to the apprehended
evil, Congress has undeniably discouraged the lawful exercise of political
freedoms as well.[29]

Douds is thus, in effect, a holding that in partial sanction cases the
constitutionality of the sanction must be tested by viewing it in *each*
of its twin aspects. Moreover, the above passage suggests that the test
for the First Amendment, or X, aspect, is more stringent that that for
the economic, or Y, aspect. Something more than "a reasonable relation to the apprehended evil" must be called for. Otherwise the answer to the economic abridgement aspect would also have been the
answer to the political freedom aspect. Whether fully intended or not,
the passage carries the promise of a preferred position treatment for
partial sanctions affecting First Amendment freedoms. As we shall see
in a moment, this is a promise Vinson is unable to keep when, having
positioned the issue with such discrimination, he finally proceeds to
resolve it.

(iii) Having thus resisted two efforts to foreclose the issue in favor
of the regulation, he proceeds to reject two proposals for foreclosing
the issue against the regulation. We noted earlier that all strategies
of direct censorship have the same status; that is, if a partial sanction
can be read as a deliberate effort to censor and suppress—to censor
X rather than to regulate Y—it presents a constitutional question
which is no different than it would be were direct sanctions used.
Vinson refuses to read the anti-Communist affidavit requirement as
a direct sanction. He accepts fully the word of Congress that the target
of the law is not Communism but *political strikes:*

Government's interest here is not in preventing the dissemination of Communist doctrine or the holding of particular beliefs because it is feared that unlawful action will result therefrom if free speech is practiced. Its interest is in protecting the free flow of commerce from what Congress considers to be substantial evils of conduct that are not the products of speech at all. Section 9(h), in other words, does not interfere with speech because Congress fears the consequences of speech; it regulates harmful conduct which Congress has determined is carried on by persons who may be identified by their political affiliations and beliefs.[30]

As Vinson sees it, the statute leaves Communists as such alone; men may go on being Communists. He will not therefore assess it as a strategy for discouraging Communism.

The baffling thing about partial sanctions keyed to subversion is whether the official motivation for employing them can be viewed in so one-dimensional a way. Certainly, when the tactic becomes more prevalent and affects many other privileges besides that of being a union official, it must at some point be weighed as an effort to limit Communism; not doing so was the great weakness of the Court's handling of the *SACB* case where the tactics were coordinated in a single statute. Yet at the date of *Douds*—1950—there is plausibility to the Court's view that the regulation was aimed at political strikes alone.

(iv) Finally, the Vinson opinion explicitly rejects the thesis of the parties that since the case involves an admitted abridgement of political freedoms, whether full or partial, the appropriate test is the clear and present danger formula. There is only one test for First Amendment questions, the argument runs, and clear and present danger is that test. The Court is not disposed to challenge the thesis that clear and present danger is the test for direct sanctions, but it does reject the notion that partial sanctions are governed by the same criteria. Rather, the Court takes its clue from the public forum cases involving such matters as the regulation of the distribution of leaflets to prevent littering:

When particular conduct is regulated in the interest of public order, and the regulation results in an indirect, conditional, partial abridgement of speech, the duty of the courts is to determine which of these two conflicting interests demands the greater protection under the particular circumstances presented.[31]

The Vinson opinion thus makes a remarkable contribution to the mapping of the partial sanction issue. The Court will not deny that the anti-Communist affidavit requirement abridges political freedom; it will not test the constitutionality of the measure as it would mere regulation of union employment; nor will it test it as it would criminal censorship against the sweep of the clear and present danger test. It has posited a *distinctive* problem that requires a *distinctive* test. But having so precisely positioned the issue, the opinion falters. The distinctive test proffered is simply the balancing of interests:

In essence, the problem is one of weighing the probable effects of the statute upon the free exercise of the right of speech and assembly against the congressional determination that political strikes are evils of conduct which cause substantial harm to interstate commerce and that Communists and others identified by section 9(h) pose continuing threats to that public interest when in positions of union leadership.[32]

The balancing process turns out to be crude and altogether predictable. On the government side of the scales he lays the interest in preventing political strikes and the likelihood that members of the Party will foment them if they are union leaders. Recalling other speech cases, he observes:

When compared with ordinances and regulations dealing with littering of the streets or disturbances of householders by itinerant preachers, the relative significance and complexity of the problem of political strikes and how to deal with their leaders become at once apparent.[33]

Turning to the speech side of the scales he notes that the statute does not limit anyone's speech or association; Communists may go on being Communists:

The "discouragements" of section 9(h) proceed, not against the groups or beliefs identified therein, but only against the *combination* of those affiliations or beliefs *with* occupancy of a position of great power over the economy of the country. [Emphasis added.][34]

The law thus has only the most narrow and discriminating impact on political freedoms:

Section 9(h) touches only a relative handful of persons, leaving the great majority of persons of the identified affiliations and beliefs completely free from restraint. And it leaves those few who are affected free to maintain their affiliations and beliefs subject only to possible loss of positions which Congress has concluded are being abused to the injury of the public by members of the described groups.[35]

The opinion works to its inevitable climax. The *Mitchell* case is offered as precedent; here the infringement is far more selective than it was in *Mitchell.* There is, he concludes, no offense to the First Amendment in section 9(h):

That Amendment requires that one be permitted to believe what he will. It requires that one be permitted to advocate what he will unless there is a clear and present danger that a substantial public evil will result therefrom. It does not require that he be permitted to be the keeper of the arsenal.[36]

In the end, the opinion does not satisfy. The justification for the limitation of political freedom is the same as that offered for the economic limitation, namely, that there is a rational relation between the proscription and the evil apprehended. What is missing is any distinctive First Amendment note. The balancing should somehow be done with a First Amendment thumb on the scales.

Moreover, the Vinson opinion veers unhappily close to the Holmes *bon mot* about the policeman. In the end, this is not so bad, he says, because the sanction is only partial; he can still be a Communist if he will forego union leadership; and other Communists not aspiring to union leadership are free to flourish. But if this is the correct logic, it is obvious that in all situations the partial will survive First Amendment challenge simply because it is partial.

Further, the opinion accepts as its rationale a premise about Communism which it neglects to scrutinize: Communists may be deposed as union leaders because they are intrinsically unreliable; they put Party objectives over union objectives; hence they are likely to call strikes to suit Communist, not union, ends. *But on this premise Communists are unreliable wherever they are placed in the society.* The apparently discriminating and limiting concern with political strikes is not a limiting factor at all. For the same reason, Communists will be "corrupt" public officials, government employees, defense contractor employees, schoolteachers, lawyers, shoe salesmen, or editorial writers.

For much the same reason, the opinion's effort to limit the decision to "only a handful of persons" is illusory. Does Vinson really mean that if more than a handful are affected the balance will be struck differently? And if not, what then is the consideration that persuades the Court that First Amendment rights have not been "unduly" abridged? Finally, since each group in the society which believes itself threatened by Communism may adopt this prophylactic tactic, who is to add up the impact of the partial sanctions?

It is the great virtue of Justice Black's prescient dissent that he so clearly sees the significance of the step the Court is taking and so clearly foresees how difficult the Court's logic will be to contain:

Under such circumstances, restrictions imposed on proscribed groups are seldom static, even though the rate of expansion may not move in geometric progression from discrimination to arm-band to ghetto and worse. Thus I cannot regard the Court's holding as one which merely bars Communists from holding union office and nothing more. For its reasoning would apply just as forcibly to statutes barring Communists and their suspected sympathizers from election to political office, mere membership in unions, and in fact from getting or holding any jobs whereby they could earn a living.[37]

Douds stands as a major datum on the Court's efforts to deal with partial sanctions under the First Amendment. The common sense of its result—"It does not require that he be permitted to be keeper of the arsenal"—is tempting. Yet it seems difficult to work out any satisfactory, limited principle for yielding it. It is instructive to recall Justice Jackson's dissent on the belief provisos in the oath. He is the most realistic, the most persuaded of the justices on the evils of Communists and their propensity to disrupt the society by tactics such as political strikes. Yet he will not tolerate the conditioning in any degree of the freedom of belief, even when designed as a prophylactic measure to keep Communists out of positions of power in labor unions. Why, given the First Amendment, are freedom of speech and association any more subservient to the prophylactic strategy? If the answer is, as it will be, that there is a difference between belief and *joining* an organization like the Communist Party, then was not the Court obligated to examine the latent premise that such an organization is a criminal conspiracy with the care and patience it was to show later when the issue was explicitly before it in *Dennis, Yates, Scales,* and *Noto?*

It is instructive, too, to juxtapose the case to *Bond v. Floyd.* In *Bond* the sanction affected only legislators who made radical speeches, yet the partialness of the sanction did not impress the Court at all. Once it established that any other citizen could say what Bond had said, it treated the case for sanctioning him with grave but not total skepticism. It asked why legislators, given their role and function, should not enjoy the same freedom as other citizens. If we ask the same question about labor leaders in *Douds*—if the ordinary citizen is free to be a Communist, why aren't they?—the answer is not so easy. It would require that we examine in a comparable way the role and function of the union leader.

In the end, as we mull *Douds* over in our minds, three points emerge. First, it is clear that the partial sanction issue cannot be handled without a *baseline* afforded by the resolution of the direct sanction issue. The impossible dilemma for the Court in *Douds* was that *at that time* it had not yet been forced to confront the direct sanction; it did not have the perspective of the necessary baseline. The second point is perhaps better stated at this stage as a hunch; it is that the solution of the partial sanction problem may turn out to be much the same as that of the direct sanction problem. The third point is the familiar one that in retrospect Justice Black's instinct for freedom appears remarkable—remarkable not only in its gallantry but also in its perceptiveness.

26

The Loyalty Oath

The partial sanction in *Douds* was cast in the form of a loyalty oath. The Taft-Hartley Act did not simply bar the benefits of the National Labor Relations Act to unions with officers who were Communists; it conditioned those benefits on the execution by union officers of an affidavit disavowing Communist Party membership. Altogether apart from the core issue of the scope of the disqualification embodied in its terms, the oath device generates controversy. In this chapter we will consider the Court's response to the issues raised by this form of regulation, as we continue to trace its experience with the partial sanction of withholding public employment.

The oath has distinctive legal properties as a regulatory device. Most regulation simply threatens sanctions if disfavored behavior occurs. So long as a person does not engage in the proscribed behavior the law will leave him alone, and even if he does engage in the behavior, the law will leave him alone unless it discovers it and can prove it. The oath, like the licensing statute, requires a positive act from everyone if he wishes to avoid a sanction, a loss of benefit. Whether or not he has engaged in the disfavored behavior, *he must come forward* and take the oath or suffer the loss of the privilege. A loyalty oath is thus a form of regulation which directly touches everyone and not simply those engaged in the disfavored behavior. Moreover, once the oath is taken, the law makes no further demands on the citizen unless it can be shown he swore falsely, in which case sanctions for perjury become available. To be effective as regulation then, the oath must be confined to cases where there is reason to believe men will not take it lightly or swear falsely.

The oath format also has a sociology all its own. The very idea of an oath, regardless of its terms, evokes from many people stubborn and bitter opposition. History furnishes numerous examples of men refusing on principle to take an oath although they could readily and honestly swear to its terms. In brief, the test oath has come down to us with a bad name. It is much as though men today react against a symbol of past indignities buried in a history long forgotten.

The behavioral puzzles do not end with the indignant response of those asked to take an oath. The puzzles are at least as great as to why the device ever commends itself to rational lawmakers. When used as a weapon against subversion, it seems contradictory in its own terms. The state seeks to ferret out people it does not trust by asking them to swear to something on which on hypothesis their oath is not to be believed. Moreover, it would appear that there is no regulation which can be accomplished through use of a test oath which could not be accomplished equally well more directly, since the only sanction behind the oath is prosecution for perjury, and a perjury prosecution must involve exactly the kind of proof that would be required for direct regulation.

One can only surmise that the oath appeals to legislators precisely because it is a ceremony. It permits the illusion that something has been done. If, as will be the case, its only predictable result will be to catch a few men of stubborn principle who will refuse to take it, that perhaps is all right too. The test oath is thus a gratuitous, unnecessary legal device, the use of which is always suspect. And it is a mark of the anti-Communist strategies of the 1950s that such heavy reliance was placed on this device.

This then is the problem in sociological terms. But do considerations such as these raise constitutional difficulties? The test oath format may be pointless and suspect, but is it therefore, apart from consideration of the substantive conditions it imposes, constitutionally vulnerable? It is this question that the Court addresses in *Douds*, [1] and the answer is no: there is nothing unconstitutional about oaths *per se.*

Chief Justice Vinson, writing for the Court, quickly disposes of the point. He notes the constitutional provision in Article VI: "no religious Test shall ever be required as a Qualification to any Office or public Trust under the United States." An argument could be mounted, as Justice Black will suggest in dissent, that this provision was meant to incorporate the lessons learned from the distasteful history of sixteenth- and seventeenth-century religious controversies, although one might counter that the provision seems aimed more at the use of conditions keyed to religion than at the oath format. The Chief Justice, however, makes neither point. He confines himself to a literal reading of the constitutional prohibition and to the observation that, whatever else it is, the anti-Communist affidavit required by section 9(h) of the Taft-Hartley Act is not a religious test. He then attempts to buttress the conclusion by arguing that since oaths of allegiance are contemplated by the Constitution, there cannot be any objection to "the mere fact that section 9(h) is in oath form."[2] This argument is unpersuasive because there is an obvious distinction between the *affirmative oath* of allegiance, which is not subject to perjury sanctions and is understood and intended as a ceremony, and the *negative test oath,* which is subject to perjury sanctions and is understood and intended to state disqualifying conditions. To pose the issue of the oath without attending to this obvious distinction is of course to miss what the objection in conscience to oaths is aimed at. But however thin the Vinson rationale for upholding the oath format, the answer is clear: "All we need hold here is that the casting of section 9(h) into the mold of an oath does not invalidate it, if it is otherwise constitutional."[3]

The grievance of those opposed to oaths in form gets a more sympathetic hearing from Justice Jackson in his concurring opinion. But he too ends up with the same answer:

I am aware that the oath is resented by many labor leaders of unquestioned loyalty and above suspicion of Communist connections, indeed by some who have themselves taken bold and difficult steps to rid the labor movement of Communists. I suppose no one likes to be compelled to exonerate himself from connections he has never acquired. I have sometimes wondered why I must file papers showing I did not steal my car before I can get a license for it. But experience shows there are thieves among automobile dealers and that there are Communists among labor leaders. The public welfare, in identifying both, outweighs any affront to individual dignity.[4]

Justice Black in dissent is primarily concerned with the substance of the oath, but in passing he aims a blow at the very idea of an oath: "Since section 9(h) was passed to exclude certain beliefs from one arena of the national economy, it was quite natural to utilize the test oath as a weapon."[5] He then goes on to cite the sources of the historical bad name:

History attests the efficacy of that instrument for inflicting penalties and disabilities on obnoxious minorities. It was one of the major devices used against the Huguenots in France, and against "heretics" during the Spanish Inquisition. It helped English rulers identify and outlaw Catholics, Quakers, Baptists, and Congregationalists—groups considered dangerous for political as well as religious reasons. And wherever the test oath was in vogue, spies and informers found rewards far more tempting than truth. Painful awareness of the evils of thought espionage made such oaths "an abomination to the founders of this nation." Whether religious, political, or both, test oaths are implacable foes of free thought. By approving their imposition, this Court has injected compromise into a field where the First Amendment forbids compromise.[6]

The formal point that regulation is not invalid simply because "cast into the mold of an oath," established in *Douds*, though without full argument, remains good doctrine today. The oath ceremony may be distasteful, it may be superfluous, it may be utterly foolish, but it is not for those reasons unconstitutional.

The next case—*Gerende v. Board of Supervisors of Elections*[7] in 1951—strengthens the impression left by *Douds*. For the Court *unanimously* upholds the oath at issue. This suggests that the oath format *per se* is simply not an issue and hence that an oath cast in sufficiently narrow terms will get the support of the full Court.[8]

Justice Black, it will be recalled, had noted with foreboding in his *Douds* dissent that the reasoning of the majority would apply equally to efforts to bar "Communists and their sympathizers from election to political office."[9] In *Gerende* the anti-subversive oath strategy *is* extended to elective office, but the Court in a brief *per curiam* opinion finds it unnecessary to discuss the point.

The explanation for the absence of controversy resides in the relatively narrow wording of the oath as construed by the state supreme court. The Maryland law at issue, as described by the Court, required that a candidate seeking a place on the ballot in a municipal election "make oath that he is not a person who is engaged 'in one way or another in the attempt to overthrow the government *by force or violence,*' and that he is not knowingly a member of an organization engaged in such an attempt."[10] This formula differs from the *Douds* formula in several respects. First, the idiosyncracies of *Douds* are gone—there is no proper name reference to the Communist Party and there is no reference to "belief." Second, the reference to "illegal and unconstitutional means" which had given rise to Justice Frankfurter's vagueness objections in *Douds* is also gone; the oath is limited to "knowing" membership. And finally the Court's selection of the verb "is engaged" in restating its understanding of the oath—an understanding explicitly adopted by the Maryland Attorney General at the bar of the Court—underscores how narrow the oath was. It reduced to a statement that the candidate was not then and there engaged in the crime of attempting violent overthrow of the government. Thus, however foolish, the oath was, on the surface at least, harmless, and the full Court accepted it.

Gerende reinforces *Douds.* It also underscores the limitations the legal etiquette imposes on how the issue is put. No one asks why the state at the height of anti-Communist feeling should go through the perfectly pointless exercise of requiring candidates for public office to declare that they are not engaged in this particular crime. It is hard to down the suspicion that Maryland envisaged the oath as barring Communists; and that, if any Communists had the hardihood to swear to it, the state anticipated that perjury sanctions would be available or that at least the individual in question would be destroyed by the public clamor over his swearing falsely.

One final word about *Gerende.* Despite its narrowness, there is one note in the oath formula that jars—the phrase "in one way or another." No one is troubled by it in 1951, but sixteen years later in *Whitehill v. Elkins* [11] it will provide the basis for invalidation by the Court of another Maryland oath modeled on this precise wording.

Scienter: Garner *and* Wieman

Garner v. Board of Public Works, [12] the third consecutive decision upholding loyalty oaths, was announced in 1951 on the same day as *Dennis.* The contrast between the two decisions is striking. The same Court that in *Dennis* had agonized over accommodating the norms of the First Amendment with the application of criminal sanctions to advocacy of violent overthrow treats the partial sanctioning of such advocacy in *Garner* as though it involved the regulation of employment and nothing more.

In *Garner* matters are complicated by a problem of retroactivity. The California legislature in 1941 had amended the charter of the

City of Los Angeles to provide that no one would be eligible for employment by the City who within the prior five years had advocated violent overthrow or had been a member of an organization that had so advocated. This provision was not self-executing, and in 1948 the City passed an ordinance requiring each city employee to take the following oath: (i) that he had not within five years of the date of the ordinance advocated violent overthrow; and (ii) that he had not within that period been a member of any organization that so advocated.[13] The *Garner* case arose as a test of the validity of the dismissal of a number of city employees for refusing to take the oath.[14] The Court upheld the oath in a 5 to 4 decision. Justice Clark wrote the opinion of the Court. Justices Black, Douglas, Frankfurter, and Burton dissented.

The *Garner* oath differs from the oath upheld in *Gerende* in several respects. First, the proscribed activity is not "engaging" but "advocating"—for the first time the referent is literally speech. Second, the oath is not limited to *knowing* membership. Third, the coverage of the oath has broadened ominously—it is required of all municipal employees. Finally, *past* as well as present activity is proscribed.

Despite these variations in the oath formula, the Court responds much as it did in *Gerende*. The oath, writes Justice Clark, is "a reasonable regulation to protect the municipal service by establishing an employment qualification of loyalty to the State and the United States."[15] Although *Dennis* is now available to the Court as a source of guidance, there is no effort to use it. The Court neither justifies the oath on the ground that *Dennis* validated the use of advocacy of violent overthrow as the boundary line for criminal sanctions nor is it troubled by the fact that the oath is worded more loosely and broadly than was Judge Medina's instruction in *Dennis*.

More striking, there is no effort to lay the case against *Douds*. Chief Justice Vinson in *Douds* had relied heavily on the circumstance that the sanction affected *only* labor leaders, "a handful of persons." It was this limited scope of the sanction which made the balancing come out in favor of the regulation. The point had been ignored in *Gerende* which had extended the device to elective office. And now in *Garner* the oath is extended to all municipal employment and by inference to all public employment, whatever the sensitivity of the job. None of the justices, however, is disposed to discuss how one squares the *Garner* decision with the *Douds* balancing rationale.

Justice Clark addresses two aspects of the oath—the proscription of past membership and the absence of a *scienter* requirement. He appears somewhat bothered by the fact that the ban is extended to advocacy or membership for five years prior to 1948, the date the oath was instituted. But he finds no merit in the claim that the ordinance violates the prohibition against *ex post facto* laws. The 1941 charter amendment gave full warning that such advocacy or membership rendered one ineligible for public employment. Hence the petitioners had been on notice for seven years of the disability; if they joined a proscribed organization after 1943, they cannot complain that the act renders them ineligible retroactively.

The dissenters, however, are not talking about retroactivity; they are talking about sanctioning past conduct. *Garner* is the first of what will be many cases to pose the puzzle of how to handle the ex-Communist, a problem that was to haunt the decade of the 1950s.

Justice Douglas, in an opinion joined by Justice Black, argues that the ordinance is a bill of attainder. Justice Clark rejects this argument on the grounds that the ordinance—"a general regulation which merely provides standards of qualification and eligibility for employment"[16]—does not impose "punishment," and, further, that it is not directed at named individuals.

It is Justice Burton who puts the point in its most poignant form. He is worried that the law leaves no room for those who have "reformed." He makes the very neat point, in which oddly no one else joins, that the deadline is not five years from the date of the oath but five years from the date of the ordinance, or 1948. Hence, as time goes on, the ban will reach further and further into the past. Thus, despite the 1941 warning, it is an unreasonable regulation of employment:

It leaves no room for a change of heart. It calls for more than a profession of present loyalty or promise of future attachment. It is not limited in retrospect to any period measured by reasonable relation to the present. In time this ordinance will amount to the requirement of an oath that the affiant has *never* done any of the proscribed acts.[17]

Justice Burton's opinion deserves, I think, to be noted and remembered as a contribution to the First Amendment tradition. Burton was never rated as a strong justice. He was an extreme conservative, especially on the Communist issue. Yet on this occasion he makes a more telling point than any of his colleagues.

The other complication which the Court acknowledges is the *scienter* issue. The *Garner* oath, unlike that in *Gerende*, proscribes membership without qualification; it does not require knowledge. Justice

Clark agrees that this is indeed a flaw, but he disposes of it by assuming that the Los Angeles officials will not place so careless and irrational a construction on their oath. He also assumes that, in light of the Supreme Court's reading of the oath, "the City of Los Angeles will give those petitioners who heretofore refused to take the oath an opportunity to take it as interpreted and resume their employment."[18] As a practical matter, Justice Clark probably has taken care of the point. The city officials are likely to accede to so explicit a message from the Court; and should they fail to do so, the Court has already informed them and the world that their oath is unconstitutional.

The issue evokes, however, an impressive dissent from Justice Frankfurter. He is too fastidious to handle it in this fashion. The oath is bad as written; there is no correcting construction by the state supreme court; it is not the job of the Supreme Court of the United States to rewrite the oath. Hence the petitioners should win their lawsuit. Let the state amend its law and try again. This may seem like a tempest in a teapot, but I suspect that it was not. In the anti-Communist atmosphere of the moment the symbol of the Court holding a loyalty oath unconstitutional would have been heartening. Once again we deal in nuances. Perhaps the Court cannot be asked to go out of its way to make heartening gestures; but surely it is proper that it not lift a finger to assist an oath which as written, it is agreed, is unconstitutional.

Justice Frankfurter contributes an illuminating essay on the *scienter* point. He repeats his thesis from *Douds:* "The validity of an oath must be judged on the assumption that it will be taken conscientiously."[19] This would mean that a truly conscientious person could subscribe only if he were "certain" that none of his affiliations were tainted. And such a condition on the privilege of public employment would be bad, because it "makes an irrational demand," because no theory of security requires "such curbs," and because it "is bound to operate as a real deterrent" to association. "These are," writes Frankfurter, "considerations that cut deep into the traditions of our people."[20]

If *scienter* is taken as seriously as Justice Frankfurter takes it in *Garner,* it would arguably impeach the loyalty oath enterprise altogether. For it would require a very close nexus between the member and the evil purpose of the organization. He must "know" in the sense a conspirator knows. But if the nexus is to be so close, the utility of the oath as a screening device is destroyed. Moreover, if the absence of this qualifying term is likely, as Frankfurter predicts, to chill and deter sensible men, it is also likely that the oath will have much the same impact whether the qualifier is added or not. Who can assess what evidence will be taken as sufficient proof of "knowledge" of the "conspiratorial" purposes of a radical political organization? Finally, amidst so much good sense, one can only wonder, uncharitably, why the *scienter* problem did not disturb Justice Frankfurter more in *Douds,* where mere membership in the Communist Party was held by him an adequate basis for an oath.

Douds, Gerende, and *Garner* represent a formidable cluster of precedent supporting the use of the loyalty oath as a device for barring subversives from public employment.[21] But the emergence of four dissents in *Garner* suggests that the justices have grown increasingly uneasy about the device. The next case—*Wieman v. Updegraff*[22] in 1952—confirms this impression.

The expansive momentum of the oath device becomes overwhelmingly evident in *Wieman.* As we have seen, the focus on engaging now in overthrow in *Gerende* expanded to advocating overthrow any time within the past five years in *Garner.* The Oklahoma oath for public employees at issue in *Wieman* retains those features of *Garner* but adds to them a disavowal of membership within the last five years in "the Communist Party" or in "any agency, party, organization, association, or group whatever which has been officially determined by the United States Attorney General . . . to be a communist front or subversive organization."[23]

The *Wieman* oath thus incorporates by reference the Attorney General's list. This is a major step. It extends the area of disqualification enormously—to members of groups that in some loose sense were tied to and sympathetic with Communist positions, a disqualification that would affect a vastly larger number of citizens than any of the measures the Court had previously considered. And the five-year time period broadens the area of disqualification still further.

Also, the incorporation of the Attorney General's list into the oath calls forth an improper partnership between the state and federal agencies pursuing subversion. The Attorney General's list was announced for the limited purpose of serving as a guide to federal employment. Moreover, when tested in the *Joint Anti-Fascist Refugee Committee* case[24] in 1951 it had been found constitutionally defective because of procedural shortcomings. The list had been compiled, it will be recalled, without providing the listed organizations with the

opportunity for a hearing. Finally, as used in the federal loyalty programs, it was evidentiary only; as used in the Oklahoma oath it has
become an automatic bar.

Wieman thus provided the Court with a major occasion to consider where loyalty oaths were leading and to reassess the constitutional analysis. It does not, however, really rise to the occasion.
Although it upsets the Oklahoma oath in a unanimous decision, it
elects not to address itself to either the "Communist front" language
or the use of the Attorney General's list. Instead, in an opinion by
Justice Clark, it adopts the argument of Justice Frankfurter in *Garner*
about *scienter.*

The concern with *scienter* in these cases, it should be noted, has
a dual aspect. From one perspective, it can be seen as a limitation on
the permissible scope of the disqualification; "knowledge," it will be
recalled, is one of the attributes of membership which *Scales* makes a
precondition for the imposition of criminal sanctions. But the *scienter*
issue can also be seen as a problem peculiar to the oath device: You
can only swear to things you know about.

Justice Clark, who had found it possible in *Garner* to assume that
the state would construe its oath so as to provide for knowing membership and that it would afford the petitioners a chance to take the
oath so narrowed, is unable to indulge in such benign assumptions
here. By quirk the Oklahoma Supreme Court has tipped the case the
other way. At the state level a question had arisen as to whether the
oath incorporated the Attorney General's list as of the date of the oath
or as of the date of the passage of the statute. The state court had
ruled that the oath was limited to organizations listed as of the date
of the statute. In theory some organizations listed as of the date of the
statute might have been dropped by the date of the oath, but it is far
more likely that any tendency over the years was in the direction of
adding organizations to the list. Hence the effect of this ruling was,
in a small way, to narrow the scope of the oath. But then the court had
perversely declined to afford the petitioners a chance to take the oath
as so narrowed. This pettiness proves too much for the Supreme
Court. Justice Clark reads the state court as having held that it does
not matter that the affiant cannot tell at the time he confronts the oath
what "front" organizations he is asked to disavow: "This must be
viewed as a holding that knowledge is not a factor under the Oklahoma statute."[25] With this premise in hand, he proceeds firmly and
rapidly to find the oath unconstitutional.

Justice Frankfurter in a concurring opinion repeats in abbreviated form the *scienter* argument he made in *Garner;* he too confines himself to the point that the proviso about "front" organizations is bad because the affiant may have been an "innocent" member. He speaks eloquently about the right of association; it is "peculiarly characteristic" of the American people; "such joining is an exercise of the rights of free speech and free inquiry."[26] And while these are rights of all citizens, the case of teachers "brings the safeguards" of the First Amendment "vividly into operation." He is almost asserting that the chill of the oath, which is tolerable for labor leaders or public employees generally, becomes intolerable when the role is the sensitive one of teacher. And he ends his essay on academic freedom with a long, and welcome, quotation from Robert M. Hutchins. Reading between the lines, we can detect his distress over the havoc the oath device seemed to be causing in the society. He begins his opinion: "The times being what they are, it is appropriate to add a word by way of emphasis."[27]

The same sense of distress permeates the concurrence of Justice Black. He pitches his opinion to quite general themes. After recalling the crisis generated by the passage of the Alien and Sedition Acts, he states:

Today however, few individuals and organizations of power and influence argue that unpopular advocacy has this same wholly unqualified immunity from governmental interference. For this and other reasons the present period of fear seems more ominously dangerous to speech and press than was that of the Alien and Sedition Laws. Suppressive laws and practices are the fashion. The Oklahoma oath statute is but one manifestation of a national network of laws aimed at coercing and controlling the minds of men. Test oaths are notorious tools of tyranny. When used to shackle the mind they are, or at least they should be, unspeakably odious to a free people. Test oaths are made still more dangerous when combined with bills of attainder which like this Oklahoma statute impose pains and penalties for past associations and utterances.[28]

The cases thus far invite one last reflection. *Douds,* the Court's first encounter with the oath device, provided a full, patient analysis of the issues. But in subsequent cases—*Gerende, Garner, Wieman*—little attention is paid to *Douds* as a precedent and as a source of analysis. It barely gets mentioned. The explanation, I suspect, is that the justification for the *Douds* decision was found in the thesis about political strikes and their impact on interstate commerce, a thesis based on the likelihood of specific wrongful action by Communists strategically placed in unions. In contrast, the justification in these public employment cases is simply the exaction, as Justice Frankfurter puts it in *Garner*, of "fidelity" from employees, a much less focused idea. The question for us is whether the fact that qualifications for employment are being set enlarges the power of the state to impose partial sanctions. I would think that the answer must be no, that the validity of such partial sanctions must also depend on their rational relations, as the Court said in *Douds*, "to the evil apprehended." The fact that the qualifications touch First Amendment freedoms should be enough to quiet any commonsense presumption about the right of an employer to have faithful employees.

The Vagueness Technique: Cramp *and* Baggett

For almost a decade after *Wieman* the Court does not have occasion to deal with the loyalty oath. During these years the important precedents on direct criminal sanctions, *Yates* and *Scales*, come down and the zone of criminality attributable to the Communist Party is appreciably narrowed. Then, beginning with *Cramp v. Board of Public Instruction*[29] in 1961, the Court confronts a sequence of oath cases and each time decides *against* the validity of the oath, thereby generating the loose impression that the loyalty oath has been *de facto* outlawed.

During this period the Court also decides several important automatic bar cases which involve the use of partial sanctions but not use of the oath. For convenience, we will first trace the story through the oath cases and then in the next chapter will pick up the non-oath partial sanction cases, as the Court seeks to extricate itself from the precedents of the anti-Communist period.

Cramp is a striking instance of the Court's technique for finding an oath unconstitutional without openly impeaching the premise that loyalty oaths *per se* are not unconstitutional. The case involves a Florida oath required of all public employees. It is suggestive of the seriousness of the whole ceremony that the recalcitrant oath taker, a schoolteacher, had been employed by the state for nine years without taking the oath before anyone discovered it.

The Florida oath is even more wretchedly drafted than the one in *Wieman*. This time the draftsmen not only require disavowal of membership "in the Communist Party," they also again use language about "not believing" in violent overthrow. The Court does not, however, find it necessary to get to either of these points. Rather, it finds the fatal flaw in still another feature of the oath, a clause which requires the affiant to swear: "I have not and will not lend my aid, support, advice, counsel, or influence to the Communist Party."

The issue is joined in a novel way. The state court had definitively construed the oath as requiring *scienter*, thereby meeting the only limitation the Court had thus far imposed on oaths for public employees and foreclosing the approach it had used in *Wieman*. Moreover, the petitioner had, arguably, pleaded himself out of court by affirming his loyalty; he had filed a sworn complaint in which he affirmed that he was not a member of the Party nor had lent it aid, support, etc., that he did not believe in violent overthrow, that he fully supported the Constitution, and that he did not decline to sign the oath out of fear of perjury for a false oath.

It is a measure of the shift of mood that the unanimous Court, in an opinion by Justice Stewart, does not find either of these points an obstacle. It cuts directly to the heart of the difficulty with this oath. It finds that the petitioner, even though he could so readily take the oath, still has a grievance worthy of the Court's attention. That grievance resides in the state's forcing him to take the risk that others will not interpret the oath as he does: "the very vice of which he complains is that the language of the oath is so vague and indefinite that others could with reason interpret it differently."[30] The risk that others might read the oath differently is in one sense ineradicable; what is required as a constitutional matter is that the oath be worded so as to avoid *unnecessary* risk of misinterpretation.[31] The remedy is to draft the oath in terms that are not in customary usage ambiguous. The point is a petty one evocative of a large general principle about the First Amendment: The rights under it cannot be subjected even to minor annoyances, if those annoyances are unnecessary. Even the lightest straw laid on the wrong side will upset the First Amendment balance.

Justice Stewart stresses that the *scienter* requirement does not cure the ambiguity. He asserts again the principle that oaths are to be read by the Court as they will be read by men of conscience who do not take them lightly; and he reaffirms the principle that the standards of permissible vagueness are more stringent where First Amendment freedoms are involved. Finally, he subjects the text of the oath to a very stringent exegesis:

Those who take this oath must swear . . . that they have not in the unending past ever knowingly lent their "aid," or "support," or "advice," or "counsel" or "influence" to the Communist Party. What do these phrases mean? In the not too distant past Communist Party candidates appeared regularly and legally on the ballot in many state and local elections. Elsewhere the Communist Party has on occasion endorsed or supported candidates nominated by others. Could one who had ever cast his vote for such a candidate safely subscribe to this legislative oath? Could a lawyer who had ever represented the Communist Party or its members swear with either confidence or honesty that he had never knowingly lent his "counsel" to the Party? Could a journalist who had ever defended the constitutional rights of the Communist Party conscientiously take an oath that he had never lent the Party his "support"? Indeed, could anyone honestly subscribe to this oath who had ever supported any cause with contemporaneous knowledge that the Communist Party also supported it?[32]

Cramp is thus a strong example of what we have called the "technical preferred position" doctrine of the modern Court. First Amendment freedoms are protected by special doctrines as to vagueness and by special sensitivity to the burden of even minor risk or annoyance.

Cramp yields a loud and clear message: Loyalty oaths are not *per se* invalid, but the Court will not lift a finger on their behalf. We may at first feel somewhat ambivalent about Justice Stewart's display of close textual analysis. Isn't it a bit too artificial and ingenious? But the feeling fades when we recall how easy it would have been for the Florida legislature to model its oath on one which the Court had already validated, such as those in *Douds, Gerende,* and *Garner.* What else were they aspiring to catch by adding those words about aid, influence, counsel, and support? To subject a hypocritical ceremony to a hypercritical reading strikes me as not a bad form of justice at all.

The technique of reading the terms of an oath with the anxious eye of a heroically conscientious man is applied again in the next oath case, *Baggett v. Bullitt*[33] in 1964. At issue are two Washington state oaths—an oath of allegiance required only of teachers and not of other public employees, and a non-subversive oath required of all.[34] Each is found bad. Justice White writes for the majority, and his exegesis of the oaths is even more ingenious than that of Justice Stewart in *Cramp.* Justices Clark and Harlan dissent.

The handling of the non-subversive oath is directly controlled by *Cramp.* The oath requires not only disavowal of membership in the Communist Party, but also—and this is the focus of the controversy—an assertion by the affiant "that I am not a subversive person." The apparent brevity of this oath is belied by the fact that it explicitly incorporates by reference the definition of "subversive person" set forth in another Washington statute. That definition is notably cumbersome and verbose, the state legislature having elaborately embroidered on the simple idea of barring those advocating the violent overthrow of the government or belonging to organizations that so advocate. The companion statute defines a "subversive person" as "any person who . . . advises or teaches by any means any person to commit, attempt to commit, or aid in the commission of any act intended to overthrow, destroy, or alter . . . the constitutional form of the government of the United States . . . by revolution, force, or violence."

Justice White finds the oath incorporating this definition intolerably vague in several respects. Since the state legislature has found that the Communist Party is a "subversive organization" engaged in activities designed to overthrow the government, White finds ambiguous the position of a teacher who has in his class known members of the Party. One cannot be confident, he argues, that the teacher has not thereby increased the resources of the Party and thus aided it in pursuing its evil purposes. Moreover, he is troubled by the reference to teaching "any person . . . to aid," which might, he surmises, reach one who teaches A who in turn passes it on to B who passes it on to C, a Communist. Although the state court had read a *scienter* requirement into the oath, White firmly rejects the argument that this cures the vagueness of the oath. "But what is it," he asks sharply, "that the Washington professor must 'know'?"[35] Thus, *Baggett,* even more clearly than *Cramp,* stands for the proposition that *scienter* will not be enough to cure an oath. Finally, White turns to the reference to altering the constitutional form of government "by revolution." This turns out to be one word too many, since "force" and "violence" are also proscribed. Hence, altering by "revolution" might cover any radical change in government even when effected by legal means. The oath, he concludes, thus suffers from "similar infirmities" to those in *Cramp.*

Justice Clark in dissent is outraged by White's exegesis of the oath:[36]

It is, of course, absurd to say that, under the words of the Washington Act, a professor risks violation when he teaches German, English, history or any other subject included in the curriculum for a college degree, to a class in which a Communist Party member might sit. To so interpret the language of the Act is to extract more sunbeams from cucumbers than did Gulliver's mad scientist. And to conjure up such ridiculous questions, the answer to which we all know or should know are in the negative, is to build up a whimsical and farcical straw man which is not only grim but Grimm.[37]

As in *Cramp*, the majority's display of ingenuity in finding ambiguities does indeed seem forced. But the sloppy lack of focus in the oath is intolerable. Justice White, perhaps responding to the needling of the Clark dissent, speaks effectively to the point:

The State labels as wholly fanciful the suggested possible coverage of the two oaths. It may well be correct, but the contention only emphasizes the difficulties with the two statutes; for if the oaths do not reach some or any of the behavior suggested, what specific conduct do the oaths cover? Where does fanciful possibility end and intended coverage begin?[38]

Moreover, Justice White emphasizes that vagueness is especially to be avoided in the First Amendment area, for it will operate as a stimulus to self-censorship. Quoting the key dictum from *Speiser v. Randall*,[39] he writes: "The uncertain meanings of the oaths require the oathtaker—teachers and public servants—to 'steer far wide of the unlawful zone.' "[40]

The novel point in *Baggett* relates to the other oath, the oath of allegiance. In general, the controversy about oaths has not in its modern form concerned oaths of allegiance. These have been commonplace for public office, army induction, etc., and most citizens have regarded them as pure ceremony with no further implications. They do not, as did the historic test oaths, require an affirmation which does violence to the beliefs of the affiant and thus provides a method of ferreting out beliefs.[41] At most they ask for a diffuse assertion of allegiance to the government. The obvious example is the oath prescribed by the Constitution for the President upon assuming office: "I do solemnly swear that I will faithfully execute the Office of the President of the United States and will to the best of my ability, preserve, protect, and defend the Constitution of the United States." Moreover, as a technical matter such oaths *once taken* cannot be subjected to sanction, other than in some instances impeachment, a sanction which does not depend on the oath for its power; they do not involve the assertion of any fact to which perjury may attach.[42]

The oath in *Baggett* may appear at first glance to be simply one more innocuous oath of allegiance, but almost immediately one's eye is caught by some variations in the wording. It reads:

I do solemnly swear (or affirm) that I will support the constitution and laws of the United States of America and the State of Washington, and will by precept and example promote respect for the flag and the institutions of the United States and the State of Washington, reverence for law and order and undivided allegiance to the Government of the United States.[43]

Justice White is appalled by the vagueness of this oath if taken seriously. Can one criticize society and government without becoming anxious lest he be viewed as breaking his promise to "promote. . . undivided allegiance"? Nor is White impressed by the state's effort to support the oath as no more than an idle ceremony: "Without the criminal sanctions, it is said, one need not fear taking this oath, regardless of whether he understands it and can comply with its mandate, however understood."[44] This argument is impeached, White notes, by the conscientiousness of the draftsmen who attached the proviso: "I understand that this statement and oath are made subject to the penalties of perjury." White then goes beyond this debater's point, good as it is. The state must, he argues, consider those who will not "solemnly swear unless they can do so honestly."[45] The point is akin to the one in *Cramp* that the citizen may not be burdened with the nuisance risk that others will interpret the oath differently than he does. He also may not be subjected to the distasteful experience of swearing lightly and without conviction. In effect, Justice White is admonishing the state that it may not bring forth a solemn device for screening loyalty and then seek to defend the excesses of that device by arguing that no one will take it seriously: "Nor should we encourage the casual taking of oaths by upholding the discharge or exclusion from public employment of those with a conscientious and scrupulous regard for such undertakings."[46]

Wieman, Cramp, and *Baggett* converge to form a powerful line of precedent subjecting loyalty oaths to the most searching scrutiny. They are, however, confined to flaws in the wording of oaths, such as vagueness and lack of *scienter.* They leave untouched and unexamined the central issue of the permissible scope of such partial sanctions if clearly worded and providing for *scienter.* And they make no use of the "revisionist" direct sanction cases, *Yates* and *Scales,* as guidelines. After so many oath cases up to 1966, only in *Douds* has the Court wrestled with the substantive merits of an oath.

The Substantive Merits: Elfbrandt

The linking of the partial sanction problem with the evolving norms for direct sanctions comes in *Elfbrandt v. Russell*[47] in 1966. This decision is the climax of the analytic patterns we have been tracing. It is the most important precedent the Court has yet rendered on the loyalty oath and is a key precedent on partial sanctions in general. Indeed, *Elfbrandt* may well have done for the partial sanction problem what *Brandenburg* did for incitement.

Its power may, however, be clouded by two circumstances. First, the Court is sharply divided. *Elfbrandt* is a 5 to 4 decision. The dissenting opinion is by Justice White, who wrote the majority opinion in *Baggett;* and it is joined by Justice Clark, the author of *Wieman,* Justice Stewart, the author of *Cramp,* and Justice Harlan, on whose opinion in *Scales* the majority relies. Second, the majority opinion by Justice Douglas, although imbued with the key insight, does not pause to argue the fundamental point it unearths about the relationship of partial sanctions to direct sanctions.

The involuted mechanics of the Arizona oath at issue in *Elfbrandt* deserve a prefatory word. In form it is a simple oath of allegiance with none of the embroidering that had troubled the Court in *Baggett.* On the surface, therefore, there is little, if any reason why anyone would object to it. There is, however, a companion statute tied to the oath. It proscribes the familiar roster of things, done "knowingly or willfully": any "act" to overthrow the government by force; any advocacy of such overthrow; membership in the Communist Party; membership in any organization "having for one of its purposes" the violent overthrow of the government At this point the legislature could have executed its intention of keeping such persons from public employment by making it a crime for them to accept public employment. Rather than proceed in a straight line, however, it provides that any person who, "at the time of subscribing the oath or affirmation, or at any time thereafter," had offended in any of the ways listed, "shall be guilty of a felony and upon conviction thereof shall be subject to all the penalties for perjury." In effect, the law makes it a crime for a subversive as defined to be a public employee and then requires all employees to come forward and swear they are not guilty of that crime. Thus the Arizona law brings to the surface the puzzle underlying any use of the oath device. Here *the crime plus the oath* can add nothing by way of deterrence to the crime standing alone. The only function the addition of the oath can perform is to catch the occasional hyperconscientious person who is troubled by oaths and will not swear lightly. Not surprisingly, the *Elfbrandt* case originates in the refusal of the petitioner, "a teacher and a Quaker," to take the oath without a chance to have its "precise scope and meaning" fixed. The Court, although prepared to go very far this time to invalidate the substance of the oath, will still not make oaths *per se* bad, and no one pays any attention to the distinctively supererogatory quality of this oath.

Despite the curious mechanics of their oath, the Arizona draftsmen were careful to meet the *scienter* requirement of *Wieman* and to avoid the excess terms that gave rise to vagueness objections in *Cramp* and *Baggett*. The Court cannot, therefore, employ either of the approaches it had used thus far to upset loyalty oaths. The majority thus elects to confront directly the substantive reach of the oath. As I read Justice Douglas's opinion, they conclude that the oath is overbroad because it does not contain the limitations on membership in subversive organizations imposed in *Scales* as a predicate for the imposition of criminal sanctions:

We recognized in *Scales v. United States* that "quasi-political parties or other groups . . . may embrace both legal and illegal aims." We noted that a "blanket prohibition of association with a group having both legal and illegal aims" would pose "a real danger that legitimate political expression or association would be impaired." The statute with which we dealt in *Scales,* the so-called "membership clause" of the Smith Act, was found not to suffer from this constitutional infirmity because, as the Court construed it, the statute reached only "active" membership with the "specific intent" of assisting in achieving the unlawful ends of the organization.[48]

The Arizona oath then is bad because it meets only one of the three limitations imposed in *Scales:* knowledge is required, but not active membership and specific intent.

Justice Douglas is thus on the brink of a major point, namely, that partial sanctions touching First Amendment freedoms are presumptively governed by the same strict criteria that apply to direct sanctions touching such freedoms. Regrettably, he does not make the point explicit; and thus a fundamental clarification of a large part of the contemporary First Amendment business of the Court is not publicly achieved. Yet the conclusion is securely implicit in the *holding* of the Court.

It will be recalled that the Court in *Scales* found the membership clause issue agonizingly close and was finally willing to impute criminal liability from association only if the three qualifications of knowledge, active membership, and specific intent were added to make membership the functional equivalent of participation in a literal conspiracy; otherwise, guilt remains personal in our system. The decision of the Court in *Elfbrandt* is that comparably stringent scrutiny of guilt through membership or association is required when partial sanctions are employed. The *Scales* requirements are not to be relaxed when the state is seeking simply to state qualifications for its employees in an effort to ensure their fidelity. Thus, the Court, recurring at long last to the direct sanction cases, has not merely found a guideline for decision; it has found something akin to the full answer.

The Douglas opinion moves to its conclusion in giant steps that brush aside the plaints of the dissent that *Scales,* a criminal case, cannot be said to foreclose this one, involving only qualifications for government employment. Moreover, Douglas does not pause to juxtapose the new ruling with the Court's prior decisions in *Douds* and *Garner.* Nor does he appear to be aware that he is breaking new ground; rather, he purports to find not only in *Scales* but also in *Aptheker v. Secretary of State*[49] and *Speiser v. Randall*[50] authority compelling the holding. Nor, finally, does he mention *United States v. Brown,*[51] decided a year earlier, although the Arizona oath contains the same fatal singling out of the Communist Party by name.

If Justice Douglas fails to explain why direct and partial sanctions should be held to the same standard, the four dissenters fail equally to explain why the standards for partial sanctions should be any less stringent. The opinion of Justice White is content to argue that "unequivocal prior holdings of this Court"[52] say that a state is entitled to deny public employment to knowing members of the Communist Party, and that these cases, such as *Garner,* have not been overruled by the majority opinion. The dissenters do not consider the impact that the revisionist doctrines of *Yates* and *Scales must* have had on earlier cases like *Garner.* Nor do they acknowledge the impact that *United States v. Brown* must have had on the Communist clause in this oath. Moreover, they rest their dismissal of *Scales* solely on the fact that it involved criminal sanctions.

Although Justice Douglas does not meet the issue as openly and explicitly as he might have, his opinion is instinct with a major insight. He quotes with discrimination from the Harlan opinion in *Scales* and fully exploits Harlan's acknowledgement that quasi-political groups differ from conventional criminal conspiracies in one important respect: They do not have a single unifying criminal purpose, but rather share "both legal and illegal aims." There is, therefore, in the careful *Scales* analysis precedent for worry about the impact on freedom of association when anything less than literal conspiracy is used by the law to impute "guilt." Douglas argues that the same cautions are relevant when we shift to government employment. The crucial sentence in his opinion reads: "Those who join an organization but do not share its unlawful purposes and who do not participate in its unlawful activities surely pose no threat, either as citizens *or as public employees*" [emphasis added].[53] To reach "the citizen" with constitutional precision, Justice Harlan argued in *Scales,* required that the law establish his nexus to the evil purpose of the group by the threefold ties of knowledge, activity, and evil intent. Justice Douglas is simply asserting that the same precision in establishing the nexus is required when the law seeks to withdraw privileges from "the public employee." Otherwise—although he does not spell out this step in the logic—the relation of the employment regulation "to the evil apprehended" is not reasonable.

The counter-argument of course is that, since we are here regulating employment and not imposing criminal sanctions, the precision need not be so great. There is a rational likelihood that persons who belong to criminal organizations with knowledge of their evil purposes will be unfaithful employees. The issue before the Court is not the imputation of criminal guilt; it is merely the imputation of employee unreliability.

What is at stake is whether the risk calculus of the prudent employer is not in a radical sense at war with the normal regard we have for the value and sensitivity of First Amendment freedoms. The calculus is by its nature probabilistic; it is not that this individual has done something wrong, but that actuarially speaking he carries a higher risk of auto accident. The actuary always imputes guilt by association. But respect for the air of freedom in the United States requires that the government as employer live dangerously.

An Uneasy Epilogue

Despite the flaws in both the majority and dissenting opinions, *Elfbrandt* emerges as a holding of great importance. When it is added to *Wieman, Cramp* and *Baggett,* it makes the line of precedent impeaching loyalty oaths overpowering indeed. It would thus seem the logically right case on which to end the sequence of oath cases. But this time the process of the law slowly working itself pure, which we have come to so admire as the essential strength of the Anglo-American tradition, does not quite run true. The process keeps churning on after *Elfbrandt*, as the Court deals with three more oath cases.[54] The first of these cases—*Whitehill v. Elkins* in 1967—is another instance of stringent scrutiny by the Court of the terms of an oath. But the other two cases—*Connell v. Higginbotham* in 1971, and *Cole v. Richardson*, first in 1970 and then in 1972[55]—stir some uneasiness. They are the first oath cases to be decided by the Burger Court; and although they are not in themselves of great significance, they leave one with the sense that what had appeared settled is in danger of being unsettled.

In *Whitehill* the Court revisits the Maryland oath it had unanimously upheld sixteen years earlier in *Gerende*. And this time to the consternation of three Justices—Harlan, White, and Stewart—the Court finds it invalid. In form the oath appears innocuous. It requires an avowal that one is not *now* "engaged in one way or another in the attempt to overthrow the Government of the United States . . . by force or violence." But Justice Douglas's opinion for the majority offers two lines of argument on the invalidity of the oath, both of which indicate how difficult it is to remove a contemporary oath from the suspicions generated by the recent past.

Although the *Whitehill* oath contains on its face no reference to any other law, Justice Douglas insists that it cannot be construed apart from the Ober Act which authorized it, and that viewed in that light it is overbroad. The Act empowered state agencies to establish procedures to screen out "subversives," broadly defined elsewhere in the statute as persons who advocate "the commission of any act intended to overthrow, destroy, or alter . . . the constitutional form of government of the United States . . . by revolution, force, or violence." The oath was the procedure devised for this purpose by the University of Maryland. Hence, Douglas argues that it must be read not in terms of what it says on its face but in terms of the aspirations of the draftsmen, who could not have intended "to do less" than they were authorized to do in getting at "subversives." Justice Harlan in dissent finds this thesis absurd—you read a document the way it is written! But surely there is some force to Douglas's view that what the draftsmen thought their oath covered will have some bearing on how it will be construed when the law is enforced.

The second Douglas argument goes to an ambiguity in the text of the oath as written, and centers on the phrase "engaged *in one way or another.*" Might not, he worries, innocent membership in a group aimed at overthrow be viewed as being "engaged in one way or another"? The upshot is that in the view of the majority not even this oath can escape grave ambiguities. Justice Harlan purports to be amazed at this ferreting out of doubt: "The only thing that does shine through the opinion of the majority is that its members do not like loyalty oaths."[56] But it would seem that his detached rationality fails to pick up the sociological coloration that gives rise to the quarrel; he plays deaf to the tone of the controversy. Since the target for decades of all oaths has been membership in the Communist Party and its affiliates, it is not farfetched to read the Maryland oath as covering "membership" as well as individual action. And certainly this oath does not meet the stringent requirements of *Scales*. Thus, *Whitehill* serves, if anything, further to limit the domain of the oath.

The other two cases—*Connell* and *Cole*—both involve affirmative oaths of allegiance rather than negative test oaths. Such oaths have always been a familiar part of American life. They amount to nothing more than a minimal, non-divisive ceremonial gesture of allegiance; there is nothing new or alarming about their use. And under normal circumstances there can be no objection to taking them. But there are two points of concern which arise when such affirmative oaths are used in the context of the anti-Communist quest of the past decades: (i) they cannot altogether escape the distrust and suspicions which the wave of loyalty oaths has generated in some of those asked to swear to them—the affirmative oaths simply do not stand alone today; and (ii) any effort by the state to embroider new terms onto the basic oath of allegiance alters the routine quality claimed on behalf of it.

The key precedent on affirmative oaths is *Baggett v. Bullitt*. There, it will be recalled, the state had not been content to ask for the familiar promise of "support" but had tacked on a pledge to "promote . . . undivided allegiance" to the government. The state had argued that the oath was little more than a ceremony and that "without the criminal sanctions . . . one need not fear taking this oath, regardless of whether he understands it and can comply with its mandate, however understood."[57] The Court, speaking through Justice White, brushed this "common sense" aside, holding that the state had an obligation toward those who would not "solemnly swear unless they can do so honestly" and warning that the state should not encourage "casual oathtaking."[58] Thus, after *Baggett* two points seemed settled: that the affirmative oath in its traditional form was not objectionable; and, conversely, that if the traditional form was varied, the affirmative oath would be subject to the same stringent exegesis as the negative test oath. Yet each of the two more recent cases seems to complicate this solution.

In *Connell* the oath has two parts. The first is the routine oath of "support," and the Court reaffirms that this presents no problems. Added to it, however, is a second provision: "I do not believe in the overthrow of the Government of the United States or the State of Florida by force or violence." The Court in a *per curiam* opinion neither treats this as surplusage, meaning in effect the same as "support"; nor does it, following the arguments of Justices Frankfurter and Jackson in *Douds* twenty years earlier, hold that the use of the idiom of "belief" invalidates the oath. Rather, it introduces a wholly new idea: the oath is bad because the petitioner was not afforded a hearing before dismissal for refusal to take it. But the very mechanics of the oath device had always called for automatic dismissal for refusal to take it; if the oath was valid, there was no issue remaining for a hearing to explore. The Court thus seemed to be mixing apples and oranges; the point of the oath was to avoid administrative loyalty proceedings. If the procedural point was good in *Connell*, it must have been good in all those prior oath cases in which it lay dormant. Possibly the Court had in mind a really new idea, namely, that the reluctant affiant should be entitled, prior to discharge, to a definitive construction from the official agency and a definitive resolution of the ambiguities that had caused him to balk. But it did not supply a rationale for the new procedure and the references to the Fifth Amendment discharge cases suggested confusion. Nevertheless, despite these shadows of confusion, *Connell*, like *Whitehill*, serves to narrow further the legitimate domain of oaths.

The "unsettling" note becomes somewhat stronger in *Cole v. Richardson*. At issue was a Massachusetts oath for public employees that contained two clauses. The first clause—"I do solemnly swear (or affirm) that I will uphold and defend the Constitution . . ."—is a routine oath of allegiance and is obviously valid. The controversy centers on the second clause: "and I will oppose the overthrow of the government. . . by force, violence, or any illegal or unconstitutional means." Does this clause add anything to the first, or does its reference to violent overthrow not import into the oath some of the lexicon of familiar anti-Communist strategies? Further, if it does not add to the first clause, can there by serious objection to permitting a reluctant affiant to swear to the first clause only?

The case arises because Mrs. Richardson, a social science researcher employed by a state hospital, refuses to take the oath and is barred from her post. She wins her challenge before a three-judge court, which holds the second clause of the oath unconstitutional. The case first reaches the Court in 1970; and it is remanded to the court below to ascertain whether it has become moot. Mrs. Richardson, presumably seeking to block appeal, had argued that her position at the hospital had been discontinued; the state, seeking to keep the appeal alive, had asserted that her job was still there, unfilled. There is one item of interest in this 1970 *per curiam* disposition—the indignant, ironic concurring opinion of Justice Harlan, in which Chief Justice Burger joins. It has been evident in prior cases that Justice Harlan has grown impatient with oath controversies; he joined the dissents in *Baggett* and *Elfbrandt* and he wrote the dissent in *Whitehill*. This time his impatience erupts and he writes a vigorous challenge to the endless search for ambiguity. He states, as well as it can be stated, one view of the oath controversies, namely, that they are foolish, time-wasting symbolic controversies on which nothing of a practical nature turns. After puzzling over the remand, he says:

I am, however, content to acquiesce in the Court's action because of the manifest triviality of the impact of the oath under challenge. . . .

. . . almost any word or phrase may be rendered vague and ambiguous by dissection with a semantic scalpel. I do not, however, consider it a provident use of the time of this Court to coach what amounts to little more than verbal calisthenics. This kind of semantic inquiry, however interesting, should not occupy the time of federal courts unless fundamental rights turn on the outcome.

I think it can be fairly said that subscribing to the instant oath subjected Mrs. Richardson to no more than an amenity. No First Amendment considerations, in my view, are at all involved in these cases. This oath does not impinge on conscience or belief, except to the extent that oath taking as such may offend particular individuals. I also think it safe to say that the signing of this oath triggered no serious possibility of prosecution for perjury or failure to perform the obligations of the oath. Indeed, I consider it most unfortunate that our past decisions in this field can be construed even to require solemn convocation of three federal judges to deal with a matter of such practical inconsequence.[59]

The *Cole* case wends its way back to the Supreme Court in 1972, the District Court having determined that the controversy was not moot and having again found the oath unconstitutional. This time the Court, in a 4 to 3 decision, with Justices Powell and Rehnquist not participating, finds the oath constitutional on the grounds that the whole oath is simply an amenity and that nothing additional was intended by the "oppose" clause. The opinion of the Court, by Chief Justice Burger, is joined by Justice Stewart, the author of *Cramp*, and Justice White, the author of *Baggett*, as well as by Justice Blackmun. Justices Douglas, Marshall, and Brennan dissent.

The *Cole* decision in itself does not disturb; the question was assuredly a close one, and this is certainly a plausible answer. One might have expected, however, that if the Court was to go this route, it would simply adopt the 1970 opinion of Justice Harlan and not spend any more effort on what he regarded as a trivial controversy unworthy of the time of the federal courts. What is disturbing is the selection of this case by Chief Justice Burger as the occasion for an extended opinion on loyalty oaths, and also to some degree the extended dissenting opinions by Justices Douglas and Marshall in reply. *Cole* is thus lent the appearance of a "big" case, and generates an illusion that the Court has at last, with the advent of the new Chief Justice, reversed the trend of decision on loyalty oaths.

The opinion of the Chief Justice is indeed remarkable. There is an elaborate review and restatement of precedent, as though the issue had the importance of that in *Dennis*. The restatement strikes me as muddied because it mixes inquiry cases with oath cases, argues that "an underlying seldom articulated concern" of the oath cases was to protect past associations,[60] and because it does not acknowledge that the one prior case most in point for present purposes was *Baggett v. Bullitt.* The Court does not find it useful to discuss *Baggett,* but spends time instead on two one-line *per curiam* affirmances of cases sustaining other oaths of allegiance. Moreover, the Chief Justice announces canons for construction which are at odds with every oath case the Court has handled. The man who does not swear to oaths lightly has been discarded, and instead there is criticism of the "highly literalistic approach" of the court below and of the effort "to give a dictionary meaning" to the words of the oath.[61] "We have," declares the Chief Justice, "rejected such rigidly literal notions."[62] And finally he concludes that the second clause is really redundant:

Such repetition, whether for emphasis or cadence, seems to be the wont of authors of oaths. That the second clause may be redundant is no ground to strike it down; we are not charged with correcting grammar but with enforcing a constitution.[63]

There is no explanation of why the refusal to answer to the *redundant* part of the oath is grounds for discharge from public employment. Although the Court has definitively read the second clause out of the oath, there is no indication, as there was in *Garner,* that Mrs. Richardson will be given a chance to take the oath as so narrowed. Nor, in the eyes of the majority, is anything added to the solemnity of the oath by the statute explicitly providing that the affiant subscribes to the oath "under the pains and penalties of perjury."

The dispute remains a tempest in a teapot, and there is of course much to be said for the commonsense impatience of Justice Harlan and Chief Justice Burger. Each side of an oath controversy seems to the other side to be almost insanely stubborn about petty points. The Court, however, cannot be so "commonsensible" about the controversy once the matter is brought to it for arbitration. It must require that the state too take seriously the ceremony it wishes the affiant to take seriously. It cannot hold that the oath is a trivial amenity, and at the same time treat the refusal of the amenity as justifying such grave consequences. And it cannot in 1972 abstract the oath and its references to violent overthrow of the government so totally from the gloss that the recent history of anti-Communism has indelibly given it. Neither Justice Harlan nor Chief Justice Burger in the end persuade by their recourse to hearty practicality. Finally, it is difficult not to see in the opinion of the Chief Justice an effort to create a sense of continued vitality in the constitutional issues generated by the use of loyalty oaths, an effort to unsettle what had been settled so as to plant seeds of doubt for future harvest. It is, I suppose, one style of judicial statesmanship.

In spite of *Cole v. Richardson,* the Court's performance in handling controversy over loyalty oaths admits of some fairly firm generalizations.

(i) In contrast to discussion at the popular level, the Court has never attended to *the format* of the oath itself, although Justice Black had valiantly tried to put the point in issue. It is safe to conclude that the Court will not openly hold that the oath format is itself unconstitutional; and this is true for negative oaths as well as for oaths of affirmation.

(ii) The oath, however, is a *disfavored device.* It will be construed with the eye of conscience, and thus held to the most exacting standards of unambiguous drafting; and held also to the most explicit limitations to those with *scienter.* Hence, while the oath format *per se* is not unconstitutional, it will be difficult in actuality to draft an oath that will pass muster.

(iii) The legality of an oath will depend not simply on the clarity of its wording, but ultimately on the content of its disqualification. That is the important lesson from *Elfbrandt,* and in this respect the oath precedents are powerfully reinforced by the non-oath precedents we will take up in the next chapter, such as *Keyishian, Robel,* and *Aptheker.*

(iv) The Court will to some extent distinguish between oaths of affirmation and negative loyalty oaths. In theory, only the latter are objectionable; the former are routine, conventional amenities of daily life. *Baggett,* however, indicates that even oaths of affirmation, if they depart from traditional formulae, might be invalid. It is only this last conclusion that the Court's gratuitous performance in *Cole v. Richardson* can, as a matter of logic, be said to unsettle.

27

The Security Calculus

Elfbrandt is not simply a decision about loyalty oaths. Its importance and reach transcend the distinctive issues of the oath and go to the analysis of partial sanctions under the First Amendment. Yet read in isolation it is unclear just what the scope of the *Elfbrandt* holding is.

There are two basic ambiguities: (i) Is the holding that *Scales* defines the limits on the degree to which membership in a disfavored group can be used as a basis for disqualification from *public employment?* Are the *Scales* requirements to be applied regardless of what the public job is? (ii) More generally, is the holding that partial sanctions affecting First Amendment freedoms, regardless of the issue, are to be measured by the standards for direct criminal sanctions? What happens to the holding if we move from public employment to other privileges? Considerable light is thrown on question (i) by two 1967 decisions, *Keyishian v. Board of Regents*[1] and *United States v. Robel*;[2] and question (ii) is illuminated by a somewhat earlier decision, *Aptheker v. Secretary of State* in 1964.[3] We will consider each in turn.

Keyishian v. Board of Regents

Keyishian, an important precedent on the First Amendment rights of public school teachers, is best read together with *Adler v. Board of Education,*[4] a 1952 decision upholding the New York loyalty scheme that *Keyishian* invalidates. Comparison of the two decisions affords a splendid chance to measure the great shift that has occurred in both the Court's attitude and analytic technique when dealing with the troublesome problem of partial sanctions. This shift can be explained by extrinsic factors such as changes in the Cold War climate and changes in personnel—only Justices Black and Douglas remain from the bench that decided *Adler*—but it can also be seen as the result of a tighter analysis of the problem, as one more example of the law slowly working itself pure.

Adler was the first of the cases to pose the problem of screening the loyalty of teachers. New York had long had on its books a statute which disqualified from public employment persons who advocated or were members of groups which advocated that the government "be overthrown . . . by force, violence, or any unlawful means," and another statute which disqualified from employment in the public school system persons who uttered "treasonable or seditious words." In 1949 the New York legislature enacted the so-called Feinberg Law, which authorized the Board of Regents to adopt rules and regulations to implement these two disqualifying provisions in the area of public education. The law directed the Board to "make a listing of organizations which it finds to be subversive in that they advocate, advise, teach or embrace the doctrine" of violent overthrow; and it provided further that membership in such listed groups should be "prima facie evidence of disqualification." The Feinberg Law was thus an echo at the state level of the Subversive Activities Control Act of 1950 in that it employed the strategy of attaching the loss of privileges to membership in suspect groups, and provided machinery for determining in advance which groups were suspect.

Adler is not precipitated by the discharge or threatened discharge of a public employee pursuant to the law; it is rather in the form of a suit for declaratory judgment of unconstitutionality. It is brought by a group of taxpayers, parents of schoolchildren, and teachers who argue that the Feinberg Law will intimidate public school employees and hence chill the exercise of their First Amendment rights. Because the regulations and procedural machinery to implement the statutory scheme have not yet been put into operation, it is, arguably, not yet clear what the parameters of the restraints projected by the law will turn out to be when it is in actual operation. There are thus serious questions of both standing and ripeness, which are ably argued by Justice Frankfurter in dissent. The Court upholds the law in a 6 to 3 decision, with Justices Black and Douglas joining Justice Frankfurter in dissent. The majority opinion by Justice Minton, in apparent eagerness to underwrite the law, does not discuss the points raised by the Frankfurter dissent.

The Minton opinion reads wretchedly in light of today's canons of criticism. He appears to be disposing of the teachers' First Amendment claims on the ground that public employment is a privilege and that a person remains free under this law to say or join what he will so long as he does not seek to be a public school teacher. Minton thus seems to embrace the right/privilege "fallacy" that Chief Justice Vinson had been so careful to avoid two years earlier in *Douds*. But it is probable that the thrust of Minton's view is that this is an utterly rational qualification scheme for teachers. His opinion is the epitome of the blunt commonsense approach to taking no risks with the corruption of education and the young. He stresses that the teacher "works in a sensitive area" and "shapes the attitude of young minds towards the society in which they live"; and he speaks of the state's power to "protect the schools from pollution."[5] He shows no sensitivity to the special importance of academic freedom, to the principle that teachers especially should be encouraged to be freely curious. Nor does he show any awareness of the overlay of political groups with conspiratorial ones which a few years later will so trouble the Court in *Yates* and *Scales*. As Minton sees it, membership in a suspect group is a compelling reason for barring a teacher: "One's associates, past and present, as well as one's conduct, may properly be considered in determining fitness and loyalty. From time immemorial, one's reputation has been determined in part by the company he keeps."[6]

In *Keyishian* fifteen years later the Court finds the same New York law in violation of the First Amendment. The majority opinion is by Justice Brennan, but significantly there are four dissenters, Justices Harlan, Stewart, White, and Clark, with Clark writing the dissenting opinion.

Although it does not formally overrule *Adler*, the Court distinguishes it in terms that have that effect. After noting that the appellants' challenge to the Act on grounds of vagueness had not been considered by the Court in the earlier case, Justice Brennan goes on to say:

Moreover, to the extent that *Adler* sustained the provision of the Feinberg Law constituting membership in an organization advocating forceful overthrow of government a ground for disqualification, pertinent constitutional doctrines have since rejected the premises upon which that conclusion rested. *Adler* is therefore not dispositive of the constitutional issues we must decide in this case.[7]

The exact grievance of the petitioners is subtle. The Board of Regents, after *Adler*, had adopted a procedure requiring each applicant for appointment or renewal to sign a so-called "Feinberg Certificate," declaring that he was not a member of the Communist Party, and that if he had ever been a member, he had communicated that fact to the president of the university. The controversy had originally arisen because the petitioners had refused to sign the Certificate. Had this procedure remained, *Keyishian* would have been one more instance of refusal to sign a loyalty oath; however, before the case reached trial, the procedure was altered and the use of the Certificate was rescinded. The applicant was simply informed that the statutes providing that utterance of "treasonable or seditious words" and membership in a group advocating violent overthrow were grounds for disqualification "constituted part of his contract." If he did not believe these disqualifications applied to him, he was free to sign the contract and no disclaimer was required. It is the constitutionality of this procedure which the case tests in the Supreme Court. It might seem that there would be no "case or controversy" in the technical sense here until the state took affirmative action to remove an employee for breach of contract. The Court, however, finds that the change in procedures has not mooted the case and that the shadow cast by the regulatory scheme is sufficiently chilling to warrant granting a declaratory judgment that it is unconstitutional.

The difference in procedures is worth a moment's further attention. As a practical matter the loyalty oath tends to be final. If the applicant declines to take it, he cannot have the job; but if he elects to take it, that will be the end of the matter and he will get the job subject to the possible risk of prosecution at some later date for swearing falsely. There is therefore arguably a certain small decency in the oath procedure; it will tend to cut off endless inquiry into the applicant's loyalty. The contract provision avoids the initial hurdle of the oath, but it leaves a lingering possibility that the applicant may be called to account in the future for violation of the contract, for a sort of breach of warranty.[8]

The Feinberg law presents two grounds for disqualification: utterance and membership. In *Keyishian* Justice Brennan pays a good deal more attention to the first ground than did Justice Minton in *Adler.* In the intervening years the Court had become far more sensitive to the ambiguities in terms like "seditious" and "advocacy of violent overthrow," thanks to decisions such as *Yates, Scales,* and *New York Times,* and it was well on the road to *Brandenburg.* Accordingly, Justice Brennan worries about whether general advocacy of violence as an "abstract doctrine" is covered by the ban. Also, in sharp contrast to Justice Minton, he articulates a key premise: "Our Nation is deeply

committed to safeguarding academic freedom, which is of transcendent value to all of us and not merely to the teachers concerned."[9]
There is, he argues, a special need for "precision" in regulating
speech in so sensitive an area. The "regulatory maze" of the New York
law lacks the requisite precision and hence is likely to encourage
self-censorship.[10] It is therefore unconstitutionally vague under the
First Amendment. In reaching this conclusion, Justice Brennan explicitly relies on the oath cases, such as *Cramp* and *Baggett* for his
canons of construction. Contracts, as well as oaths, are to be read with
the eye of conscience.

This wing of *Keyishian,* it is important to note, is on all fours with
Bond v. Floyd and *Pickering v. Board of Education.*[11] Read together, the
three cases provide a powerful nucleus of precedent on the formidable difficulties the First Amendment puts in the way of discharging a
public employee for making a speech.

It is, however, the other wing of the case dealing with group
membership that is most relevant to our immediate concerns. The
majority affirms the holding in *Elfbrandt.* It finds that the New York
provision making membership in the Communist Party a *prima facie*
disqualification violates the First Amendment because of overbreadth. The New York courts had construed the disqualification so
that it could be rebutted only by a showing of non-membership,
non-advocacy by the organization, or lack of *scienter.* The margin of
overbreadth therefore, as in *Elfbrandt,* is that some Communists who
because of lack of intent or activity would not satisfy the *Scales* test are
swept into the disqualified category. Justice Brennan advises us in a
sentence worth reading slowly and digesting: "Mere knowing membership without a specific intent to further the unlawful aims of an
organization is not a constitutionally adequate basis for exclusion
from such positions as those held by appellants."[12] *Elfbrandt* is then
cited and quoted from at length.

Keyishian thus underwrites *Elfbrandt,* but it also deepens the analysis in two respects. First, in restating the Court's holding, Brennan
writes: "legislation which sanctions membership unaccompanied by
specific intent to further the unlawful goals of the organization or
which is not active membership violates constitutional limitations."[13]
The arresting word here is "sanctions," used in the sense of imposing
sanctions. A central problem about partial sanctions, as we have
stressed, is whether we are to view them as qualifications for allocating
privileges such as employment, or whether the withdrawing of the
privilege is to be conceptualized as the imposition of a sanction.

Justice Brennan seems to have been on the verge of adopting this latter perspective.

Second, Justice Brennan is careful to leave room for possible concessions to regulation, *if the government position is sensitive enough.* He is careful *not* to say that the state may not remove from *any* government position a knowing member of the Communist Party. He speaks of "such positions as those held by appellants";[14] and at another point refers to a provision "which blankets all state employees regardless of the 'sensitivity' of their positions."[15] The view of the majority is thus not that partial sanctions, regardless of the position involved, must always be measured by the same standards as direct criminal sanctions. It is, rather, that teachers, although they have "captive audiences of young minds," do not hold positions "sensitive" enough to justify a less stringent test.

Elfbrandt and *Keyishian* together then are solid precedent that public school teachers may not constitutionally be barred from employment merely upon a showing that they are knowing members of the Communist Party. And presumably most other government employees would be entitled to the same protection. The result, translated into less technical terms, is remarkable and bears once again the trademark of Justice Brennan's statesmanship in handling First Amendment issues. Teachers may be barred from employment for "political" reasons, but *only on the very narrow ground that they are shown to be conspiratorial members of the Party who could be criminally prosecuted.* This tiny harvest is all that loyalty screening procedures may exact from teachers, and it surely powerfully reinforces the pragmatic arguments for not embarking on such ventures at all. Again the Brennan style has been to avoid absolute protection and the futile debate it is likely to engender, but to keep the jurisdiction yielded to the censor as small as possible.

As in *Elfbrandt,* Justices Clark, Harlan, Stewart, and White dissent. The dissenting opinion of Justice Clark, however, adds nothing to that of Justice White in *Elfbrandt.* Clark does not seem to understand, as White understood, that what the majority has put into issue is whether the *Scales* criteria for membership which can be made criminal are also to govern the "sanction" of loss of government employment.

United States v. Robel

The constitutional analysis of partial sanctions is further refined in *United States v. Robel,* decided about a year after *Keyishian.* This time the Court confronts one of the partial sanctions under the Subversive Activities Control Act of 1950 which Justice Frankfurter had so carefully postponed for another day in the *SACB* case in 1961. These sanctions, it will be recalled, came into play once a "Communist-action" organization was under a final order to register. At issue in *Robel* was a provision that made it a crime for any member of such a group to engage in employment at "any defense facility." The defendant, without concealing his Party membership, had worked for over ten years as a machinist at a private shipyard. Soon after the Court in *SACB* sustained the order for the Communist Party to register as a "Communist-action" organization, the Secretary of Defense, pursuant to the statute, designated the shipyard a "defense facility." A criminal prosecution was then initiated against Robel; the indictment alleged that he had "unlawfully and wilfully engaged in employment" at the shipyard with knowledge of the order against the Party and of the shipyard's designation as a "defense facility."

The Court, in a 6 to 2 decision, with Justice Marshall not participating, finds this key section of the Subversive Activities Control Act unconstitutional. The dissenting bloc has been reduced to two, Justices White and Harlan; Justice Clark is no longer on the Court and Justice Stewart has this time joined the majority. The majority opinion is by Chief Justice Warren and there is a separate concurring opinion by Justice Brennan. The dissent is once again by Justice White.

As in *Elfbrandt* and *Keyishian,* the challenge is that the Act bars from employment Communists with the wrong "quality" of membership, that is, those who lack "specific intent" to further the unlawful aims of the Party. There are two interesting moments at the outset. First, the District Court had attempted to save the statute by arguing that it must be construed narrowly so as to reach only those with "specific intent," and had relied on *Scales* as the precedent for such a narrowing construction. But the liberal majority will have none of this tactic. It insists on construing the statute more broadly so it can find it unconstitutional for overbreadth. At this technical level of the Court's operation, there is obvious leeway for political moves. In *Adler* the Court had brushed aside issues of standing and ripeness in order to get a chance to hold an anti-subversive measure constitutional; in *Robel* it brushes aside a narrowing construction in order to get a chance to hold an anti-subversive measure unconstitutional.

Second, the majority tends to look to *Aptheker,* rather than *Elf-brandt* and *Keyishian,* as the controlling precedent because it had there invalidated a companion provision of the Subversive Activities Control Act denying passports to members of designated groups. The Government in *Robel* attempts to distinguish *Aptheker* on the ground that there the Act qualified the right to travel, whereas here the Act qualifies the less basic privilege of employment in a defense facility. Thus, the Court is directly confronted with the puzzle of whether partial sanctions should be viewed as limiting the privilege being allocated or as limiting the freedom of association. The Government's argument is that we should compare cases in terms of the privilege being allocated and that travel is a more basic freedom than employment. But Chief Justice Warren elects to measure the case as essentially an interference with association and not simply with employment: "the operative fact upon which the job disability depends is the exercise of an individual's right of association, which is protected by the provisions of the First Amendment."[16]

Having disposed of these preliminaries, the Court turns to meet the core argument in support of the statute, namely, that it is a prophylactic measure aimed at reducing the risks of espionage and sabotage in defense plants. The Court acknowledges that this is not an "insubstantial" counter-interest. Indeed, the *Robel* facts recall Chief Justice Vinson's remark in *Douds* about "the keeper of the arsenal." Nevertheless the Court finds that the statute has cast its net too indiscriminately:

Thus, section 5(a)(1)(D) contains the fatal defect of overbreadth because it seeks to bar employment both for association which may be proscribed and for association which may not be proscribed consistently with First Amendment rights. See *Elfbrandt v. Russell.* . . . This the Constitution will not tolerate.[17]

The citation of *Elfbrandt* here confirms the Court's commitment to the norm that association may not be proscribed, even for non-criminal purposes, except under the most stringent and precise criteria.

Robel puts a harder case than did either *Elfbrandt* or *Keyishian.* Scienter can be said to be established from the public fact that the organization after full hearing has been adjudicated a "Communist-action" group. More important, there are stronger grounds for screening employees who may be working near classified defense materials and defense projects than there are for screening teachers, and as a concomitant, there is less intrusion into specially valued areas of freedom. Justice Brennan in *Keyishian* had not been willing, it will be remembered, to foreclose altogether the use of prophylactic disqualifications in sensitive areas, and had finally rested his decision on the judgment that teaching at least was not such an area. The opinion of Chief Justice Warren in *Robel* expresses the same caution. As I read him, he leaves open the possibility that a narrower disqualification aimed at sensitive positions within a defense plant would be constitutional; part of the overbreadth of the statute in *Robel* was that it swept together under the ban *all* employees at defense plants. Further, the Chief Justice states that a scheme that classified defense information and restricted access to it might pass constitutional muster.[18]

What emerges is a complex calculus in which the *sensitivity of the position* is weighed against the chilling impact of the *interference with political association.* The Court is taking its bearings from the criminal law standards—from the point at which political association becomes criminal conspiracy, the point Justice Harlan had struggled to define in *Scales.* Surely when that point is reached, partial sanctions may be constitutionally employed. What is at issue is whether any broader disqualification is permissible. The answer thus far—in *Elfbrandt, Keyishian,* and *Robel*—has been "no." But the genuine possibility remains that the Court will some day confront a position sensitive enough to justify a prophylactic strategy. Perhaps "the keeper of the arsenal" may still be disqualified for mere membership in the Communist Party.

Further insight into the tensions that inform the problem is furnished by Justice Brennan's concurring opinion. He is unwilling to decide this case on overbreadth. In a concise, highly useful essay at the start of his opinion he lucidly reviews the reasons for treating the ban as too indiscriminate in its failure to attend to the quality of the defendant's ties to the Communist Party and in its failure to attend to the sensitivity of his job. He carefully notes the relevance of *Keyishian, Elfbrandt,* and *Scales* as precedents. But then he reviews with equal care the reasons for saying that this is a tougher case, stressing that the impairment of employment is limited to defense facilities and that there is a genuine security risk problem involved. He concludes: "For these reasons I am not persuaded to the Court's view that overbreadth is fatal to this statute, as I agreed it was in other contexts [citing *Keyishian, Elfbrandt,* and *Aptheker*]."[19] The Brennan opinion thus serves to signal how far the Court really has gone in *Robel* toward outlawing any sanctions in excess of permissible criminal sanctions.

That Justice Brennan has in mind a calculus in which *the greater* the security risk, *the looser* the permissible disqualification is evident as he begins the main burden of his opinion, which is on the undue delegation of authority to the Secretary of Defense to designate defense facilities. He states:

Even if the statute is not overbroad on its face—because *there may be "defense facilities" so essential to our national security that Congress could constitutionally exclude all Party members from employment in them*—the congressional delegation of authority to the Secretary of Defense. . . renders this statute invalid. [Emphasis added.][20]

This time Justice White in dissent is successful in sharpening the debate between the two wings of the Court. His argument is forcefully put. He understands that the majority is conceding that Communists such as the defendant may sometimes be barred from sensitive employment and that Communists more intense than the defendant may be barred from any defense employment. What is at issue is thus a prudential calculus of the risks involved. On such a close judgment his preference is clear:

Having less confidence than the majority in the prescience of this remote body when dealing with threats to the security of the country, I much prefer the judgment of the Congress and the Executive Branch. . . .[21]

White then puts his finger on what seems to him the overwhelming difficulty with the view of the majority: "Some Party members may be no threat at all, but many of them undoubtedly are, and it is exceedingly difficult to identify those in advance of the very events which Congress seeks to avoid."[22]

This position has the ring of common sense, but it deservedly loses the argument. Three positions emerge on the Court: that of the majority, which would protect freedom of association in almost all but not quite all cases; that of the dissent, which would abdicate and leave to the legislature the calculus of association against security in presumably all cases; and finally that of Justice Brennan, who would insist on strict judicial review of the *precision* of the security calculus, but who in the present instance of employment in defense facilities would find the calculus constitutionally permissible. The weakness in Justice White's common sense is that there is no floor provided, no point at

which security would not still outweigh intrusion into freedom of
association—suppose, for example, the issue was the constitutionality
of a regulation which barred members of "Communist-front" groups
from any form of government employment whatsoever. Thus, if the
Brennan concurrence underscores the reach of the majority's liberalism, it also underscores the reach of the dissent's illiberalism.

The Security Calculus in Areas Other Than Employment

Elfbrandt, Keyishian, and *Robel* array as powerful precedent on the
issue of disqualification from public employment for membership in
the Communist Party. The differences in format—the loyalty oath in
Elfbrandt, the contract in *Keyishian,* the criminal sanction in *Robel*—do
not disturb the essential similarity. All three cases involve the tactic
of the partial sanction: you must choose, says the state, between
membership in *that* group and enjoyment of *this* government privilege. And in each instance the Court has found the choice so put to
be an impermissible interference with freedom of association. What
remains to be examined is whether the analysis changes if we vary the
nature of the government privilege. Insofar as the allocation of the
privilege is keyed to security considerations, the nature of the privilege must make a difference, for not all government privileges are
relevant to security. Thus far the privilege at issue has been government employment; suppose it were some other privilege?

The principal case for this purpose—*Aptheker v. Secretary of State*—
requires that we reverse the time sequence in which *Elfbrandt, Keyishian,* and *Robel* came to the Court and go back to pick up the 1964
decision which preceded them all. Read out of sequence in this fashion, *Aptheker* takes on added interest. The case proved more difficult
for the Court than it would have, had it come after *Elfbrandt, Keyishian,*
and *Robel;* it appears to be a somewhat primitive example of the Court
struggling with the partial sanction issue. Nevertheless, the Court
manages to work its way to a result that is congruent with the later
decisions—an example, as I see it, of how stubborn and sound the
Court's instinct for First Amendment values is. Indeed, as our repeated references to it have already indicated, *Aptheker* turns out to
have been a seminal precedent for these subsequent developments.

Like *Robel, Aptheker* involves one of the partial sanctions which the
Subversive Activities Control Act imposed upon members of "Communist-action" organizations. This time the privilege involved is the
right to a passport, the right to travel abroad. The Act makes it a crime

for a member of a designated organization, once a final order for the
group to register has been entered, even to apply for a passport. The
controversy arose when, after the order on the Communist Party to
register had become final in 1961, the State Department revoked the
passports of two prominent Party officials, Elizabeth Gurley Flynn and
Herbert Aptheker.

In a 6 to 3 decision the Court finds the passport provision of the
Act unconstitutional. The majority opinion is by Justice Goldberg;
and there are separate concurring opinions by Justices Black and
Douglas. Justice Clark writes for the dissent; he is joined by Justices
White and Harlan. The four cases—*Elfbrandt, Keyishian, Robel,* and
Aptheker—thus produce a well-defined split on the fundamental issue
of partial sanctions, with a dissenting bloc of Clark, White, and Harlan, joined from time to time by Justice Stewart. It is striking that
Justice Harlan, who was the author of *Scales,* which the majority finds
so relevant, dissents steadily from the effort to extend *Scales* to non-
criminal cases.

In the employment cases the Court had the problem "right side
up"; that is, it framed the issue primarily in terms of interference with
the freedom of association rather than interference with the right to
employment. So framed, the controversy readily put the First Amendment issues. But in *Aptheker* Justice Goldberg focuses primarily on the
distinctive quality of the government privilege being allocated and
thus treats the case as a controversy over impairment of the right to
travel. Perhaps the point is purely formal, but it does appear to have
created some special difficulties for the Court.

For one thing, the Court's focus on the right to travel gives rise
to a sharp dispute over whether the Act can be held bad on its face
or whether it must be judged simply as it applies to Flynn and Aptheker. The on-its-face technique is one of the technical preferred
positions enjoyed by First Amendment rights. In essence it permits
the individual litigant to be a vicarious champion of the rights of
others to whom the statute would apply with unconstitutional reach
even though a narrower statute would be constitutional in its application to him. Since travel is not explicitly under the First Amendment,
Justice Goldberg is hard pressed to justify his use of the on-its-face
technique in a non-First Amendment case. Over the objections of the
dissenters, he attempts to do so by arguing that freedom of travel is
so closely related to the rights of speech and association that it should
enjoy the same technical preferred position:

... since freedom of travel is a constitutional liberty closely related to rights of free speech and association, we believe that appellants in this case should not be required to assume the burden of demonstrating that Congress could not have written a statute constitutionally prohibiting their travel.[23]

It is not altogether clear why Justice Goldberg elected to focus primarily on the interference with freedom to travel rather than on the interference with freedom of association. Perhaps he was moved to do so by the awkward fact that Flynn and Aptheker, because of the active nature of their membership, could be said to satisfy the *Scales* standards. This may not in theory affect the overbreadth analysis, but it does raise tactical considerations. Presumably the Court would prefer to invalidate the statute on grounds that would also apply to the particular individuals involved; and as applied to Flynn and Aptheker, the statute is more clearly overbroad with respect to travel than with respect to association. It is thus possible that it seemed more persuasive to Justice Goldberg to document the overbreadth of the statute by putting instances of innocent, harmless travel which it would sweep within its ban rather than by limiting his impeachment to the overbreadth with respect to association which swept together subtle varieties of knowing Communists.

In any case, Goldberg makes an effort to combine both ideas in his inventory of the excesses of the statute. He first notes that it lumps together "both knowing and unknowing members," an awkward beginning, since the statute is not operative until there is a final order for the organization to register. Next he charges that the statute ignores the quality of membership by making irrelevant the degree of activity or degree of commitment to the unlawful purposes of the organization. He has thus functionally employed the three *Scales* criteria, but he does not cite *Scales* at this juncture or argue that the jurisdiction of criminal sanctions is the proper baseline for non-criminal sanctions as well. Indeed, he does not see the problem as one of prophylactic rules and speaks of the statute establishing "an irrebuttable presumption" that members of the designated group will, if given passports, engage in activity inimical to the security of the nation. Thus, he never quite puts the problem, as Justice Brennan will so clearly put it in *Robel,* as one of a calculus of security against freedom of association.

But his argument is not yet finished, and as he proceeds the advantages to him of emphasizing the interference with the freedom of travel become more evident. The statute bans travel regardless of the purpose of the travel:

Under the statute it is a crime for a notified member of a registered organization to apply for a passport to travel abroad to visit a sick relative, to receive medical treatment, or for any other wholly innocent purpose.[24]

Moreover, the statute bans travel "regardless of the security-sensitivity of the areas in which he wishes to travel":

As a result, if a notified member of a registered group were to apply for a passport to visit a relative in Ireland, or to read rare manuscripts in the Bodleian Library of Oxford University, the applicant would still be guilty of a crime; whereas, if he were to travel to Canada or Latin America to carry on criminal activities directed against the United States, he could so free from the prohibitive reach of section 6.[25]

Justice Goldberg's way of framing the argument, however, seems to me less persuasive than the form in which it matures in *Keyishian* and *Robel*. The vice is not the interference with travel; it is the interference with freedom of political association, an interference which gives the case an important commonality with other anti-subversive measures and permits arraying the precedents along a single axis. The interference with travel is relevant only insofar as limiting travel imposes partial sanctions *on association*. Hence, to upset the statute one does not have to argue that travel is any more a First Amendment right than is government employment. Moreover, put "right side up," it is possible to confront fairly the counter-tensions. May the state keep unreliable persons from foreign travel? That depends on two variables: how loosely or tightly the unreliability of the individual has been determined; and how much of a security risk to the United States is represented in foreign travel by its citizens. The Goldberg opinion offers no clue that such a calculus is involved, and hence wins an argument against straw men.

Justice Clark in dissent is thus able to score. First, he challenges the idea that the statute may be invalidated on its face. That, he insists, is a technique reserved for First Amendment rights; travel is not a First Amendment right. And if on-its-face challenge is not in order, the Goldberg examples verge on the foolish. Justice Clark reminds us that Flynn and Aptheker were principal witnesses for the Communist Party in the registration proceeding itself. He goes on:

. . . a member of the Party might wish "to visit a relative in Ireland, or to read rare manuscripts in the Bodleian Library of Oxford University. . . ." But no such party is here and no such claim is asserted. It will be soon enough to test this situation when it comes here.[26]

Second, he challenges any claim that the right to travel is an absolute. As a Fifth Amendment right, it is, he insists, clearly subject to reasonable regulation and that is all that is involved under the statute before the Court. Neither of these points could, I think, have been made, had the majority pitched their argument to the overbroad interference with the First Amendment right of association.

It is worth noting that Justice Clark also addresses himself to the relevance of the *Scales* criteria. They are not, he argues, relevant:

But that was a criminal prosecution under the Smith Act which, of course, carried stricter standards. And, in addition, this requirement, as laid down in *Scales*, was not held to be a constitutional mandate. The Court was merely interpreting a criminal statute which directly prohibits membership in organizations that come within its terms. The Act here does not prohibit membership, but merely restricts members in a field in which the Congress has found danger to our security.[27]

Justice Goldberg's reliance on the right to travel also sparks separate concurring opinions from Justices Black and Douglas. Justice Black, loyal to his basic dichotomy between speech and conduct, sees travel as conduct and hence as outside the ambit of the First Amendment. In his view, Congress may well possess broad powers to regulate the travel of citizens abroad. He cannot therefore accept a key premise of the Goldberg opinion. For him the constitutional flaw resides in the fact that the travel restriction is part of a "comprehensive statutory plan" which *as a whole* violates the Constitution[28]—the position he had argued so gallantly three years earlier in *Communist Party v. SACB.*

Justice Douglas, on the other hand, is moved in his concurring opinion not to seek separate grounds but to amplify Justice Goldberg's praise of the freedom to travel. He is very good on the theme and his opinion may well have laid the predicate, should the occasion arise, for broad protection in the future of the freedom to travel:

Free movement by the citizen is of course as dangerous to a tyrant as free expression of ideas or the right of assembly and it is therefore controlled in most countries in the interests of security. . . . That is why the ticketing of people and the use of identification papers are routine matters under totalitarian regimes, yet abhorrent in the United States.[29]

And again:

This freedom of movement is the very essence of our free society, setting us apart. Like the right of assembly and the right of association, it often makes all other rights meaningful—knowing, studying, arguing, exploring, conversing, observing and even thinking. Once the right to travel is curtailed, all other rights suffer, just as when curfew or home detention is placed on a person.[30]

Justice Douglas would protect travel as fully as he would protect speech itself; he would therefore limit control of travel to control of criminal conduct itself, to the power to detain. He states: "And no authority to detain exists except under extreme conditions, *e.g.*, unless he has been convicted of a crime or unless there is probable cause for issuing a warrant of arrest by standards of the Fourth Amendment."[31] Thus, the position of Justice Goldberg on the freedom to travel turns out to be a centrist position between Justice Douglas at one extreme and Justice Black and the dissenters at the other.

In the end, despite the skewed perspective of the majority, *Aptheker* proves a seminal precedent. The Court, once it gets the analytic frame straight in the later cases, is able to absorb *Aptheker* as directly in point on the use of partial sanctions against members of the Party. As a result, we now have, in addition to *Elfbrandt,* three major contemporary cases testing partial sanctions in contexts of varying security sensitivity and relevance: foreign travel (*Aptheker*), teaching (*Keyishian*), and employment in a defense plant (*Robel*). Each time the withdrawal of the government privilege from members of the proscribed group has been held unconstitutional because overbroad. The government has yet to put to the Court a partial sanction case in which the calculus of security against association has been precise enough to satisfy constitutional standards.

28

The Allocation of Subsidies

In theory one could generate a whole field of partial sanction problems by systematically varying the category of government privilege being allocated, much as if one were engaged in working out the ramifications of a formula in mathematics. But it would seem uselessly hypothetical to inventory government privileges and ask as to each whether denying it to Communists who did not meet the *Scales* criteria would be constitutional. Or to go further and explore what other rationales apart from risks to national security might justify a use of partial sanctions that exceeds the proper limits for criminal sanctions. The Court's experience has been concentrated and has not mapped the field. Chiefly, as we have seen, it has dealt with government efforts to allocate public employment by criteria keyed to a security risk rationale; and the basic parameters of the permissible constitutional calculus have been sufficiently indicated by the three key precedents, *Elfbrandt, Keyishian,* and *Robel,* plus *Aptheker.*

There remain, however, a handful of other partial sanction precedents that demand our attention. In this chapter we will consider two cases—*Speiser v. Randall*[1] in 1958 and *Lamont v. Postmaster General*[2] in 1965—in which the partial sanction at issue takes the form of the denial of a government *subsidy* to those who engage in disfavored speech. In *Speiser* the issue is posed by denial of a tax subsidy and in *Lamont* by a restriction that impedes access to the second-class mail subsidy. Although the government may invoke national security considerations in such cases, the essential justification for denying the subsidy does not ultimately rest on a narrow security rationale but rather on the argument that the individual, in claiming the tax exemption or availing himself of the second class mail subsidy, is appealing to the largesse of the state. First Amendment principles may bar the government from punishing, say, general advocacy of violent overthrow of the government, but surely, it is argued, those principles do not compel the government to *subsidize* such speech.

In *Speiser* the Court encounters this argument with respect to the allocation of property tax exemptions by California. The state constitution provided special tax benefits for veterans. An amendment to the constitution, however, barred tax exemptions to any person who advocated violent overthrow of the government. Pursuant to this amendment, an oath to the effect that the applicant did not so advocate was added to the property tax form. The petitioners, applicants for the exemption for veterans, refused to sign the oath and were denied the exemption. The Court, with Justice Clark the lone dissenter, found the scheme unconstitutional.[3]

The vice in the *Speiser* oath, the Court decided, was that it was not a true oath; that is, under the California procedures the oath was not *conclusive*. The tax assessor still had the responsibility on all the facts of deciding whether the applicant qualified for the exemption; he might, despite the oath, refuse to grant the exemption. Writing for the majority, Justice Brennan saw this as placing the burden of proof on the side wishing to exercise First Amendment rights and hence as a strong invitation to self-censorship: "The man who knows that he must bring forth proof and persuade another of the lawfulness of his conduct necessarily must steer far wider of the unlawful zone than if the State must bear these burdens."[4]

Speiser is thus a key precedent on the issues that arise when official inquiry and not automatic disqualification is the problem, matters we will examine later in this book. But for the moment its relevance resides not in this basic point about the misallocation of the burden of proof, but in what the Court has to say about denial of the tax exemption as a partial sanction.

Justice Clark in dissent argues that it is surely within the power of the state to decline to subsidize those engaged in advocating its overthrow:

This is not a criminal proceeding. Neither fine nor imprisonment is involved. . . . appellants are free to speak as they wish, to advocate what they will. If they advocate the violent and forceful overthrow of the California Government, California will take no action against them under the tax provisions here in question. But it will refuse to take any action *for them,* in the sense of extending to them the legislative largesse that is inherent in the granting of any tax exemption or deduction.[5]

Underlying Clark's argument is the logic of the right/privilege distinction: A tax exemption is not a matter of right; it is a "bounty" granted by the state. Hence the state possesses broad power "to attach conditions to its bounty" and to place the burden of qualifying "upon the one seeking [its] grace."[6]

The majority firmly rejects this argument. In an important clarifying passage Justice Brennan declares that the state may not allocate subsidies as a matter of grace and that discriminatory allocation will be read as a direct sanction:

It cannot be gainsaid that a discriminatory denial of a tax exemption for engaging in speech is a limitation on free speech. . . . To deny an exemption to claimants who engage in certain forms of speech is in effect to penalize them for such speech. Its deterrent effect is the same as if the State were to fine them for this speech. The appellees are plainly mistaken in their argument that, because a tax exemption is a "privilege" or "bounty," its denial may not infringe speech.[7]

The Court cannot, however, rest its decision on the ground that California has violated the constitutional standards for direct sanctions, because the state court had construed the disqualification as applying only to speech "which may be criminally punished consistently with the free speech guarantees of the Federal Constitution." Justice Brennan thus assumes "without deciding" that "California may deny tax exemptions to persons who engage in the proscribed speech for which they might be fined or imprisoned."[8] Accordingly, he shifts his attention to the *procedure* by which the exemptions are allocated. He finds the procedure unconstitutional in that by placing the burden of proof on the applicant it encourages self-censorship; that is, because they know they must convince the tax assessor that they do not advocate violent overthrow, applicants are likely to be inhibited from engaging in conduct close to the line between protected and unprotected speech and hence the California procedure, writes Brennan, "can only result in a deterrence of speech which the Constitution makes free."[9]

Our concern for the moment is not with the self-censorship point but with Justice Brennan's perception of the denial of the tax exemption as a direct sanction. Implicit in his opinion is the principle that partial sanctions intended as sanctions may go as far but no further than criminal sanctions. The clarity of this principle is underscored when near the end of the opinion he moves to distinguish such cases as *Gerende, Garner,* and *Douds:*

> While the Court recognized that the necessary effect of the legislation [in *Douds*] was to discourage the exercise of rights protected by the First Amendment, this consequence was said to be only indirect. The congressional purpose was to achieve an objective other than restraint on speech. . . . Similar considerations governed the other cases. . . . The present legislation, however, can have no such justification. It purports to deal directly with speech and the expression of political ideas.[10]

Thus, *Speiser* indicates that in cases where the partial sanction of denial of a government subsidy is supported only by "the subsidy rationale" the Court—in contrast to its approach where a narrow security rationale is involved—will not view the chilling of First Amendment rights as the unintended by-product of the pursuit of some other state purpose but rather will appraise the denial of the subsidy as a direct sanction.

In separate concurring opinions Justices Black and Douglas, loyal to their position that speech cannot constitutionally be subjected to any direct sanctions, reject Justice Brennan's concession that he will assume the state can do via tax exemptions what it can do via direct criminal penalties.

In passing, Justice Black also addresses the tendency of partial sanctions to multiply into all corners of daily life and provides an appropriate epitaph for this section of our study:

> This case offers just another example of a wide-scale effort by government in this country to impose penalties and disabilities on everyone who is or is suspected of being a "Communist" or who is not ready at all times and all places to swear his loyalty to State and Nation. Government employees, lawyers, doctors, teachers, pharmacists, veterinarians, subway conductors, industrial workers and a multitude of others have been denied an opportunity to work at their trade or profession for these reasons. Here a tax is levied unless the taxpayer makes an oath that he does not and will not in the future advocate certain things; in Ohio those without jobs have been denied unemployment insurance unless they are willing to swear that they do not hold specific views; and Congress has even attempted to deny public housing to

needy families unless they first demonstrate their loyalty. These are merely random samples; I will not take time here to refer to innumerable others, such as oaths for hunters and fishermen, wrestlers and boxers and junk dealers.[11]

Lamont v. Postmaster General reinforces the *Speiser* holding with respect to the allocation of subsidies. Decided in 1965, *Lamont* is one of those trivial controversies that sometimes reach the Court which bespeak large questions of principle. It involved an effort by the government to screen second-class foreign mail for "Communist propaganda." The sanction employed was remarkably subtle. The Government did not exclude outright such materials from the mail; rather, it simply held up delivery and notified the addressee that he could have the mail, *if* he would fill out the enclosed postcard requesting its delivery. Thus the Government would deliver mail from suspect foreign senders *only upon the request* of the addressee. Under the rule in effect when the case arose, the addressee was given an opportunity to request delivery of any "similar publication" in the future, and a list of persons expressing such a desire was maintained by the Post Office. Later—while the *Lamont* controversy was in progress—this system was replaced by a procedure under which a separate request was needed for each item of mail.

Corliss Lamont, a well-known supporter of liberal causes, refused to fill out the card. Instead, he filed a suit challenging the constitutionality of the whole scheme. The Government, hoping to moot the suit, solemnly notified Lamont that it would consider the filing of the suit the functional equivalent of the postcard as an expression of his desire to receive the mail and would so list him. Lamont then amended his complaint to challenge the constitutionality of the listing. The Court in a unanimous decision held that the screening scheme violated Lamont's First Amendment rights.

The decision is a striking datum on the Court's empathy for First Amendment values. Since the screening applied only to second-class mail, the Government's concern was not so much with national security, were such Communist messages and propaganda to spread, as it was with the allocation of the mail subsidy. Why should the United States subsidize the delivery of such hostile stuff to its citizens? It will go to the trouble only if the citizen indicates he really wants it. It is the book club technique in reverse. Thus the scheme would seem to have been supported by a commonsense rationale and would have entailed only minor inconvenience to the addressee. The Government had kept its interference with First Amendment rights to a minimum. It did not attempt to ban the publication of such propaganda directly because of its content. It did not even refuse access to the mail service. It asked only for a small "gesture of cooperation" from the addressee. The sanction was thus both tiny and partial; and the rationale was sensible. But the Court, with vigor, confidence, and unanimity, found it unconstitutional.

The postal service provides a special context for First Amendment issues. The Court has never decided the status of the postal service under the First Amendment. It has never, that is, decided whether the delivery of mail is simply an act of government grace or whether it has become over time, as Justice Holmes thought, an integral part of the publication process. This ambiguity has been aggravated by the circumstance of the second-class mail subsidy. Although the opinion of the Court by Justice Douglas does not directly engage this underlying question, it strongly suggests that the Court is disposed to extend broad First Amendment protection to communication through the mails. Douglas begins his analysis by quoting Justice Holmes, dissenting in *Milwaukee Publishing Company v. Burleson:* "The United States may give up the Post Office when it sees fit, but while it carries it on the use of the mails is almost as much a part of free speech as the right to use our tongues."[12] Moreover, implicit in the holding that the screening procedure violates the First Amendment is a stringent limitation on the government's power to deny the mails to messages it dislikes. For if it is unconstitutional to impose this slight burden on the communication of "Communist propaganda," then it wou d seem to follow that the government is without power to exclude such materials from the mails.

Justice Douglas proceeds as though all that is at issue is a clog on the exercise of First Amendment rights. The principle is firm. The Government may not burden even a little bit the exercise of such rights, where, as here, it cannot ban the speech altogether. On this approach the tiny partial sanction is perceived as being *intended* as a sanction; and when that is the case, the sanction is measured by the same First Amendment standards whether it be a criminal penalty, tort damages, as in *New York Times v. Sullivan,* [13] or the nuisance of a slight affirmative act, as in this case. Justice Douglas also adds a persuasive note of realism. The scheme, he argues, invites self-censorship: who will relish notifying the government that he wishes to receive material it has just condemned as "Communist propaganda"?

One wonders, however, whether the Douglas opinion quite

meets the distinctive issues raised by the subsidy justification for the screening. Justice Brennan, in a concurring opinion joined by Justices Harlan and Goldberg, speaks more directly to the point. He gives short shrift to the argument that "the statute is justified by the object of avoiding the subsidization of propaganda of foreign governments which bar American propaganda."[14] The government may withdraw the subsidy, but "it must do so by means and on terms which do not endanger First Amendment rights."[15] It may *not* do so by *singling out disfavored content* in response to totalitarian countries which bar American propaganda:

That the governments which originate this propaganda themselves have no equivalent guarantees only highlights the cherished values of our constitutional framework; it can never justify emulating the practice of restrictive regimes in the name of expediency.[16]

In First Amendment matters especially, two wrongs can never make a right.

Justice Brennan also makes explicit an important premise left unarticulated by the Douglas opinion. He emphasizes that the First Amendment embraces *the right to receive* communications as well as the right to disseminate them. He acknowledges that the First Amendment "contains no specific guarantee of access to publications," but argues that the right to receive is among "those equally fundamental personal rights necessary to make the express guarantees" of the First Amendment meaningful.[17] "It would," he writes, "be a barren marketplace of ideas that had only sellers and no buyers."[18]

29

The Multiplier Effect

———◆———

Perhaps the single ugliest feature of the partial sanction strategies of the 1950s was their tendency to multiply. While this was sometimes the product of design, it was also often due to the lack of coordination that characterized the wholesale imposition of partial sanctions during the anti-Communist period. No one was ever held accountable for adding up the sanctions or for responsibly tracing the consequences of what he was doing officially. The upshot was that frequently the imposition of one sanction would trigger further sanctions and thereby yield a harsher result than could have been achieved directly. In this chapter we will consider several instances of this "multiplier effect."

The first of these—*Flemming v. Nestor*[1] in 1960—is an extraordinary example of the war between logical consistency and individual equity which is always the underlying tension of any legal system. At issue is the disqualification from Social Security old age benefits of an alien deported for Communist ties. The case is made poignant by the circumstances that the petitioner was sixty-nine years old, had resided in the United States all of his adult life, and had been a member of the Communist Party only during the interval from 1933 to 1939, when the Party was legal and membership was not a ground for deportation. His "flawed associations" had thus ended some twenty years before the government action in dispute had begun. At stake are benefits of $55 per month. Speaking through Justice Harlan, the five-man majority frames the case in due process rather than First

Amendment terms and upholds the ban. Chief Justice Warren and Justices Black, Douglas, and Brennan dissent.[2]

The opinion for the Court by Justice Harlan provides a startling illustration of how unfettered government discretion in allocating partial sanctions becomes, once the protective inhibitions of the First Amendment are withdrawn and the analysis proceeds in due process terms alone. It is also a striking instance of Justice Harlan at the height of his powers supporting an astonishingly harsh result in the individual case. For those especially interested in the work of this great judge, *Flemming,* laid alongside *Cohen v. California,* [3] provides endlessly rich and perplexing material for study.

The controversy is a very narrow one: can aliens deported for past Communist ties be denied Social Security benefits? The disqualification depends upon the fact of deportation. Necessarily left unanswered are questions about the propriety of denying benefits on other grounds. At some point, surely, the logic of the subsidy cases would control. Since there can be no relationship between the allocation of such benefits and national security risks, any effort to require, say, an anti-Communist oath as a precondition to receipt of benefit payments would be viewed as a direct sanction and appraised accordingly. And even if the ban were limited to *Scales*-type membership, it might well be invalidated as an arbitrary additional penalty for conspiratorial conduct.

The disqualification in *Flemming* is a by-product of the interlocking of two complex statutory schemes. The cornerstone of the Court's logic is the premise that the government may constitutionally deport an alien for past membership in the Communist Party under a law that operates retroactively. For reasons we will examine in the next chapter, this government harshness is permitted because of what has been traditionally accepted as the extra-constitutional power of the government when acting as sovereign to determine which foreigners it will permit to enter and reside here. Those who allocate Social Security benefits are not held accountable for the wretched way the deportation power is exercised.

The upshot is that by a kind of legal algebra the government is permitted to do things with Social Security benefits through the mediation of the deportation law that it is most doubtful it would have the constitutional power to do directly. That is, I doubt, as indicated above, that the government would have the power to chill American Communism by withholding Social Security benefits from members; and I doubt also that it could chill even resident alien Communist association by the same tactic. Yet it is the conclusion of the Harlan logic, which one takes lightly always at one's peril, that in this case precisely such government action is constitutionally permissible.

As Justice Harlan moves to meet the petitioner's argument, he makes explicit the full range of possible constitutional challenges to partial sanctions, the First Amendment apart. First, there is the challenge that the rights under the Social Security Act are accrued and vested. If so, this would be the upper end of any right/privilege spectrum, and such firm privileges would be literally property which could not be taken by government without "just compensation." Justice Harlan carefully and persuasively dissects the nature of Social Security benefits: The scheme is not quite insurance; the government retains some flexibility with respect to future payments; the system by now has created serious expectations but they are not quite of the stature of vested property rights. Hence the petitioner loses his first challenge.[4]

Second, there is the challenge that, even if not vested, these expectations are nevertheless real and substantial and hence Social Security benefits cannot be allocated at whim by the government. Justice Harlan agrees and then demonstrates how slender the constitutional protections are once we are outside the First Amendment. "We must recognize," he tells us, "that the Due Process Clause can be thought to interpose a bar only if the statute manifests a patently arbitrary classification, utterly lacking in rational justification."[5] One can only wonder why the Court continues to claim some possibility of judicial review in these instances; the standard is literally that the official action passes muster unless the Court can say the government was stark raving mad when it drafted the measure! Needless to say, the allocation of benefits in *Flemming* manages to surmount so low a hurdle. One reason for cutting off benefits to those deported, says Justice Harlan, is to ensure for the sake of the American economy that the money will be spent at home and not abroad. He adds: "For these purposes, it is, of course, constitutionally irrelevant whether this reasoning in fact underlay the legislative decision."[6] Nor is it relevant that this policy has not been seriously pursued; Social Security benefits are fully available to those who elect to live abroad upon retirement. Further, in this context Harlan accepts as a second "reason" supporting the result the sort of subsidy rationale the Court had scrutinized so severely from a First Amendment perspective in *Speiser:* "Nor . . . can it be deemed irrational for Congress to have concluded that the public purse should not be utilized to contribute to the support of those deported on the grounds specified in the statute."[7]

The challenge is not yet exhausted. There remains the argument based on the special fact that the alteration of petitioner's expectations of these advantages from the government was done *retroactively*. The flawed association was terminated in 1939; it is not until 1954 that the government elects to make past membership a ground for terminating benefits. In the expectation that he would be eligible for the benefits, the petitioner has made contributions throughout his adult working life; yet near the end of that period the government changes the rules and denies him the benefits. The categories of constitutional analysis prove to be a trap here. The appeal is to the specific provisions against *ex post facto* laws and bills of attainder. Since these deal directly with retroactivity, they are taken to absorb the full possibilities of constitutional challenge predicated on this grievance. Here again the Harlan rebuttal adds to the framework for evaluating partial sanctions outside the First Amendment. To invoke these specific inhibitions and escape the bland provisions of the Due Process Clause, the crucial test is whether the withholding of the government benefit or privilege can be said to be "punishment." As long as it can be said to be aimed at "the calling and not the person,"[8] it is not punishment no matter how harsh the outcome. Justice Harlan is very clear about the guiding principle:

Where the source of legislative concern can be thought to be the activity or status from which the individual is barred, the disqualification is not punishment even though it may bear harshly upon the one affected.[9]

Unless a desire to punish is the only possible explanation of the denial of benefits, it cannot be said that there is the requisite evidence of "punitive intent."[10] The decisive circumstance here is that it is the fact of deportation, not the grounds, that triggers the disqualification, and hence the denial of benefits must be viewed as permissible rationality in administering the Social Security system. Finally, we are admonished, official motive and intent are to be derived logically from the statute itself and not from other lines of inquiry. Official motivation may not be lightly impeached. This canon will continue to plague us as we explore other examples of partial sanctioning such as congressional investigating committees.

Perhaps the chief lesson then from *Flemming* is its illustration of how very different the handling of partial sanctions is when they are not considered under the First Amendment. Whatever the case on direct sanctions, here, as we contrast *Elfbrandt, Keyishian, Robel, Aptheker,* and *Speiser* with *Flemming,* there does indeed seem to be a preferred position.

Once again it is an angry Justice Black who evokes the First Amendment echoes in the case:

The fact that the Court is sustaining this action indicates the extent to which people are willing to go these days to overlook violations of the Constitution perpetrated against anyone who has ever even innocently belonged to the Communist Party.[11]

A basic constitutional infirmity of this Act, in my judgment, is that it is part of a pattern of laws all of which violate the First Amendment out of fear that this country is in grave danger if it lets a handful of Communist fanatics or some other extremist group make their arguments and discuss their ideas.[12]

Barsky v. Board of Regents

The same multiplier phenomenon is vividly illustrated by *Barsky v. Board of Regents,* [13] a 1954 decision. Like *Flemming, Barsky* is an instance of the inability of the legal system to surmount logical rigidities. Barsky, a New York physician for over thirty years, was executive secretary of the Joint Anti-Fascist Refugee Committee. He initially got into difficulty with the law when, acting on the advice of counsel, he refused to comply with an order of the House Un-American Activities Committee to turn over various records of the organization to the Committee. He thereby precipitated a celebrated legal challenge to the constitutionality of HUAC, *Barsky v. United States,* [14] which he ultimately lost in the Court of Appeals in a close 2 to 1 decision—a decision the Supreme Court declined to review.

Barsky's "crime" of contempt of Congress was thus a very special one indeed. It involved a test case against HUAC and was an instance of adherence to principle, not ordinary criminality; it was not the kind of crime which reflected adversely on his character. He was sentenced to six months in prison. When his term had expired, the Medical Grievance Committee of New York initiated disciplinary proceedings against him because he had been convicted of a crime. The New York statute governing discipline of licensed physicians did not limit in any way the kind of crime but delegated full discretion to the Committee whether to discipline. At the hearing before the Grievance Committee, Barsky was questioned closely about this membership in the Joint

Anti-Fascist Refugee Committee and evidence was introduced to show that it was on the Attorney General's list of subversive organizations. The Grievance Committee decided to add a six-month suspension to the time Barsky had already lost due to his sentence. The New York Court of Appeals held that it was powerless to review the actions of the Grievance Committee. It is this action of the Committee, which so resembles the petty harshness of the denial of Social Security benefits in *Flemming,* that comes to the Court in the *Barsky* case. As in *Flemming,* the Court finds itself helpless to modify the action, but this time Justice Frankfurter joins Justices Black and Douglas in dissent and contributes a most useful opinion.

As in *Flemming,* it is the interlocking of two legal regimens that causes the trouble. Presumably the Court would not permit the suspension of doctors who were members of organizations listed by the Attorney General. Yet when the same result is reached circuitously, the Court will not see it as the same. Nominally, Barsky's flaw lies not in his membership but in his crime of contempt of Congress. And the Court, unwilling to deny HUAC and upset the contempt directly, can hardly be expected to be heroic enough to hold that to discipline a doctor for such a crime is to deny him First Amendment rights of association. It approaches the case therefore in terms of a *general* scheme for disciplining doctors for crimes and accordingly views it wholly as regulation of the right to practice medicine.

The Frankfurter dissent adds a special note of interest.[15] Since Barsky is already earning his livelihood as a doctor, something akin to a property right is at stake. And the Due Process Clause, in Frankfurter's view, places serious limits on how irrational the state's regulation may be:

It is one thing thus to recognize the freedom which the Constitution wisely leaves to the States in regulating the professions. It is quite another thing, however, to sanction a State's deprivation or partial destruction of a man's professional life on grounds having no possible relation to fitness, intellectual or moral, to pursue his profession. Implicit in the grant of discretion to a State's medical board is the qualification that it must not exercise its supervisory powers on arbitrary, whimsical or irrational considerations. A license cannot be revoked because a man is redheaded or because he was divorced, except for a calling, if such there be, for which redheadedness or an unbroken marriage may have some rational bearing. If a State licensing agency lays bare its arbitrary action, or if the State law explicitly allows it to act arbitrarily, that is precisely the kind of State action which the Due Process Clause forbids.[16]

There are three points to note in cases of this sort. First, here as in *Flemming,* the law somehow reaches by a process of combination a harsher result than the law would authorize were it done directly. It is tyranny by bureaucratic inadvertence and inertia. Presumably no one would have intended to deny Social Security benefits to a man after a life of work and payment of contributions simply because some twenty years earlier he had been a member of the Communist Party. And presumably no one would have intended to suspend the license to practice medicine of a physician simply because he wished to test the constitutionality of the controversial powers of the House Un-American Activities Committee. But in the one instance the mediation of the deportation and in the other the mediation of the crime of contempt of Congress yields the harsh result.

Second, there is the marked difference in the Court's degree of scrutiny depending on whether it analyzes the case as qualification of the right to a tax benefit or to earn a living and hence under the Due Process Clause or analyzes the matter as qualification of First Amendment rights of association. The difference, say, between *Barsky* in 1954 and *Robel* in 1967 is immense.

Finally, there is the difference between the due process standards employed in *Flemming,* which require a finding of virtual insanity in the legislature for the Court to impeach the state action and the due process standards in the Frankfurter dissent in *Barsky,* where the requirement that there be a *rational nexus* between the disqualification and the objective the state wishes to achieve is a requirement with some teeth in it.

Another series of cases suggestive of the multiplier effect, although not strictly analogous, may be noted here: *Sacher v. United States* (1952), *In re Isserman* (1953), *Isserman v. Ethics Committee* (1953), and *Sacher v. Association of Bar of New York* (1954).[17]

These cases were all precipitated by the *Dennis* case. Throughout the nine-month trial of the Communist leaders there was great tension between the defense counsel and the trial judge, Harold Medina, a tension which raised important questions about permissible lawyer tactics in political cases, and equally about permissible judicial indignation and irritation. At the end of the trial the judge called the counsel before him, as he had intimated during the trial he might, and sentenced them for contempt for their "conspiracy" of harassment. The Supreme Court in *Sacher v. United States,* a reluctant 5 to 3 decision in which Justice Frankfurter again joined Justices Black and

Douglas in dissent, upheld Judge Medina.

Like the deportation in *Flemming* and the contempt in *Barsky*, the contempt action by Judge Medina triggers additional consequences for the individuals—this time in the form of disciplinary action by the organized bar. In *Isserman v. Ethics Committee* the Court declines to review the action of New Jersey in permanently disbarring Isserman. In the other two instances, however, the Court is in the posture of reviewing not the action of the state in disciplining its lawyers, but the action of the federal courts over which it has supervisory power. Thus in *Sacher v. Association of Bar of New York* it is able to upset the permanent disbarment from the federal District Court in New York as "unnecessarily severe."[18]

The most interesting and poignant of these cases is *In re Isserman* where the question is simply whether Isserman will be barred from practice before the Supreme Court itself, in view of the fact that he has now been permanently disbarred in New Jersey. The Court, in a 5 to 4 decision, upholds the bar before the Supreme Court itself, and thus marks a low point in official tolerance in the United States. The moment is made memorable by the gallant dissent of Justice Jackson, in which Justices Frankfurter, Black, and Douglas join:

There has been hue and cry both for and against these lawyers for Communist defendants. There are those who think the respectability of the bar requires their expulsion. There are those who lament that any punishment of their conduct will so frighten the legal profession that it will not dare to discharge its duties to its clients. We make common cause with neither. In defending the accused Communists, these men were performing a legitimate function of the legal profession, which is under a duty to leave no man without a defender when he is charged with crime. In performing that duty, it has been adjudged that they went beyond bounds that are tolerable even in our adversary system. For this, Isserman has paid a heavy penalty.

If the purpose of disciplinary proceedings be correction of the delinquent, the courts defeat the purpose by ruining him whom they would reform. If the purpose be to deter others, disbarment is belated and superfluous, for what lawyer would not find deterrent enough in the jail sentence, the two-year suspension from the bar of the United States District Court, and the disapproval of his profession? If the disbarment rests, not on these specific proven offenses, but on the atmospheric considerations of general undesirability and Communistic leanings or affiliation, these have not been charged and he has had no chance to meet them. We cannot take judicial notice of them.[19]

Justice Jackson, who had written the majority opinion upholding Judge Medina in *Sacher v. United States,* then goes on to strike a splendidly generous note:

On the occasions when Isserman has been before this Court, or before an individual Justice, his conduct has been unexceptional and his professional ability considerable.[20]

He concludes:

. . . to permanently and wholly deprive one of his profession at Isserman's time of life, and after he has paid so dearly for his fault, impresses us as a severity which will serve no useful purpose for the bar, the court or the delinquent.[21]

Communist Party v. Catherwood[22] in 1961 provides one last example of interlocking sanctions. This time the final outcome is a happy one for the complainants. The case involves the Communist Party in the role of employer. At issue is the impact on the Federal Unemployment Insurance Tax of the provisions of the Communist Control Act of 1954 outlawing the Communist Party by name and withdrawing from it "whatever rights, privileges and immunities have hitherto been granted." Pursuant to its reading of the Act, New York terminated the Party's tax liability under the State Unemployment Insurance tax. Paradoxically the termination of a tax liability operated as a disadvantage under the circumstances, because New York gave marked reductions in tax to those employers with good "experience ratings" and apparently the Party had an exemplary employment record. The federal tax in turn gave a credit for state taxes and measured it not by the tax actually paid but by the highest rate that would have been paid had there been no reduction for "experience ratings." Thus, it was cheaper for the Party to pay a small state tax because of the rating scheme and get a sizeable credit against its federal tax than to pay no state tax at all and lose the credit. Hence the peculiar question in *Catherwood* was whether New York could constitutionally deprive the Party of this "advantage" by relieving it of any New York tax! Although Justice Harlan had found it impossible to salvage the Social Security benefits of poor Nestor, here, writing for the unanimous Court, he has no trouble in construing the federal Act so as to prevent this loss of tax advantage to the Communist Party.

Sanctions out from under the Constitution

30

Deportation

Carried to its logical extreme, the security calculus would lead to exile, to the total removal of the suspect individual from the society— to a merging, that is, of the concept of the partial sanction with that of the total sanction. If he is not reliable enough to work in a defense plant or teach school or work for the state or be a member of the bar, is there *any* position within the society where he can be trusted? Since the inexorable tendency of the calculus is to resolve doubts in favor of security and against the individual and since there will always be some doubts, the answer will be that no, there are no places within the society where the risk of his presence need be endured. The use of exile or banishment as a sanction, however, is unknown in modern democratic states and would presumably be unconstitutional in the United States. Hence, even during the height of the anti-Communist decades, the courts were never asked to confront directly, with respect to American citizens, the legal status of exile as a sanction.

Such was not the case, however, with respect to resident aliens. As applied to them, exile as an anti-subversive strategy flourished. It took the form of *deportation*—the withdrawal of the privilege of residing in the United States—and it generated a number of Supreme Court decisions. These cases are revealing as social history and as evidence of the mood of the times. Above all, they are revealing as illustrations of how the government may act to reduce the risk of subversion *when unrestrained by the Constitution.*

The series of deportation precedents starts tranquilly enough with *Kessler v. Strecker*[1] in 1939. At issue was whether an alien who had become a member of the Communist party after entry and then subsequently terminated his membership could be deported because of such past membership. At the time the relevant statute excluded from entry into the United States those who advocated violent overthrow or were members of organizations so advocating. The statute further provided that "any alien who, at any time after entering the United States, is found to have been at the time of entry, or to have become thereafter a member of any of the classes of aliens enumerated" shall be deported. The Supreme Court in a 7 to 2 decision construed the statute not to cover past membership such as Strecker's. The majority opinion was by Justice Roberts. Justice McReynolds dissented in an opinion joined by Justice Butler.

The Court's liberal handling of the case at this date is striking, for the statutory construction was not at all obvious—the administrative practice had construed the statute to permit deportation for such past membership, and a decision seven years earlier by the Court of Appeals had also so construed the statute. Justice Roberts treats the case purely as a matter of construction and does not discuss any possible constitutional implications. He does, however, display sensitivity to the harshness of deportation because of past membership:

In the absence of a clear and definite expression, we are not at liberty to conclude that Congress intended that any alien, no matter how long a resident of this country, or however well disposed toward our Government, must be deported, if at any time in the past, no matter when, or under what circumstances, or for what time, he was a member of the described organization.[2]

The dissenters, foreshadowing the mood of a later day, bemoan the fact that the Court has elected to protect "an alien who after entry has shown his contempt for our laws by deliberately associating himself with a proscribed organization."[3]

The tensions underlying the use of the deportation sanction against subversives erupt in the next case and bring the First Amendment issues vividly to the fore. The case is *Bridges v. Wixon*[4] in 1945, a 5 to 3 decision upsetting a deportation order on Harry Bridges, the nationally prominent West Coast labor leader. *Bridges* calls forth three opinions from the Court: a majority opinion by Justice Douglas, a concurring opinion by Justice Murphy, and a dissenting opinion by Chief Justice Stone in which Justices Roberts and Frankfurter join.

The opinions dramatically illustrate several points: the range of judicial styles; whether in the United States we can in the end have government action which is outside the Constitution; and whether the Court can ever acknowledge the realpolitik of the official action it is called upon to review.

Bridges was an Australian who had come to the United States in 1920 and had become an active, militant, highly visible labor organizer. Two efforts were made to deport him. The first was made under the statute which *Kessler* had limited to *present* membership in designated organizations, and was unsuccessful. After a full hearing, the hearing officer—James Landis, then the Dean of Harvard Law School—found the evidence of disqualifying ties on Bridges's part insufficient. A bill was then passed by the House, only to die in the Senate, which directed the Attorney General forthwith to take into custody and deport Harry Bridges "whose presence in this country the Congress deems hurtful." When this egregious tactic failed, the statute was amended to overrule the Court's reading in *Kessler* and to authorize deportation for *past* membership or "affiliation." The sponsor of the amendment stated on the floor of Congress: "It is my joy to announce that this bill will do, in a perfectly legal and constitutional manner, what the bill specifically aimed at the deportation of Harry Bridges seeks to accomplish."[5] A second deportation proceeding against Bridges was then initiated under the revised statute. This time the hearing officer, a former judge of the New York Court of Appeals, concluded from a complex record that there was evidence that Bridges had at one time been a member of the Communist Party and had been "affiliated" with it. The Board of Immigration Appeals unanimously rejected the hearing officer's recommendation that Bridges be deported. The Attorney General, however, reversed the Board and ordered the deportation. It is this order that the Supreme Court upsets in its 1945 decision.[6]

One additional fact is relevant. It will be recalled that in 1941 the Supreme Court in *Bridges v. California*[7] had decided in Bridges's favor the contempt by publication controversy precipitated by his public telegram to the Secretary of Labor in which he stated that there would be serious labor trouble on the West Coast if a particular judicial decision on a labor injunction then pending proved adverse to his union. The case provided the classic precedent on the role of the First Amendment in limiting a judge's power to hold for contempt by publication. The two *Bridges* cases thus dramatize a deep paradox in the legal framework. Bridges as an alien residing in the United States is entitled to the full free speech privileges of the citizen; and in *Bridges v. California* the Supreme Court went to considerable lengths to intervene to protect him from the minor fine imposed. But were the law to provide that he could be deported for an utterance such as the telegram, or even one much milder in tone, there would be no constitutional scrutiny of the imposition of so grave a penalty.

Each of the three opinions in *Bridges v. Wixon* reacts differently to this underlying paradox. The opinion of the Court by Justice Douglas reflects the constraints under which the justices operate in this area. Douglas does not challenge the blunt power of the sovereign to regulate the coming and going of aliens to its shores. Nor does he mention the background facts about the effort to "get rid of Bridges." Rather, he works to save Bridges by means of a technical argument regarding the construction of the statute and the weighing of the evidence.

Douglas separates the two grounds on which the deportation order rests—"affiliation" and "membership"—and deals with each in turn. He begins by arguing that the term "affiliation" has been misconstrued. Here the *Bridges* case supplies a precedent that is still of considerable value. The issue is what degree of attachment to an organization is required before an individual can be charged with the speech or positions of the organization. This is to be the central question in such key cases as *Scales, Elfbrandt, Keyishian,* and *Robel.* [8] Justice Douglas, employing solely the leverage of statutory construction, holds that "affiliation," while a weaker term than "membership," must be carefully limited:

We cannot assume that Congress meant to employ the term "affiliation" in a broad, fluid sense which would visit such hardship on an alien for slight or insubstantial reasons. It is clear that Congress desired to have the country rid of those aliens who embraced the political faith of force and violence. But we cannot believe that Congress intended to cast so wide a net as to reach those whose ideas and program, though coinciding with the legitimate aims of such groups, nevertheless fell far short of overthrowing the government by force and violence. Freedom of speech and of press is accorded aliens residing in this country. *Bridges v. California.* [9]

The hearing officer had found circumstantial evidence of affiliation from what he termed "a pattern which is more consistent with the conclusion that the alien followed this course of conduct as an affiliate of the Communist Party rather than as a matter of chance coincidence." [10] This is the logic that later comes to be known as proof of "fellow traveling" or "following the Communist line." It is the logic of Senator Joseph McCarthy, and, as we have noted, it received limited approval in Justice Frankfurter's opinion in *Communist Party v. Subversive Activities Control Board*[11] in 1961. It is a logic totally at war with the First Amendment. Communists are not wrong on all public issues, and it is suicidal to afford them the chance to preempt positions on public issues by adopting one side of the issue and thus frightening off other supporters. The majority opinion in *Bridges v. Wixon* thus contributes an important note of caution to the handling of "guilt by association." And on this point the Court is apparently unanimous, since the dissenters do not elect to argue this ground.

Douglas then turns to the second ground—membership. Here his argument goes to the quality of the evidence of membership which the hearing officer relied upon. There were two witnesses, Lundeberg and O'Neil. Lundeberg testified that Bridges solicited him for the Party and, somewhat implausibly, that he volunteered that he was a secret member. Justice Douglas concedes that if the hearing officer's judgment and the Attorney General's decision had rested on this item independently, it is inappropriate for the Court to second-guess it, since they were reviewing a finding by an administrative agency. The problem, however, was with the companion testimony of O'Neil. The hearing officer had relied upon prior statements O'Neil had given the FBI about being present when Bridges pasted dues stamps into his Party membership books. At the hearing O'Neil had repudiated the testimony, but the hearing officer had nevertheless admitted the prior statements not for impeachment purposes but as substantive evidence. This use of hearsay, argues Douglas, violated the regulations of the Immigration and Naturalization Service and hence violated Bridges's right to have his status determined by an authorized procedure. It thus takes no little agility on the part of the majority to save Harry Bridges from deportation.

Loyalty to long-term institutional values at the expense, if need be, of individual equities, even First Amendment equities, is the keynote of Chief Justice Stone's dissenting opinion, in which he is joined by Justices Roberts and Frankfurter. Assuredly, the dissenters are fully aware of the political realities and of the difficulty of squaring the outcome they call for with any constitutional disciplining of government action. Their point, powerfully put, is that such considerations are in this context irrelevant. Once again the perennial American debate over the proper scope of judicial review is joined:

This case presents no novel question. Under our Constitution and laws, Congress has its functions, the Attorney General his, and the courts theirs in regard to the deportation of aliens. Our function is a very limited one. In this case our decision turns on the application of the long-settled rule that in reviewing the fact findings of administrative officers or agencies, courts are without authority to set aside their findings if they are supported by evidence.[12]

On their view, the case has no more claim to the Court's attention than any other evidentiary review from this administrative agency. The Lundeberg testimony provides "some evidence" of past membership of Bridges in the Party and that is quite sufficient to trigger the serious consequence of deportation.

The equities of the case—which Chief Justice Stone treats as irrelevant and which Justice Douglas intervenes vigorously on behalf of but does not discuss—are for Justice Murphy, concurring, the only thing worth talking about. He announces the theme, with trumpets, in his opening statement:

The record in this case will stand forever as a monument to man's intolerance of man. Seldom if ever in the history of this nation has there been such a concentrated and relentless crusade to deport an individual because he dared to exercise the freedom that belongs to him as a human being and that is guaranteed to him by the Constitution.[13]

Justice Murphy then proceeds to review in detail the strikingly *ad hominem* legislative history behind the statutory provision now relied upon to deport Bridges.

Murphy challenges frontally the assumption underlying both the approach of Justice Douglas and the approach of Chief Justice Stone, namely, that "the 'plenary' power of Congress to deport resident aliens is unaffected by the guarantee of substantive freedoms contained in the Bill of Rights."[14] He declares:

From this premise it follows that Congress may constitutionally deport aliens for whatever reasons it may choose, limited only by the due process requirement of a fair hearing. . . . I am unable to believe that the Constitution sanctions that assumption or the consequences that logically and inevitably flow from its application.[15]

He then vigorously exploits the paradox of the two *Bridges* cases:

Thus the Government would be precluded from enjoining or imprisoning an alien for exercising his freedom of speech. But the Government at the same time would be free, from a constitutional standpoint, to deport him for exercising that very same freedom. The alien would be fully clothed with his constitutional rights when defending himself in a court of law, but he would be stripped of those rights when deportation officials encircle him.[16]

Murphy does not question the plenary character of the power to *exclude:* "Since an alien obviously brings with him no constitutional rights, Congress may exclude him in the first instance for whatever reason it sees fit." But he insists that once an alien has been admitted to the country, "he becomes invested with the rights guaranteed by the Constitution to all people within our borders." These include the rights protected by the First, Fifth, and Fourteenth Amendments: "None of these provisions acknowledges any distinction between citizens and resident aliens. They extend their inalienable privileges to all 'persons.'" Thus, Murphy argues, "since resident aliens have constitutional rights, it follows that Congress may not ignore them in the exercise of its 'plenary' power of deportation."[17]

Having asserted the counter-premise that constitutional restraints *do* apply to the deportation process, Murphy easily reaches the conclusion—which *on his premises* the other justices would not contest—that the statute is unconstitutional under the First Amendment, because it interferes with freedom of association in its use of mere membership or affiliation ties, and because it fails to narrow sufficiently the kind of advocacy it proscribes.

In both *Kessler* and *Bridges* then the Court manages to save the alien from deportation by means of statutory construction and an insistence on minimal procedural fairness. But when it next considers the issue—during the darkest hours of the anti-Communist period—it hands down several decisions which disclose how harsh and uninhibited by constitutional decencies the deportation law really is.

In *Harisiades v. Shaughnessy*[18] in 1952 the constitutional issues which Justice Murphy raised in his concurring opinion in *Bridges* become the explicit concern of the whole Court. Technically, the Court is called upon to pass on an issue present in *Bridges* but not used as a basis for decision: may the post-*Kessler* amendment of the statute to subject past membership to deportation, which was passed in 1940, constitutionally be used to reach past membership which was terminated *before 1940?*

The case involved three aliens, each of whom had come to the

United States prior to 1920 as a child, had married, raised a family, and lived his adult life here. Each had at some point become a member of the Party, with varying degrees of attachment and awareness. And all had terminated their memberships before 1940; indeed, in one instance the membership was terminated in 1929.

The Court reluctantly affirms the power of the Government to deport under these circumstances. In the years since *Bridges* a number of personnel changes have taken place on the Court, the most significant of which in this area is the replacement of Murphy and Rutledge by Clark and Minton. In *Harisiades* only Justices Black and Douglas dissent. The majority opinion is by Justice Jackson and there is a separate concurrence by Justice Frankfurter. We turn first to the Frankfurter opinion, because it so clearly acknowledges the harshness of the result and yet at the same time unequivocally ratifies the government power to deport aliens at whim.

Frankfurter begins by firmly placing the problem beyond the reach of the Court in an imperfect world:

It is not for this Court to reshape a world order based on politically sovereign States. . . . Ever since national States have come into being, the right of people to enjoy the hospitality of a State of which they are not citizens has been a matter of political determination by each State.[19]

He goes on to stress that this has long been an axiom of American constitutional law and that it is not now to be upset on the showing of some fresh hardship flowing from it:

The Court's acknowledgement of the sole responsibility of Congress for these matters has been made possible by Justices whose cultural outlook, whose breadth of view and robust tolerance were not exceeded by those of Jefferson. In their personal views, libertarians like Mr. Justice Holmes and Mr. Justice Brandeis doubtless disapproved of some of these policies, departures as they were from the best traditions of this country and based as they have been in part on discredited racial theories or manipulation of figures in formulating what is known as the quota system. But whether immigration laws have been crude and cruel, whether they may have reflected xenophobia in general or anti-Semitism or anti-Catholicism, the responsibility belongs to Congress.[20]

The power to expel, so the argument runs, is as broad as the power to exclude initially, and that power resides in Congress exclusively. The justices may personally detest the policies behind the deportation laws, but is it not for them to attempt amelioration: "the place to resist unwise or cruel legislation touching aliens is the Congress, not this Court."[21] Although the exercise of governmental power is offensive to constitutional norms in all the ways the dissenters spell out, the issue is simply one of allocation of powers. Hence no showing of unfair consequences is, in Frankfurter's view, relevant.

The opinion for the Court by Justice Jackson is subtly different. Jackson does not so strongly stress that Congress may, if it wishes, deport aliens at whim. Rather, he attempts a reasoned statement as to why the rule, under the circumstances of the case at hand, makes sense. He makes essentially three points.

First, the inequity is not all that great. The resident alien could always have become a citizen and he has enjoyed certain advantages as a result of his double status: "For over thirty years each of these aliens has enjoyed such advantages as accrue from residence here without renouncing his foreign allegiance."[22] Jackson here touches a mystery about the deportation problem: Why has not the alien elected to become a citizen?

Second, given the facts available to Congress with respect to the worldwide Communist conspiracy, which often works through aliens, it is prudent for a nation to retain this power to remove them from its midst. In other words, the security calculus makes good sense here: "We think that, in the present state of the world, it would be rash and irresponsible to reinterpret our fundamental law to deny or qualify the Government's power of deportation."[23]

Third, he does not find the argument for the aliens any more persuasive if it is measured against specific constitutional inhibitions such as the prohibitions against *ex post facto* laws and those contained in the First Amendment. It is not retroactive, since the aliens were aware when they entered that joining a proscribed organization would be grounds for expulsion; and even if it were retroactive, it would not fall within the coverage of the *ex post facto* provision, because deportation, "however severe its consequences,"[24] is not criminal punishment. Nor in Jackson's view can the special claims of the First Amendment save these aliens from deportation. To condition deportation on not advocating violent overthrow seems to him totally compatible with the First Amendment—it is 1952, just a few months after the decision in *Dennis v. United States.*

If we lay the two opinions side by side, we suspect that Justice Frankfurter would have found the law unconstitutional if only the Constitution had in any sense applied to it. Justice Jackson, on the other hand, appears to be holding the law constitutional because of the special facts about the threat of Communism.

Justice Douglas in a dissenting opinion joined by Justice Black sharply challenges the fundamental premise of plenary power to deport, the point he was so careful to avoid in his majority opinion in *Bridges*. He now openly embraces the position voiced by Justice Murphy, concurring in *Bridges*, that the Bill of Rights limits the power to deport. Like Murphy, he argues that it is deeply contradictory to hold, on one hand, that aliens residing in the United States enjoy the protection of the Bill of Rights and, on the other, that they are stripped of such protections when threatened with deportation: "Unless they are free from arbitrary banishment, the 'liberty' they enjoy while they live here is indeed illusory."[25]

Douglas concedes that there "may be occasions when the continued presence of an alien, no matter how long he may have been here, would be hostile to the safety or welfare of the nation due to the nature of his conduct," but he argues that Congress has not acted under such a standard here; rather, "it has ordered these aliens deported not for what they are but for what they once were."[26] In his view, there is no security calculus that can justify deportation for past membership. He flatly rejects the notion that "a person who was once a Communist is tainted for all time and forever dangerous to our society."[27] Such a view, he writes, is deeply alien to our traditions: "the principle of forgiveness and the doctrine of redemption are too deep in our philosophy to admit that there is no return for those who have once erred."[28]

Justice Jackson counters that "it is not for the judiciary to usurp the function of granting absolution or pardon";[29] that it is up to Congress and Congress has not done so. The Court thus endorses a security calculus with respect to past members that might be stated as follows: he who has once been a member of the Party and hence has subscribed to the doctrine of violent overthrow is more likely to engage in prohibited conduct than one who has never been a member. This is so for two reasons. First, despite the termination of his membership, the ex-member has disclosed something fundamental about himself. Congress, writes Jackson, "regarded the fact than an alien defied our laws to join the Communist Party as an indication that he had developed little comprehension of the principles or practice of representative government or else was unwilling to abide by them."[30] Second, the Party, after *Kessler*, had expelled all aliens from formal membership in order to protect them from deportation. It is thus possible that the ex-member did not have a true change of heart but rather had disguised his continuing allegiance to the Party. In order to insure that such individuals did not evade deportation, Congress had exposed all alien ex-members, no matter how far in the past their contact with the Party may have been, to deportation. In view of the broad power of Congress in this area, there is no need to square this costly regulatory strategy with constitutional guarantees. It is enough that "Congress may have believed that the party tactics threw upon the Government an almost impossible burden" of distinguishing "those who sincerely renounced Communist principles of force and violence from those who left the party the better to serve it."[31]

Any tiny ambiguity left after *Harisiades* that there were no, repeat no, substantive constitutional inhibitions on Congress when exercising the power to deport aliens is put to rest by *Galvan v. Press*[32] in 1954. The deportation statute at issue is a provision in the Internal Security Act of 1950 authorizing the deportation of anyone who at any time after entry "had been a member of or affiliated with the Communist Party of the United States." Under the old law it had been necessary for the prosecution to establish in each deportation case that the Communist Party did indeed advocate violent overthrow. The new provision was meant to render such proof about the Party no longer necessary on a case by case basis. We would pause to underscore the light that *Galvan* thus throws on the drafting of the 1950 Internal Security Act. The Act, it will be recalled, makes a great show of providing for a hearing before even the Communist Party may be labelled a Communist action organization and ordered to register; yet that same Act carefully provides *as to aliens* that the government may proceed to deport those who have been members without waiting for the administrative determination of the Party's status.

The *Galvan* facts tell the familiar story. This time the alien is a Mexican who has been here since 1918, has married, and raised four children. After thirty-one years of residence the government initiates deportation proceedings against him on the ground that he had been a member of the Party from 1944 to 1946. The new issue that moves the case a step beyond *Harisiades* in harshness is whether any form of *scienter* as to the unlawful purposes of the Party is required by the statute; and if not, whether the statute is still constitutional. The Court in a 7 to 2 decision holds that the answer to the first question is "no." This answer appears inescapable, since the provision of the 1950 Act dealing with membership in the Party is silent as to *scienter*, while a companion provision dealing with membership in front organ-

izations explicitly requires it. The Court then goes on to hold that the
answer to the second question is "yes": despite the absence of a
scienter requirement, the statute is constitutional. Justice Frankfurter
writes the majority opinion. Justices Black and Douglas both enter
dissenting opinions.

Justice Frankfurter, who was so eloquent about the fundamental
need for a requirement of *scienter* in *Garner*[33] and *Wieman*[34] in order
to render the security calculus rational, repeats the argument he made
in *Harisiades.* It is simply too late in the day to challenge the premise
that such decisions are left to the untrammelled judgment of the
political branches. He acknowledges "a sense of harsh incongruity"[35]
in the result and suggests that were the Court "writing on a clean
slate," the deportation might well be seen as unconstitutional. But, he
concludes, "the slate is not clean."[36]

Two details from the dissents are worth noting. First, Justice
Douglas, who, as in *Harisiades,* challenges the premise of plenary
power to deport, pointedly notes the fact that during the period of the
alien's membership in it, the Communist Party was still on the ballot
in California. Second, there is the cumulative indignation with which
Justice Black sums up the outcome:

For joining a lawful political group years ago—an act which he had no possible reason to believe would subject him to the slightest penalty—petitioner
now loses his job, his friends, his home, and maybe even his children, who
must choose between their father and their native country.[37]

Justice Black's greatest indignation, as well as perhaps the low
point of the Court's patience and tolerance in this area, comes in
Carlson v. Landon[38] in 1952, a case decided on the same day as *Harisiades. Carlson* only collaterally involves the power to deport. Rather,
it presents the question of whether the petitioners have a right to bail
pending a final determination of their deportability. The deportation
provisions of the Internal Security Act of 1950 provided that the
Attorney General had discretion to grant bail. The issue in *Carlson* is
just how broad that discretion is. Might the Attorney General withhold bail on nothing more than reason to believe the deportees were
present members of the Party, without any individualizing evidence
as to the distinctive risks they would offer if released on bail until
deported?

Carlson takes on added interest when read together with *Stack v.
Boyle,*[39] a case involving the allocation of bail pending trial to defend-

ants indicted under the Smith Act. Decided during the same term as *Carlson, Stack* provides a contrast which brings into sharp focus the vulnerability of aliens. In *Stack* the trial court, influenced by the fact that after the recently concluded *Dennis* case four of the Communist defendants had forfeited bail, had set bail uniformly high for the twelve defendants—a flat $50,000 for each. The Supreme Court in a unanimous decision upset the bail determination and sent the case back. In an opinion by Chief Justice Vinson the Court insisted, in effect, that the calculus of risk for bail must be careful and precise, even when anti-subversion is involved. It was sharply impatient in this context with any argument for guilt by association. The Chief Justice observed bitingly: "The Government asks the courts to depart from the norm by assuming, without the introduction of evidence, that each petitioner is a pawn in a conspiracy and will, in obedience to a superior, flee the jurisdiction."[40] In the absence of individual evidence that they represented a special risk of bail jumping, the Court held, the *Stack* defendants were entitled to have bail set as it would be customary for defendants who committed crimes carrying penalties comparable to those in the Smith Act.

Carlson, decided several months later by the same Court, stands in stark contrast to *Stack.* By a vote of 5 to 4, the Court affirms the power of the Attorney General to detain deportees without bail on the ground of present membership in the Communist Party. The majority opinion is by Justice Reed. Justices Douglas, Burton, Frankfurter, and Black enter dissenting opinions.

The majority makes no effort to minimize the harshness of the result. Justice Reed acknowledges that, Party membership apart, the petitioners have behaved impeccably during their long residence in America. Indeed, it is noted that one of them had two sons who served in the Army in World War II, and had himself sold $50,000 in war bonds and given blood to the Red Cross on many occasions. Moreover, the Court of Appeals, in holding that reasonable bail should be granted, had stated:

This view is more nearly in accordance with the spirit of our institutions as it relates even to those who seek protection from the laws which they incongruously seek to destroy.[41]

Justice Reed avoids confronting head-on the question of whether there are any due process restraints operative in deportation. He accepts the government position that the test under the statute is whether there was an abuse of discretion. It was, he thinks, "reason-able" for the Attorney General to conclude that membership itself made alleged Communist aliens too unreliable to release on bail pending a determination of their status and deportability. He does not find it necessary to note or distinguish *Stack v. Boyle.*

Next Justice Reed quickly dismisses the argument that the Act in leaving the bail matter to the discretion of the Attorney General without any specification of standards constitutes an undue delega-tion of legislative authority, since again presumably it would not be an abuse of discretion for him to deny bail to all alien Communist deportees.

Nor finally do the prohibitions against "excessive bail," which were thought important enough to place in the Eighth Amendment, help these petitioners. The Amendment, he concludes, leaves Con-gress free to define bailable offenses; its function is "merely to pro-vide that bail shall not be excessive in those cases where it is proper to grant bail."[42] The Court, in the most casual manner, thus makes pre-trial detention possible for any offense Congress wishes to desig-nate, and thereby renders the Eighth Amendment illogical and largely impotent. The evil of "excessive" bail is, of course, that as a practical matter it denies the right to bail; but this reading of the Amendment makes it possible to deny bail directly, and so to do that directly which is prohibited from being done indirectly! *Carlson* is thus a prime example of how preoccupation with anti-subversion corrupts the han-dling of other legal principles when they impinge.

The four dissents each reflect an emphasis characteristic of the style of the particular justice. In a brief opinion Justice Douglas pushes aside the bail controversy and, as in *Harisiades* and *Galvan,* once again challenges the premise of plenary power to deport. Justice Burton, in another brief opinion, focuses on the illogical reading of the Eighth Amendment which he argues must accomplish more than the majority intends.

The centerpieces of the dissent are the opinions of Justices Frankfurter and Black. Justice Frankfurter in a superb technical opin-ion destroys the majority's reading of the Act. Quoting heavily from *Stack v. Boyle,* which Justice Reed had so conveniently ignored, he stresses that a statute dealing with bail must be read to reflect the traditional understanding about bail, namely, that bail is an important safeguard to a defendant—or, he adds, a deportee—in preparing his defense and hence is intimately related to ideas of due process. More-

over, the granting of bail has traditionally been understood to depend
on individuating circumstances as to the particular defendant. Thus
the Act in giving the Attorney General discretion to grant or withhold
bail must have intended the traditional mode of such discretion and
that in turn meant keying the discretion to the individuating facts
about the particular individual. This the Attorney General had clearly
not done; rather, he had placed a blanket ban on all members of the
Communist Party. Further, any doubt that this was the intention of
Congress must be utterly foreclosed by the legislative history, for
Congress had expressly rejected a prior proposal to give the Attorney
General unreviewable power to detain pending deportation.

Justice Black puts his dissent in a less technical way. Like Justice
Burton, he is appalled at the construction of the Eighth Amendment:

Under this contention, the Eighth Amendment is a limitation upon judges
only, for while a judge cannot constitutionally fix excessive bail, Congress can
direct that people be held in jail without any right to bail at all. Stated still
another way, the Amendment does no more than protect a right to bail which
Congress can grant and which Congress can take away. The Amendment is
thus reduced below the level of a pious admonition. . . . I can only say that
I regret, deeply regret, that the Court now adds the right to bail to the list
of other Bill of Rights guarantees that have recently been weakened to expand governmental powers at the expense of individual freedom.[43]

Characteristically, Black's ultimate eloquence is stirred by his
perception of this technical controversy over bail as a grave affront to
First Amendment values. As he sees it, the case is an instance of
pre-trial detention for speech. The explicit ground for deportation of
aliens who are members of the Communist Party is that they vicari-
ously advocate violent overthrow. The ground for the detention without bail of these particular aliens is really the same—they are
members of a group guilty of a speech crime. The factor that makes
them too dangerous to the American community to be released on
bail pending determination of their status must then be their speech
or the speech of their group. Black quotes the District Judge, who
conceded that "there is nothing here to indicate the Government is
fearful that they are going to leave the jurisdiction" and then justified
his denial of bail by telling counsel: "I am not going to turn these
people loose if they are Communists, any more than I would turn
loose a deadly germ in this community."[44] Bad as convicting people

after trial for speech crimes may be, it is singularly offensive in Justice Black's eyes to detain them before trial because of the danger of their speech:

The stark fact is that if Congress can authorize imprisonment of "alien Communists" because dangerous, it can authorize imprisonment of citizen "Communists" on the same ground. And while this particular [Bureau of Immigration] campaign to fill the jails is said to be aimed at "dangerous" alien Communists only, peaceful citizens may be ensnared in the process. For the bureau agent is not required to prove that a person he throws in jail is an alien, or a Communist, or "dangerous." The agent need only declare he has reason to believe that such is the case. The agent may be and here apparently was acting on the rankest hearsay evidence.[45]

Justice Black is moved by his perception of the case to one of his most basic utterances of his views about free speech:

. . . the basis of holding these people in jail is a fear that they may indoctrinate people with Communist beliefs. To put people in jail for fear of their talk seems to me an abridgement of speech in flat violation of the First Amendment. . . . My belief is that we must have freedom of speech, press, and religion for all or we may eventually have it for none. I further believe that the First Amendment grants an absolute right to believe in any governmental system, discuss all governmental affairs, and argue for desired changes in the existing order. This freedom is too dangerous for bad, tyrannical governments to permit. But those who wrote and adopted our First Amendment weighed those dangers against the dangers of censorship and deliberately chose the First Amendment's unequivocal command that freedom of assembly, petition, speech and press shall not be abridged. I happen to believe this was a wise choice and that our free way of life enlists such respect and love that our Nation cannot be imperiled by mere talk. This belief of mine may and I suppose does influence me to protest whenever I think I see even slight encroachments on First Amendment liberties. But the encroachment here is not small. True it is mainly those alleged to be present or past "Communists" who are now being jailed for their beliefs and expressions. But we cannot be sure more victims will not be offered up later if the First Amendment means no more than its enemies or even some of its friends believe it does.[46]

Carlson, then, although it involves only a detail about the procedures for bail in deportation cases, is informed by the fundamental tensions which characterize First Amendment controversies where national security is the countervalue. Its denial of bail is another example, to be placed alongside the denial of Social Security benefits in *Flemming v. Nestor* [47] and the denial of the right to practice before the Supreme Court in *In re Isserman,* [48] of a pettiness, a meanness of spirit, which in the end infects government anti-subversion efforts. And in each instance the Supreme Court's unwillingness to make the small correction is disheartening.

The remainder of the story of deportation as an anti-subversive tactic can be told quickly. The Court continues to confront cases for the next decade and the deportee now wins several. But there is no new challenge to the constitutional framework settled by *Galvan:* the power to deport is plenary. Its use is an instance of a sanction the government may allocate at whim.

Rowoldt v. Perfetto [49] in 1957 affords Justice Frankfurter an opportunity to mitigate somewhat, by statutory construction, the harshness of the constitutional result he had ratified in *Galvan,* namely, that the alien could be deported for past membership without any proof of *scienter* of unlawful purpose. He had warned in *Galvan* that there were limits to the kind of minimal membership to which deportation could attach; he had spoken of "instances where membership is so nominal as to keep an alien out of the deportable class."[50] *Rowoldt* proves to be such an instance. The deportee had come to the United States in 1914 and the ground for deportation was his past affiliation with the Communist Party, which apparently lasted only one year, 1935. At the hearing he indicated only a vague sense of the purposes of the Party and emphasized that he was hungry and unemployed; there apparently was no evidence offered to counter his. Justice Frankfurter reads the record most sympathetically. "Bearing in mind the solidity of proof that is required for a judgment entailing the consequences of deportation, particularly in the case of an old man who has lived in this country for forty years," he concludes, the record does not establish "the kind of meaningful association" with the Party required by the statute.[51]

Even this modest mitigation divides the Court and Justice Frankfurter carries only four justices with him. Justice Harlan writes a reluctant dissent over the "impermissible liberties"[52] he feels Frankfurter has taken with the statute and the record. There is a small irony in this for students of judicial style. For Justice Harlan has often been thought of as a follower of Justice Frankfurter in terms of rigorous adherence to judicial restraint. His dissent charging Frankfurter with straying may be seen as an instance of "out-Heroding Herod."[53]

If we add *Rowoldt* and *Galvan* to *Elfbrandt* and *Wieman*, it is evident that the law has developed more gradations of Party membership to which constitutional consequences attach than it quite knows what to do with: there is (i) the active, knowing, evil-intending member from *Elfbrandt;* (ii) the member with *scienter* only from *Wieman;* (iii) the member with meaningful association who lacks *scienter* from *Galvan;* (iv) past members with each of these gradations of affiliation; and now (v) the member from *Rowoldt* who lacks both *scienter* and meaningful association. The Harlan dissent in *Rowoldt* presses hard the difficulty of distinguishing between (iii) and (v), and underscores once again how treacherous a predicate for legal sanctions "membership" in a group really is.

The relentless effort to ferret out ex-Communist aliens and deport them regardless of the lapse of time provides further occasions for the Court to consider the relaxation of the membership requirement Justice Frankfurter effected in *Rowoldt*. In *Niukkanen v. McAlexander,* [54] decided in 1960, the deportee had been brought to the United States in 1908 as an infant and had lived here uneventfully ever since, serving in the Army for a time. The fatal flaw in his record is the testimony of two witnesses that he had been a member of the Party for two years from 1937 to 1939. Niukkanen denies that he ever knew one of the witnesses, and their cumulative testimony shows at most attendance at meetings at which labor conditions and relief were discussed, the payment of dues of 25 cents a month, and that Niukkanen "was not an intellectual interested in 'theory' or 'political discussion.'" When questioned by the District Court, Niukkanen had somewhat evasively denied his membership. The District Court concluded he had committed perjury and ordered deportation. The Supreme Court in a 5 to 4 *per curiam* decision affirms, with Justices Frankfurter and Harlan, together again, making up the majority. Justice Douglas, dissenting, captures the gratuitous harshness of the result:

One who reads the whole of this record cannot put it down without feeling that here is a man neither conspiratorial, dangerous, cunning, nor knowledgeable. Petitioner—a painter by trade—represents a microscopic element in the ranks of our labor force who was caught up in a movement whose ideology he did not understand and whose leaders spoke in terms of bread for the hungry, and jobs for the unemployed. . . . A man who has lived here for every meaningful month of his entire life should not be sent into exile for acts which this record reveals were utterly devoid of any sinister implications. [55]

The problem of reconciling *Galvan* with *Rowoldt* plagues the Court in one last deportation case, *Gastelum-Quinones v. Kennedy*[56] in 1963. The result is another 5 to 4 decision, this time in favor of the deportee. Indeed, *Gastelum-Quinones* suggests that the distinction Justice Frankfurter had attempted in *Rowoldt* between two categories of members without *scienter*—one utterly nominal and the other substantial enough to warrant deportation—is simply too subtle for use in a legal system. In any event, the majority, speaking through Justice Goldberg, finds that a tie for perhaps two years some twenty years ago during which the alien had attended perhaps fifteen meetings of a group that met weekly was the kind of nominal association *Rowoldt* had placed beyond the reach of deportation. The four dissenters, speaking through Justice White, with Justice Harlan continuing his line of dissents in these cases, view the same data as evidence of membership within the statutory ban.

The deportation precedents form a tidy, if disheartening, universe of their own.[57] The profile of the rules governing deportation is clear. There is *plenary* power to deport aliens. And this remains true against First Amendment inhibitions. The constitutional limits on direct sanctions laid down in *Yates*[58] and *Scales*[59] in no sense provide a relevant baseline for appraising the propriety of the deportation sanction. It may be applied to resident aliens even when any sanction against citizens for comparable degrees of association would be grossly unconstitutional. It may be applied as a sanction no matter how long the alien has resided here, no matter how little awareness the alien had of the improper purposes of the association. And finally, the alien may be detained without bail pending a final determination of his status. These precedents all remain on the books to haunt us some later day.

The deportation cases also suggest several larger themes. They supply almost experimental evidence of how little Congress itself is disciplined by the traditions of political tolerance. They suggest that Congress, when freed from constitutional restraints, will pursue the logic of security relentlessly. And they demonstrate how intrinsically and dangerously expansible that logic is. From the conclusion that present active members of the Party should be deported for security reasons, the law effortlessly expands to the conclusion that former members of the Party, however long ago they terminated their memberships and however little they understood of the Party's purposes, should also be deported for security reasons.

Finally, these cases offer an interesting study in judicial tactics.

Although severely hobbled in this area, the Court has repeatedly attempted by means of statutory construction to protect resident aliens from deportation. *Kessler* (construing the deportation statute not to cover past membership), *Bridges* (narrowly construing the term "affiliation"), and *Rowoldt* and *Gastelum-Quinones* (applying the "meaningful association" limitation) are successful instances of this approach. While there may finally be little the Court can do in this area, it has done what little it can.

31

Denaturalization

The special vulnerability of the resident alien to the deportation sanction has depended in part upon his somewhat mysterious reluctance to become a citizen. It might be expected that were he to secure citizenship, he would be beyond the reach of deportation and would have precisely the same rights as native-born citizens should he engage in radical politics. That expectation, however, turns out to be not quite accurate; even after naturalization there remains a possibility that the government will reopen the matter and rescind the grant of citizenship. When concern over domestic subversion arose, this possibility of ferreting out naturalized citizens who were or had been Communists was, not surprisingly, vigorously pursued and generated a number of Supreme Court cases.

Before we turn to those cases, it will be helpful to take a quick look at the law governing naturalization, for the power to denaturalize rests ultimately on the power to naturalize. Article I, section 8, clause 4 of the Constitution confers upon Congress the power to prescribe uniform rules of naturalization. This has been read to grant Congress plenary power in this area. Congress has exercised that power to impose conditions upon naturalization that would be clearly unconstitutional if required of native-born citizens. The Nationality Act of 1906, for example, provided that anarchists were ineligible for naturalization. As concern shifted to Communists, Congress passed the Nationality Act of 1940 which barred from naturalization those who advocate or are members of organizations that advocate violent overthrow of the government. And the Internal Security Act of 1950 extended the bar to members of "Communist-action" organizations. Finally, in the Immigration and Naturalization Act of 1952 Congress flatly prohibited the naturalization of any person "who is a member of or affiliated with . . . the Communist Party of the United States."

Given the plenary power of Congress in this domain, it is only in instances where there is statutory ambiguity that the Court has been able significantly to affect the operation of the naturalization laws. The prime example is a series of cases involving the denial of naturalization to conscientious objectors. These cases present perplexities which bear some affinity to but are by no means the same as freedom of speech issues. Yet they have resonance for our purposes. This is especially true of the first of them—*United States v. Schwimmer*[1] in 1929—a case which has been kept alive chiefly by a famous Holmes dissent.

Schwimmer involved a well-known pacifist who had come to this country from Hungary in 1921 and after several years of residence had applied for citizenship. Asked in the naturalization proceedings about her willingness to take up arms in defense of the country, she had replied: "I would not take up arms personally." During the hearings she had reiterated her pacifist views, saying among other things: "I am an uncompromising pacifist." At the time of her petition she was forty-nine years old. Moreover, she had vigorously asserted her admiration and affection for the United States, her willingness to support it in any other way than by personally bearing arms, and her recognition of the government's right, in the event of war, to deal with her as it deals with male citizens who are conscientious objectors.

On these facts the District Court denied her petition. Although the naturalization statute did not explicitly bar conscientious objectors, the court upheld findings that she had not satisfied the statutory requirement of "attachment to the principles of the Constitution" and that she was unable, without mental reservations, to take the oath to "support and defend the Constitution and the laws of the United States against all enemies" prescribed for applicants. The Court of Appeals reversed and directed that her petition be granted. The Supreme Court in turn reversed the Court of Appeals and reinstated the order of the District Court. The opinion of the Court was by Justice Butler. Justices Holmes, Brandeis and Sanford dissented.

Since Miss Schwimmer was forty-nine years old and a woman and thus doubly certain not to be relied upon by the country for military duty, there was a certain awkwardness in insisting that her refusal to serve itself disqualified her for citizenship. Perhaps to obviate this, Justice Butler also emphasized her views and the likelihood of her propagating them. The fact that conscientious objectors may, due to age or sex, be unfit to serve, he reasoned, "does not lessen their purpose or power to influence others."[2]

The absurdity of the decision—"the applicant seems to be a woman of superior character and intelligence, obviously more than ordinarily desirable as a citizen of the United States"[3]—and its free speech implications trigger a splendid burst of dissent from Justice Holmes. The passage demands quotation, especially since he recurs to *Schenck*. One can, if so minded, read it as an apologia for *Schenck:*

Of course the fear is that if a war came the applicant would exert such activities as were dealt with in *Schenck v. United States*. But that seems to me unfounded. Her position and motives are wholly different from those of Schenck. She is an optimist and states in strong and, I do not doubt, sincere words her belief that war will disappear and that the impending destiny of mankind is to unite in peaceful leagues. I do not share that optimism nor do I think that a philosophic view of the world would regard war as absurd. But most people who have known it regard it with horror, as a last resort, and, even if not yet ready for cosmopolitan efforts, would welcome any practicable combinations that would increase the power on the side of peace. The notion that the applicant's optimistic anticipations would make her a worse citizen is sufficiently answered by her examination, which seems to me a better argument for her admission than any I can offer. Some of her answers might excite popular prejudice, but if there is any principle of the Constitution that more imperatively calls for attachment than any other it is the principle of free thought—not free thought for those who agree with us but freedom of thought for the thought that we hate. I think that we should adhere to that principle with regard to admission into, as well as to life within, this country. And, recurring to the opinion that bars this applicant's way, I would suggest that the Quakers have done their share to make the country what it is, that many citizens agree with the applicant's belief and that I had not supposed hitherto that we regretted our inability to expel them because they believe more than some of us do in the teachings of the Sermon on the Mount.[4]

What is so striking about this passage, its stunning literary skill and irony apart, is that Holmes is almost effortlessly assuming that we must apply the same criteria of free speech to those seeking citizenship as to those who have it. He sees the case not as a regulation of admission but as an abridgement of speech. Moreover, he sees it as so much a free speech case that he is moved to utter what is perhaps his most stirring pronouncement about the First Amendment—it protects, he reminds us, freedom for the thought we hate.

Holmes's eloquence in *Schwimmer* is reinforced in 1931 by the powerful argument of Chief Justice Hughes dissenting in *United States v. Macintosh*. [5] In an opinion joined by Justices Holmes, Brandeis, and Stone, Hughes protests the denial of naturalization to an applicant who stated that on religious grounds he would bear arms only in wars he regarded to be morally justified. Hughes does not question the plenary power of Congress to set conditions for naturalization. Rather, he insists that the issue before the Court is a narrow one of statutory construction: in view of the fact that Congress did not expressly bar conscientious objectors from eligibility for naturalization, is such an intention to be implied from the general language of the naturalization statute? Reading the "support and defend" oath and the "attachment" requirement "in the light of our regard from the beginning for freedom of conscience,"[6] Hughes argues that, in the absence of "unequivocal terms" expressing the intent of Congress, an intention to bar conscientious objectors should not be implied, for "such a construction is directly opposed to the spirit of our institutions and to the historic practice of the Congress."[7] There is, he concludes, no such evidence that Congress intended to depart from "our happy tradition" of religious liberty and the policy of avoiding "unnecessary clashes" between legislation and "the dictates of conscience."[8]

The dissenting tradition becomes majority doctrine in *Girouard v. United States*[9] in 1946. In a 5 to 4 decision, the Court reverses the denial of naturalization to a Seventh Day Adventist willing to serve in the military but not to bear arms. In the process it overrules *Schwimmer* and *Macintosh* and adopts Chief Justice Hughes's construction of the statute: Congress did not intend to bar conscientious objectors from citizenship. In reaching this conclusion, the Court does not challenge the plenary power of Congress over naturalization. The decision was possible only because the policy of denying naturalization to conscientious objectors was based on administrative rulings and not an explicit statutory command. Had Congress so desired, it could presumably have flatly barred conscientious objectors.[10]

Is the power to denaturalize equally broad? On what grounds may the government revoke a naturalization once granted? The first and most important of the cases to present these questions, *Schneiderman v. United States*[11] in 1943, was a celebrated event. It marked the beginning of the Court's dealings with modern Communism, and there is found in the dissent of Chief Justice Stone the first of the Court's attempts to write a "profile" of American Communism. The case, which is decided 5 to 3 in favor of Schneiderman, sparks almost a hundred pages of opinions and reflects a high point in the power of the liberal bloc composed of Justices Murphy, Rutledge, Black, and Douglas. The case is also made worthy of remembrance by the graceful circumstance that Wendell Willkie, who in 1940 had been the Republican candidate for President, argued the matter for Schneiderman.

The case did not involve new rules specifically tailored to meet the Communist threat; rather, existing machinery which had been used for years to rescind naturalizations suddenly became politically explosive when applied to Schneiderman. The Naturalization Act of 1906—the statute under which Schneiderman had been naturalized—provided two bases on which naturalization might be revoked: (i) that it was obtained by fraud; or (ii) that it was "illegally procured." It is illegally procured if any of the conditions prescribed for naturalization turn out subsequently not to have been satisfied in fact at the time the certificate was granted. It is analogous to a breach of warranty. There is no statute of limitations and the government retains the option at any later date of challenging the facts as to any of the prescribed conditions. In brief, a naturalization decision, even after a hearing in open court, is in no sense *res judicata* between the naturalized citizen and his adopted government. The procedure would seem in this respect an extraordinary departure from licensing procedures in general. Presumably it had not stirred controversy previously because it had been confined to objective conditions such as whether the alien had in fact resided here for the requisite five years or whether the hearing had been held in open court.

The special intensity of the *Schneiderman* case derives from the distinctive nature of the condition said to have been violated: the requirement that the applicant show that at the time of his application and for the preceding five years he was "attached to the principles of the Constitution." The 1906 Act was aimed primarily at anarchists; it did not, as would later legislation, bar members of the Communist Party or, more generally, members of groups advocating violent overthrow of the government. Hence the Government challenges Schneiderman's citizenship on the ground that he was an admitted member of the Communist Party at the time of his naturalization and therefore could not in fact have satisfied the "attachment" condition. Schneiderman, who appears to have been sophisticated intellectually and politically, contended that his membership in the Party was fully compatible with attachment to the Constitution. The trial court agreed with the Government, finding that Schneiderman's certificate of naturalization was illegally procured in that he had not satisfied the attachment condition.

The Court divides over the weight to be given the trial court's finding. The dissenters, powerfully led by Chief Justice Stone, insist that the case involves only a routine application of existing rules, long unchallenged. Stone observes sharply:

The finality which attaches to the trial court's determinations of fact from evidence heard in open court, and which ordinarily saves them from an appellate court's intermeddling, should not be remembered in every case save this one alone.[12]

Justice Murphy, writing for the Court, and Justices Douglas and Rutledge, concurring, seek to impeach Stone's contention that this is a *routine* revocation case. It appears that this is the first time lack of attachment to the Constitution has been used as a basis for revocation. In their view, that factor makes the case anything but routine.

Justice Douglas advances the technical argument that the attachment condition is distinctive and not subject to being reopened at a later date. As he reads the statute, what is called for is not the fact of attachment but a finding by the judge at the naturalization hearing that he is satisfied as to the alien's attitude. Any other construction of the statute, argues Douglas, "would mean that the United States at any time could obtain a trial *de novo* on the political faith of the applicant."[13] He continues:

If findings of attachment which underlie certificates may be set aside years later on the evidence, then the citizenship of those whose political faiths become unpopular with the passage of time becomes vulnerable.[14]

It will take clearer language than that used in the statute to persuade him that Congress intended a result so alien to American traditions.

Justice Rutledge's opinion is an eloquent soliloquy on how atrocious from a legal standpoint the scheme Chief Justice Stone would treat as routine really is. He argues that to comply with ordinary notions of adjudication and respect for courts, *the initial judgment* that the alien is entitled to citizenship must be treated with respect: "solemn decrees may not be lightly overturned."[15] Hence there must be a heavy burden of proof on the government when it attempts to overturn such a judgment. In Rutledge's view, Stone has it exactly wrong: it is the *first* judgment of the facts, not the *second,* that calls for respect.

Rutledge is also eloquent on the consequences of the rule proposed. Schneiderman had been naturalized seventeen years earlier. If his citizenship can so easily be upset after so long, "no naturalized person's citizenship is or can be secure. If this can be done after that length of time, it can be done after thirty or fifty years. If it can be done for Schneiderman, it can be done for thousands or tens of thousands of others."[16] Moreover, nothing would keep the Government from coming back again and again until it finally finds a judge who views the facts as to attachment its way. "No citizen with such a threat hanging over his head could be free. . . . Such a citizen would not be admitted to liberty. His best course would be silence or hypocrisy. This is not citizenship."[17]

Justice Murphy's opinion for the Court becomes a major effort. He begins by construing the Naturalization Act so as to require a high standard of proof. Because American citizenship is "precious" and is "conferred by solemn adjudication," he holds, it can be revoked only on a showing of "clear, unequivocal, and convincing" evidence of violation of the Act.[18] He then proceeds to review the facts to see whether the Government has met this burden.

The opinion has two wings. The first deals with whether commitment to the radical policies of the Party—socialization of the means of production, dictatorship of the proletariat, etc.—is incompatible with the principles of the Constitution. The question is strongly reminiscent of the issue of whether pacifists could honestly subscribe to the oath of allegiance and be naturalized, and Justice Murphy refers several times to Justice Holmes's opinion in *Schwimmer.* The question is, of course, easy to answer, but Murphy writes an engaging essay on the theme that the greatest variety of political, social and economic views are compatible with deep attachment to the Constitution.

He then turns to the second wing: the advocacy of violent overthrow. Schneiderman had argued elaborately that the Party did not in fact advocate violence. As Justice Murphy sees it, since there is no evidence of Schneiderman's beliefs apart from his membership in the Party, the crucial issues are whether the Party advocated violence in 1927, the year of Schneiderman's naturalization, and, if so, whether Schneiderman can be charged with it. He begins his answer by making an important statement about guilt by association:

... under our traditions beliefs are personal and are not a matter of mere association, and... men in adhering to a political party or other organization notoriously do not subscribe unqualifiedly to all of its platforms or asserted principles.[19]

This is said in 1943 at the threshold of the Court's massive confrontation with vicarious speech. The Court's first impulse is to pose the essential questions: Does the group engage in proscribed speech? What is the nexus of the individual to the illegal purposes of the group? This clarity as to the nature of the issue will soon be clouded, however, as concern shifts from speech as such to personal unreliability.

Murphy then turns to an examination of whether the Party did indeed advocate violence in 1927 and finds the record ambiguous; there is evidence pointing both ways. He agrees that a reasonable man might find that it did, but he insists that the ultimate question is whether Schneiderman personally did to such an extent that it impeaches his attachment to the Constitution. Schneiderman had insisted he interpreted Party doctrine otherwise. Justice Murphy has been much ridiculed in later opinions and commentary for being unrealistic about modern Communism. But on close reading it is clear that he comes to no conclusion about the Party, only to a conclusion about what may be imputed to Schneiderman for the purposes of a denaturalization hearing:

We hold only that where two interpretations of an organization's program are possible, the one reprehensible and a bar to naturalization and the other permissible, a court in a denaturalization proceeding. . . is not justified in canceling a certificate of citizenship by imputing the reprehensible interpretation to a member in the absence of overt acts indicating that such was his interpretation.[20]

Chief Justice Stone in dissent maintains that even under the majority's high standard of proof—a standard he insists is unwarranted—a finding of lack of attachment is inescapable. He argues on the basis of an extended survey of Communist literature that various tenets of the Party *are* wholly incompatible with attachment to the Constitution. And he stresses the active, knowing character of Schneiderman's membership: "It would be little short of preposterous to assert that vigorous aid knowingly given by a pledged Party member in disseminating the Party teachings. . . is compatible with attachment to the principles of the Constitution."[21]

But Justice Murphy carries the day. *Schneiderman* emerges as a useful precedent on the pitfalls of charging vicarious responsibility for speech. And, more important, it proves to be the controlling precedent henceforward on the construction of the denaturalization statute and on the "clear, unequivocal, and convincing" proof required to bring about a loss of citizenship.

As the ironies of world history would have it, the Court's next two encounters with the problem—*Baumgartner v. United States*[22] in 1944 and *Knauer v. United States*[23] in 1945—involve not Communists but Nazis or near-Nazis. In *Baumgartner* the Court unanimously reverses the denaturalization of a German on grounds of fraud for failure of "clear, unequivocal, and convincing" proof. The opinion is by Justice Frankfurter, who had dissented in *Schneiderman* but now restates the lessons from that decision with conviction and power.

The petitioner had been born in Germany and fought in the German Army in World War I; he had come to the United States in the late 1920s and was naturalized in 1932, just before the rise of Hitler. In the years that followed he often expressed admiration for Hitler and for the promise of the new Germany, was critical of America, and rejoiced at the fall of Dunkirk. In 1942 denaturalization proceedings were initiated against him on the ground that he had fraudulently concealed his continued allegiance to Germany when he was naturalized. The Government's case rests almost entirely on evidence of his views *after* his naturalization.

Justice Frankfurter reads the facts with notable sympathy for "old cultural loyalties" and with understanding of enthusiasm for "new strength of the land of one's nativity," which was "flamboyantly exploited before its full sinister meaning had been adequately revealed."[24] Accordingly, he finds that the Government proof fell short of showing fraudulent concealment of divided loyalty:

In short, the weakness of the proof as to Baumgartner's state of mind at the time he took the oath of allegiance can be removed, if at all, only by a presumption that disqualifying views expressed after naturalization were accurate representations of his views when he took the oath. The logical validity of such a presumption is at best dubious even were the supporting evidence less rhetorical and more conclusive. . . . The evidence in the record before us is not sufficiently compelling to require that we penalize a naturalized citizen for the expression of silly or even sinister-sounding views which native-born citizens utter with immunity.[25]

Equally striking, Justice Frankfurter now reads the law as sensitive to the rights of naturalized citizens, as Justice Murphy in *Schneiderman* had insisted it must be read:

New relations and new interests flow, once citizenship has been granted. All that should not be undone unless the proof is compelling that that which was granted was obtained in defiance of Congressional authority. . . . Nothing that we are now deciding is intended to weaken in the slightest the alertness with which admission to American citizenship should be safeguarded. But we must be equally watchful that citizenship once bestowed should not be in jeopardy nor in fear of exercising its American freedom through too easy finding that citizenship was disloyally acquired.[26]

When one lays the opinion in *Baumgartner* alongside the dissent in *Schneiderman* the difference in tone and empathy for the naturalized citizen is striking. It is not altogether clear whether the *Schneiderman* dissenters have within a year become persuaded of the views of Justices Murphy, Douglas, Black, and Rutledge, or whether they have a special set of rules when Communism is charged.

Two years later in *Knauer* a majority of the Court agree that the *Schneiderman* standards have been satisfied and affirm the denaturalization of a German-born man for fraud. The majority opinion is by Justice Douglas, and there is a separate concurrence by Justice Black. Only Justices Rutledge and Murphy remain troubled enough to dissent.

It is difficult at this distance in time to form an opinion about *Knauer*. The Court restates with force the stringent limitations on denaturalization deriving from *Schneiderman*. It restates too the cautions of Justice Frankfurter in *Baumgartner* about post-naturalization evidence: "as *Baumgartner v. United States* indicates, utterances made in years subsequent to the oath are not readily to be charged against the state of mind existing when the oath was administered."[27] And it also takes care to state that mere membership in the German-American Bund is not sufficient proof of fraud in swearing allegiance to the United States. But, insists Justice Douglas, "we have here much more than that": "there is solid, convincing evidence that Knauer before the date of his naturalization, at that time, and subsequently was a thorough-going Nazi."[28] The factor that most distinguishes *Knauer* from *Baumgartner* is the date of naturalization; it is 1937, well after Hitler had come to power and been revealed for what he was. But one is still uneasy: the Court is so open in its detestation of Nazi principles. Moreover, Justice Douglas, who had insisted in *Schneiderman* that the Government should not be permitted to go behind a finding of attachment to the Constitution is willing here to impeach several years later the good faith of an oath of allegiance to the Constitution. His prior position of reading the statute to preclude going behind a finding of attachment is not available when the Government elects to proceed on the ground of fraud rather than that of illegal procurement.

In the end, one tends to share the unease of Justices Rutledge and Murphy about the very idea of denaturalization. Going beyond their prior position in *Schneiderman* and *Baumgartner,* they argue that forfeiture of the citizenship of naturalized citizens should be restricted to the same grounds applicable to native-born citizens. Rutledge concedes that if any naturalized citizen can properly be denaturalized, it is Knauer. But to denaturalize him on the grounds and under the procedures used in this case is to reduce all naturalized citizens to second-class citizenship: "any process which takes away their citizenship for causes or by procedures not applicable to native-born citizens places them in a separate and an inferior class."[29] Rutledge challenges the assumption that the power to denaturalize is derivative of the power to set conditions for naturalization:

In my opinion the power to naturalize is not the power to denaturalize. The act of admission must be taken as final, for any cause which may have existed at that time. Otherwise there cannot but be two classes of citizens, one free and secure except for acts amounting to forfeiture within our tradition; the other, conditional, timorous and insecure because blanketed with the threat that some act or conduct, not amounting to forfeiture for others, will be taken retroactively to show that some prescribed condition had not been fulfilled and be so adjudged. I do not think such a difference was contemplated when Congress was authorized to provide for naturalization and the terms on which it should be granted.[30]

Moreover, even if denaturalization is to be permitted on grounds inapplicable to the native-born, argues Rutledge, it should be accompanied by procedures as protective of the individual as those required to take away the citizenship of the native-born:

If strings may be attached to citizenship and pulled retroactively to annul it, at least this should be done only by those forms of proceeding most fully surrounded with the constitutional securities for trial which are among the prized incidents of citizenship.[31]

Finally, Rutledge observes that adoption of his view would not render the government helpless to sanction disloyal foreign-born citizens: "there are other effective methods for dealing with those who are disloyal, just as there are for such citizens by birth."[32]

The majority opinion in *Schneiderman* is reaffirmed in a pair of 1958 cases—*Nowak v. United States*[33] and *Maisenberg v. United States*[34]—which once again involve membership in the Communist Party as the fact on which the Government seeks to predicate denaturalization. Both cases are decided in favor of the naturalized citizen by 6 to 3 votes; and perhaps the most striking fact is that the majority opinion in each is written by Justice Harlan.

The cases on their facts are almost replays of *Schneiderman*. The Government seeks to show lack of attachment because of membership and the holding of office in the Party. The denaturalization proceedings were initiated in 1952, some fourteen years after citizenship had been granted in 1938 and some forty years after the petitioners had come to reside in the United States. The pivotal questions once again are whether the Party in 1938 advocated violent overthrow; and whether, if it did, the petitioners were aware of it. It is now 1958 and Harlan approaches the matter with the sophistication and precision derived from *Yates*. He disposes of the cases on the second point—there is no satisfactory evidence that the petitioners were aware of Party advocacy of violence in the narrow *Yates* sense of illegal advocacy. Of the three instances cited of references by Nowak to "violence," Harlan says: "Read in context, they can be taken as merely the expression of opinions or predictions about future events."[35] Moreover, he calls attention to the staleness of the Government proof: "the record leaves us with the distinct impression that the testimony as to these episodes was itself quite uncertain, given as it was from 17 to 19 years after the event."[36]

Nowak and *Maisenberg* firmly reinforce *Schneiderman*. The denaturalization sequence, however, has not yet run its course. As we have noted, the liberal tradition associated with *Schneiderman* rests on statutory construction only. It is thus vulnerable to Congressional countermoves. With *Polites v. United States*[37] in 1960, it appears that such a change in the law may have, in effect, limited "the *Schneiderman* tradi-

tion" to legislation prior to 1940 and hence rendered it of little operative importance today.

The 1906 naturalization statute involved in *Schneiderman*—and in
Baumgartner, Knauer, Nowak, and *Maisenberg*—did not explicitly bar
from citizenship aliens who were members of groups advocating violent overthrow. Consequently the Government was forced to make
the complex argument that membership in the Party was incompatible
with the requirement that the applicant be "attached to the principles
of the Constitution." The liberal construction effected in *Schneiderman,* and confirmed in *Nowak* and *Maisenberg,* was thus a construction
of the attachment condition, not of an explicit membership clause. In
Polites this nuance becomes dispositive. For the statute under which
Polites was naturalized—the Nationality Act of 1940—explicitly
makes membership in a group advocating violent overthrow a ground
for denying naturalization.

Having lost a denaturalization proceeding prior to *Nowak* and
Maisenberg, Polites had taken an appeal but then had concluded because of developments in companion cases that the appeal was futile
and had agreed to dismissal with prejudice. Shortly thereafter the
decisions in *Nowak* and *Maisenberg* had come down and he had sought
to reopen the judgment in his case on the ground that it would be
"inequitable" to execute it since the law underlying it had been fundamentally changed. The Court, in a 5 to 4 decision, with Justice Harlan
joining the majority, rejects the appeal and permits the denaturalization order to stand. Justice Stewart writes the opinion of the Court.

In part, the case goes off on a technical point as to when an appeal
once waived can be reactivated. But the central point for our purposes
is that the Court firmly concludes that *Nowak* and *Maisenberg* dealt
with a different statute and a different problem: The 1940 statute at
issue in *Polites* explicitly barred naturalization to members of groups
advocating overthrow. Hence the trial court had not had to draw any
inferences about lack of attachment. Congress could, if it wished,
constitutionally make mere membership in the Party a sufficient basis
for denaturalization, as it did for deportation. *Polites* may simply mean
that by the 1940 statute it has now done so.

But a nagging detail remains. The petitioner's central point was
that membership with some sort of *scienter* must be required, as it had
been in *Nowak* and *Maisenberg.* The 1940 Act is silent on the matter.
The Court was not therefore compelled to conclude that Congress
meant to sanction so severely innocent membership, especially retroactively. It is true that the Court reached this conclusion with

respect to deportation in *Harisiades* and *Galvan*. But there it had worked seriously at the construction problem; in *Polites* it seems to take it for granted.

Yet what *Polites* suggests, above all, is how little leverage the Court finally possesses in this area. It makes apparent once again the limitations of the statutory construction tactic. *Schneiderman* remains the controlling precedent, but changes in the law have deprived it of much of its force. As the statutory terms have become more specific, the stringent *Schneiderman* standard of proof—"clear, unequivocal, and convincing evidence" of violation—has become less protective. It is easier conclusively to show membership in a group advocating violent overthrow (the 1940 Act) than it is to show lack of attachment to the principles of the Constitution (the 1906 Act). And it is easier still to show membership in the Communist Party (the 1952 Act). The career of *Schneiderman* thus underscores, as did the cases after *Kessler* in the deportation sequence, what a slender reed the statutory construction tactic can become, if there is legislative momentum to the contrary.

32

Exclusion

Working backwards, we come finally to the fundamental premise behind the power of the government to deport aliens or to rescind citizenship granted to aliens: the sheer power to exclude aliens altogether, to stop them at the borders. Until 1875 alien migration to the United States had been unrestricted. The power to exclude was established by the Court as an "incident of sovereignty" in 1889 in the *Chinese Exclusion Case*[1] which ratified exclusion based on what today would be regarded as detestable racial and ethnic discrimination. It remains to be asked whether that premise, which had survived so stringent a test case in 1889, is in any way modified when the counter-considerations come from the First Amendment. Are there *any* limits on the power of the government to exclude aliens on political grounds, no matter how offensive to First Amendment traditions?

The Court had an early encounter with this issue in *Turner v. Williams*[2] in 1904. Turner, a British alien, had apparently entered the United States only a few days before his arrest by immigration authorities. It is not clear whether the Court is treating the case as one of exclusion or of deportation; and perhaps it is immaterial since Turner had been here too brief a time to acquire any equities as a *resident* alien. The immigration statute had been amended—following the assassination of President McKinley—to bar "anarchists or persons who believe in or advocate the overthrow by force or violence of the Government of the United States or of all governments or of all forms of law." At a hearing before an immigration board, Turner was found to be "an anarchist" and ordered deported. The Supreme Court in a unanimous decision upheld the statute and affirmed the deportation order.

The case is made worthy of note by two circumstances: by the fact that Turner was represented before the Court by Clarence Darrow and Edgar Lee Masters, and by the explicit attention given to the challenge on First Amendment grounds. Turner argued that he did not advocate violent overthrow, that in fact he was simply a labor organizer; and further, that if the Act reached philosophical anarchists, it offended the First Amendment. Chief Justice Fuller inclines to a construction of the statute in which the clause about "violent overthrow" is taken to limit and define "anarchism." But he sees no constitutional difficulties if the broader meaning is given to it:

If the word "anarchists" should be interpreted as including aliens whose anarchistic views are professed as those of political philosophers innocent of evil intent, it would follow that Congress was of opinion that the tendency of the general exploitation of such views is so dangerous to the public weal that aliens who hold and advocate them would be undesirable additions to our population, whether permanently or temporarily, whether many or few, and, in the light of previous decisions, the act, even in this aspect, would not be unconstitutional. . . .[3]

It is not until the early 1970s that the exclusion of an alien is again challenged on First Amendment grounds. During the intervening decades cases testing the power to exclude arise infrequently, for it takes some exceptional circumstance to place anyone in a position to litigate the alien's rights. And the few cases that do arise are limited to technical points of procedure. In this respect, the position of the alien stopped at the border is considerably more vulnerable than that of the resident alien threatened with deportation. He may be accorded a modicum of procedural due process—e.g., if Congress so provides, he must have a hearing—but this is not a matter of constitutional right; he is regarded as wholly outside the coverage of the Constitution. Judicial review is thus limited to determining whether the procedures specified by Congress have been honored.

Knauff v. Shaughnessy[4] in 1950, a case which became a considerable *cause celebre*,[5] served to test the plenary power of government to exclude aliens not against First Amendment countervalues but against the countervalues of Home and Motherhood. Mrs. Knauff, a German, had married an American citizen in the aftermath of World

War II and sought entry to the United States under the War Brides Act, which had relaxed immigration restrictions in favor of such brides. Other immigration statutes provided that during war or national emergency the Executive could issue regulations adding such limitations on entry as he saw fit "in the interests of the United States." Regulations were accordingly issued empowering the Attorney General to exclude aliens without a hearing in special cases where he determined that the alien was excludable on the basis of "confidential" information, the disclosure of which would be "prejudicial to the public interest." Acting under this authority, the Attorney General had barred the entry of Knauff's wife, and had done so without a hearing and without disclosing the evidence on which he based his judgment. The chief issue for the Court was whether so summary a procedure was intended by Congress in the case of "war brides."

In a 4 to 3 decision the Court affirms the exclusion. Justice Minton, in a purely formal opinion for the majority, summarizes the law governing exclusion with blunt economy: "Whatever the procedure authorized by Congress is, it is due process as far as an alien denied entry is concerned."[6] And in this case, he concludes, Congress did not intend by the War Brides Act to relax the screening of aliens for security purposes: "As all other aliens, petitioner had to stand the test of security. This she failed to meet."[7]

The majority's servile obeisance to security considerations triggers angry dissents from Justices Frankfurter and Jackson. Neither questions the constitutional power of Congress to effect even this result, but both argue the familiar canon, as Jackson puts it, that "Congress will have to use more explicit language than any yet cited before I will agree that it has authorized an administrative officer to break up the family of an American citizen or force him to keep his wife by becoming an exile."[8]

Justice Frankfurter reads the majority a lecture on how to construe a statute so as to heed the ancient admonition that "the letter killeth." He is astounded that legislation such as the War Brides Act, which was explicitly intended as "a bounty" to Americans who had served honorably in the War, can be so lightly put aside as a clue to construction. "Yet it is suggested," he writes, "that the deepest tie that an American soldier could form may be secretly severed on the mere say-so of an official, however well-intentioned. Although five minutes of cross-examination could enable the soldier-husband to dissipate seemingly convincing information affecting the security danger of his wife, that opportunity need not be accorded."[9]

To the Frankfurter lecture on statutory construction, Justice Jackson adds a lecture on security and procedural decency:

Security is like liberty in that many are the crimes committed in its name. The menace to the security of this country, be it great as it may, from this girl's admission is as nothing compared to the menace to free institutions inherent in procedures of this pattern. In the name of security the police state justifies its arbitrary oppressions on evidence that is secret, because security might be prejudiced if it were brought to light in hearings. The plea that evidence of guilt must be secret is abhorrent to free men, because it provides a cloak for the malevolent, the misinformed, the meddlesome, and the corrupt to play the role of informer undetected and uncorrected.[10]

Knauff is a powerful datum for us. It deepens beyond even the *Chinese Exclusion Case* the sense of how utterly removed from constitutional checks the power to exclude aliens is. It also provides a striking instance, in a case where statutory construction allowed the Court at least a degree of freedom, of a majority driven by security considerations to exalt security over *any* other countervalues, even that of minimal procedural decency, even that of the integrity of the American family.[11]

In the next case—*Kwong Hai Chew v. Colding*[12] in 1953—the Court shows itself sensitive to the difference in equities between resident aliens and "entrant" aliens. Chew, a Chinese by birth, had after some years of residence here joined the Merchant Marine. When his ship returned to New York after a voyage, he was detained by immigration authorities and denied entry. The Attorney General, acting under the regulations which gave him the power to exclude where entry "would be prejudicial to the public interest," directed that Chew be denied a hearing and that his exclusion be made permanent. He was thus attempting to position the case squarely under the *Knauff* ruling that not even a minimum of procedural due process need be accorded to entrant aliens. The Court, with only Justice Minton in dissent, disagreed and held that for someone in Chew's position Fifth Amendment procedural due process had to be satisfied.

Justice Burton's opinion proceeds by testing what Chew's position would have been had he not taken the voyage. He would then have had the rights of a resident alien, and Burton firmly holds that, although he might be deported for security reasons, he must be accorded Fifth Amendment protections as to procedure. With this baseline firmly drawn, Justice Burton then decides that the voyage has not alchemized Chew back into an entrant alien: "We do not regard the constitutional status which petitioner indisputably enjoyed prior to his voyage as terminated by that voyage."[13]

Kwong Hai Chew thus provides an important precedent on the one constitutional limitation on deportation: whatever the substantive grounds on which resident aliens may be deported, they must be afforded a measure of procedural due process in the deportation proceedings. It is also an instance of the Court unanimously moving to avoid, if possible, the harshness of treating aliens as entrants rather than residents.

This second attitude rudely changes only a month later in *Shaughnessy v. United States ex rel Mezei,*[14] a decision the absurdity and intolerance of which is caught and preserved forever in a classic dissent by Justice Jackson. Mezei had come to the United States in 1923 and resided here for the next twenty-five years until in 1948, leaving his wife and home, he went to Rumania to visit his dying mother. Due to some difficulties both in getting into Rumania and in getting out again, Mezei did not return to the United States until nineteen months later. He was denied entry and denied a hearing by the Attorney General on the basis of information the disclosure of which, under the familiar formula, would be "prejudicial to the public interest." Thus far on its facts *Mezei* resembles *Kwong Hai Chew* and the only issue would seem to be whether Mezei had stayed away so long that, unlike Chew, he can be treated as an entrant alien.

There are, however, additional facts which give the case its distinctive flavor and which trigger the anger of Justice Jackson. Having been denied entry, Mezei was temporarily detained at Ellis Island pending the completion of arrangements to return him to some suitable foreign country. But all efforts to persuade another country to accept him proved unsuccessful and after twenty-one months he was still detained on Ellis Island. At this point he brought *habeas corpus* to force his release on bail pending arrangements for departure. It is this exquisitely narrow issue about bail under these very special facts that the Court is asked to decide. The case thus poses an issue not present in *Kwong Hai Chew,* namely, whether this prolonged detention is supportable without some minimal procedural due process being afforded Mezei.

Both the District Court and the Court of Appeals decide the bail issue in Mezei's favor, but the Supreme Court in a 5 to 4 decision— over the dissents of Justices Jackson, Frankfurter, Black, and Douglas—finds it necessary to reverse and to return Mezei to Ellis Island.

The majority opinion by Justice Clark finds no merit in either of the two issues presented by the case. First, he thinks Mezei's history "drastically differs" from Chew's and holds that his stay "behind the Iron Curtain for 19 months" broke the continuity of his residence here as an alien: "In such circumstances, we have no difficulty in holding respondent an entrant alien or as 'assimilated to [that] status' for constitutional purposes."[15] Second, he does not find that the lengthy detention changes matters or requires more procedural regularity. The alien might after all have been kept aboard ship until deported properly; his landing at Ellis Island is "a more generous course," but that act of official grace does not alter his status—he is still an alien "stopped at the border."[16] Nor is he entitled even to minimal judicial review of the decision not to release him on bail—as a deportee would be entitled after *Carlson v. Landon*.[17] Justice Clark's final paragraph merits quotation:

. . . the times being what they are, Congress may well have felt that other countries ought not to shift the onus to us; that an alien in respondent's position is no more ours than theirs. Whatever our individual estimate of that policy and the fears on which it rests, respondent's right to enter the United States depends on the congressional will, and courts cannot substitute their judgment for the legislative mandate.[18]

Justice Jackson, in a dissent joined by Justice Frankfurter, is incredulous at the outcome. He begins:

Fortunately it is still startling, in this country, to find a person held indefinitely in executive custody without accusation of crime or judicial trial. Executive imprisonment has been considered oppressive and lawless since John, at Runnymede, pledged that no free man should be imprisoned, dispossessed, outlawed, or exiled save by the judgment of his peers or by the law of the land.[19]

For Justice Jackson it is the prolonged detention that generates constitutional limitations on the official action. The realism which had moved him to indignation over the Court's tolerance of provocative speech in the public forum in *Terminiello*[20] and *Kunz*[21] now with splendid evenhandedness moves him to equal indignation over his government's relentless pursuit of security in *Mezei*. His performance is a reminder of two important characteristics of a great judge: a capacity for anger—a sense of justice and a capacity for indignation are not unconnected—and a capacity for realism as to the actual outcome of the case before him. These are difficult judicial virtues indeed; an excess of one leads to bias, an excess of the other to the destruction of any rule of law.

He writes, hurling epigrams with both hands:

This man, who seems to have led a life of unrelieved insignificance, must have been astonished to find himself suddenly putting the Government of the United States in such fear that it was afraid to tell him why it was afraid of him.[22]

And again:

Government counsel ingeniously argued that Ellis Island is his "refuge" whence he is free to take leave in any direction except west. That might mean freedom, if only he were an amphibian! . . . Despite the impeccable legal logic of the Government's argument on this point, it leads to an artificial and unreal conclusion.[23]

The Jackson dissent is an eloquent expression of what is for him and Justice Frankfurter the central value of a civilized society. Even more than freedom of speech and association, it is adherence to procedural due process. He is careful to make explicit that he has no quarrel with the exclusion of aliens for security reasons—here the power of Congress is unchallenged and would extend even to the detention in this case: "I conclude that detention of an alien would not be inconsistent with substantive due process, provided—and this is where my dissent begins—he is accorded procedural due process of law."[24] Procedural fairness, he stresses, is integrally intertwined with meaningful liberty:

Indeed, if put to the choice, one might well prefer to live under Soviet substantive law applied in good faith by our common-law procedures than under our substantive law enforced by Soviet procedural practices.[25]

He comes then to the core of his dissent:

Exclusion of an alien without judicial hearing, of course, does not deny due process when it can be accomplished merely by turning him back on land or returning him by sea. But when indefinite confinement becomes the means of enforcing exclusion, it seems to me that due process requires that the alien be informed of its grounds and have a fair chance to overcome them.[26]

The indefinite confinement is especially offensive to Jackson, so recently returned from the Nuremberg Trials, because it carries "unmistakable overtones" of the protective custody of the Nazis.[27] His parting shot, as he closes his dissent, might well stand as the epitaph for this entire section of the Court's work:

I have not been one to discount the Communist evil. But my apprehensions about the security of our form of government are about equally aroused by those who refuse to acknowledge the dangers of Communism and those who will not see danger in anything else.[28]

In one dimension of law the decision in *Mezei* is of minuscule significance; it deals only with the procedural rights of an alien under its idiosyncratic facts as to detention, a situation that may well have been unique. In another dimension of law, however, it belongs alongside cases like *Lamont v. Postmaster General*,[29] *Stanley v. Georgia*,[30] and *Cohen v. California*,[31] where homely and trivial facts are seen by the justices, in their endless dialogue about freedom under law, to embody large principles.[32]

The constitutional law as to the power of the government to exclude aliens would seem with the decision in *Mezei* to have become brutally clear and unequivocal. The rule was that there were absolutely no limits on the power of Congress to exclude aliens. Neither inhibitions against gross racial discrimination, against interference with freedom of speech and association, against breaking up the family, nor restraints dictated by notions of basic procedural fairness could stay the hand of the government. The line from the *Chinese Exclusion Case* to *Mezei* was straight and unbroken.

This harsh clarity is clouded a bit by *Kleindiest v. Mandel*[33] in 1972. Once again the Court affirms the denial of entry; this time by a vote of 6 to 3, with Justices Marshall, Douglas, and Brennan in dissent. Speaking through Justice Blackmun, the majority reviews the history we have been over and reaffirms it. Yet one senses that the seeds for future growth and revision have now been planted. For the facts in *Mandel* position the issue in a way that opens the power to exclude to direct First Amendment challenge. Although that challenge does not prevail, it is entertained by the Court and produces a precedent that quite possibly will invite efforts in the future finally to bring this area within the reach of the Constitution.

The controversy arises over an abortive effort by Ernest Mandel, an internationally known Marxist scholar and theoretician, to visit the

United States at the invitation of Stanford University to participate in a conference and to speak at a number of other universities to which he had also been invited, among them Princeton, Amherst, and Columbia. He is denied a visa by the Attorney General, acting pursuant to a statute which makes ineligible for visas aliens who advocate, write, or publish "the economic, international, and governmental doctrines of world communism or the establishment in the United States of a totalitarian dictatorship." The statute also provides that the Attorney General may at his discretion waive such ineligibility and admit the alien temporarily. The Secretary of State had in fact recommended that Dr. Mandel be permitted entry, but the Attorney General had rejected the recommendation on the ground that on a prior visit Mandel's activities "went far beyond the stated purposes of his trip" and "represented a flagrant abuse of the opportunities afforded him to express his views in this country."[34]

Mandel thus puts the issue of exclusion in a form that is fresh in two respects. First, the alien was coming only for a temporary visit and not, as in prior cases, as an immigrant. Second and more important, the arguments were couched not in terms of the rights of the alien but in terms of *the rights of the American citizens who wished to hear him.*

There has long lurked in First Amendment theory an issue as to whether freedom of speech is primarily a right of the speaker or of the audience. Under normal circumstances the issue is abstract and fruitless. Since the two sets of rights are so intimately related, it is difficult even to imagine a case in which the outcome might be different if viewed from the standpoint of the audience rather than the speaker. But the Court had on occasion touched the point. In *Martin v. Struthers*[35] it had insisted that the citizen's right to decide for himself whether he wished to receive the message could not be preempted by an ordinance designed to prevent the nuisance of having the front doorbell rung. In *Stanley v. Georgia* it had eloquently protected the citizen's right to enjoy in his library, without any government intervention, materials he had received. In *Lamont v. Postmaster General* the concurring opinion of Justice Brennan had spoken warmly of a First Amendment right to receive. And in the *Red Lion* case[36] the Court, in dealing with broadcasting, had spoken of the airwaves as existing primarily for the sake of the public and not the broadcaster.

The *Mandel* facts pose the issue more squarely than any of the previous cases: Is the refusal to permit Dr. Mandel temporary entry into the United States to make his speech unconstitutional because it abridges the First Amendment rights of his American audience? Put this way, the argument against the anti-subversive tactics applied to aliens is placed right side up for the first time.

The petitioners in *Mandel* do not, however, put the challenge in quite so bold a form. Rather, they concede that the government could have imposed a flat *ban* on aliens with Mandel's views, but argue that once waiver has been provided for, the First Amendment rights of the audience enter the picture and impose some limits on the discretion to withhold the waiver. At least, so the argument runs, the audience's right to hear the alien requires that the Attorney General offer a justification for his denial of entry, and in this case his nominal justification was wholly insubstantial.

Justice Blackmun first reviews the law on plenary power to exclude aliens and reaffirms it: "It is clear that Mandel personally, as an unadmitted and nonresident alien, had no constitutional right of entry to this country."[37] He next reviews in some detail the precedents on "the rights of the audience." He acknowledges that "First Amendment rights are implicated" in the case,[38] and that written speech is not a proper substitute for the speaker in person. But he concludes that the petitioners' argument must be rejected because "it would prove too much" and could be offered on behalf of any alien excluded,[39] since some Americans could always be found who would claim an interest in interacting with him in person. He concludes further that the argument, even when narrowed, must be rejected because the Attorney General did in fact offer a justification for his refusal to grant a waiver—Mandel's conduct on his prior visit. So long as the reason is "facially legitimate,"[40] the Court may not go behind it.

The First Amendment rejoinder is argued in the dissents of Justices Douglas and Marshall. In a brief opinion Douglas argues as a matter of statutory construction that "Congress never undertook to entrust the Attorney General with the discretion to pick and choose among the ideological offerings which alien lecturers tender from our platforms."[41] The Attorney General's discretion in these matters, he argues, should be limited to "matters commonly within the competence of the Department of Justice—national security, importation of drugs, and the like."[42]

Justice Marshall, in an opinion joined by Justice Brennan, places his dissent squarely on constitutional grounds. He rejects out of hand the majority's effort to rest the decision on the Attorney General's justification: "Even the briefest peek behind the Attorney General's reason for refusing a waiver in this case would reveal that it is a sham."[43] He also rejects the petitioners' effort to narrow the challenge. The question, as he sees it, goes not to the waiver but to the constitutionality of a flat ban. He plants doubts for a future day, saying of the plenary power precedents: "These cases are not the strongest precedents in the United States Reports, and the majority's baroque approach reveals its reluctance to rely on them completely."[44]

Marshall then shifts to his main thesis. Like other exercises of government power which may collide with First Amendment values, the power to exclude aliens must to some degree accommodate the First Amendment: "At least when the rights of Americans are involved, there is no basis for concluding that the power to exclude aliens is absolute."[45] He then cites *Robel*[46] and *Aptheker*,[47] thus attempting to bring the power to exclude aliens into the legal universe of partial sanctions.

The one shortcoming in Justice Marshall's otherwise powerful and helpful opinion is his failure to spell out just what other considerations would in his constitutional scheme outweigh the First Amendment rights of the American audience. He would not apparently use the same baseline as for American speakers. He writes:

Government may prohibit aliens from even temporary admission if exclusion is necessary to protect a compelling governmental interest. Actual threats to the national security, public health needs, and genuine requirements of law enforcement are the most apparent interests that would surely be compelling.[48]

Would his thesis apply only to temporary admissions? Who presents an "actual threat" to security?

In any event, whatever the reach of the First Amendment, it must, he thinks, apply to this case. Since there is no allegation that Mandel in person is a security risk, the Attorney General has made the case easy. There is, Marshall observes, no more danger to Dr. Mandel "live" than to his message alone.[49] The case is thus four-square with *Lamont* on the freedom to import communications from abroad.

Taken seriously, the premise embraced by Justices Marshall and Brennan would revolutionize the law as to the power to exclude and would also affect the derivative powers to deport and denaturalize. It would put the First Amendment rights of American citizens at the center of the constitutional analysis of government efforts to bar or remove aliens because of their political views and affiliations. And it would relieve American law of an awkward anomaly. At present, however, that anomaly persists: the entrant alien stopped at the border, the resident alien faced with a deportation order, and even the naturalized citizen threatened with denaturalization, though they may stand on American soil, are excluded from the domain of the First Amendment.

33

The Regulation of Passports

In the areas we have examined thus far the government claim to plenary power over movement in and out of the country by aliens has rested on the fact that they were *aliens* or naturalized aliens. There remains, however, one further corner of the law where, as an anti-subversion measure, limitations of movement across the border have been imposed on citizens—the regulation of passports.

It is axiomatic that the movement of citizens within the United States cannot be limited by government, state or federal.[1] Such movement across state lines was an important achievement of the Constitution. It is a source of both the sense of the unity of American society and the individual American's sense of personal freedom. The history of the freedom of Americans to move out of the country to foreign lands, however, has had a very different cast.

The legality of passport regulation is a surprisingly new problem. Originally a passport was an amenity of international law, an arrangement between nations whereby one nation certified that the bearer was its citizen and requested that he be permitted to "pass safely and freely." It was regarded as more a political or diplomatic matter than as a matter of law, and the issuance of passports was pretty much a discretionary dispensing of a government favor or courtesy. It was not until 1856 that legislation was passed centralizing the issuance of passports in the State Department. For the next hundred years, except when interrupted by wartime, the issuance of passports continued as a routine and non-controversial government action. The quality of the passport was changed, however, by legislation in 1952 which made it a crime for anyone to leave the United States without a valid passport. Whatever the practical inhibitions previously, after 1952 an American citizen could not legally depart the United States without the consent of the government. More or less contemporaneously, the government began to condition the issuance of passports on security criteria. The stage was thus set for posing the issue of the propriety of another partial sanction: the allocation of passports on grounds that have First Amendment resonance.

The Supreme Court first confronted the matter in *Kent v. Dulles*[2] in 1958. The case was precipitated by the refusal of the Director of the Passport Office to grant a passport to Rockwell Kent, the well-known American artist, on the grounds that he did not satisfy the regulations promulgated in 1952 by the Secretary of State in two respects: (i) he was a Communist; and (ii) he had "a consistent and prolonged adherence to the Communist Party line." The second of these conditions, it should be noted, once again expanded the interferences with freedom of speech and association substantially beyond those keyed to membership. Relatively few citizens would in fact be touched by the membership condition, but an indeterminately large fraction of the public, because of its positions on various public issues, might at some point be vulnerable to the charge of "adherence to the Communist Party line." Such a condition is deeply at odds with First Amendment values.[3] If the issuing of passports is simply within the discretion of the Secretary of State, he may impose this condition as he may impose any other, and things are much as they would be were we considering the power of the government over the movement of aliens. The Supreme Court, however, in a 5 to 4 decision upsetting the denial of a passport to Kent, refused to assume such broad discretion on the part of the Secretary of State.

The majority opinion by Justice Douglas carefully avoids direct constitutional confrontation; rather, it pursues the complementary strategy of statutory construction. Douglas first reviews the special history of passports, stressing how recently the passport had been transformed into an exit permit, "its crucial function today." He next addresses himself to the freedom to travel, a value for which he has a distinctive empathy. He argues plausibly that it is indispensable to liberty: "It may be as close to the heart of the individual as the choice of what he eats, or wears, or reads. Freedom of movement is basic in our scheme of values."[4] From these premises he readily draws his conclusion as to Congressional intention:

We, therefore, hesitate to impute to Congress, when in 1952 it made a passport necessary for foreign travel and left its issuance to the discretion of the Secretary of State, a purpose to give him unbridled discretion to grant or withhold a passport from a citizen for any substantive reason he may choose.[5]

The argument is still not home free. There remains a nagging difficulty, on which the dissent of Justice Clark chiefly relies: the prior administrative practice of long standing had been to withhold passports on a discretionary basis. Congress in reenacting the passport statute presumably had this practice in mind and did not negative it. Justice Douglas counters that, war apart, the practice of denials was narrowly restricted to improper claims of citizenship and efforts "to escape the toils of law."[6] There had been, he insists, no long-standing administrative practice of denying passports on *ideological* grounds. It will take more explicit language to persuade him that Congress intended to empower the Secretary of State to confine citizens to the United States unless he approved of their ideologies.[7]

We may profitably pause for a moment to reflect on the extension of the security calculus logic to passports. On the surface there is the intriguing point that here, in sharp contrast to deportation, the tactic is to *lock* the "unreliable" person within the community and to make it impossible for him to get out. If we pursue the logic, we are told that the risk is that conspiratorial meetings will be facilitated by permitting the suspect to go abroad. Conceivably they will, but given the unrestricted possibilities for communication by first-class mail and through intermediaries, curtailing the movement of all citizens who might be charged with adherence to the Communist line would be an extravagantly overbroad way of achieving what is at best a minor security objective. One suspects therefore that the impulse behind the passport restrictions came not from this exquisite security calculus but from symbolic considerations. The government in a sense *vouches* for the holder of a passport, and it did not want to vouch for these people. Like loyalty oaths, this logic leads to an insanely corrosive division of the community of citizens into two groups: those who are loyal and those who are suspect, those for whom the government will vouch and those for whom it will not.

Moreover, the linking of the "loyalty certification" to passports made it a wholly arbitrary, random matter. The vast majority of citizens are left undifferentiated, although among them are surely some the government would not vouch for. Only the citizen who for personal reasons wanted or needed to travel abroad would undergo the harrowing experience of discovering that his government did not trust him. I know from personal experience of a distinguished older scientist who had enjoyed a sense of reputation, respect, and security for all of his adult life until suddenly, when he needed to go abroad for a conference of scientists, he was denied a passport and awakened to the unnerving realization that his government had been busy over the years building a dossier on him to show that his positions on public issues had adhered to the Communist line.

The passport phenomenon also illustrates how easily apparently routine, non-controversial areas of daily life become intensely "politicized" by security logic. And it illustrates once again the chaotic way the government is likely to proceed. In the Internal Security Act of 1950 Congress provides that passports be taken away from members of Communist-action groups *after* a registration order on the group has become final. Virtually simultaneously the State Department decides in its 1952 regulations to deny passports to those who adhere to the Party line! This sequence underscores two important facts: first, that no officials ever assumed responsibility for the pattern and cumulative impact of such government action; second, that there were simply no norms, no traditional sense of tolerance, when First Amendment problems appeared in the guise of partial sanctions.

Six years after *Kent*, in *Aptheker v. Secretary of State*,[8] the matter moves to the constitutional plane. In *Aptheker*, it will be recalled, the Court holds invalid on their face the provisions of the Internal Security Act of 1950 prohibiting passports to members of groups required to register as Communist-action organizations. In the process it translates the statutory construction argument of *Kent* into constitutional terms.

We need not retrace our prior discussion of the opinions in *Aptheker*, but we would stress again that from our perspective the Court appears to have the problem backwards. The decision should depend not on the constitutional status of the right to travel, unless it is to be equated literally with freedom of speech, but on the propriety of excluding mere members of the Communist Party. If this view is correct, it must follow that nothing much turns on the status of the privilege the government is allocating so long as the matter is not, like the admitting of aliens, regarded as falling within the plenary discretion of the government. It is not necessary to determine, that is, whether travel abroad is more or less valued than a job in a defense

facility. This is not, we would hasten to add, to say that the *nature* of
the privilege is also irrelevant. In the end, the constitutionality of the
government action must depend on some effort to accommodate the
First Amendment values with the security considerations. Not all government privileges are equally relevant to a rational security calculus.
And travel abroad is at best only marginally relevant.

The regulation of passports presents one further complication—
the use of *restricted* passports, making travel to certain countries "off
limits." Typically such restrictions have been applied to countries
with which the United States has strained or hostile relations such as
Cuba after the Castro regime took power. The logic of this form of
regulation is to *ban the place, not the traveler.* This logic too impinges
on First Amendment values. The American public has a serious interest in learning facts about contemporary conditions in Cuba. The
government obviously could not censor articles and books reporting
on the topic, but by barring travel to Cuba it effectively deprives the
public of the relevant messages. In real life, it must be admitted, the
issue was not quite so neatly drawn, for the regulations provided
exceptions for journalists, and the dearth of reliable news from Cuba
was in large part due to the inhospitality of the Cuban government
to Americans. In any event, the Supreme Court had an opportunity
to debate these novel First Amendment issues in *Zemel v. Rusk*[9] in
1965.

The controversy is generated by the effort of Zemel, the holder
of an otherwise valid passport, to gain permission to visit Cuba as a
tourist. Zemel makes no claim that could not be made by any other
American citizen; he is not a professional journalist or scholar. As he
puts it, he wants to go in order "to satisfy my curiosity about the state
of affairs in Cuba and to make me a better informed citizen." This way
of posing the issue serves to put it most bluntly and broadly, while at
the same time diluting the First Amendment focus—there is no promise that Zemel will "go public" with his new information about Cuba.
The Secretary of State denies his request, and he seeks declaratory
and injunctive relief. The Court in a 6 to 3 decision upholds the denial
of official permission to travel to Cuba. The majority opinion is by
Chief Justice Warren. Justices Black, Douglas, and Goldberg file dissenting opinions.

One further detail should be noted. Zemel had asked that the
government be enjoined from implementing the passport restraint by
treating unauthorized travel as a crime. The Court is careful to postpone deciding whether a citizen who defies the regulation and goes

to Cuba anyway can be prosecuted. It holds that the refusal to validate the passport for Cuba is enough of a deterrent to render justiciable the issues now before it.[10]

The justices handle the First Amendment conundrum gingerly. The burden of the dissents is that Congress had not authorized the Secretary of State to impose area restrictions on passports; and further, that if the 1926 passport statute is read as a general authorization, it is unconstitutional as a blanket delegation of legislative power. It is a telltale sign of the perplexity of the First Amendment issue in this novel form that three such First Amendment enthusiasts as Justices Black, Douglas, and Goldberg should prefer to argue in these colorless terms.

Yet First Amendment nuances are discernible in the opinions of each. Justice Black, consistent with his position on symbolic speech and demonstrations, sees no First Amendment issues. For him travel is clearly not speech or speech-connected: "I repeat my belief that Congress has ample power to regulate foreign travel."[11]

Justice Douglas positions the case differently. For him travel must be viewed as a "peripheral right" of the citizen under the First Amendment:

The right to know, to converse with others, to consult with them, to observe social, physical, political and other phenomena abroad as well as at home gives meaning and substance to freedom of expression and freedom of the press. Without those contacts First Amendment rights suffer.[12]

Hence this is really a First Amendment matter and the vice in the regulations is that they are overbroad, as they were in *Aptheker*. Douglas also suggests that, while of course some limits may be placed on freedom to travel to places such as areas of pestilence, the restraints here are bottomed on a fear of dangerous ideas and hence are proximate to classic instances of censorship: "the only so-called danger present here is the Communist regime in Cuba. The world, however, is filled with Communist thought."[13]

Finally, in the third of the dissents, Justice Goldberg rests his construction argument on Congress' concern for the rights of the citizen and the press to know. He argues that, in view of "the importance and constitutional underpinnings of the right to travel and the right of a citizen and a free press to gather information about foreign countries," it cannot be presumed that Congress intended to confer "unlimited discretion upon the Executive."[14]

The answer of Chief Justice Warren, writing for the majority, is that reenactment of the statute in light of the long record of administrative practice of issuing passports with certain areas off limits indicates convincingly that Congress intended the Secretary of State to have this authority to limit passports. En route to his conclusion Warren is in several respects more explicitly responsive to the First Amendment overtones in the case than are the three dissenters. First, he is willing to treat the Secretary's refusal to validate the passport for travel to Cuba in itself—altogether apart from possible criminal liabilities were Zemel to travel to Cuba without official permission—as a sufficient deterrent to generate constitutional concerns. The case is thus strikingly like *Lamont v. Postmaster General*[15] in the subtlety of the burden imposed.

Second, he evinces no embarrassment about distinguishing *Kent v. Dulles.* He argues that the passport denial in *Kent* was not supported by a comparable record of administrative precedent. And he stresses that, in contrast to *Kent,* where the issue was whether "a citizen could be denied a passport because of his political beliefs or associations," the area restriction at issue in *Zemel* was imposed "not because of any characteristic peculiar to appellant, but rather because of foreign policy considerations affecting all citizens."[16]

Finally, he addresses the First Amendment challenge directly:

We must agree that the Secretary's refusal to validate passports for Cuba renders less than wholly free the flow of information concerning that country. While we further agree that this is a factor to be considered in determining whether appellant has been denied due process of law, we cannot accept the contention of appellant that it is a First Amendment right which is involved. For to the extent that the Secretary's refusal to validate passports for Cuba acts as an inhibition (and it would be unrealistic to assume that it does not), it is an inhibition of action. There are few restrictions on action which could not be clothed by ingenious argument in the garb of decreased data flow. For example, the prohibition of unauthorized entry into the White House diminishes the citizen's opportunities to gather information he might find relevant to his opinion of the way the country is being run, but that does not make entry into the White House a First Amendment right. The right to speak and publish does not carry with it the unrestrained right to gather information.[17]

The answer is perhaps inevitable, as the dissenters appear to have conceded, but the reasoning in support of it seems short-winded. The reliance on the distinction between speech and action seems thin and misplaced. Would the Court make the same argument if the petitioner had been an important foreign correspondent? Or suppose a given group was systematically denied access to the public libraries in the community?

The petitioner in *Zemel,* by what seems to have been a sort of wild swing, has located a new genre of First Amendment problem: how do we analyze government moves that result directly or indirectly in lowering the level of communication, in "decreased data flow"? Other recent cases have suggested the same issue.[18] We will undoubtedly hear more of it in years to come.

In less than two decades then there has been a revolution in the constitutional scrutiny of the allocation of passports. The net result of *Kent* and *Aptheker* has been to transform the citizen's claim to a passport from a request for a discretionary diplomatic gesture from the government to a government privilege which is constitutionally protected on parity with, say, a claim to teach in a public university. Moreover, two recent cases—one, *Mandel,* affecting the rights of aliens, and the other, *Zemel,* affecting area restrictions on passports— have served to put novel and refreshing First Amendment challenges about the danger of "decreased data flow," which, although rejected in the particular instances, are likely to prove seminal.

Official Inquiry

34

Legislative Investigation: The Beginnings, 1880-1956

We turn now to a new topic: the First Amendment issues posed by official inquiry—by the asking of questions about political associations. In these cases the legal confrontation is triggered by the individual's *refusal to answer*. The paradigmatic case involves the imposition of sanctions not on the man who is a member of the Communist Party but on the man who refuses to disclose whether or not he is a member.

We will begin by surveying the Court's experience with legislative investigations. This form of inquiry has provided the primary occasion for the Court to wrestle with the perplexities of evaluating *compulsory disclosure* as an interference with speech and association. We will then consider other instances of official inquiry in which disclosure is not compelled but the consequences of a refusal to answer may nonetheless be grave.

Legislative investigation is a First Amendment topic that requires considerable enriching and rounding out with sociological data. For the investigative committee "grows into" a special institution, acquiring by accretion special powers and generating special threats and a distinctive sense of grievance. In operation various committees, particularly the House Un-American Activities Committee, became *de facto* loyalty programs, bowdlerized loyalty oath procedures which touched directly or as spectators the lives of a very large number of citizens. The cases generated by such committee inquiries sharply pose the question of whether First Amendment scrutiny may not require that the Court in some way look beyond the law on the books to the law in action.

It is instructive to lay the tactics of the House Un-American Activities Committee beside the tactics of the Subversive Activities Control Act. Under the Act disclosure is one of several measures employed in a coordinated scheme. It is aimed as a sanction at a suspect group, and its use is not permitted until there has been a final adjudication of the status of the target group. The procedure, whatever its wisdom, is candid; it does in fact what it was set up by law to do. HUAC, by contrast, never dealt directly with the Communist Party; it dealt only with the individual. More important, it never established the nature of the Communist Party as a condition precedent to seeking the disclosure of its membership; rather, it employed a very loose sort of "legislative notice." Moreover, it was not consistently candid about what it was doing. It would on occasion announce publicly that its mission was to hold domestic Communism up to "the pitiless spotlight of publicity," but equally often it would state that its mission was fact-finding in aid of legislation.

Our concern here is a relatively narrow one. It is with the First Amendment dimensions of a topic that has other and possibly more important dimensions. The question that concerns us is: To what extent do First Amendment norms and principles provide limitations on the power of a legislature to compel disclosure from the individual? There are other doctrines that may serve to limit legislative inquiry, but we deal with them only by way of tracing the role, if any, of the First Amendment in this area.

Like obscenity and libel, legislative investigation furnishes a "proper-named," easily identified, and busy sector of the Court's work. There are well over forty cases dealing with the limits of legislative investigation. A number of these touch explicitly on First Amendment challenges; and almost half involve that "peculiar institution," the House Un-American Activities Committee. As we shall see, the overall impression of the Court's contribution is mixed. During the heyday of McCarthyism and HUAC in the 1950s, it repeatedly denied *certiorari* in cases seeking to test the powers of investigating committees. Very often, when it did intercede, it was only to make a technical point. Finally, there is no momentum in this line of precedent toward a *Brandenburg* or an *Elfbrandt*. [1]

It is probably true that the popular perception of legislative investigation depends on whose ox is being gored. During the 1920s and 1930s legislative inquiries into business practices were vigorously supported by liberals who were later critical of the anti-subversive investigations of the 1950s.[2] More recently, the Senate Watergate Committee seemed to many of us, who had been bitterly critical of HUAC two decades earlier, an example in a time of need of one of democracy's better institutions. The vast publicity it focused on individual witnesses was seen as performing the indispensable function of informing public opinion; the theatrical posturing of the Senator-inquisitors was perceived as the orderly process of law—at last. What criticism was heard came from a suspect quarter—the White House— which was seen as resorting to procedural points only because it had no substantive defenses to offer. If we go back two decades, the scandal was not Watergate but domestic Communism; the committees with their publicity were informing public opinion about another set of "threats to the American way of life." It is true that the Watergate investigation was an investigation of government itself and not of private individuals. It is true too that the individual witnesses in 1973 were persons who were or recently had been men of power and status, with friends in the White House itself, so that the contest was a little more on parity. Also the procedures and etiquette of the investigators had improved markedly since the days of Senator McCarthy, and counsel for the witness was allowed some role in the proceedings. Yet the parallels between the two instances of legislative investigation cannot be denied.

I have drawn the comparison as starkly as I can because I am sensitive to some inconsistency in my own view of the two committees. I thought HUAC was despicable, dangerous, and alien to American legal values; I found the Watergate Committee, in a word, splendid. I state the tension not to resolve it, but in order to underscore the chameleon nature of the phenomena we are inquiring into.

The grievance against the use of compulsory testimony by investigative committees will take one of two forms or possibly both:

(i) It may be seen in some sense as "a trial" of the individual witness, visiting informal punishments on him. One can only proceed by analogy, but the analogies here carry power. The witness's reputation is "on trial" under maximum publicity in "a court of public opinion." It is a trial by the legislative not the judicial branch, a trial before biased, politically motivated judges who also act as prosecutors. The individual is given little or no chance to have the aid of counsel, and no chance to offer evidence on his own behalf or to cross-examine hostile witnesses. There are few, if any, limits on the quality of evidence admitted, and the burden of proof is shifted to the individual. In brief, if the compelled appearance of the witness before the investigating committee can be said to be a trial, it is a perfectly wretched trial, a trial which transgresses almost all norms of procedural decency. In this aspect, the grievance against the legislative inquiry need have nothing to do with our First Amendment concerns.

(ii) In those instances where the legislative inquiry touches the opinions of the witness or his membership in various organizations, it can be seen as the imposition of a sanction on him because of his views and associations. This sanction has two aspects: the unpleasantness of the proceedings themselves and the private reactions, such as loss of employment, which compelled appearance before a committee may trigger. Men are likely to prefer to avoid the experience of being an unwilling witness in a hostile, publicized investigation, as they might prefer to avoid sitting in the stocks. One result of the investigation will be, therefore, to chill the exercise of First Amendment freedoms. Further, it will not necessarily be the case that unless one perceives the proceedings as a full-blown and unfair trial he will not perceive it as negative enough to support a First Amendment challenge. The First Amendment challenge, that is, is not redundant.

The Basic Framework: McGrain and Sinclair

The first great modern case on the powers of legislative investigations, *McGrain v. Daugherty*[3] in 1927, has no First Amendment resonance. It does, however, vividly convey the flavor of the procedural due process controversy, and it yields a precedent that still defines the basic legal architecture. It arose out of that Watergate of half a century ago, the Teapot Dome Scandal, which involved fraud by the Secretary of the Interior and the Attorney General in the sale and lease of public lands. A special Senate committee instructed to investigate the matter sought to interrogate Daugherty, the brother of the then Attorney General. When he refused to respond to subpoenas, the Senate sought to compel him. There were two routes of compulsion available. The Senate could use its inherent contempt power to have Daugherty arrested and brought before the bar of the Senate for questioning, or, it could use a statute passed in 1857 making the willful failure to respond to a congressional subpoena a federal crime. In *McGrain* the Senate resorted to its inherent contempt process and ordered its Sergeant at Arms to arrest Daugherty. It is the challenge to the validity of that arrest which put into issue the investigatory powers of the Senate.

The Supreme Court in an 8 to 0 decision firmly upheld the power of the Senate investigation. There were essentially two challenges, and their disposition has bequeathed important law for today: (i) Was there any *implied* power in Congress to perform the judicial function of compelling testimony, since there was clearly no such power explicitly designated to it in the Constitution? (ii) If there was such a power, was it nevertheless not to be implied in this instance, because the true motivation of the Senate in making this inquiry was not to get facts in order to legislate but was to "try" the Attorney General for his role in Teapot Dome?

Justice Van Devanter confidently gives an affirmative answer to the first question. He carefully marshals prior congressional practice; the use of investigating committees dates back to an inquiry into the St. Clair expedition in 1792 and includes a celebrated investigation of Brown's raid on Harper's Ferry in 1859. He cites several state court decisions which have affirmed such implied powers in state legislatures; and he cites auxiliary congressional legislation, such as the statute of 1857 making the refusal to cooperate as a witness in a congressional inquiry a crime.

Finally, he disposes of the prior Supreme Court cases that can be said to touch on the problem. Only one, *Kilbourn v. Thompson,* an 1881 decision, requires careful distinction.[4] In *Kilbourn* the House Select Committee on Bankruptcy had used its inherent contempt power to punish a recalcitrant witness in its investigation of the bankruptcy of Jay Cooke and Company. The Court upheld the position of the witness and affirmed an award of damages for false imprisonment. The opinion, by Justice Miller, favored strict construction of implied powers and found the precedent of the powers of Parliament inapposite. In the end, it did not literally pass upon whether Congress, in a proper case, would have the power to compel testimony; rather, it rested its decision on the ground that the inquiry into the Cooke bankruptcy was not a proper case—it appeared on the face of the congressional resolution to be an inquiry into the private affairs of a private citizen. Justice Van Devanter in *McGrain* is content to accept Justice Miller's principle that Congress lacks a "general power of making inquiry into the private affairs of the citizen."[5]

The decisive argument in *McGrain* comes not from practice or precedent but from function. Van Devanter argues that the power to compel disclosure is "an essential and appropriate auxiliary to the legislative function"[6]:

A legislative body cannot legislate wisely or effectively in the absence of information respecting the conditions which the legislation is intended to affect or change; and where the legislative body does not itself possess the

requisite information—which not infrequently is true—recourse must be had
to others who do possess it. Experience has taught that mere requests for
such information often are unavailing, and also that information which is
volunteered is not always accurate or complete; so some means of compulsion are essential to obtain what is needed. All this was true before and when
the Constitution was framed and adopted. . . . Thus there is ample warrant
for thinking, as we do, that the constitutional provisions which commit the
legislative function to the two houses are intended to include this attribute
to the end that the function may be effectively exercised.[7]

Justice Van Devanter thus emphatically answers the question Justice
Miller had left open in *Kilbourn:* Congress *does* have the power to
compel testimony in aid of legislation.

He then turns to the realpolitik dimension of the case. Teapot
Dome had been the great scandal of the day and the political stakes
were enormous. The Senate investigation could not but have been
motivated in part by the Democrats' desire to publicize and exploit a
Republican scandal. The Senate Resolution authorizing the inquiry
had said nothing originally about legislation and had mentioned the
former Attorney General, Harry M. Daugherty, by name. These circumstances had persuaded the trial court to decline to imply the
power to Congress in this instance:

What the Senate is engaged in doing is not investigating the Attorney General's office; it is investigating the former Attorney General. What it has done
is to put him on trial before it. In so doing it is exercising the judicial function.
That it has no power to do.[8]

The *McGrain* case a half-century ago thus put a hard test to
judicial realism, a test as stringent as those later posed in the anti-
Communist era. The Court's response, however, is unequivocal:
Surely there could be legislation on this topic; there is nothing on the
face of the Resolution itself which impeaches the congressional purpose. The Court will not go behind official declarations of the motivations of Congress:

The only legitimate object the Senate could have in ordering the investigation was to aid it in legislating; and we think the subject-matter was such that
the presumption should be indulged that this was the real object.[9]

As a parting shot, Justice Van Devanter adds: "Nor do we think it a
valid objection to the investigation that it might possibly disclose

crime or wrongdoing" on the Attorney General's part.[10]

Thus, *McGrain*, having found a power in the legislature to compel testimony, makes three important points:

(i) The power of the legislature to compel testimony is not unlimited, and it is subject to judicial review for abuse.

(ii) The power to compel testimony exists only in aid of fact-finding pursuant to legislating.

(iii) But the Court will not go behind official declarations that the compulsory inquiry is in aid of legislation.

The second of these premises deserves more careful scrutiny. Certainly a legislature needs facts in order to legislate rationally and hence must have some way of obtaining them. Certainly too the exercise of an otherwise legitimate government power cannot be unconstitutional simply because as a by-product it will generate unpleasant side effects for individuals. But the unexamined step is the assumption that facts about individuals who are unwilling to disclose them voluntarily are the kind of information that on any theory of legislation informs the lawmaking judgment. To oversimplify the point for emphasis, does the legislature need to know who committed the murder in order to know how to legislate against murder? Surely a general sense of how the facts lie, a sense that a grievance may be true in many cases, is sufficient without knowing in precisely which cases. As I wrote some years back in the course of criticizing Congress's inquiries into subversion: "But it is surely absurd to assume, as we solemnly appear to have done for years, that its best route to legislative insight is to inventory the Communists in the United States one at a time."[11]

The question then is whether *compelled* testimony is necessary to the legislative function. It may be that the reason the institution of the legislative investigation has proved so difficult to bring under the discipline of law is that it is predicated upon a radical fallacy as to the nature of facts useful for legislation. We should not pause for further debate—the thesis is admittedly not an easy one—since the point lies outside our focus on First Amendment challenges to legislative investigation. But if we are right, then all First Amendment concerns are automatically resolved, for the evils of legislative inquiries depend upon their being compulsory.

Several years after *McGrain* a second major case arising out of the Senate's Teapot Dome inquiry—*Sinclair v. United States*[12]—reached the Court.[13] Decided in 1929, *Sinclair* underscores how difficult it is to impeach official motivation. The witness, the president of one of the oil companies implicated in the Teapot Dome Scandal, had appeared before the committee five times previously and had coope-rated. This time, on the advice of counsel, he stated at the outset that he declined to testify because the matter under consideration had now been brought to a court by the Government in a civil fraud action and was also pending before a grand jury. He challenged whether under the circumstances there could be any function for the Senate inquiry and stated he "would reserve any evidence I may be able to give" for those courts to which the Government had referred the matter. Nevertheless the Supreme Court, in an opinion by Justice Butler, unanimously upheld his conviction for the statutory crime of con-tempt of Congress. The Court saw no reason why his testimony might not help inform legislative judgment and in addition noted that the committee's authority extended to the United States as *owner* of the oil lands in question as well as to any legislative function. Finally, although the witness was not simply recalcitrant but was, on the advice of counsel, stating a plausible legal objection to the power to compel his testimony, the Court found his refusal to answer done "willfully" within the terms of the statute. *Sinclair* thus yielded a rule which added considerably to the chilling impact of legislative inquiry: A witness refused to testify at his peril; he could determine his constitutional rights only by risking the commission of a federal crime.

Early HUAC Cases

Up until 1935 or so, then, legislative inquiry had been deeply contro-versial, but the controversy had centered on procedural due process and separation of powers issues. With the advent of the House Un-American Activities Committee, the focus of objection shifted to im-pairment of speech and associational freedoms. The question became: Does the First Amendment add anything to the constitu-tional grievances already stated? Does consideration of First Amend-ment values finally tip the balance against legislative investigations which compel disclosure?

    Ironically, the Supreme Court history over the next fifteen years consists largely of (i) the Court's declining to handle three Court of Appeals decisions in which HUAC had been exposed to sharp and sustained, albeit unsuccessful, First Amendment challenges, *United States v. Josephson* (1947), *Barsky v. United States* (1948), and *Eisler v. United States* (1948)[14]; and (ii) its disposition of five other cases—four of which involved HUAC—which it does review in order to "settle the law" on a series of narrow technical points, *Christoffel v. United States*

(1949), *Dennis v. United States* (1950), *Morford v. United States* (1950), *United States v. Bryan* (1950), and *United States v. Fleischman* (1950).[15]

The Courts of Appeals that decided *Josephson* and *Barsky* had been sharply divided. They had affirmed committee power by votes of only 2 to 1. Moreover, each case had provoked an eloquent dissent by a distinguished judge—Judge Charles E. Clark in *Josephson* and Judge Henry W. Edgerton in *Barsky*. The intensity of the sense of grievance engendered by HUAC is evident in the rhetoric of these dissents. The challenge to legislative investigations, in terms of their sociological reality, will not be put more strongly in the years of litigation to come. Judge Clark states:

. . . no more extensive search into the hearts and minds of private citizens can be thought of or expected than that we have before us. If this is legally permissible, it can be asserted dogmatically that investigation of private opinion is not really prohibited under the Bill of Rights.[16]

Judge Edgerton adds:

The investigation restricts the freedom of speech by uncovering and stigmatizing expressions of unpopular views. The Committee gives wide publicity to its proceedings. This exposes the men and women whose views are advertised to risks of insult, ostracism, and lasting loss of employment.[17]

And again:

No one can measure the inroad the Committee has made in the American sense of freedom to speak. There has been some suggestion that it restrains only timid people. I think it nearer the truth to say that, among the more articulate, it affects in one degree or another all but the very courageous, the very orthodox, and the very secure.[18]

Yet the Supreme Court declined to review *Josephson* and *Barsky*, thus permitting controversy over the legitimacy of congressional investigations to continue throughout the heyday of HUAC and of Senator McCarthy. Looking back, it seems ironic that the denial of *certiorari* in *Josephson,* the first case presented to the Court, carries three dissents—Justices Douglas, Murphy, and Rutledge—and that two years later the denial of a petition for a rehearing in *Barsky,* an action taken after the deaths of Murphy and Rutledge, provoked dissenting votes from Justices Black and Douglas. We are thus left with a small mystery as to why Justice Black did not join the dissent in *Josephson,* thereby providing the fourth vote necessary under Court practice to insure the granting of *certiorari.* [19]

A final tantalizing note is added by the disposition of *Eisler v. United States* in 1949. Gerhart Eisler, a well known Communist leader, had been cited for contempt for refusing to testify before HUAC unless first allowed to read a prepared statement, and at trial he had levied a sharp attack on the motives of the committee for calling him. This time the Court did accept the case and it heard argument. But with the decision pending, Eisler fled the country and efforts to extradite him were unsuccessful. The Court in a brief *per curiam* opinion ordered the case removed from the docket "pending the return of the fugitive."[20]

The Court's opinion indicates that Eisler by his own volition may have rendered the case moot. There are, however, three dissenting opinions. Justice Frankfurter, in an opinion joined by Chief Justice Vinson, argues for dismissal of *certiorari,* since the question has now become purely abstract: "If legal questions brought by the litigant are to remain here, the litigant must stay with them."[21] Justice Murphy, who presumably thought the committee had exceeded its powers, argues that the Court retains jurisdiction and should go on and decide the merits: "it is the importance of the legal issues, not the parties, which bring the case to this Court. Those issues did not leave when Eisler did."[22]

The dissent of Justice Jackson is the most arresting. He too favors having the Court decide the case. But he would do so in order to make clear to the world that the Court has no power to restrain the committee:

Decision at this time is not urged as a favor to Eisler. If only his interests were involved, they might well be forfeited by his flight. But it is due to Congress and to future witnesses before its committees that we hand down a final decision. I therefore dissent from an expedient that lends added credence to Eisler's petition, which I think is without legal merit. I do not think we can run away from the case just because Eisler has.

I should not want to be understood as approving the use that the Committee on Un-American Activities has frequently made of its power. But I think it would be an unwarranted act of judicial usurpation to strip Congress of its investigatory power, or to assume for the courts the function of supervising congressional committees. I should affirm the judgment below and leave the responsibility for the behavior of its committees squarely on the shoulders of Congress.[23]

The Court's performance in the five legislative investigation cases it does agree to review during this 1935-50 period is also worth notice. The Court's willingness to devote time and energy to the resolution of narrow technical points which are marginal at best to the controversy over the performance of HUAC brings to mind the extravagant care Justice Frankfurter is to devote a few years later to the evidentiary and procedural points in *Communist Party v. Subversive Activities Control Board*[24] while giving short shrift to the formidable constitutional issues raised. Certainly one does not want to deprecate the Court's patience with procedure. There is, as we have had occasion to note more than once, a strong argument to be made in support of the thesis that democratic, civilized values are most essentially protected by norms of procedural due process rather than by First Amendment norms. But there are occasions when meticulous attention to procedural detail can seem like caricature, because it can do so little for the real grievance. Such is the impression left by this cluster of cases.

The fault, if it be one, belongs not to the Court alone, but also to the litigation tactics of the Communist defendants. Having been unable to sustain their First Amendment challenges to HUAC in *Barsky, Josephson,* and *Eisler,* they shifted to evoking technical safeguards, as if the trial for contempt of Congress were a trial for murder. Ironically, after the *Sinclair* case, there is in a real sense no issue of fact left to try in the contempt cases. If the witness refused to answer the question put to him by the committee, that would appear to be it; and the witness is rarely defending on the ground that he did not in fact refuse to answer.

Three of the cases—*Christoffel, Bryan* and *Fleischman*—posed the narrow question of whether a quorum of the committee was required to be present when the witness committed his offense. In *Christoffel,* a 5 to 4 decision, the Court upset the perjury conviction of a witness on the ground that a quorum of the committee was not present at the time he made the false statement.[25] The issue was not constitutional; the Court rested its decision on construction of the perjury statute which defined the crime in terms of a statement before a "competent tribunal." It is conceivable that the quorum rule applied to contempt might serve to moderate somewhat the excesses of "one man committees." But a year later in *Bryan,* a contempt case arising out of the witness's refusal to answer before HUAC, the Court, because of variations in the wording of the statute, decided that no quorum need be present at the moment the witness commits his crime by declining to answer.

In *Fleischman* the Court relied on *Bryan* in disposing of the quorum issue. Also, it declined to protect the witness in refusing to produce subpoenaed documents of an organization of which she was a member, even though the Government had arguably failed to show that she had the power to do so. The documents were in the possession of the executive secretary of the organization. The defendant was one of sixteen members of the executive board with supervisory powers over the secretary. All members of the board were served with subpoenas demanding that they produce the documents. The Government theory was that the subpoena had imposed on the board members the obligation of directing the secretary to turn over the records and that their recalcitrance resided in their failure to so direct her. The Supreme Court, reversing the Court of Appeals, held that this failure was sufficient evidence of contempt of Congress to satisfy the statutory crime. The decision served to bring Justices Black and Frankfurter together in dissent, each writing an opinion.

For our purposes, the most interesting of these technical HUAC cases is *Dennis,* for the procedural challenge it advances is directly linked to the Government's anti-Communist measures. The witness-defendant argues that in a trial for contempt arising out of a HUAC hearing he should be entitled to challenge for cause all Government employees offered as jurors. The bias, he argues, arises as a matter of law and does not depend on the individual juror. It is enough that the prospective juror works for the Government, that the Loyalty Order is in effect, and that the contempt involves HUAC. In a 5 to 2 decision the Court affirms the conviction. Once again Justices Black and Frankfurter are partners in dissent, and again each writes an opinion.

The majority, speaking through Justice Minton, relies on earlier cases in which the Court had held with respect to trials for *other* federal crimes that Government employees are not automatically ineligible to be jurors. Justice Minton can see no basis for a special exemption from this general rule for Communist defendants:

In this case, no more than the trial court can we without injustice take judicial notice of a miasma of fear to which Government employees are claimed to be peculiarly vulnerable—and from which other citizens are by implication immune.[26]

Justice Jackson concurs but only because he thinks that the basic rule is wrong and that Government employees should be disqualified as jurors in *all* cases the Government prosecutes. He too, however, would not make an exception for Communist defendants: "so long as accused persons who are Republicans, Dixiecrats, Socialists, or Democrats must put up with such a jury, it will have to do for Communists."[27]

The case opens an unexpected window on the Court's concern over the anti-subversive mood of the day. Justice Black in dissent bitterly notes:

Probably at no period of the nation's history has the "loyalty" of government employees been subjected to such constant scrutiny and investigation by so many government agents and secret informers. And for the past few years press and radio have been crowded with charges by responsible officials and others that the writings, friendships, or associations of some government employee have branded him "disloyal."[28]

And Justice Frankfurter eloquently challenges the notion that any "exemption" for Communists is involved:

To recognize the existence of what is characterized as a phobia against a particular group is not to discriminate in its favor. If a particular group, no matter what its beliefs, is under pressure of popular hostility, exclusion of potential jurors peculiarly susceptible to such pressure is not an expression of regard for political opinions but recognition by law of the facts of life. . . . To take appropriate measures in order to avert injustice even towards a member of a despised group is to enforce justice. It is not to play favorites.[29]

Finally, *Morford* is an instance of self-defeating litigation tactics by the defendant. Convicted of contempt before HUAC for refusing to produce certain records of an organization of which he was an officer, Morford challenged the committee on a variety of constitutional and non-constitutional grounds. The Court in a brief *per curiam* opinion reversed on the narrow ground that the trial court had been mistaken in its refusal to permit Morford's counsel to interrogate prospective government employee jurors as to the possible influence of the Loyalty Order on their ability to render a fair and impartial verdict. Having won the jury point and been given a new trial, Morford *waived* trial by jury and was again convicted. On appeal he submitted the matter to the Court of Appeals on the same briefs filed in the earlier appeal—an appeal where the method of selecting the jury had been in issue. Not surprisingly, the Court of Appeals affirmed the second conviction and the Supreme Court denied *certiorari*.

Tenney v. Brandhove *and* United States v. Rumely

As the decade of the 1950s opens, the Court confronts problems arising out of legislative investigations in two cases of broad significance, *Tenney v. Brandhove*[30] in 1951 and *United States v. Rumely*[31] in 1953. In both cases First Amendment values are salient, but the vicissitudes of litigation in framing constitutional issues for the Court are such that in neither is the First Amendment challenge directly confronted.

Tenney involves a state replica of HUAC, the California Tenney Committee, officially known as the "Senate Fact-Finding Committee on Un-American Activities." The existence of this committee further illustrates a familiar evil of the anti-subversive measures of this period, namely, that no government agency attempted to coordinate them into a coherent strategy. Thus, everyone tended to get into the act and the measures overlapped and cumulated.

Brandhove's complaint told a complex story. After the Tenney Committee had been in operation for a year, he had petitioned the state legislature not to appropriate further funds for it, alleging that it had conspired with the successful candidate for Mayor of San Francisco in a recent election to spread "Red" charges against his opponent. The committee's response was to summon Brandhove as a witness before it. When he refused to testify, the chairman of the committee read into the record a summary of his alleged criminal record and various items impeaching his credibility. Brandhove was prosecuted for contempt, but the jury failed to return a verdict and the prosecution was dropped.

Brandhove then sued the committee under one of the civil rights acts. He sought damages for interference with his right of free speech and his right to petition for redress of grievances. He charged that the hearing had "no legitimate legislative purpose" but rather was intended to intimidate him and to deter him from criticizing the committee. The legal issue posed was whether, assuming the allegations were true, such a complaint stated a cause of action. The trial court thought not and dismissed it, but the Court of Appeals reversed. The

Supreme Court, with Justice Douglas in dissent and Justice Black filing a cautious concurrence, held that the complaint did not state a cause of action under the civil rights statute.

It should be emphasized that Brandhove's grievance was not the generic chilling of speech and associational freedoms so frequently charged to HUAC. It was far more specific to his particular situation. He charged that he was being harassed by committee inquiry *because he had criticized the committee.* In essence the charge was that the committee was using its investigative processes to punish and silence its critics, that the inquiry was a seditious libel sanction.[32]

Brandhove urged his point not as a defense to contempt charges but as part of an affirmative case seeking an award of damages. Justice Frankfurter for the majority argued powerfully that given the long-standing Anglo-American traditions of legislative freedom, as evidenced perhaps best by the Speech and Debate Clause of the Constitution, the civil rights acts cannot be construed as intended to "subject legislators to civil liability for acts done within the sphere of legislative activity,"[33] and, further, that legislative investigations are an established aspect of legislative activity.

It is not altogether clear just how broad a privilege Justice Frankfurter wishes to accord legislative investigations. He is careful not to make it absolute: "We have only considered the scope of the privilege as applied to the facts of the present case."[34] Nor is he explicit, since he need not be in this case, as to whether an abuse of the investigative process egregious enough to provide a defense to contempt of the legislature would necessarily be enough to expose the legislators to damages.

His concern appears to be not so much with the likelihood of abuse as with the likelihood that, given the mood of the day, legislators performing their investigative function will be the targets of charges of abuse of power:

In times of political passion, dishonest or vindictive motives are readily attributed to legislative conduct and as readily believed. Courts are not the place for such controversies. Self-discipline and the voters must be the ultimate reliance for discouraging or correcting such abuses. The courts should not go beyond the narrow confines of determining that a committee's inquiry may fairly be deemed within its province.[35]

The ambiguities in the Frankfurter opinion spark the separate opinions from Justice Black, concurring, and Justice Douglas, dissenting. Justice Black states: "I substantially agree with the Court's reasoning and its conclusion. But since this is a difficult case for me, I think it important to emphasize what we do *not* decide."[36] He then goes on to stress that the Court is not deciding that Brandhove might not well have a defense against contempt.

Justice Douglas alone goes to what seems to me the heart of Brandhove's grievance—the seditious libel overtones:

We are dealing here with a right protected by the Constitution—the right of free speech. The charge seems strained and difficult to sustain; but it is that a legislative committee brought the weight of its authority down on respondent for exercising his right of free speech. Reprisal for speaking is as much an abridgment as a prior restraint.[37]

As the Court's first encounter with a First Amendment grievance against legislative investigation, *Tenney v. Brandhove* provides only oblique commentary and little source for optimism as to the strength of specifically First Amendment criticism. *United States v. Rumely* in 1953, however, strikes a stronger note and intimates that compulsory disclosure pursuant to a congressional investigation *might* be limited by the First Amendment.

Rumely was the executive secretary of an organization known as the Committee for Constitutional Government (CCG). He was convicted of contempt for refusing to disclose to a House Committee on Lobbying—the Buchanan Committee—the names of certain contributors. The Court of Appeals upset his conviction, and the Supreme Court affirmed in a 7 to 0 decision. *Rumely* is thus the first decision since *Kilbourn v. Thompson* in 1881 to hold that a congressional investigating committee had exceeded its powers. Justice Frankfurter, writing for the Court, places the decision on non-constitutional grounds, but his opinion carries distinct First Amendment resonances. And Justice Douglas in a concurring opinion, joined by Justice Black, relies squarely on the First Amendment.

The Lobbying Act, enacted in 1946, required the registration of lobbyists and the reporting of all contributions of $500 or more "received or expended to influence directly the passage or defeat of any legislation by the Congress." The CCG had devised what had looked to the Buchanan Committee like a scheme to evade the Act. It would accept contributions of over $490 only if the contributor would designate that the funds be used for the purchase and distribution of books and pamphlets. The CCG would then treat the contributions as a sale and not report it. It appears that the organization had a small library of highly conservative political and economic writings to which it was able to give wide public distribution via these bulk sales to contributors. It was raising some $2,000,000 a year and distributing hundreds of thousands of books. One cannot be sure from the Court's resume of the facts whether the CCG scheme was designed primarily to secure contributions for direct lobbying in a form that would not have to be reported, or whether, indeed, the principal objective of the organization was simply to seek to influence legislation by influencing public opinion through the distribution of its literature. In any event, the Buchanan Committee thought the scheme urgently required looking into. It summoned Rumely and requested the names of those who had given $500 or more for any purpose, including the sale of books and pamphlets. It is his refusal to furnish this information that triggers the contempt citation and precipitates the litigation.

At the outset of his opinion Justice Frankfurter observes: "we would have to be that 'blind' Court . . . that does not see what 'all others can see and understand' not to know that there is wide concern, both in and out of Congress, over some aspects of the exercise of the congressional power of investigation."[38] He acknowledges the problem of accommodating "these contending principles—the one underlying the power of Congress to investigate, the other at the basis of the limitation imposed by the First Amendment."[39] It is abundantly clear, however, that he very much wants to avoid having to declare that an investigation by a congressional committee has transgressed First Amendment limits. Although *Rumely* involves the politics of the right, one senses that he is aware of the potential such a ruling would have for the politics of the left, of the threat it might create to the legitimacy of HUAC.

He finds it possible to avoid direct confrontation with the First Amendment issue by employing a ground for limiting the investigative power not touched upon in the prior cases: lack of authorization. The point derives from ordinary principles of agency. A committee can function only as the agent of the House that creates it; it has therefore only such power as the parent House gives it. The argument that a committee inquiry is in a given instance beyond the authorization of the committee is thus a basis for denying the committee the power to compel testimony in that instance.

The Resolution authorizing the Buchanan Committee stated in relevant part: "The committee is authorized and directed to conduct a study and investigation of . . . all lobbying activities intended to

influence, encourage, promote, or retard legislation." Justice Frankfurter focuses on the ambiguity of "lobbying activities," a phrase that
might mean either lobbying through *direct* contact with the legislators
or lobbying which exerts its pressure *indirectly* on legislators by acting
upon public opinion. His opinion is an exercise in the logic of judicial
restraint: The Court should avoid constitutional questions whenever
decently possible, and especially where the matter at issue is as delicate and treacherous as that of limiting the investigative powers of
Congress: "Experience admonishes us to tread warily in this domain."[40] The guiding principle is that where two constructions are
possible and one will avoid constitutional doubts, the Court should
adopt the construction that avoids the doubts and hence the necessity
for constitutional adjudication. Frankfurter thus adopts the narrow
construction of "lobbying activities" and rules that the committee was
not authorized to ask Rumely for the information he withheld.

The importance of the Frankfurter opinion lies not so much in
the illustration it provides of his well-known judicial conservatism as
in the circumstance that he is uncomfortable with the construction he
adopts.[41] There is no decisive compulsion for this construction of
"lobbying activities" in the common meaning of the words or, as the
Douglas opinion emphasizes, in the legislative history. To complete
his argument plausibly, he requires a nudge from constitutional
doubt. He has this to say:

Surely it cannot be denied that giving the scope to the resolution for which
the Government contends, that is, deriving from it the power to inquire into
all efforts of private individuals to influence public opinion through books
and periodicals, however remote the radiations of influence which they may
exert upon the ultimate legislative process, raises doubts of constitutionality
in view of the prohibition of the First Amendment. In light of the opinion of
Prettyman, J. below and of some of the views expressed here, it would not
be seemly to maintain that these doubts are fanciful or factitious.[42]

Justice Frankfurter thus acknowledges a genuine constitutional doubt
generated by the First Amendment. But just as the point becomes
interesting, he turns away from a First Amendment analysis of why
compulsory disclosure would be bad here. A closer look would have
required explaining why participating as a Communist in the dissemination of views from the left is vulnerable to compulsory disclosure,
while participating in the dissemination of views from the right triggers First Amendment concerns. If distinction is to be found in the

conspiratorial nature of the Communist Party, it would be necessary to explain when and how that conspiratorial status was officially established and just what the nexus of this witness to that conspiracy is: the questions that are to work themselves pure in the Court's analysis of cases like *Yates, Scales,* and *Elfbrandt.* [43]

The Douglas concurring opinion is the exact tactical counter to the Frankfurter opinion. Justice Douglas is anxious to establish a precedent that congressional investigations can be limited by the First Amendment. He therefore would find any narrowing construction of "lobbying activities" foreclosed by the legislative history. He examines that history in far more detail than did Justice Frankfurter and he argues persuasively that Congress did intend to authorize inquiry into indirect lobbying. Since the constitutional doubt cannot be finessed by construction, he confronts it directly: "Of necessity I come then to the constitutional questions."[44]

The ensuing two-and-a-half pages of his opinion constitute the first extended discussion at the level of the Supreme Court of an argument that the power to compel testimony is limited by the First Amendment. The analysis moves in three steps. First, the CCG itself, properly viewed, is "a segment of the American press": "We have here a publisher who through books and pamphlets seeks to reach the minds and hearts of the American people. He is different in some respects from other publishers. But the differences are minor."[45] Second, extension of the registration and disclosure requirements of the Lobbying Act itself to the kind of "lobbying" done by the press would be unconstitutional under the First Amendment. And third, since Congress cannot compel such disclosure directly through legislation, it cannot do so via investigation. Justice Douglas then proceeds to restate this last premise in a slightly different form—a form that is to be appealed to in later controversies over HUAC: "Inquiry into personal and private affairs is precluded. And so is any matter in respect to which no valid legislation could be had."[46]

The second of the Douglas premises deserves further attention. The argument is that the compulsory disclosure of who buys which books would be a deep violation of the First Amendment, even if no other sanctions were attached. It is the counterpart of the anonymity of writers and publishers accorded protection in *Talley v. California* [47] in 1960. Here it is the anonymity of purchasers and readers that is protected. If we add the principle of the privacy of one's library that emerges in the 1969 obscenity case *Stanley v. Georgia,* [48] we can discern an attractive notion of a core intellectual privacy. The disclosure is bad in Douglas's eyes because, even if it has no other consequences, it impairs the effortlessness, the confident security, that should attend the purchasing and reading of books and pamphlets:

If the present inquiry were sanctioned, the press would be subjected to harassment that in practical effect might be as serious as censorship. A publisher, compelled to register with the federal government, would be subjected to vexatious inquiries. . . . Once the government can demand of a publisher the names of the purchasers of his publications, the free press as we know it disappears. Then the spectre of a government agent will look over the shoulder of everyone who reads. The purchase of a book or pamphlet today may result in a subpoena tomorrow. Fear of criticism goes with every person into the bookstall. The subtle, imponderable pressures of the orthodox lay hold.[49]

The argument in future cases will be that political association is entitled to the same type of privacy and for much the same reasons and that inquiry about membership in the Communist Party violates such privacy.

It may be profitable to pause at this juncture to sort out some of the possible premises involved in a First Amendment analysis of the use of compulsory disclosure by legislative committees.

(i) Disclosure itself is a deterrent, a trigger of self-censorship. It is not, as the hearty would suppose, a *de minimis* harm.

(ii) In sensitive areas such as the books one reads, the ideas one espouses, the associations one joins, disclosure is therefore *presumptively* a violation of the First Amendment.

(iii) If the deterrence of speech and association by disclosure is *intended* by Government, the propriety of disclosure is to be analyzed as would be the propriety of the imposition of a direct criminal sanction.

(iv) If the deterrence is a by-product of disclosure sought for another Government purpose, its justification will depend upon the weight and precision of that purpose. It is not therefore automatically justified.

(v) It will probably not be permissible even in the context of a First Amendment argument to seek to go behind the official motivation of the government action compelling disclosure.

The Fifth Amendment Cases

Within a year or two after *Rumely,* the Court decided four further cases involving HUAC. We earlier discussed the first of these—*Barsky v. Board of Regents* (1954)—as an instance of the "multiplier effect" anti-subversive measures often generate. The three other cases— *Quinn v. United States* (1955), *Emspak v. United States* (1955), and *Bart v. United States* (1955)[50]—were precipitated by refusals to answer committee inquiries on Fifth Amendment grounds.

The *Barsky* case arose because Dr. Barsky, having lost his constitutional challenge to HUAC by a 2 to 1 vote in the Court of Appeals, a decision which the Supreme Court declined to review, was sentenced to six months in prison and a $500 fine for his contempt of Congress in failing to turn over certain records of the Joint Anti-Fascist Refugee Committee. Upon his release from prison, disciplinary proceedings were instituted against him by the Medical Grievance Committee of New York. The proceedings moved through four stages of committee and administrative review and then an appeal to the New York Court of Appeals. The initial subcommittee recommended a three-month suspension from practice; and the full Grievance Committee on review extended the suspension to six months. The Regents' Committee on Discipline, however, reversed and recommended a reprimand only and no suspension. The Board of Regents then without opinion rejected this recommendation and went back to six months' suspension. The New York court affirmed, asserting it had no jurisdiction to review the way in which the Regents had exercised their disciplinary discretion under the New York statutes regulating the practice of medicine. The Supreme Court upheld the suspension of Dr. Barsky in a 6 to 3 decision which once again found Justice Frankfurter "crossing the aisle" to join Justices Black and Douglas in dissent.

What is striking about the case in this context is the fact that the Court has little to say about the nature of Dr. Barsky's crime, although he was seeking to challenge HUAC constitutionally by the only method available to him, and although *Rumely* had strongly intimated that there might be something to his constitutional grievance. Indeed, *Barsky* on its facts is much like *Rumely*—he too is asked to turn over the names of contributors to the organization of which he is an officer. Justice Black notes the tension in a footnote:

. . . certainly since our recent holding in *United States v. Rumely,* it cannot be said that it is "fanciful or factitious" to claim that the First Amendment bars congressional committees from seeking the names of contributors to an organization alleged to be engaged in "political propaganda."[51]

Justice Douglas stresses the nature of Dr. Barsky's crime:

The fact that a doctor needs a good knowledge of biology is no excuse for suspending his license because he has little or no knowledge of constitutional law. In this case it is admitted that Dr. Barsky's "crime" consisted of no more than a justifiable mistake concerning his constitutional rights.[52]

Douglas closes his dissent with an epigram which takes judicial notice of what he finds to be the mood of the day: "When a doctor cannot save lives in America because he is opposed to Franco in Spain, it is time to call a halt and look critically at the neurosis that has possessed us."[53]

Barsky then is an example of the impotence of the Court to correct all hardships or injustices. In contrast, Quinn, Emspak, and Bart illustrate the power of the Court in using procedural tools. The principal point established by these decisions is one that will greatly affect the future function of legislative inquiries into subversion and will supply a new idiom for American culture, "Fifth Amendment Communists." The issue is: Can a witness be compelled to answer whether he is a member of the Communist Party, or is he, in light of the Smith Act, entitled to refuse to answer by reason of the Fifth Amendment privilege against self-incrimination? In Quinn Chief Justice Warren, summarizing the prior precedents, puts this basic point to rest in a few sentences:

In the instant case petitioner was convicted for refusing to answer the committee's question as to his alleged membership in the Communist Party. Clearly an answer to the question might have tended to incriminate him. As a consequence, petitioner was entitled to claim the privilege.[54]

This holding appears on the surface to be a major step toward providing constitutional limits to the power of investigating committees, but in fact it is one of the things that made it possible for committees like HUAC to flourish as long as they did. In a criminal trial the privilege of a defendant not to take the stand is a substantial safeguard; it serves to put the prosecution to its proof, without any aid from him. In the legislative investigation context, however, the constitutional privilege to refuse to answer on self-incrimination grounds tends to boomerang. It evokes in the popular mind a suspicion that the reason the witness claims the privilege is because he is a Communist. Only Communists, so runs the popular logic, will claim the privilege. Hence the successful claim of the constitutional privilege not to answer the committee's question becomes a *de facto* answer to it! Further, while criminal procedure limits the capacity of the prosecutor to comment negatively to the jury on the defendant's failure to take the stand, committee members were free to exploit the negative inference with maximum publicity, the abuse being perhaps best illustrated by the techniques of Senator McCarthy.

The upshot was a curious one with respect to the function of such committee inquiries. In the overwhelming number of instances their activity consisted of calling people who would claim the privilege. Indeed, committees like HUAC tended to measure their success by the number of claims of the Fifth Amendment they had elicited. Once assured the witness would claim the privilege, the committee would then proceed to ask him a long series of questions, often naming other people and always widening the ambit of suspicion. In effect, it was the committee members and counsel rather than witness who did the testifying.

The committees thus perfected a wretched method for testing "loyalty." There was, as we have seen, considerable ambiguity in the direct question about membership in the Communist Party. But there was enormous ambiguity to the question in this operational form: Will you claim the Fifth Amendment if asked about membership in the Party? In any event, the final outcome was an intolerable inconsistency. The chief fact-finding achievement of legislative committees investigating subversion—whose justification for existence, remember, was to supply facts in aid of legislation—was to find people who would invoke their constitutional right to decline to answer the committees' questions! No case has yet put to the courts this challenge to the legitimacy of committee operations.[55]

The chief controversy in *Quinn* and *Emspak* turns not on whether the privilege was available to the witnesses but whether they had in fact sufficiently asserted it before the committee. The Government argues that the witnesses had not done so in that they had deliberately stated their claims in "muffled terms" in an effort, as the Government's brief in *Emspak* put it, to "obtain the benefit of the privilege without incurring the popular opprobrium which often attaches to its exercise."[56] In both cases the Court, in opinions by Chief Justice

Warren, reads an ambiguous record with a high degree of sympathy and protects the witness. In *Emspak* Warren states:

> . . . if it is true that in these times a stigma may somehow result from a witness' reliance on the Self-Incrimination Clause, a committee should be all the more ready to recognize a veiled claim of the privilege. Otherwise, the great right which the Clause was intended to secure might be effectively frustrated by private pressures.[57]

In *Bart* the Court, again speaking through the Chief Justice, adds another procedural rule which undoubtedly improved the proceedings somewhat for the witness: The committee could not cite for contempt until it had explicitly rejected the witness's reasons for not answering and had directed him to answer. Thus, once again as with the points about quorum and jury selection, we find the Court taking time for narrow procedural issues while skirting the main grievance. But this time the Court decides the narrow points in favor of the witness. And, with hindsight, we may perhaps detect in Chief Justice Warren's empathetic reaction in these cases the seeds of his major 1957 opinion in *Watkins v. United States.* [58]

35

Legislative Investigation: The Period of First Amendment Challenge, 1957-1959

The Supreme Court's reticence with respect to the constitutional issues raised by legislative investigations ends explosively with Chief Justice Warren's opinion in *Watkins v. United States*,[1] a 1957 decision upsetting the contempt conviction of a witness before HUAC. The vote is 6 to 1; Justices Whittaker and Burton do not participate, and Justice Clark is the lone dissenter. Thus, one of the striking things about the outcome in *Watkins* is that Justices Harlan and Frankfurter join Justices Black, Douglas, Brennan, and the Chief Justice to produce it. Moreover, both join the Warren opinion for the Court, although Frankfurter also files a separate concurrence.

The Chief Justice's opinion ranges so widely and explicitly over various objections to committees like HUAC as to leave the impression that the Court is deciding broad constitutional issues. Read closely, however, the opinion, in the end, places the decision on narrow and essentially procedural grounds: lack of *pertinency*. The holding is thus very much in lineal descent from the Warren opinions in *Quinn, Emspak,* and *Bart.* The flavor of the *Watkins* opinion, however, is very different. In *Quinn* and *Emspak* Warren had explicitly noted at the conclusion of his opinions that, since the procedural points discussed had disposed of the cases, there was no need to reach the petitioners' First Amendment challenges. Two years later in *Watkins* he turns the etiquette on its head—he begins by discussing the First Amendment challenges and only at the end shifts to the pertinency grounds on which he ultimately rests the decision. The upshot is that he is able to deliver a lengthy sermon on the sins of legislative investigations without in the actual decision having to readjust the delicate balance of power between Congress and the Court.

Under the circumstances, the dicta prove more interesting than the rationale for the decision, but we shall consider the latter first. The federal statute defines the crime of contempt of Congress as refusal "to answer any question pertinent to the question under inquiry." Thus in theory it is not a crime to refuse to answer a question that is "not pertinent." Further, in theory, since the privacy of the witness may be invaded by compulsory disclosure only when the disclosure is public business, the very jurisdiction of the committee depends on the pertinency of its questions. Chief Justice Warren speaks of this as "a jurisdictional concept of pertinency,"[2] and his strategy—a strategy which presumably won him the support of Justices Harlan and Frankfurter—is to attempt to erect out of this concept a safeguard for the witness before a legislative committee.

The key premise of the Warren opinion is that if pertinency is jurisdictional, then the witness is entitled to screen committee questions in order to protect his right to decline to answer those which are not pertinent. In order for him to be able to do that, it must be made clear to him what the scope—or, better, the jurisdiction—of the inquiry is and why the particular question being put to him is pertinent to it. "There are," Warren notes, "several sources that can outline the 'question under inquiry' in such a way that the rules against vagueness are satisfied. The authorizing resolution, the remarks of the chairman or members of the committee, or even the nature of the proceedings themselves, might sometimes make the topic clear."[3]

The Chief Justice then patiently reviews the facts of the case before him. Watkins, a union leader, had testified fully about himself, denying membership in the Communist Party but admitting tactical cooperation with it for a period of about five years. He had also agreed to identify others he knew were still members of the Party. He refused, however, to discuss those who, whatever their past affiliations, he could not say were still members. It is the "pertinency" of this last line of questioning that is at issue.

As the parties and the Court frame the pertinency issue, however, it has nothing to do with the flavor of this particular line of questioning, with why indeed the committee needs information about former Party members. Rather, it turns on the bland question of whether the committee had made sufficiently clear to Watkins that the matter under inquiry was "Communism in labor." Chief Justice Warren finds that neither the authorizing resolution, nor the opening statement of the chairman, nor the explanation of the chairman in response to the witness's objections, nor the structure of the inquiry itself—seven of the thirty persons Watkins was asked about were not in labor—made it sufficiently clear that the inquiry was about Communism in labor.[4] The conviction cannot stand therefore, since Watkins had been deprived of an essential right under the statute—the right to decline to answer non-pertinent questions.

At first blush the solution seems an impressive one. It appears not only to honor the witness's curiosity as to the relevance to any public purpose of what he is being asked about himself, but also to be a diplomatic accommodation between the Court and Congress. Define the jurisdiction of your committees, the Court is saying to Congress, and keep their queries within it, and we will not interfere with their compulsory process.

On reflection, however, it is evident that the pertinency requirement is no solution at all. It is flawed in several respects. First, it trivializes. It makes it appear that Watkins's problem was that he did not know that the inquiry was about Communism in labor, rather than, say, Communism in Chicago, or Communism in America, and that this was the essential information he needed to defend his rights intelligently. One cannot but sympathize with Justice Clark's complaint that Watkins knew well enough what the question under inquiry was. Second, it mistakes the grievance. If the committees, once they had summoned a witness, tended to exercise idle curiosity and to ask him about anything under the sun, a pertinency requirement might possibly provide some restraint. But it is now late in the day—1957— and experience with committees like HUAC has massively shown that their pattern of inquiry is always about Communism in America. Third, the "flaw" is so easily remedied—as future committee practice is to show. All that is needed is a self-serving opening statement by the chairman as to the scope of the inquiry. In brief, so long as the scope of the inquiry is made clear, that is the end of the pertinency safeguard, no matter how objectionable the particular question.[5]

Finally, the root difficulty with a separate pertinency requirement resides in its relationship to *authorization*, the point on which the *Rumely* decision had turned. What is the difference between asking whether the particular question is authorized, as in *Rumely*, or asking whether it is pertinent, as in *Watkins*? To make pertinency an *independent* ground of objection, there must exist questions which are authorized but not pertinent, and presumably *Watkins* offered an illustration of just such a question. But if the question is authorized, it is difficult to see why it should matter that it might, for the moment, fall outside the committee's immediate agenda. Why cannot a committee *authorized* to investigate Communism in America proceed in any order it sees fit?

I suspect that the concern with pertinency in *Watkins* is animated by two genuine objections to HUAC inquiry which have little to do with the purely procedural point on which the Court ultimately comes to rest. First, there is the nature of the authorizing resolution. When it is as broad and opaque as the HUAC charter, something more than authorization seems called for. Second, there is the suspicion that the impact of HUAC inquiry on speech and association is not an unintended by-product of fact-finding pursuant to legislating but is the very purpose of the inquiry. The question is whether either of these grievances can in any degree be satisfied by a procedural requirement that the committee make clear to the witness the scope of its inquiry.

Chief Justice Warren deals extensively with each of these grievances for the first twenty-eight pages of his thirty-six-page opinion. It was this circumstance that lent the opinion the appearance of having imposed far more sweeping restrictions on legislative investigations than was actually the case.

HUAC had begun originally as a select committee which meant that its authorization had to be renewed each year thus giving Congress some control over its mission. But in 1942, when Representative Martin Dies of Texas became chairman, it was made a standing committee and given its famous authorizing resolution. Perhaps this shift in status from select to standing committee more than any other single circumstance accounted for the difficulty of securing congressional control over HUAC.

The authorizing resolution read:

The Committee on Un-American Activities, as a whole or by subcommittee, is authorized to make from time to time investigations of (1) the extent, character, and objects of un-American propaganda activities in the United States, (2) the diffusion within the United States of subversive and un-American propaganda that is instigated from foreign countries or of a domestic origin and attacks the principle of the form of government as guaranteed by our Constitution, and (3) all other questions in relation thereto that would aid Congress in any necessary remedial legislation.[6]

If HUAC had done what it was authorized to do, it seems clear that its inquiries would have violated the First Amendment. The vice of the HUAC resolution is much the same as the vice in *Rumely:* It authorizes inquiry into the general formation of opinion very broadly defined, and it has the added feature, to which *New York Times v. Sullivan* has made us sensitive today, of strong overtones of seditious libel. The great irony is that HUAC escaped that fate by eschewing inquiry into propaganda, even Communist propaganda, and concentrating on inventorying individual Communists instead. It was thus perceived by its supporters not as an investigation of speech and press but as an investigation of a criminal conspiracy.

The Chief Justice has this to say about the HUAC charter:

It would be difficult to imagine a less explicit authorizing resolution. Who can define the meaning of "un-American"? What is that single, solitary "principle of the form of government as guaranteed by our Constitution"?[7]

He goes on to intimate that there was a time when it would have been an open question whether the resolution authorized HUAC to investigate individual Communists: "At one time, perhaps, the resolution might have been read narrowly to confine the Committee to the subject of propaganda."[8] But he quickly adds: "The events that have transpired in the fifteen years before the interrogation of petitioner make such a construction impossible at this date."[9]

What then is one to do at this date—1957—with the HUAC resolution? The Chief Justice attacks it for its breadth and vagueness. He sketches a series of criticisms that *might* have been made the basis for the Court's decision. He notes that the "preliminary control" which Congress would normally exercise over a committee in authorizing it is in this instance "slight or non-existent."[10] "The Committee," he adds, "is allowed, in essence, to define its own authority, to choose the direction and focus of its activities."[11]

Chief Justice Warren here puts his finger on a critical point. Suppose a committee were authorized to investigate whatever it pleased? The rationale for compulsory process in the legislative committee is that it is needed to aid legislation. It would seem indispensable then that the use of compulsion be supported by a judgment of the responsible legislative body that the information is needed. But if the responsible body *defaults* on exercising that judgment and, in Warren's phrase, allows the committee to define its own authority, the only judgment in support of compulsion will be that of a few committee members. Judicial restraint in deference to separation of powers presupposes the responsible exercise by each branch of its powers. Thus, it would seem possible to have built a formidable argument against the HUAC resolution not only on grounds of vagueness but also by impeaching the institutional logic through which the power to compel testimony from individuals was derived.

All prior cases had affirmed the proposition that legislative investigations into the affairs of individuals were not unlimited, but had jurisdictional parameters and were therefore subject to judicial review. Chief Justice Warren notes that so broad an authorization renders judicial review impossible; there is no way for a court to decide whether a committee has exceeded its authorization. Thus, it would seem that the unfettered nature of the HUAC authorization is a radical defect which would warrant denying it compulsory process until it was brought under the discipline of Congress. But although he sets out the premises, the Chief Justice will not take the step and draw the conclusion. At least not yet.

He elects rather to attempt to limit the committee's power by means of the pertinency requirement. The Committee is left free to do what it wants so long as it makes clear to the witness what it is it wants! But this strategy cannot work. So long as the committee is free to set the scope of its inquiry, a requirement that its questions must be within the scope of its inquiry is necessarily an empty one.

Like his discussion of the HUAC resolution, Chief Justice Warren's First Amendment analysis articulates powerful premises but then stops short of the expected conclusion. He begins with a firm declaration that the First Amendment *does* limit congressional investigations. He sees no difficulty raised by the circumstance that no statute is involved: "The First Amendment may be invoked against infringement of the protected freedoms by law or by lawmaking."[12] This dictum, when read together with *Rumely,* yields a firm promise that there are indeed circumstances under which an investigation would violate the First Amendment.

Warren then describes the pressures generated by the investigative process—pressures which "may imperceptibly lead to abridgement of protected freedoms."[13] There is the impact on the witness himself; the impact on those the witness may name who are "thereby placed in the same glare of publicity";[14] and there is the "subtle and immeasurable" effect on those spectators in the general public who may "tend to adhere to the most orthodox and uncontroversial views and associations in order to avoid a similar fate at some future time."[15] Nor does it matter that the chilling of speech and association arises in part from the reaction of a hostile public rather than from direct government action. The government remains responsible for "initiating the reaction."[16]

The Chief Justice is particularly sensitive to behavioral nuance in profiling the impact on the witness himself:

> The mere summoning of a witness and compelling him to testify, against his will, about his beliefs, expressions or associations is a measure of governmental interference. And when those forced revelations concern matters that are unorthodox, unpopular, or even hateful to the general public, the reaction in the life of the witness may be disastrous. This effect is even more harsh when it is past beliefs, expressions or associations that are disclosed and judged by current standards rather than those contemporary with the matters exposed.[17]

The Warren analysis of the First Amendment grievance against legislative investigation calls forth two observations. First, these are brave words. The criticism is put so strongly one expects that condemnation as unconstitutional must logically follow of the government activity which so chills the exercise of First Amendment rights. We shall return in a moment to why it does not. Second, the critique, although sensitive, detailed, and realistic, is curiously off target. It reads as if the committee questioning went primarily to unorthodox views that the witness had and did not wish to make public—that he was a single Taxer, believed in astrology, or was convinced that the earth was flat. There is no attention to the fact that the questioning which for years had been under challenge went simply to whether or not the witness was or had been a member of the Communist Party. The ambiguity of such membership, which one side saw as political and the other as conspiratorial, was surely the root difficulty. The Chief Justice makes no effort to deal with this difficulty and his admirable strictures on legislative investigations thus take on some of the abstract quality that marred the opinions of Justice Black in the obscenity cases. It will be the achievement of the Court during the next decade, in cases like *Scales, Elfbrandt, Keyishian, Robel* and *Aptheker,*[18] to confront the ambiguity of being a Communist in the United States. But the opinion in *Watkins*—a decision announced on the same day as *Yates*[19]—makes no effort to engage and wrestle with this critical ambiguity.

This weakness in Warren's analysis suggests a paradox that has hobbled efforts to mount a First Amendment argument against legislative investigations. The opinions that most clearly and persuasively need protection are in the nature of things opinions not at all likely to trigger the damaging public reaction if disclosed; and conversely, the belief or association that would most probably trigger a negative reaction was membership in the Communist Party. It may well be that it is only in the NAACP membership cases that the law has had occasion to deal with compulsory disclosure of innocent, but nevertheless highly prejudicial, association.

Why, to return to the first point of observation, given the stringency of the Warren criticisms, does the Court decline to hold there has been an abridgement of First Amendment rights? It is explicit about its mode of analysis. What is called for is "accommodating" the two competing interests, the witness's interest in privacy and Congress's interest in information. Striking the proper accommodation, observes Warren, is "an arduous and delicate task for any court."[20] He adds: "The critical element is the existence of, and the weight to be ascribed to, the interest of the Congress in demanding disclosures from an unwilling witness."[21] Once again, however, the opinion defaults just as it becomes interesting. There is no effort to explain why the "accommodation" in this case comes out favorably to the government, if only the pertinency of the question is made clear to the witness. In the end, one suspects that the "delicate" task of accommodation reduces to comparing in gross the legislative need for information about Communism to this witness's need for privacy and security in selecting his associations. And since the accommodation comes down on the government side in this case, it will presumably do so in any case where the inquiry concerns Communism.

The Court's failure to concern itself with the facts of the case before it in evaluating the strength of the congressional need for information is especially troubling, because *Watkins* had so explicitly put into issue the propriety of compelling a witness to inform on *the past connections of others*. The Court might have paused to confront how strong the need for information as to *past* ties really was. Indeed, it may well be that the chief problem during the anti-Communist decades was the problem of the ex-Communist being judged publicly, to borrow Warren's phrase, "by current standards."[22] And it is almost certainly true that the chief business of committees like HUAC was to stir up curiosity about former Party members who were poignantly vulnerable to the mood of the day.[23]

There is one last strand to Warren's First Amendment dicta. The defendant had argued strenuously that the chilling effects on speech and association were not in this case a by-product of government action for another purpose but were "the sole purpose of the inquiry"[24]; and he had quoted several passages from congressional sources in support of the thesis that the committee conceived its role to be disciplining Communism by focusing "the spotlight of publicity" upon it.[25] The chief thrust of the argument is that legislative committees lack the power to compel testimony for this purpose. The argument does not and need not reach the question of whether the government through some other agency or means has the power to discipline and control Communism by compulsory disclosure, a matter which will finally surface in *Communist Party v. Subversive Activities Control Board*[26] in 1961 and be answered affirmatively.

Chief Justice Warren stoutly agrees with the defendant's major premise: "We have no doubt that there is no congressional power to expose for the sake of exposure."[27] Further, in a helpful footnote he puts to rest the notion that Congress has, in Woodrow Wilson's phrase, "an informing function."[28] It might make sense to inform public opinion about the dangers of domestic Communism, but Congress has no power to do so through the device of the investigating committee. The informing function is limited, the footnote states, to publicizing "corruption, maladministration or inefficiency in agencies of the Government."[29] Presumably the Watergate hearings were an instance. This is an important point. Throughout its existence HUAC, and comparable committees, have justified to the public their use of power to compel testimony of private individuals on a premise which the Court has explicitly rejected.

Once again, however, the opinion does not draw the expected conclusion. The Court will not undertake serious inquiry into the actual motives of Congress:

But a solution to our problem is not to be found in testing the motives of committee members for this purpose. Such is not our function. Their motives alone would not vitiate an investigation which had been instituted by a House of Congress if that assembly's legislative purpose is being served.[30]

It is instructive to lay *Watkins* alongside *McGrain v. Daugherty.* Thirty years have elapsed. There has been repeated and intense public controversy over the conduct of congressional investigating committees. Senator McCarthy, armed with nothing more than committee subpoena power, did for a time "bestride the narrow world like a colossus." Furthermore, a First Amendment grievance has been added to the arsenal of criticism. Chief Justice Warren is openly and vigorously critical of committee performance and decides the case in favor of the witness. Yet in the end the legal architecture has not really changed much. The reality of the committee performance and purpose remains irrelevant. Its negative impact on individuals is a by-product of government action for another purpose. And the Court will not permit inquiry into official motivation.

We should also note the complex analogy that is evolving between investigation cases like *Watkins* and membership cases like *Elfbrandt, Keyishian, Robel,* and *Aptheker.* Although the sanction in investigation cases is somewhat different—it is imposed by private reaction as well as government action—such cases resemble the partial sanction cases in two essential respects: The sanctions are partial; and they are ostensibly not sanctions at all but by-products of government action directed to another purpose. The question which is slowly forming is this: If the government is to be limited in barring people from public employment to a narrow definition of nexus to Communist activities, should there not be an analogous limiting of its power to *inquire into* the degree of nexus of a given individual to Communist activities?

Sweezy v. New Hampshire

Considerable light is thrown on the Court's difficulties in finding a satisfactory method for disposition of these legislative investigation cases by *Sweezy v. New Hampshire,*[31] a companion case to *Watkins* handed down on the same day, June 17, 1957. Once again the witness wins, but, as in *Rumely* and *Watkins,* the Court declines to place the decision on First Amendment grounds. Ironically, it is Justices Frankfurter and Harlan, concurring in the result, who invoke the First Amendment, while Chief Justice Warren and Justices Black, Douglas, and Brennan eschew the First Amendment rationale and place their decision, in another opinion by the Chief Justice, on procedural grounds. Justice Whittaker does not participate, and Justices Clark and Burton dissent.

Sweezy puts a new fact situation—one that falls outside the familiar pattern of resistance to the standard question about Party membership. The controversy involves a legislative investigation at the state level. In 1951 New Hampshire had enacted an elaborate law against subversion. In 1953 the state legislature adopted a resolution empowering the Attorney General to investigate whether the law had been complied with or whether there were still "subversives" at large in the state and to report legislative recommendations back to it. The state court treated this scheme as "a one-man legislative committee." In the course of his investigation the Attorney General subpoenaed Paul Sweezy, a well-known Marxist writer who had taught at several universities. Sweezy made a very atypical witness.[32] He denied he was a Party member, and his reputation, which was not inconsiderable, depended on his sophisticated support for Marxist theory. There could be no embarrassment to him in exposure of his "unorthodox, unpopular views." At the outset of the hearing he declared that he would not answer questions which were not pertinent to the subject under inquiry or which violated his First Amendment rights.

The Attorney General subjected Sweezy to extensive inquiry about his past, his views, and his associations. Sweezy answered a majority of the questions but finally balked at three of them. He was brought by the Attorney General before a court and when he continued to refuse to answer the questions was held in contempt. The contempt was upheld by the state supreme court. The three questions he refused to answer were: whether he believed in Communism; what his activities and those of others, including his wife, were in the Progressive Party; and what the subject matter of a lecture he had given upon invitation at Dartmouth College was. The question about belief in Communism appears to have dropped out of the area of contention by the time the case reached the Supreme Court, and the justices confine their discussion to the other two questions—about activities in the Progressive Party and the content of the Dartmouth lecture.

The case thus involved atypical questions posed by an atypical means to an atypical witness. The Warren opinion for the Court finds its clue for decision in the atypicality of the means; the Frankfurter concurring opinion finds its clue in the atypicality of the questions.

Chief Justice Warren focuses on the breadth of discretion left to the Attorney General to decide what to subject to compulsory inquiry in the name of the legislature. He notes that one line of questioning invaded political freedom and the other invaded academic freedom, two sensitive and deeply valued areas of freedom in American life, but that the New Hampshire Supreme Court had nevertheless found that the abridgement of these freedoms was justified by "the legislature's judgment, expressed by its authorizing resolution, that there exists a potential menace from those who would overthrow the government by force and violence."[33] The state court concluded, writes Warren, "that the need for the legislature to be informed on so elemental a subject . . . outweighed the deprivation of constitutional rights that

occurred in the process."[34] He expresses grave doubt that this strikes
the proper balance of the competing interests but then quickly shifts
grounds so as to avoid judicial review of the balance struck by the state
court: "But we do not need to reach such fundamental questions of
state power to decide this case."[35]

Instead, the Chief Justice finds the constitutional flaw in the circumstance that the balancing was done entirely by the Attorney General. It did not reflect judgment or deliberation by the state
legislature, which, by giving the Attorney General "such a sweeping
and uncertain mandate," had "insulated itself."[36] The Supreme
Court cannot, on these facts, be certain that the legislature "wanted"
the information the Attorney General is bent on exacting from the
witness on its behalf. Hence "the judiciary are thus placed in an
untenable position."[37] There is no way of telling what should be
placed on the state side of the scales. The Court will give great deference to the state's judgment of its need for information, even when
precious rights are endangered by compulsory inquiry, but the state
legislature must take "responsibility"[38] for the judgment.

The upshot is that the Warren opinion carefully withholds judgment on whether the state legislature would be entitled to compel
disclosure of this same information, had it asked for it directly. Moreover, a parallel difficulty had arisen in *Watkins* with respect to the
breadth of the HUAC authorizing resolution which gave great discretion to the committee itself to determine what to investigate. In the
end, Warren had elected not to place the *Watkins* decision on the
parallel failure to have a serious judgment from Congress as to the
need for the information about *past* Communist ties. Yet the only
difference is that in the one case it is the Attorney General and in the
other it is a few members of the House who are giving the final
judgment on the state's need for the particular information. The
inference is very strong that the Chief Justice wishes to see this as the
crucial difference. He thus bequeaths us in *Sweezy*, despite its promis-
ing fact situation, a decision which almost certainly can have little or
no precedential value, for it rests on the odd circumstance that the
Attorney General was functioning as a one-man legislative committee.

Justice Frankfurter's concurring opinion effectively impeaches
the rationale put forward by the Chief Justice. The Supreme Court,
he argues, must accept as final the state court's judgment that the
inquiries to Sweezy came within the authorization to the state Attorney General. It can no more review this point than it can alter a state
court's construction of its own statute. Thus, the Court must judge

the matter "as though the whole body of the legislature had demanded the information of petitioner."[39]

Given this formidable logical difficulty, the mystery of the *Sweezy* case is why Chief Justice Warren and Justices Black, Douglas, and Brennan, the most sensitive protectors of First Amendment rights on the Court, should have stubbornly held to their narrow rationale and declined to join Justices Frankfurter and Harlan in a rationale squarely limiting congressional investigations on First Amendment grounds. The answer, I surmise, resides in the distinction Justices Frankfurter and Harlan see between the facts in *Watkins* and the facts in *Sweezy,* a distinction drawn at the expense of cases involving compulsory inquiry into membership in the Communist Party.

Since Justice Frankfurter finds the narrow Warren rationale for protecting the witness so inadequate, he is forced to broader grounds and must confront the task Warren so carefully sidestepped: a review of whether the state court had balanced the interests properly. He takes up the questioning about the lecture first. The symbol of the government solemnly inquiring into what was taught at a university is too much for him. The state court had offered three reasons for inquiring into Sweezy's Dartmouth lecture as a potential instance of teaching the violent overthrow of New Hampshire: that he was avowedly a socialist; that he had a record of association with front groups cited on the Attorney General's list or by HUAC; and that he had co-authored an article which, while deploring violence, expressed the view that it was less to be deplored when used by the Soviet Union than when used by capitalist countries. Justice Frankfurter concludes: "When weighed against the grave harm resulting from governmental intrusion into the intellectual life of a university, such justification for compelling a witness to discuss the contents of his lecture appears grossly inadequate."[40] He goes on to praise with considerable eloquence the importance for a free society of free universities, and quotes at length from a report on the imperiled state of South African universities. He grants that the situation in New Hampshire is in no sense comparably grave, but adds: "in these matters of the spirit inroads on legitimacy must be resisted at their incipiency. This kind of evil grows by what it is allowed to feed on."[41]

The passage is important. In Frankfurter's view, the coercive questioning of Sweezy about his lecture is unconstitutional not because it will humiliate him in public and invite hostile reaction to him. The questioning is bad because it is conducted under government aegis and presupposes some legitimate interest on the part of the government in what is taught at universities, some jurisdiction. Once again, as in *Rumely* and *Stanley v. Georgia,* we encounter the notion of a core intellectual privacy.

Yet the Frankfurter analysis reserves the possibility that there could be circumstances under which the question of what was taught in a lecture at a university would be proper in pursuit of those urging the overthrow of the government by force and violence. The flaw in this instance is that it is so unlikely that the questioning of Paul Sweezy would turn up anything, and correlatively, it was so likely it would be read by others as a concern on the part of the state with socialist doctrines.

The privacy note is even stronger in Justice Frankfurter's discussion of the other questions put to Sweezy, those concerning the Progressive Party, which under Henry Wallace had been a salient force in the 1948 Presidential Election. The New Hampshire court found justification for this intrusion into political freedom in reports that Communists had been active in the formation and direction of the Progressive Party. Justice Frankfurter is indignant: "In the political realm, as in the academic, thought and action are presumptively immune from inquisition by political authority."[42] He notes the analogy of the deep tradition of the privacy of the secret ballot and argues: "For a citizen to be made to forego even a part of so basic a liberty as his political autonomy, the subordinating interest of the State must be compelling."[43] Then in a memorably angry passage he rejects out of hand the New Hampshire court's balancing of the competing interests:

But the inviolability of privacy belonging to a citizen's political loyalties has so overwhelming an importance to the well-being of our kind of society that it cannot be constitutionally encroached upon on the basis of so meagre a countervailing interest of the State as may be argumentatively found in the remote, shadowy threat to the security of New Hampshire allegedly presented in the origins and contributing elements of the Progressive Party and in petitioner's relations to these.[44]

The Frankfurter-Harlan affirmance of the First Amendment as a limit to legislative inquiry is thus dramatic and eloquent. Why then did Chief Justice Warren and Justices Black, Douglas, and Brennan decline to join it? The answer is found in a further passage in Frankfurter's opinion where he addresses in passing the question of why it is permissible to intrude upon political privacy with questions about membership in the Communist Party. The Communist Party is different:

> Whatever, on the basis of massive proof and in the light of history, of which the Court may well take judicial notice, be the justification for not regarding the Communist Party as a conventional political party, no such justification has been afforded in regard to the Progressive Party.[45]

The state has a "compelling" interest in information about the Communist Party; hence compulsory inquiry directed to that end outweighs the individual's interest in political or academic privacy or in avoiding stimuli to self-censorship. But the moment, as in *Rumely* or in *Sweezy*, we are outside the Communist orbit, the balance shifts dramatically and the questioning collides with the First Amendment.

The answer, although blunt and clear, leaves some puzzles. The status of the Party, on which so much now depends, has never been officially adjudicated; that will not happen until the *SACB* case in 1961. Justice Frankfurter, however, tells us that the matter has been taken care of by judicial notice. Moreover, if political privacy is so inviolate, there are the nagging ambiguities in any given case about the quality of membership in the Party. If it was grossly inappropriate to ask Sweezy the topic of his lecture, might it not also be inappropriate to ask a witness whether he was a member of the Party?

The Warren, Black, Douglas, Brennan strategy is, I think, now apparent. Justices Frankfurter and Harlan are willing to buy First Amendment protection for Sweezy by distinguishing his case sharply from *Watkins* and other Communist-tie cases. They will concede that there is no First Amendment problem present when Communism is under inquiry. The other four justices, I suspect, are unwilling to make such a concession; they are not ready to give up altogether on the First Amendment possibilities even in the Communist cases. Their strategy is thus to protect the witness by means of procedural safeguards, while saving the First Amendment challenge for some later day.

Barenblatt v. United States

The First Amendment considerations that have emerged by degrees as we have moved from the construction tactic in *Rumely* to the dicta in *Watkins* to the Frankfurter-Harlan concurring opinion in *Sweezy* are finally confronted by the full Court in *Barenblatt v. United States*[46] in

1959.[47] For the first time the Court renders a decision squarely on the First Amendment challenge. Unfortunately, the answer is in the negative: There is no First Amendment infirmity in legislative investigations into Communism. Thus, the cautious strategy of Chief Justice Warren and Justices Black, Douglas, and Brennan of marking time with procedural protections until some later day backfires. The "later day" arrives too soon, and the four find themselves in dissent where they now openly rest their objections on the First Amendment grounds they had so carefully eschewed in *Sweezy*.

A deep division emerges in the Court. Although the high point of HUAC has already passed by the time *Barenblatt* is decided, the problem of disciplining congressional investigations obviously remains important and intense for the justices. *Barenblatt* provides the occasion for a classic debate between those "friendly adversaries," Justice Harlan and Justice Black. The former writes at length for the five-man majority, the latter for the four-man dissent.[48]

The witness was a college teacher who had just finished a term of teaching at Vassar but was not so employed at the moment he appeared before HUAC. He refused to answer a series of questions about whether he was, or ever had been, a member of the Party, and more specifically about whether he had been a member of a Communist Club while a graduate student and teaching fellow at the University of Michigan a few years earlier. He explicitly based his refusal to answer on First Amendment grounds.

For our purposes, the importance of *Barenblatt* as a precedent is to be measured by comparing it not so much to *Watkins* as to *Sweezy*. There are, however, two issues from *Watkins* which require attention: the pertinency requirement and the status of the HUAC resolution. Justice Harlan disposes of each firmly and with dispatch; and Justice Black provides an interesting counterpoint to the Harlan discussion of each issue.

The outcome in *Barenblatt* makes clear that the pertinency requirement is a slender reed indeed, an absurd safeguard to endow with constitutional dimensions. At the opening of the hearing the chairman, taking his clues from *Watkins*, had stated that the committee was investigating "Communists and Communist activities within the field of education," just as it had previously investigated Communism in entertainment, labor, government, newspapers, and the professions. This "clarification" presumably gave the witness all the protection he was entitled to under the pertinency safeguard. The problem is not with this conclusion; it is with the *Watkins* conclusion, in which, it must be remembered, Justice Harlan joined. It is difficult to detect any difference between the awareness of Watkins and the awareness of Barenblatt as to what was going on. Both knew the committee was inquiring into Communism in America. There is to my eye no sense in which Watkins can be said to have had a grievance which the committee cured in *Barenblatt.*

It will be recalled that Chief Justice Warren's opinion in *Watkins* had contained formidable dicta critical of the breadth and vagueness of the authorizing resolution setting up HUAC. In *Barenblatt* the defendant seeks to reopen the challenge to the HUAC charter. He argues that *Watkins* should be read as having found the resolution unconstitutionally vague; that, in any event, it *is* unconstitutionally vague and the Court should now so hold; and, finally, that nothing in the resolution could be taken to authorize an inquiry into education.

Justice Harlan rejects each of these contentions. He states correctly that *Watkins* did not in the end decide anything about the HUAC resolution but only about pertinency. He makes no effort to defend the language of the resolution, but finds in the long legislative history of continued approval of HUAC in the context of its "unremitting pursuits"[49] of Communism in American life "a persuasive gloss"[50] of the resolution. It is simply too late in the day to challenge the wording of the charter. The committee's authorization is to be defined in terms of what it has actually been doing for so many years. Finally, he can see no basis for construing the committee's authorization so as to exclude inquiries into education: "the legislative history affirmatively evinces House approval of this phase of the Committee's work."[51] Thus, concludes Harlan, the questioning of Barenblatt was authorized by Congress.

Justice Black in dissent treats both pertinency and the HUAC charter as aspects of a single issue. For him the crucial flaw in the vague, broad charter lies in its incompatibility with any serious requirement of pertinency. The problem, as he sees it, is not whether the Court can piece together an inference of congressional intent and authorization from bits of legislative history, but whether the witness himself, by recourse to the charter, can get any guidance in exercising his valuable privilege to refuse to answer questions which are not pertinent. The vagueness of the charter makes it impossible, he charges, for the witness to exercise his rights intelligently. Implicit in Black's argument is the attractive norm that free men should not yield to compulsory inquiry an inch more than they have to. He also suggests that in an area as sensitive as this Congress cannot properly proceed by such loose, undue delegation of legislative power. If Congress wants such delicate matters inquired into, "it must be prepared to say so expressly and unequivocally."[52]

The majority's response to the First Amendment issues is almost exactly that of the Frankfurter-Harlan concurring opinion in *Sweezy*. Justice Harlan's framework of analysis is perfectly clear: Legislative investigations are limited by the First Amendment. The test of whether those limits have been transgressed "always involves a balancing . . . of the competing private and public interests at stake in the particular circumstances."[53] In this instance "the balance between the individual and the governmental interests . . . must be struck in favor of the latter."[54] Thus, "the provisions of the First Amendment have not been offended."[55]

Presumably political and academic privacy are entitled to the same high presumption of inviolability granted to them so eloquently in *Sweezy*. But that presumption is offset by the state's weighty need for information about efforts to overthrow it by force. Further, there is a high probability of discovering relevant and useful information about this, and correlatively, little chance of the inquiry being misunderstood as an intrusion into other matters, *if* the questioning is about associations and activities of the Communist Party. This is so, because, as in *Sweezy*, judicial notice will be taken of the conspiratorial nature of Communist activities. Citing the Subversive Activities Control Act of 1950, Justice Harlan notes "the long and widely accepted view that the tenets of the Communist Party include the ultimate overthrow of the Government of the United States by force and violence, a view which has been given formal expression by Congress."[56] Thus inquiries into Communism have a distinctive gravity which will invariably outweigh any infringements of valued privacies or any stimuli to self-censorship which the compulsory process might entail. The balancing formula, for all of its appearance of discriminating nicely among competing interests, reduces down to a blunt rule of thumb: The need for information about Communism outweighs any First Amendment concerns.

Justice Black challenges both the mode of analysis through balancing and the crucial premise that the Communist Party is different. *Barenblatt* marks a key engagement in his famous debate with Justice Harlan over balancing and the First Amendment. That argument is, I believe, narrower than many commentators have taken it to be. Both justices agree that when *direct sanctions* are employed—as in *Yates*, for example, or *New York Times v. Sullivan*[57]—the constitutional analysis does not reduce to a bland balancing of the government's interest in security against the individual's interest in speech and association. Moreover, Justice Black in *Barenblatt* qualifies his major premise by use of the adjective "direct": "I do not agree that laws directly abridging First Amendment freedoms can be justified by a congressional or judicial balancing process."[58]

After criticizing balancing in general terms, Black goes on to argue that "even assuming what I cannot assume"[59]—that balancing is proper in this case—the majority "mistakes the factors to be weighed."[60] In his view, the majority has both sides of the scale wrong. It has exaggerated the government interest in such information, because the possibilities of valid legislation touching speech and association in the field of education are so narrow. And it has radically understated the First Amendment interests. It has failed to acknowledge that what is at stake is not Barenblatt's individual right to silence, but, as Black so eloquently puts it, "the interest of the people as a whole in being able to join organizations, advocate causes and make political 'mistakes' without later being subjected to governmental penalties for having dared to think for themselves."[61] He adds: "It is this right, the right to err politically, which keeps us strong as a Nation."[62] Hence, he argues, the balancing has been so insensitive to the items on the scale, so lacking in rigor or precision, as to reduce to "a mere play on words."[63]

The Black opinion suggests another little-noticed complexity of the problem of constitutional challenge. If he is right as to how to balance, virtually *any* investigation by HUAC will be found unconstitutional. It is the existence and operation of the institution that shakes our sense of security in political tolerance. Justice Black is, in effect, arguing that HUAC is unconstitutional *on its face.* The majority, on the other hand, will apply the First Amendment to HUAC only on a case by case basis; it will not concern itself with the "sweep" of the institution in other cases not before it as it would were a statute under attack.

The *Sweezy-Barenblatt* analysis, which involves distinguishing so sharply between the Communist Party and other groups, leaves some uneasiness about two points: first, the casual determination by judicial notice of the conspiratorial status of the Party; and, second, the apparent indifference of the majority to the ambiguities of Party membership, which the Court will be so attentive to in other contexts, such as *Scales, Elfbrandt,* and *Schware.* Justice Black vigorously challenges the majority on both grounds. The distinction between the Party and other political groups, he argues, is tantamount to outlawry of the Party, a step we had refused to take overtly:

The Court implies, however, that the ordinary rules and requirements of the Constitution do not apply because the Committee is merely after Communists and they do not constitute a political party but only a criminal gang. . . . This justifies the investigation undertaken. By accepting this charge and allowing it to support treatment of the Communist Party and its members which would violate the Constitution if applied to other groups, the Court, in effect, declares that Party is outlawed. It has been only a few years since there was a practically unanimous feeling throughout the country and in our courts that this could not be done in our free land. Of course it has always been recognized that members of the Party who, either individually or in combination, commit acts in violation of valid laws can be prosecuted. But the Party as a whole and innocent members of it could not be attainted merely because it had some illegal aims and because some of its members were lawbreakers.[64]

It is a singular strength of the Black dissent in *Barenblatt,* as in *SACB* in 1961, that he asks the Court to confront squarely what it is ratifying. The Constitution may permit outlawry of a party when it becomes equivalent to a conspiracy, but Justice Black passionately urges that we should not tolerate various anti-Communist measures on an implicit, unexamined assumption that the Communist Party could validly be outlawed. We should confront the question openly, and if we would hesitate to outlaw the Party, then we should hesitate— even for the purposes of Congressional investigations—to treat it as an outlaw group.

Both the majority and the dissent address themselves to the issues of motivation so salient in popular discussion of HUAC. Justice Harlan briskly dismisses the challenge. He acknowledges that an absence of legislative purpose would make the balancing come out in Barenblatt's favor, but emphasizes that the Court cannot in our scheme of government undertake to scrutinize the motives of other branches of government. It cannot upset a statute which is otherwise valid because it was passed for bad motives; and it can no more upset for that reason an investigation which could be useful to lawmaking. Nor does he feel the Court is compelled on this record to doubt the conclusion of the Court of Appeals that "the primary purposes of the inquiry were in aid of legislative processes."[65]

Justice Black, however, mounts a serious attack on the committee's motivation. With neat irony to which Justice Harlan does not rise to reply, he too appeals to "legislative history," adding an appendix of quotations from committee reports to the effect that its purpose is "to expose and ferret out Communists."[66] There is also a sharp exchange of charges of blindness. To the Harlan remark that to treat the Party as an ordinary political party would be "to ask this Court to blind itself,"[67] Justice Black counters: "the Court today fails to see what is here for all to see—that exposure and punishment is the aim of this Committee and the reason for its existence. . . . I cannot believe that the nature of our judicial office requires us to be so blind."[68]

Justice Black argues that the committee is literally inflicting punishment on individuals, and that it intends to do so:

The punishment imposed is generally punishment by humiliation and public shame. There is nothing strange or novel about this kind of punishment. It is in fact one of the oldest forms of governmental punishment known to mankind: branding, the pillory, ostracism and subjection to public hatred being but a few examples of it.[69]

Legislative investigation as practiced by HUAC is thus a radically defective procedure because it inflicts punishment on individuals without trial and without judicial safeguards.

There are several issues at stake in this powerful rhetoric. First, is there a limit to how much realism a court can utilize? I suspect there both is and should be. The difficulties go beyond the bad etiquette of inquiry into official motivation of the actions of a coordinate branch of government. They go to the question of how the Court can *test* propositions such as those Justice Black puts forward, of how the parties can offer proof on one side or the other.

Second, suppose HUAC was explicitly authorized to do what Justice Black, and many others, insist it has in fact been doing—compelling witnesses "to testify as to Communist affiliations in order to subject them to ridicule and social and economic retaliation."[70] Would this be unconstitutional? Black says firmly that it would be when done by a legislative committee because of the lack of due process. Certainly it would also forfeit the conventional rationale for legislative subpoena power. But suppose it were done by a separate agency created for the purpose of inflicting shame and exposure on Communists. Presumably the Court would then be openly confronted with much the same issue it handles with care in *Yates* and *Scales* as to the First Amendment limits on the imposition of direct sanctions on radical political association.

Finally, there is a puzzle as to whether HUAC simply presents the question of compulsory disclosure or whether the grievance is that it is a "virulent ceremony" of disclosure because the committee context and trappings almost invite ridicule, shame, and retaliation on the witness. Does, that is, the affirmation of the compulsory disclosure of membership lists from the Party in the *SACB* case two years later foreclose any lingering doubts about the result in *Barenblatt?*

It risks oversimplification to reduce the Harlan rationale to reliance on the difference between the Party and other groups. He has not forgotten the precision he insisted on just a few years earlier in *Yates.* He distinguishes *Barenblatt* from *Yates* on the ground that there we dealt with criminal sanctions and here we deal with *investigation.* Investigation requires by its very nature a certain amount of leeway. One cannot, he admonishes, employ "a too constricted view of the nature of the investigatory process"[71]:

The strict requirements of a prosecution under the Smith Act, see *Dennis v. United States* and *Yates v. United States,* are not the measure of the permissible scope of a congressional investigation into "overthrow," for of necessity the investigatory power must proceed step by step.[72]

This is an important observation. It unquestionably reflects a firm distinction in Justice Harlan's perceptions of the various anti-subversive tactics. But given the risks to the witnesses involved in starting with loose, ambiguous, and damaging questions about undifferentiated membership in the Party, *should* investigation in this instance still be permitted to proceed step by step or should it be forced to ask its *target question* at the outset? Justice Black does not comment on this aspect in his dissent.

Although the Court will handle another dozen cases challenging legislative investigations in the period from 1959 to date, *Barenblatt* remains both the authoritative answer and the high point of analysis of the First Amendment issues in this context. The Court has not yet worked through to a stable solution of the problem, and it is difficult to predict how developments in related areas, such as *Scales, Elfbrandt,* and the bar admission cases, will affect legislative inquiries when the problem next arises. In a fashion somewhat analogous to its experience in the deportation, denaturalization, and exclusion cases, the Court has been unable in this special context to derive from the First

Amendment and its tradition an effective way of disciplining political intolerance.

The First Amendment issues posed by efforts to discipline membership in the Communist Party were, as we have seen, subtle and difficult when put in terms of direct criminal sanctions as in *Scales*. The subtlety and difficulty increase a dimension when they are posed, as in *Elfbrandt*, by the use of partial sanctions qualifying the grant of government privileges such as public employment. But the subtlety and difficulty become still greater when the issue of sanctioning Communist membership is posed in the context of legislative investigation, as in *Sweezy, Watkins,* and *Barenblatt*.

In one sense the Court has arrived at a point of considerable promise and power in its use of the First Amendment in this area. If we add the four *Barenblatt* dissenters to the two concurring justices in *Sweezy*, it is apparent that as of 1959 there are *six* justices—Warren, Black, Brennan, Douglas, Frankfurter, and Harlan—who would find that compulsory disclosure in the circumstances of *Sweezy* violates the First Amendment. That represents a considerable achievement. The promise and power dwindle, however, when the Court turns to compulsory disclosure of membership in the Communist Party. It has thus answered bravely the idiosyncratic non-recurring question, while answering shabbily the question that keeps arising and disturbing the climate of freedom in the society.

36

Legislative Investigation:
The Law Unable
to Work Itself Pure

In retrospect it is clear that *Barenblatt* marked the critical moment for the First Amendment controversy over legislative investigations. Over the next few years the Court hands down a number of decisions in investigation cases, but their effect is to underscore the controlling status of the *Barenblatt* precedent. Chief Justice Warren and Justices Black, Douglas, and Brennan, having just failed to carry the day in *Barenblatt,* now converge into a stubborn voice of dissent.

Uphaus v. Wyman,[1] a decision announced on the same day as *Barenblatt,* underscores the impression that the Court has become impatient with challenges to legislative inquiries into Communism. Another 5 to 4 decision upholding compulsory disclosure, *Uphaus* is valuable largely because of a remarkable dissenting opinion by Justice Brennan which puts as strongly as is possible the challenge to official motivation in seeking disclosure.

Once again the controversy is generated by the New Hampshire procedure under which the Attorney General operates as a one-man subcommittee to investigate subversion in the state. As in *Sweezy,* the witness is atypical and the inquiry does not involve direct questions about membership in the Party. Dr. Uphaus was the Executive Director of World Fellowship, Inc., an organization which maintained a summer camp in New Hampshire where it presented discussion programs, open to the public, on political, economic, and social themes. Various guest speakers came to the camp to participate in these programs. Uphaus testified about his own activities but refused to turn over to the Attorney General upon subpoena the names of those who had attended the camp in 1954 and 1955. He was found in contempt by the state courts for his refusal. When his appeal first reached the Supreme Court in 1957, the Court remanded the case for reconsideration in light of *Sweezy*. On the remand the New Hampshire court again affirmed, and in 1959 the case returned to the Court on the constitutional merits.

The majority opinion by Justice Clark is brief. The state court had effectively foreclosed the ground utilized by the Court in *Sweezy* by explicitly finding as a matter of state law that the legislature "did and does desire" the information requested of Uphaus. The case thus moves to the First Amendment grounds, upon which, it will be recalled, the Frankfurter-Harlan concurring opinion in *Sweezy* had so eloquently rested. If not a formal university enterprise, the World Fellowship summer camp is surely recognizable as a venture in adult education and would therefore seem to evoke comparable presumptions of privacy. But Justice Clark finds that "the academic and political freedoms discussed in *Sweezy v. New Hampshire* are not present here in the same degree, since World Fellowship is neither a university nor a political party."[2]

Clark then proceeds to balance "the public interests" against the "conflicting private ones."[3] He characterizes the governmental interest in information about who attended the summer camp as "self-preservation" and concludes, not unexpectedly, that this interest "is sufficiently compelling to subordinate the interest in associational privacy."[4] He is satisfied that "the nexus between World Fellowship and subversive activities disclosed by the record furnished adequate justification for the investigation."[5] Apparently he is persuaded of this because the record contains evidence that Uphaus had participated in "Communist-front" activities and that a number of the speakers invited to lecture at the camp were members of the Party or of various "front" organizations listed on the Attorney General's list. He does not discuss the difference between this kind of nexus and the charges of Communist influence in forming the Progressive Party which were held "too remote" in *Sweezy*. Compliance with the subpoena, he acknowledges, will result in the "exposure" of those named, but this is "an inescapable incident of an investigation into the presence of subversive persons within a State."[6]

The Clark opinion is thus untroubled by the First Amendment countervalues. It leaves the impression that the five-man majority no longer sees any issues in legislative investigations into subversion that require debate. And the silent concurrence of Justices Frankfurter and Harlan in this opinion has the effect of trivializing in retrospect their fine opinion in *Sweezy.*

The serious, sustained dissent of Justice Brennan highlights the weakness of the majority opinion. Brennan opens with a helpful summary of the structure of the problem of compulsory disclosure in the context of legislative investigations. He notes that the Court has only recently begun to explore the problem and that it differs from the use of direct criminal sanctions and from the withholding of privileges such as public employment. The dilemma is that modern government has a weighty need for information and hence for investigation, but exercise of the investigatory power will often have as inescapable concomitants adverse effects of "unwanted publicity" and "exposure" which will trigger self-censorship and hence inhibit the exercise of First Amendment rights. What is called for is the accommodation of the two interests "with minimum sacrifice of either."[7] Such accommodation requires scrutiny of the state's need for the information, that is, of the connection between the investigation and a "discernible" legislative purpose.[8] Scrutiny of this sort imposes a delicate task on a court; and this is especially so since in the nature of things "the specific interest of the State and the final legislative means to be chosen to implement it are almost by definition not precisely defined at the start of the inquiry."[9] Thus, Justice Brennan, in contrast to Justice Black in *Barenblatt,* accepts with some empathy the majority's framework of analysis and advances his argument against compulsory disclosure within that framework.[10]

The *Uphaus* facts enable Brennan to put the motivation argument sharply. In 1951 the legislature had enacted a broad sedition law which provided severe criminal sanctions for subversive activities; and in 1953 it had directed the Attorney General to make a "full and complete investigation" of violations of that law and to determine whether there were "subversive persons" in the state. Drawing on a report the Attorney General filed with the legislature in 1955, Brennan establishes that he conceived his purpose to be exposure of "subversive persons" and executed it accordingly, compiling a list of individual names with their associations. Since the legislature renewed the Attorney General's authority on the basis of his report, Brennan argues, it has ratified this use of disclosure and has thus officially defined the state's need for disclosure in this instance.

Brennan argues persuasively that the state cannot forever leave open the possible legislative use it might someday make of the information gathered. It must at least state a "discernible" use for the data in legislation. Otherwise it must carry the burden of justifying the disclosure solely for the sake of exposure. And that burden is a heavy one: Disclosure for the sake of exposure can be justified only, he argues, if it meets "the traditional standards that the common law in this country has established for the application of sanctions to the individual or a constitutionally permissible modification of them."[11] In this instance, he concludes, the state has utterly failed to meet such standards. Hence its need for disclosure for the sake of exposure is outweighed by the interferences with First Amendment rights that the disclosure entails.

The Brennan argument draws on detailed familiarity with the record in the case and is put with painstaking care. Justice Clark, however, does not really rise to answer it. The majority simply will not inquire realistically into legislative investigations into Communist activities. After *Uphaus* it is indelibly clear than any challenge keyed to the absence of a genuine legislative purpose will lose.[12]

The majority's disinclination to question official motivation is further illustrated by two 1961 cases, *Wilkinson v. United States*[13] and *Braden v. United States.*[14] Both cases arise out of hearings held by HUAC in Atlanta, Georgia and involve refusals to answer the direct question about membership in the Communist Party. In each the petitioner directly challenges the motivation of the committee. The five-man majority, relying on *Barenblatt,* flatly rejects these challenges. Chief Justice Warren and Justices Black, Douglas, and Brennan continue to voice angry dissents.

Wilkinson, which comes before the Court three years prior to *New York Times v. Sullivan,*[15] presents distinct overtones of seditious libel. Wilkinson had for several years been active in several organizations which were vigorously critical of HUAC and were openly seeking its abolition. He went to Atlanta in his role as public critic of HUAC to assist the local fight against the hearings. Within an hour of his registration at his hotel he was served with a committee subpoena. He claims that the committee called him primarily for the purpose of silencing its critics and that therefore the inquiry lacked legitimate legislative purpose and violated the First Amendment.

The majority, speaking through Justice Stewart, professes to see nothing novel in the circumstance that the committee has called one of its chief public critics and asked him if he is a Communist. Justice Stewart notes that the questioning of Wilkinson was prefaced by a statement by the committee's staff director which revealed the sub-committee's awareness of Wilkinson's opposition to the hearings and indicated that he was not summoned to appear until after he had arrived in Atlanta as the representative of a group campaigning for the abolition of the committee. Yet, despite the suspicions this raises, the Court refuses to go behind official motivation. Stewart repeats the formula from *Watkins:* "A solution to our problems is not to be found in testing the motives of committee members for this purpose . . . Their motives alone would not vitiate an investigation which had been instituted by a House of Congress if that assembly's legislative purpose is being served."[16] Nor does the fact that Wilkinson is engaged at the moment in criticizing government institutions and policy generate any presumption of privacy as in *Sweezy.* Presumably whatever he was doing, whether in politics, education, or public criticism, he could appropriately be asked by his government about his membership in the Communist Party. As Justice Stewart puts it: "we cannot say that, simply because the petitioner at the moment may have been engaged in lawful conduct, his Communist activities in connection therewith could not be investigated."[17] Further, argues Stewart, this is an investigation and the question is "preliminary": "Indeed, it is difficult to imagine a preliminary question more pertinent to the topics under investigation than whether petitioner was in fact a member of the Communist Party."[18] He thus concludes that Wilkinson's claims are "indistinguishable from those considered in *Barenblatt.*"[19]

Justice Black, dissenting, agrees that "so far as petitioner's constitutional claims are concerned, *Barenblatt* is 'indistinguishable.' "[20] But he draws a different conclusion from the parallels between the two cases: "Unlike the majority, however, I regard this recognition of the unlimited sweep of the decision in the *Barenblatt* case a compelling reason, not to reaffirm that case, but to overrule it."[21] Justice Douglas's dissent highlights the anomaly in American life of government being able to pursue its critics. He would narrowly construe the basic HUAC authorization "so as to exclude criticism of the Committee."[22] And Justice Brennan's dissent notes that Wilkinson had been called nineteen months earlier by HUAC and had refused to answer, that there could be no practical expectation he would answer this time, and "accordingly that the Committee's purpose could not have been the legitimate one of fact gathering."[23]

Braden involves much the same considerations. Braden and his wife had been active in the civil rights movement in the South and had been indicted in 1954 in a nationally visible racial incident when

Kentucky sought to apply its sedition statute to, as Justice Black puts it, the "events surrounding petitioner's helping a Negro family to purchase a home in an all-white suburb in Louisville." Braden had drafted and circulated a petition to Congress opposing a law which would reinstate state sedition laws by legislatively overruling *Pennsylvania v. Nelson,* [24] a 1956 decision in which the Court invalidated such laws on the ground that Congress in enacting the Smith Act had preempted the field. State sedition laws, Braden contended, were easily perverted locally into weapons against integration efforts. He was also thought to have drafted a petition to Congress signed by two hundred Negro leaders opposing the HUAC hearings in the South. Before the committee he refused to answer the question of whether "at the instant" of drafting these documents he was a member of the Party. The issues are precisely as in *Wilkinson.* The fact that Braden was engaged in petitioning for a redress of grievances does not insulate him from inquiry into his Communist affiliations.

Taken together, *Wilkinson* and *Braden* leave the impression that, in the Committee's view, criticism of the House Un-American Activities Committee is in itself un-American activity and hence a proper target of investigation. Also, *Braden* introduces a new note which will become stronger a year or so later in *Gibson v. Florida Legislative Investigation Committee* [25]—the use of committee inquiry into Communist influences as a way of defaming civil rights organizations.

As we have traced the course of Supreme Court adjudication in the area of legislative investigation, marked trends of decision have emerged. These trends suggest an inviting topic for study in terms of behavioral factors extrinsic to the compulsions of legal reasoning. Thus, during the six years after *Rumely* in 1953 the Court handles eight further challenges to investigations and decides all of them in favor of the witness. Then *Barenblatt* in 1959 introduces a sharp change in direction which is followed in *Uphaus, Wilkinson,* and *Braden.*

With *Deutch v. United States* [26] in 1961, the Court launches what proves to be a new trend, again moving in favor of the witness. If the 1959 reversal of direction is to be explained in part by the move of Justices Frankfurter and Harlan from the *Watkins-Sweezy* majority to the *Barenblatt* majority, the new trend is to be explained initially by the move of Justice Stewart, which suddenly transforms the solid four-man dissent into a five-man majority. Although it is tempting to reduce the issue to a matter of "either you like HUAC or you don't" and to see all formal reasoning about it as rationalization, we will resist the temptation and will pursue the possibilities of intellectual analysis of the hard problem of disciplining, on behalf of First Amendment values, legislative investigations.

Once again in *Deutch,* as Justice Stewart pointedly notes in the opening sentence of his majority opinion, HUAC is before the Court. As in *Barenblatt,* the witness is asked about his Communist affiliations while a graduate student, this time at Cornell. He freely admits his own membership and offers an appealing account of it, but he refuses to name others involved at the time. The case thus suggests two major issues: (i) whether the Court should continue to endorse inquiries into education or should re-examine the rationale in *Barenblatt;* and (ii) whether it should openly distinguish the situation of the witness who, as in *Watkins* and here, will be open and candid about himself but will not inform on others. The Court, although moved to decide the case in Deutch's favor, addresses neither issue but rather places its decision squarely on lack of pertinency.

The subcommittee that questioned Deutch was ostensibly investigating "Communism in the Albany area" and was focusing in particular on labor and industry, not education. The flaw in the Government's case, as Justice Stewart sees it, is that the chairman at the hearing and the Government at the contempt trial utterly failed to connect the questioning of the witness about his graduate student activities at Cornell with this definition of the scope of the hearing. The witness knew nothing about labor conditions or about conditions in Albany. Indeed, Justice Stewart seems more disturbed by the fact that Cornell is not in the Albany area—"we may take judicial notice of the fact that Ithaca is more than one hundred and sixty-five miles from Albany"[27]— than he is by the fact that labor is different from education. Having found this weakness in the prosecution's case, he notes, with a sigh of relief, that it is unnecessary for the Court to "reach the large issues stirred by the petitioner's First Amendment claims."[28]

The absurdity of having a significant matter of political freedom turn on whether or not Cornell is in the Albany area is highlighted by the dissents. Justice Harlan, in an opinion joined by Justice Frankfurter, argues that when, as was the case here, the witness does not question pertinency during the hearing, the Government should be allowed more leeway in connecting the question up at time of trial, and, as in *Barenblatt,* he emphasizes that investigation is an unfolding process which must be allowed to proceed "step by step."[29] The puzzle again is not so much over why Harlan finds the questioning pertinent here but rather why he agreed that it was not pertinent in

Watkins. In any event, he joins the geography controversy and, as a New Yorker, observes: "I think it fair to suggest that in common usage, at least among New Yorkers, 'Albany area' would be regarded as aptly descriptive of 'upstate New York.' "[30]

Justice Whittaker in a dissent joined by Justice Clark relies on statements the chairman had made to the witness as he was called indicating that there had been testimony about a Communist group at Cornell, that he had been named, and that they want to ask him about it. Whittaker thus comes perilously close to arguing that the "subject under inquiry" was whether Deutch was a Communist and therefore that asking him whether he was a Communist was pertinent to the subject under inquiry!

Russell v. United States,[31] decided in 1962, is an even more dramatic instance of the Court's penchant for protecting the witness while not reaching "the large issues stirred" by First Amendment claims. At issue are a series of contempt convictions growing out of investigations by HUAC and the Senate Internal Security Committee in 1955 and 1956 of Communist influence in the press. Some thirty of the thirty-eight witnesses called in 1955 and fifteen of the eighteen called in 1956 were past or present employees of *The New York Times.* Thus the issue which had been touched upon with respect to Communists engaged in university life in *Barenblatt,* engaged in criticism of government in *Wilkinson,* and engaged in petitioning for redress of grievances in *Braden* here emerges in its most dramatic form: Communists engaged in editing a newspaper. Is a legislative committee free to inquire into Communism wherever it finds it or are there some contexts in which First Amendment values outweigh the need for inquiry? A case could hardly pose this issue more sharply. Yet the Court, although it decides the case 4 to 2 in favor of the witness, chooses to remain silent about "the large issues stirred," and rests its decision on a technical defect in the indictments.

Only Justice Douglas, in a helpful concurring opinion, addresses himself to the dissonance for American traditions of subjecting the press to legislative investigation. He argues that the congressional power to investigate is coextensive with the power to legislate; that in view of the First Amendment, Congress has no power to legislate in this area; and hence that it has no power to investigate. "Since the editorials written and the news printed and the policies advocated by the press are none of the Government's business," writes Douglas, "I see no justification for the Government investigating the capacities, leanings, ideology, qualifications, prejudices or politics of those who collect or write the news."[32]

Justice Stewart, speaking for the Court, eschews such broad premises and instead utilizes a variant of the pertinency requirement. This time the focus is not on making the pertinency of the question evident to the witness at the time he is asked it but on making it evident by spelling it out in the indictment. The fatal flaw in *Russell* is that the indictment simply charges a refusal to answer "pertinent questions" without indicating the subject matter of the inquiry. Since there appears to be no complaint that the pertinency of the questions was not made clear to the witness at the hearing and since the indictment sets out the time and place of the hearing and the actual questions the defendant refused to answer, the grievance seems hypertechnical. Moreover, as Justice Clark and Harlan argue in dissent, it has no foundation in prior law and rests on a defect never before noticed in the numerous contempt convictions the Court has passed upon.

Gibson v. Florida Legislative Investigation Committee[33] in 1963 continues the trend of protecting the witness. Another 5 to 4 decision, *Gibson* discloses once again the extreme lack of consensus among the justices. There are five opinions in all. The majority opinion is by Justice Goldberg, who had recently replaced Justice Frankfurter, and is joined by Chief Justice Warren and Justices Black, Douglas, and Brennan. It is sharply contested by Justice Harlan in a dissent joined by Justices Clark, Stewart, and White. In addition, Justice Douglas writes a lengthy concurring opinion in which he voices a view of political privacy not fully articulated in his prior opinions. Finally, neither Justice Black nor Justice White is fully satisfied by the opinions on his side; Black adds a short concurring opinion and White a short dissent.

During the late 1950s and early 1960s, while the Court struggled with the problems of disciplining legislative inquiry into Communist affiliations, it was also dealing with the series of cases in which the South sought disclosure of NAACP membership. We discussed these cases in Chapter 19. The South's efforts proved to be so egregiously clumsy and hypocritical as to pretty much dull any excitement about comparing the two sets of cases. Yet the differences in decision are so pronounced that one cannot altogether quiet the suspicion that the true operating principle was: the Communists cannot win; the NAACP cannot lose. We note this again in order to focus on a special tension in the *Gibson* fact situation: It involves both Communism and the NAACP.

The case arises out of an effort by the Florida Legislature, starting in 1956, to obtain via an investigating committee the entire membership list of the Miami Branch of the NAACP. The Florida courts supported the NAACP's refusal to turn over the full list but held that the committee could require information as to specific individuals. In a subsequent hearing in 1959 the committee ordered the petitioner, the president of the Miami NAACP chapter, to bring the membership list to the hearing so he could inform the committee whether some fourteen named individuals were NAACP members. What makes the case interesting, and difficult, are the further facts that each of the fourteen is identified by the committee as a person who was a member of the Communist Party or of a "front" organization, and that the inquiry about membership is directed not at the individual but at the group.

An additional fact, however, introduces an awkwardness into this dramatic fact situation. The witness's refusal to cooperate with the inquiry is curiously partial. He agrees to answer "from memory" whether the named individuals were members and indeed he does so—he says he does not recognize any of them—but he firmly refuses to bring the membership records to the hearing. For this refusal he is held in contempt by the Florida courts. In upsetting the contempt conviction, the majority ignores the embarrassment created by the willingness of the petitioner to disclose. Justice Harlan, however, devotes a brief, acid comment to it in his dissent:

In effect what we are asked to hold here is that the petitioner had a constitutional right to give only partial or inaccurate testimony, and that indeed seems to me the true effect of the Court's holding today.[34]

Gibson proves to be a singularly frustrating precedent, because neither the majority nor the dissent can, within the legal traditions, find a way realistically to debate the true grievance against the inquiry by the Florida committee. That grievance has an element of novelty. Hitherto the argument for protecting the witness from inquiry into either NAACP or Communist Party membership was that disclosure of his membership would invite a negative response from the public. Thus the ceremony of disclosure could be said to have a chilling impact on freedom of association. In *Gibson*, however, it is unlikely that the fourteen individuals already designated by the committee as Communists or fellow travelers would be humiliated by disclosure that they were also members of the NAACP. It cannot be this fact of membership that the majority so urgently wishes to protect. Hence the case does not seem genuinely to implicate the values of privacy for NAACP membership. Yet the members of the majority argue as if this were the case. On the other hand, it is not true, as the dissenters suggest, that because the case involves Communism more than it does the NAACP, there is no grievance. The grievance, one would surmise, is the *defamatory thrust* of official inquiry into Communist infiltration of the NAACP. The vice is not the exposure of members of the NAACP to local hostility because of that membership; it is rather the innuendo created in the public mind by the fact of official inquiry itself, with its accompanying newspaper fanfare, that there is "a Communist problem in the NAACP" to inquire into. Moreover, if it turns out that these fourteen individuals were NAACP members, there can be little doubt that the committee will vigorously pursue further inquiry into the degree of impact they may have had on the organization. This, however, states a grievance in "sociological" terms which the Court simply cannot openly evaluate.

Presumably the justices are realistic enough to see what is really at stake. The majority are moved to protect the NAACP and to discourage similar forays in the future, but they must find some other ground on which to place their decision. They do so by finding a lack of "nexus." The dissent confines its rebuttal to arguing against the nexus analysis of the majority. It is thus difficult to discern how the dissenters view the unspoken concerns that appear to have moved the majority. Are they less persuaded of the reality or gravity of the harm to the NAACP threatened by the inquiry? Are they more concerned about "infiltration" of the civil rights movement? In any event, the ironic result of the Court's inability to directly address the underlying issue posed by the facts is that the *Gibson* opinions produce a considerable increment of new doctrinal analysis on the theme of nexus.

The majority opinion by Justice Goldberg exploits an ambiguity which has been lurking since *Barenblatt* in the idea of nexus between the state interest and the particular inquiry. On a close reading of the cases, it is apparent that the Court has been using "nexus" in two different senses. The dominant sense has been that used in the balancing of interests; it refers to the connection between the state's ostensible need for the information and the content of the question asked. In order for the state interest to weigh in properly, the state must connect the question up to the need. This is the step the state fails to make in the NAACP disclosure cases; it can establish no rational connection between the NAACP membership lists it seeks and the various innocent purposes it offers as the reason for wanting them.

Hence each time the state's interests are outweighed in the balancing. Similarly in *Sweezy,* as Justices Frankfurter and Harlan viewed it, the state failed to show a rational connection between its interest in self-preservation from violent overthrow and the questions about the Dartmouth lecture or the Progressive Party. They were, said Justice Frankfurter, "too remote." When the question is explicitly about membership in the Communist Party, however, the nexus problem is solved. For on the majority's view, there is always a rational connection between questions about Party membership and the state's need to preserve itself from violent overthrow.

There is discernible, however, a second related but distinct use of "nexus." Presumably not just anybody can be summoned and asked if he is a Communist. There is an element of harassment in the summoning; and the question, even if the witness answers it in the negative, carries a measure of innuendo. Hence there appears to be a need for a "foundation" for the question to the particular witness, that is, some reason for thinking the witness may have information about Communist activities. Justice Harlan spoke to this type of nexus in a casual dictum toward the end of his *Barenblatt* opinion. Referring to the fact that a prior witness before the committee had testified that Barenblatt had been a Communist while they were graduate students together at the University of Michigan, Harlan observed: "Nor did petitioner's appearance as a witness follow from indiscriminate dragnet procedures, lacking in probable cause for belief that he possessed information which might be helpful to the Subcommittee."[35] This sentence is carefully repeated by Justice Stewart in *Wilkinson* and again in *Braden.* The "probable cause" phrase appears to have been borrowed from Fourth Amendment doctrine; the idea seems to be that there must be "probable cause" for "searching and seizing" the witness by summoning him to the investigation.

Justice Black, dissenting in *Wilkinson,* saves some of his strongest words for condemnation of this form of "protection" for witnesses. The friendly witnesses before the committee, he charges, have in general been paid informants whose allegations are welcomed and are not subjected to any scrutiny; and in any event, it is all too easy to find people these days willing to call a person a Communist: "Every member of this Court has, on one occasion or another, been so designated."[36] He concluded: "If the mere fact that someone has been called a Communist is permitted to satisfy a requirement of probable cause, I think it is plain that such a requirement is wholly without value."[37]

Returning to the situation in *Gibson,* the first issue is whether the question about the membership of a Communist, X, in the NAACP bears a sufficient nexus to the state's need to protect itself by inquiry into Communist activities to outweigh the intrusion into associational privacy. On this issue the dissent seems, in light of the prior cases, to win the day. The topic of the inquiry is Communist *infiltration.* If that reflects a legitimate state interest, as *Barenblatt, Wilkinson, Braden, Deutch,* and *Russell* would indicate, then the nexus between the question and the state interest is established. Certainly it would seem that if X had been a known member of the NAACP—as Barenblatt had been a known graduate student at the University of Michigan—he could, under the prior precedents, have been compelled to disclose whether he was a Communist at the time. Is there a real difference between that question and the one asked in *Gibson?* The dissenters vigorously protest that there is not. Justice Harlan states:

. . . until today, I had never supposed that any of our decisions relating to state or federal power to investigate in the field of Communist subversion could possibly be taken as suggesting any difference in the degree of governmental investigatory interest as between Communist infiltration *of* organizations and Communist activity *by* organizations.[38]

Justice Goldberg does not, as I understand his opinion, contend that there is a lack of nexus in this primary sense. Rather, he shifts his attention to the second meaning of "nexus"—the lack of probable cause for "searching" this witness's mind with the question.[39] What Goldberg finds missing in the foundation laid by the Florida committee for its inquiry into NAACP membership is any basis for thinking the fourteen individuals were ever active or influential members of the NAACP. Hence there was, to borrow Harlan's phrase from *Barenblatt,* "no probable cause" for bothering the NAACP with questions about its membership. The foundation for the question was no better than it would have been, had inquiry about the named individuals been directed at, say, the Republican Party instead of the NAACP.

As a preliminary to asking the petitioner whether any of the fourteen were ever NAACP members, the committee had had two witnesses testify about the connections of the fourteen with the NAACP. Justice Goldberg meticulously dissects the ambiguities in the foundation thus laid. The contact of one of the two witnesses with the NAACP antedated 1950. The other witness loosely charged that each of the fourteen had been a member or "attended meetings" of the

NAACP, but there was no firm indication that any had done more than attend a public meeting and no indication of how long ago that might have been. Accordingly, Justice Goldberg holds that there has been an "utter failure"[40] to connect the inquiry about NAACP membership with any serious state interest in Communist infiltration.

Justice Harlan does not argue these facts, but he is incredulous that the majority is resting its decision on lack of nexus in this second sense of lack of foundation:

> Given the unsoundness of the basic premise underlying the Court's holding as to the absence of "nexus," this decision surely falls of its own weight. For unless "nexus" requires an investigating agency to prove in advance the very things it is trying to find out, I do not understand how it can be said that the information preliminarily developed by the Committee's investigator was not sufficient to satisfy, under any reasonable test, the requirement of "nexus."[41]

It is not clear how significant this new source of limitation on legislative investigations is. The probable cause requirement remains good law, but the Court has not had occasion since *Gibson* to comment on it. It would seem to apply to situations where the witness is asked directly about his membership in the Party, and thus in theory to be available to protect some witnesses from answering even that question. But this is not likely to come up often in real life. It requires a witness as to whom the committee has made a major error, whom it nevertheless does not excuse in executive session, and who when called in public would prefer to assume the role of vicarious champion of privacy and refuse to answer because of insufficient foundation rather than simply to deny that he had ever been a member.[42]

In practice it is likely that the probable cause requirement will reduce to another procedural protection for the witness which, like the pertinency requirement, is essentially trivial. For the reasons Justice Harlan urges, the threshold preliminary proof required that the witness will have relevant information will either be kept low or it will run afoul of virtually requiring the Committee to know in advance what it is trying to find out. Indeed, to vary Harlan's conundrum, a probable cause requirement taken seriously would seem to impeach the basic premise upon which legislative committees have been granted subpoena power. If the committee knows enough to justify its asking this particular witness, it already knows enough to inform legislative judgment, and there is no reason for it to pursue the exact truth about the individual case.

The formal debate in *Gibson* sparks an interesting set of larger reflections from Justice Douglas, which are countered in turn by Justice White in dissent. Douglas goes back to the first sense of nexus and vigorously asserts the grave potential for harm to freedom of association, if the government is permitted to investigate "infiltration" of unlawful groups, if it may inquire into Communism wherever it finds it. As he sees it, all groups however peaceful and lawful are suddenly *brought within the jurisdiction of government by the allegation that there is a Communist among them.* He does not believe that the questioning, once allowed, can be limited to the inquiry of whether particular members of the organization are Communists. He would therefore make absolute the privacy of membership in lawful organizations, and in *Gibson* there is no suggestion that the NAACP is not a wholly lawful organization. He states:

If, in its quest to determine whether existing laws are being enforced or new laws are needed, an investigating committee can ascertain whether known Communists or criminals are members of an organization not shown to be engaged in conduct properly subject to regulation, it is but a short and inexorable step to the conclusion that it may also probe to ascertain what effect they have had on the other members. For how much more "necessary and appropriate" this information is to the legislative purpose being pursued![43]

Douglas returns again and again to the theme that the inquiry into associational privacy, once allowed, will prove unlimitable:

But there is no showing here that the N.A.A.C.P. is engaged in any criminal activity of any kind whatsoever. . . . Whether it has members who have committed crimes is immaterial. One man's privacy may not be invaded because of another's perversity. If the files of the N.A.A.C.P. can be ransacked because some Communists may have joined it, then all walls of privacy are broken down. By that reasoning the records of the confessional can be ransacked because a "subversive" or a criminal was implicated. By that reasoning an entire church can be investigated because one member was an ideological stray or had once been a Communist or because the minister's sermon paralleled the party line. By that reasoning the files of any society or club can be seized because members of a "subversive" group had infiltrated it.[44]

If Justice Douglas risks overstating the possible harmful consequences of such inquiries for associational freedoms, Justice White in dissent risks ignoring them altogether. In his view, the inquiry *benefits* the organization by helping it rid itself of Communist influence:

I would have thought that the freedom of association which is and should be entitled to constitutional protection would be promoted, not hindered, by disclosure which permits members of an organization to know with whom they are associating and affords them the opportunity to make an intelligent choice as to whether certain of their associates who are Communists should be allowed to continue their membership.[45]

The vitality and polarity of the debate among the justices in *Gibson* is striking. It shows that after the long, arduous dialectic of cases over the almost forty years since *McGrain v. Daughtery* in 1926 the constitutional law governing legislative investigation has been unable to work itself pure.

In the aftermath of *Gibson,* the Court decides three more cases arising from legislative investigations: *Yellin v. United States* in 1963, and *DeGregory v. Attorney General of New Hampshire* and *Gojack v. United States* in 1966.[46] Each touches on an interesting aspect of the problem and in each the witness wins, thereby extending the trend of decision favoring the witness which began with *Deutch* in 1961 and ran through *Russell* in 1962 and *Gibson* in 1963.

As we have seen, the holding in *Gibson* might be regarded as a gloss on First Amendment balancing, or simply as a technical procedural rule defining the foundation the Government must lay before it may bother a witness with compulsory disclosure. *Yellin,* however, like *Deutch* and *Russell,* selects an unequivocally technical ground for decision and explicitly sidesteps any re-examination of the First Amendment issues, although urgently requested to do so by the petitioner. The Court upsets the contempt conviction by a 5 to 4 vote. Chief Justice Warren writes the majority opinion and is debated at length by Justice White. Justice Stewart, who had provided the key vote in *Deutch* and *Russell,* rejoins the dissent; and Justice Harlan firmly continues his long practice in this sequence of cases of supporting the investigation.

The tactic of the majority in *Gibson,* and especially in *Yellin,* of not seeking to reopen the First Amendment challenge is puzzling. Since *Watkins* and *Sweezy* in 1957 the four adamant critics of legislative investigation—Warren, Black, Douglas, and Brennan—have moved together. When outvoted during the next few years in *Barenblatt, Uphaus, Wilkinson,* and *Braden,* they articulated in dissent a forceful First Amendment position. The appointment of Justice Goldberg adds a sympathizer to their number, giving them a crucial fifth vote in *Gibson* and now in *Yellin.* Yet having regained control of the Court,

they revert to their pre-*Barenblatt* strategy of finessing the First
Amendment issues.

Once again in *Yellin* the setting is a witness summoned before
HUAC. A few days before he is due to appear, his lawyer wires the
committee requesting that he be permitted to testify in executive
session because "testimony needed for legislative . . . purposes can
be secured in executive session without exposing witnesses to publicity." The Chairman and the counsel of the committee are not in
Washington when the telegram is received, and it is considered and
denied by the committee's staff director, who is without authority to
decide such issues on behalf of the committee. When Yellin is called
he declines to testify on other grounds, principally the First Amendment. The Chairman cuts short an effort by Yellin's counsel to introduce the telegram into the record, and it is apparent that the
committee has never known of the specific request for an executive
session and has never acted on it. Yellin contends that the Committee
had violated one of its own rules which provides that when a majority
of the Committee believes that the public interrogation of a witness
"might endanger national security or unjustly injure his reputation,
or the reputation of other individuals," his testimony shall be received
in executive session in order to determine "the necessity or advisabil-
ity of conducting such interrogation thereafter in a public hearing."

Chief Justice Warren invokes the important rule that government
bodies and agencies are bound by their own rules, even where there
is no constitutional compulsion to have the rule in the first place. The
principle of such self-imposed limitation on sovereign power is an
attractive one and can apply in a wide variety of situations. The dissenters do not question this principle, but they do question whether
it can be validly applied to the situation presented in *Yellin.* They
argue that the rule was not intended for the protection of the witness,
that it was waived since the witness did not urge it as the reason for
refusing to testify, and that, in any event, it was not violated, since the
committee must have considered whether or not to call Yellin in
executive session when it first decided to subpoena him and since it
had a valid reason for believing it would not unjustly injure his reputation to testify in public because "he was a known Communist."

There are three things to note about *Yellin.* First, the central
grievance against the committee has arisen from its use of exposure
and publicity. The Court has been unable to confront this grievance
squarely. It will, however, consider it in the peculiarly oblique form
it takes in *Yellin.* Yellin's telegram went to the heart of the committee

procedure. If the committee could get the information it needed in executive session, what was the justification for exacting that information over again in public—not merely in Yellin's case, but in any case? Second, the committee's rationale for not calling Yellin first in executive session is revealing. Justice White in dissent endorses that rationale. As he puts it:

There was sworn testimony or other proof to back up the questions to be asked. There would be no "unjust injury" to the reputation of the witness Yellin. Publicly interrogating a witness if the Committee's foundation for its questions rests only upon suspicion or rumor falls within the area of unjust injury to reputation. But public revelation of the truth does not.[47]

Third, it takes considerable ingenuity and effort for Chief Justice Warren to maintain his rationale in the teeth of the dissent's objections. One can only puzzle again as to why a majority which felt so strongly motivated to protect the witness should have preferred this ground to the First Amendment.

In *DeGregory v. Attorney General of New Hampshire* in 1966 the Court does go to First Amendment grounds to protect the witness and in the process produces an important precedent on the problem of the ex-Communist. *DeGregory* confronts the Court for the third time with a controversy arising from New Hampshire's use of its Attorney General as a one-man subcommittee to investigate subversive activity in the state. In the mid-1950s the New Hampshire legislature had repealed the statute empowering the Attorney General to investigate subversives. Then in 1957 it had re-enacted a comparable statute. Taking the date of the new statute as his baseline, the petitioner answers all questions about Communist affiliation in the period since 1957, denying that he has had any. He refuses, however, to answer any of the questions put to him about affiliations prior to 1957 (e.g., "Have you ever been a member of the Communist Party?"). For this refusal he is held in contempt. The Court upsets the contempt conviction in a 6 to 3 decision, with Justices Harlan, Stewart, and White in dissent. In addition to the adamant four—Warren, Black, Douglas, and Brennan—the *DeGregory* majority includes Justice Fortas, who had recently replaced Justice Goldberg, and, surprisingly, Justice Clark.

The majority opinion is by Justice Douglas. This time he does not argue from inviolate political privacies, as he had with eloquence in *Gibson, Russell,* and *Rumely,* but rather finds by means of balancing that compulsory disclosure under these circumstances violates the First

Amendment. In his view, there are two reasons why the state interest is not sufficiently compelling to outweigh the adverse impact on associational freedoms which, he recalls, the Court in *Uphaus* had characterized as "an inescapable incident"[48] of the New Hampshire investigation. First, the inquiry is limited to Communism in New Hampshire, Communism as a national problem having been preempted by the federal government, and "there is no showing whatsoever of present danger of sedition against the State itself."[49] Second, there is, in Douglas's phrase, "the staleness of both the basis for the investigation and its subject matter."[50] How substantial can the state interest in such stale information be? "The information being sought," notes Douglas, "was historical, not current."[51] He thus concludes—in the idiom adopted in *Barenblatt*—that "New Hampshire's interest on this record is too remote and conjectural to override the guarantee of the First Amendment."[52]

Once again, Justice Harlan, writing for the dissent, gives voice to his perception that *investigation* is somehow different. It cannot be circumscribed too narrowly in advance:

. . . given that the subject of investigation in this case is a permissible one, the appellant seems to me a witness who could properly be called to testify about it; I cannot say as a constitutional matter that inquiry into the current operations of the local Communist Party could not be advanced by knowledge of its operations a decade ago.[53]

It is striking that the only two substantive victories over legislative investigations—the Frankfurter-Harlan concurring opinion in *Sweezy* and now the decision in *DeGregory*—have involved the New Hampshire procedure. Will the logic of *DeGregory* work when applied to a committee like HUAC engaged in investigating Communism on a national scale? Will "staleness" become a constitutional criterion of proper questioning, or will it always be possible to argue that inquiries into past Communist affiliations are relevant to a rational interest in current Communist activities? May the witness insist that the question "Are you now or have you ever been . . . ?" be broken into its parts? The New Hampshire procedure is so idiosyncratic, and by now so suspect in the Supreme Court, that one hesitates to invest too much significance in *DeGregory* as a general precedent. But it is placed squarely on First Amendment grounds. And it touches a genuine problem: For years the anti-Communist crusades indiscriminately swept former Communists together with present members. *DeGregory* offers hope that a way can be found to bar the pursuit of disclosure and exposure of past political mistakes.

Gojack v. United States in 1966 is the last word from the Supreme Court on the vexed issues of disciplining legislative investigations by judicial review. It is an appropriate last word, for it touches on many of the points the Court has established in this area. The contempt conviction at issue arose out of a HUAC hearing in 1955. Gojack had refused to answer questions about his Communist affiliations on the grounds that the inquiry was improperly motivated and that it violated the First Amendment. Initially the conviction was among those upset in *Russell* in 1962 for failure to state the subject of the investigation in the indictment. Gojack was then re-indicted and the subject under inquiry was set forth in the indictment as "Communist Party activities within the field of labor." The Court reverses this second conviction and, remarkably, the decision is unanimous. The opinion of the Court is by Justice Fortas.

The First Amendment resonance of the decisions in *Gibson* and *DeGregory* carried a suggestion that *Barenblatt* might no longer be so secure as a precedent. Indeed, the petitioner in *Gojack* explicitly asks the Court to "reconsider" the *Barenblatt* decision. But once again the Court eschews First Amendment analysis for more technical grounds. It repeats the familiar refrain: "Since we decide the present case on other grounds, it is not necessary nor would it be appropriate to reach the constitutional questions."[54] Not unexpectedly, Justice Black, while joining the Court's opinion, appends a note that he "would prefer" to reverse *Barenblatt* and hold HUAC unconstitutional.[55]

The "other grounds" on which the Court rests its decision involve two technical points. The first of these goes to a committee rule which requires that "major investigations" be approved by a majority of the committee. The investigation of Communist activities in labor is a "major investigation," but there is no evidence that the majority of the committee ever approved it. Hence, as in *Yellin*, the committee is without jurisdiction to compel testimony because it was acting in violation of its own rules. There is no indication that a committee need have such a rule, but once it has adopted the rule, the committee is stuck with it.

There are several things worth noting about the Court's handling of this apparently narrow issue. First, it appears that the Court has now developed enough technical requirements so that it can whipsaw a committee within them. Here, to avoid the defect in the indictment found in *Russell,* the committee flatly announces a topic of inquiry. But by committing itself to a particular topic it opens the possibility of pertinency challenges, as in *Watkins,* or of violation of its own rules in launching inquiry into a new topic.

Second, Justice Fortas is able to make use of statements by the Chairman and members of the committee indicating that their intention is to expose. For example, the Chairman had characterized the hearings as part of a "plan for driving Reds out of important industries," and had expressed confidence that once the committee had exposed witnesses as Communists, "the loyal Americans who work with them will do the rest of the job." It will be recalled that comparable evidence of motivation was urged in vain in cases like *Uphaus, Barenblatt, Wilkinson,* and *Braden* in an effort to show an absence of "legislative purpose." In *Gojack* Justice Fortas finds a way to exploit such evidence without challenging the principle that the Court will not go behind statements of official motivation. Since there was no evidence that a majority of the committee had formally approved this "major investigation" into the labor field, the Government sought to argue that such approval could as a matter of common sense be "inferred" as part of the widespread continuing investigation by HUAC. Presumably there is little doubt that a majority would have approved, had they been asked. Justice Fortas, however, counters that the actual statements of the committee members are so broad and so ambiguous as to legitimate purpose that they defeat any inference. He states:

We do not characterize these statements or appraise their legal effects. They are relevant here only to demonstrate the insuperable hurdle of "inferring," as the Government suggests, the authorization of the inquiry in the absence of a specific statement and the particularized authorization required by the Committee's own rules.[56]

The upshot is that if the Court is to follow the etiquette of not inquiring into official motivation, it must be afforded a specific official statement of that motivation.

Finally, Justice Fortas is also able to utilize the breadth of the HUAC charter itself, another datum appealed to in vain in prior cases such as *Watkins* and *Barenblatt.* The committee rule requiring prior approval by a majority of the committee, he argues, is particularly important in the case of a committee like HUAC:

The Committee is a standing committee of the House, not a special committee with a specific, narrow mandate. Its charter is phrased in exceedingly
broad language. . . . To support criminal prosecution under [the contempt
statute], this generality must be refined as Rule I contemplated.[57]

The second ground for upsetting the contempt conviction turns
on the fact that the investigation was being conducted by a subcommittee. Justice Fortas finds that the Committee had failed "to specify
the subject of inquiry that the Subcommittee was to undertake"[58]:

Neither the resolution nor any minutes or other records of the Committee
stated the subject matter committed to the Subcommittee or otherwise described or defined its jurisdiction in terms of subject matter.[59]

The subcommittee thus lacks the power to compel testimony, for
there has been no "lawful delegation of authority" to it by the parent
committee.

In effect, what Justice Fortas has done is to turn the effort to cure
the *Russell* defect in the indictment into something of a trap. When
the new indictment is drawn so as to state a topic of inquiry, the Court
asks sharply: How do you *know* that this is the topic of inquiry? *Who*
said so? There are two ways to interpret *Gojack*. It can be read as a
further sign of the erosion of *Barenblatt*. Since *Wilkinson* and *Braden*
in 1961 there has been an unbroken sequence of cases reversing
contempt convictions—*Deutch, Russell, Gibson, Yellin, DeGregory,* and
now *Gojack*. Moreover, *Gojack* is unanimous, suggesting that the dissenters have given up the fight and the legislative investigating bodies
like HUAC have fallen into universal disfavor among the justices.

Alternatively, *Gojack* can be read more modestly as indicating a
preference on the part of the Court for having the problem handled,
if possible, through *political* channels. It has been apparent that the
Court has found it difficult, as we have, to formulate a limitation in
First Amendment terms. In the end, the First Amendment harvest has
been sparse. There are only five cases to note—*Rumely, Watkins,
Sweezy, Gibson,* and *DeGregory*—and each admits of a ready explanation
narrowing its scope. In numerous other cases the Court has been
moved to intervene on behalf of the witness and has employed technical procedural points to upset contempt convictions. But the defects—lack of pertinency, failure to state the topic in the indictment,
failure to give the witness an unequivocal order to answer the question, failure of the committee to obey its own rules—have all been

readily cured, leaving intact the grievance against the committee process. Hence the attractiveness to the Court of finding some *general* way to limit committee excesses. The Court may be indicating in *Gojack* a desire to return the problem of disciplining legislative investigations to the legislature. The Fortas opinion emphasizes the need for a "clear chain of authority."[60] The investigation in *Gojack* is infirm because of two breaks in such a chain: There is no authorization from a majority of the committee and there is no delegation to the subcommittee. Topics of inquiry must be officially chosen and specifically delineated. What the Court is saying, I think, is that the balancing of the competing interests of the need for information and the need for political and associational privacy must be made, in the first instance at least, by the legislature. It is moving toward insisting on *political responsibility* for the course charted by legislative inquiry.

A summary of the elaborate body of law we have surveyed in the last three chapters cannot be tightly stated; it can only be sketched.

Legislative investigation poses a problem pushing against the outer limits of judicial review of government action under the criteria of the First Amendment. It may indeed be a First Amendment problem which the First Amendment cannot solve.

The Court has unanimously accepted the perception that compulsory disclosure of beliefs, ideas, and associations can prove prejudicial and consequently inhibit First Amendment freedoms. It is especially clear about this with respect to freedom of association. Two related ideas have emerged in the Court's discussions of the issue: the notion of inviolate or presumptively inviolate *privacies* like the secret ballot; and the familiar idea of triggering self-censorship because of the stigma disclosure might entail.

It is acknowledged by all that a legislative investigation could violate the First Amendment. We lack, however, a seminal example of such violation. The strongest instance thus far is furnished by *DeGregory*.

The basic framework of analysis is now firmly established.

(i) It is agreed that the power to compel testimony exists only in aid of the legislative function. There is no power to inquire into private affairs; and there is no power to compel testimony in order to "inform the public," at least where the investigation is of private persons and not government officials.

(ii) But so long as there is an official statement of the legislative purpose of the investigation, the Court will assume that any information sought is being gathered as an aid to lawmaking. The Court will not permit evidence to be brought in to impeach the official statement of purpose. This principle has been repeatedly tested and states what may well be a necessary policy for a court to follow.

(iii) Accordingly, the negative impact of compulsory disclosure in the investigation context upon freedom of speech and association will be evaluated by the Court as an inescapable by-product of government action directed to another end and not as a deliberate sanction.

(iv) It is not clear just how decisive step (iii) is. The *SACB* decision[61] indicates that exposure of Communists as a control tactic does not violate the First Amendment because exposure of something akin to political fraud is involved. If HUAC had been explicitly authorized to do what it in fact did, namely, to expose Communism in order, to borrow their phrase, "to place it in the pitiless spotlight of publicity," it would have been improper not so much because of the First Amendment but because Congress has no subpoena power for that purpose. (In the case of a state legislature, it would be up to the state to allocate the powers.)

(v) The critical step is the next one: Since any chilling of First Amendment freedoms generated by legislative investigation is an unintended by-product of legitimate government action directed to other ends, some accommodation of the competing interests must be effected. Hence the authoritative mode of analysis has been to apply a balancing test. There must be a "compelling state interest" shown to justify subordinating the political privacies. This need to justify invasion of presumptively inviolate privacy is often spoken of as the "nexus" requirement; there must be a rationale connection, or nexus, between the need for the information sought and a serious state interest.

(vi) When the disclosures involve matters other than Communism, such as membership in the NAACP or in the Progressive Party, the balancing test can work with considerable power to protect privacy. In the overwhelming number of instances, however, the questions have involved membership in the Communist Party. Here the state's interest in learning more about Communism so as to legislate intelligently in its own protection has been held to outweigh the witness's claim to privacy as an individual and presumably as a vicarious champion of the privacy of others. Hence in general there is no First Amendment obstacle to compulsory inquiry by a legislative committee into membership in the Party; and this remains true, although the context may involve a university, the civil rights movement, a newspaper, or public critics of the committee.

(vii) The Communist question must be answered in its *indiscriminate* form. There has been no insistence that it be refined to spell out conspiratorial Communism. Legislative investigation has thus been allowed to inquire into degrees of affiliation with Communism which the state under contemporary law would be powerless to sanction. This extra reach of investigation has been justified on the ground that it is in the nature of investigation to be open-ended and to proceed step by step.

(viii) Even when the question is about Communism, the First Amendment under a balancing test has imposed some limits. *Gibson* introduced the requirement that some foundation must be laid for asking the question of this particular witness. More important, in *DeGregory* the Court was willing to consider the staleness of the information sought in weighing the state's interest. The emerging rule appears to be that old "historical" information about Communist ties will not outweigh the interest in privacy.

(ix) As yet the Court has not found a way to consider the constitutionality of institutions like HUAC "on their face" so as to make the challenge less dependent upon the exact questions asked the particular witness.

(x) The Court's efforts to develop an analytic scheme for the problem has undoubtedly been handicapped by the circumstance that so many of the cases have involved a single legislative investigating committee, the House Un-American Activities Committee.

(xi) The case sequence is marked by two unusually steady factions among the justices. Since Justice Brennan joined the Court in 1956, there have been nineteen cases involving legislative investigations, from *Watkins* in 1957 to *Gojack* in 1966. In this interval Chief Justice Warren and Justices Douglas, Black, and Brennan have formed a solid bloc in unwavering opposition to investigations and have decided the issues in favor of the witnesses in all nineteen cases. Equally striking is the record of Justice Harlan whose exposure to the problem covers twenty-two cases, from *Quinn* in 1955 through *Gojack* in 1966. In this interval he has decided in favor of the power to compel testimony and against the witness in sixteen cases. These numbers are illuminating not so much about the predilections of the justices as about the structure and difficulty of the issue. In view of these two sequences, it is not surprising that the Court in the twenty-three cases since *Rumely* in 1953 has been unanimous in only four cases and has split 5 to 4, 4 to 4, or 6 to 3 no less than thirteen times. The unanimity achieved in the last case, *Gojack,* is thus a significant datum.

(xii) Central to the pattern of these precedents is the Court's perception that inquiries into affiliation with the Communist Party are different in kind from inquiries into any other political or intellectual associations. This difference is predicated in turn upon assumptions about the criminal nature of the Party. There are two disturbing features in the Court's approach: First, it has been willing to rest its knowledge that the Party is in fact different upon an informal judicial notice and has not required proof of these facts about the Party. Its procedure is thus in sharp contrast to the importance it attaches in the *SACB* case to adjudication of the status of the Party as a preliminary to compelling disclosure of its membership. Second, during the decade from 1955 to 1965 the Court in cases like *Yates* and *Scales* worked seriously at refining the nature and narrowing the scope of a Communist conspiracy sufficient to permit the application of criminal sanctions to it. None of that rigor and patience is transferred to the inquiry into the Communist conspiracy via the legislative investigation.

37

The Principle
of *Speiser v. Randall*

The legislative inquiry has been the most prominent form of official inquiry into subversive speech and association. But the issue arises in other contexts as well, and the constitutional evaluation may depend on nuances of the exact context. We turn now to cases in which the refusal to answer is in response to an inquiry undertaken as a preliminary to allocating a government privilege. Such inquiries differ from loyalty oaths in that they are not conclusive; the information sought is relevant to, but not automatically determinative of, eligibility for the privilege. And they differ from legislative investigations in that they are not compulsory; there are no criminal penalties for refusal to answer.

Garner v. Board of Public Works of Los Angeles, [1] decided in 1951, is an early example of the issues raised by this sort of inquiry. The law at issue required public employees to execute a loyalty oath *and* a non-Communist affidavit. Both provisions were upheld in a 5 to 4 decision, with Justices Black and Douglas in dissent. We had occasion earlier to discuss the loyalty oath aspect of *Garner.* Our interest here is in the Court's handling of the affidavit.

The *Garner* oath did not mention the Communist Party by name; it required the employee to swear that he was not a member of a group that advocated violent overthrow. The affidavit, on the other hand, called for an answer to the question of whether the employee was a member of the Party. In theory therefore an affirmative answer to the affidavit would not automatically bar one from employment. Justice

Clark, writing for the majority, relies on this difference in confidently dismissing the challenge to the affidavit:

> The affidavit raises the issue whether the City of Los Angeles is constitutionally forbidden to require that its employees disclose their past or present membership in the Communist Party or the Communist Political Association. Now before us is the question of whether the city may determine that an employee's disclosure of such political affiliation justifies his discharge.
>
> We think that a municipal employer is not disabled because it is an agency of the State from inquiring of its employees as to matters that may prove relevant to their fitness and suitability for public service. Past conduct may well relate to present fitness; past loyalty may have a reasonable relationship to present and future trust. Both are commonly inquired into in determining fitness for both high and low positions in private industry and are not less relevant in public employment. The affidavit requirement is valid.[2]

Justices Black and Douglas in their dissenting opinions do not address themselves separately to the merits of the affidavit, but treat it as subject to the same infirmities they find in the oath. That was probably the realistic view of the matter, since it was likely that an affirmative answer to the affidavit would in itself have resulted in discharge.

Justice Burton, however, while dissenting from the Court's affirmance of the oath, agrees with Justice Clark's distinction between the oath and the affidavit:

> Such refusal does not now present the question of whether the Constitution permits the City to discharge them from municipal employment on the basis of information in their affidavits. We have before us only the question of whether municipal employees may be required to give to their employer factual information which is relevant to a determination of their present loyalty and suitability for public service.[3]

Garner thus dramatizes the dilemma presented by these inquiry cases. Unwilling to impeach official motivation, the Court accepts the state's contention that the inquiry is not conclusive, that an affirmative answer would not automatically result in disqualification. Hence, in contrast to the loyalty oath situation where its analysis goes to the propriety of the substantive condition, it is limited to considering the propriety of the refusal to answer. The Court's dilemma then is this: Acceptance of the state's framing of the issue yields the anomalous result that the individual is punished more harshly for his refusal to answer than he would be for an affirmative answer. But suspicions that an affirmative answer would in fact result in denial of the privilege—making the asking of the question tantamount to conditioning the privilege on the execution of an oath—collide with the etiquette of not impeaching official motivation.

Speiser v. Randall, [4] decided in 1958, offers a means of largely resolving this dilemma and of doing so without directly challenging official motivation. In a creative opinion by Justice Brennan it launches a principle about the allocation of the burden of proof in inquiries touching First Amendment concerns that may prove germinal.

We have had occasion to look at *Speiser* before. It supplies an important precedent on First Amendment limitations on the allocation of subsidies. We are concerned with it here as a precedent on official inquiry. California, through its Constitution, had provided special property tax exemptions for veterans, but had also conditioned the granting of all tax exemptions upon the taking of the following oath:

I do not advocate the overthrow of the Government of the United States or of the State of California by force or violence or other unlawful means, nor advocate the support of a foreign government against the United States in event of hostilities.[5]

The petitioners refused to subscribe to the oath, and accordingly their claims for tax exemptions were denied by the assessor. The California courts upheld the assessor. The Supreme Court in a 6 to 1 decision reversed, holding that the procedure for implementing the exemption provision violated the First Amendment.

At first blush *Speiser* seems to be one more loyalty oath case. Viewed in that light, the one novel question posed is whether the constitutional principles apply differently when tax subsidies are being allocated. Justice Brennan, writing for the majority, indicates that the analysis is different in the subsidy case since there is no security risk calculus involved, but he stops short of deciding whether or not California could validly deny subsidies to those who did advocate violent overthrow. He is willing to assume *arguendo* that such a condition is valid: "For the purposes of this case we assume without deciding that California may deny tax exemptions to persons who engage in the proscribed speech for which they might be fined or imprisoned."[6] What makes *Speiser* relevant to our discussion at this point is the rationale he goes on to offer for nevertheless finding the California oath unconstitutional.

The critical point for Justice Brennan is that the California provision is not a pure oath. It is not conclusive. The pure oath procedure is not an inquiry. If the subject swears to the fact requested, that conclusively satisfies the condition set by the oath; there is no credibility or other data for the oath-giver to weigh. If it is later discovered that the oath was sworn to falsely, there may be perjury sanctions, but at the moment the taking of the oath in and of itself makes the affiant eligible for the government privilege. Under the California property tax exemption procedure, however, the oath was regarded as simply the taxpayer's assertion of one of the facts relevant to the determination of his tax and it had the same status as his assertion of the other relevant facts. The taxpayer was left with the burden of persuading the assessor he fell within the exempt class. As Justice Brennan summarized the procedure: "The declaration required by [section] 32 is but a part of the probative process by which the State seeks to determine which taxpayers fall into the proscribed category."[7]

Justice Brennan invokes a major premise of broad significance linking procedural safeguards to the protection of First Amendment rights. He suggests a new kind of balancing formula: "the more important the rights at stake the more important must be the procedural safeguards surrounding those rights."[8] Speech rights are of the highest importance; they are "essential to the workings of a free society."[9] It follows that procedures regulating them must carry special burdens. "It becomes essential, therefore, to scrutinize the procedures by which California has sought to restrain speech."[10]

When subjected to such exacting scrutiny the California procedure is found wanting because of the way it allocates the burden of proof. With only Justice Clark in dissent, and with Justices Harlan and Frankfurter joining him, Justice Brennan expounds the thesis that where matters are this close to the line between protected and unprotected speech, due regard for the First Amendment requires that the government carry the burden of proof both in the sense of producing evidence and the burden of persuasion. After observing that the line between protected and unprotected speech is "finely drawn" and that there is in litigation always "a margin of error" in fact-finding,[11] he writes:

Where one party has at stake an interest of transcending value—as a criminal defendant his liberty—this margin of error is reduced as to him by the process of placing on the other party the burden of producing a sufficiency of proof in the first instance, and of persuading the factfinder at the conclusion of the trial of his guilt beyond a reasonable doubt. . . . Where the transcendent value of speech is involved, due process certainly requires in the circumstances of this case that the State bear the burden of persuasion to show that the appellants engaged in criminal speech.[12]

Unless the burden is placed on the government, Justice Brennan argues, the risks of exercising First Amendment rights close to the line will tend to chill the freest exercise of those rights. It will, in brief, lead to self-censorship. He has full command of a genuine and fruitful insight:

The vice of the present procedure is that, where particular speech falls close to the line separating the lawful and the unlawful, the possibility of mistaken factfinding—inherent in all litigation—will create the danger that the legitimate utterance will be penalized. The man who knows that he must bring forth proof and persuade another of the lawfulness of his conduct necessarily must steer far wider of the unlawful zone than if the State must bear these burdens.[13]

The analysis is subtle. California had agreed to narrow the line of improper advocacy of violent overthrow to that set in *Yates,* but this concession does not save the law. The vice in a law inducing self-censorship is that, although its nominal censorship is kept within strict constitutional limits, the self-censorship will extend its reach into the domain of legitimate speech. Justice Brennan is very clear about this point:

In practical operation, therefore, this procedural device must necessarily produce a result which the State could not command directly. It can only result in a deterrence of speech which the Constitution makes free.[14]

Implicit in Brennan's logic is the principle that laws affecting speech are not permitted a penumbra of convenience in defining their targets as are other laws. The citizen is to be encouraged to exercise his free speech to its utter limits, up to the very frontier of legitimate censorship.

One might question how realistic this behavioral analysis is. Would people really alter their speech in order to avoid the risk of losing a property tax exemption? Justice Brennan is not called upon to speak directly to this challenge, but it is, I think, clear what his answer would be. It is not a question of numbers. It is sufficient that this law has the potential of inducing such self-censoring behavior. No chances for the exercise of free speech should be wasted. The California law has a bias, whatever its weight, which lies in the wrong direction. And the risk to free speech is gratuitous, since it can so readily be cured by shifting the burden of proof to the government. Thus this is not like other problems where the chilling of speech is an unintended but inevitable concomitant of government activity pursued for some other end: The self-censorship may be unintended, but it is not inevitable. Hence no accommodation, no balancing of competing interests is called for; what is called for is shifting the burden of proof to the government.

The opinion still has one final step to take. It must connect the improper allocation of the burden of proof to the petitioners' refusal to sign the oath. The step is an easy one. *Until* the state has satisfied its burden, it can attach no significance to the petitioners' refusal to sign; it can generate no obligation upon the petitioners to speak. Hence it cannot deny them the exemption because they refused to speak when they were not obligated to speak: "Since the entire statutory procedure, by placing the burden of proof on the claimants, violated the requirements of due process, appellants were not obliged to take the first step in such a procedure."[15]

Justice Clark in his dissent challenges the logic of the Brennan opinion at several points. First, he argues that it is by no means clear that California does place the burden of proof on the taxpayer. Without this step, of course, the elaborate edifice of the Brennan opinion collapses. Second, he contends that in any case there is only an "exceedingly flimsy"[16] difference between a conclusive oath and the "inconclusive" type involved here. In both the claimant has the burden of coming forward and making the requisite declaration: "So far as impact on freedom of speech is concerned, the further burden of proving the declaration true appears close to being *de minimis.*"[17] Further, he argues that, even if the burden is on the claimant, the state's interest justifies leaving it there, since we are dealing with the conditions the state may impose when there is "appeal to the largesse of the State."[18] Finally, he wryly acknowledges the originality of the Brennan approach by calling the shifting of the burden of proof because "the transcendent value of speech" is involved "a wholly novel doctrine, unsupported by any precedent."[19]

There is some force to the Clark dissent. The grievance Justice Brennan has responded to can scarcely be the one perceived by the aggrieved parties. Yet the Brennan opinion is a triumph of judicial statesmanship. He has found a way to avoid the impasse created by what is so often a stubbornness on both sides over symbols—the state stubbornly insisting on the symbol of the oath, the claimant stubbornly insisting on the symbol of freedom. *Speiser v. Randall* thus emerges as a prime example of what might be called the modern First Amendment case both in the complexity of its issues and in the subtlety of its analysis.

Even among those who applaud the result it yields, Justice Brennan's statesmanship may not be universally admired. It may seem too meticulous, too legalistic, and a failure to go to high enough ground. Thus both Justice Black and Justice Douglas, while concurring and joining the Brennan opinion, elect to file separate opinions. Douglas argues that *all* oaths—conclusive as well as inconclusive—are unconstitutional because they misallocate the burden of proof; and Justice Black launches a broad, ironic attack on the proliferation of loyalty oaths "for hunters and fishermen, wrestlers and boxers, and junk dealers."[20] *Speiser* is thus another datum on the interesting tension that runs throughout their many years together on the bench between these three most stalwart enthusiasts for the First Amendment—Justice Brennan on the one hand and Justices Black and Douglas on the other.

It is not yet clear what the reach of the *Speiser* principle about allocating the burden of proof will be in other situations. Although Brennan's language about self-censorship—"steer far wider of the unlawful zone"—has often been quoted in later cases, the burden of proof holding has not yet seen much use. As we shall see in the next chapter, an attempt to apply it to the inquiry pursuant to admission to the bar was abortive. But its potential generality would seem corroborated by two somewhat analogous developments:

(i) In recent years the Court in prior licensing cases has emphasized that a cardinal weakness of the prior restraint procedure is that it allocates the burden of proof improperly. In *Freedman v. Maryland,*[21] a 1965 obscenity decision, it relied on *Speiser* in holding with respect to a motion picture licensing system that the licensor must bear the burden of proof if he wishes to deny the license.

(ii) In the legislative investigation area the Court required in *Gibson v. Florida Legislative Investigation Committee*[22] in 1963 that, before a witness would be obligated to respond to a question, the committee must show probable cause for asking *him.* Although the context is very different, this requirement of a nexus in the sense of laying a foundation for the question seems akin to shifting the burden of proof to the government before it can obligate the witness to answer.

It appears, however, that Justice Brennan intends his point to be literally and precisely about the burden of proof. He thus rejects the analogy put forth in Douglas's concurring opinion that loyalty oaths, even when conclusive, offend by shifting the burden of exoneration to the claimant who must step forward and take the oath.

On the same day it announced its decision in *Speiser,* the Court handed down two other decisions in cases involving refusals to answer official inquiries: *Beilan v. Board of Public Education* [23] and *Lerner v. Casey.* [24] In sharp contrast to the analytic subtlety and liberal result of *Speiser,* these decisions are egregious instances of the Court ratifying what might be described as "tax avoidance tactics" in the pursuit of subversives.

Beilan involved a teacher who had taught in the Philadelphia public school system for twenty-two years. In June 1952 he was called before the Superintendent of Schools who indicated that he had certain information adverse to Beilan which he wanted him to affirm or deny. Beilan was then asked about a Communist Party affiliation dating back to 1944. He declined to answer without a chance to consult counsel. This was granted and he was again similarly interrogated by the Superintendent in October 1952. This time he flatly declined to answer. Some thirteen months later dismissal proceedings were initiated against him under the School Code for "incompetency."

The case presented three issues: (i) whether the question was constitutionally proper to put to a school teacher; (ii) whether it was in this instance improperly motivated in that after months of inaction the dismissal procedure was begun just five days after Beilan had claimed the Fifth Amendment before HUAC; (iii) whether the dismissal was not really for disloyalty, hence entitling Beilan to the special procedures of the Pennsylvania Loyalty Act under which the state carried the burden of proof.

The Supreme Court, again by a 5 to 4 vote, upheld the dismissal. Justice Burton, writing for the majority, mentions in a footnote that the Board had specified Beilan's invocation of the Fifth Amendment before HUAC as one of the grounds of "incompetency." He does not, however, find it necessary to consider the issue thereby posed. The state court had found Beilan's refusal to answer the Superintendent's questions to be sufficient evidence of "incompetency" to justify dismissal and had rested its decision on that ground alone. Hence Burton limits his consideration of the case to the refusal to answer the Superintendent.

Burton finds the case, so framed, to be easy. It is, as he sees it, controlled by *Garner*. Teachers work in sensitive areas and hence their loyalty is relevant to fitness; and Communist affiliations are relevant to assessing loyalty. Nor does it matter that the question relates to activities in 1944, since Beilan had cut off further questions and "it was apparent . . . that the Superintendent had other questions to ask."[25] There was no need to apply the Loyalty Act, since the Board had explicitly based the dismissal simply on the refusal to answer: "It found him insubordinate and lacking in frankness and candor—it made no finding as to his loyalty."[26] The case thus illustrates a "clever" new way to handle the puzzle of a refusal to answer in a proceeding where the questioner lacks contempt power—simply rename the refusal "incompetency."

Justice Frankfurter adds a concurring opinion which goes out of its way to endorse this shabby tactic. He admonishes against attributing to the State "determinations" it has not made. This happens, he tells us, "because persons who do not make distinctions that are important in law and the conduct of government may loosely infer them."[27] He professes to be unable to see why anyone would think a dismissal for refusal to answer about Communist affiliations had anything to do with loyalty when the state has said it did not. Once again there is interposed the absolute barrier to impeaching official motivation.

There are dissenting opinions by Chief Justice Warren, Justice Brennan, and Justice Douglas. Each focuses on a different issue. The Chief Justice argues that Beilan's claim of the Fifth Amendment before HUAC was "so inextricably involved" that the discharge cannot be evaluated without consideration of it, and that under the 1956 Court's decision in *Slochower v. Board of Higher Education*[28] a claim of the Fifth Amendment before another body cannot be used as a ground for discharge from public service. Justice Brennan argues that the case made more demands upon fair procedure than would a routine discharge for incompetency: "it is the simultaneous public labeling of the employees as disloyal that gives rise to our concern."[29] It was therefore constitutionally required that the procedures of the Loyalty Act be used before Beilan could be discharged under this degree of stigma. Also, as an offset to the Frankfurter opinion Justice Brennan has a few comments about "palpable evasion" and "transparent denials."[30] Finally, Justice Douglas, in an opinion joined by Justice Black, attacks the whole endeavor of screening the loyalty-security of public employees in terms of beliefs and associations as a violation of the First Amendment.

In *Lerner v. Casey* the petitioner, a subway guard in New York, is officially questioned under the State Security Risk Law about membership in the Party and he keys his refusal to answer to a claim of the Fifth Amendment privilege against self-incrimination. He is dismissed, under the statutory formula, as a person of "doubtful trust and reliability," because of the refusal to answer.

The Court, again by a 5 to 4 vote, affirms the state's action. Chief Justice Warren, Justice Douglas, and Justice Brennan extend their dissenting opinions in *Beilan* to cover their objections in this case as well. The majority opinion is by Justice Harlan and again reflects the Court's perception that a refusal to answer is very different from an affirmative answer and does not call for the same constitutional analysis.

Justice Harlan has no trouble with the extension of a security risk calculus to so routine a position as subway guard:

Nor can we say that it was so irrational as to make it constitutionally impermissible for New York to apply this statute to one employed in the major artery of New York's transportation system, even though appellant's daily task was simply to open and shut subway doors.[31]

The petitioner, however, argues that the dismissal was based either on an inference of Party membership "without regard to the character of such membership" or was based simply on the fact that he had claimed the Fifth Amendment. Justice Harlan finds both contentions mistaken. He was dismissed "because of the doubt created as to his 'reliability' by his refusal to answer a relevant question put by his employer, a doubt which the court held justifiable quite independently of appellant's reasons for his silence."[32] The refusal to answer which is alchemized into "incompetency" in *Beilan* is here turned into a "lack of candor which provided evidence of appellant's doubtful trust and reliability."[33]

38

The Principle
of *Shelton v. Tucker*

As we have seen, the Negro civil rights movement has had benign consequences for First Amendment doctrine. Moved by the Negro equities, the Court has on occasion been forced to high ground in order to decide the case before it with an appearance of neutrality and in the process has generated First Amendment principles of considerable scope.[1] The great example is *New York Times v. Sullivan*[2] in 1964, in which the Court, moved to protect the *Times* from a huge libel judgment arising out of its publication of an editorial advertisement sponsored by civil rights groups, undertook to rethink the relevance of the 1798 Sedition Act experience for the free speech tradition. Another instance is *Gibson v. Florida Legislative Investigating Committee*[3] in 1963, in which the Court, in order to protect the NAACP in a legislative inquiry, refined the degree of nexus or foundation required before a question could compel an answer. We turn now to a third illustration of the theme: *Shelton v. Tucker*[4] in 1960. In *Shelton* the Court, by a 5 to 4 vote, finds a First Amendment flaw in an Arkansas questionnaire required of all public school teachers. The realpolitik of the case strongly suggests that it is moved to intervene because NAACP membership was in reality at stake. The result of its intervention was the articulation of a new principle of some generality limiting disclosure.

Shelton is especially interesting because it is decided during the 1959-61 period when the Court was handing down a series of decisions, starting with *Barenblatt*,[5] upholding compulsory disclosure in the legislative investigation context. Justice Stewart, whose position so often proves decisive in these 5 to 4 cases and who wrote the majority opinions in *Braden* and *Wilkinson*,[6] this time votes to place limits on the official demand for disclosure.

The case arises out of a dispute over a 1958 revision of the Arkansas statutes regulating the conditions of employment of public school teachers. In Arkansas public school teachers do not have tenure, but are hired strictly on a year-to-year basis. To qualify, a teacher must annually file an affidavit "listing all organizations to which he at the time belongs and to which he has belonged during the past five years." Failure to file renders the employment contract void; and filing a false affidavit is treated as perjury. The petitioners refused to answer the question and accordingly their contracts were not renewed.

Two appeals were combined for argument before the Supreme Court, one from a state court proceeding and one from a federal court proceeding. While the teachers refused to answer the broad question, they did furnish some information. For example, Carr, a university professor, listed all of the professional organizations to which he belonged and denied ever being a member of any subversive organization. Shelton, another of the teachers, had been employed in the public school system for twenty-five years; at the trial below evidence showed that he *was not* a member of the Communist Party and that he *was* a member of the NAACP.

The issue in *Shelton* is thus arrestingly different from that in the other disclosure cases we have examined. In the usual case the information sought is focused; it is membership in a specifically named or characterized organization—the Communist Party, the NAACP, groups advocating overthrow, etc. Here, by contrast, the inquiry is on the face of the statute neutral; it is not explicitly aimed at particular organizations.

One additional fact is relevant, although it is not technically before the Court: the affidavit requirement did not stand alone; it was accompanied by a statute "making it unlawful for any member of the NAACP to be employed by the State of Arkansas or its subdivisions." The lower court had found this statute unconstitutional.[7] Thus it seems that the state's apparently colorless query as to how many organizations its teachers belong to was much more pointed than it appeared on its face. Once again we come upon the dilemma of impeaching official motivation. The strategy of Justice Stewart's majority opinion is to find a constitutional flaw in the question without relying explicitly on the connection of the question to the anti-NAACP tactic. The existence of the anti-NAACP statute receives only a brief, bland footnote in his opinion and does not figure in his argument. It is not noted at all in the dissenting opinions of Justices Frankfurter and Harlan.

The Stewart opinion is concise and well structured. He acknowledges that the state has a valid interest in information about the outside activities of its teachers: "Fitness for teaching depends on a broad range of factors."[8] Hence he concedes that this sets the case apart from other disclosure cases, like *Bates*,[9] where the state was unable to show a rational connection between the nominal state interest and the kind of information sought.

He takes as a counter-premise that "to compel a teacher to disclose his every associational tie is to impair that teacher's right of free association."[10] This is especially true in the present situation where the teacher's employment is at will and can be terminated "without bringing charges, without notice, without a hearing, without affording an opportunity to explain."[11] Moreover, the chilling effect of the disclosure is heightened by the circumstance that there is no assurance the information will be kept confidential:

Public exposure, bringing with it the possibility of public pressures upon school boards to discharge teachers who belong to unpopular or minority organizations, would simply operate to widen and aggravate the impairment of constitutional liberty.[12]

Having thus framed the issue, Stewart proceeds to resolve it by articulating an elegant First Amendment principle of economy. The vice of the Arkansas statute is that it is *so wasteful* of the teacher's associational privacy. He is forced to disclose many relationships which "could have no possible bearing upon [his] occupational competence or fitness."[13] Stewart then states the controlling principle:

In a series of decisions this Court has held that, even though the governmental purpose be legitimate and substantial, that purpose cannot be pursued by means that broadly stifle fundamental personal liberties when the end can be more narrowly achieved. The breadth of legislative abridgment must be viewed in light of less drastic means for achieving the same basic purpose.[14]

Justice Stewart then examines in detail such disparate precedents as *Lovell v. Griffin*, *Schneider v. State*, and *Talley v. California* and persuasively demonstrates that each is illustrative of his generalization.[15]

The *Shelton* principle introduces a new complexity into the balancing of interests. What is placed in the balance here is the degree of infringement weighed against the ease of achieving the state purpose "more narrowly." If it turns out there is no way of achieving the state purpose more economically, then the stage is set for the customary balancing of the state interest against the by-product interference. It is still possible that, although the means are drastic, the law will be valid because there are no less drastic means. But the new point introduced by *Shelton* is that even though the state interest will in a pinch outweigh the degree of by-product infringement of personal freedoms, the state will still lose, if there are other ways to achieve its purpose which are less expensive in personal liberty.

The passage is resonant and suggests a dimension along which various First Amendment concepts can perhaps be congenially arrayed—overbreadth, precision in drafting, self-censorship, less drastic means. Justice Stewart adds a helpful footnote: "In other areas, involving different constitutional issues, more administrative leeway has been thought allowable in the interest of increased efficiency in accomplishing a clearly constitutional central purpose."[16] At this point he cites *Schlesinger v. Wisconsin,*[17] a 1926 decision in which Justice Holmes spoke of "a penumbra" of administrative convenience. It is precisely in this reversal of attitude toward legislative or administrative convenience in law-making that the distinctive position of First Amendment rights resides. In these matters the law must hit its target.

If there is anything to fault in an otherwise admirable performance, it is that Justice Stewart does not pause to indicate by what less drastic means Arkansas might have achieved its purposes. He notes that it would be permissible to ask all teachers about certain associations, or to ask them how many organizations they belong to, or how much time they spend at it, but he does not pursue the matter further. It is this aspect of his analysis that both Justice Frankfurter and Justice Harlan focus on in dissent. The Harlan dissent sounds a realistic and conciliatory note. He refers to "the context of the racial situation in various parts of the country" and notes that neither of the cases "actually presents an issue of racial discrimination."[18] He also states:

I do not mean to say that alternatives such as an enquiry limited to the names of organizations of whose character the State is presently aware, or to a class of organizations defined by their purposes, would not be more consonant with a decent respect for the privacy of the teacher, nor that such alternatives would be utterly unworkable.[19]

His chief objection to the Stewart view is forcefully put:

> I am unable to subscribe to this view because I believe it impossible to determine *a priori* the place where the line should be drawn between what would be permissible inquiry and overbroad inquiry in a situation like this. Certainly the Court does not point that place out.[20]

The Frankfurter opinion underscores the "bite" of the Stewart principle which accords a kind of new preferred position to First Amendment interests. Whereas Stewart implies that there is an obligation on the legislator to use "the less drastic means" in the First Amendment area, Justice Frankfurter insists there is no novel test for such problems: "This is not because some novel, particular rule of law obtains in cases of this kind."[21] The availability or unavailability of alternatives is always part of the reasonableness of a given state action. Reasonableness remains the standard and the Court must take a generous view of what constitutes reasonable means. The question is whether "it is reasonable for a legislature to choose that form of regulation rather than others less restrictive."[22]

Justice Frankfurter is not willing to leave it at that. He devotes the remainder of his dissent to spelling out why it was not unreasonable for the state to seek information as to all organizations whatsoever to which the teachers belonged during the past five years. The effort, to my ear, verges on the ludicrous:

> Granted that a given teacher's membership in the First Street Congregation is, standing alone, of little relevance to what may rightly be expected of a teacher, is that membership equally irrelevant when it is discovered that the teacher is in fact a member of the First Street Congregation *and* the Second Street Congregation *and* the Third Street Congregation *and* the 4-H Club *and* the 3-H Club *and* half a dozen other groups?[23]

But if the point of the state's inquiry is to find out whether teachers are overcommitted to outside activities, this interest would seem readily satisfied by asking the teacher how many organizations he belongs to and how much time they take. To this obvious rejoinder, Justice Frankfurter replies: "the answer to such questions could reasonably be regarded by a state legislature as insufficient . . . because the veracity of the answer is more difficult to test, in cases where doubts as to veracity may arise."[24] Even taking this answer at face value, the state interest, which is to be weighed against the undeniable intrusion into associational privacy, has now shrunk to an interest in a somewhat more efficient testing of the veracity of the answers. Surely it is dubious that this attenuated interest still outweighs the abridgement of political privacy.

The difference between the position of Justices Frankfurter and Harlan and the majority derives not only from their greater concern with not transgressing the proper bounds of judicial review, from their disinclination to give any sort of preferred position to freedom of speech and association, and their unwillingness to impeach official motivation; it also derives from what might be called their greater patience. They too realize that the information sought may well be used improperly by the state. They would, however, wait until the discriminatory use of the information became a matter of record and then act. "All that is now here," says Justice Harlan, "is the validity of the statute on its face, and I am unable to agree that in this posture of things the enactment can be said to be unconstitutional."[25] Justice Frankfurter, after noting that there is nothing in the record showing unfair use by the state of the information requested, states: "It will be time enough, if such use is made, to hold the application of the statute unconstitutional."[26] The point at issue here—and present as well in numerous other controversies—is whether in the First Amendment area the Court should intervene before the matter comes fully to a head. It is the philosophy of Justices Frankfurter and Harlan as judges not to cross any bridges, even First Amendment ones, until they come to them.

39

Wondrous Complexity: The Bar Admission Cases

It has become apparent that there are three closely related types of cases in which questions about subversive affiliations are put to individuals who refuse on constitutional grounds to answer, thus confronting the Court with the puzzle of how, in First Amendment terms, to evaluate the question and the refusal to answer. The three models are: (i) the loyalty oath which requires the individual, as a condition to his obtaining the government privilege, to swear that he does not have the suspect affiliation; (ii) the legislative inquiry which seeks to compel the individual to answer questions about his affiliations; and (iii) the official inquiry which as a preliminary to allocating a government privilege—public employment, a tax exemption, etc.—seeks answers to questions about affiliations which are relevant to, but not automatically determinative of, eligibility for the privilege. *Garner v. Board of Public Works, Beilan v. Board of Education, Lerner v. Casey,* and *Speiser v. Randall* were subtle, and apparently infrequent, examples of this third category.[1] We move now to a richer instance: the inquiries posed pursuant to screening applicants for admission to the bar.

Lawyers are not public employees; they earn their living by marketing services in the private sector of the economy. Yet tradition makes them something more than private businessmen; they are, in a favorite metaphor, "officers of the court," and they require a state license before they can sell their services. It has long been conceded that a lawyer's character is relevant to his qualifying for a license. Thus there has been by tradition a kind of administrative procedure via bar committees set up to test not specifically the loyalty or security risk aspect of a lawyer but his character. A comparable set of character qualifications for, say, those who wished to write for a living would be rejected as flagrantly unconstitutional.

The fertility of the legal order in generating cases to test principles can be seen by juxtaposing the legislative investigation and the bar admission inquiry. The situations, although similar in many respects, prove legally, and sociologically, to be subtly different. The bar committees operate in relative privacy, without the glare of publicity employed by the legislative committee. They are not *ad hoc;* they are merely continuing to perform a time-honored function: the screening of "the character and fitness" of applicants to the profession. And in fact they have become a routine minor ceremonial step to admission and have no tradition of rigorous investigation, the Communist question apart. They are not committees on un-American activities; they are committees on character and fitness. On the other hand, their behavior, though not fully public, is being closely watched by a sensitive audience—generations of young lawyers.

The Court does not confront the problem of a refusal on First Amendment grounds to answer an inquiry of a bar committee until *Konigsberg v. State Bar of California*[2] in 1957. Then in 1961 it revisits the problem in the second *Konigsberg* case[3] and *In re Anastaplo.*[4] Finally in a cluster of three cases in 1971—*In re Stolar, Baird v. State Bar of Arizona* and *Law Students Civil Rights Research Council v. Wadmond*[5]—it deals for a third time with disclosure in the bar admission setting. In a fashion reminiscent of the loyalty oath problem, and quite unlike the Court's experience with the legislative investigation, the law in this very special sector appears in the 1971 cases to have largely worked itself pure.

Before turning to the sequence of cases involving refusals to answer bar inquiries, we should note three early cases that touch on the question of what substantive conditions may be placed upon admission to the practice of law: *Ex parte Garland* in 1867, *In re Summers* in 1945, and *Schware v. New Mexico* in 1957.[6]

The *Garland* case arose in the aftermath of the Civil War. It involved a federal statute barring from federal office and from the federal bar all who would not take an oath disclaiming participation in the Confederacy. Garland had been a member of the Supreme Court bar but had gone with his home state, Arkansas, in the Civil War. In 1865 he received a full Presidential pardon and then sought readmission to the federal bar without taking the oath. The Supreme

Court in a 5 to 4 decision held that the statute was invalid as a bill of attainder and that Garland was entitled to readmission. The case is ironically almost too old to be directly useful as a precedent today; then too there are the obvious distinguishing factors of the prior pardon and the retroactivity of the condition. Nevertheless, *Garland* offers an instance of the state demanding a special measure of loyalty from lawyers and of the Court intervening to veto that demand on constitutional grounds.

In re Summers, decided some eighty years later, in 1945, comes down the other way. It approves in a 5 to 4 decision a curious attempt by Illinois to exclude conscientious objectors from admission to the practice of law on the ground that they could not in good faith take the oath to support the Illinois Constitution. Although never reexamined, *Summers* must be treated as very doubtful authority today in view of *Girouard v. United States* [7] in 1948, in which the Court reversed itself on the similar issue of the denial of naturalization to conscientious objectors and in the process overruled two precedents relied on in *Summers.* [8]

Nevertheless, *Summers* is a disturbing datum. It shows the ease with which the state's interest in character can become the expansive predicate for other regulation. Justice Reed—in an opinion joined by Chief Justice Stone and Justices Frankfurter, Jackson, and Roberts— approves the ban even though there is no rational connection between a sincere belief in pacifism and fitness to practice law; and even though, as Justice Black argues in dissent, the likelihood that Summers will ever be needed to serve in the Illinois militia is infinitesimal—it had not drafted men since 1864. "The responsibility for choice as to the personnel of its bar," writes Justice Reed, "rests with Illinois." [9]

Justice Black in dissent observes:

The conclusion seems to me inescapable that if Illinois can bar this petitioner from the practice of law it can bar every person from every public occupation solely because he believes in non-resistance rather than in force. For a lawyer is no more subject to call for military duty than a plumber, a highway worker, a Secretary of State, or a prison chaplain. [10]

Schware, decided in 1957, is the case most directly relevant for our purposes, since it involves a concern with subversive affiliations. It dramatically puts to rest any doubts *Summers* may have stirred about the Court's commitment to serious judicial review of the power of a

state to select the personnel of its bar. In a unanimous decision the
Court upsets an effort by New Mexico to deny an applicant admission
to its bar because of *past* Communist Party membership. The opinion
of the Court is by Justice Black, and there is a concurring opinion by
Justice Frankfurter in which Justices Harlan and Clark join. Both
opinions patiently dissect the record and reflect a realistic and tolerant view of what it meant to be a Communist in the United States in
the early 1930s.

   Schware involves neither a loyalty oath nor a refusal to answer a
relevant question of an official inquiry. Rather, it involves the assessment of a complex biography. Schware was thirty-nine years old at the
time of his application to the New Mexico bar in 1954 and hence his
life story was far more complex than that of the usual applicant. It
reads like a saga of American Communism in the early 1930s. Born
of poor immigrant parents, he began to work at the age of nine. He
and his family experienced the depths of the Depression, and in 1932,
when he was eighteen years old and a senior in high school, he joined
the Young Communist League. During the next decade he worked in
a variety of jobs and was periodically unemployed; among his jobs
during this period was work in a glove factory and as a longshoreman.
He was active in union organizing and in 1934 participated in the
great maritime strikes on the West Coast in the course of which he was
twice arrested on "suspicion of criminal syndicalism." On another
occasion he was arrested and charged with violating the Neutrality Act
by attempting to recruit people to serve on the Loyalist side of the
Spanish Civil War. In 1940 he quit the Communist Party in disgust
over the Nazi-Soviet Pact of 1939. He joined the army in 1944 and had
a creditable record of military service. Upon his discharge in 1946 he
went to college and then in 1950 entered the New Mexico Law School.
At the start of his law studies he had gone to the Dean and disclosed
his past associations with the Party.

   Before the New Mexico Character and Fitness Committee, he
answered all questions fully and disclosed not only his past Communist ties but also his use of aliases in the past and his several arrests.
His record before the committee contained much affirmative evidence
from his fellow law students, his teachers, and his rabbi. The committee, however, voted to deny him admission for failure "to satisfy the
Board as to requisite moral character." It stated that it was particularly
troubled by the aliases, the arrests, and the past Communist Party
membership.

Justice Black states the principle for evaluating the substantive conditions a state may properly impose on the practice of law:

A State can require high standards of qualification, such as good moral character or proficiency in its law, before it admits an applicant to the bar, but any qualification must have a rational connection with the applicant's fitness or capacity to practice law.[11]

He then proceeds to weigh with care the negative inferences that can rationally be drawn from each of the three items that troubled the bar committee. The use of aliases was readily explained by a desire to avoid anti-Semitism and to facilitate his efforts to organize his fellow workers; the arrests were dismissed prior to trial; the membership in the Communist Party is now fourteen years into the past and "there is nothing in the record that gives any indication that his association with that Party was anything more than a political faith in a political party."[12] Each item considered separately proves to be without significance; moreover, even when all three are considered together, as the State contends they should be, they fall short of raising "substantial doubts" about Schware's moral character.

The Black opinion does not rest on explicit First Amendment considerations but simply on the arbitrariness of the evidentiary judgment of character in this particular case. It does not supply a precedent of any generality, since the idiosyncratic details of Schware's life are so important. Yet the Court's investment of this much care and patience in a single non-precedent-making decision is heartening indeed.

The decision is lent more precedential value and vigor by the concurring opinion of Justice Frankfurter, which differs only in nuance from that of the Court. Frankfurter, in order to accommodate his notions of federalism, stresses the importance the New Mexico court attached to the past Communist affiliation. And on this point he pens a memorable contribution to the Court's high tradition of protecting political dissent:

This brings me to the inference that the court drew from petitioner's early, pre-1940 affiliations. To hold, as the court did, that Communist affiliation for six or seven years up to 1940, fifteen years prior to the court's assessment of it, in and of itself made the petitioner "a person of questionable character" is so dogmatic an inference as to be wholly unwarranted. History overwhelmingly establishes that many youths like the petitioner were drawn by the mirage of communism during the depression era, only to have their eyes later opened to reality. Such experiences no doubt may disclose a woolly mind or naive notions regarding the problems of society. But facts of history that we would be arbitrary in rejecting bar the presumption, let alone an irrebuttable presumption, that response to foolish, baseless hopes regarding the betterment of society made those who had entertained them but who later undoubtedly came to their senses and their sense of responsibility "questionable characters." Since the Supreme Court of New Mexico as a matter of law took a contrary view of such a situation in denying petitioner's application, it denied him due process of law.[13]

Thus, *Schware*—especially in the Frankfurter opinion—provides important documentation of how poignant the overlap of political action with conspiracy was in American communism, and it underscores how agonizing and delicate the problem of a decent screening out of the conspiracy was. It also marks a high point of tolerance by the Court for *past* Communism, a point the law has not always been able or willing to isolate. Arguably, the great problem for America vis-à-vis Communism was with *former* Communists; it was this discrimination particularly that clamored for constitutional correction. In *Schware* the Court displays insight and understanding toward the former Communist. What remains a great puzzle in its overall performance during the anti-Communist decades is its general failure in other areas— loyalty oaths, loyalty programs, legislative investigations—to protect him.

Because the affirmative evidence of good character is so strong in *Schware,* it is not clear how broad the Court's holding is. Certainly it has intimated nothing about loyalty oaths for bar applicants or lawyers keyed to *present* membership in the Party. But it does seem to hold that a flat ban on past Communists would be unconstitutional and so provides an important parameter for screening the bar. The state's sole interest in limiting membership of those with the requisite intellectual training and abilities from the practice of law is, says the Court, its interest in the "character" of its lawyers. The disqualification of lawyers on loyalty grounds thus requires the showing of a rational connection between membership in a suspect group and personal character. And the burden of Justice Frankfurter's eloquence in *Schware* is to argue that there is no such connection when inferences about present character are drawn from past associations.[14]

Finally, we would note that *Schware* leaves unexplored the constitutional status of efforts to screen out subversives from those already admitted to the practice of law. This would frame the issue in terms of permissible grounds for disbarment and arguably something more intimately concerned with the individual's behavior as a lawyer would be required. In any event, it is worth noting that even during the height of anti-subversive emotion, a period when the organized bar was hardly heroic, no effort was ever made to screen the loyalty of those already practicing law.[15]

The analysis and evaluation of a refusal on First Amendment grounds to answer the familiar question about membership in the Communist Party when asked by a Committee on Character and Fitness proves wondrously complex in the Court's first encounter with the issue, *Konigsberg v. California,* a decision announced in 1957 on the same day as *Schware.* By a vote of 5 to 3, the Court upsets the refusal of California to admit to its bar an applicant who had declined to answer. The majority opinion is by Justice Black and is countered by a deeply felt thirty-six-page dissent from Justice Harlan. It is quickly apparent that the issue is far more difficult in this form, i.e., when the refusal is before a bar committee than when it is before a legislative investigating committee.

On its facts *Konigsberg* is much like *Schware.* There is again the complex biography of an applicant who is atypical in age. Konigsberg is forty-two years old when he applies to the bar. After graduating from college in 1931, he had taught high school, done graduate study, and worked as a social worker for public agencies in the District of Columbia and Ohio. During World War II he volunteered for military service and rose to the rank of captain. After the War he returned to social work, and finally in 1950 entered law school at the University of Southern California. He presented to the committee testimonials as to his character from forty-two persons "in all walks of life."

Indeed, Konigsberg's biography is, if anything, less clouded than Schware's—with one critical exception. He declined on constitutional grounds to tell the committee whether he was or had ever been a member of the Communist Party. He did, however, emphatically and repeatedly deny that he advocated *violent* political change.

There are two additional facts which help position the controversy. First, the committee hears testimony in Konigsberg's presence from a former member of the Party who identifies him as having attended some meetings of a Communist group back in 1941. Second, the California law governing bar admissions provides that applicants must meet *two* requirements: good moral character and non-advocacy of violent overthrow. The non-advocacy requirement is not in the form of a loyalty oath; it is treated as a fact about the applicant which the committee is to certify. The committee is thus able to argue that its inquiries regarding Communist Party membership were intended to test Konigsberg's denial of advocacy.

As will be the case in *Barenblatt*, *Konigsberg* provides a stage for an elaborate debate between Justices Black and Harlan. It also affords Justice Frankfurter, who has just written with eloquent sympathy about the ex-Communist in *Schware*, an occasion to endorse the institutional values he cares about so deeply. The state supreme court had affirmed the committee's action by a 4 to 3 vote without rendering an opinion. The State solemnly argued before the United States Supreme Court that the denial of Konigsberg's appeal might have been based on state rather than federal grounds and that, therefore, the Court lacked jurisdiction. The state ground on which, it was argued, the California court might have relied was a purely formal failure in Konigsberg's brief to list points and authorities. Justice Black dismisses the contention, impatiently noting that the state court would scarcely honor so formal a point with so sharply split a vote. Justice Frankfurter, however, places his dissent wholly on this ground. In his view, the legitimate functioning of the Court as well as values of federalism are jeopardized if the Court becomes impatient with the niceties of federal jurisdiction. He would remand the case for a certification of the basis on which the appeal had been denied. As a result, we are deprived of his seasoned judgment on the matters in dispute between Justices Black and Harlan.

Justice Black handles the case much as he did *Schware*. He distinguishes between two situations: (i) where the refusal to answer a relevant question is in and of itself a basis for rejecting the applicant; (ii) where the refusal and any inferences from it are simply items of evidence to be weighed with the entire record in determining the applicant's fitness. The distinction is not a play on words. If the refusal is *per se* sufficient to support exclusion, it operates on analogy to contempt and makes answering the question in effect compulsory. In such instances it will not matter what other facts are in the record. But if the refusal is evidentiary only, the outcome depends critically on what else is in the record. Justice Black obviously intends the distinction to be exhaustive. As we shall see in a moment, it is the thrust of Justice Harlan's dissent to deny that it is exhaustive and to posit a third possibility, which he insists is the one California had adopted.

Within the framework provided by the distinction, the Black

opinion moves with firm steps. He first establishes to his satisfaction that California has not chosen to make exclusion automatic upon refusal to answer. He finds nothing in the committee's comments to the applicant to indicate that this is its rule. Moreover, he argues, were such a rule in operation, "elemental fairness"[16] would require that the applicant be given very explicit notice. He adds significantly that if California had an automatic exclusion rule for failure to answer about Communist affiliations, "then we would be compelled to decide far-reaching and complex questions relating to freedom of speech, press and assembly."[17] Such questions he reserves for another day.

Justice Black then devotes the remainder of his opinion to evaluating the evidentiary record. He focuses primarily on the requirement of good moral character. He finds the testimony of the ex-Communist witness thin, since it relates only to attendance at meetings and Konigsberg has denied ever seeing her before. Moreover, since it dates back to 1941, even if it is accepted as true, it has little more weight than the past membership in *Schware*. He easily dismisses a second item concerning editorials critical of public officials and public policies. Finally, he is unable to see what inferences *as to character* can under the circumstances be drawn from the refusal to answer; it was based on a constitutional claim that was sincere and "not frivolous."[18] Hence, adding up the evidence in the *Konigsberg* record, including the refusal to answer and the massive affirmative evidence of good character, he comes out as he did in *Schware*: the particular record cannot rationally support a finding of lack of good moral character.

Justice Black then turns to the requirement of non-advocacy of violent overthrow. Since Konigsberg has explicitly denied advocacy of violent overthrow, none of the perplexities of a refusal to answer are present in this wing of the case. Black can find in the record only an editorial in which Konigsberg had spoken of "militant" support for American ideals to suggest the contrary about his position.

The opinion closes with some words of admonition:

A bar composed of lawyers of good character is a worthy objective but it is unnecessary to sacrifice vital freedoms in order to obtain that goal. It is also important both to society and the bar itself that lawyers be unintimidated— free to think, speak, and act as members of an Independent Bar.[19]

Black's handling of the case leaves four issues of general interest unexplored. First, he explicitly eschews considering the propriety of the questions Konigsberg refused to answer; and hence does not engage the question of the constitutional limits to a loyalty program for lawyers. In this respect, he, uncharacteristically, declines going to the heart of the matter. Second, he does not quite respond to the circumstance—which will be stronger a few years later in *In re Anastaplo*—that the refusal to answer seems to be a gesture of civil disobedience or conscientious objection. The puzzle in these bar admission cases is whether the Court can find a way to use this perception. If the inquiry is essentially into character, a refusal to answer keyed to conscience would seem paradoxical as evidence of *poor* character. Third, there is no sensitivity to the point Justice Brennan will make a year or so later in *Speiser v. Randall* about allocating the burden of proof to the state in inquiries touching on First Amendment freedoms. Justice Black appears to be saying that the balance of evidence in the record before him is so clearly in favor of Konigsberg that it does not matter who has the burden of proof. Finally, he does not respond to or utilize Konigsberg's own point before the committee, that once the target question about advocacy of overthrow has been answered squarely, there is no justification for asking further questions about it.

Although there is no indication Justice Harlan thinks the evidence against Konigsberg any stronger than does Justice Black, he is deeply disturbed by the result. He sees the case very differently in two respects. First, unlike Black, he treats the evidence on membership in the Party as going not so much to character as to the requirement of non-advocacy: "At least it seems apparent to me that Communist Party membership is relevant to the question of forcible overthrow."[20] Second, as we have noted, he rejects Black's framework in which the refusal to answer is *either* the basis for automatic exclusion in and of itself *or* is merely an additional item of evidence to be weighed with the whole record. He agrees that California has no automatic exclusion rule: "Of course California has not laid down an abstract rule that refusal to answer under any circumstances *ipso facto* calls for denial of admission to the Bar."[21] He also agrees that the inferences from Konigsberg's refusal to answer do not amount to much as evidence. But these, he insists, are not the only possibilities, or perhaps more precisely put, the automatic exclusion rule is not a *real* alternative—it elides necessarily into this third possibility: "We have here a case where a state bar committee was prevented by an applicant from discharging its statutory responsibilities in further investigating the applicant's qualifications."[22] Harlan argues that under the circumstances of this record, the applicant has failed to meet his burden of going forward with the evidence, and his refusal has blocked the committee's efforts to test the credibility of his denial of non-advocacy by cross-examination on Party membership. He then makes a very lengthy examination of the transcript of the hearings to demonstrate that the committee was posing the Communist question in an effort to test credibility.

It is not, he argues, that the committee *finds* Konigsberg unqualified on the basis of the record; it is rather that they are *prevented from reaching a conclusion* on his qualifications, because he had failed to carry his burden of going forward with the evidence. The political sensitivity of the Communist question is irrelevant:

The principle here involved is so self-evident that I should have thought it would be accepted without discussion. Can it really be said that a bar-admissions committee could not reject an applicant because he refused to reveal his past addresses, or the names of his former employers, or his criminal record?[23]

Thus on Harlan's view, the refusal to answer may bar when the answer itself would not.

It is perhaps not profitable to push the conflicting patterns of the Black and Harlan analyses further. Black has attempted to capture the controversy in a logical framework which Harlan rejects as an unrealistic and forced way to look at what California was actually doing. It is evident that to dispose of the bar applicant who refuses to tell a committee on character and fitness whether he is a Communist the legal system is pushed to its analytic limits.

The contrast between the unanimity reached in *Schware* and the perplexities stirred in *Konigsberg* is startling. It underscores once again how different *the asking of questions* about Communist affiliations is from *the imposing of sanctions* because of Communist affiliations. And once again it is evident, as it was in the legislative investigation cases, that this is especially true for Justice Harlan. This is an investigation; it must be allowed to unfold "step by step." He is impatient with Konigsberg's position that once he has answered *the target question* about forcible overthrow, the committee has no further power to question him along that line:

I think this position is untenable. There is no conceivable reason why the Committee should not attempt by cross-examination to ascertain whether the facts squared with petitioner's bare assertion that he was qualified for admission.[24]

Undoubtedly Justice Black has not responded fully enough to the points Justice Harlan raises to be altogether persuasive. Yet it is not clear that Harlan has escaped the Black categories. When would a refusal to answer not be regarded by him as a failure to meet the burden of going forward with the evidence? And if it would be so regarded in every case, since credibility always remains to be tested, would not the elegant Harlan rule turn out in fact to be a rule of automatic exclusion, a rule he does not attempt to justify directly? Moreover, can the Court be as heroically insensitive to the real life situation as Justice Harlan aspires to be? This is not a refusal to give one's name and address; it is a refusal on principle to answer what is felt to be a question improperly intrusive into valued political privacies.

In *Konigsberg* Justice Black, in a style quite exceptional for him, sought to avoid the larger issues raised by screening the loyalty of the bar and elected instead to treat the case narrowly as an evidentiary problem only. Presumably he did this to win a fifth vote—that of Justice Burton. The tactic not only provokes a storm of technical protest from Justice Harlan, but it also leaves in obscurity the underlying issue: When may an applicant to the bar be asked whether he is a member of the Party and when may he refuse to answer?

Appeals to judicial statesmanship in order to finesse confrontations on fundamental issues have a way of establishing short-lived precedents. Thus Chief Justice Warren's effort in *Watkins* in 1957 to avoid First Amendment evaluation of congressional investigation by relying on a technical requirement of pertinency collapses just three years later in *Barenblatt*. The same fate awaits Justice Black's tactic of treating *Konigsberg* as an evidentiary dispute.[25] It does not even survive to the next case. The *Konigsberg* controversy itself comes back to the Supreme Court in 1961, after California upon the remand again denied him admission to its bar. And the Court, by a vote of 5 to 4, affirms. In *Konigsberg* II, as in *Barenblatt,* the "villain" who undoes the momentary victory is Justice Harlan. Again, there is an elaborate debate between Justices Harlan and Black. This time, however, the debate directly engages the First Amendment considerations.

It is easy to explain *Konigsberg* II simply in terms of changes in the composition of the Court. The new five-man majority, this time against Konigsberg, is made up of Justices Harlan, Clark, Frankfurter, Justice Whittaker (who had not participated in the first case), and Justice Stewart, who has replaced Justice Burton. There is, however, another factor. California on the remand changed the positioning of the case. Having been told by the United States Supreme Court that it had evaluated Konigsberg's record with unconstitutional arbitrariness, the California bar does not simply yield and admit him. Upon his reapplication for admission, it holds a further hearing and again asks him about Communist affiliations. It takes care to warn him that it will consider his refusal to answer a sufficient basis for denying him admission. In short, it adopts an automatic exclusion rule, thus precipitating "the far-reaching and complex questions relating to freedom of speech, press and assembly"[26] which Justice Black had been so careful not to reach in the first case.

At the outset there is the question of whether California has not acted inconsistently with the Supreme Court's mandate. There is, to be sure, some embarrassment. Justice Black notes that the prior adjudication of Konigsberg's character is back before them "unimpaired."[27] But Justice Harlan, relying on the distinction he professed to be unable to follow when Justice Black drew it in *Konigsberg* I, correctly points out that the adoption of the automatic exclusion rule raises "an issue that is not foreclosed by anything in this Court's earlier opinion which decided a quite different question."[28] We note the point not because of the legal quirk involved but because it furnishes so striking a datum about the idle and relentless ceremony that the pursuit of subversives sometimes degenerates into.

The debate between the justices is now over the validity of an automatic exclusion rule upon a refusal to answer. Justice Harlan breaks the issue down into four components: (i) Was there adequate warning to the applicant that a refusal to answer would be treated so gravely by the committee? (ii) Did the application of such a rule in this case result in *arbitrarily* barring Konigsberg from admission? (iii) Should the principle of *Speiser v. Randall* have been followed and the burden of proof shifted to the committee in deference to First Amendment values? (iv) Was the question about Communist affiliations an infringement of Konigsberg's First Amendment rights?

Justice Harlan disposes of the first two items quickly. With respect to the first, he finds that there was sufficiently explicit warning of the rule. And with respect to the second he restates the thrust of his dissent in *Konigsberg* I: there is enough in this record to support the State's conclusion that it was prevented by applicant's refusal to answer from making up its mind about his character and non-advocacy and therefore to bar him from obstructing its inquiry. Harlan apparently will not quite endorse a rule that would treat refusal as fatal to the applicant regardless of what was in the record. There is a suggestion that there must be some basis for doubt in the record. He notes that the Court in *Konigsberg* I had held that "neither the somewhat weak but uncontradicted testimony, that petitioner had been a Communist Party member in 1941, nor his refusal to answer questions relating to Party membership, could rationally support any substantive adverse inferences as to petitioner's character qualifications."[29] He then goes on to state his final assessment with almost unbearable elegance:

> That was not to say, however, that these factors, singly or together, could not be regarded as leaving the investigatory record in sufficient uncertainty as constitutionally to permit application of the procedural rule which the State has now invoked. . . .[30]

This extraordinarily anemic standard of judicial review for a case embodying so deeply felt a controversy over political tolerance is, I think, attributable to Justice Black's tactical effort to turn the case into an evidentiary dispute and nothing else. For that purpose the First Amendment overtones are irrelevant; and if that is to be the game, Justice Harlan will handle the evidence point without regard to them.

This is a convenient juncture at which to turn to the possible relevance of *Speiser v. Randall.* Clearly the Harlan logic which treats the refusal to answer not as the basis for negative inference as a matter of evidence but simply as obstruction of the committee investigation depends crucially on allocating to the applicant the burden of producing evidence. It was precisely where questioning intruded into politically sensitive areas that *Speiser* held that First Amendment considerations required shifting the burdens of going forward and of proof to the State. If this principle were applied in *Konigsberg,* the petitioner would be under no obligation to produce evidence on non-advocacy unless and until the State had met its burden. Hence his refusal to answer could not be considered obstruction of the bar committee investigation. *Speiser* thus offered a way of giving some First Amendment "flavor" to the procedural rules for evaluating evidence. Indeed, the analogy had seemed so strong that Justice Traynor of the California Supreme Court, dissenting in *Konigsberg* II, had urged the court to adopt it as common law.

Justice Brennan, the author of *Speiser,* files a separate dissenting opinion relying solely on what he understood to have been decided in that case: "unless mere whimsy governs this Court's decisions in situations impossible rationally to distinguish, such a procedure is

indeed constitutionally required here."[31] And Justice Black in his
dissent accuses the majority of cutting "the heart out of one of the
very few liberty-protecting decisions that this Court has rendered in
the last decade."[32] He argues that if anything this is the "stronger"
case for application of the *Speiser* principle, "for here Konigsberg
agreed to take the oath required [that he did not advocate violent
overthrow] and he refused to answer only when the State insisted
upon more."[33]

Why then does Justice Harlan, who had joined the majority in
Speiser, reject its application here? He offers two distinctions. First, he
reads *Speiser* as limiting its shifting of the burden of proof to cases in
which there is "an intent to penalize political beliefs."[34] This is an
artificial, ungenerous reading of *Speiser.* It is true that one of the
grounds on which Justice Brennan in *Speiser* had distinguished cases
like *Garner, Gerende,* and *Douds*[35] had been a difference in terms of
intent between conditioning public employment and conditioning tax
exemptions. But he had then gone on to advance a second wholly
sufficient ground of distinction which Justice Harlan chooses to ignore. Said Justice Brennan in *Speiser:*

Moreover, the oaths required in those cases [*Garner, Gerende, Douds*] performed a very different function from the declaration in issue here. In the
earlier cases it appears that the loyalty oath, once signed, became conclusive
evidence of the facts attested so far as the right to office was concerned. If
the person took the oath he retained his position. The oath was not part of
a device to shift to the officeholder the burden of proving his right to retain
his position.[36]

Justice Harlan's other basis for distinguishing *Speiser* is that there
is "no unequivocal indication that California in this proceeding has
placed upon petitioner the burden of proof of non-advocacy of violent
overthrow."[37] But in *Konigsberg* I Harlan, after noting carefully that
California imposed *two* requirements—good character and non-advocacy—had stated: "The applicant has the burden of proof in showing that these requirements have been met."[38] It is an unusually
unpersuasive performance by one of the most rigorous justices in the
Court's history. As with his repeated dissents in the legislative investigation cases, one can only infer that there is something about the
position of a witness refusing to cooperate in an official inquiry that
he finds wholly and uniquely unsympathetic.

It is obvious now that the analysis of bar admission inquiries takes a different road than does the analysis of legislative investigation. In the latter instance there is direct compulsion to answer and disclose in the form of criminal penalties for contempt, and equally important, the committee purports to make no findings of fact about the individual witness. There is therefore no reason to talk of the burden of proof and every reason to talk of the constitutional validity of exacting compulsory disclosure of Communist Party membership. In the bar admission inquiry these two points are virtually reversed: There is no compulsion to answer unless the refusal leads to automatic rejection of the applicant, turning the question, in effect, into a loyalty oath; and there is an obligation on the bar committee to make findings of fact about the applicant. Hence it is plausible to talk of it in evidentiary terms and to defer consideration of the root policy issue of whether the state can constitutionally deny Communists the privilege of practicing law if they are otherwise qualified. The layman presumably would have gone directly to this issue if put the facts of the *Konigsberg* case. It takes, as we have seen, Justices Black and Harlan "a case and a half" to finally get there.

And they really never quite do get there. The final subtlety of the case is that, although the decisive fact is Konigsberg's refusal to answer the question about membership in the Party, the issue for First Amendment purposes is set by the requirement of non-advocacy of violent overthrow. Justice Harlan states that Konigsberg does not challenge the constitutionality of the provision "forbidding certification for admission to the practice of those advocating the violent overthrow of government."[39] As the justices join in First Amendment debate, the issues tend to fall between them. Justice Harlan does not pass on the constitutionality of *barring* Communists from the practice of law merely on the constitutionality of *inquiring* into such membership. He confines himself to justifying the constitutionality of barring advocates of violent overthrow. Justice Black, on the other hand, does not much challenge the barring of advocates of violent overthrow; rather, he directs his fire at the barring of Communists.

Justice Harlan thinks it self-evident that the state can bar lawyers committed to violent change:

It would indeed be difficult to argue that a belief, firm enough to be carried over into advocacy, in the use of illegal means to change the form of the State or Federal Government is an unimportant consideration in determining the fitness of applicants for membership in a profession in whose hands so largely lies the safekeeping of this country's legal and political institutions.[40]

The issue would, I think, have been worth debating. For one thing, Justice Harlan is ignoring the critical ambiguities in formulas about the advocacy of violence to which he was so splendidly attentive four years earlier in *Yates v. United States.* [41] For another, he makes no effort to examine whether or how a "security risk" analysis applies *distinctively* to lawyers. Finally, he pays no attention to the breadth of the premise being asserted. Are lawyers' views on other public issues— socialism, distributive justice, imprisonment, racial discrimination— now also relevant?

Justice Harlan needs a second premise in order to reach his result that the inquiry into Party membership with consequences attached to the refusal to answer is constitutional under the First Amendment, namely, that the appropriate mode of analysis for this type of case is to apply a balancing test. He supplies an elegant preface in support of this view, and Justice Black devotes most of his energy to a criticism of "balancing." We shall pick up that general debate in a moment.

Given his two premises, the Harlan argument is firm, and follows familiar lines. There is a recognized connection between the Party and advocacy of overthrow. Hence inquiries into membership in the Party are relevant for findings on non-advocacy. There is thus a clearly defined state interest in exacting such information from bar applicants. On the other side the deterrent impact of disclosure in this context on freedom of association is likely to be slight; the bar admission inquiry is in private, and hence there is "no likelihood that deterrence of association may result from foreseeable private action." [42] He comes then to the balance:

With respect to this same question of Communist Party membership, we regard the State's interest in having lawyers who are devoted to the law in its broadest sense, including not only its substantive provisions, but also its procedures for orderly change, as clearly sufficient to outweigh the minimal effect upon free association occasioned by compulsory disclosure in the circumstances here presented. [43]

Harlan does not pause to acknowledge that Konigsberg has, after all, repeatedly answered the question of interest to the state; he has denied advocacy of violence. Hence the state's interest in pursuing the matter via questions about Communist membership is reduced to an interest in testing the veracity of his denials by this one line of cross-examination. What remains unsatisfying about Justice Harlan's analysis, despite its clarity and rigor, is that it is so abstracted from any contemporary reality. He is engaged in solving a geometry problem. He never permits himself to wonder publicly why Konigsberg or any applicant would vehemently deny advocacy of violence and yet decline to answer about Party membership.

Justice Black devotes his opinion largely to challenging Harlan's premise that balancing is the appropriate mode of analysis of the First Amendment issue involved, a debate we will turn to in a moment. He also challenges, however, the way the balance is struck, assuming *arguendo* that balancing is proper. He sees little need for the state to know about Konigsberg's Communist membership since he has answered the target question about non-advocacy. He doubts that the inquiry would in fact be kept private, and "would not rapidly leak out."[44] Moreover, he would weigh more heavily the society's interest in an independent bar:

It seems plain to me that the inevitable effect of the majority's decision is to condone a practice that will have a substantial deterrent effect upon the associations entered into by anyone who may want to become a lawyer in California. If every person who wants to be a lawyer is required to account for his associations as a prerequisite to admission into the practice of law, the only safe course for those desiring admission would seem to be scrupulously to avoid association with any organization that advocates anything at all somebody might possibly be against. . . .[45]

Justice Black then comes to *his* balance:

The interest of the Committee in satisfying its curiosity with respect to Konigsberg's "possible" membership in the Communist Party two decades ago has been inflated out of all proportion to its real value—the vast interest of the public in maintaining unabridged the basic freedoms of speech, press and assembly has been paid little if anything more than lip service—and important constitutional rights have once again been "balanced" away.[46]

Justice Black does not address Harlan's first premise that non-advocacy of violent change can be made a condition for admission to the bar. At most he challenges in a sentence or two the conclusion that advocacy of violent overthrow can be reached by the criminal law:

I realize that there has been considerable talk, even in the opinions of this Court, to the effect that "advocacy" is not "speech." But with the highest respect for those who believe that there is such a distinction, I cannot agree with it.[47]

The challenge is thin and oddly put. Whether advocacy is speech was hardly the point at issue in the cases like *Yates* which held that at some point of proximity to action this kind of speech could constitutionally be censored. Moreover, criminal sanctions for such advocacy are not in issue here; qualifications for admission to the bar are.

Black saves his fire for challenging whether the non-advocacy condition is really the committee's premise. He takes it as given that no one is contending that California may validly bar all Communists from the practice of law and that California has not attempted to do so. He then insists that the real motivation of the committee in pursuing the Communist inquiry is to bar Konigsberg because it believes he is or was a Communist. Hence, since the inquiry into Communist membership is, as he sees it, really predicated on the desire to bar Communists, the question itself is improper and not supported by a valid state interest. Once again, as in legislative investigations, there arises the stubborn issue of impeaching official motivation:

> . . . And yet it seems to me that this record shows, beyond any shadow of a doubt, that the reason Konigsberg has been rejected is because the Committee suspects that he was at one time a member of the Communist Party. I agree with the implication of the majority opinion that this is not an adequate ground to reject Konigsberg and that it could not be constitutionally defended.
>
> The majority avoids the otherwise unavoidable necessity of reversing the judgment below on that ground by simply refusing to look beyond the reason given by the Committee to justify Konigsberg's rejection.[48]

This blindness on the part of the Court, Justice Black continues, leads it to the anomaly of treating Konigsberg's refusal to answer more gravely than it would have treated an affirmative answer.

That anomaly is a reminder that Justice Harlan has succeeded in framing the issue as not whether the State can bar Communists from the practice of law but whether the State can bar applicants who refuse to answer whether they are Communists.

We turn now to the debate over balancing. *Konigsberg* was the occasion for perhaps the fullest debate ever between Justices Harlan and Black over balancing. There has been a tendency among commentators to take this exchange out of the context of the case and turn it into a general debate over First Amendment theory—a debate between those who favor "absolutes" and those who favor balancing.

Indeed, there is much in Justice Black's lengthy dissent on this point to suggest that he views the controversy as underlying all First Amendment decisions. But on inspection the issue between them turns out to be narrower and more technical. Justice Black would not reject balancing in all situations nor would Justice Harlan balance in all situations. The disagreement is really over how big the category of cases is for which some sort of balancing is appropriate.

Justice Black's argument against balancing ranges over a considerable field. He revisits the clear and present danger test and the opinions of Holmes and Brandeis; he again criticizes the handling of *Beauharnais v. Illinois*[49]; he expresses doubt that "a 'literal reading of the First Amendment' would . . . invalidate many widely accepted laws"; and he argues that balancing will inevitably lead to "balancing away."[50] But his quintessential view is stated at the outset:

> . . . I believe that the First Amendment's unequivocal command that there shall be no abridgment of the rights of free speech and assembly shows that the men who drafted our Bill of Rights did all the "balancing" that was to be done in this field.[51]

Once he has rejected balancing, Justice Black is able to reduce the case to a simple syllogism. Justice Harlan had acknowledged some minimal chilling of freedom of association but had found it outweighed by the state's interest in disclosure. For Black, "the recognition that California has subjected 'speech and association to the deterrence of subsequent disclosure' is, under the First Amendment, sufficient in itself to render the action of the State unconstitutional."[52]

In rebuttal Justice Harlan provides a lucid, helpful summary of his view of the prior law. The First Amendment is not an "absolute"; there have always been acknowledged, if limited, areas of regulation. He distinguishes between two different sorts of regulations: those which are directly aimed at the content of speech; and those which are intended to serve some other legitimate state purpose but which, as a by-product, impinge on speech. It is in the latter category of cases that he sees a need to balance the purpose of the regulation against the inadvertent restraint on speech. He cites many cases that fall within this category, including those involving non-content regulation in the public forum, such as the littering and sound truck cases. And he argues that it is in this category "that this Court has always placed rules compelling disclosure of prior association as an incident of the informed exercise of a valid governmental function."[53]

Such cases necessarily entail some accommodation of conflicting claims, some balancing:

Whenever, in such a context, these constitutional protections are asserted against the exercise of valid governmental powers a reconciliation must be effected, and that perforce requires an appropriate weighing of the respective interests involved.[54]

As his citations to *Watkins, Barenblatt, Braden* and *Wilkinson* at this point indicate,[55] the parallel to disclosure in the legislative investigation context is quite exact. In both instances the negative effects are unintended by-products of the pursuit of an otherwise legitimate government objective—there the objective is gathering information for the purpose of legislating; here it is testing the veracity of the denial of advocacy of violence. In both cases the measure of First Amendment protection can be judged only by some comparison of the degree of negative effect with the importance of the state objective.

Justice Black concedes that the Court has used balancing in the cases involving general regulation of the public forum, but argues that it was to maximize speech protection:

When those cases came before this Court, we did not treat the issue posed by them as one primarily involving First Amendment rights. Recognizing instead that the streets are avenues of travel which must be kept open for that purpose, we upheld various city ordinances designed to prevent unnecessary noises and congestions that disrupt the normal and necessary flow of traffic. In doing so, however, we recognized that the enforcement of even these ordinances, which attempted no regulation at all of the content of speech and which were neither openly nor surreptitiously aimed at speech, could bring about an "incidental" abridgment of speech. So we went on to point out that even ordinances directed at and regulating only conduct might be invalidated if, after "weighing" the reasons for regulating the particular conduct, we found them insufficient to justify diminishing "the exercise of rights so vital to the maintenance of democratic institutions" as those of the First Amendment.[56]

Justice Black and Harlan can thus be said to agree that there is a category of cases for which balancing is the proper mode of analysis. They disagree sharply, however, as to the breadth of that category. The immediate question is whether a case such as the one before them involving disclosure not for its own sake but pursuant to the exercise of some government function is to be viewed as imposing direct sanctions on speech and association and evaluated accordingly or is, like the public forum cases, to be evaluated by accommodation of the competing interests. Each asserts a firm position. Justice Harlan sounds a note of incredulity that some weighing of the factors is not required:

With more particular reference to the present context of a state decision as to character qualifications, it is difficult, indeed, to imagine a view of the constitutional protections of speech and association which would automatically and without consideration of the extent of the deterrence of speech and association and of the importance of the state function, exclude all reference to prior speech or association on such issues as character, purpose, credibility, or intent.[57]

Justice Black is equally adamant that there is nothing in the prior cases which compels balancing in a case like that at bar:

But those cases never intimated that we would uphold as constitutional an ordinance which purported to rest upon the power of a city to regulate traffic but which was aimed at speech or attempted to regulate the content of speech. . . . Those cases have only begun to take on that meaning by being relied upon, again and again as they are here, to justify the application of the "balancing test" to governmental action that is aimed at speech and depends for its application upon the content of speech.[58]

If we must judge the matter simply as we would a debate or a moot court, we must adjudge Justice Harlan the winner. His argument is structured and clean, and he is in complete control of it. Justice Black seems off balance throughout his dissent and unable to marshall his counterthrusts. But, as always, Justice Black's admirable *instinct* for freedom grievances and for what the case is really about breaks through. There *is* a content aspect in the case. The anomaly that we end up penalizing a refusal to answer more severely than we would an affirmative answer cannot be altogether pushed aside. The vice in the Harlan scheme of things is that the Court is relieved of the obligation of deciding the scope of a loyalty program for the bar. It is not so much that balancing is wrong in this situation; it is that the wrong things are being balanced. We need a balance drawn on whether Communists as such may be barred from law practice. Only if we are persuaded they may be is the result in *Konigsberg* II fully satisfactory. If, however, we are persuaded that it is too great an inroad on political freedom and the ideal of an independent bar to apply a security risk analysis so loosely to lawyers, then Justice Black seems right that we cannot attach so much weight to the refusal to answer about Communist affiliation. The matter cannot be left in limbo, as Justice Harlan would have us do. Black's instinct is on target: The disruption caused by the Communist query cannot be viewed as a neutral, incidental by-product of a government effort which is so much concerned with screening out subversives.

The two *Konigsberg* cases are worth special study, especially by lawyers. They illustrate again how precarious it is to attempt to homogenize First Amendment problems. Even the two disclosure situations found in legislative investigations and bar admission inquiries turn out upon analysis to be very different. Justices Harlan and Black were both men of high intelligence, great good will, and serious commitment to their roles as judges. Their struggle over the more than one hundred pages of discussion in the two cases to locate their disagreement and justify their positions vividly illustrates the perennial tensions that sweep First Amendment controversies at the level of the Supreme Court. Finally, the organized bar should be reminded of how much California's inglorious, relentless pursuit of Konigsberg resembles in retrospect the imposition of a trivial flag salute ceremony.

If the performance of the California bar in *Konigsberg* can be characterized as inglorious, the performance of the Illinois bar in *In re Anastaplo* in 1961 is more inglorious still. But once again the Supreme Court, by a 5 to 4 vote, affirms the barring of the applicant from the practice of law. The decision is announced on the same day as *Konigsberg* II. And Justice Harlan is again the spokesman for the Court.

On its facts *Anastaplo* is very similar to *Konigsberg*. In both instances an otherwise qualified applicant gets enmeshed in an atypically elaborate investigation into his fitness by the bar committee, is put the question about membership in the Communist Party, and is barred from admission because of his refusal to answer that one question. And in both instances the applicant is an articulate expositor of his reasons for declining on principle to cooperate. But our interest in *Anastaplo* for present purposes resides precisely in those details in which it *differs* on its facts from *Konigsberg*. There are four differences: (i) There is nothing in the record comparable to the testimony that Konigsberg had attended some Communist Party meetings in 1941; there is absolutely nothing to occasion the committee asking Anastaplo about Communist affiliation—except a somewhat quixotic answer on his written application to the effect that the "right of revolution" was a basic principle of the American Constitution. The Illinois Bar Committee, displaying its illiteracy and ineptness, is sufficiently alarmed by this talk of revolution to launch its inquiry into Communist Party membership. (ii) There is in Illinois law nothing comparable to the California requirement of non-advocacy of violence; there is only a good character requirement. (iii) There is a very spotty record on whether the committee had warned Anastaplo adequately that it had, in effect, an automatic exclusion rule, even though it is questioning him after the *Konigsberg* I decision had made the matter salient; moreover, it is not at all clear that Illinois regards itself as having such a rule. (iv) The final vote against Anastaplo in his second appearance before the Illinois committee was only 11 to 6. It appeared from the committee's final report that "certain members of the Committee (who are included within the majority . . .)" were influenced by his position on a right of revolution, a ground the Court disallows. Hence arguably the committee majority was "corrupted" by its erroneous view on this point and might have decided differently had it understood that this ground was not available to it. These differences all fall on Anastaplo's side of the line, and at least points (i) and (ii) require some extension of the holding in *Konigsberg* II. Nevertheless, Justice Harlan treats the case as essentially "settled" by the decision in *Konigsberg* II,[59] and thus exposes some further difficulties with the rationale of that decision.

The *Konigsberg* II theory appeared to have been that the committee in the course of its investigation into Konigsberg had come upon material—the testimony about attendance at Party meetings in 1941—which could possibly have generated some doubts about the credibility of his denial of advocacy of violent overthrow; and that therefore it was unable to make up its mind about non-advocacy. Surely it is a different case, if there is nothing in the record to cause the applicant's credibility to be in issue. *On what points did the committee deem it necessary to test and probe Anastaplo's credibility?*

If then Illinois had an automatic rule excluding the applicant upon refusal to answer any question, the rule was unconstitutionally arbitrary as applied to Anastaplo in contradistinction to Konigsberg. Justice Harlan does comment on the challenge put in this form:

It is sufficient to say in answer to the first contention that even though the Committee already had before it substantial character evidence altogether favorable to Anastaplo, there is nothing in the Federal Constitution which required the Committee to draw the curtain upon its investigation at that point. It had the right to supplement that evidence and to test the applicant's own credibility by interrogating him.[60]

The First Amendment balancing analysis is also in trouble. On the state's side of the scale there is now only the severely attenuated interest in testing not credibility in general but the credibility of an applicant whose credibility cannot rationally be in doubt.

In brief, the rule Justice Harlan endorses in *Anastaplo* turns the questioning into a non-Communist loyalty oath for bar applicants. Moreover, the Illinois procedure compares unfavorably to conventional oaths. It is not applied uniformly and evenhandedly to *all* applicants; and it is not evaluated as a substantive condition limiting the privilege of law practice but is evaluated as only a step in the investigatory process and is not conclusive.

We have remarked previously on how strangely alienated Justice Harlan seems to be by the refusal to cooperate in an investigation. There is a passage at the end of the *Anastaplo* opinion which may throw some light on his reaction, at least in the context of a bar inquiry. He does not think Illinois will continue to bar Anastaplo "any longer than his refusal to answer." "In short," he writes, "petitioner holds the key to admission in his own hands."[61]

The applicant, as Justice Harlan sees it, is justified in testing his constitutional rights by refusing to answer. But once the validity of the question has been authoritatively established, there is nothing admirable in continuing to refuse to answer. The practical problem of the *Anastaplo* case has now been settled; he has had his test day in court; he should now answer the question and proceed with his career at the bar. Whatever can be said on behalf of civil disobedience, it does not generate any legal immunities.

In fact, however, the case has left an impasse which today remains unresolved. Anastaplo will not approach the committee with a willingness to answer the question. And the committee, it might be noted, having won its point, has not approached him with a willingness to admit him without again insisting on the ceremony of its utterly pointless and expensive question.[62]

It is only now fully apparent how stubbornly distinctive the disclosure issue becomes in the context of the bar admissions inquiry. It is not, as we have noted, quite like the loyalty oath. Nor is it like disclosure intended in itself to act as sanction or a remedy for the evil apprehended, as in the statute requiring lobbyists to register or the Subversive Activities Control Act requiring "Communist-action" groups to disclose their membership and their sponsorship of mail or broadcasts. Nor—and this is the point *Anastaplo* finally makes evident—is it like disclosure in the legislative investigation context. There the chilling effect on First Amendment freedoms comes from the behavioral consequences of the public ceremony of disclosure. In the bar admission context these consequences are, as Justice Harlan argues, considerably lessened and the impact on First Amendment freedoms arises from the conditioning of admissions. The distinction is elusive. Perhaps it can be clarified by this example: Suppose a state makes membership in the Party a ground for rejecting the applicant. If he is then asked whether he is a member, the objection goes not to the chilling effect of the question and the disclosure as in the legislative investigation but to the condition itself.

Finally, a few words about Justice Black's dissent in *Anastaplo*. If he was thrown off balance in *Konigsberg*, he is fully in command of his views in *Anastaplo*. His opinion is highly effective and flavorsome. He examines the record in great detail and gives a full picture of Anastaplo's personal dignity and eloquence as well as of the bar committee's ineptness. The committee, we discover, was so upset by Anastaplo's talk about a "right of revolution" in the natural law sense of the Declaration of Independence that it asked him not only about Communism but also about belief in God, finally desisting only when Anastaplo pointed out the old Illinois case on which it was relying had long ago been overruled.

Further, Justice Black is sharply critical of the notion that the committee was in a posture of needing to test the credibility of Anastaplo's prior answers:

Thus, it is against the background of a mountain of evidence so favorable to Anastaplo that the word "overwhelming" seems inadequate to describe it that the action of the Committee in refusing to certify Anastaplo as fit for admission to the Bar must be considered. . . . it is difficult to see what possible relevancy answers to the questions could have had in the minds of these members [of the majority] of the Committee after they had received such completely overwhelming proof beyond a reasonable doubt of Anastaplo's good character and staunch patriotism.[63]

He also pungently and concisely repeats his criticism of balancing:

If I had ever doubted that the "balancing test" comes close to being a doctrine of governmental absolutism—that to "balance" an interest in individual liberty means almost inevitably to destroy that liberty—those doubts would have been dissipated by this case.[64]

In the end, what is moving about Justice Black's dissent is its special generosity toward Anastaplo personally. He comes very close to embodying Black's idea of what a lawyer should be. Black quotes at length and with evident approval Anastaplo's statements to the committee about the proper role of the bar in American democracy. Black sees him as rejected in reality because he believed too much in the principles of the Declaration of Independence. His final praise is put ironically: "The very most that fairly can be said against Anastaplo's position in this entire matter is that he took too much of the responsibility of preserving that freedom upon himself."[65] Thanks to the dissent of Justice Black, the *Anastaplo* case has in a very real sense a happy ending, although Anastaplo is still not a member of the Illinois bar. He earns the distinctive reward of being enshrined in the pages of the United States Reports in a living opinion by one of the most cherished of justices.

Konigsberg II and *Anastaplo* yield a rule that an applicant for admission to the bar could constitutionally be rejected for refusal to answer an undifferentiated query about membership in the Communist Party. Thus the applicant appeared to have ended up in a position less favorable than that finally reached by the witness asked the same question before a legislative investigation committee who could claim the protection of *Gibson* and *DeGregory*[66]; and in a position considerably less favorable than that of the person required, in order to obtain a government privilege, to swear to a non-Communist oath, who could claim the protection of *Elfbrandt.*[67]

The *Konigsberg-Anastaplo* rule undergoes major revision and narrowing, however, in the cluster of three 1971 cases—*Baird, Stolar* and *Wadmond*—all of which are decided on the same day. Read together, these cases bring the results in the bar admissions area roughly in line with those worked out in *Elfbrandt.* In *Baird* and *Stolar* the challenge of the applicant prevails; in *Wadmond* it fails. All three cases are decided by 5 to 4 votes. In each Justices Black, Brennan, Douglas, and Marshall vote with the bar applicant and Chief Justice Burger and Justices Blackmun, White and Harlan vote with the bar committee which rejected him. The decisive vote in each instance is cast by

Justice Stewart, who finds the situation presented in *Wadmond* significantly different from that in *Baird* and *Stolar*. Justice Stewart, it might
be recalled, had also supplied the crucial fifth vote in *Konigsberg* II and
Anastaplo.

We pause for a moment to underscore how remarkable the
Court's voting pattern has been in the disclosure cases. Disclosure has
posed a uniquely divisive First Amendment issue for the justices.
Since *Konigsberg* I in 1957, there have been six Supreme Court cases
on refusals to answer in bar admissions inquiries: All six have been
decided by 5 to 4 votes. Since *Barenblatt* in 1957 there have been
thirteen legislative investigation cases involving refusals to answer.
Seven of these have been by 5 to 4 votes, one by a 4 to 4 vote, and
twelve of the thirteen by votes with at least two in dissent. When we
add *Speiser, Beilan, Lerner,* and *Shelton,* we have three more 5 to 4
decisions. Hence, out of twenty-three recent cases involving refusal to
answer an official question, the Supreme Court has split 5 to 4 no less
than seventeen times. This remarkable pattern testifies, I think, not
to the fact that the Court lacks a consistent, persuasive First Amendment theory but rather to the nature and structure of the issue. It is
obviously a matter of durable difficulty and subtlety to work out a free
speech analysis of official questioning. Finally, the voting pattern is
one more bit of evidence on the degree to which Justices Black and
Harlan dominated the Warren Court: The dispute in these cases is a
steady dispute between them.

The only differences between *Baird* and *Konigsberg* II or *Anastaplo*
are that the question about Communist affiliation is put by questionnaire prior to interview and hence presumably is required evenhandedly of all applicants, and that the question covers not only
membership in the Party but also membership in any organization
that advocates violent overthrow. Upon the applicant's refusal to answer the question, the bar committee declines to process her application further. But this time the Supreme Court, as it had in *Konigsberg*
I, finds the denial of admission to the Arizona Bar on this basis to be
unconstitutional state action.

The petitioner had acknowledged that the case was highly similar
to *Konigsberg* II and *Anastaplo* and had argued that those cases "warrant . . . delimiting, and perhaps even overruling in light of the trend
since 1961." The response of the justices to this frontal attack on
Konigsberg II and *Anastaplo* is varied.

Justice Black's opinion for four members of the Court is confusing. He does not explicitly overrule *Konigsberg* II or *Anastaplo;* nor

does he go back to the evidentiary analysis he had used in *Konigsberg*
I. He sounds querulous and professes to be confused by the lengthy
prior debate he had engaged in on the very question before him. He
advocates a stunningly simplistic approach:

The foregoing cases and others contain thousands of pages of confusing
formulas, refined reasonings, and puzzling holdings that touch on the same
suspicions and fears about citizenship and loyalty. However we have concluded the best way to handle this case is to narrate its simple facts and then
relate them to the 45 words that make up the First Amendment.[68]

It is the advocacy of the overthrow aspect of the question that
troubles Justice Black. The question requires the applicant "to guess"
about the position of organizations she has belonged to; the information cannot be said to be needed by the state in view of her full answer
to all other questions (including one requiring her to list all organizations to which she had belonged since the age of sixteen); and most
important, the question is being asked pursuant to the imposition of
an improper condition for admission to the bar. Again his tone is
querulous:

Much has been written about the application of the First Amendment to cases
where penalties have been imposed on people because of their beliefs. Some
of what has been written is reconcilable with what we have said here and some
of it is not. Without detailed reference to all prior cases, it is sufficient to say
we hold that views and beliefs are immune from bar association inquisitions
designed to lay a foundation for barring an applicant from the practice of
law.[69]

It is 1971—Justice Black's final year on the Court. Perhaps what his
opinion in *Baird* says most loudly of all is that he has become just too
old for the wondrous complexity with which the Court has worked out
an analysis of the bar admission inquiry cases.

Baird is saved for future utility, I suspect, by the concurring
opinion of Justice Stewart. He is clear about how he fits the prior
precedents together. *Konigsberg* II and *Anastaplo* remain good law on
the consequences for bar applicants of refusals to answer questions
about Communist Party membership. The current inquiry, he feels,
goes further. The question asks whether the applicant "ever belonged
to any organization that advocates overthrow of the United States
Government by force or violence." It is too indiscriminate. Member-

ship as such is "quite different from knowing membership . . . on the part of one sharing the specific intent to further the organization's illegal goals."[70] What is most arresting about his opinion is the citation at this juncture of *Scales.*[71] The implicit suggestion is that such inquiries are permissible only if the question asked is tailored closely to *the target question.*

The Stewart opinion, although it connects up with the past and offers promise for the future, is itself puzzling on one score. The Communist question approved in *Konigsberg* II and *Anastaplo,* and now endorsed by him, was undifferentiated with respect both to knowing membership and specific intent. If a broad question can be asked as a preliminary step in investigation there, it is puzzling why it may not be asked as a preliminary step here.

Justice White directs his dissenting opinion to this point:

> I also believe that the State may ask an applicant preliminary questions that will permit further investigation and reasoned, articulated judgment as to whether the applicant will or will not advise lawless conduct as a practicing lawyer.[72]

The opinion of Justice Black is almost perfectly offset in tone by the dissent of Justice Blackmun. If Justice Black sees the asking of the question by the state as a direct affront to the forty-five words of the First Amendment, Justice Blackmun sees the refusal to answer on the part of the young applicant to the bar as an impertinence.

Blackmun correctly objects that the holding is in direct conflict with *Konigsberg* II and *Anastaplo* and quotes shrewdly from those opinions. He locates precisely the issue that is dividing the Court: How much breadth can be conceded to preliminary questioning about affiliations on the assumption they will be connected up more precisely as the investigation unfolds? But he is not quite content to rest his opinion on the prior holdings that preliminary questioning is to be accorded considerable tolerance. He concedes that the question is not ideally drafted:

> Although Question 27, concededly, would have been better phrased had it gone on to inquire as to the applicant's own knowing participation in, and promotion of, illegal goals, a realistic reading of the question discloses that it is directed not at mere belief but at advocacy and at the call to violent action and force in pursuit of that advocacy.[73]

The concession, it seems to me, is fatal. If, as he sees it, the state's interest would have been as well served by a question drafted with attention to "knowing participation and promotion," then surely the First Amendment requires that the state draft its question with economy and precision. This is all the more true because it is precisely from the "surplusage" of the question that the conscientious objector dissent to it arises—it looks more than it needs to like an inquiry into political association and belief. We stumble here onto an important difference in the facts of *Konigsberg* and *Baird*. In *Konigsberg* Justice Harlan could attempt to justify the undifferentiated question about Communist membership on the ground that it would be useful in testing the veracity of the applicant's denial of advocacy of violence. When, however, the undifferentiated question is about the advocacy of violence, as in *Baird*, it has arguably lost any justification as a way of testing veracity.

Justice Blackmun in the course of elaborating his reasons for dissenting drops two other remarks worth noting. First, in rejecting the applicant's claim that by listing all the organizations she has belonged to in answer to another question she has in effect already answered the question she is refusing to answer, he says with irritation: "She gives the appearance of playing a game. The importance of the subject deserves better than that."[74] One has a twinge of sympathy for this reaction. As we noted in discussing loyalty oaths, there is something stubborn and pettifogging about many of those who refuse to take oaths. But if we are to note the stubbornness of those who resist, we must attend equally to the stubbornness of those who impose the requirements. If Mrs. Baird gave the appearance of "playing a game," so did the bar committee. "The importance of the subject deserves" better drafted questions, and some effort on both sides to avoid unnecessary First Amendment quarrels.

Justice Blackmun's second remark gives a clue as to what the bar's actual interest in ceremonial inquiry about violent overthrow was at this late date:

We have seen, of late, an overabundance of courtroom spectacles brought about by attorneys—frequently those who, being unlicensed in the particular State, are nevertheless permitted, by the court's indulgence, to appear for clients in a given case—who give indications of ignoring their responsibility to the courts and to the judicial process. Question 27 bears upon this facet of an applicant's character.[75]

If Arizona had more straightforwardly pursued this interest in not having trials politicized, it would have posed a difficult but genuine issue of constitutional policy on which one could argue both about the desirability of the end and the suitability of the means.[76]

In re Stolar is almost identical to *Baird*. It differs in just four details: The applicant has already been admitted to practice in New York and now seeks admission in Ohio; in his New York application he had answered without protest a question about non-advocacy of violence at which he now balks; and in an interview before the Ohio committee he had explicitly denied membership in the Communist Party or any organization on the Attorney General's list. His situation is thus the exact reverse of Konigsberg's. He will answer the Communist question but he balks at the general question about advocacy; Konigsberg had freely denied advocacy but balked at the Party membership query. Finally, Stolar also declines to answer questions asking that he list all organizations of which he has ever been a member and that he list all organizations of which he has been a member since registering as a law student.

Once again the majority opinion is by Justice Black. Justice Stewart files a one-paragraph concurrence; and Justice Blackmun writes a dissent. This time Justice Harlan appends a separate dissent.

All of the justices agree that the questions asking for "total recall" of all organizations one has ever joined are unconstitutional under the principle of *Shelton v. Tucker*. Hence the controversy among them reduces down, as in *Baird*, to the non-advocacy question. It might be noted, as a commentary on the technical skill of bar committees, that *Shelton v. Tucker* was decided in 1960 and *Stolar* arose in 1969, yet the Ohio Bar was still using a form of question that had become palpably invalid after *Shelton*.

Because the *Shelton* ground is so readily available to him, Justice Black need not put his opinion as sweepingly as he did in *Baird*. He does, however, venture one broad statement. Looking back, at the end of his long career on the bench, over the decades of First Amendment controversies involving advocacy of overthrow of the government by force, he observes of *Stolar* and its companion cases:

These cases, which concern inquisitions about loyalty and government overthrow, are relics of a turbulent period known as the "McCarthy era". . . . We have just referred in our opinion in *Baird v. State Bar of Arizona* to the confusion and uncertainty created by past cases in this constitutional field. The central question in all of them has been the same, whether involving lawyers, doctors, marine workers, or State or Federal Government employees, namely: to what extent does the First or Fifth Amendment or other constitutional provision protect persons against governmental intrusion and invasion into private beliefs and views that have not ripened into any punishable conduct?[77]

Justice Stewart puts his concurrence with spectacular conciseness. Two of the three contested questions are "plainly unconstitutional" under *Shelton*[78]; the other is bad under *Baird*.

Justice Blackmun, after conceding the *Shelton* point about two of the questions, devotes his dissenting opinion to the refusal to answer the advocacy question. He emphasizes the "inconsistency" in Stolar's position—his "willingness to respond orally and his unwillingness to respond in writing."[79] And, as in *Baird*, he "readily" concedes that the question "could have been better phrased," but deems it "unrealistic" to quibble over the wording since the state's objective is to get "at knowing membership" and "willingness to participate in the forceful destruction of government."[80]

Justice Harlan's dissenting opinion is addressed to all three cases. He expresses concern lest the Court be understood to have treated the states as denying admission to those whose membership in "so-called subversive organizations" is "born of a purely philosophical cast of mind."[81] He reiterates what has for him been the cardinal distinction—the cases do not deal with conditions upon entry to the bar: "They show no more than a refusal to certify candidates who deliberately, albeit in good faith, refuse to assist the Bar-admission authorities in their 'fitness' investigations by declining fully to answer the questionnaires."[82]

Harlan's tone, in his final words about the bar admission controversy, has become mellow. There is a suggestion of empathy for those who refuse on principle to answer and a suggestion of impatience with the foolishness of the bar in pursuing these methods of screening applicants, but as always he is scrupulously aware of the limits on his role:

I could hardly believe that anyone would dispute a State's right to refuse admission to the Bar to an applicant who avowed or was shown to possess a dedication to overthrowing governmental authority by force or to supplanting the rule of law by incitement to individual or group violence as the best means of attaining desired goals. One could question the efficacy or wisdom of questionnaires of the kind involved in these cases as a means of weeding out occasional misfits from the general run of Bar candidates, or criticize as unduly complicated or pervasive some aspects of such questionnaires. And one may also be understanding of the considerations which in this day and age breed lawsuits like these. But we should nonetheless take care lest the indulging of such points of view lead us into warped constitutional decision.[83]

   Baird, Stolar, and *Wadmond* are all decided on the same day. In terms of the scope and intensity of the challenge and the degree of attention it commands from the Court, *Wadmond* emerges as the "big case." The decision cannot be read as a setback, although this time, to be sure, the challenge fails and Justice Black finds himself again in dissent.

   The important fact in *Wadmond* is that Justice Stewart shifts his vote to form the five-man majority, and thus has occasion to write the opinion for the Court. He shifts because he finds that the overbreadth in the questions to which he objected in *Baird* and *Stolar* has been corrected in *Wadmond*. He is thus in a position to give authoritative voice to the constitutional limitations he sees on inquiries into association. Given Stewart's role as spokesman for the Court in *Wadmond*, his three opinions together—*Baird, Stolar, Wadmond*—can, I think, be fairly taken as the statement of the current constitutional requirements for bar admission inquiries. There remain, as we shall see, some inconsistencies and confusions to iron out, but one senses that the law in this special sector has now been significantly clarified and brought more into line with the *Elfbrandt, Keyishian, Robel* sequence.

   The setting in *Wadmond* differs from the companion cases in four respects. First, the challenge is in the form of a suit for declaratory and injunctive relief and does not depend on a literal denial of admission for refusal to answer. Second, it is brought as a class action on behalf of law students, giving salience to the critical audience in these bar admission cases. Third, the case comes to the Court with the New York law having undergone correction and narrowing in several respects at the hands of the three-judge court below; the Court faces, in Justice Marshall's phrase, "the residuum of the appellants' original challenge."[84] Fourth, the appellant's argument not only tracks *Baird* and *Stolar* in objecting to specific questions about advocacy of overthrow but also poses a radical challenge to the whole scheme of screening the loyalty and character of applicants to the bar.

   The New York scheme needs a word of explanation in order to

locate the precise point at which the appellants challenge it. New York required of applicants proof of citizenship, proof of six months' residence, an oath to support the Constitution, and in Rule 9406 proof that he "believes in the form of the government of the United States and is loyal to such government." It is this provision and the effort of the bar committee to implement it with two questions on the questionnaire furnished applicants (Nos. 26 and 27) that is the target of the challenge.

Justice Stewart notes that if Rule 9406 stood alone, it would raise serious constitutional doubts for two reasons: the breadth of the inquiry into political beliefs and the apparent placing of the burden of proof upon the applicant. His citation of *Speiser v. Randall* at this point is heartening in that it suggests that, despite *Konigsberg* II, *Speiser* retains continued vitality in this area.

Rule 9406 does not, however, stand alone. It has been given a narrow construction by the bar committee. Hence Justice Stewart is disposed, in effect, to read it out of the case. The committee would place no burden of proof upon applicants beyond answering Questions 26 and 27; and it would read the broad language of Rule 9406 as referring simply to the Constitution and to a willingness to take the oath of affirmation and to take it in good faith. Thus Justice Stewart sees Rule 9406 as on a par with the taking of an oath to support the Constitution, a requirement he regards as beyond challenge. Similarly he finds Question 27, which requires the applicant to affirm that he could "without any mental reservation" support the Constitution, to be unobjectionable: "The question is simply supportive of appellees' task of ascertaining the good faith with which an applicant can take the constitutional oath."[85]

The argument between the justices breaks down then into two issues: (i) whether Rule 9406 is rendered innocuous by the committee construction; and (ii) whether Question 26 is overbroad. We first turn to this second issue, because it is on this point that *Wadmond* is directly continuous with the issues we have been discussing in *Konigsberg* I and II, *Anastaplo, Baird,* and *Stolar.*

Question 26 is in two parts and reads as follows:

(a) Have you ever organized or helped to organize or become a member of any organization or group of persons which, during the period of your membership or association, you knew was advocating or teaching that the government of the United States or any state or any political subdivision thereof should be overthrown or overturned by force, violence or any unlawful means? . . .

(b) If your answer to (a) is in the affirmative, did you, during the period of such membership or association, have the specific intent to further the aims of such organization or group of persons to overthrow or overturn the government of the United States or any state or political subdivision thereof by force, violence or any unlawful means?[86]

It is evident that the question asked in *Wadmond* differs in two respects from the parallel question asked in *Baird* and *Stolar:* it requires "*knowing* membership" and it requires "*specific intent.*" Justice Stewart finds these differences crucial:

Question 26 is precisely tailored to conform to the relevant decisions of this Court. Our cases establish that inquiry into associations of the kind referred to is permissible under the limitations carefully observed here. We have held that knowing membership in an organization advocating the overthrow of the Government by force or violence, on the part of one sharing the specific intent to further the organization's illegal goals, may be made criminally punishable. *Scales v. United States.* [87]

The shift in idiom since *Konigsberg* II and *Anastaplo* is striking. There is explicit concern with the overbreadth of questions as distinguished from sanctions; there is no nod to the familiar Harlan point that leeway must be allowed in investigation which unfolds step by step; and the citing of *Scales* suggests that it not only defines the limits of criminal sanctions on association but may also serve to set the limits on questions as to association.

Yet the matter cannot quite be said to be put to rest for two reasons. Logically, Justice Stewart has worded his comment so as to assert that an inquiry narrow enough to satisfy *Scales* must be constitutional; he is not asserting in so many words that unless it is kept that narrow it is unconstitutional. Moreover, he continues to endorse *Konigsberg* and *Anastaplo:* "It is also well settled," he writes, "that Bar examiners may ask about Communist affiliations as a preliminary to further inquiry into the nature of the association and may exclude an applicant for refusal to answer."[88] But, to repeat a point already noted, it is difficult to see why the undifferentiated question about association with the Communist Party should not also be limited to asking about knowing membership with specific intent.

Hence we reach what paradoxically may either be regarded as a point of total confusion, or as a point of the law working itself pure, as it finally did in *Elfbrandt, Keyishian,* and *Robel.* I incline strongly to the latter interpretation, aided perhaps by Justice Blackmun's concession in *Baird* and *Stolar* that the questions would have been better phrased had they included the knowledge and intent limitations. The Court, due to developments in other areas during the 1960s, has become aware of the possibility of *overbreadth in questions.* Moreover, if the bar committees will confine themselves to asking the target question a considerable social cost may be avoided—the question will then not permit ready confusion with political association, and the basis for objection in principle to the question will be greatly weakened. Hence, if we lay *Wadmond* side by side with *Scales* and *Elfbrandt,* there is considerable basis for feeling that the Court has here too worked its way to a tolerable solution.

The dissenters are not, however, pleased with the outcome. Justice Black states his position in such a way as to indicate that his war has been with the *Scales* baseline itself. He argues that even if inquiry into association is tailored to the *Scales* requirements, it still violates the First Amendment: "I do not think that a State can, consistently with the First Amendment, exclude an applicant because he has belonged to organizations that advocate violent overthrow of the Government, even if his membership was 'knowing' and he shared the organization's aims."[89] He then turns to the precise wording of Question 26. He argues, and Justice Marshall joins him in urging the point, that while the membership component may now be tailored to meet *Scales,* the advocacy component is still bad because it fails to meet the stringent incitement requirements of *Brandenburg,* as indeed it does: "for their failure to meet the *Brandenburg* requirements, the New York questions are overbroad."[90] *Wadmond* is thus a striking instance of recent developments in criminal sanction cases being utilized to argue that the law in partial sanction situations must be updated.

Finally, Justice Black, not giving an inch in his opposition to such screening of the political reliability of the bar, advances a point that makes one wonder uneasily whether the whole enterprise—bar committee inquiry, objection on principle to answering questions, and judicial review under the canons of the First Amendment—has not become faintly ridiculous. He objects that Question 26(a), taken alone, is impermissibly broad since it does not include the "intent" limitation found in Question 26(b):

Since even on the majority's theory New York cannot exclude an applicant unless *all* these requirements are met, why is the State permitted to ask Question 26(a) which makes no reference to "specific intent"?[91]

The point seems to elevate punctuation to constitutional status. Presumably it was cumbersome to combine both limitations into a single sentence, so two sentences were used. Had the two points been combined in a single question there would have been no objection! In any event, since the answers are given in writing, there is no ambiguity about where Question 26(a) leads and no chance that it will be left hanging in the air with the thought incomplete. Justice Black is not, however, assuaged:

It may be argued, of course, that Question 26 is sufficiently specific under the majority's standard because parts (a) and (b) *taken together* do include a "specific intent" requirement. But the Court's holding permits the knowledge and specific intent elements of Question 26 to be split into two parts. This allows the State to force an applicant to supply information about his associations, which, even under the majority's rationale, are protected by the First Amendment.[92]

Yet, if Black's intransigence seems curious, so does the drafting of Question 26. It is almost a caricature of the lawyer's art of drafting with lucidity. On rereading, (a) seems pretty cumbersome as it stands. Would it have been appreciably worsened if the specific intent qualification had been added? Moreover, is it conceivable that (b) will serve to eliminate *anyone* not already taken out by (a), that is, someone who would conscientiously answer, yes, he had been a knowing member of such organizations but without the specific intent to further their illegal purposes?

Justice Marshall, though he too takes some shots at the drafting of Question 26, places his dissent largely on the implications of Rule 9406, which Question 26 is intended to implement. Justice Stewart, it will be recalled, read the Rule out of the controversy, because of the narrow construction given it by the committee. Justice Marshall is disturbed by the premise it embodies and is far less certain than Justice Stewart just how authoritatively the Rule has been narrowed, and if so, what its current meaning is. The premise behind the Rule is not, he feels, "politically neutral"; it fastens not on conduct or even

on speech "but on personal belief itself."[93] Moreover, insofar as it is
limited to testing *the sincerity* with which the affirmative ceremonial
oath of support is taken, it ratifies a logic of turning affirmative oaths
into test oaths, a logic rejected by the Court in *Bond v. Floyd.* [94] Finally,
it supplies a background against which the ambiguities in Question 26
become more troublesome. Hence he would conclude that the challenge to the New York bar admissions scheme *as a whole* was well
founded: "I believe that appellants' basic First Amendment complaint, transcending the particulars of the attack, retains its validity."[95]

A final word on this generic attack. We noted in discussing legislative investigations that it was never quite possible to attack, say,
HUAC not in terms of specific questions put to specific witnesses but
somehow *on its face.* The applicants in *Wadmond* seem to have levied
just such an attack on the entire bar admission scheme. As Justice
Stewart restates their argument:

They suggest that, whatever the facial validity of the various details of a
screening system such as New York's, there inheres in such a system so
constant a threat to applicants that constitutional deprivations will be inevitable. The implication of this argument is that no screening would be constitutionally permissible beyond academic examination and extremely minimal
checking for serious, concrete character deficiencies.[96]

Appellants have, I think, put their finger on the structural defect
in the current bar practices. A relatively moribund inquiry into "character" is tolerated because it is prefunctory and time-honored. It
provides, however, in moments of political stress a ready-made "loyalty program." It is tempting therefore to suggest breaking the easy
linkage from inquiry into moral character to inquiry into political
reliability. The appellants have at least succeeded in planting their
argument indelibly in the pages of the Reports. And perhaps we can
detect a note of admonition to other bars in Justice Stewart's words
as he rejects the generic challenge to the New York scheme: "We are
not persuaded that careful administration of such a scheme as New
York's need result in chilling effects upon the exercise of constitutional freedoms."[97]

Looking back over the Court's experience with various forms of official inquiry, several formal principles emerge. Each serves to limit
official demands for disclosure and to protect individuals who refuse

to answer. The principle articulated in *Gibson v. Florida Legislative Investigation Committee* requires that there be some foundation, some nexus, some reason for singling out *this* particular witness to answer *that* particular question. The *Speiser* principle requires the shifting of the burden of producing evidence to the state. The *Shelton* principle requires strict economy in invading basic privacies with a question, no matter how relevant. To these we should add the principle of *Wadmond* that questions too can suffer from overbreadth. All four ideas can be said to be aspects of the contemporary reach and meaning of the First Amendment.

Editor's Afterword

My father's study was at the top of the stairs. It was an unusual study.
A large room with French doors and many windows, it had been used
by earlier occupants of the house as a ballroom. Although it contained
much furniture—a desk, two sofas, filing cabinets, a long table, as-
sorted chairs, end tables, lamps—one's dominant impression was of
space and light. His typewriter sat on a small table in the middle of
the room.

Bookshelves lined the walls interrupted here and there by
photographs: my mother at nineteen; the children; a studio portrait
of his father with a grandchild on his knee. On another wall, near
the desk, were portraits of two teachers with whom he had become
a colleague—Malcolm Sharp and Charles Gregory. A color snap-
shot, carefully framed, held the faded image of him and Alexander
Meiklejohn, erect and alert at ninety-one, walking arm in arm down
a green lane.

The size of the room allowed him the luxury of a horizontal filing
system. (The filing cabinets were all but empty.) Piles of paper covered the floor. Manuscripts and notes. Briefs and reprints. Newspaper
clippings on various topics: the King assassination, the moon landing,
Churchill's funeral, the appointment of Edward Levi as President of
the University of Chicago, Watergate, the retirement of Willie Mays.
Piles of correspondence, answered and unanswered. Student exams
and papers, graded and ungraded.

There was an underlying order to all this paper, but its basis was
not immediately apparent. Always moving on to the next project, he
rarely winnowed through the material generated by the last. The

paper in that room thus constituted, layer upon layer, a sort of geology of his career. The deepest substrata included the journal he kept during his first year in college, papers he wrote as an undergraduate, exams he took in law school.

Evidence of his passion for the First Amendment was embedded in every strata. Throughout his career, whatever his primary professional involvement at the moment, he never failed to respond to the claims of the First Amendment, to its "charisma." His work in the field was thus the product of a series of passionate engagements rather than of a carefully plotted campaign. Yet it was also the work of a man who carried in his mind from the start a vision of the book on freedom of speech he "always wanted to write."

All around him, on the day he died, were materials pertaining to that book. The manuscript in a series of binders. Notes in folders and piles. Relevant books and articles, his own and those of others. Thick volumes of *U.S. Reports*—a complete set from 1919 to 1974—dominated a large bookshelf. On his desk a paperback copy of *The Negro and the First Amendment,* a book he had written a decade earlier, lay open to the discussion of the case *NAACP v. Button.*

When he was alive and at work, what we referred to as "the book" was the manuscript plus the contents of his mind—a mind immersed in its subject and absorbed in the process of composition. That mind animated and enlarged the essay. It filled the manuscript with promise and possibility, gave body to sketchy fragments and force to cryptic margin notes. When it was stilled, "the book" contracted down to the words on the page. Standing alone—left behind—the manuscript seemed, in the afterglow of his life, at once an emblem of loss and a repository of hope.

I

This must be a common occurrence. A scholar or writer who is productive until the end will almost inevitably leave work-in-progress. Yet there is no established procedure, no readily accessible body of shared experience to guide one in handling this situation. There are too many variables; one cannot generalize. A great deal turns on the precise condition of the particular manuscript.

HK wrote as he talked: in an unforced, unrestrained flow of language. His general practice was to rewrite relatively little; one does not find among his papers numerous drafts of various articles. His conversational ease, his tolerance of the proximate, his readiness to risk error and overstatement in pursuit of fresh perceptions—these were closely allied to his originality. His style was a loosely woven net for catching large truths. He did not aspire to be definitive. His trust of first utterance was grounded on the knowledge that one could always say more. This was a feature of his conversation often recalled by friends: just as one was about to take one's leave, he would say, "One more thing," and be off on a new tangent. The point is not that he was verbose; one never tired of talking with him. It is rather that his impulse was always to add to what had been said—to enlarge upon it, to qualify it, to locate the questions inside assertions.

These qualities play through his manuscript. It is literally a *first* draft. I would be surprised if he crumpled up and discarded more than half a dozen sheets of paper in the course of producing it. Initially the writing was uncharacteristically halting and uncertain. He seemed cramped by threshold questions of form. In view of the scale and diversity of the field, the task he had set himself—to encompass the entire tradition in a single essay—required strategies of compression and summary; it required a sure sense of literary architecture. HK's great gift, by contrast, was his rich, seemingly inexhaustible capacity for response. So much of his writing, so much of his best writing, was produced in headlong response to a decision just handed down, to a controversy of the moment. The mismatch between his gifts and his chosen task recalls the character in Proust—a writer he adored—who is said to have had the misfortune to fall in love with a woman who was not his type.

At first HK tried to maintain a strict sense of form. (For example, he initially conceived of each "minor jurisdiction" chapter as centering on a single paradigmatic case.) But soon he reverted to the style of approach most congenial to him. He surrendered to his fascination with the material, tackling the cases, one by one, as if they had just been handed down. He thus exercised to the utmost the freedom a first draft affords.

Yet the resulting manuscript is, in two respects, a most unusual first draft. First, there are the marginalia. Each summer, while on vacation, he would reread the manuscript—"amidst swans, rabbits, and egrets"—and sketch his reactions in the margins. There are roughly six hundred margin notes scattered through the manuscript. They range from question marks to full pages of commentary on the backside of manuscript pages. Most suggest revisions and additions;

some raise difficult substantive questions. Taken together, they testify to his intention to extensively rework the manuscript. Indeed, there are chapters in which more analytic perceptions reside in the margins than in the text.

The second distinguishing feature of the manuscript is its relationship to HK's published work and his teaching. This may have been a first draft, but it was also the culmination of decades of teaching and writing about First Amendment issues. The manuscript was thus surrounded by much relevant material. There were scores of articles and reviews. There were masses of notes: eight hundred pages of handwritten notes outlining the salient points in some three hundred First Amendment cases; four hundred pages of random notes—quickly sketched perceptions, questions, hunches. Most important, there were his lecture notes for the course on the First Amendment he taught throughout his career. These, in turn, generated yet another category of notes: those of his students. After his death, I solicited several sets of notes from students in the 1974 course and prepared a composite account of the substance of the classes. This resource was especially helpful, for there was a close kinship between the essay and the course. "The book will be like the course would be," HK once remarked to a student, "if I was coherent all the time."

These outside resources created a context for evaluating the manuscript and for making editorial decisions. They were especially valuable because of the unity and continuity of HK's thought over time. Although his writing and his teaching always had a fresh, firsthand quality, he did not in the course of his career change his mind much about these matters. His thinking deepened and advanced, but there were no sharp breaks or turns.

The condition of the manuscript thus necessitated editorial intervention and at the same time gave reason to hope it would be possible. The loosely woven first draft texture, the marginalia, the context created by HK's other work—these nourished the hope that the process of composition, arrested by death, might somehow be advanced.

II

The aim was to carry on: to make available to readers, insofar as possible, the book HK would have given them, had he lived. This was hardly a matter of picking up where he left off. Our relationship to the manuscript was very different from his. Words he put down with such a light touch took on, after his death, resistant weight. For him, they were part of an ongoing flow that would be augmented and modified by what came after. For us, they were his last words. Under his hand, the manuscript was full of movement, a work-in-progress; for us, it was a vast, intricate puzzle. He had inhabited it; we were on the outside looking in.

To have read the manuscript—even with the intensity and heightened lucidity of grief—was hardly to have entered it. Yet certain broad problems were immediately apparent. There were structural difficulties he had identified but not resolved. There were internal gaps. The texture of the writing was uneven; some chapters were fully realized, others only lightly sketched. And there were the marginal notes—scattered clues holding out the promise that there might be a way back toward HK's mind.

At the threshold, I formulated broad editorial guidelines. Beyond editing for clarity and style, I would, where possible and desirable, act on his marginal "instructions." I would not, however, attempt to "complete" the essay. A substantial part of HK's overall design remained unwritten. There was to have been a section on prior restraint and a large section on non-content regulation. (The latter was to have included chapters on regulation of the public forum keyed to the time, place, and manner of expression; regulation of symbolic conduct; regulation of voting and political activity; regulation of the business of communication; the newsman's privilege; the issue of access and other special problems of broadcasting.) The absence of these chapters did not affect the existing manuscript. Hence we simply reconceived the shape of the book not to include them.

We were also, at the outset, intensely concerned about the impact of the passage of time. Would cases handed down after HK's death drain the essay of interest and timeliness? It was clear that some updating would be required—there were instances in which the essay was dated as of the time of his death. But would it be necessary—would it be appropriate—to add discussion of developments *since* his death? We decided to defer that question, to carry it forward with us.

In general, it was my hope that appropriate editorial criteria would emerge from our interaction with the manuscript. The substance of editorial policy thus took shape slowly, incrementally, page by page; it was the product of countless discrete choices. The *form* of the effort, by contrast, crystallized at the start; and we sustained it throughout. It had two essential features: (i) I articulated in writing the rationale for all significant changes; and (ii) at every stage, the

editorial process was exposed to the critical scrutiny of others—
chiefly Professor Owen Fiss of the Yale Law School with whom I have
over the years discussed virtually every line in the manuscript. (Early
in the project I also had the benefit of a series of conversations about
the manuscript with Staughton Lynd.)

The process of editing a chapter had several phases. After preparing a clean, lightly edited draft, I would try to determine what HK's
intentions were beyond the draft. The point of departure for this
inquiry was his marginalia. Although time-consuming and laborious,
the pursuit of his marginal clues and leads often yielded fruit. We
were able to make sense of virtually all the notes and in many instances to execute the revisions they suggested.

We could not, however, assume in every case that a given note
was a expression of his intentions. Nor could we assume that the
notes, taken together, constituted a full critique of the manuscript, a
complete blueprint for revisions. Had we acted on that assumption,
it would be a very odd book indeed. It was thus necessary to make an
independent critique of the chapter. This was a matter of reading the
draft against the relevant cases. Above all, it was a matter of evaluating
the manuscript in light of HK's other writings and notes on the subject—of reading him against himself.

The product of this phase of the process was a memo, often
exceeding the length of the chapter, which addressed the problems
and possibilities that resided in the draft. Once I had prepared the
draft and memo, I discussed them with Owen Fiss. He would read the
draft against the original and the memo against the draft. In addition
to responding to the points raised in the memo, he would make
independent criticisms and suggestions. Finally, I would write a draft,
incorporating those revisions and additions that had survived discussion and reflection. I would also write another memo, generally a
good deal shorter than the first, which would provide an agenda for
further discussion with Owen and a blueprint for another draft of the
chapter. Each chapter went through this process at least twice.

Both the memos and my talks with Owen were centrally concerned with issues of editorial license. Editing under normal circumstances is a matter of addressing suggestions and questions to the
author. The ultimate responsibility for decision is his. But there was
no one to whom we could address our queries except one another.
In a sense, we assumed the responsibility of the author but did not
claim his freedom. Clarity about the intellectual merits did not resolve
the issue of the propriety of editorial intervention. That question was

independent. Some of the hardest decisions, absorbing the most time and effort, were decisions not to intervene. For better or worse, nothing reflects the character of this project more than the amount of intellectual effort and moral intensity that went into decisions not to do anything.

The design of the editorial process was initially prompted by concern about the limitations and vulnerabilities I brought to the project as a non-lawyer, apprentice-writer, and son. Over time the forms we adopted proved to serve other important functions as well. Besides opening the editorial process to the scrutiny of others, the draft/memo approach enforced awareness and conscious choice. It enabled us to keep a record of changes made. In a sense, it functioned as a sort of body of law—a way of keeping track of evolving questions. At the same time that it insulated the manuscript from ill-considered interventions, it released me from the sort of self-censorship—the cramping of thought by doubt—I would have suffered, had I implemented changes directly in the manuscript without first developing them in memos. In the memos I could freely explore possibilities and alternative strategies. They also provided a vehicle for my ongoing education. Indeed, that was perhaps their primary purpose early in the project, as I sought my bearings in the field and in my father's writings.

Similarly, the functions served by my ongoing conversation with Owen proved something other—something more—than originally conceived. His contribution was essential; the project simply would not have been possible without it. I am not now talking about his expertise and judgment; nor about the combination of patience and unyielding standards that make him such a powerful teacher; nor finally about the bracing effect of the utter seriousness he brought to a venture many saw as quixotic. All those things enriched the process and improved the product, but they were not essential. What was essential was how the dynamic between us provided a means of managing the tensions that inhabited the project, a way of playing out those tensions—without being completely stymied by them or seeking to escape them. This is not to suggest that we recreated the tension, the dialectic, between author and editor; nor that one of us was the advocate of intervention, the other of restraint. Those roles shifted back and forth virtually from moment to moment. Indeed, that is the point: it was the conversation that dramatized the competing values implicated in the project—that kept them in play.

Ironically, one of the most important functions of our conversation was to discipline the rich mix of feelings we brought to the project. The emotions that compelled the effort also had power to skew it. We were at once, each in his own way, apprentices seeking to come to terms with HK and the stewards of his last words. The ardor of the apprentice can be a distorting lens. It was our function to be critical, but to do so in the service of the manuscript and not in the service of our own self-definition. The challenge was thus to draw upon powerful emotional currents, not fully understood, yet keep them from overflowing their banks and flooding the manuscript. It may be that the fact that I am the literal and not the symbolic son of the author of this work alerted us from the start to tensions that would have inhabited the project for anyone moved to undertake it. In any case, for us, given the feelings that summoned us to the task, clarity could only be the product of passionate engagement and struggle, never of dispassion.

III

The editorial policy that emerged over time from this strenuous process cannot be tightly summarized. We proceeded page by page, working through each problem in its turn. Our responses to diverse problems cannot be harmonized into a single general statement. In this respect, the editorial work the manuscript demanded resembles the legal processes it describes: the questions can be framed in general terms, but they can only be answered in particulars.

Yet readers have a right to know something about what was done to the manuscript in the course of preparing it for publication. We considered somehow rendering the editorial presence visible on the page—through the use of brackets, different typefaces, or an elaborate system of footnoting—but decided against it. Such an approach would burden the text; it would defeat one of the chief ends to which the editorial process was directed—the fluent, unimpeded movement of the essay. Also, it would not really meet the need. It would not convey the many changes—some quite sensitive—that take the form of deletions or word changes. Finally, it would be distracting. The editorial process, once entered into, is a fascinating puzzle which might draw the attention of readers away from the substance of the essay.

It has seemed preferable to pursue editorial candor by other means. Copies of the original manuscript have been placed in the

Library of Congress and the law libraries of Stanford University, the University of Chicago, and Yale University. The presence of the original in the public domain is intended to allow for informed criticism of the editing and for competing interpretations of the papers we found in HK's study on the day he died.

This afterword is another means of making known the character of the editorial process. While it is not possible here to give a full record of changes made, I will try to convey something of the flavor of the process through specific examples of different genres of changes. For the most part, I will draw examples from one part of the book—the section on subversive advocacy—in order to lend continuity to the discussion and to suggest how editorial interventions came to interact with one another.

Structure

HK conceived of the book as an effort to "map" the Court's experience under the First Amendment. In order to preserve his sense of the geography of the field, we were conservative about altering the structure of the essay. Thus, for example, we generally maintained his chapter divisions, even when the resulting chapter was only a few pages long and could easily be absorbed into a neighboring chapter. We did not want to obscure points he saw on the intellectual landscape.

This conservatism with respect to structure also prompted us to act contrary to his intentions in one of our first major editorial decisions. Not long before he died, he physically reorganized Part One; that is, he took the bulk of the "minor jurisdictions" section and placed it at the end of Part One, after the discussion of "subversive advocacy." The rationale for this move appears to have centered on the "libel" chapter and, more specifically, on *New York Times v. Sullivan*. The general principle associated with *Times*—rejection of the crime of seditious libel—was a star by which HK navigated, a reference point to which he frequently recurred. Perhaps because of its centrality in his thinking, he was stumped by the question of where to present it. Initially he discussed the general implications of *Times* in "the consensus" chapter. But on reflection he decided it did not belong there and shifted it to the "libel" chapter. A margin note at the end of "the consensus" asks: "Q: How handle 'seditious libel' now that we've excised pp. 37 ff for libel chapter?" Finally, he shifted the "minor jurisdictions" section as a whole to the end of

Part One. A margin note opposite the opening of the final "subversive advocacy" chapter indicated that he did so in order to add "NYT corroborations" and to present a "libel climax."

On the evidence of this sequence of moves, HK appears to have been weighing several considerations. It seemed necessary to present the seditious libel point early on because of its centrality in his thinking. Yet it would distort the discussion to present such a hard-won principle as an element of "the consensus." Further, he wanted to discuss the point in the context created by the subversive advocacy narrative.

Because HK did not have an opportunity to rewrite the manuscript, the structural changes he intended had not been realized. He had simply moved the blocks of material around. He had not fashioned new transitions; nor had he reorchestrated internal references. As a result, there were jarring discontinuities between chapters; and the essay recurred to themes and cases that had not yet been introduced. Also, the move had an adverse impact on "the regulation of groups" section. Those chapters are continuous with the subversive advocacy discussion—in substance, in style, in analytic texture. The intrusion of "the minor jurisdictions" at that point broke the movement of the essay and resulted in an unnecessarily complex structure.

We decided to restore the original sequence. Because the reorganization went against the grain of the manuscript as written, it would have required a great deal of editorial intervention to realize. Moreover, we had doubts about the merits of the move, even if HK were alive to implement it. Yet this solution did not satisfy. While it served to present the *New York Times* case early in the essay and to do so in an appropriate context, it frustrated HK's impulse to discuss the case in connection with the subversive advocacy narrative. As was often the case, we moved on, carrying with us a sense of dissatisfaction. The question remained open.

Happily, in this instance developments elsewhere in the manuscript presented a solution. In the original the final chapter of the "subversive advocacy" section struck us as thin and disappointing. A note at the head of the chapter suggested HK felt the same way: "This needs reworking to catch exact harvest of long journey." One of the problems was that the essay moved so quickly and abruptly from *Yates* in 1957 to *Brandenburg* in 1968 that it left the impression the latter was little more than a footnote to the former. Something was missing: the era between *Yates* and *Brandenburg* during which *Times* and kindred decisions fixed the countervalue involved in subversive advocacy cases and so facilitated the *Brandenburg* resolution. The interaction of this problem with the unresolved "seditious libel" question yielded a solution to both: place a discussion of the general implications of *Times* between *Yates* and *Brandenburg*. Although HK had not specifically directed that this be done, we were confident it was true to his intentions: it had emerged from the internal logic of his manuscript.

Editing for clarity and style

At the outset I assumed my primary task was to tighten and polish HK's language, to clear away first draft debris, to remove the sort of scaffolding that gets erected in the course of a first draft. I was only too aware of the sensitivity of what I had undertaken. Yet I did not anticipate just how difficult such routine editorial work would prove. I soon discovered that, under the circumstances of this project, there were no trivial changes.

Under normal circumstances editing at all levels—from copy editing to the deepest rethinking of substance—is an interaction. The editor suggests, the author responds, either accepting or rejecting the suggestion. In many instances the phrasing finally settled on will be neither the author's original nor the editor's suggested revision but something that has emerged from the interaction. A good editor will be sensitive to the distinctive qualities of the writer's style but will also be guided by his own sense of language, of the common language, secure in the knowledge that the author can talk back, that he will reject suggestions that distort his meaning or make his voice alien to his ear.

No such interaction was possible in this case and that generated tensions even at the level of routine copy editing. On one hand, there was the temptation to preserve HK's characteristic misspellings simply because they were *his*. It was painful to delete a word he had appropriated and made his own—"stunning," say, or "gallant"—even if it appeared three times on the same page. Yet to preserve his misspellings and the stylistic equivalents of misspellings would have been an indulgence and a disservice. On the other hand, there was the danger that the cumulative effect of my revisions would be to flatten his distinctive accents, to muffle his voice: the danger that, word by word, I would impose my voice upon his.

The aim from the start has been for the book to speak with a single voice and for that voice to be recognizably his. That is not to say that I have attempted to mimic his voice. It is one thing to recognize and seek to preserve the distinctive qualities of a voice, quite another to try to reproduce them. I found I had no alternative but to rely on my own taste and ear. It may have helped that my sense of language was powerfully shaped by his; although by no means the same, there is perhaps a sense in which our styles are kindred.

The essential issue, however, was not a matter of style but of meaning. Early on I entertained a distinction between "literary" and "substantive" dimensions of the project and saw my efforts as addressing the former. That distinction did not survive long; it simply did not exist in practice. Again and again small cracks in the manuscript—an awkward sentence, a congested passage—broadened under scrutiny to disclose difficult substantive questions. Once such a question emerged into view, it had to be engaged. We might decide not to intervene, but we must *decide*. We could not cease to see the question.

The margin notes

The margin notes vary. Some are emphatic and decisive. Others are tentative and exploratory. A number are just debris; they have already been acted on or have been obviated by other moves. In many instances the location of a note is revealing; in others it only indicates where HK's hand was when an idea struck. Most of the notes contain explicit instructions:

"Revise to underscore general advocacy insight."

"Add NYT!!!"

"Transfer to start of next chapter."

"Drop to footnote."

"Add other WWI cases in note to complete coverage."

"Revise opening."

"Expand this theme—intro to problem of 'overlay' of legal and illegal— political conspiracy."

"Add! *Hartzel v. US*-322 US (1944)—Esp. Act again like Schenck."

"Clumsy—revise transition."

Some of the notes are charming but non-operational: "This is a swell chapter." Some are charming and can be incorporated into the text. For example, beside the discussion of Judge Hand's restatement in

Dennis of the clear and present danger test as "gravity discounted by improbability," HK wrote, "Suppose wording were reversed! Improbability augmented by gravity!" We preserved this as a footnote.

Then there are notes that are ambitious and provocative—notes that suggest a basic rethinking of a portion of the essay:

Rework. Add oddity of size of speaker as variable when NY Times or CBS counts as one!
    Is this simply bequest of *Dennis?*
    Also do more on *why answer* should be different for group and individual.
    $64: Is there a more *direct* way to put *political conspiracy* issue?

Whether or not we acted on a note depended on a number of considerations. Some were simply too general—others too cryptic— to implement with any confidence. Yet in many instances a note which standing alone was an insufficient basis for intervention would interact with other notes and with outside materials in such a way that HK's intentions were illuminated. And then there were instances in which a note, though general, was simply too important not to act on.

Some notes were neither directions nor clearly crystallized perceptions but rather were reminders to himself to think about something. Here is an example of one such note which led us to perceptions we might not otherwise have had. In the original HK concludes a passage critical of Justice Holmes's example of a man falsely shouting "fire" in a crowded theater with these sentences:

Moreover, because the example is so wholly apolitical, it lacks the requisite complexity for dealing with any serious speech problem likely to confront the legal system. The man shouting "fire" is unique in that he is urging action without offering premises.

This seems an elegant way of making a point that is central to HK's discussion of subversive advocacy: The problem of incitement arises exclusively in a political context and hence involves a uniquely important countervalue—radical criticism of the society and the government. The revolutionary does not simply shout "revolt"; he offers premises in support of that conclusion, and those premises embody criticism which should be heard. The essential problem confronting the legal system is thus to protect the premises of the revolutionary, while curbing his conclusion as it approaches the threshold of action. The "fire" example betrays Holmes's insensitivity to the nature of the problem. It is inapt.

Why, then, did HK write "watch this" in the margin beside the second of the sentences quoted? Prompted by his note to stare at that sentence for a while, one realizes that "fire" is the premise and that it is the conclusion "run for your lives" that is unspoken. This may be a small point; in context HK's meaning is clear and most readers would probably just pass over that sentence. But once you have seen it, it triggers a series of further perceptions. If "fire" is the premise, then the Holmes example is even more disturbing in its application to political speech. It is the false shouting of "fire" that is criminal; presumably to shout "fire" when there is in fact a fire would be a service. Thus, within the terms of the example, everything turns on the truth or falsity of the premise. The parallel in a political context would be to shout "racism" or "injustice."

After much discussion, we revised the sentence as follows:

The man shouting "fire" does not offer premises resembling those underlying radical political rhetoric—premises that constitute criticism of government.

Thus, at some cost in elegance and compression, we addressed the problem HK's note had alerted us to. Was the change warranted? Was it responsive to what was bothering him when he wrote "watch this" in the margin? Having had the analytic perception, were we justified in making the change, even if this was not in fact what prompted the note? These are the sorts of questions of editorial propriety that occupied us after we had worked through the intellectual merits of a particular point.

The measure of a note's importance was not its length or degree of detail. A question mark or a single word could have implications reaching far beyond its immediate setting. For example: HK's strategy in the "subversive advocacy" section was to begin with *Brandenburg,* the Court's most recent major precedent; he then returned to its first encounters with the issue during the World War I period and traced the development of the law back to *Brandenburg.* (In a note he commented: "Begin with the *funeral,* as in O'Hara story.") The first case he discussed after *Brandenburg* was *Masses v. Patten* in 1917, the occasion for an opinion by Judge Learned Hand which he much admired. In his view, Hand in 1917 had an important insight into the nature of the problem which would soon be eclipsed by Justice Holmes's clear and present danger approach. HK remarks in a sentence characteristic in its generosity and sweep:

As I see it, what *Brandenburg* does in its inelegant *per curiam* opinion is to bring the law back at long last to the point where Learned Hand's elegant opinion had left it fifty-two years earlier.

In the margin, beside this sentence, he wrote: "qualify?"

When this note is viewed in the context of the manuscript as a whole, it becomes apparent why HK was uneasy. *Brandenburg* announced the principle that the constitutional line is located where advocacy of violence or law violation "is directed to inciting or producing imminent lawless action and is likely to incite or produce such action." That is, it combines the Hand emphasis on the content of the message with the Holmes emphasis on the surrounding circumstances. HK notes this in passing several pages later as a sort of afterthought at the end of a passage comparing the Hand and Holmes approaches, but he never again recurs to the point, though it would seem an important one.

We revised the sentence as follows:

Indeed, as I see it, part of the achievement of the inelegant *Brandenburg per curiam* opinion is that it recovers an insight into the nature of the problem of speech triggering action first advanced by Learned Hand's elegant opinion fifty-two years earlier.

This revision was not the end of the matter. For here we touch upon a deep current flowing through the subversive advocacy section—HK's intense dislike for the clear and present danger test. This is not an isolated instance; it is the burden of the argument; and it drives the plot. Acknowledgment that *Brandenburg* does more than simply recover the Hand approach—that it also incorporates the clear and present danger test—is thus of fundamental importance to HK's interpretation of *Brandenburg,* to his analysis of the subversive advocacy issue, and to the lines of his narrative. The one word written in the margin—"qualify?"—ramifies. And ramifies.

Additions

There were several different bases for making additions to the manuscript. Many—perhaps most—of HK's margin notes directed that material be added. Sometimes when we read a chapter against the outside resources absences became apparent. And there were gaps— some identified by HK, some forced on our attention by the internal logic of the manuscript—that demanded to be filled.

The general principle governing additions was that my words could be added, if they served as vehicles for relevant thoughts of HK's which would otherwise have to be excluded. The key criteria were the clarity of HK's instructions and whether the outside resources made clear the substance of the intended addition. Ideally, the outside resources would also provide language with which to execute the addition. This was not, however, essential. I was prepared to use my own words, if I was confident I had a secure grasp of the substantive point.

Most of the major additions were concentrated in Part One. That is where the unevenness of the manuscript was most pronounced. The early chapters were thin and fragmentary; HK had not yet hit his stride. The marginal instructions in that part of the manuscript were generally quite extensive and explicit. In part, this reflected his concern about the thinness of these chapters. In part, it reflected a more general pattern: the earlier the chapter, the more critical readings it went through, hence the more opportunity there was for marginalia to accumulate.

The "obscenity" chapter, for example, was an instance in which we determined that substantial additions were warranted. The original chapter was only fifteen pages long and dealt with just one case. HK's marginalia provided a clear and thorough diagnosis of what needed to be done. And there was a wealth of relevant outside material: several articles, four full class sessions devoted to the subject in the 1974 course, a great many notes. (It may be that one reason for the thinness of the chapter was that HK had already had his say on the subject and so was not engaged by it.) It was thus possible, guided by his instructions and drawing on the outside resources, to supplement "obscenity" with a fair degree of confidence as to the substance of his views.

There was, by contrast, another set of situations in which we found it necessary to make substantial additions, despite the fact that there was little or no specific direction from HK and few, if any, outside resources. The most significant instance of this was a projected but unwritten chapter in the "subversive advocacy" section. The gap fell in the middle of the account of the evolution of doctrine from the World War I cases to *Brandenburg* in 1969. It came between Chapter 12-"Speech Starts to Win" and Chapter 14:"The Great Confrontation— *Dennis v. United States.*" Although the essay did not miss a beat—the narrative did not stop and then start up again—it was clear that HK intended a chapter there. It was in his outline, and he had placed a title page between Chapters 12 and 14 and written on it: "The Heyday of Clear and Present Danger." There was, however, little indication of his specific intentions apart from a margin note which read: "Heyday of c/pd—*Thornhill, Thomas v. Collins, Bridges* again, *Taylor, Barnette.*"

At this point the essay is tending toward a development which has been clearly foreshadowed—the acceptance by the majority of the Court of the clear and present danger test—but instead HK skips over the decade of the 1940s to the *Dennis* case in 1951. Why did he leave this chapter unwritten? For one thing, the cases during the 1940s are difficult to accommodate within the analytic framework of the discussion because all but a few fall outside the subversive advocacy genre. Also, HK was eager to get to *Dennis*—and what he saw as the demise, once and for all, of the clear and present danger test. He recognized the need to deal with the cases of the 1940s, but seems to have seen this as little more than a housekeeping detail. They were not part of the story he was intent on telling. So, full of narrative appetite and momentum, he skipped over them.

The cases of the 1940s, however, were very much part of the story. Having skipped over them, HK slipped into a skewed perspective. Viewing *Dennis* against *Gitlow,* without reference to the intervening "heyday of clear and present danger," he saw it as a doctrinal advance (albeit in the context of a debacle). But *Dennis* looks very different when viewed from the perspective of the precedents of the 1940s which established the clear and present danger test as majority doctrine.

Similarly, HK was puzzled about the logic of the Court's opinion. Why, he asks, did it not simply rest on *Gitlow?* He suggests that the dissenting tradition has become more powerful than the official tradition and that the Court eschews *Gitlow* and adopts clear and present danger out of deference to Holmes and Brandeis. But then, having burdened itself with clear and present danger, the Court must restate the test in order to convict. HK wrote:

Chief Justice Vinson, having first gratuitously bound the Court to the Holmes-Brandeis view, now gratuitously restates that view so as to dilute the rigor of their test. He has indeed travelled the long way around the barn.

But Vinson's deference to the Holmes-Brandeis view is hardly "gratuitous," for that view is now majority doctrine. Moreover, the "heyday" cases blocked easy access to *Gitlow*. Indeed, there is a sense in which the *Dennis* Court was attempting to get back to *Gitlow*—around the obstacle presented by those decisions. The route it takes, though circuitous, is not "gratuitous."

The "heyday" chapter was not merely a gap that needed to be filled in the interest of completeness; it was an absence that distorted. It had to be filled in the interest of the subversive advocacy section as a whole. Apart from the chapter heading, this was not a matter of following directions from HK. Nor was it possible to draw on his other writings for this purpose. Rather, it was a matter of taking my bearings from the contours of the gap and filling it on the basis of an independent reading of the cases. Again, the addition ramified through the balance of the subversive advocacy discussion. The main lines of HK's plot remain, but in a variety of ways they have been softened; qualifications have been entered; the distribution of emphasis has been adjusted.

Deletions

A piece of writing takes shape as much from what is excluded as from what is included. To delete is a creative act; it can demand a deeper intellectual effort than to write. This can be the distinctive contribution of an editor: to suggest bold deletions which the author is too close to the work to conceive himself. Yet, ironically, in the case of this manuscript, it generally seemed less of a presumption to add my words than to delete HK's; that is, it was easier to justify making additions intended to facilitate access to his mind than to justify substantial deletions. Were he alive, we would have strongly recommended that major deletions be made as part of a larger rethinking of the analysis. This project, however, was dominated by the fact that these are his last words.

The problem was not with repetitious passages or with the occasional passage that simply did not go anywhere. (We used to joke: "He is just clearing his throat." Or: "He has just come back to the typewriter after a heavy lunch.") Such passages were easy to delete. The difficulties peculiar to this manuscript arose when the question was whether—in the service of some other intellectual or aesthetic value—to delete material that was of interest. In most instances, under the circumstances of this project, there simply was no higher value than preserving HK's voice.

I did, however, find it necessary to make one major deletion. The original manuscript includes a short chapter titled "commercial speech." This chapter contains two subsections. The first deals with the First Amendment status of commercial advertising. The principal case discussed is *Valentine v. Chrestensen,* a 1942 decision in which the Court held that advertising is not protected by the First Amendment. The second is devoted to the theme that "the fact that speech is sold for profit—and is in that sense 'commercial'—does not deprive it of First Amendment protection." It is advertising, not commercial publishing, that is denied protection under *Valentine.*

The "commercial speech" chapter presented two problems. First, it was without a clear position in the essay; it was a loose piece in the structural puzzle. It appears that HK may have intended this chapter and the one on "the child audience" to serve an introductory function; that he saw them as introducing general points of perspective (as opposed to surveying distinctive genres of speech problems). In any case, "commercial speech" was loosely grouped with the minor jurisdictions chapters. Second, commercial speech proved a busy area during the Burger Court years. In a series of decisions handed down after HK's death the Court moved by degrees toward the conclusion that commercial speech is within the protection of the First Amendment.

At first these developments seemed to offer a possible solution to the structural problem. A unifying theme of the minor jurisdictions section is HK's celebration of the recovery of various categories of speech from the domain of the censor. The extension of First Amendment protection to commercial advertising could thus be seen as bringing the chapter within that theme. At this stage the "updating" question—whether or not to add material on cases decided after HK's death—was still open. So, on the strength of developments since his death, we integrated the chapter into the minor jurisdictions section. We did so provisionally and with misgivings. Over time those misgivings grew. We were concerned that inclusion of the chapter within the minor jurisdictions framework created an uncritically approving context for developments HK might well have found questionable. At the same time, we were coming to the conclusion that, as a general matter, updating of the manuscript beyond the time of HK's death was neither necessary nor appropriate. The alternative of deleting the chapter altogether presented itself. We went back and forth on this; at different times each of us argued both sides of the question. We resisted deleting the chapter because it would mean removing a point on HK's map and excising material of interest. Yet to include it would have risked seriously misrepresenting him. In the end, virtually on the eve of sending the manuscript to the publisher, we concluded that the chapter should be deleted. Although we do not know what HK would have said about the commercial speech developments, we do know that he would not have said what this chapter, presented in the context of the minor jurisdictions section, would have conveyed.

IV

To talk of different genres of editorial changes is somewhat artificial. Most of the problems presented by the manuscript did not stand alone; nor did our responses. Almost invariably, as the work on a block of material progressed, we would find that broad tensions in HK's thinking underlay various problems we had initially addressed, in isolation, one at a time. This could be an intense experience: a sudden surge of current as the connection between manuscript and mind was restored. There was the satisfaction of reaching the depth at which the choices were made—a sense of touching solid ground. It was as if the editing was a sort of ongoing reconnaissance which, little by little, yielded an ever more detailed map of his mind. That map, in turn, then guided the editing.

As the project progressed, HK's mind—his mind as it survives in the medium of language—emerged as the central value. That perception oriented us; it served to clarify both the purposes of the project and the dangers that attend it. And it had an impact on certain questions of editorial policy we had carried forward with us. For example, it came to seem inappropriate—indeed, beside the point—for us to update the manuscript by adding material on developments after HK's death. We were helped in reaching this conclusion by the odd historical circumstance that the areas of law which centrally concerned him have seen little activity at the level of the Supreme Court in the years since his death. Yet the decisive factor was our deepening perception that what is original and enduring and timely about the manuscript resides in the qualities of mind it embodies.

Have we kept faith with HK's mind? I remain uncertain. The great challenge has been to distinguish between tensions that obscure his mind and tensions that are expressions of his mind. It has been to pursue internal consistency—coherence—while preserving the unresolved chords in his thinking. This was the most sensitive sort of editorial problem we faced. To what extent could we properly take on his confusions as our own? How far could we press toward their resolution? Could we properly act on the assumption that we could persuade him, if he was alive? Should we mute the unresolved chords in the text? Or, on the contrary, should we highlight them?

Sometimes the unresolved tensions in the manuscript were like a sprung bow: energy we could release. This could be immensely satisfying. At such times, the manuscript seemed a living thing, developing according to an internal logic HK had set in motion. There were many other times, however, when the effort to gain access to his mind yielded not clarity but confusion. This did not necessarily mean the editorial process had derailed. It may indeed have run true; it may have achieved access to his mind, but it was access to an area of active confusion in his mind. In one's own work this can be the decisive moment; so often in a piece of writing it is that which resists one that is most alive. But under the circumstances of this project, it was a wall, a barrier, the end of the line.

The irony is that HK's mind—actively baffled, puzzled, in play— never seemed closer at hand than it did at those moments. The sensation was one of coming close, so close, yet with no way to get any closer: oh, for an opportunity to talk with him, to press the point, to provoke a response. The danger was that our enthusiasm for a particular point and our frustration at not being able to urge it upon him would lead us to overreach—to revise his mind by way of his prose. In a sense, what happened at such moments was that the critical process outran the editorial process. I could write an essay on the tensions and unresolved chords in HK's thinking on a particular point—sometimes I did so in the memos—but I could not justify making changes in *his* essay. I could justify editorial interventions that made his mind more accessible, but I could not justify changing his mind.

I am deeply marked by the knowledge that it is possible, through language, in Auden's lovely phrase, "to break bread with the dead." Yet that realization does not stand alone. It cannot be separated from the hard knowledge that this is only possible up to a point, that the connection is at best partial and intermittent. I have found that difficult to accept. Looking back, I can see now that I deferred completion in the hope I would somehow become wiser, able to see further, to go deeper; beneath the surface turbulence of my life, I waited.

The passage of time brought no answers, no breakthroughs, but it did bring unexpected gifts. Early on, I experienced the project as an isolated struggle to wrest something away from death. I approached it as a crisis, an emergency. With time, this changed. My understanding of tradition ripened. In large part, this was due to the generosity of those around me. The responsive chord the project struck in others and the good will it elicited both sustained and instructed me. I began to discern certain familiar motifs in the world around me. The refusal, through language, to accept death as final; the unfinished texture of things; the importance of fidelity to form (the discipline of one's passion) as a means of acting appropriately in the midst of mystery—these themes, so explicit in my life by virtue of this project, proved to be present in lives all around me. I came to see the project as part of a larger community of effort, a larger conversation. Absorbed into the ongoingness of life, it became possible to bring to a close that which could never be finished.

The generosity that has meant most—sustaining the project and gracing my life—is that of my wife, Patricia Evans. Her life, no less than mine, has been caught in the web of love and language radiating out from my father's words. I am grateful for her love and her support, for her patience *and* her impatience. Above all, I am grateful for her insistence that life has its claims. What we have created together is at the center of my understanding of this effort.

My first thought upon learning of my father's death was, "But who will I *talk* with now?" Our ongoing conversation was for me a domain of freedom and delight; I loved talking with him. Little did I know at that moment that the conversation had not ended but rather had altered its terms; that it would not only continue but would, in some respects, deepen and intensify. My father's last words—the wealth of questions he bequeathed—have enriched my life. At once a burden, a riddle, and a gift, this inheritance demanded a concentrated effort which, with the grace of time, disclosed spacious possibilities. The conversation will continue; the questions will remain in play. That is part of what I have learned: the work is always unfinished. Yet, mercifully, there are also endings. This phase of my conversation with my father is over. So, it is with the deepest gratitude and affection that I now, with these words, take my leave.

Notes

———————————◆———————————

Editor's Introduction

1. Chapter 2, p. 23.
2. *Ibid.*
3. Chafee, *Free Speech in the United States* (Cambridge, Mass.: Harvard University Press, 1941).
4. Meiklejohn, *Free Speech and Its Relation to Self-Government* (New York: Harper & Row, 1948).
5. Kalven, *The Negro and the First Amendment* (Columbus: Ohio University Press, 1965), pp. 5–6.
6. 376 U.S. 254 (1964).
7. Kalven, "The New York Times Case: A Note on the Central Meaning of the First Amendment," 1964 *Supreme Court Review* 191.
8. Kalven, "Tradition in Law," in *The Great Ideas Today* (R. Hutchins and M. Adler, eds.) (Chicago: Encyclopedia Britannica, 1974).
9. *Id.* at 22.
10. *Id.* at 32.
11. *Id.* at 33.
12. 341 U.S. 123, 162–63 (1951).
13. Kalven, "Tradition in Law," p. 33, quoting Llewellyn, *The Common Law Tradition* (Boston: Little, Brown & Co., 1960).
14. Eliot, "Tradition and the Individual Talent," in *Selected Prose of T. S. Eliot* (New York: Harcourt, Brace, Jovanovich; and Farrar, Straus and Giroux, 1975) (first published 1919).
15. *Id.* at 38.
16. Kalven, "Professor Ernst Freund and *Debs v. United States,*" 40 *University of Chicago Law Review* 235, 236 (1973).

17. Eliot, *Selected Prose,* p. 39.
18. MacIntyre, *After Virtue: A Study in Moral Theory* (Notre Dame: Notre Dame University Press, 1981), p. 222.
19. Memorial tribute, Rockefeller Memorial Chapel, the University of Chicago, December 6, 1974.
20. Kalven, "Alexander Meiklejohn," memorial tribute, January 31, 1965 [privately printed].
21. Kalven, "The Metaphysics of the Law of Obscenity," [1960] *Supreme Court Review* 1, 45.
22. Kalven, "Tradition in Law," p. 27.
23. 395 U.S. 444 (1969).

Preface

1. 244 F. 535 (1917).
2. *Id.* at 543.
3. A suggestion of this approach was made in Justice Black's concurring and dissenting opinion in *Cox v. Louisiana,* 379 U.S. 536 (1965), a case ostensibly involving the non-content regulation of public issue picketing. In finding the statute's flat ban on obstructing public passageways unconstitutional in that it exempted labor unions, Justice Black argued:

> . . . I have no doubt about the general power of Louisiana to bar all picketing on its streets and highways. Standing, patrolling, or marching back and forth on streets is conduct, not speech, and as conduct can be regulated or prohibited. But by specifically permitting picketing for the publication of labor union views, Louisiana is attempting to pick and choose among the views it is willing to have discussed on its streets. It thus is trying to prescribe by law what matters of public interest people whom it allows to assemble on its streets may and may not discuss. This seems to me to be censorship in a most odious form, unconstitutional under the First and Fourteenth Amendments. And to deny this appellant and his group use of the streets because of their views against racial discrimination, while allowing other groups to use the streets to voice opinions on other subjects, also amounts, I think, to an invidious discrimination forbidden by the Equal Protection Clause of the Fourteenth Amendment.

> *Id.* at 581. See also *Chicago Police Department v. Mosley,* 408 U.S. 92 (1972).

Chapter 1: The Consensus on Untouchable Content

1. 310 U.S. 296 (1940).
2. *Id.* at 310.
3. *Burstyn v. Wilson,* 343 U.S. 495 (1952).
4. *Id.* at 528-9.

5. 393 U.S. 97 (1968).

6. 154 Tenn. 105, 289 S.W. 363 (1927). See Kalven, "A Commemorative Case Note: *Scopes v. State,*" 27 *University of Chicago Law Review* 505 (1960); Kalven, " 'Please, Morris, Don't Make Trouble': Two Lessons in Courtroom Confrontation," 27 *Journal of Social Issues* 219 (1971).

7. 393 U.S. at 103-4.

8. 367 U.S. 488 (1961).

9. *Id.* at 495.

10. Mill, *On Liberty* (Indianapolis: Bobbs-Merrill, 1956) (first published 1859), pp. 28-9.

11. 360 U.S. 684 (1959).

12. *Id.* at 688.

13. *Id.* at 688-9.

14. 394 U.S. 576 (1969).

15. *Id.* at 591.

16. The consensus in this area is somewhat qualified by the special case of broadcasting.

17. 327 U.S. 146 (1946).

18. The Supreme Court affirmed the judgment of the Court of Appeals in *Esquire v. Walker,* 151 F. 2d 49 (D.C. Cir. 1945). The opinion of the Court of Appeals was by Judge Thurman Arnold, who quoted the trial record at length in an effort to demonstrate "the kind of mental confusion" that ensues when a government agency takes upon itself the task of resolving "the age old question when a scantily clad lady is art, and when she is highly improper." *Id.* at 52.

19. 327 U.S. at 157-8.

20. 333 U.S. 507 (1948).

21. *Id.* at 510.

22. *Cohen v. California,* 403 U S. 15 (1971).

23. *Id.* at 18.

24. *Ibid.*

25. *Ibid.*

26. *Id.* at 19.

27. *Id.* at 20.

28. *Id.* at 21.

29. *Id.* at 23.

30. *Id.* at 24-5.

31. 315 U.S. 568 (1942).

32. *Id.* at 573.

33. *Id.* at 571-2.

34. 354 U.S. 476 (1957).

35. *Id.* at 484.

Chapter 2: Contempt by Publication

1. There is a striking analogy between this strategy of regulation and that attempted in the field of obscenity in the interest of protecting the child audience. In the latter area the Court has firmly rejected efforts to shield children from unsuitable material by prohibiting it more generally.
2. 366 U.S. 717 (1961).
3. *Id.* at 730.
4. 384 U.S. 333 (1966).
5. *Id.* at 358.
6. 314 U.S. 252 (1941).
7. *Id.* at 279.
8. *Id.* at 291.
9. *Id.* at 268-9.
10. *Id.* at 269.
11. *Id.* at 270.
12. *Id.* at 270-1.
13. *Id.* at 273.
14. *Id.* at 303.
15. *Id.* at 278.
16. 328 U.S. 331 (1946).
17. *Id.* at 350.
18. *Id.* at 347.
19. 331 U.S. 367 (1947).
20. *Id.* at 391.
21. *Id.* at 376.
22. 370 U.S. 375 (1962).
23. *Id.* at 394.
24. *Id.* at 389.
25. Justice Harlan did not accept the Chief Justice's reasoning with respect to the general character of the grand jury inquiry. He pointed out that individual indictments might have been forthcoming and stressed that, though the statements "would tend to aid rather than to prejudice implicated individuals . . . the State as well as the individual is entitled to a day in court." *Id.* at 398.
26. *Id.* at 392.

Chapter 3: Obscenity

1. The most striking, and depressing, contemporary evidence of the political potency lurking in the obscenity issue is to be found in the Senate hearings on the nomination of Abe Fortas to the Chief Justiceship in 1968. In the course of the hearings the senators received extended testimony from anti-obscenity groups and even went so far as to view one

of the movies which the Court, with Fortas in the majority, had found to be protected by the First Amendment. In effect, the senators used criteria that would have served to bar promotion of *all* the justices then on the Court. It is of course possible that the senators were not really serious about obscenity but were simply using it as a device to block Fortas. Nevertheless, it is revealing that they thought obscenity such good ammunition for their purposes.

Another episode which serves to illustrate the political potency of the issue is the fate of *The Report of the Commission on Obscenity and Pornography. The Report,* issued in 1970, recommended, among other things, that obscenity laws aimed at consenting adults be repealed. President Nixon responded by "categorically" rejecting the *Report* and by characterizing its conclusions as "morally bankrupt." The Senate's reponse was equally emphatic. By a vote of 60 to 5, it rejected various of the Commission's findings and recommendations and declared that "the Commission has not properly performed its statutory duties."

2. Arnold, *Fair Fights and Foul: A Dissenting Lawyer's Life* (New York: Harcourt, Brace & World, 1965), p. 184.
3. 354 U.S. 476 (1957).
4. 335 U.S. 848 (1948).
5. The possibility of such a division had arisen because Justice Frankfurter, a personal friend of Wilson's, had disqualified himself.
6. 352 U.S. 380 (1957).
7. *Id.* at 383-4.
8. 354 U.S. at 481.
9. *Id.* at 484-5.
10. *Chaplinsky v. New Hampshire,* 315 U.S. 568 (1942).
11. 354 U.S. at 491.
12. L.R. 3 Q.B. 360 (1868).
13. 354 U.S. at 489.
14. 370 U.S. 478 (1962).
15. *Id.* at 490.
16. *Id.* at 482.
17. 378 U.S. 184 (1964).
18. *Id.* at 194-5, quoting *Pennekamp v. Florida,* 328 U.S. at 335.
19. 383 U.S. 413 (1966).
20. *Id.* at 418.
21. *Id.* at 415-16.
22. *Id.* at 419-20.
23. 378 U.S. at 197.
24. 383 U.S. at 433.
25. *Id.* at 481.
26. Justice Douglas adds a fillip to his opinion by appending a sermon titled "Dr. Peale and Fanny Hill" in which a Reverend John R. Graham argues

with zest that *Fanny Hill* preaches a truer morality than does Dr. Peale. It is a thesis for which I, like Justice Douglas, cannot altogether suppress my sympathy.

27. Justice Clark offers a capsule plot review, which concludes:

> In each of the sexual scenes the exposed bodies of the participants are described in minute and individual detail. The pubic hair is often used for a background to the most vivid and precise descriptions of the response, condition, size, shape, and color of the sexual organs before, during and after orgasms. There are some short transitory passages between the various sexual episodes, but for the most part they only set the scene and identify the participants for the next orgy, or make smutty reference and comparison to past episodes.

Id. at 446. Although I suspect he has been highly selective in his excerpting, Clark's critique of the expert testimony is deadly. Three instances caught my eye. One expert finds that Fanny is "an intellectual . . . someone who is extremely curious about life and who seeks . . . to record with accuracy the details of the external world, physical sensations, psychological responses . . . an empiricist." Another finds in the following description an example of the skillful writing that characterizes the book: "Phoebe who is 'red-faced, fat, and in her early 50's, who waddles into a room.' She doesn't walk in, she waddles in." Still another cites the giving of a silver watch to a servant; he describes it as "an odd and interesting custom that I would like to know more about." *Id.* at 447-50. These instances of expert testimony are, to be sure, a bit unnerving. Yet I suspect the decisive point is that there are many examples of commercial pornography on behalf of which one could not solicit *any* public expressions of expert opinion.

28. *Id.* at 441.
29. 383 U.S. 502 (1966).
30. 383 U.S. 463 (1966).
31. *Id.* at 468-9 n.9.
32. *Id.* at 480-1.
33. 386 U.S. 767 (1967).
34. *Id.* at 769.
35. 394 U.S. 557 (1969).
36. *Id.* at 564-5.
37. *Id.* at 565-6.
38. *Id.* at 568.
39. *Id.* at 566-7.
40. *Id.* at 567.
41. *Ibid.*
42. 402 U.S. 351 (1971).
43. *Id.* at 355-6.
44. *Id.* at 360.
45. *Ibid.*

46. 413 U.S. at 20.
47. 413 U.S. 49 (1973).
48. 413 U.S. 15 (1973).
49. *Id.* at 23.
50. *Id.* at 57-8.
51. *Id.* at 58.
52. *Ibid.*
53. *Id.* at 63.
54. *Id.* at 21.
55. *Id.* at 22.
56. *Id.* at 24.
57. *Id.* at 73-4.
58. *Id.* at 97.
59. *Id.* at 98.
60. *Id.* at 94.
61. *Ibid.*
62. *Id.* at 101.
63. *Id.* at 103.
64. *Id.* at 112-13.

Chapter 4: The Child Audience

1. Mill, *On Liberty* (Indianapolis: Bobbs-Merrill, 1956), pp.13-14.
2. 352 U.S. 380 (1957).
3. 390 U.S. 629 (1968).
4. *Roth v. United States,* 354 U.S. 476 (1957).
5. 390 U.S. at 650.
6. *Id.* at 673-4.
7. 391 U.S. 462 (1968).
8. 390 U.S. 676 (1968).
9. 391 U.S. at 462-3.
10. 333 U.S. 507 (1948).
11. *Kingsley International Pictures v. Regents,* 360 U.S. 684 (1959).
12. 397 U.S. 728 (1970).
13. *Id.* at 734.
14. *Id.* at 741.

Chapter 5: Libel

1. 376 U.S. 254 (1964).
2. Courtney, "Absurdities of the Law of Libel and Slander," 36 *American Law Review* 552 (1902).
3. 343 U.S. 250 (1952).
4. *Id.* at 252.
5. *Chaplinsky v. New Hampshire,* 315 U.S. 568 (1942).

6. *Roth v. United States,* 354 U.S. 476 (1957).

7. 343 U.S. at 286.

8. Several factors contribute to the impression that Alabama pounced on this opportunity to punish the *Times* for its support of the civil rights movement. First, the newspaper was all but invisible in the community in which the plaintiff was claiming harm to his reputation: of the 650,000 published copies of the issue containing the advertisement, only 394 were distributed in Alabama, of which only 35 were circulated in Montgomery County. Second, given the mood of the day, there was something disingenuous about the argument that the advertisement's allegations of vigorous measures to counter the civil rights movement would be regarded as defamatory by a Southern audience. Third, several other officials, including the Governor of Alabama, had libel suits pending against the *Times,* claiming that the same advertisement had defamed them and seeking an additional 2.5 million dollars in damages.

9. 376 U.S. at 280.

10. *Id.* at 273.

11. 1 Stat. 596 (1798).

12. 250 U.S. 616 (1919).

13. 40 Stat. 553 (1918).

14. 250 U.S. at 630.

15. 376 U.S. at 273.

16. *Id.* at 275.

17. *Id.* at 276.

18. *Ibid.*

19. *Id.* at 270.

20. 360 U.S. 564 (1959).

21. 376 U.S. at 282.

22. *Id.* at 292.

23. 383 U.S. 75 (1966).

24. *Id.* at 83.

25. Justice Brennan did observe that the fact that the plaintiff was no longer supervisor of the recreation area when the column appeared was of no "decisional significance here," for "the management of the Area was still a matter of lively public interest; propositions for further change were abroad, and public interest in the way in which the prior administration had done its task continued strong." *Id.* at 87 n.14.

He also noted the irony that the argument by which the plaintiff sought to show that the statement applied specifically to him tended to support the conclusion that he was a public official: "to prove the article referred to him, he showed the importance of his role; that same showing, at the least, raises a substantial argument that he was a 'public official.'" *Ibid.*

26. *Id.* at 85.

27. *Id.* at 95.
28. *Id.* at 92-4.

Chapter 6: Reflexive Disorder: The First Encounter

1. The countervalue of maintaining public order should be distinguished from the countervalue of facilitating competing uses of the public forum. The latter underlies the non-content regulation of the time, place, and manner of speech. See Kalven, "The Concept of the Public Forum," 1965 *Supreme Court Review* 1.
2. *Cantwell v. Connecticut,* 310 U.S. 296 (1940); *Chaplinsky v. New Hampshire,* 315 U.S. 568 (1942); *Terminiello v. Chicago,* 337 U.S. 1 (1949); *Feiner v. New York,* 340 U.S. 315 (1951); *Kunz v. New York,* 340 U.S. 290 (1951); *Beauharnais v. Illinois,* 343 U.S. 250 (1952).
3. Professor Zechariah Chafee, a great champion of free speech and a Boston gentleman, explained the rationale for such regulation this way in a passage cited by the Court:

> Words of this type offer little opportunity for the usual process of counter-argument. The harm is done as soon as they are communicated, or is liable to follow almost immediately in the form of retaliatory violence. The only sound explanation of the punishment of obscenity and profanity is that the words are criminal, not because of the ideas they communicate, but like acts because of their immediate consequences to the five senses. The man who swears in a street car is as much of a nuisance as the man who smokes there. Insults are punished like a threatening gesture, since they are likely to provoke a fight.

Free Speech in the United States (Cambridge, Mass.: Harvard University Press, 1941), p. 150.
4. 315 U.S. at 569-70.
5. It should also be noted that the words were addressed to a *policeman. Chaplinsky* thus introduces an issue that has been much in the news in recent years: Is it a breach of peace to address "fighting words" to a policeman on duty? Certainly the culture has coined some new "classical epithets" for the police!
6. Such a narrow statute is present in *Chaplinsky* two years later. Hence the two decisions are wholly consistent. Moreover, Justice Roberts in *Cantwell* anticipates the fighting words formula. After noting that a speaker may commit a breach of peace by provoking violence and disturbance of good order, he adds:

> Decisions to this effect are many, but examination discloses that, in practically all, the provocative language which was held to amount to a breach of the peace consisted of profane, indecent, or abusive remarks directed to the person of the hearer. Resort to epithets or personal abuse is not in any proper sense

communication of information or opinion safeguarded by the Constitution . . .

     310 U.S. at 309-10.

7. 376 U.S. 254, 270 (1964).
8. 310 U.S. at 310.
9. 337 U.S. at 3.
10. *Id.* at 13.
11. *Id.* at 23.
12. *Id.* at 32.
13. *Id.* at 33.
14. *Id.* at 37.
15. 340 U.S. at 294.
16. *Id.* at 285.
17. *Ibid.*
18. *Id.* at 305.
19. *Id.* at 298.
20. *Id.* at 299.
21. 340 U.S. at 319-20.
22. *Id.* at 321.
23. *Id.* at 275.
24. *Id.* at 330.
25. *Ibid.* at 324 n. 5.
26. *Id.* at 288.
27. *Id.* at 289.
28. *Ibid.*
29. *Id.* at 326.
30. *Ibid.*
31. 343 U.S. at 251.
32. *Id.* at 276.
33. *Id.* at 258
34. I have had occasion elsewhere to discuss *Beauharnais* in connection with the problem of group libel and as an instance of the two-level theory. See Kalven, *The Negro and the First Amendment* (Columbus, Ohio: Ohio State University Press, 1965).
35. 343 U.S. at 303-4.
36. *Id.* at 267.

Chapter 7: Reflexive Disorder: The Civil Rights Cases

1. 372 U.S. 229 (1963).
2. *Id.* at 235.
3. *Id.* at 236.
4. *Id.* at 237.

5. *Id.* at 236.
6. 379 U.S. 536 (1965).
7. *Id.* at 549-50.
8. *Id.* at 551.
9. *Id.* at 552.
10. 394 U.S. 111 (1969).
11. *Id.* at 111-2.
12. *Id.* at 113.
13. *Ibid.*
14. *Id.* at 117.
15. *Ibid.*
16. *Id.* at 118.
17. *Id.* at 124.
18. Mailer, *Miami and the Siege of Chicago* (New York: New American Library, 1968).
19. 394 U.S. at 124.
20. 382 U.S. 87 (1969).
21. *Id.* at 90-1.
22. 379 U.S. at 579.
23. 394 U.S. at 120.
24. 376 U.S. 254, 270 (1964).

Chapter 8: Reflexive Disorder: *Chaplinsky* Redux

1. 403 U.S. 15 (1971).
2. Prior to *Cohen,* Justice Harlan addressed the question of the scope of *Chaplinsky,* albeit briefly, in *Street v. New York,* 394 U.S. 576, the 1969 case of a man who, upon learning that James Meredith had been shot, burned his American flag on a street corner and said, "We don't need no damn flag." Writing on behalf of a five-member majority, Harlan tersely dismissed the possibility of interdicting Street's comment on the ground that it might invite retaliatory violence:

> Though it is conceivable that some listeners might have been moved to retaliate upon hearing appellant's disrespectful words, we cannot say that appellant's remarks were so inherently inflammatory as to come within that small class of "fighting words" which are "likely to provoke the average person to retaliation, and thereby cause a breach of the peace." *Chaplinsky v. New Hampshire.*

Id. at 592.
3. 403 U.S. at 18.
4. *Id.* at 20.
5. *Ibid.*
6. *Id.* at 21.

7. *Ibid.*

8. *Ibid.*

9. *Ibid.* at 22-3.

10. *Id.* at 23.

11. *Ibid.*

12. *Id.* at 25.

13. *Id.* at 26.

14. *Ibid.*

15. *Ibid.*

16. 315 U.S. at 572.

17. 403 U.S. at 27.

18. 405 U.S. 518 (1972).

19. *Id.* at 521.

20. *Id.* at 524.

21. *Id.* at 529.

22. *Id.* at 537.

23. 408 U.S. 901 (1972).

24. 408 U.S. 913 (1972).

25. 408 U.S. 914 (1972).

26. *Ibid.*

27. *Id.* at 913.

28. In 1974 the *Lewis* case returned to the Court, 415 U.S. 130. On remand the state court had sustained the conviction on the ground that the statute applied only to "obscene and opprobrious words" addressed to policemen on duty. The Court, in an opinion by Justice Brennan, reversed. It found the statute overbroad in that it included within its scope words "that do not 'by their very utterance inflict injury or tend to incite an immediate breach of the peace.'" *Id.* at 133. The Court noted—but found it unnecessary to decide—the point about the possibility that a great degree of restraint is to be expected from a policeman. This time Justice Powell, concurring, joined in the Court's application of the overbreadth technique, an approach he had eschewed in the first *Lewis* case.

   Justice Blackmun in a dissent joined by Chief Justice Burger and Justice Rehnquist criticized the majority's use of the overbreadth and vagueness doctrines in speech cases:

   Overbreadth and vagueness in the field of speech, as the present case and *Gooding* indicate, have become result-oriented rubberstamps attuned to the easy and imagined self-assurance that "one man's vulgarity is another's lyric."

   Id. at 140.

29. 408 U.S. at 902.

30. *Id.* at 905.

31. *Ibid.*
32. *Id.* at 906.
33. *Id.* at 909.
34. *Id.* at 914.
35. 403 U.S. at 21.
36. *Id.* at 21.
37. Apart from the offensive speech cases, there were two other noteworthy street corner speech cases during this period: *Bachellar v. Maryland,* 397 U.S. 564 (1970), and *Coates v. Cincinnati,* 402 U.S. 611 (1971).

    Bachellar involved a disorderly conduct conviction for events growing out of an anti-Vietnam demonstration in front of a recruiting station. The statute under which the demonstrators were charged prohibited "the doing or saying or both of that which offends, disturbs, incites or tends to incite a number of people gathered in the same area." In his instructions to the jury the trial judge quoted the statute and added that "refusal to obey a policeman's command to move on when not to do so may endanger the public peace, may amount to disorderly conduct." The jury returned a guilty verdict. The Supreme Court unanimously reversed, in an opinion by Justice Brennan, on the ground that the jury charge left the jury several possibilities, one of which would infringe the defendants' constitutional rights: to find that their anti-Vietnam sentiments came within the statutory clause about "doing or saying that which offends, disturbs, incites or tends to incite" others. Because the verdict was a general one, the Court concluded, it must be reversed, for it may have rested on the unconstitutional ground.

    Coates involved a challenge to a city ordinance making it an offense for "three or more persons to assemble . . . on any of the sidewalks . . . and then conduct themselves in a manner annoying to persons passing by." The Court upset the conviction in a 6 to 3 decision. The dissenters—Chief Justice Burger and Justices White and Blackmun— argued that the ordinance was clear enough for the regulation of conduct including picketing and that if and when it was applied too broadly, the application could be struck down. But Justice Stewart, writing for the majority, found the prohibition of "annoying" conduct unconstitutionally vague and overbroad; he could conceive of no set of facts that would "serve to validate" it. *Id.* at 616.
38. *New York Times v. Sullivan,* 376 U.S. 254 (1964).
39. 403 U.S. at 20.

Chapter 9: The Core Issue and the *Brandenburg* Answer

1. Mill, *On Liberty* (Indianapolis: Bobbs-Merrill, 1956), pp. 67-8.
2. It might be an instructive exercise to compare with some rigor the problems of pornography and radical rhetoric. One point is immediately

clear: there is no equivalent in radical rhetoric to hard-core pornography.

3. 395 U.S. 444 (1969).
4. 274 U.S. 357 (1927).
5. 395 U.S. at 446.
6. *Id.* at 447-9.
7. *Kingsley International Pictures v. Regents,* 360 U.S. 684 (1959).
8. *Epperson v. Arkansas,* 393 U.S. 97 (1968).

Chapter 10: The Beginnings

1. 244 F. 535 (1917).
2. 249 U.S. 47 (1919).
3. 40 Stat. 217 (1917).
4. 244 F. at 538.
5. *Id.* at 539.
6. *Id.* at 539–40.
7. *Id.* at 540.
8. *Id.* at 536.
9. *Id.* at 541.
10. *Id.* at 541–2.
11. *Id.* at 542–3.
12. 249 U.S. 211 (1919).
13. The full text of the *Schenck* leaflet can be found in Anastaplo, *The Constitutionalist* (Dallas: Southern Methodist University Press, 1971), pp. 296-300.
14. 249 U.S. at 51-2.
15. *Id.* at 52.
16. *Goldman v. United States,* 245 U.S. 474 (1918). Goldman and Berkman were convicted of conspiring to "induce" others to disobey the Selective Draft Act by failing to register. The Court unanimously affirmed the convictions, holding that conspiracy is in itself a substantive offense whether or not the object of the conspiracy has been accomplished.
17. 249 U.S. at 51.
18. For example, in the play *Rosencrantz and Guildenstern Are Dead* (New York: Grove Press, 1967) by Tom Stoppard, one of the characters comes to the front of the stage and shouts at the audience, "Fire!" Another asks in baffled tones, "Where?" And the first replies, "It's all right—I'm demonstrating the misuse of free speech. To prove that it exists."
19. The issue is one on which constitutional law cannot yet be said to be fully settled, but the tenor of recent cases, decided while the nation was at war in Vietnam, is firmly contrary to the Holmes premise in *Schenck*. The most striking of these decisions is *New York Times v. United States,* 403 U.S. 713 (1971), the Pentagon Papers case, in which the Supreme Court

refused to enjoin the publication of classified documents about the war, publication intended to fuel public criticism of the war. See Kalven, "Foreword: Even When a Nation Is at War, The Supreme Court, 1978 Term," 85 *Harvard Law Review* 3 (1971). See also *Bond v. Floyd*, 385 U.S. 116 (1966), *Watts v. United States*, 394 U.S. 705 (1969), *Cohen v. California*, 403 U.S. 15 (1971), *Bachellar v. Maryland*, 397 U.S. 564 (1970).

20. *Brandenburg v. Ohio*, 395 U.S. 444 (1969).

21. 249 U.S. at 213-14.

22. *Id.* at 215.

23. *Id.* at 216.

24. Chafee, *Free Speech in the United States* (Cambridge, Mass.: Harvard University Press, 1941). Professor Chafee was not unappreciative of Judge Hand's efforts in *Masses*. Indeed, he dedicated the first edition of his book (1920)—though not the second (1941)—to Hand. Revealing correspondence between Hand and Chafee, as well as Hand and Holmes, is presented in Gunther, "Learned Hand and the Origins of Modern First Amendment Doctrine: Some Fragments of History," 27 *Stanford Law Review* 719 (1975).—*Ed.*

25. Chafee, *Free Speech*, pp. 80-1.

26. *Id.* at p. 82.

27. *Ibid.*

28. *Id.* at 84.

29. Chafee goes on to cite and quote a powerful critique of *Debs* by Professor Freund in *The New Republic*. See Kalven, "Ernst Freund and the First Amendment Tradition," 40 *University of Chicago Law Review* 235 (1973).

30. Chafee. *Free Speech*, p. 86.

31. *Abrams v. United States*, 250 U.S. 616 (1919).

32. For Chafee, the *Abrams* case was the great injustice of the World War I period, and he had written an eloquent law review article condemning the trial. This article became something of *cause celebre* when Harvard University, pressured by angry alumni, conducted an inquiry and required Chafee to defend his thesis. It is not easy for us at this distance in time to appreciate what an extraordinary ally Justice Holmes must have been when he lent his prestige to the Chafee side in his *Abrams* dissent.

33. 40 Stat. 553 (1918).

34. "A Contemporary State Trial—*The United States v. Jacob Abrams et al*, 33 *Harvard Law Review* 747 (1920).

35. 250 U.S. at 620.

36. *Ibid.*

37. *Ibid.*

38. *Id.* at 620-1.

39. *Id.* at 621-2.

40. *Abrams* suggests a type of problem we have not yet had occasion to

confront: direct advocacy of concrete action which action itself is not a crime. Can the inciting to anything short of crime be censored? Can it be made a crime to incite people, say, not to buy War Bonds, not to volunteer for the Armed Forces, or, as in *Abrams,* to urge them to strike their jobs in a munitions factory?

The question is puzzling. On one hand, there may well be weighty social values which the society has an interest in protecting from words which are triggers of action even though the target action itself cannot be made criminal. On the other hand, if the target of the incitement can be adjusted in this fashion, the barrier that free speech policy seeks to interpose between censorship and radical criticism will dissolve. The Court has never passed on the issue in this precise form, and in *Abrams* it receives little attention from either the majority or the dissent.

The issue resurfaces in *Taylor v. Mississippi,* 319 U.S. 583 (1943).

41. 376 U.S. 254 (1964).
42. 250 U.S. at 618-19.
43. *Id.* at 626.
44. *Ibid.*
45. *Id.* at 627.
46. *Id.* at 627-8.
47. *Id.* at 628.
48. *Id.* at 628-9.
49. *Id.* at 629.
50. *Id.* at 629-30.
51. *Id.* at 630-1.
52. Chafee, *Free Speech,* p. 136.
53. 251 U.S. 466 (1920).
54. 252 U.S. 239 (1920).
55. 254 U.S. 325 (1920).
56. 255 U.S. 407 (1921).
57. 254 U.S. at 327.
58. *Id.* at 332.
59. *Id.* at 333.

Chapter 11: The Great Debate: Sanford in *Gitlow* vs. Brandeis in *Whitney*

1. 268 U.S. 652 (1925).
2. *Id.* at 665.
3. *Ibid.* at 673.
4. *Id.* at 661.
5. *Id.* at 663.
6. *Id.* at 670.
7. *Id.* at 669.

8. *Id.* at 656.
9. Justice Sanford marshals impressive precedent for this view. *Abrams, Schaefer, Pierce* and *Gilbert* all involved speech statutes proper and all sustained the statutes.
10. *Id.* at 671.
11. *Id.* at 673.
12. *Ibid.*
13. *Ibid.*
14. 274 U.S. 357 (1927).
15. *Id.* at 373.
16. *Id.* at 371.
17. *Id.* at 373.
18. *Id.* at 374.
19. Although the Court makes no direct reference to the First Amendment, *Fiske v. Kansas,* 274 U.S. 380 (1927), a decision handed down the same day as *Whitney,* shows that the majority was capable of protecting radical speech. The defendant was charged under the Kansas criminal syndicalism statute with advocating criminal syndicalism by recruiting members for the I.W.W. The *only* evidence that the I.W.W. so advocated was a copy of the preamble to its constitution which called for the industrial organization of workers for the purpose of taking possession of the machinery of production and abolishing the wage system. The Court unanimously reversed, because of the utter absence of evidence in the record of violation of the statute. It held that the preamble standing alone simply was not evidence that the I.W.W. advocated the terror and violence of criminal syndicalism.

   Fiske deserves to be remembered for several things. It is an early example of judicial sensitivity in reading radical rhetoric. It is perhaps the first instance of the Court extending special technical protections—in this instance the stringency of review of the evidence at trial and the employment of the "utter failure of evidence" tactic—in the First Amendment area. Finally, it should be noted that the opinion is by Justice Sanford, the author of the majority opinions in *Gitlow* and *Whitney.*
20. *Id.* at 374.
21. *Id.* at 375.
22. *Id.* at 375-6.
23. *Id.* at 376.
24. *Ibid.*
25. *Ibid.*
26. *Id.* at 377.
27. 254 U.S. at 333.
28. 274 U.S. at 374.
29. *Id.* at 377-8.

30. *Id.* at 378-9.
31. Justice Brandeis's exposition of the test here seems to contemplate evidence and trial on the issue of danger. One can only wonder then how the Court knew the danger in *Schenck* and *Debs,* or how Holmes and Brandeis knew the lack of it in *Gitlow* and in the World War I cases in which they dissented.
32. 274 U.S. at 379.
33. *Ibid.*
34. *Id.* at 376.

Chapter 12: Speech Starts to Win

1. 283 U.S. 359 (1931).
2. *Id.* at 362.
3. 391 U.S. 367 (1968).
4. 283 U.S. at 361.
5. *Id.* at 368-9.
6. 301 U.S. 242 (1937).
7. Chafee, *Free Speech,* p. 397.
8. See *Herndon v. Georgia,* 295 U.S. 441 (1935).
9. 301 U.S. at 246 n. 2.
10. The Georgia statute also contained a section aimed at the circulating of any writing "for the purpose of inciting insurrection, riot, or conspiracy, or resistance against the lawful authority of the State." Had Herndon been indicted under this section, the case would have posed an intelligible speech issue.
11. 301 U.S. at 258.
12. *Id.* at 260-1.
13. *Id.* at 254-5.
14. *Id.* at 262.
15. *Id.* at 256.
16. *Id.* at 258.
17. *Id.* at 261.
18. Chafee, *Free Speech,* p. 392.
19. 376 U.S. 254 (1964).
20. 283 U.S. 697 (1931).
21. 297 U.S. 233 (1936).
22. 299 U.S. 353 (1937).
23. 303 U.S. 444 (1938).
24. 307 U.S. 496 (1939).
25. 304 U.S. 144 (1938).
26. 308 U.S. 147 (1939).
27. 304 U.S. at 152.
28. *Id.* at 152 n.4.
29. 308 U.S. at 161.

Chapter 13: The Heyday of Clear and Present Danger

1. 310 U.S. 88 (1940).
2. *Id.* at 104-5.
3. 319 U.S. 624 (1943).
4. *Id.* at 633.
5. *Cantwell v. Connecticut,* 310 U.S. 296 (1940); *Bridges v. California,* 314 U.S. 252 (1941); *Pennekamp v. Florida,* 328 U.S. 331 (1946); *Craig v. Harney,* 331 U.S. 367 (1947).
6. This is apparent in Justice Black's restatement of the test in *Bridges:*

   What finally emerges from the "clear and present danger" cases is a working principle that the substantive evil must be extremely serious and the degree of imminence extremely high before utterances can be punished.

   314 U.S. at 263. In this statement "gravity" has displaced "clear . . . danger."
7. In order to reject "gravity," while continuing to speak for Holmes and Brandeis, Frankfurter must, in effect, read the *Whitney* concurrence out of the tradition. See, for example, his concurrence in *Pennekamp v. Florida,* 328 U.S. 331, 350 (1946).
8. To some degree, this may have been a matter of choice. In 1943 the Court declined to consider *Dunne v. United States,* 138 F. 2d 137 (1943), a case involving the convictions under the advocacy provisions of the Smith Act of eighteen members of the Socialist Workers Party, a Trotskyist organization. The Court's denial of *certiorari* left standing a Court of Appeals decision which relied on *Gitlow* in sustaining the convictions.
9. *Taylor v. Mississippi,* 319 U.S. 583 (1943); *Schneiderman v. United States,* 320 U.S. 118 (1943); *Hartzel v. United States,* 322 U.S. 680 (1944).
10. Justice Roberts's handling of the issue also suggests another line of possibilities. The Jehovah's Witnesses can be viewed, in the flag salute controversy, as engaging in pure civil disobedience, that is, as openly violating a law in protest against it and on grounds of conscience. Justice Roberts stresses the conscience factor:

    If the state cannot constrain one to violate his conscientious religious convictions by saluting the national emblem, then certainly it cannot punish him for imparting his views on the subject to his fellows and exhorting them to accept those views.

    319 U.S. at 589. Two questions rush to mind here. Does the sincerity of the speaker's convictions have any relevance for measuring the degree to which the state may censor his utterances? Granting that one cannot commit civil disobedience with impunity, may one advocate with impunity that others commit it?
11. *Id.* at 589-90.

12. The denaturalization proceedings against Schneiderman were initiated in 1939. By the time the cases reached the Court, the United States and Russia were wartime allies. In an apparent effort to avoid strains in its relationship with Russia, the Government informally approached the Court and asked that it postpone consideration of the case. The Court refused. See Liss, "The *Schneiderman* Case: An Inside View of the Roosevelt Court," 74 *Michigan Law Review* 500 (1976).—*Ed.*

13. 320 U.S. at 122-5.

14. *Id.* at 157-8.

15. 322 U.S. at 683.

16. *Id.* at 693.

17. During these years the Court decided another case bearing on the advocacy issue, *Musser v. Utah,* 333 U.S. 95 (1948). This case posed the issue of speech triggering action in a novel context—the defendants were charged with the advocacy of polygamy. The majority did not confront the issue head on, but instead remanded to the state court to pass on an issue unearthed in oral argument—whether the Utah statute was unconstitutionally vague. The dissenters—Rutledge, Douglas and Murphy—wanted to confront the First Amendment issue, and did so in terms that hark back to *Masses.* Justice Rutledge notes that the state court, by setting aside the convictions of several defendants who had done no more than attend meetings and discuss polygamy, had drawn the line "between discussion and advocacy." The true boundary, he argues, lies elsewhere:

> At the very least the line must be drawn between advocacy and incitement, and even the state's power to punish incitement may vary with the nature of the speech, whether persuasive or coercive, the nature of the wrong induced, whether violent or merely offensive to the mores, and the degree of probability that the substantive evil actually will result.

    Id. at 101.

18. 339 U.S. 382 (1950).

19. *Id.* at 396.

20. *Id.* at 395.

21. *Id.* at 396.

22. *Ibid.*

23. *Id.* at 399.

Chapter 14: The Great Confrontation— *Dennis v. United States*

1. 341 U.S. 494 (1951).

2. For a detailed discussion of the legislative history of the Act, see Chafee, *Free Speech,* pp. 439-90.

3. 341 U.S. at 496.

4. 274 at 372-3.
5. 341 U.S. at 497.
6. *Id.* at 582.
7. *Ibid.*
8. 354 U.S. 298 (1957).
9. 341 U.S. at 506.
10. *Id.* at 507. In a footnote keyed to this passage Vinson cites, among other decisions, *Bridges, Thornhill, Thomas v. Collins, Taylor,* and *Barnette.*
11. *Id.* at 508.
12. *Ibid.*
13. *Id.* at 509.
14. *Id.* at 510. Suppose the wording were reversed: improbability augmented by gravity.
15. A puzzling feature of *Dennis* is the role played by Judge Hand, the author of *Masses.* He contributes the "gravity discounted by improbability" formula—a standard considerably less speech-protective than the "incitement" standard he articulated in *Masses.* A partial explanation may reside in his position as a lower court judge. Bound by the clear and present danger doctrine developed by the Supreme Court during the three decades since *Masses,* he was not free to revive his "incitement" approach. Yet, as of 1950, clear and present danger doctrine included several statements of First Amendment policy one would have expected the author of *Masses* to applaud, such as Justice Brandeis' *Whitney* concurrence, which had been adopted as majority doctrine during the 1940s, and Justice Murphy's opinion in *Schneiderman,* arguably the single precedent most directly relevant to *Dennis.* Both opinions resonate to Hand's *Masses* approach, and both anticipate *Brandenburg* by combining the Hand focus on content with the Holmes focus on the imminence of the danger. But Hand passes over the *Whitney* concurrence without subjecting it to close exegesis and he dismisses *Schneiderman* on the ground that the Court was divided 5 to 3: "We should feel bound to await a more definitive declaration before accepting a doctrine which, with deference, seems to us so open to doubt." 183 F. 2d 201, 210.—*Ed.*
16. 341 at 510-1.
17. *Id.* at 511.
18. *Id.* at 588-9.
19. *Id.* at 584.
20. *Id.* at 579.
21. *Ibid.*
22. *Id.* at 580.
23. *Id.* at 581.
24. *Id.* at 564-5.
25. *Id.* at 568.
26. *Id.* at 568-9.

27. *Id.* at 570.
28. *Ibid.*
29. *Id.* at 571.
30. *Id.* at 572.
31. *Id.* at 577.
32. *Ibid.*
33. *Id.* at 576.
34. *Id.* at 518.
35. *Id.* at 519.
36. *Id.* at 527.
37. *Id.* at 528.
38. It is tempting to go over his reading of the cases closely, but two details will have to suffice. First, he attempts to categorize "six different types of cases." I find his choice of categories indicative of the lack of any common perspective among the justices in 1951 on the contours of an analytic map for the speech issues they have been considering. The categories are: speech in public places; labor picketing; deportation and denaturalization; free press *vis a vis* taxation and contempt by publication; the *Douds* case; and speech which "has a tendency to lead to crime." Second, as in his dissents during the 1940s, he passes over *Whitney* without any discussion of the Brandeis concurrence. One could never detect from his review of the precedents that Brandeis had issued a lengthy, eloquent, and enormously prestigious opinion on behalf of clear and present danger in *Whitney*.
39. *Id.* at 543.
40. *Id.* at 544.
41. *Id.* at 541.
42. *Ibid.*
43. *Id.* at 550.
44. *Id.* at 556.
45. *Id.* at 549.
46. *Ibid.*

Chapter 15: The *Yates* Revision

1. 354 U.S. 178 (1957).
2. 354 U.S. 234 (1957).
3. 354 U.S. 363 (1957).
4. 354 U.S. 298 (1957).
5. The allusion is Professor Kurland's. He used it to describe *Shelley v. Kraemer*. "Foreword: 'Equal in Origin and Equal in Title to the Legislative and Executive Branches of the Government,' The Supreme Court, 1963 Term," 78 *Harvard Law Review* 143, 148 (1963).
6. 283 U.S. 359 (1931).

7. 354 U.S. at 307-8.

8. The Smith Act had been amended in 1948 in minor respects with the result that the conspiracy section which had been used in *Dennis* was eliminated. Consequently, in *Yates* the conspiracy after 1948 was charged under the general federal conspiracy statute which requires an "overt act."

9. 341 U.S. at 511-2.

10. 354 U.S. at 315.

11. *Id.* at 313 n.18.

12. *Id.* at 321-2.

13. *Id.* at 324-5.

14. *Id.* at 327.

15. *Id.* at 328.

16. *Ibid.*

17. *Id.* at 329.

18. *Id.* at 329-30.

19. *Id.* at 330.

20. *Id.* at 331.

21. *Id.* at 345 n.1.

22. *Id.* at 331.

23. *Ibid.*

24. *Id.* at 332.

25. In requesting dismissal of the charges against the remaining nine defendants, the Government stated: "we cannot satisfy the evidentiary requirements laid down by the Supreme Court in its opinion reversing the convictions in this matter." *The New York Times*, December 3, 1957.

    As we shall see, the Court will again have occasion to consider the Smith Act in *Scales v. United States* and *Noto v. United States*, both decided in 1961, but the prosecutions in those cases were commenced before the *Yates* decision.

26. 354 U.S. at 345-6.

27. *Id.* at 346.

28. *Id.* at 349.

29. *Id.* at 349-50.

30. *Id.* at 350.

31. *Id.* at 340.

32. 367 U.S. 203 (1961).

33. It is worth noting that Scales, who was charged only with membership, was given a six-year sentence, while the top-echelon leaders in *Dennis* were given five-year sentences. In part this may be attributable to the fact that a 1956 amendment increased the maximum penalty for violation of the Smith Act from ten to twenty years.

34. 367 U.S. at 235.

35. *Id.* at 232.

36. *Id.* at 233.
37. *Id.* at 252-3.
38. Just possibly *Brandenburg*, which gives constitutional status to the statutory analysis, may have altered the law on this point.
39. 367 U.S. 290 (1961).
40. *Id.* at 299.

Chapter 16: *Brandenburg* Revisited

1. 376 U.S. 254 (1964).
2. *Id.* at 270.
3. *Ibid.*
4. *Id.* at 273.
5. See, e.g., *Watts v. United States*, 394 U.S. 705 (1969) and *Street v. New York*, 394 U.S. 576 (1969).
6. 385 U.S. 116 (1966).
7. *Id.* at 120.
8. *Id.* at 124.
9. *Id.* at 136.
10. *Id.* at 134.
11. 395 U.S. at 447-8.
12. *Ibid.*
13. And they leave Justices Black and Douglas gasping. Concurring in a decision wholly silent as to the clear and present danger formula, Black can only add:

> I agree with the views expressed by Mr. Justice Douglas in his concurring opinion in this case that the "clear and present danger doctrine" should have no place in the interpretation of the First Amendment. I join in the Court's opinion, which, as I understand it, simply cites *Dennis v. United States,* but does not indicate any agreement on the Court's part with the "clear and present danger" doctrine on which *Dennis* purported to rely.

Id. at 449-50. Justice Douglas is stirred to more elaborate reflection. He prefaces his views with a five-page essay in which he reviews once again the precedents from *Schenck* through *Dennis* and concludes that the test has always been prone to misuse:

> My own view is quite different. I see no place in the regime of the First Amendment for any "clear and present danger" test, whether strict and tight as some would make it, or free-wheeling as the Court in *Dennis* rephrased it.

Id. at 454.
14. *Id.* at 448.
15. *Kingsley International Pictures v. Regents*, 360 U.S. 684 (1959).

Chapter 17: Sanctions Against Groups

1. *Dennis v. United States*, 341 U.S. 494 (1951); *Yates v. United States*, 354 U.S. 298 (1957).
2. *Scales v. United States*, 367 U.S. 203 (1961).

Chapter 18: The Nexus Issue: Is Membership Enough?

1. *Whitney v. California*, 274 U.S. 357 (1927); *Dennis v. United States*, 341 U.S. 494 (1951); *Yates v. United States*, 354 U.S. 298 (1957); *Brandenburg v. Ohio*, 395 U.S. 444 (1969).
2. 367 U.S. 203 (1961).
3. We should note that Miss Whitney was charged not simply with membership but with assisting in organizing the group. Hence *Whitney* is a "leadership" case like *Dennis* and *Yates*.
4. *Herndon v. Lowry*, 301 U.S. 242 (1937).
5. 299 U.S. 353 (1937).
6. *Id.* at 362.
7. *Id.* at 365.
8. 367 U.S. at 209.
9. This accommodation between the Smith Act and the SACA is to prove short-lived. Four years later in *Albertson v. Subversive Activities Control Board*, 382 U.S. 70 (1965), the Court concludes that under the Fifth Amendment no one can be forced to incriminate himself by registering the Communist Party, thereby paralyzing the SACA compulsory disclosure procedures.

   The sequence of events that culminates with *Albertson* is a striking illustration of how erratically important issues may arise in our scheme of things. The Smith Act is enacted in 1940. The Court does not adjudicate its propriety until 1951, and does not reach the membership provision, which alone would lay a predicate for wholesale prosecutions, until 1961. But by 1950 Congress had come to prefer compulsory disclosure as the way to fight domestic Communism and had passed the Subversive Activities Control Act, thereby giving rise to the self-incrimination dilemma. To make the ironies of timing complete, in *Communist Party v. Subversive Activities Control Board*, 367 U.S. 1 (1961), handed down on the same day as *Scales*, the Court, speaking through Justice Frankfurter, decides that this precise question of the degree to which the self-incrimination privilege inhibits compulsory disclosure is not yet ripe for decision! Finally, four years later in *Albertson* the privilege is held applicable. Hence over a full quarter of a century from 1940 to 1965 the government and the Court were notably unsuccessful in synchronizing their moves.
10. *Id.* at 220.

11. *Id.* at 224-5.
12. *Id.* at 226-7.
13. *Id.* at 227.
14. *Id.* at 227-8.
15. *Id.* at 228.
16. *Ibid.*
17. *Id.* at 229.
18. *Ibid.*
19. *Id.* at 229-30.
20. *Id.* at 265.
21. *Barenblatt v. United States,* 360 U.S. 109 (1959); *Konigsberg v. State Bar of California,* 353 U.S. 252 (1957); *Konigsberg v. State Bar of California,* 366 U.S. 36 (1961).

Chapter 19: Compulsory Disclosure as a Group Sanction: The Civil Rights Cases

1. 362 U.S. 60 (1960).
2. *Id.* at 70.
3. *Id.* at 71.
4. *Id.* at 64-5.
5. 278 U.S. 63 (1928).
6. *Id.* at 71.
7. *Id.* at 72.
8. *Ibid.*
9. *Id.* at 75.
10. *Ibid.*
11. 347 U.S. 483 (1954).
12. 357 U.S. 449 (1958).
13. *Id.* at 460-1.
14. *Id.* at 461.
15. *Id.* at 462.
16. *Ibid.*
17. The source of this language is Justice Frankfurter's concurring opinion in *Sweezy v. New Hampshire,* 354 U.S. 234 (1957).
18. 361 U.S. 516 (1960).
19. *Id.* at 523.
20. *Id.* at 524. In a third encounter with the compulsory disclosure tactic against the NAACP, *Louisiana v. NAACP,* 366 U.S. 293 (1961), the Court again unanimously upholds the First Amendment challenge. But perhaps because the case comes to the Court over the propriety of a temporary injunction protecting the NAACP issued by a three-judge court below, the controversy is at too preliminary a stage to evoke vigorous use of the stringent balancing formula fashioned in *Alabama* and *Bates.* Also, it is not clear what the state purpose in requiring disclosure

was. The case thus supplies only a fuzzy footnote to the prior precedents.

21. 364 U.S. 479 (1960).
22. *Shelton v. McKinley*, a 1959 federal district court case, discloses the legislative history of the statute involved in *Shelton v. Tucker*. It was passed in 1958 during a special emergency session of the Arkansas legislature. A companion statute, which is invalidated in *Shelton v. McKinley*, barred all members of the NAACP from public employment and required a non-NAACP affidavit as a condition of employment. These provisions were preceded by a preamble which stated that the NAACP was guilty of stirring up racial strife in the state and that the organization "is captive of the international communist conspiracy." 174 F. Supp. 351 (1959).
23. *Id.* at 485.
24. *Lovell v. Griffin*, 303 U.S. 444 (1938); *Schneider v. State*, 308 U.S. 147 (1939).
25. 364 U.S. at 488.
26. *Id.* at 490.
27. 367 U.S. 1 (1961).

Chapter 20: Compulsory Disclosure as a Group Sanction: The *SACB* Case

1. 367 U.S. 1 (1961).
2. The Act also provides that in the event the organization fails to register within a prescribed period, the duty to do so falls upon its officers. Further, in the case of action groups, if both the organization and the officers fail to register, individual members are required to register themselves. Each day of failure to register by the officers and, in the case of action groups, the individual members is treated as a separate offense subject to a maximum punishment of a $10,000 fine and imprisonment for five years.
3. 351 U.S. 115 (1956).
4. 367 U.S. at 106.
5. Among the arguments advanced by the defendants was the claim that the legislative findings of the SACA and of the 1954 Communist Control Act (which flatly stated that the Party "is in fact an instrumentality of a conspiracy to overthrow the Government") had denied them due process by predetermining the facts on which application of the Act depends. Justice Frankfurter discounts the impact of the legislative findings on the administrative adjudication of the Party's status under the Act:

> While we must, of course, assume that the Board was aware of them, we cannot say that their very annunciation by Congress—in the absence of any showing that the Board took them into account—foreclosed or impaired a fair administrative determination.

Id. at 115. Compare his concern about the impact of an out-of-court comment on the impartial administration of justice in *Bridges v. California,* 314 U.S. 252 (1941).

6. 303 U.S. 419 (1938).
7. 367 U.S. at 78-9.
8. *Id.* at 144.
9. *Id.* at 55.
10. *Id.* at 56.
11. *Id.* at 131.
12. *Id.* at 132.
13. *Ibid.*
14. *Id.* at 133.
15. 382 U.S. 70 (1965).
16. 318 U.S. 236 (1943). In his *Viereck* dissent Justice Black argues that the disclosure requirements of the Foreign Agents Registration Act, far from offending First Amendment values, actually serve those values·

> Resting on the fundamental constitutional principle that our people, adequately informed, may be trusted to distinguish between the true and the false, the bill is intended to label information of foreign origin so that hearers and readers may not be deceived by the belief that the information comes from a disinterested source. Such legislation implements rather than detracts from the prized freedoms guaranteed by the First Amendment.

Id. at 251. Compare his eloquence on behalf of anonymity in *Talley v. California,* 362 U.S. 60 (1960).
17. 367 U.S. at 139-40.
18. *Id.* at 141.
19. Only Justice Black touches on the issue. He observes in passing:

> If there is one thing certain about the First Amendment it is that this Amendment was designed to guarantee the freest interchange of ideas about public matters and that, of course, means the interchange of *all* ideas, however such ideas may be viewed in other countries. . . .

Id. at 148.
20. *Id.* at 65-6.
21. *Id.* at 82.
22. *Id.* at 83.
23. *Id.* at 85.
24. *Id.* at 83.
25. *Id.* at 84-5.
26. *Id.* at 148.
27. *Id.* at 141.
28. *Id.* at 142.
29. *Ibid.*

30. *Id.* at 147.
31. 376 U.S. 254 (1964).
32. 367 U.S. at 88-9.
33. *Id.* at 90-1.
34. Ironically, Justice Harlan in *NAACP v. Alabama* cites as the source of this language Justice Frankfurter's concurring opinion in *Sweezy v. New Hampshire*, 354 U.S. 234 (1957).
35. 367 U.S. at 91. Frankfurter never gives up. He cites as authority for this proposition *Schenck*, *Douds*, and *Dennis*.
36. *Id.* at 95.
37. *Id.* at 97.
38. *Id.* at 101-2.
39. *Id.* at 102-3.
40. Chief Justice Warren pointedly notes the absence of evidence regarding the *purposes* of Party secrecy. Among the criteria listed by the Act for determining whether a group is a Communist-action organization is the extent to which it uses secrecy to conceal foreign domination and to promote its objectives. The Board's first report concludes that the Party practiced secrecy for both of these purposes. The Court of Appeals held that, while the evidence established that the Party engaged in secret practices, it was insufficient to support the Board's conclusions as to the purposes served by those secret practices. In subsequent reports the Board deleted the conclusion regarding concealment of foreign domination but reiterated the conclusion regarding the promotion of Party objectives. The Court of Appeals again ruled that this conclusion was unsupported by the evidence. It rejected, however, the Party's claim that the case should therefore be remanded, and it affirmed the order to register on the ground that the record as a whole supported the Board's conclusion that the Party was a Communist-action organization. Justice Frankfurter endorses the Court of Appeals' handling of this point. He characterizes the secrecy finding as merely "one subsidiary finding." Its infirmity, in his view, does not call into question the Board's conclusion as to the status of the Party under the Act. Chief Justice Warren disagrees: "It is unrealistic to characterize the Board's secrecy finding as insignificant and subsidiary." *Id.* at 134. He would remand the case for reconsideration in the absence of the secrecy finding.
41. *Id.* at 172.
42. *Id.* at 172-3.
43. *Id.* at 104.
44. *Id.* at 105.
45. *Aptheker v. Secretary of State*, 378 U.S. 500 (1964); *United States v. Robel*, 389 U.S. 258 (1967).

After it was barred from compelling registration and disclosure, the Subversive Activities Control Board became for all practical purposes inoperative. In 1967 Congress passed legislation designed to resuscitate it by repealing the registration provisions. The 1967 amendments left the Board with the power to issue orders designating organizations as "action" groups, "front" groups, etc; these orders were to be kept in public files and to be reported annually to Congress. In 1969 the Court of Appeals held invalid under the First Amendment orders of the Board that certain named individuals be designated members of a "Communist-action" organization. In 1971 President Nixon made another attempt to revive the Board by issuing an executive order empowering it to determine what groups should be placed on the Attorney General's list. Finally, in 1973, the Board was disbanded.

46. 367 U.S. at 137.

Chapter 21: Stigmatization as a Group Sanction

1. *Joint Anti-Fascist Refugee Committee v. McGrath,* 341 U.S. 123 (1951); *American Committee for Protection of Foreign Born v. Subversive Activities Control Board,* 380 U.S. 503 (1965); *Veterans of the Abraham Lincoln Brigade v. Subversive Activities Control Board,* 380 U.S. 513 (1965); *DuBois Clubs of America v. Clark,* 389 U.S. 309 (1967).
2. 341 U.S. 918 (1951).
3. *Id.* at 141.
4. *Id.* at 202.
5. *Id.* at 200.
6. The concurring opinion of Justice Jackson offers another variant. He argues that the organizations themselves have suffered no injury and so do not have standing to seek relief, but that individual members who may be denied government employment because of the designation of the group are exposed to harm by the loyalty program procedures. Hence the organization has standing to "vindicate unconstitutional deprivation of members' rights." *Id.* at 186.
7. *Id.* at 160-1.
8. *Id.* at 162-3.
9. *Id.* at 142.
10. *Id.* at 143.
11. 380 U.S. at 505 n. 2.
12. *Id.* at 511.
13. *Id.* at 512.
14. *Id.* at 513.
15. *Id.* at 514.

Chapter 22: Sanctions Against Individuals as a Group Sanction

1. 378 U.S. 500 (1964).
2. *Id.* at 518.

Chapter 23: The Partial Sanction: A General Analysis

1. *McAuliffe v. Mayor of New Bedford,* 155 Mass. 216, 29 N.E. 517 (1892).
2. 155 Mass. at 220, 29 N.E. at 517-18.
3. See, e.g., *Wieman v. Updegraff,* 344 U.S. 183, 192 (1952); *Keyishian v. Board of Regents,* 385 U.S. 589, 605 (1967); *Pickering v. Board of Education,* 391 U.S. 563, 568 (1968); *Board of Regents v. Roth,* 408 U.S. 564, 571 (1972); *Perry v. Sinderman,* 408 U.S. 593, 597 (1972).
4. 330 U.S. 75 (1947).
5. In 1973 the Supreme Court again upheld the Hatch Act against First Amendment challenge in *United States Civil Service Commission v. National Association of Letter Carriers,* 413 U.S. 548. Justice White, speaking for the Court, declared: "We unhesitatingly reaffirm the *Mitchell* holding." *Id.* at 556.
6. 330 U.S. at 94-5.
7. *Id.* at 100.
8. *Id.* at 96.
9. *Ibid.*, citing *Ex parte Curtis,* 106 U.S. 371 (1882).
10. *Id.* at 98.
11. *Id.* at 102.
12. *Id.* at 102-3.
13. *Id.* at 126.
14. *Ibid.* Justice Black makes a similar statement:

> Certainly laws which restrict the liberties guaranteed by the First Amendment should be narrowly drawn to meet the evil aimed at and to affect only the minimum number of people imperatively necessary to prevent a grave and imminent danger to the public.

Id. at 110.
15. *Id.* at 106-7.
16. *Id.* at 108-9.
17. *Id.* at 112-14.
18. *Id.* at 113-14.
19. 308 U.S. 147 (1939).
20. 330 U.S. at 115.
21. 367 U.S. 488 (1961).
22. *Id.* at 495.
23. *Ibid.*
24. Cf. the sequence of cases in which the Court considered the scope of the exemption from the military draft for those opposed to participation in war by reason of "religious training and belief." *United States v. Seeger,* 380 U.S. 163 (1965); *Welsh v. United States,* 398 U.S. 333 (1970); and *Gillette v. United States,* 401 U.S. 437 (1971).
25. 385 U.S. 116 (1966).

26. *Id.* at 132-3.
27. *Id.* at 135-7.
28. 391 U.S. 563 (1968).
29. Justice White concurred in part and dissented in part.
30. 391 U.S. at 567.
31. *Id.* at 569.
32. *Id.* at 570.
33. *Ibid.*
34. *Id.* at 573.

Chapter 24: Partial Sanctions Keyed to Membership in Disfavored Groups

1. *Keyishian v. Board of Regents*, 385 U.S. 589 (1967); *United States v. Robel*, 389 U.S. 258 (1967); *Aptheker v. Secretary of State*, 378 U.S. 500 (1964); *Law Students Research Council v. Wadmond*, 401 U.S. 154 (1971).

Chapter 25: The Denial of Employment

1. 328 U.S. 303 (1946).
2. 339 U.S. 382 (1950).
3. 328 U.S. at 311.
4. See, e.g., his opinions in *Communist Party v. Subversive Activities Control Board*, 367 U.S. 1 (1961), and *Joint Anti-Fascist Refugee Committee v. McGrath*, 341 U.S. 123 (1951).
5. 328 U.S. at 315.
6. *Id.* at 316-17.
7. *Id.* at 324-5.
8. There was one intervening case between *Lovett* and *Douds: Parker v. Los Angeles County*, 338 U.S. 327 (1949). In *Parker* Justice Frankfurter is once again the spokesman for avoidance of the constitutional questions. This time the entire Court agrees that the issues are not ripe, and the decision to dismiss the writs of *certiorari* heretofore granted is unanimous. The facts, however, are worth a brief word.

   Los Angeles County had adopted, as Frankfurter puts it, "what is colloquially known as a loyalty test" for its employees. The test consisted of a four part affidavit. Part A was a conventional oath of allegiance; Part B was an oath that one did not advocate violent overthrow and since 1941 had not been a member of a group so advocating; Part C dealt with the use of aliases; and Part D was an oath that one "had never been a member of or directly or indirectly supported or followed any of the listed organizations except those checked." There followed a list of approximately 150 organizations that probably was based on the Attorney General's list. Employees who had declined to fill out the form brought suit to enjoin enforcement of the loyalty program. The case thus bristled with First Amendment issues, including the critical one about applying sanctions to membership in alleged "front" organizations.

The posture of the litigation, however, was such that the issues were imperfectly presented for adjudication. There was no indication in the record of what sanction, if any, followed disclosure, as in Part D, of affiliations. Moreover, while this case was pending, the employees who had refused to take the oath were dismissed and another suit was begun in the California courts testing the constitutionality under California law of the dismissals. That suit was still pending. The Court thus decided to postpone the confrontation over loyalty programs and oaths.

9. A month later the Court was presented with precisely the same issues in *Osman v. Douds*, 339 U.S. 846 (1950). This time eight members of the Court participated. The *per curiam* opinion reports that the justices who took part in *Douds* adhere to their opinions in that case and that Justice Whittaker joins Chief Justice Vinson's opinion in *Douds*. Justice Douglas, we are told, joins the dissenting opinions of Justices Black, Frankfurter, and Jackson in *Douds* "insofar as they hold unconstitutional the portion of the oath dealing with beliefs, and being of the view that provisions of the oath are not separable votes to reverse. He therefore does not find it necessary to reach the question of the constitutionality of the other part of the oath." *Id.* at 847-8. Thus, the *Osman* vote is 4 to 4 with respect to the belief portion of the oath and 6 to 1 with respect to the rest of the statute.

10. 339 U.S. at 413.

11. *Id.* at 422.

12. *Id.* at 433.

13. *Ibid.*

14. *Id.* at 450-1.

15. 381 U.S. 437 (1965).

16. *Id.* at 461.

17. *Id.* at 458. Cf. *Flemming v. Nestor*, 363 U.S. 603 (1960).

18. 381 U.S. at 460.

19. For another instance of an oath cast in the idiom of "belief," see *Connell v. Higginbotham*, 403 U.S. 207 (1971).

20. See also the position of Justice Douglas in *Osman v. Douds*, 339 U.S. 847 (1950).

21. 339 U.S. at 444.

22. Chief Justice Vinson argues that these terms are saved from vagueness in "the particular context" by the fact that the criminal sanctions provided by the statute are limited to false statements made "knowingly or willfully." As he sees it, the requirement of *scienter* "removes the possibility of constitutional infirmity" due to vagueness:

. . . since the constitutional vice in a vague or indefinite statute is the injustice to the accused in placing him on trial for an offense, the nature of which he is given no fair warning, the fact that punishment is restricted to acts done with knowledge that they contravene the statute makes this objection untenable.

Id. at 413. Cf. *Cramp v. Board of Instruction,* 368 U.S. 278 (1961), and *Baggett v. Bullitt,* 377 U.S. 360 (1964).

23. 339 U.S. at 420.
24. *Id.* at 421.
25. *Id.* at 390.
26. *Ibid.*
27. *Board of Governors v. Agnew,* 329 U.S. 441 (1947).
28. 339 U.S. at 392.
29. *Id.* at 393.
30. *Id.* at 396.
31. *Id.* at 399.
32. *Id.* at 400.
33. *Id.* at 401.
34. *Id.* at 403-4.
35. *Id.* at 404.
36. *Id.* at 412.
37. *Id.* at 449.

Chapter 26: The Loyalty Oath

1. *American Communication Association v. Douds,* 339 U.S. 382 (1950).
2. *Id.* at 414.
3. *Id.* at 415.
4. *Id.* at 434-5.
5. *Id.* at 446-7.
6. *Id.* at 447-8. Justice Black here quotes from his own dissenting opinion in *In re Summers,* 325 U.S. 561 (1945):

Test oaths, designed to impose civil disabilities upon men for their beliefs rather than for unlawful conduct, were an abomination to the founders of this nation. This feeling was made manifest in Article VI of the Constitution which provides that "no religious test shall ever be required as a Qualification to any Office or public Trust under the United States."

Id. at 576.
7. 341 U.S. 56 (1951).
8. But note the argument advanced by Justice Douglas, concurring in *Speiser v. Randall,* 357 U.S. 513 (1958), that the oath device is unconstitutional in that it improperly places the burden of proof on the affiant.
9. 339 U.S. at 449.

10. 341 U.S. at 56-7.

11. 389 U.S. 54 (1967).

12. 341 U.S. 716 (1951).

13. The employee was also required to swear that he would not, while employed by the City, advocate violent overthrow or become a member of a group that so advocated. None of the justices addresses this prospective aspect of the oath.

14. *Garner* also involved an inquiry. In addition to the oath, the ordinance required all employees to execute an affidavit stating "whether or not he is or ever was a member of the Communist Party" and specifying the dates of such membership. The Court upholds the affidavit requirement by a vote of 7 to 2, with Justices Frankfurter and Burton joining the majority on this point. As the majority sees the case, no element of automatic bar is involved, since there is no indication in the record of the consequences of an affirmative answer to the inquiry: "Not before us is the question whether the city may determine that an employee's disclosure of such political affiliation justifies his discharge." *Id.* at 720.

15. *Id.* at 720-1.

16. *Id.* at 722.

17. *Id.* at 729.

18. *Id.* at 724.

19. *Id.* at 726.

20. *Id.* at 727-8.

21. See also *Adler v. Board of Regents*, 342 U.S. 485 (1952), a roughly contemporaneous decision upholding a New York statute which made the utterance of "treasonable or seditious words" and membership in groups which advocate overthrow of government "by force or violence, or by any unlawful means" grounds for dismissal from public employment.

22. 344 U.S. 183 (1952).

23. The *Wieman* oath is staggering in its sheer length and complexity:

I, _____, do solemnly swear (or affirm) that I will support and defend the Constitution of the United States and the Constitution of the State of Oklahoma against all enemies, foreign and domestic; that I will bear true faith and allegiance to the Constitution of the United States and the Constitution of the State of Oklahoma; that I take this obligation freely, without any mental reservation or purpose of evasion; and that I will well and faithfully discharge the duties upon which I am about to enter.

And I do further swear (or affirm) that I do not advocate, nor am I a member of any party or organization, political or otherwise, that now advocates the overthrow of the Government of the United States or of the State of Oklahoma by force or violence or other unlawful means; That I am not affiliated directly or indirectly with the Communist Party, the Third Communist International, with any foreign political agency, party, organization or Government, or with any agency, party, organization, association, or group whatever which has been officially determined by the United States Attorney General or other authorized agency of the United States to be a communist front or subversive organization; nor do I advocate revolution, teach or justify a program of sabotage, force or violence, sedition or treason, against the Government of the United States or of this State; nor do I advocate directly or indirectly, teach or justify by any means whatsoever, the overthrow of the Government of the United States or of this State, or change in the form of Government thereof, by force or any unlawful means; that I will take up arms in the defense of the United States in time of War, or National Emergency, if necessary; that within the five (5) years immediately preceding the taking of this oath (or affirmation) I have not been a member of the Communist Party, the Third Communist International, or any agency, party, organization, association, or group whatever which has been officially determined by the United States Attorney General or other authorized public agency of the United States to be a communist front or subversive organization, or of any party or organization, political or otherwise, that advocated the overthrow of the Government of the United States or of the State of Oklahoma by force or violence or other unlawful means;

And I do further swear (or affirm) that during such time as I am—(*Here put name of office, or, if an employee) insert "An employee of" followed by the complete designation of the employing officer, office, agency, authority, commission, department or institution.*

I will not advocate and that I will not become a member of any party or organization, political or otherwise, that advocates the overthrow of the Government of the United States or of the State of Oklahoma by force or violence or other unlawful means.

Id. at 184-5 n. 1.

24. *Joint Anti-Fascist Refugee Committee v. McGrath,* 341 U.S. 123 (1951).

25. 344 U.S. at 190.

26. *Id.* at 195.

27. *Id.* at 194.

28. *Id.* at 193.

29. 368 U.S. 278 (1961).

30. *Id.* at 284.

31. A question: would vagueness impeach an oath even though both interpretations would give it constitutional scope?

32. *Id.* at 286.

33. 377 U.S. 360 (1964).

34. Two of the *Baggett* petitioners had earlier challenged the non-subversive oath by means of a suit seeking a declaratory judgment that the state loyalty statute was unconstitutional on a variety of grounds. They argued, among other things, that the statute, which provided that refusal to take the oath "on any grounds shall be cause for immediate termination," did not afford a hearing at which the employee might explain or defend his refusal. In *Nostrand v. Little,* 362 U.S. 474 (1960), the Court in a *per curiam* opinion found that the state court in upholding the statute had not passed on this point and hence remanded the case. Justices

Douglas and Black dissented in an opinion by the former: "The command of the statute is clear: refusal to take the oath 'on any grounds' is cause for discharge. That command poses the critical issue for us. A remand for a determination of whether there will be a hearing therefore seems to me to be a remand for an irrelevancy in the setting of the case." *Id.* at 478.

On remand the state court held that those who refused to take the oath are entitled to a hearing. Then in *Nostrand v. Little,* 368 U.S. 436 (1962), the Supreme Court in a one sentence *per curiam* order dismissed the appeal of the decision upholding the statute against other points of constitutional challenge for want of a substantial federal question. Presumably the unstated rationale of the Court's action was that the state court's decision on the hearing point afforded petitioners administrative relief. Again, Justices Douglas and Black dissented.

Finally in *Baggett*—petitioners having been terminated after hearing for refusal to take the oath—the Court considers their constitutional challenge.

35. 377 U.S. at 369.
36. Justice Clark also complains that the oath invalidated in *Baggett* is identical to the one upheld in *Gerende.* He contends that the oath affirmed in *Gerende* incorporated the definition of "subversive person" given by Maryland's Ober Act, and that the Washington statute had in turn been modelled on this language. "It is unfortunate," he laments, "that *Gerende* is overruled so quickly. Other state laws have been copied from the Maryland Act—just as Washington's 1955 Act was—primarily because of our approval of it, and now this Court would declare them void." *Id.* at 382.

Justice White denies that the Court has overruled *Gerende.* He emphasizes that the Court in *Gerende* did not affirm—or even pass on—the constitutionality of the Ober law's definition of "subversive person"; rather, the Court took pains to make clear that it only endorsed the Maryland oath as narrowly construed by the state court to require the affiant to swear that he is not "engaged" in "overthrow of the government by force or violence" and that he is not a member of a group so "engaged." *Id.* at 368 n. 7.

37. *Id.* at 382-3.
38. *Id.* at 373.
39. 357 U.S. 513 (1958).
40. 377 U.S. at 372.
41. But compare the flag salute cases, *Minersville School District v. Gobitis,* 310 U.S. 586 (1940) and *West Virginia State Board of Education v. Barnette,* 319 U.S. 624 (1943).

Oaths of allegiance have on occasion been converted into test oaths by means of the argument that the individual's views render him unable to take the oath in good faith. In *Bond v. Floyd*, 385 U.S. 116 (1966), the Court condemned this practice. The Georgia legislature had barred Bond from taking his seat as a duly elected representative on the ground that anti-war statements he had made showed him to be unable to take the oath to support the Georgia Constitution in good faith. The Court declared:

> . . . we do not quarrel with the State's contention that the oath provisions of the United States and Georgia Constitutions do not violate the First Amendment. But this requirement does not authorize a majority of state legislators to test the sincerity with which another duly elected legislator can swear to uphold the Constitution. Such a power could be utilized to restrict the right of legislators to dissent from national or state policy or that of a majority of their colleagues under the guise of judging their loyalty to the Constitution.

Id. at 132. See also the use made of oaths of allegiance in *In re Summers*, 325 U.S. 561 (1945), where a pacifist was barred from the practice of law in Illinois on the ground that he could not, in light of his pacifism, take the oath to support the state constitution; and in the sequence of cases, beginning with *United States v. Schwimmer*, 279 U.S. 644 (1929), involving the denial of naturalization to conscientious objectors on the ground they could not take the oath to support and defend the Constitution without reservation.

42. This has not stopped the draftsmen of certain oaths of allegiance from appending perjury sanctions. Such was the case, for example, in *Baggett*, and in *Cole v. Richardson*, 397 U.S. 238 (1970).

43. 377 U.S. at 361-2.

44. *Id.* at 374.

45. *Id.* at 373-4.

46. *Ibid.* The dissenters do not speak to the merits of the oath of allegiance; rather, they argue that the Court has declared the oath void "without the benefit of an opinion of either a state or federal court." "I dissent," writes Justice Clark, "because the Court refuses to afford the State an opportunity to interpret its own laws." *Id.* at 380. Thus, the dissents of Clark and Harlan in *Baggett* do not necessarily represent judgments on their parts that the oath of allegiance is constitutional.

47. 384 U.S. 11 (1966).

48. *Id.* at 15.

49. 378 U.S. 500 (1964).

50. 357 U.S. 513 (1958).

51. 381 U.S. 437 (1965).

52. 384 U.S. at 19.

53. *Id.* at 17.

54. During this period the Court also hands down three one-line *per curiam*

affirmances of oaths of allegiance: *Knight v. Board of Regents,* 269 F. Supp. 339 (SDNY 1967), aff'd, 390 U.S. 36 (1968); *Hosack v. Smiley,* 276 F. Supp. 876 (Colo. 1967), aff'd, 390 U.S. 744 (1968); and *Ohlson v. Phillips,* 304 F. Supp. 1152 (Colo. 1969), aff'd, 397 U.S. 317 (1970).

55. *Whitehill v. Elkins,* 389 U.S. 54 (1967); *Connell v. Higginbotham,* 403 U.S. 207 (1971); *Cole v. Richardson,* 397 U.S. 238 (1970), 405 U.S. 676 (1972).
56. 389 U.S. at 63.
57. 377 U.S. at 374.
58. *Id.* at 373-4.
59. 397 U.S. at 240-1.
60. 405 U.S. at 681.
61. *Id.* at 683.
62. *Id.* at 684.
63. *Ibid.*

Chapter 27: The Security Calculus

1. 385 U.S. 589 (1967).
2. 389 U.S. 258 (1967).
3. 378 U.S. 500 (1964).
4. 342 U.S. 485 (1952).
5. *Id.* at 493.
6. *Ibid.*
7. 385 U.S. at 595.
8. Under the New York scheme, as described by Justice Brennan, there is "an annual review of every teacher to determine whether any utterance or act of his, inside the classroom or out, came within the sanctions of the laws." *Id.* at 601-2. The chilling effect of this ongoing inquiry is augmented, Brennan observes, by a memorandum warning employees that " 'subversive' activities may take the form of 'the writing of articles, the distribution of pamphlets, the endorsement of speeches made or articles written or acts performed by others.' " *Id.* at 602.
9. *Id.* at 603.
10. *Id.* at 604.
11. *Bond v. Floyd,* 385 U.S. 116 (1966); *Pickering v. Board of Education,* 391 U.S. 563 (1968).
12. 385 U.S. at 606.
13. *Id.* at 608.
14. *Id.* at 606.
15. *Id.* at 607.
16. 389 U.S. at 263.
17. *Id.* at 266.
18. Note the possibility that such a classification scheme would recast the employment issue in other terms: The suspect individual might be de-

nied the particular job on the ground that the classification scheme denied him access to the information necessary to perform the job.

19. *Id.* at 271-2.
20. *Id.* at 272.
21. *Id.* at 285.
22. *Id.* at 287.
23. 378 U.S. at 517.
24. *Id.* at 511.
25. *Id.* at 512.
26. *Id.* at 525.
27. *Id.* at 529.
28. *Id.* at 518.
29. *Id.* at 519.
30. *Id.* at 520.
31. *Ibid.*

Chapter 28: The Allocation of Subsidies

1. 357 U.S. 513 (1958).
2. 381 U.S. 301 (1965).
3. See also *First Unitarian Church of Los Angeles v. County of Los Angeles,* 357 U.S. 545 (1958), a companion case in which the Court, relying on *Speiser,* finds unconstitutional the denial of a tax exemption for property used for religious worship to two churches which had refused to execute the California oath.
4. *Id.* at 526.
5. *Id.* at 540-1.
6. *Id.* at 541.
7. *Id.* at 518.
8. *Id.* at 520.
9. *Id.* at 526.
10. *Id.* at 527.
11. *Id.* at 530-1.
12. 255 U.S. 407, 437 (1921).
13. 376 U.S. 254 (1964).
14. 381 U.S. at 310.
15. *Ibid.*
16. *Ibid.*
17. *Id.* at 308.
18. *Ibid.*

Chapter 29: The Multiplier Effect

1. 363 U.S. 603 (1960).
2. Compare *Bell v. United States,* 366 U.S. 393 (1961), unanimously holding

that American soldiers taken prisoner during the Korean War who cooperated with their captors and after the war refused repatriation and went for a time to Communist China are entitled to back pay accumulated during their detention.

3. 403 U.S. 15 (1971).

4. There is perhaps an analogy between Social Security benefits and postal services as examples of government largesse. Each has acquired over time a kind of sociological weight of its own. The expectation of Social Security benefits might seem even stronger than of postal services since contributions have been made for the former over time. Yet the services evoke First Amendment considerations which the benefits do not, and the scrutiny of government action is accordingly more stringent.

5. 363 U.S. at 611.

6. *Id.* at 612.

7. *Ibid.*

8. *Id.* at 614.

9. *Ibid.*

10. Compare the broad construction of "punishment" by Chief Justice Warren writing for the Court in *United States v. Brown,* 381 U.S. 437 (1965).

11. 363 U.S. at 622.

12. *Id.* at 628.

13. 347 U.S. 442 (1954).

14. 167 F. 2d 241 (1948).

15. See his similar opinion in *Schware v. Board of Bar Examiners of New Mexico,* 353 U.S. 232 (1957), in which the practice of law is at issue.

16. 347 U.S. at 470-1.

17. *Sacher v. United States,* 343 U.S. 1 (1952); *In re Isserman,* 345 U.S. 286 (1953); *Isserman v. Ethics Committee,* 345 U.S. 927 (1953); *Sacher v. Association of Bar of New York,* 347 U.S. 388 (1954),

18. 347 U.S. at 389.

19. 345 U.S. at 293-4.

20. *Id.* at 294.

21. *Ibid.*

22. 367 U.S. 389 (1961).

Chapter 30: Deportation

1. 307 U.S. 22 (1939).

2. *Id.* at 30.

3. *Id.* at 38.

4. 326 U.S. 135 (1945).

5. *Id.* at 158-9.

6. The Court's decision in *Bridges v. Wixon* did not end the pursuit of Harry Bridges. In 1945 Bridges was naturalized. Then in 1949 he was indicted under the Nationality Act of 1940 for testifying falsely at his naturaliza-

tion hearing that he had never been a member of the Communist Party. The indictment also charged that two men who had testified on his behalf had knowingly aided him to obtain naturalization by fraud; and, finally, all three were charged with conspiring to defraud the United States. They were convicted on all counts. Bridges received a five-year sentence, and the other two were given two-year sentences. The Court of Appeals affirmed.

The Supreme Court in *Bridges v. United States,* 346 U.S. 209 (1953), reversed and ordered the indictment dismissed on the grounds that the three-year statute of limitations had run and that various wartime measures extending the statute of limitations for fraud against the United States were inapplicable in this instance. The majority was composed of Justices Burton, Black, Douglas and Frankfurter. Chief Justice Vinson and Justices Reed and Minton dissented. Justices Jackson and Clark did not participate.

In the wake of *Bridges v. United States,* the government made one last effort. It initiated denaturalization proceedings against Bridges. In 1955 it lost in District Court and took no appeal. *United States v. Bridges,* 133 F. Supp. 638 (Cal. 1955).

  7. 314 U.S. 252 (1941).
  8. *Scales v. United States,* 367 U.S. 203 (1961); *Elfbrandt v. Russell,* 384 U.S. 11 (1966); *Keyishian v. Board of Regents,* 385 U.S. 589 (1967); *United States v. Robel,* 389 U.S. 258 (1967).
  9. 326 U.S. at 147-8.
10. *Id.* at 144-5.
11. 367 U.S. 1 (1961).
12. 326 U.S. at 166.
13. *Id.* at 157.
14. *Id.* at 160.
15. *Id.* at 160-1.
16. *Id.* at 162.
17. *Id.* at 161.
18. 342 U.S. 580 (1952).
19. *Id.* at 596.
20. *Id.* at 597.
21. *Id.* at 598.
22. *Id.* at 585.
23. *Id.* at 591.
24. *Id.* at 594.
25. *Id.* at 600.
26. *Id.* at 601.
27. *Id.* at 598.
28. *Id.* at 601.
29. *Id.* at 595.

30. *Id.* at 593-4.

31. *Id.* at 595-6.

32. 347 U.S. 522 (1954).

33. *Garner v. Board of Public Works*, 341 U.S. 716 (1951).

34. *Wieman v. Updegraff*, 344 U.S. 183 (1952).

35. 347 U.S. at 530.

36. *Id.* at 530-1.

37. *Id.* at 533.

38. 342 U.S. 524 (1952).

39. 342 U.S. 1 (1951).

40. *Id.* at 5-6.

41. *Id.* at 533.

42. *Id.* at 545.

43. *Id.* at 556-8.

44. *Id.* at 550.

45. *Id.* at 552.

46. *Id.* at 555-6.

47. *Flemming v. Nestor*, 363 U.S. 603 (1960).

48. *In re Isserman*, 345 U.S. 286 (1953).

49. 355 U.S. 115 (1957).

50. 347 U.S. at 527.

51. 355 U.S. at 120. See Justice Frankfurter's concurring opinion in *Schware v. Board of Bar Examiners of New Mexico*, 353 U.S. 232 (1957), another sympathetic reading of the record in a case involving past membership.

52. 355 U.S. at 121.

53. In *Bonetti v. Rogers*, 356 U.S. 691 (1958), decided the following year, the Court again effects a marginal mitigation of the deportation scheme by statutory construction. This time the vote is 6 to 3, as Justice Frankfurter closes ranks and joins Justices Harlan and Clark in dissent. Bonetti had entered the United States in 1927 and had been a member of the Party from 1932 to 1936. Then, in 1937, he had left the country to go fight for the Loyalists in the Spanish Civil War. He was admitted again as a quota immigrant in 1938 and remained here. Twenty years later deportation proceedings were brought against him under a statute proscribing membership "at the time of entry or any time thereafter." The Court in an opinion by Justice Whittaker finds the term at the time of entry ambiguous, and following the canon that "ambiguity should be resolved in favor of leniency," concludes that it is the later—the 1938—entry that is relevant. Hence the alien cannot be deported, for he was not a member in 1938 or thereafter. *Bonetti* deserves to be remembered, if at all, as an occasion where joining the Loyalist side in the Spanish Civil War served to purge a man's record!

54. 362 U.S. 390 (1960).

55. *Id.* at 393-5.

56. 374 U.S. 469 (1963).

57. One additional case should be noted here, *Kimm v. Rosenberg*, 363 U.S. 405 (1960). In *Kimm* a Korean alien who had been in the United States since 1928 is asked at the deportation hearing if he is a member of the Party and claims the Fifth Amendment. There is apparently no affirmative government evidence of membership and his record is otherwise impeccable. In still one more 5 to 4 decision the Court affirms the order of deportation.

58. *Yates v. United States*, 354 U.S. 298 (1957).

59. *Scales v. United States*, 367 U.S. 203 (1961).

Chapter 31: Denaturalization

1. 279 U.S. 644 (1929).

2. *Id.* at 651.

3. *Id.* at 653.

4. *Id.* at 654-5.

5. 283 U.S. 605 (1931).

6. *Id.* at 631.

7. *Id.* at 627.

8. *Id.* at 634.

9. 328 U.S. 61 (1946).

10. The *Girouard* Court's interpretation of the intent of Congress was ultimately vindicated by the passage of the Immigration and Naturalization Act of 1952 which preserved the "support and defend" oath requirement but provided that in the case of an applicant with religious scruples against bearing arms the oath would be satisfied by a willingness to perform non-military or non-combatant service in defense of the United States.

11. 320 U.S. 118 (1943).

12. *Id.* at 170.

13. *Id.* at 164.

14. *Id.* at 165.

15. *Id.* at 169.

16. *Id.* at 166.

17. *Id.* at 167.

18. *Id.* at 125.

19. *Id.* at 136.

20. *Id.* at 158-9.

21. *Id.* at 195-6.

22. 322 U.S. 665 (1944).

23. 328 U.S. 654 (1946).

24. 322 U.S. at 674.

25. *Id.* at 677.

26. *Id.* at 675-6.
27. 328 U.S. at 659.
28. *Id.* at 660.
29. *Id.* at 677.
30. *Id.* at 678.
31. *Ibid.*
32. *Id.* at 679.
33. 356 U.S. 660 (1958).
34. 356 U.S. 670 (1958).
35. *Id.* at 666.
36. *Id.* at 667. *Nowak* and *Maisenberg* also contain a fraud count. It was based on petitioners answering "no" to the question: "Are you a believer in anarchy?. . . Do you belong to or are you associated with any organization which teaches or advocates anarchy or the overthrow of existing government in this country?" Justice Harlan, parsing the question with care, found it unclear whether it referred to Communism as well as "anarchy" and concluded that there was no basis for the petitioners in 1938 to have understood it as encompassing more than anarchy. Hence their answers were truthful and the fraud count falls.
37. 364 U.S. 426 (1960).

Chapter 32: Exclusion

1. 130 U.S. 581 (1889).
2. 194 U.S. 279 (1904).
3. *Id.* at 294.
4. 338 U.S. 537 (1950).
5. See Ellen Knauff, *The Ellen Knauff Story* (New York: W. W. Norton, 1952).
6. *Id.* at 544.
7. *Id.* at 547.
8. *Id.* at 551-2.
9. *Id.* at 548.
10. *Id.* at 551.
11. Ultimately, after much public protest, the Attorney General granted Mrs. Knauff a regular exclusion hearing at which the Board of Immigration Appeal concluded that the evidence did not justify exclusion.
12. 344 U.S. 590 (1953).
13. *Id.* at 600.
14. 345 U.S. 206 (1953).
15. *Id.* at 214.
16. *Id.* at 215.
17. 342 U.S. 524 (1952).
18. 345 U.S. at 216.
19. *Id.* at 218.

20. *Terminiello v. Chicago,* 337 U.S. 1 (1949).

21. *Kunz v. New York,* 340 U.S. 290 (1951).

22. 345 U.S. at 219.

23. *Id.* at 220.

24. *Id.* at 224.

25. *Ibid.*

26. *Id.* at 227.

27. *Id.* at 226.

28. *Id.* at 227.

29. 381 U.S. 301 (1965).

30. 394 U.S. 557 (1969).

31. 403 U.S. 15 (1971).

32. After winning its case in the Supreme Court, the government gave Mezei a hearing before a special board of inquiry. The board upheld the exclusion but recommended that he be paroled into the United States.

33. 408 U.S. 753 (1972).

34. *Id.* at 759. Justice Douglas in his dissent observes that "the activities which the Attorney General labeled 'flagrant abuses' of Dr. Mandel's opportunity to speak in the United States appear merely to have been his speaking at more universities than his visa application indicated." *Id.* at 773 n. 4. Justice Blackmun contests this. "The asserted noncompliance," he argues, is "broader" than that. *Id.* at 758 n.5. It also includes violation of a limitation on Mandel's visa which forbade him to appear where contributions were solicited for political causes. He had, it appears, been present at a meeting at which money was solicited for French students involved in the 1968 demonstrations.

    The State Department in recommending to the Justice Department that Mandel be permitted entry had noted that he may not have been apprised on his prior visit of the limitations imposed on his visa.

35. 319 U.S. 141 (1943).

36. *Red Lion Broadcasting Co. v. FCC,* 395 U.S. 367 (1969).

37. 408 U.S. at 762.

38. *Id.* at 765.

39. *Id.* at 768.

40. *Id.* at 769.

41. *Id.* at 774.

42. *Ibid.*

43. *Id.* at 778.

44. *Id.* at 781.

45. *Id.* at 782.

46. *United States v. Robel,* 389 U.S. 258 (1967).

47. *Aptheker v. Secretary of State,* 378 U.S. 500 (1964).

48. 408 U.S. at 783-4.

49. An aesthetic detail about legal patterns. In the soundtrack cases, *Saia v.*

New York, 334 U.S. 558 (1948) and *Kovacs v. Cooper,* 336 U.S. 77 (1949), the problem can be framed as the propriety of the message coming in when the speaker himself could not. Here the problem is whether if the message can come in, the speaker himself can be kept out!

Chapter 33: The Regulation of Passports

1. See *Shapiro v. Thompson,* 394 U.S. 618 (1969). Also see the concurring opinions of Justices Douglas and Jackson in *Edwards v. California,* 314 U.S. 160 (1941).
2. 357 U.S. 116 (1958).
3. Justice Douglas pointedly observes that Kent had "a hearing at which the principal evidence against him was from his book It's Me O'Lord, which Kent agreed was accurate." *Id.* at 119.
4. *Id.* at 126.
5. *Id.* at 128.
6. *Id.* at 127.
7. A companion case to *Kent, Dayton v. Dulles,* 357 U.S. 144 (1958), suggests that the procedures by which the Passport Office reached its conclusions of unreliability were often as much departures from due process as the procedures at issue in *Knauff* and *Mezei.* The ground for denial of the passport in *Dayton* rested not on membership or "Party line" criteria but on suspected complicity in the Rosenberg spy ring. (The Secretary of State's findings indicated at most association with some of the people suspected but never charged with being involved in the Rosenberg case.) The challenge went primarily to the reliance of the Secretary of State on confidential files not disclosed to the petitioner. The Court, however, found it unnecessary to reach this issue. In another 5 to 4 decision it summarily upset the denial on the statutory construction grounds of *Kent.*
8. 378 U.S. 500 (1964).
9. 381 U.S. 1 (1965).
10. In 1967 the Court was confronted with the issue it postponed in *Zemel:* Given that the area restriction is constitutional, is it a criminal offense to travel to Cuba without official permission, i.e., without a specially validated passport? In two companion cases—*United States v. Laub,* 385 U.S. 475 (1967), and *Travis v. United States,* 385 U.S. 491 (1967)—the Court unanimously held that such travel had not been made criminal under the existing statutes and regulations. In construing the law the Court went back to the twin functions of a passport, as voucher of government protection and as exit permit. It elected to read the passport regulations as involving only the loss of the voucher of government services if one went to Cuba without permission. "Crimes," wrote Justice Fortas in *Laub,* "are not to be created by inference." *Id.* at 487.
11. 381 U.S. at 22.

12. *Id.* at 24.

13. *Id.* at 25.

14. *Id.* at 39.

15. 381 U.S. 301 (1965).

16. *Id.* at 13.

17. *Id.* at 16-17.

18. The Pentagon Papers case, *New York Times v. United States,* 403 U.S. 713 (1971), the controversy over reporters' privilege, and the controversy over the access of reporters to prisoners all raise in one way or another questions of negative impacts on communications.

Chapter 34: Legislative Investigation: The Beginnings, 1880-1956

1. *Brandenburg v. Ohio,* 395 U.S. 444 (1969); *Elfbrandt v. Russell,* 384 U.S. 11 (1966).

2. See Frankfurter, "Hands Off the Investigations," *The New Republic,* May 21, 1924; Landis, "Constitutional Limitations on the Congressional Power of Investigation," 40 *Harvard Law Review* 153 (1926); Black, "Inside a Senate Investigation," *Harper's,* February 1936. Cf. Coudert, "Congressional Inquisition vs. Individual Liberty," 15 *Virginia Law Review* 537 (1929).

3. 273 U.S. 135 (1927).

4. 103 U.S. 168 (1881). The other cases discussed by Justice Van Devanter dealt with the inherent contempt power of Congress but not in conjunction with compelling testimony. *Anderson v. Dunn,* 6 Wheat 204 (1821), held that the power was not limited to use against members of the House. *Marshall v. Gordon,* 243 U.S. 521 (1917), the case closest to our First Amendment theme, held that there was no implied power to punish for contempt of Congress by publication. And *In re Chapman,* 166 U.S. 661 (1897), held that the passage of the 1857 statute creating a statutory contempt of Congress did not serve to eliminate the inherent power to bring the recalcitrant before the bar of the House.

5. 103 U.S. at 190.

6. 273 U.S. at 174.

7. *Id.* at 175.

8. *Id.* at 177.

9. *Id.* at 178.

10. *Id.* at 179-80.

11. Kalven, "Mr. Alexander Meiklejohn and the Barenblatt Opinion," 27 *University of Chicago Law Review* 315, 327 (1960).

12. 279 U.S. 263 (1929).

13. In the decade following *McGrain* the Court dealt with the power of legislative committees to compel testimony in two other cases: *Barry v. United States ex rel Cunningham,* 279 U.S. 597 (1929), and *Jurney v. McCracken,* 294 U.S. 125 (1935). These are the last cases to deal with use

of the *inherent contempt power* of Congress. Henceforward all cases will involve the federal statutory crime of contempt of Congress.

14. *United States v. Josephson*, 165 F. 2d 82 (1947); *Barsky v. United States*, 167 F. 2d 241 (1948); *Eisler v. United States*, 170 F. 2d 273 (1948), 338 U.S. 189 (1949).

15. *Christoffel v. United States*, 338 U.S. 84 (1949); *Dennis v. United States*, 339 U.S. 162 (1950); *Morford v. United States*, 339 U.S. 258 (1950); *United States v. Bryan*, 339 U.S. 323 (1950); *United States v. Fleischman*, 339 U.S. 349 (1950).

16. 165 F. 2d at 93.

17. 167 F. 2d at 254.

18. *Id.* at 255.

19. Was it because the defendant refused to appear altogether? Josephson refused even to be sworn; Barsky, by contrast, appeared before the committee but refused to produce the subpoenaed records of an organization of which he was an officer.

20. 338 U.S. at 190.

21. *Id.* at 192. Later in the term the Court adopted Justice Frankfurter's view and dismissed *certiorari*.

22. *Id.* at 194.

23. *Id.* at 196.

24. 367 U.S. 1 (1961).

25. Justice Jackson entered a vigorous dissent in *Christoffel.* He argued that the rule was intensely impractical, as the number of members in the room customarily fluctuated while a hearing was in session, and it was pure happenstance how many members would be present at any given moment. Further, he argued that if the witness saw the quorum as protection, his remedy was to request a quorum before the hearing proceeded, thus giving the committee a chance to correct the matter.

26. 339 U.S. at 172.

27. *Id.* at 175.

28. *Id.* at 180.

29. *Id.* at 183-4.

30. 341 U.S. 367 (1951).

31. 345 U.S. 41 (1953).

32. See Kalven, "Congressional Testing of Linus Pauling: The Legal Framework," 16 *Bulletin of the Atomic Scientists* 383 (1960), and "Congressional Testing of Linus Pauling: Sourwine in an Old Bottle," 17 *Bulletin of the Atomic Scientists* 12 (1961).

33. 341 U.S. at 376.

34. *Id.* at 378.

35. *Ibid.*

36. *Id.* at 379.

37. *Id.* at 382.

38. 345 U.S. at 44.

39. *Ibid.*
40. *Id.* at 46.
41. One difficulty for the Frankfurter construction of the resolution is that in voting the contempt of Rumely the House ratified on a close vote the scope of its authorization of the committee. Justice Frankfurter now argues persuasively that the House can *now* be in error about what the House at an earlier date had intended.
42. 345 U.S. at 46.
43. *Yates v. United States,* 354 U.S. 298 (1957); *Scales v. United States,* 367 U.S. 203 (1961); *Elfbrandt v. Russell,* 384 U.S. 11 (1966).
44. 345 U.S. at 56.
45. *Ibid.*
46. *Id.* at 58.
47. 362 U.S. 60 (1960).
48. 394 U.S. 557 (1969).
49. 345 U.S. at 57.
50. *Barsky v. Board of Regents,* 347 U.S. 442 (1954); *Quinn v. United States,* 349 U.S. 155 (1955); *Emspak v. United States,* 349 U.S. 190 (1955); *Bart v. United States,* 349 U.S. 219 (1955).
51. 347 U.S. at 457.
52. *Id.* at 473-4.
53. *Id.* at 474.
54. 349 U.S. at 162.
55. But see Sullivan, Kamin, and Sussman, "The Case Against HUAC: The Stamler Litigation," 11 *Harvard Civil Rights-Civil Liberties Law Review* 243 (1976); and Zeisel and Stamler, "The Case Against HUAC: The Evidence: A Content Analysis of the HUAC Record," 11 *Harvard Civil Rights-Civil Liberties Law Review* 262 (1976).
56. *Id.* at 194.
57. *Id.* at 195.
58. 354 U.S. 179 (1957).

Chapter 35: Legislative Investigation: The Period of First Amendment Challenge, 1957-1959

1. 354 U.S. 179 (1957).
2. *Id.* at 206.
3. *Id.* at 209.
4. Justice Frankfurter, in his concurring opinion, adds:

> . . . the actual scope of the inquiry that the Committee was authorized to conduct and the relevance of the questions to that inquiry must be shown to have been luminous at the time when asked and not left, at best, in cloudiness.

Id. at 217.

5. Also, Justice Clark, dissenting, suggests that the pertinency requirement would be no bar to the House using its inherent contempt power.
6. *Id.* at 201-2.
7. *Id.* at 202.
8. *Ibid.*
9. *Ibid.*
10. *Id.* at 203-4.
11. *Id.* at 205.
12. *Id.* at 197.
13. *Ibid.*
14. *Ibid.*
15. *Id.* at 197-8.
16. *Id.* at 196.
17. *Id.* at 197.
18. *Scales v. United States,* 367 U.S. 203 (1961); *Elfbrandt v. Russell,* 384 U.S. 11 (1966); *Keyishian v. Board of Regents,* 385 U.S. 589 (1967); *United States v. Robel,* 389 U.S. 258 (1967); *Apetheker v. Secretary of State,* 378 U.S. 500 (1964).
19. *Yates v. United States,* 354 U.S. 298 (1957).
20. 354 U.S. at 198.
21. *Ibid.*
22. *Id.* at 197.
23. *Watkins* suggests another possible First Amendment grievance against legislative investigation: In view of the widespread feeling that a man of honor does not inform, it can be argued, the threat that one may be placed in a position where he will be asked to inform is a real and substantial restraint on his freedom of speech.
24. *Id.* at 199.
25. The following is an example of the sort of statement quoted by the defendant. It was culled from a report of the committee to the House: "While Congress does not have the power to deny to citizens the right to believe in, teach, or advocate, communism, fascism, and nazism, it does have the right to focus the spotlight of publicity upon their activities." *Id.* at 199 n. 32.

    An effort to document committee motives by means of a content analysis of the official HUAC transcripts for the years 1947-67 is reported in Zeisel and Stamler, "The Case Against HUAC: The Evidence: A Content Analysis of the HUAC Record," 11 *Harvard Civil Rights-Civil Liberties Law Review* 262 (1976).—*Ed.*
26. 367 U.S. 1 (1961).
27. 354 U.S. at 200.
28. *Id.* at 200 n.33.
29. *Ibid.*
30. *Id.* at 200.
31. 354 U.S. 234 (1957).

32. He submitted an eloquent personal statement on behalf of his refusal to answer certain questions which the Court quotes in full in a note. *Id.* at 239-42. His counsel before the Supreme Court was Professor Thomas Emerson of the Yale Law School.

33. *Id.* at 251.

34. *Ibid.*

35. *Ibid.*

36. *Id.* at 253.

37. *Id.* at 254.

38. *Id.* at 255.

39. *Id.* at 256.

40. *Id.* at 261.

41. *Id.* at 263.

42. *Id.* at 266.

43. *Id.* at 265.

44. *Ibid.*

45. *Id.* at 266.

46. 360 U.S. 109 (1959).

47. During the period between *Sweezy* and *Barenblatt* the Court firmly decides three cases in favor of the witness, *Sacher v. United States,* 356 U.S. 576 (1958), *Flaxer v. United States,* 358 U.S. 147 (1958), and *Scull v. Virginia,* 359 U.S. 344 (1959). The decisions are unanimous, except for a lone dissent by Justice Clark in *Sacher.*

   Flaxer reaffirms the procedural point laid down in *Quinn* that the witness must be unequivocally ordered to answer before he can be held in contempt for not doing so. *Sacher* and *Scull* are of somewhat broader interest. *Sacher* involves a two-man subcommittee of the Senate Internal Security Committee authorized to inquire into the circumstances leading to the recantation of Harvey Matusow, a Communist informer who later changed his story. The subcommittee asked Sacher, a lawyer, certain questions about proposed federal legislation to bar Communist lawyers from the federal bar which he refused to answer. The Court in a *per curiam* opinion held that the questions were not pertinent and freed the witness from the contempt. It is apparent in this instance that non-pertinency means the same thing as lack of authorization. The Court speaks of "a subject not within the subcommittee's scope of inquiry as authorized by its parent committee." 356 U.S. at 577. The case thus highlights the perplexity of treating pertinency as an *independent* ground of objection.

   Scull illustrates that the pertinency requirement may on occasion serve to protect a witness from harassment. It arises out of an investigation conducted by a committee of the Virginia legislature—the Committee on Law Reform and Racial Activities—established in the aftermath of *Brown v. Board of Education.* The witness charges that the committee was set up as part of a legislative program of "massive resistance" to the desegregation decision "in order to harass, vilify, and publicly embarrass members of the NAACP and others who are attempting to secure integrated public schooling in Virginia." 359 U.S. at 345. A printer who had been active in publishing newsletters on the integration issue, he had been called before the committee and asked a lengthy series of questions: Are you a member of the NAACP? Are you a member of the Fairfax County Council on Human Relations? Have other organizations—the ACLU, the B'Nai B'rith, the Friends Service Committee, the Communist Party, etc.—used the post office box listed in your newsletter? He asked for clarification of the pertinency of these questions to the committee's scope of inquiry, and although its authorization included as a subject the impact of integration on the Virginia school system and on the general welfare of Virginia, the committee chairman was wholly unable to connect up the questions with any purpose of the committee. The Court is thus able by means of the pertinency requirement to protect Scull without having to wrestle with the hard question posed by his challenge to official motivation.

48. There is also a one paragraph dissent by Justice Brennan. He finds it "sufficient" to express his "complete agreement" with Justice Black that "no purpose for the investigation of Barenblatt is revealed by the record except exposure purely for the sake of exposure." 360 U.S. at 166.

49. *Id.* at 119.

50. *Id.* at 118.

51. *Id.* at 121.

52. *Id.* at 140.

53. *Id.* at 126.

54. *Id.* at 134.

55. *Ibid.*

56. *Id.* at 128.

57. 376 U.S. 254 (1964).

58. 360 U.S. at 141

59. *Id.* at 144.

60. *Ibid.*

61. *Ibid.*

62. *Ibid.*

63. *Id.* at 145.

64. *Id.* at 146-7.

65. *Id.* at 133.

66. *Id.* at 163-6.

67. *Id.* at 129.

68. *Id.* at 162.

69. *Id.* at 153-4.

70. *Id.* at 159.

71. *Id.* at 130.
72. *Ibid.*

Chapter 36: Legislative Investigation: The Law Unable to Work Itself Pure

1. 360 U.S. 72 (1959).
2. *Id.* at 77.
3. *Id.* at 78.
4. *Id.* at 81.
5. *Id.* at 79.
6. *Id.* at 80-1. Justice Clark also notes that a New Hampshire statute requires all hotel keepers and managers of tourist camps, cabins and the like to maintain a register signed by each guest and open to inspection by the police. It appears that World Fellowship had complied with this statute and that most of the names sought by the Attorney General had been recorded in this fashion.
7. *Id.* at 84.
8. *Id.* at 106.
9. *Id.* at 85.
10. Although Justices Black and Douglas join Justice Brennan's dissenting opinion in *Uphaus,* they do not give his argument their unqualified support. A note appended to Brennan's opinion indicates that they would prefer to decide the case on the First Amendment grounds "developed in" their dissenting opinions in *Adler v. Board of Education,* 342 U.S. 485 (1952), and *Beauharnais v. Illinois,* 343 U.S. 250 (1952), but that they join in Brennan's opinion "because he makes clear to them" that the New Hampshire scheme violates the prohibition against bills of attainder.
11. 360 U.S. at 101.
12. The Court's peculiar lack of empathy for the *Uphaus* situation is further illustrated when the case comes back to it in 1960 in *Uphaus v. Wyman,* 364 U.S. 388. In the initial case the state court had held Uphaus in contempt under an "indefinite sentence," that is, *until* he produced the information requested. While he was in jail the legislature repealed the Act under which the Attorney General had acted. Uphaus sought release on the ground that there was no continuing state need for the information. The New Hampshire court rejected the argument, finding that the state legislature still wanted the information. The Supreme Court in a brief *per curiam* opinion, in which Justice Brennan joins, affirms, treating it as a point of state law. Chief Justice Warren and Justices Black and Douglas file dissenting opinions. The upshot is that, because of the compulsions of the federal system, the Court leaves the seventy-year-old Dr. Uphaus, who has already been there for eleven months, in jail for the

indefinite future for his failure to satisfy the state's need for the names of those who attended the summer camp in 1954 and 1955.

13. 365 U.S. 399 (1961).
14. 365 U.S. 431 (1961).
15. 376 U.S. 254 (1964).
16. 365 U.S. at 412, quoting 354 U.S. at 200.
17. *Id.* at 414.
18. *Id.* at 413.
19. *Id.* at 415.
20. *Id.* at 416-7.
21. *Id.* at 417.
22. *Id.* at 428.
23. *Id.* at 430.
24. 350 U.S. 497 (1956).
25. 372 U.S. 539 (1963).
26. 367 U.S. 456 (1961).
27. *Id.* at 470.
28. *Id.* at 471-2.
29. *Id.* at 473.
30. *Id.* at 474.
31. 369 U.S. 749 (1962).
32. *Id.* at 777.
33. 372 U.S. 539 (1963).
34. *Id.* at 582.
35. 360 U.S. at 134.
36. 365 U.S. at 419-20.
37. *Id.* at 420.
38. 372 U.S. at 579.
39. Note the kinship between this requirement and the principle of *Speiser v. Randall,* 357 U.S. 513 (1958), that the burden of proof is to be allocated to the government in "sensitive" inquiry cases.
40. *Id.* at 554.
41. *Id.* at 580.
42. Such situations—and such individuals—are rare but by no means nonexistent. See *In re Anastaplo,* 366 U.S. 82 (1961).
43. 372 U.S. at 565-6.
44. *Id.* at 572-3.
45. *Id.* at 584.
46. *Yellin v. United States,* 374 U.S. 109 (1963); *DeGregory v. Attorney General of New Hampshire,* 383 U.S. 825 (1966); *Gojack v. United States,* 384 U.S. 702 (1966).
47. 374 U.S. at 145.
48. 383 U.S. at 828.
49. *Id.* at 829.

50. *Id.* at 828-9.
51. *Id.* at 829.
52. *Id.* at 830.
53. *Ibid.*
54. 384 U.S. at 706.
55. *Id.* at 717.
56. *Id.* at 711.
57. *Id.* at 711-2.
58. *Id.* at 714.
59. *Id.* at 713.
60. *Id.* at 716.
61. *Communist Party v. Subversive Activities Control Board,* 367 U.S. 1 (1961).

Chapter 37: The Principle of *Speiser v. Randall*

1. 341 U.S. 716 (1951).
2. *Id.* at 720.
3. *Id.* at 730.
4. 357 U.S. 513 (1958). See also *First Unitarian Church v. Los Angeles,* 357 U.S. 545 (1958), a companion case in which the Court relies on *Speiser.*
5. *Id.* at 515.
6. *Id.* at 519-20.
7. *Id.* at 522.
8. *Id.* at 520-1.
9. *Id.* at 521.
10. *Ibid.*
11. *Id.* at 525.
12. *Id.* at 525-6.
13. *Id.* at 526.
14. *Ibid.*
15. *Id.* at 529.
16. *Id.* at 542.
17. *Ibid.*
18. *Id.* at 543.
19. *Id.* at 541.
20. *Id.* at 531.
21. 380 U.S. 51 (1965).
22. 372 U.S. 539 (1963).
23. 357 U.S. 399 (1958).
24. 357 U.S. 468 (1958).
25. *Id.* at 405.
26. *Id.* at 406.
27. *Id.* at 410.
28. 350 U.S. 551 (1956).
29. 357 U.S. at 418.

30. *Id.* at 419.

31. *Id.* at 474.

32. *Id.* at 475.

33. *Id.* at 476. The status of *Beilan* and *Lerner* as precedents has been placed in doubt by subsequent developments:

In *Lerner* the Court held that the Fifth Amendment privilege against self-incrimination did not apply to the states. But in *Malloy v. Hogan,* 378 U.S. 1 (1964), it held that the Fifth Amendment *does* apply to the states by way of the Fourteenth Amendment.

In *Spevack v. Klein,* 385 U.S. 511 (1967), the Court, reversing its 1961 decision in *Cohen v. Hurley,* 366 U.S. 117 (1961), held that a lawyer may claim the Fifth Amendment in disbarment proceedings. Justice Fortas concurred on the ground that public employees are in a different position than a lawyer who "is not an employee of the State." Justice Harlan, dissenting, would have applied the analysis of *Beilan* and *Lerner* to the refusal to testify so long as no inference of guilt is drawn from it.

In *Garrity v. New Jersey,* 385 U.S. 493 (1967), police officers were forced to testify in an investigation of traffic ticket fixing on threat that they would lose their jobs if they refused, although the questions might be incriminating. Their testimony was subsequently used in a prosecution of them which resulted in their conviction. The Court reversed on the ground that it was unconstitutional to thus induce them to forego the privilege against self-incrimination; hence the testimony was coerced and should have been inadmissible.

In *Gardner v. Broderick,* 392 U.S. 273 (1968), a police officer was called upon to testify in an investigation of bribery and informed of the privilege but advised that unless he signed "a waiver of immunity" he would be discharged. He declined to sign the waiver and was discharged. The Court held that the discharge was improper, but that if he had refused to testify without waiving immunity, the refusal would have supported a valid discharge even though the refusal was based on a claim of privilege. The policeman, said Justice Fortas, had a greater duty to respond to relevant inquiries than did the lawyer: "Unlike the lawyer who is directly responsible to his client, the policeman is either responsible to the State or to no one."

In *Uniformed Sanitation Men Association v. Commissioner,* 392 U.S. 280 (1968), the Court applied the principle of *Gardner v. Broderick* to other public employees; and in *Leftkowitz v. Turley,* 414 U.S. 70 (1973), it reaffirmed the *Gardner* principle with respect to public contractors.

Chapter 38: The Principle of *Shelton v. Tucker*

1. It does not always work, however. Cf. *Wilkinson v. United States,* 365 U.S. 399 (1961), and *Braden v. United States,* 365 U.S. 431 (1961).

2. 376 U.S. 254 (1964).

3. 372 U.S. 539 (1963).

4. 364 U.S. 479 (1960).

5. *Barenblatt v. United States,* 360 U.S. 109 (1959).

6. *Braden v. United States,* 365 U.S. 431 (1961); *Wilkinson v. United States,* 365 U.S. 399 (1961).

7. *Shelton v. McKinley,* 174 F. Supp. 351 (1959).

8. 364 U.S. at 485.

9. *Bates v. Little Rock,* 361 U.S. 516 (1960).

10. 364 U.S. at 485-6.

11. *Id.* at 486.

12. *Id.* at 486-7.

13. *Id.* at 488.

14. *Ibid.*

15. *Lovell v. Griffin,* 303 U.S. 444 (1938); *Schneider v. State,* 308 U.S. 147 (1939); *Talley v. California,* 362 U.S. 60 (1960).

16. 364 U.S. at 488 n.8.

17. 270 U.S. 230 (1926).

18. 364 U.S. at 496-7.

19. *Id.* at 499.

20. *Id.* at 498.

21. *Id.* at 493.

22. *Id.* at 494.

23. *Ibid.*

24. *Id.* at 495.

25. *Id.* at 499.

26. *Id.* at 496.

Chapter 39: Wondrous Complexity: The Bar Admission Cases

1. *Garner v. Board of Public Works,*, 341 U.S. 716 (1951); *Beilan v. Board of Education,* 357 U.S. 399 (1958); *Lerner v. Casey,* 357 U.S. 468 (1958); *Speiser v. Randall,* 357 U.S. 513 (1958).

2. 353 U.S. 252 (1957).

3. *Konigsberg v. State Bar of California,* 366 U.S. 36 (1961).

4. 366 U.S. 82 (1961).

5. *In re Stolar,* 401 U.S. 23 (1971); *Baird v. State Bar of Arizona,* 401 U.S. 1 (1971); *Law Students Civil Rights Research Council v. Wadmond,* 401 U.S. 154 (1971).

6. *Ex parte Garland,* 71 U.S. (4 Wall) 333 (1867); *In re Summers,* 325 U.S. 561 (1945); *Schware v. Board of Bar Examiners of New Mexico,* 353 U.S. 232 (1957).

7. 328 U.S. 61 (1946).

8. The decisions overruled were *United States v. Schwimmer,* 279 U.S. 644 (1929), and *United States v. Macintosh,* 283 U.S. 605 (1931).

9. 325 U.S. at 570-1.
10. *Id.* at 575.
11. 353 U.S. at 239.
12. *Id.* at 244.
13. *Id.* at 251.
14. *Schware* stands in sharp contrast to the Court's inability to review the federal administrative loyalty program. Is the critical difference to be found in the difference between admission to the bar, *i.e.*, to a means of livelihood, and employment by the federal government? Is it to be found in the procedural rule on confidential informants which has the effect in the loyalty program cases of denying the courts access to the full record? Or is it to be found in the difference in standards—in the one case, rejection as a loyalty-security risk; in the other, as a man of questionable character?
15. Three other cases bear tangentially on the state's power to impose substantive conditions on the practice of law: *In re Isserman*, 345 U.S. 286 (1953), *Isserman v. Ethics Committee*, 345 U.S. 927 (1953), and *Sacher v. Association of Bar of New York*, 347 U.S. 388 (1954). We discussed these cases earlier as examples of the "multiplier effect" of anti-Communist sanctions. All three involve efforts by bar grievance committees to discipline the defense lawyers in *Dennis v. United States*, 341 U.S. 494 (1951), after they had been found in contempt by Judge Medina. In *Isserman v. Ethics Committee* the Court declines to disturb the disbarment of petitioner imposed by New Jersey; and in *In re Isserman* it also affirms barring him, since he has lost his state base, from practice before the Supreme Court. However, in *Sacher*, under its supervisory power over federal courts, it upsets a permanent disbarment from the federal courts in New York as "too severe."
16. 353 U.S. at 261.
17. *Ibid.*
18. *Id.* at 270.
19. *Id.* at 273.
20. *Id.* at 310.
21. *Id.* at 281.
22. *Id.* at 310.
23. *Id.* at 311.
24. *Id.* at 310.
25. Its fate is foreshadowed by two cases in 1958 in which the Court by 5 to 4 votes affirms the discharges of public employees who, in official inquiries, refuse to answer questions as to Communist affiliations: *Beilan v. Board of Public Education*, 357 U.S. 399, and *Lerner v. Casey*, 357 U.S. 468.
26. 353 U.S. at 261.
27. 366 U.S. at 57.
28. *Id.* at 43.

29. *Id.* at 45-6.
30. *Id.* at 46.
31. *Id.* at 80-1.
32. *Id.* at 75.
33. *Id.* at 77.
34. *Id.* at 54.
35. *Garner v. Board of Public Works,* 341 U.S. 716 (1951); *Gerende v. Board of Supervisors of Elections,* 341 U.S. 56 (1945); *American Communication Association v. Douds,* 339 U.S. 382 (1950).
36. 357 U.S. at 528.
37. 366 U.S. at 55.
38. 353 U.S. at 277.
39. 366 U.S. at 51.
40. *Id.* at 51-2.
41. 354 U.S. 298 (1957).
42. 366 U.S. at 52.
43. *Ibid.*
44. *Id.* at 73.
45. *Id.* at 73-4.
46. *Id.* at 74.
47. *Id.* at 70.
48. *Id.* at 59-60.
49. 343 U.S. 250 (1952).
50. 366 U.S. at 64.
51. *Id.* at 61.
52. *Id.* at 60-1.
53. *Id.* at 51.
54. *Ibid.*
55. *Watkins v. United States,* 354 U.S. 178 (1957); *Barenblatt v. United States,* 360 U.S. 109 (1959); *Wilkinson v. United States,* 365 U.S. 399 (1961); *Braden v. United States,* 365 U.S. 431 (1961).
56. 366 U.S. at 69.
57. *Id.* at 51.
58. *Id.* at 69-70.
59. Justice Harlan does discuss in some detail, however, the adequacy of the warning and the impropriety of the question about the right of revolution. The Harlan opinion suggests the gravest doubt that rejecting Anastaplo for his views on revolution would have been constitutional. But it also rejects Justice Black's conclusion that this was the real reason the Committee had rejected him.
60. 366 U.S. at 95.
61. *Id.* at 97.
62. Since these words were written the committee has, on its own initiative, approached Anastaplo. In 1978 the committee reopened the matter,

heard testimony as to Anastaplo's good character, and voted 13 to 4 to recommend him to the Illinois Supreme Court for admission to the bar. The Court informed the committee that "it would be inappropriate to act on this matter in its present posture" and recommended that Anastaplo apply anew for admission to the bar. This Anastaplo has declined to do.—*Ed.*

63. 366 U.S. at 107-8.

64. *Id.* at 111.

65. *Id.* at 114.

66. *Gibson v. Florida Legislative Investigation Committee,* 372 U.S. 539 (1963); *DeGregory v. Attorney General of New Hampshire,* 383 U.S. 825 (1966).

67. *Elfbrand v. Russell,* 384 U.S. 11 (1966).

68. 401 U.S. at 4.

69. *Id.* at 7-8.

70. *Id.* at 9.

71. *Scales v. United States,* 367 U.S. 203 (1961). The Arizona committee in explaining its position stated it was concerned with discovering whether the applicant "truly and sincerely *believes* in the overthrow of the Government of the United States by force and violence." Justice Stewart singles out this explicit reference to belief as an additional flaw in the Arizona procedure: "And the respondent's explanation of its purpose in asking the question makes clear that the question must be treated as an inquiry into political beliefs." 401 U.S. at 9. Thus, we meet again the Court's special sensitivity to any governmental touching of beliefs even in the peculiar and atypical form found here. Cf. the Jackson and Frankfurter dissents in *American Communication Association v. Douds,* 339 U.S. 382 (1950).

72. 401 U.S. at 10.

73. *Id.* at 17.

74. *Id.* at 16.

75. *Id.* at 21.

76. See Kalven, Introduction, *Contempt: Transcript of the Contempt Citations, Sentences, and Responses of the Chicago 10* (Chicago: Swallow, 1970).

77. 401 U.S. at 24-5.

78. *Id.* at 31.

79. *Id.* at 33.

80. *Id.* at 33-4.

81. *Id.* at 34.

82. *Id.* at 35.

83. *Ibid.*

84. *Id.* at 186.

85. *Id.* at 166.

86. *Id.* at 164-5.

87. *Id.* at 165.

88. *Id.* at 165-6.
89. *Id.* at 175.
90. *Id.* at 184.
91. *Id.* at 182.
92. *Id.* at 182-3.
93. *Id.* at 188.
94. 385 U.S. 116 (1966).
95. 401 U.S. at 186.
96. *Id.* at 167.
97. *Ibid.*

Table of Cases

A Book Named "John Cleland's Memoirs of a Woman of Pleasure" v. Attorney General of Massachusetts, 38, 39–40, 41, 43, 44, 45, 48, 49, 51

Abrams v. United States, 64–64, 138, 139, 143–145, 146, 148, 152, 156, 162, 182, 183, 196, 207, 227

Adler v. Board of Education, 368–372

Albertson v. Subversive Activities Control Board, 273, 286–287

American Committee for Protection of Foreign Born v. Subversive Activities Control Board, 288, 294

American Communications Association v. Douds, 187–189, 196, 197, 319, 332–339, 340, 341, 342, 343, 344, 345, 347, 348, 350, 353, 356, 358, 363, 370, 375, 387, 562

Anastaplo, *In re*, 549, 557, 570–574, 575, 576, 577, 578, 582, 583

Aptheker v. Secretary of State, 287, 298, 317, 359, 367, 368, 375, 376, 379, 381–383, 384, 395, 447, 452, 454, 456, 489, 492

Baggett v. Bullitt, 353–356, 357, 358, 360, 361, 364, 365, 367, 374

Bailey v. Richardson, 289, 290

Baird v. State Bar of Arizona, 549, 574, 575, 576, 578, 579, 580, 581, 582, 583, 584

Barenblatt v. United States, 253, 497–505, 506, 508, 509, 510, 511, 512, 513, 516, 517, 518, 522, 524, 525, 526, 542, 555, 559, 568, 575

Barr v. Matteo, 67

Barsky v. Board of Regents, 395–399, 466, 467, 469, 479

Bart v. United States, 479, 480, 482, 483

Bates v. Alabama, 281

Bates v. Little Rock, 261, 262, 263, 544

Baumgartner v. United States, 431–432, 433, 435

Beauharnais v. Illinois, 61, 78, 89, 92, 96, 110, 116, 117, 567

Beilan v. Board of Public Education, 539–541, 548, 575

Bond v. Floyd, 123, 229, 309–311, 314, 338–339, 372, 586

Braden v. United States, 509, 510, 511, 517, 518, 521, 526, 527, 543, 560

Brandenburg v. Ohio, 121, 122–123, 124, 125, 129, 135, 138, 162, 164, 165, 166, 185, 216, 227–236, 243, 357, 371, 460, 584, 598–599, 602, 603, 604

Bridges v. California, 26–27, 30, 31, 180, 184, 405, 406, 605

Bridges v. Wilson, 404, 406, 407, 410, 412, 422

Brown v. Board of Education, 259

Brown v. Oklahoma, 112, 113, 114–115

Brown, United States v., 327–329, 359

Bryan, United States v., 467, 469, 470

Bryant v. Zimmerman, 256–258, 282, 283, 285

Burleson, United States ex rel. Milwaukee Social Democratic Publishing Company v., 147, 149

Burstyn v. Wilson, 8, 9, 11, 12, 13, 14, 19

Butler v. Michigan, 35–36, 55

Cantwell v. Connecticut, 7, 78, 80–81, 86, 88, 97, 117, 118, 180

Carlson v. Landon, 414, 415, 416, 442

Carolene Products, United States v., 176, 179

Chaplinsky v. New Hampshire, 17–18, 19, 36, 61, 78–80, 88, 94, 97, 106, 107, 108, 110, 111, 112, 113, 114, 115

Chinese Exclusion case, 437, 440, 444

Christoffel v. United States, 466, 469

Cohen v. California, 15–16, 17, 18, 19, 106–110, 112, 114, 115, 118, 392, 444

Cole v. Richardson, 361, 362, 363–367

Communist Party v. Catherwood, 399

Communist Party v. Subversive Activities Control Board, 263–289

Connell v. Higgenbotham, 361, 363

Cox v. Louisiana, 98–99, 103, 117

Craig v. Harney, 30, 180

Cramp v. Board of Public Instruction, 351–353, 354, 355, 356, 357, 358, 360, 365, 372

Debs v. United States, 130, 135, 136, 137, 138, 139, 140, 143, 145, 148, 158, 196

DeGregory v. Attorney General of New Hampshire, 521, 523–525, 527, 530

DeJonge v. Oregon, 123, 175, 177, 183, 244–245

Dennis v. United States, 122, 190–210, 211, 212, 214, 215, 216, 217, 219, 220, 221, 222, 228, 229, 230, 231, 232, 233, 234, 242, 243, 249, 250–251, 258, 264, 284, 285, 289, 292, 323, 325, 338, 345, 365, 397, 415, 467, 470, 601, 604, 605, 606

Deutch v. United States, 511, 512, 513, 518, 521, 527

Doubleday v. New York, 35

Dubois Clubs of America v. Clark, 288, 294, 295–296

Edwards v. South Carolina, 96, 99, 117

Eisler v. United States, 466, 468, 469

Electric Bond & Share Company v. SEC, 270–271

Elfbrandt v. Russell, 357–360, 361, 364, 367, 368, 372, 373, 374, 375, 376, 378, 379, 383, 395, 406, 419, 460, 477, 489, 492, 501, 504, 505, 574, 581, 584

Emspak v. United States, 479, 480, 481, 483
Epperson v. Arkansas, 9, 10, 12, 124
Ex Parte Garland, 549–550

Feiner v. New York, 78, 89–92, 97, 98, 100, 104, 107, 116, 118
Fiske v. Kansas, 122, 177
Fleischman, United States v., 467, 469, 470
Flemming v. Nestor, 391–395, 396, 398, 419
Freedman v. Maryland, 538

Galvan v. Press, 412, 413, 419, 436
Garland, *Ex parte*, 549–550
Garner v. Board of Public Works of Los Angeles, 344–348, 350, 351, 353, 358, 359, 366, 387, 414, 532–534, 540, 548, 562
Gastelum-Quinones v. Kennedy, 412, 422
Gerende v. Board of Supervisors of Elections, 343–344, 346, 348, 350, 353, 361, 387, 562
Gibson v. Florida Legislative Investigation Committee, 511, 514–521, 523, 525, 527, 530, 538, 542, 587
Gilbert v. Minnesota, 147–149, 151, 152, 162
Ginsberg v. New York, 55–57
Ginzburg v. United States, 42, 43, 44, 45
Girouard v. United States, 426, 550
Gitlow v. New York, 150–156, 157, 159, 161, 169, 171, 174, 176, 177, 178, 180, 182, 183, 189, 191, 195, 196, 197, 198, 201, 204, 208, 210, 227, 228, 245, 605, 606
Gojack v. United States, 521, 525, 526, 527, 528, 530, 531
Goldman v. United States, 132
Gooding v. Wilson, 110–112
Gregory v. Chicago, 99–102, 103
Grosjean v. American Press Company, 175, 177

Hague v. CIO, 175
Hannegan v. Esquire, 13–14, 15
Harisiades v. Shaughnessy, 409–413, 414, 436
Hartzel v. United States, 182, 185
Herndon v. Lowry, 123, 169–175, 179, 183, 244

In re Anastaplo, 549, 557, 570–574, 575, 576, 577, 578, 582, 583
In re Isserman, 397, 398, 419
In re Stolar, 549, 574, 579, 581, 582, 583, 584
In re Summers, 549, 550
Interstate Circuit, Inc. v. Dallas, 57
Irvin v. Dowds, 25
Isserman v. Ethics Committee, 397, 398

Jacobellis v. Ohio, 38, 40
Joint Anti-Fascist Refugee Committee v. McGrath, 288, 289–292, 306, 323, 348
Josephson, United States v., 466, 467, 469

Kent v. Dulles, 450, 455, 456

Kessler v. Strecker, 404, 405, 409, 412, 422, 436

Keyishian v. Board of Regents, 317, 367, 368–374, 375, 376, 378, 379, 380, 383, 384, 395, 406, 492, 581, 584

Kilbourn v. Thompson, 463, 464, 474

Kingsley International Pictures v. Regents, 58, 123, 236

Kleindiest v. Mandel, 444–445, 446

Knauer v. United States, 431, 432, 435

Knauff v. Shaughnessy, 438–440

Konigsberg v. State Bar of California (Konigsberg I & II), 253, 549, 554–570, 571, 574, 575, 576, 577, 578, 582, 583

Kunz v. New York, 78, 81, 86–88, 89, 94, 203, 205, 442

Kwong Hai Chew v. Colding, 440–441

Lady Chatterley's Lover, Kingsley Pictures v. Regents, 11–12, 13

Lamont v. Postmaster General, 384, 388–390, 444, 445, 447, 455

Law Students Civil Rights Research Council v. Wadmond, 317, 549, 574, 575, 581, 583, 584, 586, 587

Lerner v. Casey, 541, 548, 575

Lewis v. New Orleans, 112

Lovell v. Griffin, 175, 177, 262, 544

Lovett, United States v., 319–323, 325, 326, 328

Macintosh, United States v., 426

Maisenberg v. United States, 434, 435

Manual Enterprises v. Day, 37–38

Martin v. Struthers, 445

Masses Publishing Co. v. Patten, 4, 125–130, 133, 134, 137, 161, 162, 228, 229, 456, 602

McAuliffe v. Mayor of New Bedford, 301

McGrain v. Daugherty, 462–465, 491, 521

Memoirs Case, 38, 39–40, 41, 43, 44, 45, 48, 49, 51

Miller v. California, 48–53

Milwaukee Publishing Company v. Burleson, 389

Mishkin v. New York, 42, 44

Morford v. United States, 467, 471–472

NAACP v. Button, 590

Near v. Minnesota, 175, 177

New York Times v. Sullivan, 60, 61, 62, 63, 68–73, 81, 105, 117, 141, 175, 228, 229, 230, 236, 280, 310, 312, 313, 371, 389, 487, 501, 509, 542, 597, 598–599, 601

Niukkanen v. McAlexander, 420

Nixon v. Condon, 177

Nixon v. Herndon, 177

Noto v. United States, 123, 225–226, 228, 232, 234, 249, 325, 338

Nowak v. United States, 434, 435

O'Brien v. United States, 168

Paris Theatre I v. Slaton, 48–53
Patterson v. Colorado, 132
Pennekamp v. Florida, 30, 180
Pennsylvania v. Nelson, 511
Pickering v. Board of Education, 311–314, 372
Pierce v. United States, 147, 149, 152
Polites v. United States, 434–436

Queen v. Hicklin, 37
Quinn v. United States, 479, 480, 481, 483, 530

Rabeck v. New York, 57
Red Lion case, 445
Redrup v. New York, 44–45, 46
Reidel, United States v., 47
Robel, United States v., 287, 317, 367, 374–378, 379, 380, 383, 384, 385, 395, 397, 406, 447, 492, 581, 584
Rosenblatt v. Baer, 68
Rosenfeld v. New Jersey, 112, 113, 114, 115
Roth v. United States, 18–19, 35, 36, 37, 38, 41, 42, 43, 44, 45, 47, 48, 49, 51, 53, 56, 61, 110
Rowan v. United States Post Office, 58
Rowold v. Perfetto, 419–420, 421
Rumely, United States v., 472, 474–479, 485, 487, 488, 492, 496, 497, 511, 523, 527, 530
Russell v. United States, 513, 514, 521, 523, 525, 526, 527

Sacher v. Association of the Bar of New York, 397, 398
Sacher v. United States, 397
Scales v. United States, 222–2?4, 228, 242, 244, 246–253, 254, 269, 285, 289, 323, 325, 338, 349, 351, 356, 357, 358–359, 360, 362, 368, 370, 371, 372, 373, 374, 376, 378, 380, 382, 384, 392, 406, 421, 477, 489, 501, 503, 504, 505, 531, 577, 583, 584
Schaefer v. United States, 147, 148, 149, 152
Schenck v. United States, 125, 130, 133, 134, 135, 136, 137, 138, 139, 140, 143, 145, 146, 147, 148, 153, 154, 155, 156, 158, 159, 160, 163, 183, 185, 186, 187, 191, 192, 196, 201, 227, 234, 425
Schlesinger v. Wisconsin, 545
Schneider v. State, 176, 262, 308, 544
Schneiderman v. United States, 182, 184, 185, 187, 426–431, 432, 433, 434, 435, 436
Schware v. New Mexico, 501, 549, 550–551, 554, 555, 556, 558
Schwimmer, United States v., 424, 426
Scopes case, 9
Service v. Dulles, 211
Shaughnessy v. United States ex rel. Mezei, 441–444

Shelton v. Tucker, 262–263, 542–547, 575, 579, 580, 587
Sheppard v. Maxwell, 25–26
Shuttlesworth v. Birmingham, 102–103
Sinclair v. United States, 465–466, 469
Slochower v. Board of Higher Education, 540
Speiser v. Randall, 355, 359, 384, 385–388, 393, 395, 532, 534–539, 548, 557, 561, 575, 582, 587
Stack v. Boyle, 414–419
Stanley v. Georgia, 45, 47, 48, 49, 444, 445, 477, 496
Stolar, *In re*, 549, 574, 579, 581, 582, 583, 584
Stromberg v. California, 123, 167–169, 173, 174, 175, 177, 212, 213
Street v. New York, 12–13
Summers, *In re*, 549, 550
Sweezy v. New Hampshire, 211, 492–497, 498, 500, 501, 505, 507, 510, 511, 521, 524, 527

Talley v. California, 255, 477, 544
Taylor v. Mississippi, 182–183, 184, 185, 605
Tenney v. Brandhove, 472
Terminiello v. Chicago, 78, 81–86, 89, 94, 97, 99, 105, 107, 116, 203, 442
Thomas v. Collins, 605
Thornhill v. Alabama, 179–180, 605
Torcaso v. Watkins, 10, 308–309, 311
Turner v. Williams, 437–438

United Public Workers v. Mitchell, 303–308, 309, 311, 318, 337
United States *ex rel.* Milwaukee Social Democratic Publishing Co. v. Burleson, 147, 149
United States v. Brown, 327–329, 359
United States v. Bryan, 467, 469, 470
United States v. Carolene Products Co., 176
United States v. Fleischman, 467, 469, 470
United States v. Josephson, 466, 467, 469
United States v. Lovett, 319–323, 325, 326, 328
United States v. Macintosh, 426
United States v. Reidel, 47
United States v. Robel, 287, 317, 367, 374–378, 379, 380, 383, 384, 385, 395, 397, 406, 447, 492, 581, 584
United States v. Rumely, 472, 474–479, 485, 487, 488, 492, 496, 497, 511, 523, 527, 530
United States v. Schwimmer, 424, 426
Uphaus v. Wyman, 506–509, 511, 521, 524, 526

Valentine v. Chrestensen, 607
Veterans of the Abraham Lincoln Brigade v. Subversive Activities Control Board, 288, 289, 292, 293, 294, 295, 297, 298, 306, 316, 317, 321, 323, 374, 382, 407, 469, 491, 497, 502, 504, 529, 531
Viereck v. United States, 274

Watkins v. United States, 211, 482, 483–492, 494, 495, 497, 498, 499, 510, 511, 512, 521, 526, 527, 530, 559, 568

West Virginia Board of Education v. Barnette, 180, 182

Whitehill v. Elkins, 344, 361, 362, 363, 364

Whitney v. California, 122, 123, 156–166, 169, 171, 177, 178, 179, 180, 182, 183, 184, 191, 192, 195, 196, 198, 201, 210, 227, 228, 229, 231, 232, 233, 243, 244, 249

Wieman v. Updegraff, 348–351, 356, 357, 360, 414, 419

Wilkinson v. United States, 509, 511, 512, 517, 518, 521, 526, 527, 568

Winters v. New York, 14–15, 19, 57

Wood v. Georgia, 31

Yates v. United States, 123, 195, 211, 212, 213, 215, 216, 217, 218, 233, 224, 225, 228, 229, 230, 232, 233, 234, 236, 242, 243, 246, 249, 250, 272, 274, 280, 285, 286, 289, 323, 325, 338, 351, 356, 359, 370, 371, 421, 434, 477, 489, 500, 503, 504, 521, 522–523, 525, 527, 531, 536, 564, 566, 598–599

Zemel v. Rusk, 453–456

Index

abrasive speech, categories of, 235–236
academic freedom invaded by legislative
    inquiry, 493, 500
action triggered by speech, 183
actual malice standard for defamation,
    228
actual malice test, libel and, 63
adherence to Communist Party lines as
    grounds for passport denial, 450,
    451
ad hominem deportation statutes,
    408–409
admission to the bar, *see* bar admission
adultery portrayed in motion pictures,
    11–12
"advocating," 213
advocacy
    by groups, 192
    defined, 220–221
    of action, 224
    of forcible overthrow of government,
        232
    of violence
        as tactic for social change, 236
        generally, 216, 220
        subversive, 221
affidavit requirement of Taft-Hartley Act,
    324
affidavits
    listing membership in organization
        542–547
    of non-allegiance to Communist Party,
        187
    of non-Communism, 532

affidavits *(cont.)*
    of organizations affiant belongs to,
        543–547
affiliation with a group, 406–407
affirmative oath of allegiance, 342,
    362–363, 367
aliens, *see also* exclusion; denaturalization;
    held in detention, 442–444
allegiance, affirmative oath of, 342,
    362–363, 367
allocation of subsidies as partial sanction,
    384–390
American Communist Party, see also
    Communist Party, 212, 220
American race policy, 230
American tradition, the consensus of
    untouchable content and, 9–10
anarchists, 213, 437–438
Anderson, Sherwood, featured in *The
    Masses*, 126
anonymity in political disclosure, 256–261
anonymous speech, no freedom of, 255
Anti-Communism
    generally, 250, 264, 316
    in the 1950s, 217
    legal strategies, 319
Anti-Communist
    affidavit requirement of Taft-Hartley
        Act, 324
    cases, 187–189
anti-war speech, 106–112
Aptheker, Herbert, 379, 380, 381
Arnold, Thurman, 34

assembly
  freedom of, 245
  in public places, 175
  right of, 241
association
  freedom of, 241–242, 260–261, 264
  regulation of, 237
  right of, 257, 350
associational privacy
  generally, 259–260, 281, 520
  of teachers, 544, 547
atheism, withholding from public office
    and, 308–309
atheists, no state purpose to disfavor, 311
attachment to Constitution, naturalization
    and, 426–431, 433, 434, 435
Attorney General
  as one-man investigative committee,
    494, 506, 523
  discretion to exclude aliens, 446–447
audience, First Amendment right to,
    445–446
automatic exclusion from bar admission
    for refusing to answer question on
    Communist Party membership,
    560–571

bail
  as a matter of discretion of Attorney
    General, 415–417
  Eighth Amendment and, 416–417
  pending deportation, 414
  pending trial, 414–415
balancing of interests test
  applied to partial sanctions for
    membership in disfavored groups,
    335–336
  used in NAACP cases, 281
balancing test
  applied to refusal to answer questions
    for bar admission, 373–374,
    566–570, 572
  in NAACP v. Alabama, 261–262
  used in requiring teachers to sign
    disclosure affidavits, 545
  used on partial sanctions, 305, 306, 314
  used when disclosure is used as a direct
    sanction, 282
bar admission
  applicant's burden of going forward
    with evidence, 557–558, 561
  automatic exclusion from for refusing
    to answer questions about
    Communist Party membership,
    560–571
  burden of proof on denial of, 557, 562,
    563
  character and fitness requirements for,
    548–587

bar admission (cont.)
  conscientious objectors excluded from,
    550
  denied
    because of Communist Party
      membership, 551–587
    for advocating violent overthrow of
      government, 575–587
    for refusal to answer questions about
      membership in Communist Party,
      554–587
  generally, 548–587
  overbreadth of questions put to
    applicants, 584
  past membership in Communist Party
    and, 553
  questioning about Communist Party
    membership, official motivation and,
    566
  refusal to answer questions, balancing
    test and, 566–570, 572, 573–574
  substantive conditions on, 549, 587
belief
  freedom of, 332
  in God, declarations of, 308
  in overthrow of government by force,
    329–332
beliefs, sanctioning, 330
Bellow, George, featured in The Masses,
    126
benign conspiracy, 136–138
Berkman, Alexander, 126
bills of attainder
  constitutionality of, 329
  defined, 321
  generally, 293, 319, 322, 323, 326,
    327–329, 550
  loyalty oath as, 346
  mentioning Communist Party, 328–329
  prohibition against, 321, 328
  Taft-Hartley Amendments to National
    Labor Relations Act as, 325
Black, Justice
  dissenting opinion in
    American Committee for Protection of
      Foreign Born v. Subversive Activities
      Control Board, 295
    American Communication Association v.
      Douds, 326–327, 338, 342–343
    Anastaplo, In re, 573–574
    Barenblatt v. United States, 502, 503
    Communist Party v. Subversive Activities
      Control Board, 271, 279–280, 281
    Dennis v. United States, 201–203, 471
    Ginzburg v. United States, 44
    Stack v. Boyle, 417, 418
    Summers, In re, 550
  opinion in
    Aptheker v. Secretary of State, 298

Black: opinion in *(cont.)*
    Baird v. State Bar of Arizona, 576,
        577–578, 579–580, 585
    Barksy v. Board of Regents, 479–480
    Bridges v. California, 27–28, 29
    Cox v. Louisiana, 103
    Epperson v. Arkansas, 9
    Feiner v. New York, 91
    Flemming v. Nestor, 395
    Galvan v. Press, 414
    Gregory v. Chicago, 100–101, 102,
        103–104
    *Joint Anti-Fascist Refugee Committee v.
        McGrath,* 293
    Konigsberg v. State Bar of California, 556,
        565, 567, 568, 569
    *Lady Chatterley's Lover, Kingsley Pictures v.
        Regents,* 11
    Rosenblatt v. Baer, 70
    Schware v. New Mexico, 552
    Speiser v. Randall, 387–388
    Talley v. California, 256
    Torcaso v. Watkins, 10, 308–309
    United Public Workers v. Mitchell,
        306–308
    United States v. Lovett, 321
    Viereck v. United States, 274–275
    Wieman v. Updegraff, 350
blasphemy, 7, 8
Bond, Julian, 229, 318
Brandeis, Justice, opinion in *Whitney v.
    California,* 158–160, 161, 162,
    163–164, 165, 166, 192–193
Brandenburg Test for subversive advocacy,
    166
Brennan, Justice
    dissenting opinion in *Miller v. California,*
        51–52, 53
    opinion in
    Keyishian v. Board of Regents, 370
    Lamont v. Postmaster General, 390
    Memoirs case, 38, 39–40
    New York Times v. Sullivan, 66, 67,
        68
    Rosenblatt v. Baer, 69–70
    Roth v. United States, 18–19, 36
    Rowan v. United States Post Office, 58–59
    Speiser v. Randall, 386, 562
    United States v. Robel, 377
Bridges, Harry, 405
broadcasting, 593
Brown's raid on Harpers Ferry in 1859,
    inquiry into, 463
Buchanan Committee, 474
burden of going forward with evidence,
    bar applicants and, 557–558, 561
burden of proof
    denial of bar admission and, 557, 562,
        563

burden of proof *(cont.)*
    failure to take loyalty oath and,
        535–539
Burger, Chief Justice
    dissenting opinion in
    Gooding v. Wilson, 111–112
    Rosenfeld v. New Jersey, 113
    opinion in
    Cole v. Richardson, 365
    *Garner v. Board of Public Works of Los
        Angeles,* 346, 532
    Paris Theater I v. Slaton, 48–49
business of communications, regulation
    of, 593

California Criminal Syndication Act, 192,
    250
California Tenney Committee, 472
Captive audiences, 92
Carolina District Communist Party, 223
category of speech proscribed, 196
censor, jurisdiction of, 193
censorship, *see also* self-censorship
    clear and present danger as condition
        for, 134, 138
    countervalue of risk of disorder and,
        100
    generally, 4
    major jurisdiction of, 75–236
    minor jurisdiction of, 21–74
    of general advocacy of violence, 228
    of group speech, 254
    of groups advocating violent overthrow
        of government, 280
    of out-of-court comments, 24
    of radical political groups, permissible
        censorship, 287
    of radical speech, 227, 231
    of street corner speech, 86–95
    of wholly permissible content, 90
    prior, 202
    religion as motivation for, 7
censor's power, boundaries of, 250
Chafee, Professor, 136, 137, 138, 139,
    146, 170, 174–175
character and fitness requirements for bar
    admission, 548–587
children, obscenity and, 54–59
chilling effect of disclosure of
    membership in a disfavored group,
    285
citizenship, 184
civil disobedience, 572
civil rights cases, 96–105
Clark, Justice
    dissenting opinion in
    Aptheker v. Secretary of State, 381, 182
    Baggett v. Bullitt, 354–355
    Talley v. California, 255–256

Clark *(cont.)*
  opinion in
    Abrams v. United States, 140
    Burstyn v. Wilson, 8–9
    Garner v. Board of Public Works of Los Angeles, 533
    Lady Chatterley's Lover, Kingsley Pictures v. Regents, 11
    Shaughnessy v. United States ex rel Mezei, 442
    Sheppard v. Maxwell, 25–26
    Speiser v. Randall, 385–386
    Yates v. United States, 219, 220–221
clear and present danger as a condition for censorship, 134, 138
clear and present danger test
  after *American Communication Association v. Douds,* 188–189
  applied to obscenity, 36
  applied to out-of-court comments, 28
  applied to subversive advocacy, 132–133, 137, 138
  Brandenburg Court's silence on, 232–233
  conspiracy and, 165
  conspiracy doctrine and, 200–201
  degree of evil necessary to abridge free speech, 163–164
  Dennis case version of, 233
  effect of *Dennis v. United States,* 190–210
  evidence of danger and, 164–165
  generally, 149, 154, 157, 159, 161–162, 174, 196, 205–206, 227–228, 601, 604
  gravity of the evil requirement, 180–181, 198
  how imminent action must be, 160–163
  inapplicable where regulation has indirect impact on speech, 197
  judicial critics of, 181
  judicial support for, 181
  lack of Constitutional status of, 206–207
  out-of-court publication and, 30, 31, 32
  subversive advocacy and, 179–189
  wartime and, 165
Cleland, John, 38, 39
Cold War, 187–189, 211
commercial speech, 607
Committee for Constitutional Government, 474
common law of defamation, 60–61, 64
communication, business regulation of, 593
Communism
  American, 220
  generally, 167–175, 200, 202, 203, 264–289
  in America, 484–485

Communist
  doctrine of forcible overthrow, 218
  infiltration, 518–521
  influence on labor unions, 323–324
  labor leaders, barring, 325, 327, 333, 337
  newspaper, 219
  organizations, regulating, 282
Communist-action organizations
  generally, 265, 268, 269, 272, 273, 274, 275, 294, 374
  partial sanctions imposed on, 378–379
  passports taken from members of, 452
  sanctions on, 267
  scienter established by, 375–376
Communist-action parent, 294
Communist advocacy
  generally, 193
  in the 1950s, 187–189
Communist China seated in the United Nations, 276
Communist clause in loyalty oath, 359
Communist conspiracy
  direct criminal sanctions applied to, 316
  generally, 220, 244
Communist Control Act of 1954, 399
Communist-front cases, 294–296
Communist-front organizations
  barring employment of members of, 378
  generally, 265, 267–268, 274, 294, 295, 507
Communist-front supporters, 36
The Communist Manifesto, 194
Communist Party
  advocacy, effect on clear and present danger test, 228
  affidavits of non-membership in, 532–541
  allegiances in the 1950s, 190
  as Communist-action organization, 268–269
  California branch, 211
  compelling interest of State in information about, 497
  conspiracy of, 268
  criminal conspiracy, 326
  efforts to outlaw, 277–280
  generally, 202, 213, 215, 218, 220, 223, 224, 243, 245, 246, 259, 263, 284
  group speech and, 242
  growth of, 220
  incitement standard and, 234
  intent to further unlawful aims, 374
  legislating about by name, 328
  legislative investigations into not subject to First Amendment, 497–505

Communist Party *(cont.)*
lines, adherence to as grounds for
passport denial, 450
loyalty oaths against membership in,
532–541
membership
as target of loyalty oath, 362
bar admission denied for refusal to
answer questions about, 554–587
cases and, 222
cause of denial of bar admission,
551–587
gradations of, 420
partial sanctions and, 368–383
refusal to disclose, 459, 506–531,
532–541, 548–587
Noto case and, 225
outlawing, attempts at, 317
outlawry of, 502
positions on public issues as proof of
Soviet domination, 275–277
registration of members
generally, 280
required registration, 269–270
response to threat believed created by,
315
teachers as members of, 373
Communist Political Association, 212
Communist speech
dangers of, 200
generally, 210
proximity of danger from, 205
Communists
as subject of legislative inquiry, 461,
469–474, 476, 480–482, 484–505,
506–531
barring from labor unions, 324
criminal sanctions applied to, 252
generally, 181, 184, 185, 187–189
stigmatization of, 292
Communist threat of the 1950s, 190–210
compelled testimony, necessity of for
legislative function, 465, 487–488
compelling interest of the state in
information about Communist Party,
497
compelling testimony, power of
investigative legislative committees,
461–482, 484–505, 506–531
compulsory disclosure
as a group sanction
generally, 254–287
SACB case, 264–289
First Amendment limitations on,
476–482, 484–505, 512, 513
of members in unfavored group, Fifth
Amendment and, 286–287
compulsory disclosure of membership
as group sanction, 297

compulsory disclosure of membership *(cont.)*
generally, 280–286, 316
in a group
as sanction, sufficiency of evilness of
group to impose sanction, 285–286
balancing test for, 261–262
justification for, 284, 285
used to prevent political fraud by
subversive groups, 282–283
Comstock, Anthony, 34
concealment of membership in group,
sinister purposes of, 282–283
concreteness of subversive advocacy, 224
concreteness requirement for incitement
generally, 216–217
membership cases and, 226
conduct as speech, 15–16
conflicts of interest, regulations designed
to avoid, 333
congressional subpoena, failure to
respond to, 462, 470–471
conscientious objectors
denying naturalization to, 426
excluded from bar admission, 550
conspiracy
grades of, 268
group, speech and, 241
membership in political organizations
and, 243–253
of the Communist Party, 268
personal guilt incurred through joining,
326
political, 199
to advocate overthrow of government,
191, 192, 193, 213
to obstruct the draft, 192
to organize, 193, 212
to overthrow the government, 199
twin aspects of, 193
within the larger conspiracy of the
Communist Party, 219–220
conspiracy doctrine
clear and present danger test and,
200–201
generally, 202, 205, 220
contempt
by publication, 23–32
of Congress, crime of, 484
content
censorship of wholly permissible
content, 90
of communications, when may be
interdicted by law, 235
of group speech, 243
of speech
generally, 15–16, 24
untouchable, 235
Cornell University, 512, 513
Corrupt Practices Act, 282

counter-speech as remedy for evil speech, 162
criminal conspiracy
  Communist Party as, 326
  treating a group as, as group sanction, 297
criminal sanctions
  applied to Communists, 252
  applied to Communist conspiracy, 316
  applied to groups, 254–287
  Communist conspiracy and, 244, 246
  for affiliation with disfavored group, 301
  for group speech, 243
  for organizing groups, 242
  to penalize advocacy of terrorism, 157
criminal syndicalism, 157, 245
criticism
  of government, 28
  of judicial action, 26–30
  of public officials, restraining, 175
Cuba, prohibition against travel to, 543

The Daily People's World
dangerous speech, categories of, 161–162
Darrow, Clarence, 438
defamation, *see also* libel
  common law of, 60–61, 64
  criticism of government, 69–70
  impact of *New York Times v. Sullivan*, 68–73
  liability for, rule in *New York Times v. Sullivan*, 228
  protection of individual reputation and, 71
  tension between criticism of public matters and protection of individual reputation, 71
  Times privilege and, 71–73
defense facilities
  barring employment from, 287
  employment at, 374
defense of free speech, 167
denaturalization
  advocacy of violent overthrow of government as grounds for, 435
  fraudulent concealment of divided loyalty and, 431
  generally, 316, 423–436
  government power of, 423
  showing needed for, 429
  standards for, 431
denial of employment as partial sanction keyed to membership in disfavored group, 318–339
deportation
  as anti-subversive tactic, 403–419
  as sanction, 403–422
  ex post facto laws, 411

deportation *(cont.)*
  of aliens, 316
  power of the government, 392, 410–11, 413
  without proof of scienter, 413, 419
de Tocqueville, 64
detain, authority to, 383
Dies, Representative Martin, 319, 320, 486
direct incitement, 150–151
disbarment of lawyers as sanction, 398–399
disclosure
  by teachers, of membership in organizations, 543
  compelling, 459–505, 506–531, 532–541, 567–568, 548–587
  compulsory, *see* compulsory disclosure
  for sake of exposure, 509
  NAACP and, 258–261
  of evidence outside the record, 25–26
  of membership in a group, compulsory, *see* compulsory disclosure of membership in a group
disclosure and exposure of past political mistakes during legislative investigation, 524–525
disclosure of membership intended as sanction, 280
disloyalty, criteria for, 318
dismissal, loyalty-security, 211
disorderly and unfair administration of justice, 28–29
disrespect for the judiciary, 28
distribution
  of obscenity, 47
  of leaflets
    generally, 175
    regulating, 335
doctors, license to practice revoked, 395–399
doctrine
  of criminal syndicalism, 245
  of forcible overthrow, Communist Party and, 218
  of violent revolution, 224
Douglas, Justice
  dissenting opinion in
    Barsky v. Board of Regents, 480
    Beauharnais v. Illinois, 62
    Communist Party v. Subversive Activities Control Board, 282
    Niukkanen v. McAlexander, 420–421
    Scales v. United States, 252
  opinion in
    Aptheker v. Secretary of State, 382–383
    Bridges v. Wixon, 406
    Craig v. Harney, 31

Douglas: opinion in *(cont.)*
  Dennis v. United States, 194, 195,
    199–201
  Elfbrandt v. Russell, 358
  *Gibson v. Florida Legislative Investigation
    Committee,* 520
  Hannegan v. Esquire, 14
  Kent v. Dulles, 450–451
  Tenney v. Branddhove, 474
  United Public Workers v. Mitchell, 306
  United States v. Rumely, 478
  *Veterans of the Abraham Lincoln Brigade v.
    Subversive Activities Control Board,* 295
  Zemel v. Rusk, 454
draft, criticism of, 15–16
draft card burning, 230
due process, *see also* Fifth Amendment
  obscenity statutes and, 37
  violations
    caused by stigmatization, 292–293
    disclosure of evidence outside the
      record, 25
    generally, 176

Eastman, Max, featured in *The Masses,* 126
Eighth Amendment, bail and, 416–417
employment, *see also* public employment
  denial of as partial sanction for
    membership in disfavored group,
    318–339
  keyed to employee's loyalty, 318
Engels, 194
entrant alien, 440–442
Equal Protection Clause, 4
Eros magazine, 43
Espionage Act of 1917, 65, 126, 131, 133,
    135, 137, 139, 147, 173, 185, 186
Establishment Clause
  construed in *Epperson v. Arkansas,* 9–10
  freedom of speech and, 10
Evans, Patricia, 610
evidence, disclosure of outside the record,
    25–26
excessive bail, 414–416
exclusion of aliens
  bail for detainees, 441
  discretion of Attorney General,
    446–447
  entrant aliens versus resident aliens,
    440–442
  Fifth Amendment implications, 440–448
  First Amendment challenges to, 438
  from United States, 437–448
  government power to, 438, 446, 447
  habeas corpus and, 441
  prolonged detention and, 442–444
  security considerations and, 439
  without hearings, 439–448

executive session requested instead of
  legislative investigation, 522–523
explicitness of subversive advocacy,
  224
ex post facto laws, *see also retroactivity*
  on deportation, 411
  prohibition against, 346

fair comment privilege, 61
fair trial, right to, 24, 25
false doctrine, 11–13
Fanny Hill, 38–39, 40, 41, 42, 43
Federal Unemployment Insurance Tax,
  399
Federalist Papers, 256
Feinberg certificate, 371
Feinberg Law, 369, 370, 371
Fifth Amendment, *see also* due process,
  compulsory disclosure of
    membership in a disfavored group
    and, 286–287
fighting words
  absence of, 99
  generally, 16, 17–18, 78–95, 110–115,
    116
  ideological, 80–95
"filled milk," 176
Finnegans Wake, 24
"fire" shouted in a theatre, 133–134, 142,
    160, 602
First Amendment, *see also* freedom of
  speech
  applicable via Fourteenth Amendment
    to the states, 151
  limitations on legislative investigations,
    476–482, 483–505, 512, 513
  rights of audience, 445–446
Fiss, Professor Owen, 594, 595
flag burning, 12–13
flag saluting ceremonies, 180, 182–183
Flynn, Elizabeth Gurley, 379, 380, 381
forcible overthrow of government,
  advocacy of, 232
Foreign Agents Registration Act, 274
Foreign Registration Act, 282
Fortas, Justice
  dissenting opinion in *Ginsberg v. New
    York,* 56–57
  opinion in
    Epperson v. Arkansas, 9–10
    Gojack v. United States, 526, 527
Foundations of Leninism, 194
Frankfurter, Justice
  criticism of clear and present danger
    test, 181
  dissenting opinion in
    Barsky v. Board of Regents, 396
    Bridges v. California, 27, 29

Frankfurter *(cont.)*
  opinion in
    *American Communication Association v.
      Douds,* 331
    Baumgartner v. United States, 431–432
    Burstyn v. Wilson, 8
    Butler v. Michigan, 35–36
    *Communist Party v. Subversive Activities
      Control Board,* 270, 271, 276,
      277–278, 280–281, 283, 284–285
    Dennis v. United States, 203–209, 471
    Harisiades v. Shaughnessy, 410
    Irwin v. Dowds, 25
    *Joint Anti-Fascist Refugee Committee v.
      McGrath,* 292–293
    Schware v. New Mexico, 552–553
    Shelton v. Tucker, 546
    Sweezy v. New Hampshire, 496, 497
    Tenney v. Brandhove, 473
    United States v. Lovett, 322–323
Free Speech in the United States, 136
freedom
  of assembly, 175, 245
  of association, 241–242, 260–261, 264
  of belief, 332
  of movement, *see also* travel; passports;
    382–383
  of speech, *see also* First Amendment;
    Establishment Clause and, 10
"fuck the draft" used as slogan, 15–16
Fuller, Chief Justice, opinion in *Turner v.
  Williams,* 438

general advocacy of violence
  as tactic of social change, 236
  censorship of, 228
German-American Bund, 432
Gitlow-Whitney standard of general
  advocacy, 178, 198, 210, 227
God
  belief in, 10–11
  declarations of belief in, 308
Goldberg, Justice, opinion in *Aptheker v.
  Secretary of State,* 368, 380, 381
Goldman, Emma, 126
government criticism as defamation,
  69–70
government employees as jurors sitting in
  judgment of Communists, 470–472
government privileges, refusal to answer
  inquiries preliminary to allocation
  of, 532–541
gravity element applied to clear and
  present danger test, 180–181
gravity of the evil requirement to clear
  and present danger test, 198
group activity, proscribed, individual
  nexus to, 244–253

group advocacy
  effect of *Dennis v. United States* on, 243
  generally, 216, 217
  of violent overthrow of government,
    censorship of, 280
  permissible, 222, 225, 243
group fighting words, 117
group membership as a crime, 242
groups
  and conspiracies, sanctions on, 267
  organizing, criminal sanctions for, 242
  registration of, 280
  regulation of, 598
  sanctions against, 241–242
group sanctions
  compulsory disclosure of membership,
    297
  generally, 254–287
  official stigmatization, 297
  sanctions against individuals as
    sanction, 297–298
  stigmatization as, 288–296
  treating group as a criminal conspiracy,
    297
group speech
  censorship of, 254
  Communist Party and, 242
  conspiracy and, 241
  content of, 243
  freedom compared with individual
    speech, 241–242
  generally, 241
  Jehovah's Witnesses and, 242
  membership cases and, 225
  NAACP and, 242
  radical industrial groups of the 1920s
    and, 242
  socialist-pacifists of World War I period
    and, 242

Hand, Justice
  opinion in
    Dennis v. United States, 198
    Masses Publishing Co. v. Patten, 126–130
Hand legacy in subversive advocacy,
  125–130
handbills
  ban on distributing, 262
  distributing, 255
hard-core pornography, 40–41
Harlan, Justice
  dissenting opinion in
    *DeGregory v. Attorney General of New
      Hampshire,* 524
    *Gibson v. Florida Legislative Investigation
      Committee,* 515, 518, 519
    Shelton v. Tucker, 545–546

Harlan *(cont.)*
  opinion in
    Anastaplo, In re, 571–572
    Baird v. State Bar of Arizona, 580–581
    Barenblatt v. United States, 504
    Cohen v. California, 15–16, 107–110
    Cole v. Richardson, 364
    Flemming v. Nestor, 394
    Konigsberg v. State Bar of California, 558,
      561, 563, 564, 568, 569
    Lerner v. Casey, 541
    NAACP v. Alabama, 260
    Noto v. United States, 225
    Scales v. United States, 224, 247–248,
      249, 250, 251–252
    Street v. New York, 13
    Wood v. Georgia, 31–32
    Yates v. United States, 215–216, 217,
      218, 219–220
Hatch Act, 303, 304, 306, 307
heckler's veto, 89–90, 91, 97–98, 101
heresy, 7, 9, 10
History of the Communist Party of the
  Soviet Union, 194
Hitler, 431
Holmes, Justice
  dissenting opinion in
    Gitlow v. New York, 155–156
    United States v. Schwimmer, 425
  opinion in
    Abrams v. United States, 65, 142–143,
      144–145
    Debs v. United States, 131–132, 136
    McAuliffe v. Mayor of New Bedford, 302
Holmes legacy in subversive advocacy,
  130–136
House Select Committee in Bankruptcy,
  463
House Un-American Activities Committee
  application of First Amendment to, 501
  challenges to, 509–510
  generally, 319, 320, 321, 395, 459, 460,
    461, 466, 467, 468, 469, 470, 471,
    472, 473, 475, 477, 479, 480, 481,
    483, 485, 486, 487, 488, 489, 491,
    494, 495, 498, 499, 501, 502, 503,
    504, 509–510, 511, 512, 513, 522,
    524, 525, 526, 527, 529, 530, 539,
    540, 586
Hughes, Charles Evans, 167
Hughes, Chief Justice, opinion in *DeJonge
  v. Oregon,* 245
Hutchins, Robert M., 350

ideas, regulation of, 18–19
ideological fighting words, 80–95
ideological speech causing audience
  unrest, 78–95

immediacy of incitement
  generally, 216–217
  membership cases and, 226
immediacy requirement of incitement, 231
incitement
  as type of abrasive speech, 236
  concreteness requirement, 216–217
  direct, 150–151
  generally, 156, 161–162, 214, 221,
    231
  immediacy of, 216–217
  immediacy requirement of, 231
  membership cases and, 222
  of crime, 157
  of mobs, 235
  of violence, 14–15
  Scales case and, 225
  standard, Communist Party and, 234
  test, 129–130
  to overthrow government by unlawful
    means, 169
  to violence, 216
incitement-to-future-action
  generally, 216, 217, 222, 243, 250
  membership cases and, 226
  standard of *Brandenburg,* 234
  test in Yates, 228
incitement to lawless action test
  generally, 124
  history of, 227–228
  of *Brandenburg,* 227
inciting
  insurrection, 169–175
  overthrow of government by unlawful
    means, 152–153
  violence, *see* subversive advocacy
individual, charging with speech of
  organization, 406
individual nexus to proscribed group
  activity, 244
individual speech, subversive advocacy
  and, 233–234
individual speech freedom compared with
  group speech freedom, 241–242
inflicting offense on a captive audience,
  16
insurrection, inciting, 169–175
intellectual privacy, 496
intent
  subversive advocacy and, 143–144, 145,
    186
  to further unlawful aims of the
    Communist Party, 374
intent requirement, sanctions and,
  372–373
Internal Security Act of 1950, 413, 414,
  424, 452
International Worker's Order, 290

interstate commerce, 176, 188
intrastate movement of citizens, 449

Jackson, Justice
  dissenting opinion in
    Eisler v. United States, 468–469
    Kunz v. New York, 87–88
    Isserman, In re, 398–399
    Shaughnessy v. United States ex rel Mezei,
      442, 443–444
    Terminiello v. Chicago, 84–86
  generally, 9
  opinion in
    *American Communication Association v.
      Douds,* 331, 342
    Dennis v. United States, 203–204
    Harisiades v. Shaughnessy, 41
    Knauff v. Shaughnessy, 440
    *West Virginia Board of Education v.
      Barnette,* 180
Jehovah's Witnesses
  generally, 17, 182–183
  group speech and, 242
Joint Anti-Fascist Refugee Committee,
  290, 395, 396, 479
judicial action, criticism of, 26–30
jurisdiction of censorship
  generally, 28, 193
  minor, 21–74
  of subversive advocacy, 121
jurors, government employees, sitting in
    judgment of Communists, 470–472

Kennan, 209
Kerr Committee, 322
knowing membership
  as a crime, 254
  in illegal organization, 248–249
Korea, peace in, 276
Krutch, Joseph Wood, 190
Ku Klux Klan, 121, 122, 256, 258

labor leaders, barring Communists as,
  325, 327, 333, 337
labor unions
  barring Communists from, 324
  Communist influence on, 323–324
lacking serious literary, artistic, political,
    or scientific value test for obscenity,
    50
Lady Chatterley's Lover, 39
Lamont, Corliss, 388
lawyers, disciplinary action taken against
    as partial sanction, 398–399
leaflets, distribution of
  generally, 175, 308
  regulating, 335
legislative investigation
  academic freedom invaded by, 493, 500

legislative investigation *(cont.)*
  authorization for, 527–528
  burden of proof, 461
  challenging, 472–482, 483–531
  committees exceeding their power,
    474–478, 487–488
  Communist infiltration, 518–521
  Communist Party investigation not
    subject to First Amendment,
    497–505
  compelled testimony, necessity of for
    legislative function, 465, 487–488
  compelling, 461–482, 506–531
  court not to look into official motivation
    for, 526
  disclosure and exposure of past political
    mistakes, 524–525
  disclosure for sake of exposure, 509
  domestic Communism, 461, 469–474,
    476, 480–484, 484–505, 506–531
  First Amendment challenges to,
    483–531
  First Amendment limitations to,
    476–482, 483–505, 512, 513
  generally, 506–531
  invasion of intellectual privacy, 496
  lobbying, 472–478
  membership in groups, 459–531
  motivation of, court's disinclination to
    question, 509
  NAACP membership, 514–521, 529
  nexus between state interest and
    particular inquiry, 516–521
  quorum requirement when witness
    refuses to answer, 469–471
  past connections of others, 490
  pertinancy of, 483–489, 490, 493, 498,
    499, 512, 513, 514, 519
  political freedom invaded by, 493, 500,
    512
  probable cause requirement, 519
  refusal to answer questions, 459, 469,
    484–505
  request of executive session instead of,
    522–523
  subcommittee inquiry, 527
  summary of body of law of, 528–531
  the beginnings, 459–482
  Watergate, 491
legislators, standards for speech applied
    to, 310–311
Letter of Junius, 256
Levi, Edward, 589
libel, *see also* defamation
  actual malice applied to public officials,
    63
  criticism of government, 67
  generally, 60–73
  old law of, 60–61

libel *(cont.)*
  privilege of fair comment, 61
  privilege offered under old law of libel,
    61
  public officials' privilege, 62–63
  sedition, *see* seditious libel
license to practice medicine, revoking,
  395–399
licensing public speakers, 86–87
Liliburne, John, 256
limitations on speech, motivations for, 6
littering, as rationale for banning leaflets,
  308
Lobbying Act, 282, 474–477
longshoremen's strike, 245
loyalty
  of employee, employment keyed to, 318
  of teachers, 365–373
loyalty oaths
  affirmative oaths of allegiance, 362, 367
  as anti-Communist strategy, 341
  as bill of attainder, 346
  as disfavored device, 366
  as partial sanction, 340–367
  as regulatory devices, 340–367
  automatic dismissal from employment
    for failure to take, 363
  barring Communists from the ballot, 344
  Communist clause in, 359
  Communist Party membership as target
    of, 362
  distinction between affirmative and
    negative oaths, 367
  failure to take, burden of proof and,
    535–539
  firm generalizations about, 366–367
  format of, 366
  for teachers, 535
  generally, 318, 319, 324, 371, 532
  legality of, 366–367
  negative test oath, 363, 367
  perjury prosecution for violation of,
    341
  proscribing membership in a disfavored
    group, 344–351
  public employment and, 344–351
  retroactive clauses in, 344–351
  scienter and, 344–352, 354, 356, 358,
    372
  vagueness technique, 351–356
Loyalty Program for federal employees,
  289
loyalty screening, 289–290
loyalty-security dismissal, 211
Lynd, Staughton, 594

mail
  screening, 388–390
  subsidies, 384–390

Mailer, Norman, 101
Mandel, Ernest, 444
margin notes in manuscript for this book,
  600–603
Marshall, Justice, opinion in
  Kleindiest v. Mandel, 447
  Stanley v. Georgia, 46–47
Marx, Karl, 194
Marxist
  literature, 184–185
  theory as subject of legislative inquiry,
    492–497
Marxist-Leninist
  classics, teaching, 223
  doctrine, 194
The Masses, 126
Masters, Edward Lee, 438
Mays, Willie, 589
McCarthy, Senator Joseph, 217, 275, 407,
  461, 467, 481, 491
McCarthyism, 315, 460
McKenna, Justice, opinion in *Gilbert v.
  Minnesota*, 148–149
McKinley, President, assassination of, 437
Medical Grievance Committee of New
  York, 395, 396, 479
Medina, Harold, 194
Meiklejohn, Alexander, 67, 162
membership
  compulsory disclosure of, 280–286
  disclosure as non-criminal sanction, 242
  generally, 243–253
  knowing, 254
  in a disfavored group, loyalty oath
    proscribing, 344–351
  in a group as a crime, 242
  in groups, legislative investigation into,
    459–531
  in illegal organization, knowing
    membership, 248–249
  in organizations, affidavit listing,
    542–547
  in political organizations, conspiracy
    and, 243–253
  subversive advocacy and, 222–226
membership cases
  concreteness requirement of incitement
    and, 226
  immediacy of incitement and, 226
  Scales and *Noto* cases and, 222–225
membership clause of Smith Act, 246–253
Memoirs of Hecate County, 35
Memoirs tripartite test for obscenity, 45,
  49
Miami and the Siege of Chicago, 101–102
milk, 176
Mill, John Stuart, 11, 23, 54, 119, 235
Miller/Paris Theatre I test for obscenity,
  48–53

Mindszenty, Cardinal, case of, 276
Minton, Justice, opinion in *Dennis v. United
    States,* 470–471
The Miracle, 8
Mosely, Dr., 275
"motherfucker" as offensive speech, 112
motion pictures, adultery portrayed in,
    11–12
Murphy, Justice, opinion in
    Bridges v. Wixon, 408–409
    Chaplinsky v. New Hampshire, 17–18, 79
    Schneiderman v. United States, 429–430
    Thornhill v. Alabama, 179–180

NAACP
    cases, 286
    disclosure and, 258–261
    generally, 259–263, 542, 543, 544
    group speech and, 242
    membership, legislative investigation
        into, 514–521, 529
    membership cases, 281
National Council of Soviet-American
    Friendship, 290
Nationality Act of 1906, 423, 427, 435,
    436
Nationality Act of 1940, 423, 435, 436
National Labor Relations Act
    generally, 187, 266, 333, 340
    Taft-Hartley Amendments to, 323, 324,
        325, 327
National Labor Relations Board, 187, 324
Nat Turner's Rebellion in 1832, 170
naturalization, denial of, 424–431
Naturalization Act of 1906, 184
Nazis
    denaturalization and, 431
    generally, 444
Nazi-Soviet Pact of 1939, 551
negative test oath, 342, 363, 367
The Negro and the First Amendment, 590
Neutrality Act, 551
newsman's privilege, 593
newspaper, trial by, 25
New York Bar Admission Question 26,
    582
The New Yorker, 214
New York Rule 9406, 582
New York State Security Risk Law, 541
New York Times privilege, ambit of, 71–73
non-content regulation, 304, 593
non-criminal sanctions, 316
North Atlantic Pact, 276
Nuremberg Trials, 444

oaths, *see also* loyalty oaths
    affirmative, 342
    generally, 230
    historical bad name of, 343

oaths *(cont.)*
    how construed, 331
    negative test, 342
    of allegiance, 309, 355–356
    of belief in God, 10
Ober Act, 361
obscenity
    anti-social behavior and, 49
    Burger Court revisions, 48–53
    child audiences and, 33
    children and, 54–59
    clear and present danger test applied
        to, 36, 37
    consenting adults and, 48, 51, 52
    danger to children, 33, 47
    definition of, 37
    distributing, 47
    evils of, 33–34, 44
    generally, 13–14, 17–19, 33–53, 604
    impact on adults, 35, 36
    lacking serious literary, artistic, political,
        or scientific value test for, 50
    laws
        due process and, 37
        regulating, 34–35
        vagueness of, 57–58
    legitimate state interest in regulating,
        48–49
    Memoirs tripartite test for regulating,
        45–49
    Miller/Paris Theatre I test for, 48–53
    not protected by First Amendment,
        36–37, 48, 49, 52
    pandering and, 43, 45
    patently offensive test for, 37–38, 39,
        49–50
    possession of, 46–47
    protecting the vulnerable against, 35–36
    prurient interest test and, 37, 38, 39,
        42, 49
    rational basis test for regulating, 49
    regulation of, 33, 41, 44, 45, 52–53
    Roth-Memoirs definition of, 45
    three-prong test for, 18
    utterly without social value test and, 36,
        38, 39–40, 50
    vulnerable audience concept and, 55
offensive speech, 106–118
officership in unions, 323
official motivation
    for instituting loyalty oaths and
        affidavits of non-membership in
        Communist Party, 532
    generally, 543, 547
    questioning about Communist Party
        membership for bar admission, 566
official inquiry
    generally, 457–588
    motivation for, 532

O'Neill, Eugene, 190
On Liberty, 11, 23, 54–55, 235
"organize," 213
outlawing the Communist Party, efforts
    to, 277–280
outlawry
    challenges to Subversive Activities
        Control Act, 277–280
    of Communist Party, 317, 502
    of political parties, 502
out-of-court comments, regulation of, *see*
    regulation of out-of-court comments
out-of-court expression of opinion on a
    pending case, 26–32
overbreadth
    doctrine, 111, 112
    in questions for bar admission, 584
    of laws making membership in
        Communist Party grounds for
        disqualification, 372, 375, 376, 380,
        383
overt acts, 213

pandering
    advertising, 58
    generally, 43, 45
    to children, 56
partial sanctions
    allocating subsidies, 384–390
    anti-Communist inheritance and,
        299–401
    applied to individuals because of
        membership in disfavored groups,
        315–317
    balancing test and, 305, 306, 314
    Communist Party membership and,
        368–383
    denial of property tax subsidy, 385–388
    denial of Social Security benefits to
        deportees, 391–395
    for membership in disfavored group
        balancing test applied to, 335–336
    denial of employment for, 318–319
    generally, 244, 301–314, 368–383
    imposed on members of
        Communist-action group, 378–379
    keyed to membership in disfavored
        group, 315–317
    keyed to political association, 332–339
    loyalty oath as, 340–367
    merits of, 332–339
    multiplier effect of, 391–399
    objective of, 302
    passport bans, 378–379
    withholding public employment as
        sanction, 303–309, 340
passports
    ban on applications for, 378–379
    ban on as partial sanction, 378–379

passports *(cont.)*
    crime for U.S. citizens to leave U.S.
        without, 450
    denied subversive group members, 266
    interdiction against applying for, 287
    loyalty certification of, 451–452
    1952 regulations concerning, 449
    prohibition against members of
        subversive groups applying for, 298
    regulation of, *see* regulation of
        passports
    restricted, 453
    taken from members of
        Communist-action groups, 452
    travel without as crime, 450, 453, 455
past membership
    deportation statutes reaching, 409
    generally, 408
patently offensive test for obscenity,
    37–38, 39, 49–50
Pennsylvania Loyalty Act, 539, 540
Penry, John, 256
penumbra doctrine not applicable to laws
    affecting speech, 536
penumbra of administrative convenience,
    545
perjury prosecution for violating oath,
    341
permissible group advocacy, 225, 243
personal guilt incurred through joining a
    conspiracy, 326
pertinancy as jurisdictional basis for
    Legislative investigation, 484, 489,
    490, 493, 498, 499, 512, 513, 514,
    519
picketing residential areas, 99–102
picket line violence, 224
Playboy magazine, 34
police orders, refusal to obey order as
    offense, 102
political
    activity, regulation of, 593
    association, partial sanctions keyed to,
        332–339
    censorship, 214
    conspiracy, 199, 204–205
    freedom
        interfered with, 317
        invaded by legislative investigation,
            493, 500, 512
    groups, regulation of, 239
    mistakes, disclosure and exposure of
        past political mistakes, 524–525
    partisanship of federal employees,
        303–306
    speech, 228
    strikes
        avoiding, 327–328

political: strikes *(cont.)*
   risk of, 333–335
pornography, hard-core, 40–41
possession of obscenity, 46–47
Powell, Justice
   dissenting opinion in *Rosenfeld v. New Jersey,* 114
   opinion in *Lewis v. New Orleans,* 113
presumption of constitutionality, 176–177
pre-trial detention for speech of aliens, 417–419
prior censorship, 202
prior licensing, 11–12
prior restraint, 86, 131, 175, 176, 593
privacy, associational, 259–260, 281, 544, 547
privacy for organization, 281
privilege
   enunciated in *New York Times v. Sullivan,* ambit of, 71–73
   newsman's, 593
probable cause requirement, legislative investigation and, 519
Progressive Party, 493, 496, 497
proper name reference, 327
property tax subsidy, denial of as partial sanction, 385–388
Proust, 591
proximate cause test for subversive advocacy, 173
proximity of danger from Communist speech, 205
prurient interest test for obscenity, 37, 38, 39, 42, 49
public comment, 26–32
public employees, few rationales for limiting First Amendment rights of, 311, 312
public employment
   as a privilege, 370
   generally, 316, 317
   loyalty oath and, 344–351
   state limitation of, 318–319
public
   forum, protecting, 92
   officials, libel of, 62–63
   places, assemblies in, 175
public-issue picketing, 96–97
Public Utilities Holding Company Act, 270–271
pure speech test of "reasonable apprehension of danger," 171

quorum requirement at legislative investigation when witness refuses to answer, 469–471

race and religion as "suspect" criteria for classification, 4
race policy in America, 230
radical
   censorship, 231
   industrial groups of the 1920s, group speech and, 242
   speech
      boundaries of 228–229
      censorship of, 227
      generally, 122–124, 227
rational basis test
   for regulating obscenity, 49
   for restrictions on speech, 177
reasonable apprehension of danger test for pure speech, 171
Reed, John, featured in *The Masses,* 126
Reed, Justice
   dissenting opinion in *Hartzel v. United States,* 186–187
   opinion in
      Joint Anti-Fascist Refugee Committee v. McGrath, 291
      Pennekamp v. Florida, 30
      United Public Workers v. Mitchell, 304–305
      Winters v. New York, 15
reflexive
   disorder, 75–124, 180
   violence problem, 100
refusal
   of bar applicant to answer questions about Communist Party membership, 554–587
   to answer an inquiry preliminary to allocating a government privilege, 532–541
   to answer questions on Communist Party membership, automatic exclusion from admission to bar and, 560–571
   to obey police orders, 102–105
registration
   of Communist Party members, 286–287
   of groups, 280, 281
   of members of subversive groups, 296
   provisions used to outlaw Communist Party, 277–278
   statutes, purpose of, 275
regulation
   non-content, 304
   of Communist organizations, 282
   of groups, 598
   of non-content, 593
   of obscenity
      generally, 41, 44, 52–53
      justification for, 45
   of out-of-court comments, 24–32

regulation *(cont.)*
of passports
First Amendment challenges to,
455–456
generally, 449–456
grounds for, 450
in discretion of Secretary of State,
451–455
security logic of, 452, 453
of political groups, 239
of symbolic content, 593
of the business of communication, 593
of travel, 378–383
of voting and political activity, 593
regulation of association, 237
regulations designed to avoid conflicts of
interest, 333
regulations of 1952 concerning passports,
449
religion as motivation for censorship, 7
religion clauses, 7
requisite danger, subversive advocacy and,
143–144
resident aliens
deportation of for past membership,
403–422
generally, 440–442
right of, 409
residential picketing, 99–102
responsibility for the speech of another,
192
restricted passports, 453
retroactivity, *see also ex post facto;* bills of
attainder
retroactive clauses in loyalty oaths,
344–351
retroactive denial of Social Security
benefits, 394
revoking license to practice medicine,
395–399
revolution, violent, doctrine of, 224
revolutionary
speech, value of, 209
techniques, teaching, 223
right
of assembly, 241
of association, 257, 350
of resident aliens, 409
to fair trial, 24
to receive communication, 390
to travel, *see also* passports, 379–383
right/privilege
distinction, 386
fallacy, 370
Roberts, Justice, opinion in
Cantwell v. Connecticut, 81
Cantwell v. Roberts, 7
Herndon v. Lowry, 171–172, 173, 174

Roberts, Justice, opinion in *(cont.)*
Kessler v. Strecker, 404
Schneider v. State, 177–178
Taylor v. Mississippi, 183
Robert's Rules of Order, 24, 104
Roth-Memoirs definition of obscenity, 45
Rutledge, Justice, opinion in *Knauer v.*
United States, 433, 434

sacrilege, 8, 9, 12, 14, 19
sadomasochism, 42
St. Clair expedition in 1792, inquiry into,
463
sanctioning beliefs, 330
sanctions
against groups, 241–242
against individuals as a group sanction,
297–298
by the Subversive Activities Control
Act, 265–267
criminal, *see* criminal sanctions
deportation as, 403–422
direct, balancing test used on, 282
disclosure of membership intended as,
280
group, *see* group sanctions
intent requirement and, 372–373
non-criminal, 316
on Communist-action groups, 267
on groups as conspiracies, 267
partial, *see* partial sanctions
satellite sanctions, 297–298
Sanford, Justice, opinion in *Gitlow v.*
United States, 152–153, 154–155
satellite sanctions, 297–298
scienter
deportation without proof of, 413, 419
established when organization is a
Communist-action group, 375
loyalty oaths and, 344–352, 354, 356,
358, 372
requirement for deportation statutes,
413–414
screening of mail, 388–390
second-class mail subsidy, 383–390
security risks, employment of Communist
Party members and, 368–383
Sedition Act of 1798, 63, 65, 66, 67, 139,
141, 542
seditious libel
generally, 63–67, 94, 95, 109, 228, 229,
235–236, 597, 598
subordinate libeling his superiors, 312
teachers and, 312–314
Selective Draft Act, 132
self-censorship, 355, 372, 385, 386, 478,
497, 500, 508, 528, 536, 537, 538,
545

Senate Internal Security, 513
Senate Watergate Committee, 461
separation of Church and State, 7
Shakespeare, 190
Sharp, Malcom, 589
silencing the speaker, 89–95
Sloan, John, featured in *The Masses*, 126
Smith Act
  as applied to the Communist Party,
      208–209
  decisions
    effect of *Brandenburg* case on, 243
    effect of *Whitney* case on, 243
    generally, 191, 194, 195, 196, 201, 202,
        211, 212, 213, 214, 215, 216, 217,
        220, 224, 228, 231, 232, 233, 248,
        254, 267, 271, 272, 274, 415, 511
    membership cases, *Scales* case and, 244
    membership clause, 246–253
    prosecutions, 221
    Scales case and, 222, 246–253
Social Security Act, 266
Social Security benefits
  denial of for Communist ties, 391–395
  nature of, 393
  retroactive denial of, 394
socialist-pacifists of World War I period,
    group speech and, 242
Socialist Party, 192
Socratic dialogue on meaning of freedom
    of speech, 23
Soviet domination, Communist Party
    positions on public issues as
    evidence of, 275–277
Soviet Union, 275–276
speakers, silencing, 89–95, 116–117
speech
  abrasive, categories of, 235–236
  of aliens, pretrial detention for,
      417–419
  of another, responsibility for, 192
  of organization, charging individual
      with, 406
  revolutionary value of, 209
  that excites other to disorder, 77–95
  triggering action, 183
  vicarious responsibility for, 431
  with ideological content causing
      audience unrest, 78–95
  worthless and offending, 88
Stalin, 194
State and Revolution, 194
statute of limitations, 212
Stewart, Justice, opinion in
  Baird v. State Bar of Arizona, 586
  Bates v. Little Rock, 261–262
  Cramp v. Board of Public Instruction,
      352–353
  Edwards v. South Carolina, 97

Stewart, Justice, opinion in *(cont.)*
  Epperson v. Arkansas, 9
  Ginsberg v. New York, 56
  Jacobellis v. Ohio, 40–41
  *Lady Chatterley's Lover, Kingsley Pictures v.
      Regent*, 12
  Rosenblatt v. Baer, 70–71
  Shelton v. Tucker, 262–263, 544
  Shuttlesworth v. Birmingham, 102–103
stigma used to outlaw Communist Party,
    277–278
stigmatization
  as a group sanction, 288–296, 297
  generally, 274–275, 316
  of Communists, 292
  of members of disfavored group, 287
  procedural due process violations and,
      292
Stone, Chief Justice, dissenting opinion in
  Bridges v. Wilson, 408
  Schneiderman v. United States, 428,
      430–431
street corner speech, 106–124
Student Nonviolent Coordinating
    Committee (SNCC), 229–230
subcommittees, legislative, investigations
    by, 527
subpoena, congressional, failure to
    respond to, 462, 470–471
subsidies
  allocation of as partial sanction,
      384–390
  denial of, security rationale for, 385
Subversive Activities Control Act
  generally, 246, 264, 272, 274, 275, 279,
      286, 287, 288, 289, 290, 294, 295,
      296, 297, 315, 316, 324, 325, 369,
      374, 378–379, 460, 500, 573
  outlawry challenges to, 277–280
  sanctions by, 265–267
Subversive Activities Control Board, 265,
    335
subversive activity defined, 320
subversive advocacy
  as a political tactic, 120
  Brandenburg case and, 227–236
  Brandenburg test for, 166
  categories of, 151–152
  clear and present danger test applied
      to, 132–133, 179–189
  confrontation of *Dennis v. United States*,
      190–210
  generally, 119–124, 125–161, 598
  group speakers, 233–234
  Hand legacy, 125–130
  Holmes legacy, 130–136
  inciting overthrow of government by
      unlawful means, 152–153
  individual speakers, 233–234

subversive advocacy *(cont.)*
  intent and, 133, 135, 143–144, 145
  jurisdiction to censorship, 121
  membership cases, 222–226
  proximate cause test for, 173
  requisite danger and, 143–144
  Sanford and Brandeis legacy, 150–166
  specific intent and, 186
  speech starts to win, 167–178
  Yates revision, 211–226
symbolic content, regulation of, 593
syndicalism
  criminal, 245
  generally, 192
syndicalists, 213

Taft-Hartley Act, 187, 340, 342
Taft-Hartley anti-Communist affidavit
  generally, 224
  requirement, 324
taste, 13–19
tax subsidy, 384
teacher's
  affidavits of membership in
    organizations, 542–547
  loyalty, 369–373
  membership in Communist Party, 373
teaching
  Marxist-Leninist classics, 223
  revolutionary techniques, 223
Teapot Dome Scandal, 462, 464, 465
terrorism, 157
travel
  as Fifth Amendment right, 382
  as peripheral right, 454
  freedom to, 450–456
  reasonable regulation of, 382
  right to (*see also* passports), 379–383
treason, 230
trial by newspaper, 25
Truman, President
  Executive Order 9835, 289, 291
  veto message of, 294–296

Udal, John, 256
unions, officership in, 323
untouchable content of speech, 6–19, 235
utterly without social value test, obscenity
  and, 36, 38, 39–40, 50

vagueness
  generally, 168, 173, 176, 183
  of obscenity statutes, 57–58
  techniques used in loyalty oaths,
    351–356
Van Devanter, Justice, opinion in *McGrain*
  v. Daugherty, 463–464
verbal assaults, 114

vicarious liability for speech, 241
vicarious responsibility for the speech of
  another, 243, 431
Vietnam War, 229–230, 309
Vinson, Chief Justice
  dissenting opinion in *American*
    Communication Association v. Douds,
    188, 325–326, 334, 335, 336, 337
  opinion in
    Dennis v. United States, 194, 196,
      198–199
    Feiner v. New York, 90
    United States v. Brown, 328
violence
  advocacy of, 216, 220
  incitement of, 14–15
  incitement to, 216
violent overthrow of government
  advocacy of as grounds for
    denaturalization, 435
  belief in, naturalization and, 429–431
  censorship of groups advocating, 280
  denial of bar admission for advocacy of,
    575–587
  membership in group that advocates,
    222
The Virginian, 17
visa, denial of, 444–445
voting, regulation of, 593
vulnerable audience concept, obscenity
  and, 55

Wallice, Henry, 496
War Brides Act, 439
war brides, exclusion of without hearing,
  439–440
Warren, Chief Justice, opinion in
  Bond v. Floyd, 230–231, 310–311
  Communist Party v. Subversive Activities
    Control Board, 272
  Emspak v. United States, 482
  Gregory v. Chicago, 99–100
  Quinn v. United States, 480
  Watkins v. United States, 487–489
  Wood v. Georgia, 32
  Zemel v. Rusk, 455–456
wartime effect on freedom of speech,
  142–143, 147
Watergate
  Committee, 461
  hearings, 491
White, Justice
  dissenting opinion in
    Baird v. State Bar of Arizona, 577
    United States v. Robel, 377
    Yellin v. United States, 523
  opinion in
    Baggett v. Bullitt, 355

White: opinion in *(cont.)*
  Gibson v. Florida Legislative Investigation
    Committee, 500–521
  United States v. Reidel, 47
Wilkerson, Doxey, 223, 224
Wilkie, Wendell, 427
Wilson, Edmund, 35, 53
withholding employment as partial
    sanction, 303–309
World Fellowship, Inc., 506, 507

World War I subversive advocacy cases
  after *Abrams,* 146–149
  generally, 169, 229, 281
worthless speech, 17, 18, 19

Young, Art, featured in *The Masses,*
    126
Young Communist League, 551
Yugoslavia, election of to the Security
    Council, 276